The Emerging Elementary Curriculum

The Authors

Albert H. Shuster (Ed.D., University of Virginia), is Professor and Chairman of the Department of Elementary Education at Ohio University. His experience includes several years as a practicing elementary school teacher and administrator. Dr. Shuster is the author of the book, *Leadership in Elementary Administration and Supervision,* and writes numerous articles for professional publications.

Milton E. Ploghoft (Ed.D., University of Nebraska), is Professor of Education and Director of the Center for Social Science Education at Ohio University. He has also served as Director for the Nigerian College of Education (1962-64), the Center of International Programs at Ohio University (1965-66), and the Literature section of Project English, University of Nebraska (1961-62). He also writes numerous articles for professional publications.

The Emerging Elementary Curriculum
Methods and Procedures

Albert H. Shuster
Ohio University

Milton E. Ploghoft
Ohio University

CHARLES E. MERRILL PUBLISHING CO.
A Bell & Howell Company
Columbus, Ohio

Standard Book Number: 675-09377-5
Library of Congress Catalog Card Number: 70-103327
1 2 3 4 5 6 7 8 9 10 - 75 74 73 72 71 70
Printed in the United States of America

Preface to the
Second Edition

This book will provide modern, practical understandings, attitudes, and skills that will improve the preservice as well as the inservice elementary teachers' efficiency in providing sound learning experiences for children. The theme of the book lies in the authors' philosophy of the curriculum and its organization: i.e., from a curriculum design, *per se*, will flow the ways of working with children; the *emerging* curriculum design, however, must consider first the *experiences of children*. Textbooks, courses of study, curriculum guides, and the like are of value only so long as they focus on the child. In the same way, the methods of teaching are important, constituting as vital a segment of the curriculum as the content which is to be learned. These are the essential features presented in this book to guide the teacher in the elementary school.

The text is divided into three logical parts: (1) the bases for the emerging curriculum design; (2) the content of the curriculum; and (3) the bases for curriculum modifications in the elementary school.

Part I presents philosophical foundations for teaching the basic values that contribute so significantly to the development of the child. These foundations are examined in the light of the findings of child development and learning theory. Early childhood intervention is considered an essential part of public education. Nursery school, Head Start, and kindergarten are recognized as the starting point for planning the child-centered curriculum. A large group of prospective teachers may find that their interests lie with this age group; these persons will be further stimulated and encouraged to concentrate upon this major field of endeavor. However, the Early Childhood chapter will be useful to all students as it should assist in helping preservice teachers to gain a perspective of the total school program as well as to help set the stage for continued learning. Individual differences are considered through discussions of individualized learning programs. Continuous progress in such learning programs is dealt with through the strengths of the team form of instructional organization.

Part II of the book concentrates on the subject matter which makes up the curriculum. The language arts, science, social studies, and mathematics present the findings of major national curriculum projects and provide guides for considering curriculum change in the content fields with implications for *the emerging curriculum*. Individualized learning in each curriculum area is considered with appropriate guides for beginning teachers to move into this kind of teaching.

The *inquiry approach* is dealt with as it relates to science, mathematics, and the social sciences. Attention is given to concept-oriented programs which make use of the inquiry process since the authors believe these will emerge in schools in the years ahead.

Each curriculum area is described in such a way that the reader is more than simply introduced to a subject matter content. New issues and trends are considered in the light of current demands. Consistent with the philosophy of the book, discussions are aimed at explaining teaching goals, sequential experiences, and implications for more effective organizational practices of teaching children.

Part III focuses upon other problems and responsibilities confronting the classroom teacher. Reliable procedures in classroom control, guidance, and evaluation, including the reporting of pupil progress to parents, are set forth in practical ways.

Good teaching will not simply result because an emerging curriculum design is clearly defined and even present within a given school system. The authors have drawn upon their own experiences and research efforts to provide useful guides that demonstrate more efficient ways of working in the classroom. Each curriculum area is handled in such a way that realistic suggestions and understandings take on meaning. And with its definite grounding in theory, the book offers teachers consistent and sensible ideas and instructional practices as seen within the emerging curriculum design.

The authors wish to express their sincere appreciation to the many professors who have used the book in their undergraduate and graduate programs and who have made many suggestions for its revision. In addition, the comments which have come from students and practicing teachers who have used the book have been most encouraging.

The writers are indebted to Dr. Wilson F. Wetzler, Dean, Manatee Junior College, and co-author with A. H. Shuster in *Leadership in Ele-*

mentary School Administration and Supervision, for his many contributions and constructive criticisms for improving the manuscript. Indebtedness is also acknowledged to Dr. Robert G. Underhill, Assistant Professor of Education at Ohio University, for his contribution of the mathematics chapter. Gratitude should be expressed to the publishers and other organizations for permission to reproduce material and to quote from manuals and books, and to the many public school systems that permitted description and illustration of their procedures and materials.

To Mrs. Tate Baird for typing and assisting in editing the authors express their gratitude.

Photo Credits

Contents

The Emerging Elementary Curriculum

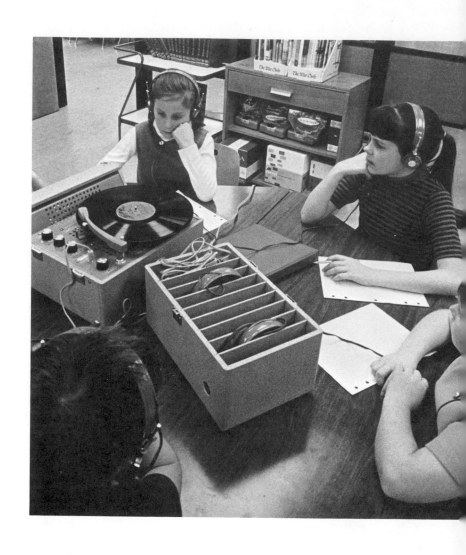

PART I

Bases for the
Emerging Curriculum

prologue to part I

Progress in the realms of technology and human behavior has presented numerous challenges to twentieth century society in the United States, and, indeed, throughout the world. The life conditions of the human being present new demands as a result of the advances which are being made along a broad front which extends from purely technological developments to those which involve new approaches to the study and guidance of human behavior.

Today the individual is confronted by the fact that man is encountering new environments in the vastness of space. The machines which have been produced by the imaginative science and the expert technology of the age have taken man into situations which challenge his potentialities for dealing with an array of environmental problems, both human and natural. Of a subtler nature, but with awesome implications, is the challenge of the age which demands that men seek new insights and understandings with respect to the nature and value of the individual in the increasingly complex social structures of the twentieth century.

It is against this background of change and challenge that those who work with the children and youth of a democratic society strive to provide the educational experiences which will most effectively prepare for the human conditions which exist today, and which are anticipated for the future.

Part One of *The Emerging Elementary Curriculum* provides the foundations whereby the student in professional education may move to an understanding of the many forces and factors, social, psychological, technological, and philosophical, which must be considered in any plan for the education of the children of a nation. In the first section of this book, the reader will become familiar with the concept of a dynamic approach to education, the emergent nature of curriculum. The growth and development characteristics of the children for whom the curriculum is created, as well as the nature of the learning process, are other important concerns of Part One. It is within the framework established in Part One that the balance of the emerging curriculum should be studied and assessed.

CHAPTER 1

The Emerging
Curriculum Design

INTRODUCTION

It has been said that each new generation looks upon its challenge as the most difficult and the most crucial ever to confront mankind. The citizen of the United States in the middle decades of the twentieth century is no exception, and his conception of the difficult tasks which face man is shared with equal, and perhaps greater, intensity by the professional educators of his time. If indeed the average citizen is anxious about his readiness and ability to live in an age of automation, space exploration, cultural crises, and conflicting world ideologies, what must be the anxieties of the teacher who is in great measure responsible for preparing children for life in this age?

In these years when rapid change has occurred in so many aspects of man's environment, how can the elementary school provide a foundation of learning experiences for boys and girls with any notion that this foundation will prove to be realistic ten or twenty years hence? There are many persons, both within and outside of the field of professional education, who are ready to propose plans and formulas for an educational program to do the job. In some instances, the recipe calls for a "return" to basic education, which implies that basic education has been long neglected. Other planners wish to introduce a more vigorous requirement of homework, a longer school day, a longer school year, and more subjects in the school program.

Yet others propose that the elementary school must radically revise its teaching materials and techniques. Programmed textbooks, teaching machines, tape recorders, and televised instruction are suggested as necessary features of a forward-looking program. On another front there is a call for reorganizing the teaching staff into teaching teams selected to do specialized jobs within the instructional program. Then there are the vast numbers of teachers and laymen who believe that the schools should continue with the present programs.

It is from the context of such issues that the curriculum emerges.

WHAT IS THE CURRICULUM?

The term curriculum has been defined variously, depending upon the view which is held concerning its content, purposes, and implementation. At the present time, curriculum is commonly defined by educators as all the learning experiences which are planned and sponsored by the school. Earlier definitions had suggested that the curriculum was the written plan of education for the school children, much like the course of study. Other definitions considered the curriculum to be comprised of the "academic" subjects of the school, thus excluding physical education, art, and other such learning areas.

Ragan has proposed that the curriculum comes into actual existence only in the experiences of children, and nowhere else.[1] According to this concept, it would follow that teachers, administrators, and children are always in a process of creating the curriculum. Until the responsibility for planning and implementing the educational program is borne by persons outside the school, it seems appropriate to accept the definition of curriculum as the learning experiences which are sponsored and guided by the school (regardless of locale, source of the experience, or the clock hour at which it occurs). Ragan's view is useful, also, to the extent that it emphasizes the experience and the internalization of the curriculum by the child. The use of both definitions provides a needed alternative to an older and short-sighted concept that the quality of the curriculum could be assessed by reading the courses of study and scrutinizing the teachers' lesson plans.

THE EMERGING CURRICULUM DESIGN

For as long as societies have aspired to provide formalized learning experiences for their young, there have been emerging curricula. The ever-changing conditions and situations of human existence have re-

---

[1] William B. Ragan, *Modern Elementary Curriculum* (New York: Holt, Rinehart & Winston, Inc., 1960), p. 4.

quired that man adapt, and his efforts at adaptation to social and physical realities have been expressed in these educational programs. Since
the curriculum emerges from the many forces within the social fabric at
any given time, its details vary extensively as it comes into being.

How Has the Curriculum Changed Over the Years?

The modern curriculum of the elementary school can be viewed in
terms of an historical perspective which mirrors the structure of a growing, changing society and the thinking of its people at various times.
Certainly no single summary can reveal every important aspect, but a
brief description of history's influence upon the curriculum will illustrate
how significant changes have taken place when the people have desired
new purposes and goals for the elementary school.

Changing in community life. Perhaps one of the most penetrating
approaches toward the understanding of curriculum design is the consideration of the changes that have taken place in community life. Four
periods of community development should furnish a framework for
viewing these changes in the goals of the elementary school.[2] The first
period emphasized the religious training of the child. During the Colonial
era, from 1647 to 1776, the children were required to attend the common schools that favored an authoritarian concept in the curriculum
and in educational practice. Within the limited confines of these developing colonies there were some variations from a basic "curriculum" reading, writing, spelling, some arithmetic and language, together with various religious subjects. Because children learned to read and understand
the Bible and their religion, or because the Southern aristocrat became
more polished and able to move confidently within his restricted circle,
the curriculum of the school had certain meaning. To understand the
narrow objectives for children during this first period is to know the
scope and breadth of the curriculum of the early colonial days, though
elementary schools were in existence before 1647.

The new nation that won its independence in America was composed of people who were convinced that literacy must be universal
if freedom is to be appreciated and maintained. Thus the second period
of community development expanded the design of the curriculum from
the narrow pattern of colonial days to the broader designs influenced
by political ideals. Whereas all children were to pursue learning with

---

[2] Adapted from William C. Reavis, Paul R. Pierce, Edward H. Stulken, and
Bertrand L. Smith, *Administering the Elementary School* (Englewood Cliffs, N. J.:
Prentice-Hall, Inc., 1953), pp. 3-5.

religious overtones, there was no mistaking the demands of this new emphasis on educating people for a newly-won freedom and independence. The curriculum did not vary widely from that of the classical emphasis given in the European schools, for people logically seek those "models" with which they are most familiar. A system of free public schools became a reality only after much opposition by some private and sectarian schools. As more children enrolled in the schools, subjects such as geography and history were added to the curriculum. It should be noted that in spite of the dominant philosophy that a curriculum must be designed to educate every child to live in a free society, there were many instances of neglect in adhering to this principle. That is to say, the bright children and the economically favored classes of people found it easier to take advantage of the educational program.

The third period of community development was characterized by a kind of Jacksonian democracy. People were moving westward to new homesteads and the territories, establishing communities and states. Many immigrants from foreign countries mingled with the shifting population movement to the west, and the dominant philosophy was that no one was bound by birth or name to an unchanging status or position in society. A person advanced and prospered according to his desires and abilities. Thus an education was a necessity if one were to take full advantage of one's opportunities. Even a higher education became a reality for more people as land grant colleges, state colleges, and universities came into being through the sponsorship of both state and federal governmental legislation. The increased emphasis upon higher education had at least two effects upon the curriculum of the elementary school. First, the increase in enrollment made larger demands upon the schools. Building facilities and teaching personnel were both inadequate, and both experienced many radical changes during this era as the needs for improved educational advantages were being met. Second, there was an apparent need to expand the offerings of the elementary school subjects. Thus between the years 1800 and 1900 at least thirteen subjects were commonly found in the elementary school program: arithmetic, language, spelling, history, civics, geography, nature study or science, art, music, literature, cooking, sewing, and manual training.[3] The schools were now regarded as allies in helping the individual to achieve his station in life, and the elementary level of education was a necessary part of the total pattern in preparing the person for the position he would like to attain. The curriculum design

---

[3] Henry J. Otto, "The Over-crowded Elementary School Curriculum," *Texas Outlook*, 28 (May, 1944), 40.

was changing because the people found new goals and objectives in life itself, and the schools were to assist them in achieving what they wanted and considered most important to their way of life.

The fourth period merged with the third in this sense: America was still expanding in its cities and in the growth of an industrialized society. These social and economic problems which were arising formed baffling situations and created a new emphasis upon personality, citizenship, and character development. The curriculum would need to be centered upon such problems that people considered meaningful and important. Perhaps the morality lessons for children were to be stated in practical terms. To be sure, the person needed improved skills and abilities to cope with the social problems of the changing society. Again, the struggle of the schools to meet these problems meant more changes on the elementary level.

What Are Some Implications of History for the Elementary School Curriculum?

It will be noted that many influences and changes in American culture have had some implications for the development of the elementary school and its curriculum. The public elementary school began to make even more radical changes in many ways during the period from 1870 to 1929, the year of the great Depression. Again, pupil enrollments, new subjects, pupil expenditures, and length of school terms were materially increased and lengthened. The teachers and administrative staff personnel were now considered more as professional career persons. By the start of the Civil War normal schools were in existence in every older, established state in the Union. Even if certification requirements insured little or no professional training,[4] the curriculum for teacher education was being expanded to include special methods courses, curriculum work, psychology courses concerned with educational practices and child development, educational measurement, history and philosophy of education, and even apprentice teaching. The increased emphasis upon the preparation of teachers paved the way for improvements in the use of tests, the evaluation of individual progress, and work with the individual child. As the demands and needs of society helped to alter the structure of the elementary school, it soon became evident that reforms were needed in school practices and curricular designs.

---

[4] Ross L. Finney, *The American Public School* (New York: The Macmillan Co., 1921), p. 165.

The elementary schools before 1930 were unique in several respects. For one, the break with the classical approach, as evidenced in the European concept of education, had never been made completely. In many instances the formalized and regimented programs in America were poor duplications of those in Europe. Children were often encouraged to continue their schooling only when they showed promise of scholarship, and the less gifted found no curriculum organized to meet their interests and needs. In addition, the pressure from the high schools upon the elementary schools supported the theory that a curriculum design must promote and foster basic skills and facts before admittance was given to the high school. The colleges were increasingly placing similar demands upon the high schools for adequate preparation to an institution of higher learning.

It is interesting to note that the faculty psychology theory strengthened the emphasis on drill and repetition as a means of educating the child satisfactorily. School personnel were fascinated with the idea that they could put children into an "assembly line" procedure and turn out a more finished product. Thus the elementary school curriculum was conceived as a series of subjects that were too much concerned with the skills and knowledge to be learned and neglected to help children acquire desirable behavior skills in terms of social, creative, and personal factors. Of course educators such as Dewey, Kilpatrick, Horn and others were leading the way by emphasizing the importance of developing the child who had good work habits, initiative for self direction, and proper attitudes about himself and others. These men were ahead of the educational practice of their time, but the curriculum of the elementary school was still due for another more radical change after the 1930's.

The period since the stock market collapse in 1929 has had perhaps as much to do with changing the life of the American people as any previous era. The depressed economic conditions brought into being the realistic fact that people can be in want even when wealth from land, raw materials, and productivity lie within quick if not easy grasp. Even as social, political, and economic institutions were beginning to modify their machinery and purposes, the public schools began a reorganization of curriculum to meet the demands of an ever changing society. In the past, schools had emphasized that education could better equip a person to meet competition and to advance himself. Now a new framework was needed to insure all people that a greater degree of economic security would practically be guaranteed. Thus the curriculum of the elementary school broadened its base to embrace certain principles that are social and psychological in nature and led the child to solve actual problems within a desired framework. A few changes within the elementary school curriculum may be stated in the following terms and illustrate some current trends:

1. The separate school subject matter areas are more directly related to those actual problems of life outside of the school. As a matter of fact, there are generally some six broad areas of instruction instead of at least twenty separate subjects: the language arts, science, arithmetic, social studies, arts and crafts, and health and physical education.

2. The unit of work that has little regard for subject matter lines is being favored as a means of carrying out learning experiences over a period of time. The dull, wearisome recitation and drill of repetitive work have not captured the interest of the pupil, nor has there been any provision for pupil participation and variety within such a rigid framework.

3. The problems of promotion, grade standards, evaluation and the like are receiving attention. If the curriculum design is to be consistent, it should be clear that an increased emphasis is required that will consider all the needs and characteristics of the child. That is, a curriculum is not simply designed for the child, but each child is first considered in terms of his level of maturity and achievement and how work may be planned according to his interests and abilities.

4. Teachers and administrators are receiving better professional training, more intensive work orientation, and increased in-service aid and instruction. The elementary teacher is not penalized with respect to salary, prestige, or professional benefits. In short, the curriculum for the elementary school has evolved from many professional sources and signifies the need for a high type of person to carry out its objectives.

5. Inspite of recent attacks upon the public school by those who believe that the elementary curriculum is designed merely to provide basic skills and facts, the work of the child- and social-centered educators has had a powerful implication for curriculum practices. The child is the focus of learning; he is also living his school experiences within a socially oriented and directed framework. The teacher has learned to rely upon the psychological principles of learning that encourage group participation in problem solving as well as more individual participation according to interests and abilities. It should be noted that the attacks upon education and the ever recurring attempts to bring the curriculum back to traditional practices of emphasizing only the three R's are nothing new on the educational scene. Undoubtedly whenever people are adequately

informed about their school program their communities will be immune from the professional critic as such.

In summary, the curriculum of the elementary school has developed slowly in relation to the goals of society and the institution itself. The four periods of community development mentioned in the foregoing discussion point out the changing emphasis placed upon the elementary school and have had certain implications for the curriculum, school, and administrative practices. Apparently, only when the people themselves felt a need for changes in educative practices were efforts made to give new or different directions within the program itself. Chart I summarizes the phases of curriculum development since 1647 and also presents the modern elementary school's attempt to reconcile certain differences and criticisms made about its educational program.

What Is the Emerging Curriculum?

It was pointed out in the preceding sections that plans for the education of a society's children and youth have always been emergent in nature, with a large scheme observable from classroom to classroom, from village to village, from province to province. The crucial level of emergence of the specifics within the design of the educational plan, or curriculum, is represented by teacher and pupil, and the educative experiences emerge as unique to the individual.

Considered in a rather analytic fashion, it may be said that the program of educational experiences finds its beginnings in the ideals and values of its society, its roots deeply imbedded in the history of its culture, and its pressures and directions drawn from the sociological conditions of the time in which it exists. It is obliged to be concerned with the nature of the organism for whom it is provided, the human being. These sources are presented in Chart II, together with the levels at which the factors appear that serve to shape and direct the curriculum.

Examples of the emerging nature of the curriculum may be drawn from any of the sources which stimulate, direct, and control human effort. The accomplishment of rapid air transportation has made its impact upon the social learnings of children, and has had its effect upon the socioscientific complex of modern life. Another great impact upon the curriculum resulted from the Sputnik breakthrough of the Soviets in 1957, an impact which was felt at the international and national levels. National goals of the United States were affected, and the concern became a contagion among laymen and professional educators alike.

In recent years the growing problems of the poor, the alienation of minority ethnic groups, and the failure of school experiences to bring many young people into the mainstream of American society have given rise to many special efforts at national, state, and local levels. Job Corps, Teacher Corps, Head Start, and Upward Bound are but a few examples of programs which have operated outside of the typical curriculum. Why might you expect that these problems and programs will eventually effect the emerging curriculum?

The interpretation which one finally makes at the local school level and the resulting action or inaction is an example of yet another phase of the emerging curriculum design. Many schools in the United States have interpreted the rapid development of science and technology in the Soviet Union as a challenge to the programs in science which are provided in American schools. As a result of such an interpretation (one which various officials at the national level have vigorously asserted), many schools have taken action to improve and extend the science and mathematics opportunities for children. In other communities where the political and sociological orientation is isolationist or otherwise provincial, the schools will have taken either a different course of action or no action at all. Thus the rural community schools may interpret the issues and demands which arise in a light different from that of the city or urban groups.

The shape and direction of the schools' curricula are constantly developing, cast in a mold which reflects the greater forces of the human situation, world-wide and nation-wide. This mold leaves much room for local innovation, for creation of unique teaching situations and the individual learning experiences of each child. There are seemingly overpowering forces of international crisis and national interest which press into the curriculum design; but those forces which arise from the sociology of the community, from the philosophy of the teacher, and from the nature and needs of the child—forces that appear mild by contrast—are near the point and moment of the educational process. They are vital to emerging curriculum design.

Why Is the Concept of Emergence Important?

A great deal has been said here concerning the proposition that the curriculum is a dynamic, evolving, emerging plan for the education of children, and the reader may aptly observe that this is no more than a statement of fact. The careful student of education in any society would soon confirm the realism and the naturalness of the emerging plans for

CHART 1[5]

Three Hundred Years of Community and Curriculum Development

Period	Colonial—1647	National—1776	Jacksonian—1800's	Modern—1900's
Purpose of Education	Religious instruction	Appreciate political freedom	Personal and economic advancement	Social appreciations
Content of Curriculum	Reading, writing, spelling, arithmetic, related religious subjects.	Reading, writing, spelling, arithmetic, physiology, hygiene, grammar, history, geography, drawing, music, agriculture, deportment	Reading, writing, spelling, arithmetic, physiology, hygiene, English, grammar, language, history, Constitution of the U.S., geography, music, arts and crafts, citizenship, manual training, homemaking, civics, physical education, nature study, literature, deportment	Language arts, social studies, arithmetic, science, arts, crafts, health, physical education.
Administrative Organization	Ungraded	Ungraded	Graded, departmental, platoon	Graded, some grade divisions disappearing, ungraded primaries, team teaching
Types of Schools	Dame schools, apprentice schools, reading and writing schools, ciphering schools	Kindergartens, 8 year elementary schools	Nursery schools, kindergartens, 8 year elementary schools	6 and 8 year elementary schools with primary, intermediate, and upper elementary divisions

Methods of Instruction	Emphasis on individual memorization	Monitorial group instruction	Recitation, supervised study, units and project method (individual and group)	Recitation, experience units, group committees
Organization of the Curriculum	Separate subjects	Separate subjects	Separate subjects, correlation, fusion	Separate subjects, correlation, fusion, integration
Teacher Preparation	None	Normal schools	Teachers colleges, schools of education, in-service education	Expanding departments and schools of education, experimentation in functional types of teacher education preparation
Control of Curriculum	Local	Local, state	State departments of education, national committees	National committees, state committees, local committees
Materials of Instruction	Hornbook, New England primer	Ungraded textbooks	State adopted texts for separate subjects	Multiple adopted texts, libraries, audio visual, varied community resources, teaching machines, programmed learning materials.

---

5 Adapted with modifications from William B. Ragan, *Modern Elementary Curriculum* (New York: Henry Holt & Co., 1960), pp. 16-17.

CHART II

The Emerging Curriculum Design

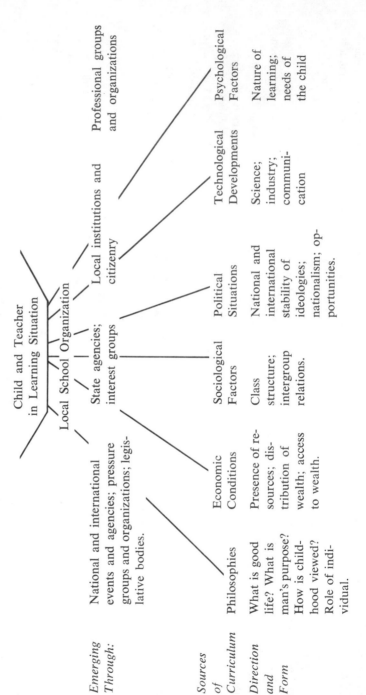

education. Why, then, is it so important to elaborate upon what may be obvious to many persons?

In the first place, it is not easy for parents and teachers in any community to maintain a broad outlook of the sources and forces that shape the curriculum unless there is a point of view which contains the concept of emergence. It is too easy to see the school program as beginning and ending in the local district. The constantly changing situations in the greater national and world community may seem remote to the educator who fails to consider the relationships which prevail between cultural groups, nations, and individuals in an age of aero-space travel.

Another requisite in curriculum planning and implementation is that of seeing the changing nature of human events over a period of time. The inclination to accept a curriculum scheme as "basic" and, therefore, of timeless worth, is to be deceived by an inability to think beyond the present. This necessity for a sharp perspective may be illustrated by calling attention to one of the gross differences in the psychological environment of youngsters in the 1960's compared to their environment in the early 1940's. Youngsters today know that they live in a tentative condition in view of the possibilities of national destruction by use of atomic weapons: they feel the threat at their very doorstep rather than at the coastline of the nation. How have the needs of children changed as a result of the developments in modern warfare? Is the teacher sensitive to this as a factor to be considered as she works with children? Does this have implications for the schools' approach to mental health?

Probably the most important need is to understand the crucial roles played by principals, supervisors, and teachers, for the curriculum design emerges *through* people as well as from events, values, and needs. When the dynamic nature of curriculum is understood, it is apparent that the teacher's role is important not only as one involving methodology, but (equally important) as one including the selection of learning experiences within the broader framework of the total school plan. The school principals and supervisors who regard the curriculum as relatively fixed are serving to confuse the role of the teacher. It is essential that teachers be concerned with and involved in the broader aspects of curriculum planning if the curriculum created at the classroom level is to incorporate adequately the implications and objectives of a broadly conceived plan.

Is an Emerging Curriculum a Planned Curriculum?

It is unthinkable that the educational experiences of children should, in any situation, be unplanned. The most inept teacher must give thought to her work with children. Alternative courses of action which are available many times each day in every classroom make planning imperative, crude though it may be.

In another sense, it may be thought that an emerging curriculum is composed of incidental learning situations that arise from mere impulse. This is not the case, as one may see from the information provided in Figure I. Thoughtful planning is essential when the emerging nature of the curriculum is understood by the teachers, administrators, and others who are concerned with the details of the design and who finally implement it through the learning experiences of boys and girls.

By nature of its content and function the curriculum is dynamic and emerging, and continuous attention must be given to it. The curriculum in which planning is neglected may depend too much upon history and tradition as sources of its content, though a single focus upon the immediate needs of children may result in a neglect of urgent sociological factors. A case in point may very well be the continuation of elaborate programs in agriculture instruction in farming communities where fewer than 20 per cent of the students go on to become farmers. What was, in 1920, a recognition of a need to prepare youth for efficient farming has become in the 1970's a traditional aspect of the curriculum. The sociological and economic factors of the latter decades of this century may be unrecognized or disregarded in school programs where planning and evaluation is not broad and continuous.

Regardless of the quality of the educational planning, the curriculum exists as an emerging design. However, as we can see from the example just cited, the design may be imbalanced or outdated because of the neglect of one or more of the sources from which the curriculum emerges. Were it not for the vitality of the teaching-learning experience itself, and if the philosophical, sociological, psychological, and historical factors were not subject to change and revised interpretation, then indeed the curriculum could be planned to serve for years ahead. The complexities of life conditions are not fixed, however, and the educational plans for the youth of a nation will continue to emerge in many dimensions from basic sources, and these plans will require careful formulation and modification in an on-going process.

Recently emerging forces. One of the more difficult challenges to educators is to be sensitive to the emerging problems and needs of the society so that school programs may be modified accordingly. As the reader must realize from his own study of history, it is fairly safe and comfortable to study a problem a century or two after it has been resolved through conflict, compromise, and action. Modern educators may benefit from the experiences of the past, but they cannot wait fifty years to move on the problems of today.

FIGURE 1

An Emerging Force: From Source to Child

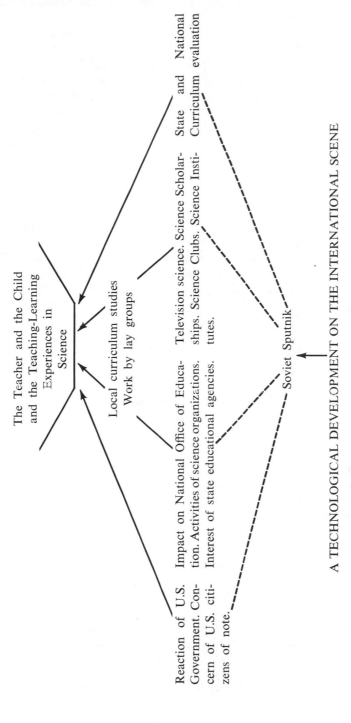

A TECHNOLOGICAL DEVELOPMENT ON THE INTERNATIONAL SCENE

Since 1960, there has been a growing concern for the problems presented by those youth who are called "disadvantaged." Considerable effort has gone into the analysis of the many facets of disadvantagement in our society and shows that the dimensions of the problem include economic deprivation, isolation and alienation from the larger society, and educational deficiency, to name but a few. How have these problems manifested themselves in our schools and society? Why have they emerged to the level of national concern only in the past few years?

Another factor has been the work of behaviorist psychologists, such as B. F. Skinner, who has had an impact upon the planning and the materials used in learning situations. The teaching machines and programmed materials have emerged in response to the belief that certain human learnings are subject to conditioning and reinforcement and that these experiences can be quite structured and highly routinized. The recent concern for observable behavioral outcomes as vital parts of the educational program may have been influenced by the behaviorists. There has been a growing conviction among many educators that the schools must be able to provide visible evidence of changed pupil behavior if the public is to believe that education in fact improves the person. It may no longer be enough for a teacher to tell Johnny's parents that she "believes" he is doing better in reading or science. What observable evidence does she have?

Forces that affect curriculum move on a broken front. For example, technology and government funds provided some schools with sophisticated equipment long before the teaching staffs were prepared to use them wisely. Some teachers will use films and projectors because they have them, although the curriculum may be largely stagnant. Is it likely that the products of our technology stimulate curriculum change?

Harold Taylor, former president of Sarah Lawrence College, has been critical of American educators for their failure to be at the front of the changing political and social scene. In essence, Taylor argues that the educators join the battle long after the issue is settled and they know which side has won. If this criticism is accurate, what reasons do you believe lie behind the educational lag? Do problems have to become very obvious and severe before the curriculum can be modified in response to the problem? In the chapter "Emerging Programs in Social Science Education," we will consider this area of study further. In any event, it is a problem that confronts the educator in all aspects of his effort to plan *relevant* experiences for boys and girls in a changing world.

What Are the Purposes of the Emerging Curriculum?

The objectives of education in the United States have been set forth in numerous statements ranging from the Seven Cardinal Principles

(1918), to the objectives enunciated by the Educational Policies Commission (1938), and to the recent statements of the Yale-Fairfield Study (1956). Broadly conceived, the objectives here included self-realization, human relationships, economic efficiency, and civic responsibility.[6] In detail, the objectives have included physical health, mental and emotional health, communication, quantitative understandings, social relationships, understanding the social environment, moral and spiritual values, understanding the physical world, critical thinking, and aesthetic and creative development.[7]

The curriculum design which is emerging in the 1960's and 70's will recognize as its major educational objective the guidance of children and youth toward *becoming effective in the process through which they seek to understand the social and physical environment of the human condition, and wherein they relate themselves to the human enterprise.* This is an age when man's traditional concepts of his universe and his relation to it are being changed by the impelling forces of aero-space exploration; when his function as a worker and producer is challenged by the advent of automation; and when his long-standing cultural and social images are being rapidly antiquated by the impact of necessary social contacts. So it is essential that the people of a democracy conceive the role of education as one in which the individual is encouraged, guided, and sustained as he seeks to understand and relate to the human conditions of his age. All other objectives must support this larger objective if education is to serve mankind honestly and adequately in the latter decades of this century. The curriculum must accommodate the process.

In the final analysis, it may be seen that the significant differences between the hopes and ideals of the totalitarian society and the democratic society must be reflected in the ultimate objectives which are held as well as in the means by which these objectives are attained. Cast in this light, the objectives which pertain to economic efficiency, civic competence, human relationships and self-realization are quite as much desired in the Soviet society as in the United States. The cliché, *Democracy is a way of life* is something of a truism. Communism, also, is a way of life. So are Fascism and all other political and social ideologies. The curriculum obtains its basic direction from a philosophy which asserts that *democracy is a good way of life for man because in it the quest by the individual for self-value and social value is encouraged and sustained.* The curriculum provides early opportunities wherein the child may start this quest.

---

[6] Educational Policies Commission, *The Purposes of Education in American Democracy* (Washington, D.C.: N.E.A., 1938).

[7] C. M. Hill *et al.*, *Yale-Fairfield Study of Elementary Teaching* (New Haven: Yale University, 1956), Chapter 6.

The purposes set forth in these several statements are general and inclusive. The determination of immediate and intermediate goals within the statements of broad purposes is, of course, additional evidence that forces and directions for curriculum appear at various levels. Inevitably, the critical level of decision and action is found to be in the local school system and in the individual classroom.

When the curriculum design is recognized as being unique in each school community, the teachers, principals, supervisors, and laymen will encounter the need to specify the purposes they envision for their school programs. The general statement of objective which pertains to critical thinking, for example, will not be functional unless and until it is translated into specific learning experiences and behavior characteristics. In situations where the emerging nature of the curriculum is unrecognized or neglected, general statements of purposes for education are adopted and forgotten. Somehow, it is assumed that the adoption of a set of objectives which has been formulated by a competent committee is tantamount to implementation. Although general statements of objectives are valuable for providing a commonly shared frame of reference for curriculum planning, the community and its educators must build their own plan.

The teacher's role.   The classroom teacher must implement the plan through opportunities for learning. She may be regarded as working with boys and girls at the crucial point of "educational contact," the point at which the curriculum comes into being in the experiences of children. When the curriculum is looked upon as being an emerging plan which comes to reality in the individual lives of boys and girls, then the role of the teacher is recognized as being extremely crucial. The days when the paternalistic administrator "produced" a curriculum and ordered the teachers to "teach it" become more and more remote as the teacher is seen to be at the vital point of creation of opportunity rather than in the position of duplication and imitation.

Reference was made previously regarding the forces and sources of curriculum which are relatively removed from the learning situations in the classroom. For example, take the plea from military leaders for more emphasis on loyalty and duty to country. However valid and persistent such a plea may be, it is not in close proximity to the situation where teaching and learning occur. The teacher, in the most influential and *affective* position, may or may not translate valid suggestions into action.

It is nothing new to state that the teacher is a key person in the educational scheme of things, but the usual reason given is not sufficient. As a presenter of information, a custodian of children, and a grade giver, the teacher is replaceable by teaching machines, by educational television, by parent monitors, by standardized tests and computing machines. An emerging curriculum design includes the pupils as a group, and as individuals to be recognized and accounted for in selecting and adapting learning opportunities for pupils. Learning situations do not emerge from presentations alone, nor can they be adequately evaluated by tests and computers. Interaction between children and teachers, integration and reaction by children, behavior modification—all are components in the teaching-learning environment. In the emerging curriculum design the able teacher is not a replaceable element.

What Is a Balanced Curriculum?

Much has been said and written concerning a balanced program of learning experiences for children and youth. To some persons this has meant that school time would be allocated for instruction in the several areas of the curriculum to the end that no area would be overemphasized and no area neglected.

To other educators a balanced curriculum was one which attempted to complement the form and direction of informal learning opportunities in the community by providing a "rounded out" program. Thus, in deprived urban areas there have been provided out-of-doors activities in camping and nature study in an effort to provide a balance which was needed in a particular locality by certain children.

At this point it is understood that balance may be approached from a content centered view or from a child-need centered view, and it should be noted that many schools attempt to encompass both views in their program.

Balance in an emerging design. In a curriculum that is recognized to be emerging in design (and all curriculum designs are in fact emerging), balance may be viewed by looking first at the sources of curriculum. It is from these sources that direction, purpose, and form are created in the school program.

In achieving a balanced curriculum, satisfactory answers to these appropriate questions should be sought:

1. Do our purposes and objectives reflect the beliefs which are contained in our philosophy of education in a democracy?

2. Is sufficient attention given to those aspects of education which contain traditional values of education?

3. Are the events and information of the aero-space age studied and assessed in terms of their implications for educational planning?

4. Has the local community been considered with respect to the opportunities it provides, to the needs that it has, to the values and goals it represents?

5. Has the individual been considered to the extent that there is the room and freedom within which his needs and capabilities can be accommodated?

As groups of teachers, parents and principals work together on the school's program they will doubtless raise other questions. In no instance should the five questions posed here be omitted.

There are today school programs in which the desires of the local community have been so strongly emphasized in the school program that the individual pupil has been subjugated to the position of a cog in the community's educational machine. Examples of this may be found in highly industrialized areas where far too few able youth proceed to college and far too many leave technical schools to enter the factories where their fathers work. In other economically favored neighborhoods the individual pupil may be forced into status-seeking experiences when mothers and fathers demand foreign language instruction without a soundly developed philosophy as to its values for children.

Balance in the curriculum is a goal. Balance in the curriculum is never attained; it is always a goal. This is an essential fact in any curriculum plan, but it may not be recognized by many persons who do not view the curriculum as highly dynamic and ever-emerging. Again, the point of view from which the educator looks at curriculum makes the difference at the point of educational contact. As an example, the writer worked with a kindergarten teacher who always introduced the five-year-olds to painting with tempera at the beginning of the second semester, never earlier. This she did because the kindergarten "guide" which had been developed some years before had made this suggestion. To introduce tempera in first semester would throw the program out of balance, the teacher reasoned. The children who came to this teacher each year were really not considered as factors to be reckoned with in providing balance.

More and more the contemporary educator looks upon curriculum as alive, growing, and changing. The thoughtful teacher is aware of the world in which her pupils live today and anticipates the world in which they will live tomorrow. She views her responsibility to pursue balance as one that is most nearly fulfilled when *each child is pursuing balance* in terms of his needs, interests, and abilities. This the child can most readily do when the educational opportunities that are offered are intended as the means to balanced growth.

In the emerging curriculum design the opportunities for balance of educational experience do not preclude the possibility that a child may develop deep and specific interests. In fact, the child may find himself thwarted if his attempts to pursue desirable interests are denied. Balance in the emerging curriculum design suggests, however, that the skills and information which each youngster needs to serve as the "yeast buds" for his continued education are not neglected. The point here, however, is that the goal of balance is not well served when the challenge inherent in highly individual learning interests are omitted.

How Does the Teacher Face Conflicting Views in an Emerging Curriculum?

The teacher who recognizes the emerging nature of the curriculum is aware of the many conflicting forces that must be considered in planning and implementing the educational program. A number of examples have been mentioned to illustrate the sources from which the curriculum emerges and it should be readily understood that, although there may be agreement as to the major purposes of education in a democracy, the means to that end are often disagreed upon.

Those educators who believe that the objectives of education are most efficiently realized through the child's study and mastery of various *subjects* may be regarded as *subject-centered* in their choice of the means whereby they hope to gain the *end*.

Other educators believe that the child must be given first consideration in terms of the *needs* which he must strive to satisfy if he is to live successfully as a child, and ultimately as an adult.[8] These educators are identified as holding a *child centered* approach to education with the information and skills of various subject fields being used to help meet the apparent needs of the children.

Yet other educators would look at life situations of the people in this society and attempt to identify the recurring demands which life places upon people; hence their curriculum would be planned to prepare children to cope successfully as children and as adults with such *recurring life demands.*[9] The emphasis here may be upon meeting the demands which are made within the *social environment* of the individual, or they may be regarded as mainly psychological needs which the individual must strive to satisfy if he is to be valuable to himself and to others.

Conflicting points of view may then arise in differences of philosophy held regarding education: (1) differences in the interpretation of the current social and political implications for education; (2) differences in

---

[8] See Robert J. Havighurst, *Development Tasks and Education* (New York: Longmans, Green & Co., Inc., 1952), for discussion of this approach.

[9] For discussion of this view of curriculum see Florence Stretemeyer *et al.*, *Developing A Curriculum for Modern Living* (New York: Bureau of Publications, Teachers College, Columbia University, 1947).

beliefs concerning the nature of children with respect to their needs, abilities, and potentials; and (3) differences concerning the best ways to attain the goals sought.

So it may be seen that differences are to be expected when curriculum is viewed as an emerging design within which the child will finally create the educational experience. This serves to emphasize the role of the teacher as one who must be acquainted with the various points of view regarding the purposes and nature of education; the means and methods of education; the role of the individual child in the process; and, indeed, the responsibilities of the teacher. In the final analysis, the classroom teacher will make vital choices concerning learning opportunities, learning environment, and evaluation of the learning process and product. Her own ideas and procedures will be in a state of development and emergence in the educational program. The scope of her outlook will be broad and tentative in the emerging curriculum, and only her commitment to the greatest possible development of individual human potentiality will remain absolute.

Why Should Curriculum Be Studied?

The student may ask why it is that the curriculum should be studied at all. Would not a separate consideration of the several areas of the elementary school program be sufficient? Curriculum study is important to the extent that it offers a total view of the foundations, developments, and problems which are involved in planning and producing the educational experiences in the school. It is largely through a study of curriculum that the sources and forces that shape and direct it are seen, and considerations of balance and emphasis are brought more sharply into focus.

Through the study of curriculum the teacher will come to realize her key position not only as a teacher of seemingly separate skills and topics, but as one who is in a central position where society's scheme for human fulfillment is translated into learning experiences for boys and girls.

A PREVIEW

In the chapters which follow, the specific areas of content and skill development will be discussed as related parts of the whole emerging curriculum. As the reader becomes acquainted with various problems which are common to reading instruction, he will appreciate the sources from which factors that must be considered in the reading program arise: the high value which society accords to the reading process, the nature and needs of the child, and the more immediate impact of parents and community values as they are reflected in the efforts of the child as he seeks to become a mature reader.

At no point in the chapters which follow is it intended that the concept of the emerging curriculum be neglected or overshadowed. As the effective approaches to evaluation and guidance of children are presented, it is desired that the reader view them as points of progress which have been made in many schools, goals yet to be realized in still other schools, and in all instances that they be regarded as suggestive of greater opportunities to be explored and provided to children and youth.

Teachers must work within the framework of what is presently conceived to be adequate information concerning child growth and learning. Materials of instruction and methods of teaching which promise the best outcomes must be used today, to be sure. All of this is necessary if education is to be active at all, but none of this detracts from the emerging nature of the curriculum as it comes into creation in each community, each classroom, and each child with the guidance of perceptive teachers. Regard the discussions which follow as providing the large background within which will be created the learning plans and experiences of pupils across the land.

SUMMARY

The curriculum of the elementary school has been viewed and discussed as more than a plan or a prescribed set of experiences whereby the children of the United States will become educated. Curriculum has been examined here as a dynamic complex which comes into existence in the opportunities for learning which are created and realized in the many communities and classrooms throughout this nation.

Traditions, social values, economic factors, international situations, the nature and needs of the young human being—all contribute to the curriculum as it "emerges" through the people, lay and professional, who react to and interpret the forces that serve to create and direct it.

From a historical position, it has been shown that the bolder outlines of the curriculum design have emerged in ever changing patterns since the beginning of this nation's attempts to educate its children. The more subtle elements which emerge to give the curriculum its unique design have their sources in the more immediate elements of society such as the developments in technology, in evolving social relationships, in community interests and needs, and in the numerous individual characteristics of teacher and child. The sources are historical, philosophical, psychological, and sociological in nature. The emerging design is variable and complex within a general framework of unity across the nation.

The teacher who views curriculum as an emerging educational experience will, of necessity, see her role as being much more vital, much more involved, and certainly more demanding of her creativity and perception than if she were to view the curriculum as a "fixed" plan for education of children.

SUGGESTED ACTIVITIES

1. Request the students to obtain from various references three or four definitions of curriculum, and ask them to identify the major points of difference when compared to the "emerging curriculum" concept.

2. Discuss the school curriculum with which most of the students are familiar, due to their own experiences, in terms of how it reflects the influences of local community values, current economic situations, and traditional content.

3. Plan with the class for visitation and observation in several elementary classrooms. Suggest that they attempt to identify those aspects of the teaching-learning environment which were quite different from room to room. Such an activity should help students become sensitive to the emerging nature of the program as it is influenced by various groups of pupils and teachers.

4. Invite, at different times, persons from outside the school to talk with your class in an informal manner concerning their views of what education should do for children. (Don't invite only professional people or community leaders.)

5. Read the references listed below that were written in the middle 1950's. Have the changes predicted then become realities yet? What problems and changes does your class expect in the decade ahead?

SELECTED READINGS

Beck, R. H., W. W. Cook and N. C. Kearney. *Curriculum in the Modern Elementary School.* Englewood Cliffs, N. J.: Prentice-Hall, Inc., 1960, Chapter I.

Bruner, Jerome. *The Process of Education.* Cambridge, Mass.: Harvard University Press, 1960.

Chase, F. S. "The Changes Ahead for our Schools," *School Review,* 65 (March, 1957), 3-11.

Eddy, L. K. "The American School and Its Social Context," *Educational Leadership,* 14 (April, 1957), 413-17.

Enlaw, R. "Organizing Schools for the Future," *Educational Leadership*, 14 (February, 1957), 288-92.

Fawcett, H. P. "Curricular Values of the Future," *Progressive Education*, 33 (January, 1956), 1-4.

Getzels, J. W. "Changing Values Challenge the Schools," *School Review*, 65 (March, 1957), 92-102.

Gordon, J. W. "Individual Growth: The Basis for Curriculum Planning," *Instructor*, 66 (December, 1956), 16.

Hauser, P. M. "The Implications of Social Change for Public Schools," *American School Board Journal*, 33 (September, 1956), 82.

Larsen, R. E. and H. Toy, Jr. "The Forces Affecting Curriculum Improvements," *National Council of Social Studies Yearbook*, 1955, pp. 5-15.

Mayer, Frederick. *A History of Educational Thought.* 2nd ed., Columbus, Ohio: Charles E. Merrill Publishing Co., 1966, Chapters I and II.

MacLean, M. S. and D. W. Dodson. "Educational Needs Emerging from the Changing Demands of Society," *National Society for the Study of Education*, Part I, 1956, pp. 11-40.

Phenix, Philip H. *Realms of Meaning.* New York: McGraw-Hill Book Company, 1964.

CHAPTER 2

Focus On Child Development

INTRODUCTION

Understanding the child is a prime requisite in arranging the kinds of learning situations that will enhance pupil progress. Many teachers are keenly aware of their role in planning meaningful experiences that are based upon their knowledge of children, although there is evidence that they admit they do not know enough about children.[1] In fact, teacher morale, quality of instruction, and rate of teacher turn-over are definite problems that can be traced in part to poor understandings about the elementary child. Then teachers may well ask such questions as: In what ways do children grow and develop? What behavior can be generally expected at various age levels? What can the teacher do with the knowledge he possesses about the child in the classroom? Since some beginning teachers have reported that they are not completely satisfied with certain unrealistic courses in college, perhaps more practical principles of understanding children are needed, as well as the development of a philosophy "concerning the nature and meaning of infancy and childhood."[2]

Professional competence in the classroom is required if teachers are to meet individual needs, since the amazing uniqueness of each child demands the acquisition of knowledge of his growth and development. Parents are also growing in their awareness of these problems. In any process of curriculum construction the focus must be on the nature of the individual learner and on the learning process, not simply on teaching methods or content.[3]

The teacher faces may difficulties in arriving at a set of workable principles, since there are often misunderstandings and different interpre-

---

[1] Albert H. Shuster, "A Study of the Advantages and Disadvantages of the Collegiate Certificate in Virginia" (unpublished doctor's dissertation, University of Virginia, Charlottesville, Virginia, 1955).

[2] Arnold Gesell and Frances L. Ilg, *Child Development*, Part I (New York: Harper and Brothers, 1949), p. 288.

[3] J. Weber, "Childhood Development Implications for Curriculum Building," *Educational Leadership*, 2 (March, 1954), 343-46.

tations of recognized generalizations and principles. Research in some areas may also be lacking. In addition, it is easy for the time-pressed teacher to fail to see the implications of much that is read, especially if there is a fuzzy concept of the goals desirable in gaining understandings of the child. Thus it may be that teacher preparation is such that "mistaken interpretations of children's motivations and needs are constantly being made."[4] The teacher must also work with the principal, who represents the school system, and with parents, who represent the community. A diversity of their philosophies and demands often hampers the meeting of the child's needs. Considering other factors—large classes, inadequate space, poor preparation in teacher education—the instructor may find that understanding the child is indeed a difficult task.

Teachers need a point of view in their organization of the learning situation, since there is further evidence that certain common practices found in the elementary school may interfere with the normal development of personality.[5] This chapter is concerned with furnishing a practical and realistic approach to that unique, living organism—the child. The following topics are considered in detail: (1) the physical and social factors in understanding the child, (2) the psychodynamic factors in child development, (3) ways of working with the child from the developmental point of view.

Since the knowledge of children required by teachers and parents is so vast, and the skills in securing and interpreting data so complex, emphasis here is confined to the kindergarten, primary, and elementary school child. Much valuable and interesting information concerning the pre-school child, as well as the more complete details generally found in textbooks on child and adolescent psychology must be omitted. This chapter deals with those developmental aspects that should be useful and practical to the elementary school teacher. The following illustration serves to point up the scope of understandings needed by the teacher as it suggests how varied and complex the problems are.

This is the story of a classroom episode that could and does happen in just about the same way in numerous classrooms throughout the country: As Miss Cooper calls upon Jane to react to a question, she is disturbed (again) by Johnny who interrupts the session with his version of the answer that is completely off the subject and contrary to the class

---

[4] Daniel A. Prescott, *The Child in the Educational Process* (New York: McGraw-Hill Book Company, Inc., 1957), p. 9.

[5] Helen Heffernan *et al.*, "The Organization of the Elementary School and the Development of a Healthy Personality," *California Journal of Elementary Education*, 20 (February, 1952), 129-53.

practice of breaking in upon another person's right to speak. The teacher is forced to deal with Johnny in the usual squelching way, but she is also becoming more aware that he must first be understood. She may ask the following questions to guide her thinking concerning his behavior to find out why he acts as he does:

1. Is he entering early adolescence? Could he be calling attention, as it were, to his growth?

2. Does he possess a high energy level or output?

3. Are major physical changes taking place, causing difficulty in accepting such changes?

4. Is there a lack of good interpersonal relationships with his family?

5. Is he competing? With his family?

6. Is he seeking a better interpersonal relationship with his family?

7. Does he have low status with his group? Is he striking back in the only way he knows?

8. Is this the beginning of an interest in the boy-girl relationship?

9. Does he come from a cultural pattern that encourages this kind of behavior?

10. Is the school expecting too much from him? Confusing him? Does he feel academically inferior? Bored?

11. Does his behavior suggest that this might be language experimentation?

12. Does he have an adequate self-concept of himself and of the adult he expects to be?

13. Is this his way of employing psychological weapons for ego support?[6]

To answer these questions and others, it is clear that the teacher must know what the child does, when he does a certain thing, where he does it, with whom, and why. That is to say, observation of interpersonal relationships, study of motives and purposes, and a knowledge of the physical, intellectual, emotional, and social factors all should be combined in designing a curriculum for individual growth and shaping the processes the teacher will use in working with children.

THE PHYSICAL AND SOCIAL FACTORS IN UNDERSTANDING THE CHILD

The teachers of children who are 6 to 12 may expect to work with boys and girls who are entering into new periods of social and physical growth. Since rates of growth are different, it is clear that only generaliza-

---

[6] H. G. Morgan, "Toward Understanding Children," *Education*, 77 (March, 1957), 430-34.

tions must be made about behavior and interests. As some children reach maturity earlier than others, because of sex differentiations, teachers can anticipate definite shifts in behavior and learn to accept any generalization in light of many altering conditions. It is believed that the following questions can orient the teacher in approaching the problems of understanding the child, as they provide a framework for securing and interpreting pertinent data about him:

1. What conditions seem to stimulate growth? Enhance growth? Actually hinder or lower growth?
2. What reasons may there be for variations? (For example, a change in positive attitudes, or a seeming shift in intelligence, etc.)
3. What could possibly be done about a particular condition?

Although it is true that individual patterns are unique to each child, it is still important to know that as structure and function develop, they are varied and progress is made at different rates. The teacher should recognize that "an adequate frame of reference for understanding change, or differentiation in growth, must include individual differences in temporal processes, as well as structural and functional processes."[7] This section is designed to furnish a frame of reference to the teacher in understanding certain physical and social factors.

What Should the Teacher Know About the Physical Needs of the Child?

There is a vast amount of data concerning the preschool and elementary school child that deals with such problems as factors in physical growth and development, growth rates, influencing factors, health, muscular co-ordination, and so on. Many biological aspects of development have direct implications for instruction. Thus, in order to present a more simplified approach in understanding the physical needs of the child, this section considers the following aspects:

1. What are some of the general patterns of growth for the elementary school child?
2. How may the problem of intellectual development be approached?
3. What can the teacher use as a suggested checklist in a practical, general approach to the physical needs problem of the child?

---

[7] N. Bayley, "Individual Patterns of Development," *Child Development*, 27 (March, 1956), 46.

Growth and development patterns. As each child matures, he finds new abilities and capacities for achievement. With such maturations his skill development improves in every phase of his development. It is important for the teacher to keep in mind certain growth trends which have implications for instruction.

Physical growth. Generally, the teacher is most concerned with height and weight. In some instances, the teacher measures these two aspects of body growth regularly, even though there may be no consideration of why these records are kept. Meredith[8] suggests that the teacher consider these three items: (1) Use a norm in describing the measurement, not as an instrument of appraisal but for descriptive and screening purposes only. (2) To appraise the child, determine whether or not this measurement states an unsatisfactory or satisfactory condition. Does it *fit* the child? That is to say, though the child is of short stature, he may still be perfectly normal and developing according to his pattern of growth. (3) Use measurement data about the child for screening purposes and look for possible deviations. A careful and accurate measuring of growth that is used with selected norms and standards[9] should confirm the fact that growth during this period is in terms of breadth rather than height, and is at a slower pace than during the pre-school years. For some children, at nine or ten, there is a spurt of growth, generally preceded by a period of relative stability and rest.

Motor development. As the child grows in size, he also makes gains in motor skills. When he begins his first year in the kindergarten, he is usually able to make some use of crayons, paints, or pencils. At the first grade level he can copy certain simple figures. Some generalizations are now summarized: the first grade child is improving in motor control; by seven, he is using more of the large and small muscles and can write; by eight, he manipulates more skillfully and his writing is more legible; by nine, he is aware of certain skills and begins practicing for improvement; from ten to twelve he may reach near adult maturity in certain hand skills. Girls excel in manual dexterity, while boys excel in muscular strength, speed, and coordination of gross movements.

The teacher views the growing child as one who may excel other children in some respects, but may fall short in other ways. The individual differences in children are quite noticeable and may tend to disturb or distress a child:

> On the playground Jimmy observes his age mates playing softball and wishes to join in the fun. However, he does very poorly in "batting" and

---

[8] H. V. Meredith, "Measuring the Growth Characteristics of School Children," *Journal of School Health,* 25 (December, 1955), 267-73.

[9] See Selected Readings for further references in analyzing growth progress.

"fielding the ball." He knows this, and so do his playmates who are impatient with him. Thus it is more convenient and safer to leave him on the sidelines where he could run after the stray balls. Jimmy worries over his inability to perform more adequately, but he may not realize that physically he is still less mature than boys of his age. There is no reason to believe that within a year or so he will not "catch up" and with practice take his place on the ball field. It should be noted that Jimmy may excel in reading, whereas the home-run hitter can be classed as doing no better in reading than Jimmy does in ballplaying. The poor reader has developed in terms of motor skills, but he is less mature or advanced in reading ability. This is not to imply that a boy or girl who excels in some physical feat will not excel in academic learning.

It will be noted that such problems as school achievement, immaturity, and even misbehavior are to be viewed in relation to the change in bodily proportions and nervous system as the child progresses through the grades. Frandsen then is correct in stating:

> . . . development is a product of maturation and environmental stimulation . . . it is highly important, in providing the conditions for effective learning, that the learning tasks and activities be adjusted to each child's level of maturity and pattern of abilities.[10]

Intellectual development. If the teacher is to work with the child as an individual, it is necessary to go beyond understanding the general physical and motor trends. Mental development takes in such symbolic processes as reasoning, memory, language, perceptions, concepts, judgments, imagination, and the like. It is generally known that the infant makes rapid growth in intelligence and levels off gradually during childhood until maturity is reached. It is interesting to note that spurts in physical growth during pre-adolescence are not matched by intellectual development. Even as the child exhibits differences in the physical growth aspects, it is also true that intelligence can be measured by various tests to show that each child may possess several different abilities comprising what is commonly known as his intelligence quotient.

For most practical purposes the teacher may study Jenkins, Shacter, and Bauer's conclusions in their discussion of intellectual growth,[11] particularly as the child engages in many and varied activities. *The six-year-old* uses symbols and language more widely; he is engaging in a variety of activities, as he learns to read, to count, and to be creative. *The seven-*

---

[10] Arden N. Frandsen, *How Children Learn* (New York: McGraw-Hill Book Co., Inc., 1957), p. 56.

[11] Jenkins, G. G., Shacter, H. and Bauer, W. W., *These Are Your Children* (3rd ed., Chicago: Scott, Foresman, & Company, 1966), pp. 129-181.

year-old becomes even more goal-seeking in his behavior in contrast to his pre-school days; he is thinking more critically and is more easily encouraged to do some independent work. *The eight-year-old* begins to expand more in his intellectual interests and activities; he is especially concerned with acquiring items that are of particular concern to him. *The nine-year-old* concentrates more intensely on things that are beyond his immediate environment; he can be encouraged to read more widely and deeply than previously. *The ten-to-twelve-year-old* reaches a state where he can be on his own intellectually as he seeks answers to interesting problems; he is sometimes well-prepared to do constructive work, simple research, and follow through in a rather well-defined and organized way. Thus teachers may find an increasing amount of data about the intellectual development of elementary school children, but the two generalizations given should prove helpful. *Generalization number one:* Think of intelligence as being made up of several abilities and capitalize on those aspects that promise significant results for the child or lead to his best development. Then as the teacher plans learning experiences in terms of mental development, another viewpoint is to be considered. *Generalization number two:* Regard the shifts in thinking that will occur as the child goes up through the grades. As he is subjected to many influences, he will change his views, ideas, and attitudes. There are many factors that enhance or lower his intellectual abilities, and the teacher may take note of shifts in thinking, employing them for the child's optimum personal achievement. It is important that intelligence tests be given and interpreted carefully. Single tests are not conclusive, nor should an intelligence quotient assigned to a child be the only determinant in planning an optimum learning experience for him. A considerable spread in intelligence may generally be found in the average classroom.

A suggested checklist for the teacher in understanding the physical needs of children. The following questions are designed as guides to the teacher in organizing an approach toward understanding the physical needs of the child. By using certain questions as points of departure in exploring further particular physical factors, the teacher may collect pertinent data for gaining a more complete perspective of the child:

1. Is there an understanding of any particular features of the child's genetic endowment?
2. Have the environment and the interactions between it and heredity been investigated?
3. Is there a recognition that the child's inner forces both balance and regulate the direction of the growth trend toward maturation and readiness?

4. Has the effect of the endocrine glands upon health and development been considered?

5. Have there been any prolonged or acute illnesses that may have changed the course of physical growth or caused emotional problems?

6. Are there any physical defects limiting the child?

7. Have there been thorough investigations made of the child to discover the less evident physical conditions such as allergies, nutrition, and the like?

8. Are the health practices and habits of the child known to be satisfactory, or in need of correction?

9. Is the pattern of growth in height and weight understood?

10. Is there a knowledge of the skeletal development of the child?

11. Does the child exhibit satisfactory progress in terms of endurance, posture, motor skills, and the like? Is the progress commensurate with his own rate of development?

12. Is there an understanding of the growth of sense perceptions, judgments, memory, imagination, etc., in terms of the intellectual development of the child?

This twelve-point checklist should be considered only as a guide to the teacher for supplying deeper insights into the child's physical growth factors. To be realistic, the amount of data concerning the child's genetic endowment, functioning of the glands, and skeletal development will, at best, be sketchy indeed. The medical doctor is professionally competent to supply this information, but at least the teacher should be conversant with these factors and recognize that growth and development are considered in such terms, and so on.

What Are the Social Factors to be Considered in Understanding the Child?

The socializing of the child is a process that begins at birth, since there is no human nature[12] prior to that time. There are many forces contributing to the socialization of the individual as he acquires ways of behaving according to his culture and society. His family, the play groups, the church, particular daily experiences, and even his views of himself and the kind of an adult he thinks he may become are all definite forces which transform the child into the kind of social person he should be.

---

[12] T. R. Shaffler, "The Process of Socialization," *Phi Delta Kappan*, 34 (March, 1953), 225-28.

However, there is a definite need for his receiving continued instruction if "social development may be thought of as that which the child acquires or builds into himself as he moves toward maturity in his various human relations."[13] It would be interesting and informative to show the formal and informal kinds of instruction that shape the individual, and to trace the social development of the person from infancy to maturity. However, our discussion of this wide area is confined to three topics: (1) a description of the social development of the elementary school child; (2) some definite objectives of the teacher for the social education of children; and (3) a guide to the teacher in developing a program for social development.

Social development of the elementary school child. The socialization of the child is a gradual process, and growth is dependent upon maturation, intellectual development, emotional nature, and environmental experiences. Therefore, no single description of the social development of the elementary school child will fit any individual except in a general way.

Play activities seem to give evidence of increasing social consciousness,[14] and by the time the child is in the elementary school he exhibits some ability to plan and organize. Boys are more concerned with the active sports, while girls are interested in the more quiet, home-like forms of activity. There is some segregation in play activities, but it is still common for both sexes to share certain play experiences.

The teacher may expect some teasing to occur. Recognition of two factors[15] should help the teacher to better understand this form of social development. First, the child learns how other people react to his initiated annoyances and, secondly, the child begins to discover his own powers of securing responses from and influencing others. Of course, the instructor must be aware of any malicious intents that could underlie some teasing.

By the time the child is in the fourth grade he is capable of developing rather strong friendships.[16] It is well to encourage friendships, since the social development of the child is furthered as he gains feelings of inner security and brings into better focus the awareness of social consciousness. By the time the child is in the fourth or fifth grade he is being prepared socially for peer group participation. It is through this latter association that he may be best viewed as he progresses socially. Within a

---

[13] Henry J. Otto, *Social Education in Elementary Schools* (New York: Holt, Rinehart & Winston, Inc., 1956), p. 12.

[14] Lester D. Crow and Alice Crow, *Human Development and Learning* (New York: American Book Company, 1956), p. 85.

[15] *Ibid.*, pp. 86-7.

[16] *Ibid.*

peer group the needs of the child are met in the following ways:[17] (1) The child finds models for behavior and achievement among his peer group members and their activities. (2) The peer group makes it possible for him to secure attentions that he discovers he needs and wants. (3) He learns to view himself in different ways as he identifies with the group. (4) The group furnishes him a support in asking or doing certain things; he is growing toward maturity with the help of the peer group as he learns to rely less upon his parents.

Objectives for the social development of children. One approach that teachers have in gaining understandings about the social factors in the development of the child is to have certain classroom objectives that suggest competencies desirable for the child. These competencies are listed below to assist the teacher in understanding the child and particularly in guiding his development:[18]

1. Acquiring skills, habits, and attitudes for meeting successfully person-to-person relationships. In his classroom the elementary school child should find situations for social learning, since "the way to become really a member of society is by living and experiencing within it."[19]

2. Developing competencies in and active participation with social groups and institutional organizations. Whether the child has many formal, direct contact opportunities or not, the school may be his one realistic opportunity for acquiring significant understandings of institutions.

3. Gaining understandings and control of factors and forces in the physical world. Social development is certainly enhanced as the child becomes increasingly competent in dealing with the world about him.

4. Becoming competent in understanding and working with problems of goods and services. Firsthand experiences in the school and home point up many phases of human relations as the child grows in understanding production and distribution factors of goods and services.

It should be clear that as the teacher arranges learning situations that are designed to promote and foster social development, she comes

---

[17] William E. Martin and Celia Burns Stendler, *Child Development; The Process of Growing Up in Society* (New York: Harcourt, Brace & World, Inc., 1953), pp. 450-55.

[18] Otto, *op. cit.*, pp. 12-29.

[19] W. R. Niblett, "Education and Individuality," *Educational Forum,* 17 (March, 1953), 272.

to recognize the complexity of the task. She may be able to describe social behavior that is desirable for any grade-level pupil, and she may be cognizant of such objectives described above; but it is believed that there is no single approach for studying or analyzing social development in an isolated way. The social differences found among children are so varied that teachers face difficulties in guiding social learning. For example, some of these difficulties may be traced to homes where mothers may work, or where relationships with parents are poor.[20] The problems of desegregation, migrant workers, and foreign-born children, are a few more of the difficulties, posing challenges to the teacher. The next topic serves as a practical guide for the teacher in organizing and evolving a program for the social development of elementary school children. It also serves as an aid in gaining further insights and understandings of the child.

A guide for the teacher from the developmental point of view. Although the primary purpose of this section is to suggest some practical guides[21] for the teacher in fostering children's social development, it suggests implications for every phase of his growth. The teacher should attempt to:

1. Know and understand as much as possible about the child.

2. Help him to go through his various stages by arranging deliberate ways of involving him with his culture.

3. Provide as many outside sources of stimulation and help as possible.

4. Accept the child for what he is and understand his feelings even though there are plans for changing certain behaviors.

5. Help him to develop an insight into himself and acquire a more acceptable picture of himself, if needed.

6. Give him feelings of responsibility, a role to play, and help him in the special ways he may need.

7. Encourage and work with peer groups.

8. Help him to understand the adult world and its expectations of him; assist him in meeting the pressures and demands that may be made of him.

9. Examine values from teacher-student-school-community viewpoints and help child to think through conflicts.

---

[20] Evelyn D. Adlerblum, "The Social Differences Among Children," *Childhood Education*, 32 (January, 1956), 214-18.

[21] Doris Klaussen, "How Children Differ—Working With Exceptions: The Physically Different," *Childhood Education*, 32 (January, 1956), 209-11.

To summarize: the teacher must learn much about the physical, mental, and social characteristics of children in order to plan carefully for optimum learning experiences. It is not expected that all facts will be uncovered, but there is a workable approach to every classroom problem: state your child's problem as definitely as possible; gather all the facts you can relating to the situation; decide what you think may be a cause for behavior; check on your tentative solution; and proceed in a constructive way.

THE PSYCHODYNAMIC FACTORS IN CHILD DEVELOPMENT

Probably one of the most baffling tasks of the teacher is that of going beyond the observation of the outward behavior of children and considering *how* and *why* a person inwardly organizes his experiences. Though there are techniques for inquiring into the inner life of an individual, complete insight is not possible. Yet the teacher should become familiar with certain psychological processes in reaching understandings about the child. It is believed that the three topics to be discussed will furnish the teacher certain principles in working with the psychodynamic factors present in the developmental processes. These three topics are stated as follows:

1. A general approach to the problems of psychodynamics in childhood is needed for practical purposes by the classroom teacher.
2. Teachers should at least be conversant with the theory of psychoanalysis and the socio-psychological point of view.
3. The emotional needs of children should be understood by the elementary school teacher.

What Is a General Approach to the Problems of Psychodynamics?

The theme of Dreikurs[22] is that every person basically desires to be an accepted and functioning member of a group. With this principle as a guide, the teacher may then attempt to understand how well the child fulfills or fails in satisfying this desire. Perhaps for practical purposes an explanation of social behavior may be helpful to the teacher in approaching the problem of psychodynamics in grade school children. Dreikurs furnishes a framework for the following discussion that at-

---

[22] Rudolf Dreikurs, *Psychology in the Classroom* (New York: Harper and Row, Publishers, 1957), p. 3.

tempts to suggest some principles by explaining the child's development from the psychological point of view.[23]

First, the child comes into the world endowed with certain bodily characteristics or hereditary properties. He is surrounded by an environment not of his choosing, and he is particularly influenced by his mother. However, even as he is shaped by these two forces, he begins early to react to life about him and to create patterns of response.

Second, his interactions with his environment cause him to form his life style or pattern.[24] Perhaps this is really the key for unlocking the individual or discovering his personality. By the age of 4 or 5 his life pattern or style is fairly well established.[25] He has acquired an attitude toward solving certain problems: he may confront or evade them; or he may seek to compensate, over-compensate, rationalize, or otherwise follow his developed scheme of action.

Third, it is inevitable that each child must face obstacles that may bar his realization for achievement and group participation. The calibre or "quality" of his life style will, in part, determine how well he manages his feelings of inferiority. If he is considered to have a strong life pattern, the inferiority feelings will serve to spur him on to surmount the barriers. There is the possibility that his life style cannot ward off these feelings, and he may then develop a sense of hopelessness or an inferiority complex. It should be noted that as the child begins to develop his life style, his choice of that style will certainly depend upon the advantages that were his and how successfully he was able to meet various obstacles.

Fourth, the child is brought up within some kind of family atmosphere and occupies a certain position within that group. The general trend of the child's behavior will be determined by the child's individual reaction to the relationship that exists between the parents. The position of the child in the family should also be considered as the teacher understands the dynamics of behavior. Rivalry for parental affections, competition between siblings for power, compensation by the youngest for attention, are a few of the complications that the teacher may work with to learn how the personality traits of children may have stemmed from one or more of these responses. It should be added that to gain further insight, the methods of training the child should be examined since the child may have been spoiled or suppressed in various ways by parents. In many ways, a child's repertoire of responses are reflections of the manner in which parents have treated him.

---

[23] *Ibid.,* Chapter I, pp. 3-20.
[24] *Ibid.,* p. 4.
[25] *Ibid.,* p. 6.

Fifth, the teacher may find the disturbing behavior of a child of most concern, but he should know that the same principle (viz., his behavior is his way of finding social status or acceptance) is operative as the child misbehaves or appears to be poorly adjusted. In fact, it probably is the only way he knows how to behave, and he is convinced it will get him results, even though he is labelled "the problem child." Dreikurs[26] believes there are four goals that may explain why a child behaves in a certain way. Various techniques are used in reaching a goal, but no matter which goal is desired or which techniques are employed the purpose seems to be the same: to gain social status by the way the child knows best. An explanation of these four goals now follows and should help the teacher to understand more clearly some of the dynamics of behavior patterns that may be exhibited in the elementary school classroom:

1. *The techniques of attention-getting.* Perhaps the life style of the child has been formed by his belief that he gains status through affection or attention demonstrations, and not by his own contributions. Self-reliance and confidence are constantly maintained by new proof that he is wanted, even if he has to press people into *his* service or simply get attention through personal charm or more dramatic techniques.

2. *The demonstrations of power and superiority.* Whether the child is struggling with parent, teacher, or other adults, there are instances when he must prove he can win out over that adult. Usually, the child can win his point even if the adult believes that the victory was his. When that happens, the child is more firmly convinced that power is more valuable than ever, and the next struggle may be that much more difficult.

3. *The desire for revenge or retaliation.* A corollary of the struggle for power is the desire of adult and child to retaliate. If the child particularly fails in his bid for superiority, then he can resort to gaining status by being hated. In effect, he becomes successful in the ways he is able to strike back and inflict hurt and pain.

4. *The display of inferiority feelings.* If the child finds both the struggle and retaliating efforts too difficult, in that success may still not be his, he may then turn either to imagined or real feelings of inferiority. In hiding behind this protective curtain he finds he does not have to contribute nor participate. He avoids being placed in a

---

[26] *Ibid.*, pp. 12-17.

humiliating position of any kind, since he knows that defeat is inevitable and the way to meet it must be in his refusal to do anything at all.

As the teacher understands the child, he may consider how active the student is in pursuing a particular goal. Some children may demonstrate a definite aggressiveness as they seek social status. On the other hand, the teacher should be alert to that child who does not seem to be very much interested, but who, in a quiet way, is still achieving his ends or adopting one of the goals mentioned above. In addition, teachers should regularly note that some children are neither aggressive, poorly adjusted, nor actively concerned with any particular problems. These complacent, happy, and secure persons do not seem to present any difficulties except that they do not get interested, excited, or involved in their work. In some instances they may even avoid doing the class work even though they have the ability. Assuming that the child has ability, is free from unreasonable fears and anxieties, and has no handicaps, the teacher is confronted with a real motivational problem. It is true that this rather negative attitude toward work is his life pattern or style and reflects personality and behavior traits formed during early periods of training. Nevertheless, this child can be motivated and impressed by a work-oriented classroom atmosphere. By understanding that all children seek social status through the ways they know best, it is believed that the over-complacent child can be led into better work habits and attitudes by the teacher's insistence upon sensible work standards and parent support and encouragement. Supplemented by good teaching practices over a period of years, the poorly motivated child will come to see and accept the virtues of working for realistic ends and purposes.

What Does the Teacher Need to Know About the Emotional Needs of Children?

The school has the responsibility of helping children to learn and live together in every phase of their relationships with other persons. The teachers face the important task of meeting the child's emotional needs even as they seek to gain insight into these needs. It must be stated that meeting emotional needs of children from the viewpoint of the teacher should emphasize the kind of attitude and classroom atmosphere provided by the instructor. The serious and deep-rooted emotional problems constitute areas of endeavor by the trained psychiatrist, psychologist, and social worker. Therefore, the teacher may best profit in understanding the emotional factors in children by approaching the task through recognizing emotional needs as they are expressed by the child. Certain emotional needs are presently to be discussed from the developmental point of view. Emphasis is given to indicate at what grade levels teachers may expect to encounter a particular emotional need as the child grows toward maturity. The last section of this chapter will suggest some principles of working with children in light of their emotional needs.

An examination of the literature shows that there are different ways of describing the emotional needs of the child. It is believed that D'Evelyn[27] has defined these needs in clear and understandable terms, for practical purposes of the elementary school teacher, and furnishes an approach to the following discussions.

The emotional need of feeling accepted. Everyone must believe that he receives the support and acceptance of some one person. This emotional need of being accepted for what one is begins, of course, in the home and continues throughout life. As this need is met, the individual learns to relate himself to other people more satisfactorily.

The emotional need of feeling successful. It is not enough for a child to secure praise and approval from someone; he must also experience a sense of progress or accomplishment. When the child sees that he has done something in a satisfactory manner, he is building up a reservoir of self-esteem and confidence. It is true that failures are inevitable, but even failure to achieve can be turned into a profitable and valuable experience. Still, the child must have more successes rather than an overwhelming number of repeated, frustrating failures.

The emotional need of feeling independent. As the child acquires feelings of acceptance and experiences success, he is ready to become more independent. He needs better understandings of his inner forces, but especially he needs to develop an improved system of inner controls. The need to feel progressively more independent is surely predicated upon the child's ability to handle situations more adequately; hence, he needs security and confidence in himself as he seeks the more desirable status of being an independent person.

The emotional need of feeling and being a peer group member. The identification with age mates is a step forward toward sound mental health and social adjustment. A good peer relationship is evidence that emotional growth is progressing and that the child is learning to live with people. He also finds a certain kind of status as a member of a peer group.

---

[27] Katherine D'Evelyn, *Meeting Children's Emotional Needs* (Englewood Cliffs, N. J.: Prentice-Hall, Inc., 1957), Chapters 2, 3, and 4.

CHART III

THE CHILD'S EMOTIONAL NEED OF FEELING:	THE PRIMARY LEVEL NEEDS REQUIRE:	THE INTERMEDIATE LEVEL NEEDS REQUIRE:
Accepted	—Firm, sympathetic parental support. —Definite, early teacher support, acceptance, and praise. —Acceptance on child's own merit, not by competing nor being "nice" in themselves. —First steps to be taken in seeking his own acceptance of other people.	—That he feel liked by teacher and grown members. —The fostering of self-confidence through teacher-group participation and support.
Successful	—An early sense of accomplishing something. —A turning of failure into a learning experience, if possible. —The close cooperation with parents to further the development of confidence.	—An increasing amount of school success; it is important and significant that success engender self-power and mastery. —That competition be minimized in school life.
Independent	—Recognition of fact that fostering of independence begins early. —Active support by teacher as child acquires more independence; the proper kind of support at the right time. —That the child be led to accept and manage his independence by building inner controls.	—A growing awareness for more independence; but complete freedom is still not desirable nor wanted. —A strengthening of the self-concept through guidance and inner controls.
Identified with peer group	—Some weaning away from parents toward accepting and being accepted by peers. —Only partial identification with peer groups.	—More group feelings of solidarity; possible, but greater need for peer acceptance and still some definite need of teacher support are present. —That he does not lose face, with group particularly.
Creative	—At least a start in this direction, even if only partially successful. —Adequate materials and permissive atmosphere conducive to creativity, and its encouragement. —Definite cultivation by the teacher in fostering creativity and knowing how to work with parents.	—Recognition that the child is desirous of many more new experiences. —More ways of getting the child to live creatively be provided.

The emotional need of feeling free to be creative and to enjoy new experiences.   Children are creative in that they can express themselves and their feelings through many mediums. A child is doing something original whenever it is a "first" experience for him. Children must feel free to express themselves and to be creative as they seek satisfying new experiences. Of course, these expressions and desires for new experiences must be acceptable in themselves and gauged according to the child's age, abilities, and even certain environmental conditions.

Summary Chart III indicates briefly the developmental perspective for the teacher who is concerned with the emotional needs of children. These needs are considered from the primary and intermediate levels. The main purpose of this presentation is to suggest that even though each emotional need is present at every growth stage, the teacher can recognize immediately that in most cases the need may assume a different emphasis at the various grade levels.

How Can the Developmental Approach Be Summarized?

So far, the discussion has emphasized the physical, social, mental, and psychological understanding of children that teachers should consider in the developmental approach to learning. To bring these areas into sharper perspective a diagram is shown on a later page. First are the biological drives and urges, the immediate needs after birth which compel the person to seek necessary satisfactions. This drive is one of the factors in creating a goal-seeking type of person and, in fact, initiates in many instances this goal-seeking trait as well as those drives acquired by the individual through his experiences. Thus, in time, the social needs appear as the child finds he desires both approval and acceptance by other persons and some mastery or achievement, success feelings. The maturational pattern is thought of as growth in all areas— physical, motor and sensory, and mental. As a result of heredity each child has his own unique rate of growth. Because of different rates of maturation, there are limits to what an individual child can accomplish at any given time.

Now as the child adjusts and moves toward certain satisfactions because of goal-seeking behavior, these questions are asked: What causes his striving toward a particular kind of behavior (satisfaction)? Is it basically to satisfy a biological drive (hunger, etc.)? Is it a social drive (to win approval of others, etc.)? In the process of drive, tension will surely arise to some degree. The kinds of adjustment the child will make in acquiring satisfaction will depend on many factors—his life pattern, intelligence, the type of obstacle, and so on. Most children will attempt to meet their problems intelligently if they have been given opportunities to exercise their reasoning faculties. Some will solve their problems in due time, while others will compensate or compromise in some way. There are those children who will "retreat" or withdraw by denying themselves the drive and refusing to move forward. One intelligent course of action is substituting for the original satisfaction a new one that may be more reasonable and attainable.

In summary, the teacher can see that each child has needs arising out of his hereditary assets and liabilities, his environment, and particularly his ways of meeting and solving his problems. Whatever kind of activity or behavior is manifest, there is always a cause for it that may often be traced and understood. By understanding the developmental life tasks of children at any given period in their lives, the teacher may well assist them in making a more successful adjustment. For those children in grades one through six, these life tasks may be summarized as learning and developing:[28]

—the physical skills in play activities,
—the proper attitudes about oneself,
—the skills of getting along with age mates or peer group members,
—the fundamental skills in the three R's,
—the concepts needed for daily living,
—the right understanding of one's sex role,
—the proper value system and appropriate moral values,
—the proper attitude and understanding toward society and its institutions.

WORKING WITH CHILDREN FROM THE DEVELOPMENTAL POINT OF VIEW

Inasmuch as educators believe that effective instruction is based upon knowledge of the child, it follows that children must be studied carefully. Then it can be expected that a philosophy should develop so that the attitude of the adult toward the child and *how* he works with him will mean improved classroom practices. However, little or no change in teacher behavior[29] generally takes place in the instructional program merely because teachers have studied children or completed

[28] R. J. Havighurst, *Developmental Tasks and Education* (Chicago: University of Chicago Press, 1948), pp. 6, 8.

[29] V. E. Herrick, "Approaches in Helping Teachers Improve Their Instructional Practices," *School Review*, 62 (December, 1954), 527-34.

a particular college course in education. Therefore, this section can assist the in-service teacher or the prospective instructor in gaining not only a philosophy about planning learning experiences geared to the developmental approach, but in obtaining specific suggestions for ways in which knowledge about the child can be put into practice. Teachers may amass certain data about children, but they are often unsure how to apply such information. The specific objectives now are:

1. To give emphasis to the planning and organizing of a child study program,

2. To suggest some general implications of child growth and development for classroom practices,

3. To define how teachers may use the causal approach in working with children,

4. To note how the use of certain psychological processes are employed in the classroom based upon child growth,

5. To suggest how the teacher may work more effectively with children in terms of their emotional needs.

How May a Child Study Program Be Planned and Organized?

The study of children cannot be reduced to a simple formula or a series of steps to be followed. A professional and scholarly approach to child study is needed and should be under the leadership of competent instructors combined with library and laboratory facilities. However, the emphasis here is upon the teachers or school system personnel who are concerned with practical procedures and desire help in launching a practical, realistic research program. The teacher can use a pattern for obtaining information about the child and can also employ certain organizational features in working with the data.

Obtaining significant information. As has been suggested, the teacher should collect all the information possible about the child. In order to simplify this task, seven sources or ways to be followed are here submitted:

1. Observe the child within the total school situation. As he performs in and outside the classroom, write down anecdotal comments that are characteristic of his behavior.

2. Study the cumulative records of the child. Record pertinent material from them for the record now being compiled.

3. Visit the home situation and encourage parental visits to the school. List certain observations and conversational matters to be included in the child's record.

4. Observe the child's life style or life space and describe it carefully in terms of classroom functioning. The meaning of life space is how the child views his universe, through those experiences which have shaped him as an individual. The term life style has already been discussed and is included here to extend the meaning of the experience background inferences of life space.

5. Talk with teachers who have taught the child in the past. It is more important to secure facts rather than personal opinions or evaluations that may not be based upon such things as norms, recurring patterns of behavior and the like.

6. Collect and analyze representative samples of the classroom work of the child. Include characteristic samples for the study record.

7. Talk freely with the child in as many different settings as possible and record pertinent conversations.[30]

In using this framework for collecting information, the teacher is able to secure current illustrative material. There should be stress and emphasis upon doing these things as accurately and scientifically as possible. In addition, each instructor should be in a position to get suggestions, inferences, and evaluations from other staff members, as they exchange ideas and approach the study of children with concerted efforts.

Organizing the information. It has been stated that many teachers have studied children or collected a great deal of information about them but may have made no corresponding changes in behavior in working with them. Therefore, teachers need a guide to help them catalogue the data about the child. This guide assists the teacher in recognizing the dynamics that are operating to shape the adjustment and behavior of the child, and assessing whether or not sufficient information is present. Furthermore, the teacher will have particular information that will indicate how to deal with these forces in arranging a classroom experience. The framework offered here is one that has been used in some child-study programs[31] but contains only the broad headings with some details:

1. The physical factors and processes: growth and maturity rate-levels, energy and fatigue; health; defects and limitations; body skills; physical attractiveness and impact upon others and self.

2. The love relationships: with parent and sibling, particularly how expressed; how parents express their relationships; with other adults in

---

[30] Prescott, *op. cit.*, Chapter 6.
[31] Prescott, *op. cit.*, pp. 205-08.

home; with pets; how difficulties in home relationships are managed; with individuals outside the home.

3. The cultural background and process of socialization: characteristics of his sub-cultures; how the child internalizes certain cultural factors; how he functions in the various institutions; his feelings and concepts of society in various aspects; inconsistencies, conflicts, and pressures that may affect the child in his culture.

4. The peer group status and processes: characteristics of his group; his role and status; his successes and failures; how he is affected; how he manages himself.

5. The self-development factors and processes: concepts and feelings about himself; how he looks at situations, the universe, and the like; his potentials, his mental attacks upon problems; his goals for himself; concepts of others about him.

6. The self-adjustive factors and processes: feelings of adequacy; quality of feelings about love relationships, social situations, and status among peers; concept of total self; how he acts, re-acts, distorts, or appears in need of professional help.

To summarize: the teacher has techniques of collecting data and can follow a guide in organizing the information about the child. In practice, there must be other steps taken as well: interpreting, recognizing gaps in the data; planning how to help the child with his developmental tasks and adjustment; and continuing the child study work. A child study program can be profitable if it is conducted properly. The evidence of a study from a controlled situation[32] makes it clear that the traditional in-service reading of material about children produces little change in behavior. It takes time for teachers to change attitudes and learn about children. Still another study[33] confirms the fact that teachers must become sensitive to the factors that affect learning, and especially the feelings, needs, and goals of the learner. This emphasis means that understanding children is paramount to good teaching. Again there is evidence[34] that when teachers use child developmental approaches they do better teaching. They change their own attitudes and make better value judgments about the child because they are more scientific in their study of him.

---

[32] R. L. Henderson, "Do Teachers Profit from Self-Directed Child Study?", *Elementary School Journal*, 56 (December, 1955), 152-57.

[33] H. V. Perkins, "The Effects of Climate and Curriculum on Group Learning," *Journal of Educational Research*, 44 (December, 1950), 269-86.

[34] H. V. Perkins, "Teachers Grow in Understanding Children," *Educational Leadership*, 7 (May, 1950), 549-55.

What Are Some General Implications for the Teacher in Understanding the Child for Improved Teaching?

Some implications for classroom practices have already been noted, and the following comments are made to bring together a more complete list of suggestions for the teacher. The items contained in this section are designed to aid the teacher in summarizing what the organized data about the child can mean for better teaching, as well as to stimulate thinking that should lead to changing ways of behavior. It is hoped that the teacher or prospective instructor may view actual past performance, or ways of having been taught, in light of the following comments and see new approaches that are based upon knowledge of the child.

Implication for better teaching—1: View the total situation of the child with emphasis on what is said, done, and known by and about the child. This insightful approach certainly focuses upon the learning activities, but there is a definite awareness of the uniqueness of each child.[35] Thus, teaching is geared to the developmental tasks of children in light of individual capacities, environmental factors, social, and emotional conditions that have shaped him and are still modifying the personality.

Implication for better teaching—2: See the relationships that exist. The many inter-relationships between the physical, environmental, and emotional factors are viewed. Such techniques as sociometry are employed to discover positions of persons in the group.

Implication for better teaching—3: Use research and action research to develop a guiding philosophy based upon a theory of curriculum that is child-centered. Available evidence is gathered to shed light on a realistic classroom problem, and attempts are made to secure and employ a variety of resources and persons in understanding the child better or providing him with better classroom experiences.

Implication for better teaching—4: Be practical and thorough in the child study efforts. Teachers can consider working more closely with colleagues and parents. Better records can be kept for use by other staff members. Improved teacher self-understanding may be sought. Self-evaluations by teacher-pupil may be a new objective and secure mutual understandings. Different grouping procedures may not only give further understandings but increase class participation and improve performance.

It is clear that this listing of four implications for better teaching is not exhaustive. They serve their purpose in summarizing what the

---

[35] Viola Theman, "Emerging Concepts of Child Growth and Development: What They Suggest for Classroom Practices," 13th Yearbook of the John Dewey Society, *The American Elementary School* (New York: Harper and Row, Publishers, 1953), Chapter 4.

teacher may do in the classroom if child understandings are to be stressed. Perhaps Figure II may help to clarify the task of the teacher in working with the developmental patterns of children to improve teaching. Only five aspects are presented in Figure II, and the teacher may well wish to extend the number of factors to include such items as carpal age, grip, teeth, height, weight, socio-economic status, certain achievement items, and so on. The comparison of Jimmy and Jack shows that Jimmy is a gifted child who is socially and emotionally well adjusted. Jack possesses below average mental capacity but is adjusted

FIGURE II

*Some Different Behavior and
Development Patterns in Children*

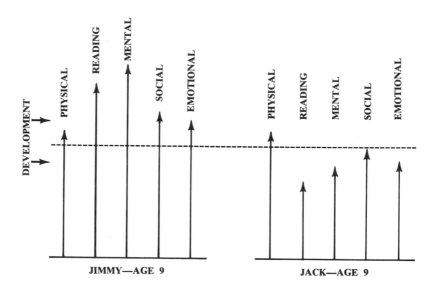

JIMMY—AGE 9   JACK—AGE 9

and fairly free from psychological problems. Physically the two boys are about the same. Thus, each boy may face the same school environment, but in light of developmental patterns one will master some tasks more rapidly and efficiently than the other. The teacher should study each child's growth and behavior patterns and try to estimate the success the child will have in mastering his developmental tasks. The teacher must be prepared to give the right kind and amount of assistance.

How May Teachers Use the Causal Approach in Working With Children?

The contents of this chapter are devoted to the theme that teachers need to know and understand children better. Pertinent points are stated to give these basic understandings in so far as possible within the compass of a single chapter. In addition, it has been firmly stressed that teachers must change their attitudes and behavior in providing learning tasks from the developmental point of view. One approach to teaching that deserves particular attention is that of working with children to help them as they approach people and specific problems in terms of behavior dynamics. The teacher uses the "causal approach"[36] in all phases of teaching. Although this procedure involves getting the child to think in terms of causes, it means also that the teacher must know a great deal about the child. Children should be constantly led to think and discover "cause" and "feeling" within specific classroom situations. Questions are asked, discussions are directed, and thinking is done to find answers to problems. As answers are secured, the causes behind the answers and the feelings of those involved should also be determined by similar methods. Environmental and cultural influences as well as certain emotional needs must be considered; and, above all, children must be aided in expressing their feelings in constructive ways.[37] Many adults believe that what the child feels about himself, other persons, or situations may not really be important. The evidence[38] of this is revealed in an experiment which compared a teacher who was causally trained with one who was, traditionally, concerned only with teaching specific content. The results showed that in the class where the children were taught to think in terms of causes there was less authoritarianism, more willingness to assume responsibility, easier acceptance of people, and, of course, a greater tendency to think of causes and feelings. An illustration of an actual situation indicates how the causally oriented teacher works with children in every phase of the curriculum:

> Mrs. Reap was talking with her sixth grade class about a student teacher from a local college that would be teaching and working with them. She knew the special handicap of this teacher and was confident that her group would appreciate and understand that the student teacher's slight speech defect of stuttering would not have to be a barrier to good

---

[36] R. H. Ojemann, "Changing Attitudes in the Classroom," *Children*, 3 (July, 1956), 130-34.
[37] *Ibid.*
[38] *Ibid.*

teaching. She knew her class well and was able to direct a few tactful
questions at key persons to get the discussion going. Within 30 minutes
she was able to view with some satisfaction that this class would make a
very special effort to work hard and cooperate with a student teacher that
could succeed in spite of a handicap. Mrs. Reap employed the approach
that brought in feelings and causes that were applied to a teaching situation. However, her class was used to this, since even in social studies the
children were encouraged to express feelings and see reasons and causes
in every appropriate topic.

The causal approach receives further discussion in Chapter 3, but
it should be clear that attitudes of children can be changed when they
are taught to think causally. Reading and study materials must also be
prepared carefully to contribute to this desired behavior, but the teacher
must first understand the dynamics of child behavior before she can
teach them in terms of these dynamics.

How Does the Teacher Influence the Child by Employing Certain Psychological Processes?

Whether the teacher is dealing with an emotionally upset or disturbed
child or with the more common everyday problems, there is a need to
employ certain skills and to have special information about the psychological mechanisms. It is believed that the difficult cases naturally
require professional help, but the teacher may find that it is easier to
influence the child than may have been imagined. This is not to say that
understandings of children are to be minimized, but there are definite
and specific ways by which the teacher may influence children.[39]

First, children need to be won over through *friendly, warm relationships.* The teacher must know the child well and work hard sometimes
to accomplish this end. It may mean a change of behavior for the teacher
in terms of mutual faith and respect for each other. There are many
ways of winning cooperation, but no single formula can be given.

Second, children need to be *encouraged.* Many times the child may
have faced a bleak, discouraging situation and may have experienced a
series of frustrations and failures. He may expect the teacher to treat
him as he has been handled in the past. Thus, firm attitudes against
learning may be the only way of retaliation by the child. Again, teacher
encouragement must fit the child and his temperament. There should

---

[39] Dreikurs, *op. cit.,* Chapter 3.

be a knowledge of how much to expect of him, what kinds of signs he looks for from the teacher that are encouraging, how much praise to give and when to offer it, and particularly how to avoid unfair competition with other children. It should be added that children should compete with each other only in limited situations. There would be no reason to encourage all children to read at the same level, since there may be a wide range of abilities and mental ages present within a given classroom. A child with a mental age of 7 years, for example, would have difficulty in keeping pace in reading with a child who possesses a mental age of 8 years or more.

Third, the teacher must help the child to *see himself* in a better perspective. It is important that the child find causes for his behavior, instead of being sermonized or told about them. As the child saves face the teacher is able to use a non-directive approach in getting the child to express himself more completely. This mechanism may be thought of as being related to the causal type of classroom management discussed in the previous section. That is to say, the child is led to think through situations and "discover" for himself instead of being directed and "told" by the teacher.

Fourth, the teacher should *use the group* as a means of working with the child. Children are accustomed to moving within a group structure and are greatly influenced by group actions and decisions. Much skill is required, but even discipline can be more effective where group dynamics are operating.

Fifth, one of the prime objectives of all teachers is getting children to *consider new beliefs* and to *change attitudes and behavior*. The resourceful teacher needs to know what is behind certain thinking or behavior and then find different ways by which the child himself discovers the futility of his thinking or efforts and the need to change his goals.[40] This principle must be observed whether the child is struggling with improper reading techniques or is concerned about gaining power or superiority. It makes a difference in the teacher's approach in terms of whether the child sees himself as a success or a failure, is accepted by his peers, and so on.

It is not sufficient to be enthusiastic and interested in children when no special techniques for understanding and working with the child are in evidence. These psychological mechanisms may be considered as ways of arranging classroom situations because they are the skills needed to help children grow and develop.

---

[40] Dreikurs, *op. cit.*, p. 54.

What Are Some Practical Ways of Working With the Emotional Problems of Children?

In another section of this chapter the developmental tasks of children from the emotional viewpoint were considered. It is now appropriate to suggest some practical guides to the teacher in dealing with the emotional aspects of the child.

How May the Teacher Be More Effective in Understanding the Emotional Aspects of Children?

The realistic teacher in the elementary school classroom realizes that many emotional problems of children are beyond his professional knowledge and area of preparation for adequate diagnosis or treatment. Yet the teacher does have ways and means of meeting a majority of the emotional needs of the child; and the contributions to the emotional adjustment and personality development of the child are innumerable for the instructor. A series of suggested guides are now offered that can serve to point the way both in meeting the emotional needs of the child and providing some principles for arranging more effective learning experiences that contribute to emotional maturity.

1. The teacher must understand the developmental aspects of the basic emotional needs of children.

2. The understandings of children's emotional needs should serve as points of departure for counseling, the organization of learning experiences, and all other phases of school life.

3. The symptoms of emotional development that suggest an unsatisfactory kind of adjustment should be known and applied to children who may have special needs as well as to all normal children. Such symptoms may be thought of in terms of stealing, tattling (particularly in the intermediate and upper elementary grades), withdrawal behavior, aggressiveness, phobias of certain kinds, fear of school, learning disabilities with an emotional core, speech problems, truancy, tantrums, clowning, nervousness, and so on.

4. The parent-teacher conferences should encourage the meeting of emotional problems of the child.

5. The teacher should call upon professional help in diagnosing special problems and acquiring suggestions for working with the child.

6. All community resources should be brought to bear upon understanding the child and in meeting his emotional needs.

Although these principles are general in nature, it should be stated again that the elementary school teacher is in a strategic position for meeting the emotional needs of the child. From the first year of school the child is ready to accept the teacher with respect and concern. As the teacher provides the right kind of support and environment the child develops emotionally and gains self-control, assurance and insight. A carefully planned program by the teacher can insure an emotional growth, even as planned learning experiences in arithmetic may produce the ability to solve certain problems.

SUMMARY

Since there is evidence that beginning teachers especially see a need for understanding children better in order to be more effective in teaching, emphasis here has been on presenting some basic principles of child development, together with suggested guides for furthering child study and for working with children. The physical, intellectual, and motor development of the child point up the principle that though each person follows a pattern, every individual is unique and requires special attention by the teacher. The competencies for the social development of children are listed as objectives for the teacher in the classroom. These objectives serve a dual purpose of helping the teacher in arranging learning situations to foster such competencies, and furnishing clues for better understanding of the child's progress in social development. Guides for the teacher in appraising the physical and social development of the child are furnished.

The psychodynamic factors in child development are discussed in terms of some general approaches to the problem; brief reviews of psychoanalysis and the socio-psychological theory are given. The emotional needs of children are also discussed. As the teacher understands more about the child's psychological development, it is clear that such concepts are needed for more intelligent planning of classroom experiences.

The last section is devoted to a discussion of suggested ways of working with children from the developmental point of view. Since there is evidence that studying children does not necessarily change the behavior of teachers in the classroom, it is believed that this discussion may contribute to the actual changing of teacher attitude and behavior. Some practical suggestions are given to aid in obtaining and organizing information about the child. Four implications for better teaching in light of child understandings are presented to stimulate further thinking. The causal approach in working with children indicates that the teacher understands children by preparing reading and study materials that are designed to help children to think causally. Five psychological principles are offered to show how the teacher, through understanding of child behavior, may influence the child in the classroom. Finally, the emotional problems of children are discussed in terms of how the teacher may deal with them.

SUGGESTED ACTIVITIES

1. Find an actual classroom problem in a local situation and apply as far as possible the 13 questions listed on p. 33. Discuss the case in terms of how much must be learned about the child.

2. Make a brief case study of a child, using the guides suggested in this chapter, and discuss certain features, i.e. the special physical, intellectual, social, or motor characteristics. Include any salient emotional factors. Use the suggestions for collecting and organizing data. This may be either an individual or group project.

3. Observe a classroom and learn which child is a disturbing influence. Study him and try to understand the dynamics of his behavior patterns in light of the four competencies given on page 40. Report your conclusions to the class.

4. Assign a class report about psychoanalysis that will summarize the main principles, point up its contributions, and note its weaknesses. Secure any implications for modern day teaching.

5. Contrast the socio-psychological theory with the psychoanalytic theory in understanding children.

6. Observe a group of children and note what emotional needs are apparently being met, and which, if any, are being denied. Suggest what changes could be made to meet various emotional needs. Use the suggestions listed in this chapter as a guide.

7. Summarize the things that the elementary school teacher should know about the adolescent. Discuss how such knowledge should be helpful to the teacher in the elementary school.

8. Review the implications for better teaching given on pages 52 and 53 and examine for practicality. Extend the list.

9. List a number of different things that can be done in the classroom to help children to think causally. Show how understanding of the child must be in evidence.

10. Examine the five suggestions on page 57 that discuss how the teacher may influence children. Indicate what understandings of the child are needed under each item.

11. After completing Chapter 2 have all students who have never taught in an elementary school submit a list of questions about further understandings they would like to have about children. Either submit these questions to

members of the class who are experienced, to a panel of in-service teachers, or to someone qualified to react to them in a practical way. This concluding experience may well serve to summarize the chapter, as well as to point up what information has been or will be secured in certain physical growth and development courses and in educational psychology.

SELECTED READINGS

Almy, Millie. *Child Development*. New York: Holt, Rinehart & Winston, Inc., 1955, Chapters 9, 10, 11, and 12.

Bernard, Harold W., and Wesley C. Huckins. *Readings in Human Development*. Boston: Allyn and Bacon, Inc., 1967, Sections V, VIII.

Crow, Lester D., and Alice Crow. *Human Development and Learning*. New York: American Book Company, 1956, Chapters 3, 4, and 5.

Dreikurs, Rudolf. *Psychology in the Classroom*. New York: Harper & Row, Publishers, 1957, Chapters 1, 2, and 3.

Jenkins, Gladys G., Helen S. Shacter, and William W. Bauer. *These Are Your Children*. 3rd ed.; Glenview, Ill.: Scott, Foresman and Company, 1966.

Jersild, Arthur T. *Child Psychology*. 4th ed.; Englewood, N. J.: Prentice-Hall, Inc., 1954.

Landreth, Catherine. *The Psychology of Early Childhood*. New York: Alfred A. Knopf, Inc., 1958, Chapters 1 and 2.

Lane, Harvard A. and Marg Beauchamp. *Understanding Human Development*. Englewood Cliffs, N. J.: Prentice-Hall, Inc., 1959.

Martin, William E. and Celia B. Stendler. *Child Development*. New York: Harcourt, Brace & World, Inc., 1953, Chapters 1, 2, 7, 11, and 12.

Millard, Cecil V. *Child Growth and Development*. Boston: D. C. Heath & Company, 1958.

Olson, Willard C. *Child Development*. 2nd ed.; Boston: D. C. Heath & Company, 1959.

Prescott, Daniel A. *The Child in the Educative Process*. New York: McGraw-Hill Book Company, 1957, Chapters 1, 4, 5, 6, and 7.

Sarason, Seymour, Kenneth S. Davidson, Frederick K. Lighthall, Richard R. Waite, and Britton K. Rulbush. *Anxiety in Elementary School Children*. New York: John Wiley & Sons, Inc., 1960.

Theman, Viola. "Emerging Concepts of Child Growth and Development: What They Suggest for Classroom Practices," 13th Yearbook of the John Dewey Society, *The American Elementary School*. New York: Harper & Row, Publishers, 1953, Chapter 4.

Thompson, G. C., E. F. Gardner, and F. J. Di Vesta. *Educational Psychology*. New York: Appleton-Century-Crofts, 1959, Chapter 18.

Waetjen, Walter B. (ed.). *New Dimensions in Learning: A Multidisciplinary Approach*. Papers and reports from the Sixth Curriculum Research Institute; Washington, D.C.: Association for Supervision and Curriculum Development, 1962.

CHAPTER 3

Focus on Learning

INTRODUCTION

Classroom teachers who work effectively with children are constantly aware of the factors which affect learning. They recognize that the desired outcomes of classroom experiences are achieved to the extent that the learner and the learning environment are wisely assessed and planned as part of the teaching procedure.

It is the purpose of this chapter to direct attention to the factors that influence learning and to the characteristics of desirable learning situations as they are known to exist in typical classrooms. The concern here is not with the exploration of learning theories, but the consideration of the outcomes of learning and the conditions which affect these outcomes. For the student who desires to familiarize himself with theories of learning as advanced by the several schools of psychological thought, pertinent references are included at the end of the chapter.

WHAT IS LEARNING?

A rather commonly accepted concept of learning states that "learning is the modification of behavior as a function of practice in motor, ideational, or affective responses."[1] In other words, as the child encounters and responds to different situations in his environment, he acts or behaves in a certain manner as a result of these experiences. Thus, the

---

[1] Louis Thorpe, *Child Psychology and Development* (New York: The Ronald Press Company, 1955), p. 547.

child is in a continuous state of change as far as his mental and physical behavior is concerned. As these changes become part of the individual's behavior, learning is said to occur. According to this concept of learning, behavior which results from the child's experiences may be desirable or undesirable. Since the school is concerned with helping the child develop desirable patterns of behavior in accord with his own individual needs and the demands of society, it is important that the child's relationships with other children and with adults contribute to stable emotions and cooperative attitudes. Emotional stability, personality adjustment, and social attitudes have been regarded by many persons as relatively unimportant in the learning experiences of children. However, since learning involves feelings as well as ideas and physical behavior, the teacher must be concerned with all aspects of learning.

The future teacher may be more concerned with listing the outcomes of learning rather than defining the learning process. Thus, memorization of a large number of facts may be one outcome of learning. Perhaps proficiency in rope skipping or proper use of eating utensils may also represent other outcomes of learning. Then the learning process itself has to do with "a sequence of mental processes which leads to changes in the learner."[2] Changes which may occur in the learner as a result of mental processes may be in the form of ideas, attitudes, physical activities, or combinations of all of these.

There is some objection to regarding the learning process as one which results only in behavior changes, since there is a tendency to define "behavior" as something, such as physical activity, that can be seen. If behavior is regarded as including emotional activity and ideational responses, as well as visible reactions to stimuli in the environment, then perhaps the concept is adequate.

In any learning situation it is difficult to separate the outcomes into attitudes, ideas, or skills. In arithmetic class the child may learn certain addition "facts." He may also learn attitudes about other children, about the value of arithmetic, and about the teacher. Learning, then, is a process which leads to a variety of *changes* in an individual and his mental development (a term used frequently as a synonym for learning, but more accurately described as a part of the learning process.) As learning brings about the extension of reading or other skills, it contributes to the child's mental development.

---

[2] W. C. Cummins and Barry Fagan, *Principles of Educational Psychology* (New York: The Ronald Press Company, 1954), p. 39.

Changes in the outward behavior of a child result from certain learnings, and these changes may in turn lead to further learnings. Thus a child who has come to recognize the letters of the alphabet may move on toward the developing of skills in spelling. These are the changes that indicate learning has occurred. Another kind of learning may be illustrated by the child who becomes oriented to a new classroom situation, as in kindergarten, and overcomes certain problems, such as the presence of strange adults and contacts with relatively large numbers of other children. This adjusting to a new environment signifies the child has been learning.

What Is Learning by Doing?

"Children learn by doing" is a statement that has been misinterpreted far too often. In the thinking of many teachers and parents, learning by doing implies a great amount of moving about in the classroom with confusion and disorganization as the result. The terms "activity" and "doing" should also be applied to mental activity (thinking) and to less conspicuous types of physical activity (listening). Depending upon the learning situation and the objectives to be secured, physical activity, to the extent that there is much moving about the classroom, may promote or hinder efficient learning. The classroom teacher provides prudent guidance in planning for the most efficient learning experiences for children so as to make use of that type of physical activity which is appropriate.

Constructing an Eskimo dwelling may constitute a desirable learning experience if the children have some ideas why Eskimos live in dwellings different from most of those found in the United States. If the children intend to gain a visual concept of an Eskimo dwelling and understand why it is functional in certain parts of the world, the physical activity may be rewarding.

As children read about life in America during the nineteenth century they may want to churn butter, make candles, and the like in order to gain appreciation of the ways of living before the advent of modern conveniences.

What Is Mechanical Learning?

Mechanical learning activities of the "cite" and "recite" types have been so strongly criticized in some quarters that many teachers may doubt the value of "practice" or "drill." Usually, learning activities of the so-called mechanistic type are centered largely upon the memory aspect of learning. Certainly, drill and practice, as a means for securing facts for the child's use, have a place in the school program. The misuse of mechanistic methods of teaching and overemphasis on the mechanistic aspect of learning led teachers to ignore the fact that children's attitudes, emotions, and interests are affected by the learning process.

In order that the child may be able to locate information in an encyclopedia, for example, it is a requisite for the child to become familiar with the names and order of the letters of the alphabet. Memorizing by repetition of the alphabet may aid the child in this instance, but the question to be decided by the classroom teacher is: When should drill and practice sessions occur? If drill or practice is to be most effective, the teacher takes into account (1) the reason for which drill is used; (2) the meaning which drill contains for the child in any given situation; (3) the further learnings which are to follow the drill sessions; and (4) the opportunities which the child will have through drill to develop insight into the learning task. Drill as an end in itself is not justified, but it may be quite necessary as readiness for further learning tasks. In all circumstances where drill is indicated the child must be given ample opportunities to acquire the insight into the learning problem for which the drill is being used.

An example of purposeful practice or drill was observed by one of the authors upon a visit to a fifth grade classroom. In the situation which is here described, children practiced with enthusiasm because there was an acceptable goal in view.

> Miss Doan's fifth grade pupils had invited their parents to a classroom tea. In preparing for the occasion, the children found it necessary to determine the number of cookies that would be needed and to compute the cost. It was important, also, that they determine how many boxes of tea would be needed, depending, of course, on how many cups of tea can be prepared from a given box of tea. Review of multiplication facts was needed by some of the pupils, while practice on division processes was required by others as they found the problem of dividing up the cost of the tea among the children in the room. In such situations, the matter of purchasing tea and cookies is no longer relegated to the story book—it becomes an important concern of children who want their party to be handled properly and correctly.

Miss Doan could have taken care of all the financial matters which arose in connection with the classroom tea. She recognized, however, that children can find in real life situations the reasons for practicing the arithmetic skills. It is true that teachers may not always find convenient situations for purposeful drill. However, the teacher who is aware of the possibilities and effectiveness of purposeful drill will certainly be in a position to sense the opportunities when they exist.

The use of drill-dominated learning experiences may continue to be a matter of concern to those who feel that the brain "muscle" needs exercising in long drill sessions even though the drill material has little relevancy to the learning problems of children. This is quite likely an influence of the faculty theory of learning. In the use of drill situations the teacher may do well to ask herself: how will drill help children perform more effectively in the learning and living situations which they encounter?

FORCES THAT AFFECT THE LEARNING PROCESS

Teachers today recognize that there are a number of factors which seem to influence the learnings of children. No longer may the teacher assume that placing children in straight rows, insisting upon absolute quiet, and preparing lessons will result in effective learning. Because of the presence of many forces in the lives of children, there are certain approaches and considerations that teachers must make as they plan and work with children.

Some of the factors which influence learning have been thoroughly studied by psychologists in recent years. Classroom teachers have also taken an active interest in making careful observations of the learning activities of children. Thus, out of this increased attention to the factors which affect learning have come certain findings of definite interest. "Basic needs" of children have been identified as being important to the learning process; "readiness" is another factor that has been recognized; the "maturation" and "intelligence" of the child are still other concerns in the child's learning performance; and the "previous experiences" and "purposes" of the learner are also thought to have considerable effect upon the learning process.

As psychologists and teachers continue to devote themselves to the study and observation of the learner and the learning situation, other forces which play important roles in the learning process will doubtless be identified.

What Are Some Basic Needs of Children?

As the child attempts to adjust himself satisfactorily to the changing situations of his world, it becomes apparent that there are certain "needs" which must be met. These "needs" have been described in numerous ways by educators, psychologists and sociologists. In most cases the basic needs involve:

1. Physical well being,
2. A satisfying home life,
3. Acceptance by others in one's own age group,
4. Experiencing success,
5. A feeling of self-worth.

Some writers on the problem of basic needs have attempted to arrange the needs in the order of their importance to the existence of the individual. For example, the need for food, clothing, and shelter as prime requisites for physical well-being would be at the top of the list. No attempt has been made to ascribe rank importance here inasmuch as the teacher must be aware of and concerned with all of the needs of children.

The need for physical well-being includes security from violence as well as satisfaction of basic bodily needs. The child who is afraid of being physically mistreated by his age mates or by adults will be hindered in his efforts to make a satisfactory schoolroom adjustment. Certainly, his learnings will be affected adversely, and, at worst, it may be expected that undesirable social attitudes will be learned.

The case of Anne illustrates the fact that failure to satisfy basic needs in one area may have harmful effects upon efforts made by the child to satisfy needs in other areas. Acceptance by one's fellows, a feeling of self-worth, and success in some areas of achievement are certainly closely related needs.

> The case of Anne is an example of the problems brought about by failure to satisfy the need for physical well-being. Anne lived with her mother and a younger sister in a basement apartment with no plumbing facilities. Bathing was infrequent and clothing was seldom laundered. Anne was hindered in making friends with her second grade classmates because they found her to be physically repulsive. No one wanted to be seated near Anne. As a result of this social ostracism, Anne did not like to go to school. Her teacher recognized the problem as one that required the help of the school nurse and the mother. Needless to say, an improvement in Anne's personal appearance and bodily cleanliness created an improved attitude toward school and made the establishment of friendships easier.

One of the paradoxical aspects of man's attempt to satisfy his need for social acceptance is the fact that he must subjugate his individuality in many instances. As they plan for a wholesome learning environment, the teachers' thought and attention should center on the implications and dangers involved when the individual socializes and the expense of individual expression. Further discussion will be devoted to this problem in a later chapter, and an excellent treatment of this topic may be found in the writings of Fromm.[3]

What Is Readiness?

Readiness is a comparatively new concept in education, having received much attention during the past twenty years. Readiness was initially regarded as that state of mental receptiveness wherein the learner was disposed to approach the situation at hand. More recently it has come to be looked upon as a composite of several factors; and such concepts as social readiness, emotional readiness, and physical readiness have come to be recognized as important in the child's educational life.

Readiness may also be regarded as that period during which the conditions affecting learning are favorable for effective performance by the child. Lack of opportunity to learn that which is expected of the child at the "appropriate" time may have unfavorable effects upon the later learnings of the child in the specific area.

The relatedness of the various types of readiness has come to be recognized. A child may appear to be mentally mature to the extent that he should succeed in reading. However, if the child has impaired vision, defective speech, or other physical difficulties[4] such conditions may interfere with the child's readiness for reading.

Emotional instability due to an insecure home life may interfere with the child's educational readiness to the extent that he cannot give sufficient attention to a task, and hence, does not learn efficiently.

Readiness to engage in one particular learning activity does not imply that the child is ready to engage in all other activities common to the child's age group. A child of first grade age may be ready for the social learnings to be experienced in the group, although he may not be ready for manuscript writing because of poor muscle coordination.

Readiness, like certain other forces which influence the learning process, is the result of hereditary patterns of development and the previous experiences of the individual. It is in this respect that the impor-

---

[3] Erich Fromm, *Escape from Freedom* (New York: Holt, Rinehart & Winston, Inc., 1941); Erich Fromm, *Man for Himself* (New York: Holt, Rinehart & Winston, Inc., 1947).

[4] Margaret G. McKim, *Guiding Growth in Reading* (New York: The Macmillan Co., 1955), p. 62.

tance of early childhood experiences is brought to light in the case of Larry.

> Larry entered first grade without the benefit of kindergarten. Although he gave evidence of being sufficiently mature mentally to begin reading, he was distracted by the presence of the other children in the room. He seemed to be overly concerned about his safety from the aggressiveness of other children. On the playground, Larry would not play on the "jungle gym" or use the swing. He avoided any active play with others. After several weeks, Larry's teacher learned that the boy had been afraid to play actively with others, almost since birth, due to the fact that his mother had told him repeatedly that he would be hurt. For Larry adjustment to the active environment of the classroom and playground was a slow process during which he had to overcome the effects of undesirable learnings.

A state of reading readiness may exist for the typical 6½-year-old. In fact, the social pressures placed upon the first grade child with regard to beginning reading is a factor in reading readiness. A number of children who are eagerly awaiting the first grade and the opportunity to begin reading may lack necessary control of the eye muscles. A deficiency in one aspect of reading readiness may bring about frustration if the child is ready in other important aspects. Certainly, it is important that the teacher provide interesting and challenging learning activities for all children, inasmuch as the child who is not ready for a learning task cannot be expected to sit quietly by and wait for "readiness."

There is, likewise, little doubt that some children are quite ready to read before first grade. The fact that kindergarten teachers provide stimulating opportunities for learnings in other areas probably draws the child's interest away from reading. However, insofar as reading is a basic skill that opens the gateway to infinite experiences through books, there must remain some question as to whether the child who is ready to read should be delayed.

Commins and Fagin[5] draw an interesting comparison between what they term the "pacing" method of instruction and the older "forcing" methods. In the former, the educational experience is geared to the developmental level of the child; in the latter, the child is pressed into very challenging activities with small regard for readiness factors.

In classroom situations where "forcing" is the rule, the teacher may well expect a low rate of retention and utilization of facts and skills by the children. Insofar as the child lacks maturity to the extent that he is

---

[5] Commins and Fagin, *op. cit.*, p. 162.

not ready for a specific learning situation, there is much doubt that the learning experiences will come to be incorporated into behavior patterns.[6] Then, readiness for any learning task, whether of a physical, social, or mental nature, involves the state of physical, social, emotional, and mental maturity of the individual.

How Is Readiness Appraised?

In order to organize the classroom for any form of learning activity, it is essential that the teacher possess some information concerning the readiness of the individual pupils for the various learning experiences. Ordinarily the classroom teacher will find it convenient and informative to draw upon three methods for appraising readiness. These methods are (1) obtaining information from parents, from previous teachers, and from cumulative pupil records; (2) observing the pupils directly in classroom and playground situations; and (3) using standardized tests including intelligence tests, achievement tests, and readiness tests.

Readiness is properly the concern of teachers of all youngsters, even though a great deal of attention to first grade readiness problems may lead one to assume that readiness begins and ends with the first year of school. With each new learning task the teacher will need to be aware of the readiness of the child for that experience. The teaching of multiplication will likely be quite effective if the child is ready as a result of mental maturity and previous successful experiences with numbers. This will be treated in more detail in Chapter 9.

How May Readiness Be Fostered?

To the extent that maturation as a natural process cannot be hastened by artificial stimulation, readiness for a learning experience may not be hurried. However, in situations where the child lacks readiness due to a dearth of certain experiences in the home or in previous school life, it is possible to plan a number of activities which will promote readiness. An example may be found in the case of Vernon, a five-year-old.

> Vernon came to kindergarten with very little experience with books of any kind. The customary picture books were new to him. He was apparently unaware of the fact that books might contain stories of interest to him. In other classroom situations, as in playing with blocks, Vernon revealed evidence of normal intelligence. As the teacher planned a de-

---

[6] Gertrude Hildreth, *Readiness for School Beginners* (New York: World Book Company, 1950), p. 6.

velopmental program for Vernon, she provided time for him to occupy himself with pictures and picture books. She encouraged Vernon to tell what he liked about stories which were read to him. The teacher encouraged Vernon to tell the other children about interesting happenings outside of school. She gave Vernon opportunities to tell stories which he saw in sequential arrangements of pictures. Vernon's parents were provided suggestions as to books they might provide for reading to him at home.

Vernon had sufficient mental maturity and language background to benefit from the experiences which his teacher planned in an effort to promote reading readiness. Kindergarten may well be looked upon as a place replete with opportunities for promoting readiness to the extent allowed by the child's physical and mental maturity. It is a thoughtful proposal of many kindergarten teachers that the social adjustments of kindergarten are often sufficiently challenging to the five-year-old to preclude formal reading instruction, even though the child appears ready in other respects.

Readiness, then, for any learning task involves a number of factors ranging from organismic maturation to the influences of past and present environmental conditions. In many instances readiness may be promoted through pertinent experiences in and out of school. In other instances, readiness to engage in a specific learning activity may have to await maturation of physical or mental factors which are not subject to external acceleration. In order to work effectively with children the teacher must make decisions as to the readiness status of individual children. He must also decide on suitable programs of readiness development when a lack of readiness is indicated.

In summation, then, it may be said that readiness is not a unique stage of development which is separate from the preceding or later experiences of the child. Readiness is, as Mursell has pointed out, "a part of the continuous growth process."[7] It is not so much a question of the child's readiness for reading; rather, it is a question of the child's readiness for a *specific* phase of reading experience. The three-year-old may obtain information and meaning from contact with pictures, and in the sense that he may be reading pictures, he gains meaning from printed symbols. Likewise, the three-year-old may select the larger of two pieces of candy or he may choose the plate containing three cookies rather than the dish containing only one. In such situations, then, we may find the

---

[7] James L. Mursell, *Principles of Democratic Education* (New York: W. W. Norton and Co., Inc., 1955) p. 228.

child using certain reading processes and certain aspects of quantitative thinking long before he will participate in a formal learning program in reading and arithmetic. The proper concern of the teacher must be directed toward the child's readiness for further growth in certain phases of learning because readiness is a part of the total growth of the child and cannot be regarded as a period to be provided only for five-year-olds and never considered again.

How Does Intelligence Affect Learning?

Intelligence has been regarded as a mental factor that "manages the learning processes"; it has been looked upon by some as a composite of many mental factors, and by others as that which is observable in the adaptive behavior of a person.[8] Bischof[9] has suggested that intelligence be regarded as "the ability to solve problems of all kinds." He has further proposed that of the many definitions of intelligence, all have a common element in that they regard intelligence as the ability to solve problems in the academic and social areas.

The teacher should rely upon observations of actual pupil performance and the results of group and individual intelligence tests for clues and information as to the child's mental capacities. With the information procured by careful observation and formal testing, the teacher may plan educational activities appropriate to the child's capacity. It is in this regard that mental maturity in terms of mental age, rather than intelligence quotient, may be looked upon as an important element in readiness for certain learning tasks.

In other words, an intelligence quotient of 110 for a four-year-old child would not, in and of itself, suggest a level of mental maturity sufficient to attempt formal reading instruction. The teacher needs to consider mental age, among other things, in such instances. Again it is necessary to point out that mental age must also be considered in the light of other factors. The child who is chronologically ten years old but who has a mental age of 7 years should not be considered analogous to the six-year-old who has a mental age of 7 years. Many factors should be included with intelligence quotient and mental age when one attempts to assess the educational status of an individual child.

---

[8] Carrol A. Whitmer, "Has Man Measured His Intelligence?" *University of Pittsburgh Quarterly* (Autumn, 1941), 38-40. George D. Stoddard, "On The Meaning of Intelligence," *Psychological Review* (1941), 250-60.

[9] L. J. Bischof, *Intelligence, Statistical Concepts of Its Nature* (Garden City, N. Y.: Doubleday and Co., Inc., 1954), p. 1.

Good has stated that "language is a highly sensitive indicator of intelligence and, barring specific handicaps, there is no evidence that those who cannot understand or use their native language with facility are likely to be endowed with some special kind of 'general mental ability'."[10] The teacher may make careful and frequent observations concerning the child's language development. This should not be limited to reading performance alone, but should consider oral language, listening comprehension, and written expression—all forms of language as a means of communication.[11] It is important that the influences of the home be included in any judgment of intelligence based on language ability.

Do Previous Experiences Affect Learning?

All children bring to school backgrounds of abundant experiences. Since all children are in states of interaction with the persons and things of the environment, it is not a question of whether the child has had many and varied experiences; rather it is a question of the types of experiences involved. Even the child who comes from a home barren of books, pictures, records, radio, television, and trips to various points, has had, nonetheless, experiences of many types. The teacher is concerned with the nature of previous experiences and their contribution to the child's readiness to engage in particular school activities.

Obviously, the school cannot attempt to control the pre-school activities and environment of the child in order to insure those experiences which will promote readiness for learning tasks of the classroom. The teacher must recognize the influence of experiences outside of the school, and in cases where readiness appears to be lacking because of a dearth of appropriate experiences, the instructor should make every effort to enrich the school program with firsthand experiences. A trip to the local post office may do more to aid children in developing understandings of the postman's job than any number of stories about him. A visit to the bank may be invaluable to the sixth or seventh grade pupils who are concerned with "interest" problems in arithmetic. When the child has some meaningful concepts of the actual operations of banks and other similar businesses, he is able to enter into the abstract learning

---

[10] Warren R. Good, "Misconceptions About Intelligence Testing," *Test Service Bulletin No. 79* (New York: Harcourt, Brace & World, Inc.), p. 4.

[11] Richard Gunderson and Leonard S. Feldt, "The Relationship of Differences Between Verbal and Nonverbal Intelligence Scores to Achievement," *The Journal of Educational Psychology*, 51 (June, 1960), 115-21.

situations with greater confidence and understanding. Readiness may present a challenge to the sixth grade arithmetic teacher quite as often as to the first grade reading teacher.

What Is the Role of Purpose in Learning?

The role of purpose in the learning process has been the subject of study and research for a considerable period of time. Certain writers referred to *purpose* as being the driving force behind any type of behavior. Other writers looked upon purpose as being synonymous with motive. In the early part of this century, a great deal of thought and experimentation was devoted to "purposive" behavior.[12] In many instances, *purpose was regarded as being that part of a specific behavior pattern which provided the impetus of movement or action toward attainment of a goal.*

The implications of *purpose* as a factor in learning in the school setting may be realized if it is accepted that children will have increased interest toward and exert more energy in an activity or problem which is of importance to them.[13]

Whether the child is at all times conscious and aware of all the purposes behind his behavior is not pertinent at this point. It is important, however, that the teacher recognize that purposes and interests are present in all children.[14] The teacher who fears that "interest" cannot be created among children may be ignoring the fact that everyone has interests and purposes that are closely related to his personal life. An important function of the teacher is to recognize these existing purposes and interests in order that the learning experiences of the school may build upon them.

In view of the many issues in educational practice which center around purpose, interest, and motivation, it is necessary that the teacher be familiar with some of the extensive research which has been carried on in this area. The person who suggests that teachers should not waste their valuable time in familiarizing themselves with existing pupil pur-

---

[12] See C. H. Judd, "Practice Without Knowledge of Results," *Psychological Monographs*, 1905-1906, pp. 185-98; C. C. Ross, "An Experiment in Motivation," *Journal of Educational Psychology*, 18 (1927), 337-46; T. H. Briggs, "Praise and Censure as Incentives," *School and Society*, 26 (1927), 596-8; E. C. Tolman, *Purposive Behavior in Animals and Men* (Berkeley, Cal.: University of California Press, 1949.)

[13] Edward William Dolch, *Methods In Reading* (Champaign, Ill.: The Garrard Press, 1955), pp. 28-42.

[14] John Dewey, *Interest and Effort in Education* (Boston: Houghton Mifflin Co., 1913), p. 19.

teachers with much data in support of their important role in providing
interest, purpose, and motivation in learning tasks[15] for children.
poses and interests is, quite obviously, disregarding the research findings
of psychologists. It is evident that the activities of most adults are carried
on in view of immediate and future purposes. Research has provided
teachers with much data in support of their important role in providing
interest, purpose, and motivation in learning tasks[15] for children.

Thorpe has stated the effects of interest upon learning thus:

> Learning proceeds most effectively and tends to be most permanent
> when the learner is motivated, that is, when he has an interest, a stake, as
> it were, in the activity being undertaken.[16]

It may be that some teachers find themselves giving considerable
thought to those ways of building pupil interest by artificial means. Such
procedures in stimulating pupil interest will likely be far less effective
than if the ever-present interests of children were explored and related to
school learnings. The classroom store situation, which of course must
be carefully planned, is an example of the manner in which pupil interests can be drawn upon as a basis for school learnings. Eisen[17] has reported on the economic concepts, arithmetic skills, and social learnings
that were involved as third grade children operated a classroom store.
It should be stated that the classroom "store," which contains only empty
cans, used boxes, and the like, does not truly represent an activity based
upon existing genuine interests of children.

Purpose, interest, and the motivation to pursue some desired form
of activity are definitely related to the amount of effort and the persistence
with which an individual engages in the task. This fact has important
bearings upon the activity of the teacher, whether he is guiding children
in acquiring the skills involved in hop-scotch, or in developing the concepts of distances in the realm of outer space.

Retention, or remembering, is related to the meaning and purpose
which the learner associates with the learning task. In order to avoid
inefficient or "wasteful" learning, it is necessary to insure that meaning
and purpose are parts of the learning situation.[18]

Forms of motivation.   In any discussion of the forms of motivation
it is not unusual for the terms "extrinsic" and "intrinsic" to be introduced.

---

[15] A. T. Jersild and R. J. Tasch, *Children's Interests and What They Suggest
for Education* (New York: Columbia University, Bureau of Publications, Teacher's
College, 1949).

[16] Thorpe, *op. cit.*, p. 554.

[17] Agnes Eisen, "Economic Education Through a School Store," *The Elementary School Journal*, 58 (February, 1958), 287-89.

[18] Commins and Fagin, *op cit.*, pp. 651-55.

From a psycho-biological point of view it is difficult to determine the differences between these forms of motivation. Seagoe[19] has suggested that the intrinsic forms of motivation are those which exist in ordinary life situations within the experiences of the learner and which are similar to the problem at hand. Extrinsic forms of motivation would be those that are introduced from sources quite apart from the learner and have little or no relation to the present experiences of the child. The promise of gold stars for excellence in spelling or arithmetic would more than likely constitute an extrinsic form of motivation, inasmuch as the awarding of stars has little relationship to the child's actual needs and experiences in the areas mentioned. An activity in which the children are writing stories to be read to pupils in other rooms may provide considerable intrinsic motivation, since children are familiar with the enjoyment of stories and may take pains to write legibly for the benefit of the readers.

Warden and Cohen[20] studied the use of several forms of motivation with children and observed that external forms of motivation are not as effective as many educators would believe. It is not uncommon, however, to find high school and college students who are so accustomed to the external forms of motivation that they have difficulty in adjusting to learning situations which lack such forms of motivation.

Munn has concluded that learning is inefficient, if not absent, unless motivation to learn is present; but he has stated further that it is not possible to say which kind of motivation or incentive is most effective.[21] Praise may be more effective than blame in many situations, but it may not be as effective as a reward of candy or an extra recess period. The classroom teacher will want to be aware of the need for different kinds of motivation for individual pupils and that there are no recipes for pupil motivation that will work for all children.

Other studies of motivation have suggested that the teacher must be concerned with the emotional motivation of children quite as much as with their intellectual motivation.[22] Human beings do not perform in a rational manner merely as the result of intellectual motivation; emotional factors enter in. Studies by Sears and others have indicated that

---

[19] May V. Seagoe, *A Teacher's Guide to the Learning Process* (Dubuque, Iowa: Wm. C. Brown Co., 1956), p. 22.

[20] C. J. Warden and A. Cohen, "A Study of Certain Incentives Applied under School Room Conditions," *Journal of Genetic Psychology*, 39 (September, 1931), 320-27.

[21] Norman L. Munn, *Psychology* (Boston: Houghton Mifflin Co., 1951), pp. 177-78.

[22] John A. Blake, "Comprehension Versus Motivation in Child Behavior," *Understanding the Child*, 24 (June, 1955), 77-9.

achievement and self-esteem are two powerful forces of human motivation although various individuals will react in various ways according to differing self-concepts, personal goals, and the like.[23] How a child *feels* about arithmetic may be quite as important as what he *knows* about arithmetic; his emotional motivation may be as effective as his intellectual motivation. The performance that a child expects of himself, his own ambitions and goals, may likewise be powerful motivating factors. Thus it becomes clear that the teacher cannot expect to motivate the slow learner and the rapid learner in identical manners, but she must know as much as possible about individual interests, ambitions, and capabilities in order that motivation may be provided that will reach the individual child.[24]

It is true that gold stars, awards, badges, and the like may provide a rather temporary incentive, but it seems that the child is apt to find himself at the end of his purposes once the prizes have been won. The teacher could be in the position of operating a gigantic educational lottery, with an endless assortment of prizes to be exchanged for efforts and accomplishments in the classroom.

In summary, research on the various forms of motivation has indicated that:[25]

1. Extrinsic motivation often results in temporary learning.
2. Extrinsic motivation seems to be more effective with the egocentric child than with the emotionally stable child.
3. Extrinsic motivation usually ends with the winning of the award.

Motivation through group activities.   It is apparent that the child in a classroom situation will be influenced by the activities and the accomplishments of the other children. That is, the child may be motivated to greater effort due to his acceptance of group goals. The competition with other pupils in the class may cause the child to strive toward the goals at hand. However, if the goals to be sought are unrealistic to the child in terms of his ability, then competitive or teacher-imposed incentives may result in the child's withdrawal and refusal to participate in a given activity.

---

[23] Pauline S. Sears, "Problems in the Investigation of Achievement and Self-Esteem Motivation," *Nebraska Symposium on Motivation* (Lincoln: University of Nebraska Press, 1957), pp. 265-67.

[24] See Don E. Hamachek, *What Research Says to the Teacher: Motivation in Teaching and Learning.* Washington, D. C.: Association for Supervision and Curriculum Development, 1968, p. 7.

[25] Seagoe, *op. cit.*, p. 30.

Cooperative group action has been regarded by certain sociologists and anthropologists as representing advanced forms of social development.[26] Classroom activities which require cooperation rather than competition by children as they move toward commonly held objectives result in higher qualities of interpersonal relationships.[27] Competition tends to cause greater effort than does cooperation, but results more often in negative social attitudes among the children.[28]

There are many opportunities for the teacher to direct competitive efforts into individual channels. An example of this is found in the following illustration:

> In the building where Miss J. taught fifth grade, it was a common practice among the teachers to display only those samples of pupil work which were outstanding for the grade. It was possible for an entire year to pass with some of the pupils never having the opportunity to see their work displayed. Miss J. planned her displays of pupil work so that five or six samples of one child's work in spelling or writing were exhibited together for one specific purpose: to show the improvement the child had made. Children were encouraged to select their own samples of work to be displayed on the classroom bulletin board. The bulletin board carried the caption, HOW WE HAVE IMPROVED. Competition between pupils was minimized in order that each child might concentrate upon improvement of his own skills rather than being absorbed in the problems of another child who was superior.

The structure or composition of American society has been considered by many persons to be highly competitive in nature. This concept may have definite affects upon the aggressiveness of children as they strive for recognition by surpassing the other children. However, if the goal is only to do better than certain other children in the room, it is likely that the exceptionally bright child will find it possible to drift along easily. He may lead the group with little real effort on his part, and receive the acclaim of the teachers and pupils for an excellence not commensurate with his real potentialities. Society and the individual alike will be better served when children strive for self-improvement in keeping with their capacities.

---

[26] H. S. Sullivan, *Conceptions of Modern Psychiatry* (Washington, D. C.: William Alanson White Psychiatric Foundation, 1947), pp. 14-21.

[27] C. Stendler, D. Damrin, and A. C. Haines, "Studies in Cooperation and Competition:" "I. The Effects of Working for Group and Individual Rewards on the Social Climate of Children's Groups," *Journal of Genetic Psychology*, 79 (Dec., 1951), 173-97.

[28] Seagoe, *op. cit.*, p. 121.

Certain persons have suggested that the best way to motivate children in school is to inject the same type of competition which they claim exists in adult life. These suggestions frequently fail to point out that the adult generally has some choice in selecting his field of endeavor. In most cases the adult will enter an occupation or profession in which he feels there are possibilities for success. Thus, the plumber does not vie with the attorney for clientele; the college president does not compete with the architect for a position; the postman does not attempt to outshine the auto mechanic.

In the classroom there are certain educational experiences which are deemed valuable for all children. In terms of effective learning it seems reasonable that each child should be introduced to such experiences as multiplication, spelling, and the like when they are ready and able to profit from them. Then, motivation in the classroom must be geared to the individual child. As a matter of fact, some lay observers of public education seem to be accepting the idea that it is important to recognize and provide for the differing needs of individuals in terms of motivation within the classroom.[29]

Motivation through success. It has been said that, "Nothing succeeds like success." There is probably considerable truth in this statement for one concerned with motivating children. In a situation where success seems to be not only improbable but almost impossible, the child is apt to become emotionally involved and retreat from the situation. This is undesirable in terms of the child's approach to the problem at hand and may be instrumental in later failures to attack learning problems. Success and chances for success are important in planning the learning experiences for children in the school.

A number of studies relating to the effects of failure on learning activities and future motivation have been conducted.[30] Thompson and Hunnicutt[31] among others, have reported that the use of praise or blame as a means of motivation depends very much upon the personality of the child. Generally, it appears that *efficient learning is fostered more by praise and success than by punishment and failure.* Where praise and success are used as motivating factors, attitudes are usually more satisfactory in terms of relationships with the teacher and other pupils.

---

[29] See *Time* (May 5, 1958), 39.

[30] W. W. Cook, *op. cit.;* V. Klene and E. P. Branson, "Trial Promotion Versus Failure," *Educational Research Bulletin*, Los Angeles City Schools, 8 (1929), 6-11.

[31] G. G. Thompson and C. W. Hunnicutt, "The Effect of Repeated Praise or Blame on the Work Achievement of Extroverts and Introverts," *Journal of Educational Psychology*, 35 (May, 1944), 257-66.

Occasionally one may encounter the argument which suggests that failure is a desirable condition as it causes children to face the realities of life. Proponents of a "failure" philosophy seldom take into account the fact that there is a difference between doing poorly when success should have resulted and doing poorly when success is beyond the individual's ability. In the former situation the child may intelligently criticize his poor performance; in the latter he is more likely to be frustrated. The "failure" advocates, also, seem to believe that the slow learner needs more of this valuable "failing" experience than does the bright child. At any rate, in many school situations the slow learner receives a huge portion of the "failing" experience.

Sarason and others have reported that pupils will respond differently to identical forms of motivation depending upon the level of anxiety with which they approach a problem situation.[32] As a result of experimentation, these researchers have stated that, if frustrating factors are introduced, individuals who approach a test situation with high levels of anxiety concerning successful performance will do more poorly than those individuals who have lower anxiety levels. For example, an impossible time limit on a test will affect the performance of the high anxiety pupil more than it will the performance of the low anxiety individual.[33] Again, this seems to point out that the goals of the child, in terms of self-concepts and desires for success, enter into motivation for performance to a great degree, and that the child who is not particularly worried about his performance does not find it affected so readily by adverse conditions.

Much remains to be learned about human motivation for learning, but the information which is now available suggests that teachers will definitely want to employ various approaches to pupil motivation in terms of such individual factors as:

1. Levels of aspiration,
2. Areas of interest,
3. Abilities and aptitudes,
4. Emotional and temperamental characteristics.

In certain situations a negative approach may be employed in order to weaken an undesirable habit.[34] The typist who finds herself reversing

---

[32] Seymour B. Sarason, George Mandler, and Peyton G. Craighill, "The Effect of Differential Instructions on Anxiety and Learning," *Studies In Motivation*, ed. David C. McClelland (New York: Appleton-Century-Crofts, 1955), pp. 400-47.

[33] *Ibid.*

[34] K. Dunlap, *Habits: Their Making and Unmaking* (New York: Liveright Publishing Corp., 1949).

the *t* and the *h* in *the*, may intentionally type *hte* in order to make way for the correct form. However, the use of such negative approaches must be applied carefully with elementary school children.

In summary, the motivation of children is then one of the major concerns of teachers. In most cases, it appears that motivation should be intrinsic in form; it should foster desirable social attitudes, and it should be based upon the positive or success aspects of the task at hand. As with any other phase of the learning process, the classroom teacher must be aware of the individual problems of children as she attempts to motivate them toward educational achievement.

Why Is Conditioning a Factor in Learning?

One of the best known and classic experiments dealing with conditioning is that of Pavlov in which the simultaneous ringing of a bell and offering meat to a hungry dog conditioned the response of the dog to the extent that he would salivate upon the sound of the bell even though no meat was offered. It appears that experiments with animals have implications for persons who work with human behavior only insofar as later work with human subjects confirms original hypotheses. For example, the dog in Pavlov's experiment apparently had few choices to make with respect to the presentation of the meat insofar as he was hungry, and the subsequent ringing of the bell recalled the earlier response to the same stimulus. Although it is believed that conditioning plays a large part in the formation of attitudes and emotional responses to certain situations, it must be recognized that the human creature has open to him, generally, a variety of choices as to the response made.

Conditioning probably plays a part in the development of early childhood attitudes toward certain things, such as a fear of going to kindergarten if the mention of school has been frequently accompanied by the remark that children get spanked by the teacher when they start to school. Another example of the effect of conditioning may be in the area of rote responses, such as do-re-mi-fa-so-la-___-__. The youngster, with no insight or understanding of the scale, may easily respond with the verbal symbols to the scale as played on a piano. In other situations, such as the rapid response to certain number combinations, the child may respond to the printed 1 plus 1, with a verbal "two." Garrett has suggested the conditioned responses may often be undesirable as they often lack a basis in reasoning.[35] It seems certain that conditioning will continue to be a factor in learning, however, and it is important that the

---

[35] H. E. Garrett, *Psychology* (New York: American Book Co., 1951), p. 143.

teacher be alert to the learnings that may occur in the classroom in a contiguous manner. Certainly the assignment of a long list of spelling words as punishment for unacceptable behavior may result in an unreasoned dislike for spelling, although spelling may not be particularly difficult for the individual.

In terms of attitudes which children hold toward people of other races or religions, the teacher must be aware of the fact that the children may have been verbally conditioned against certain groups. For example, the mention of "Gypsies" may have produced warnings about children being kidnapped or about things being stolen by people who travel about the country with no apparent home. Likewise, fear of animals may be the result of a conditioned learning.

A few conditioned responses of a negative nature seem to be justified in instances where they operate to safeguard the child. The three-year-old who associates "street" and "dangerous cars" may avoid injury even though she has not been able to understand all the reasons why she is apt to be hurt if she wanders into the street. The teacher should be cautious in the use of conditioned responses in view of the fact that an important aim of democratic education is to guide children toward a reasonable approach to their problems.

EMPHASES ON LEARNING

With increased interest and research into the nature of the learning process, there has been a corresponding increase in the attention given to the evaluation of pupil growth and achievement. This appears to be a rather logical development as psychologists and educators have come to consider as valuable and acceptable only those teaching procedures which give rise to desirable learnings. The performance of the child as a learner is of course of greater importance than any discussion of a single teaching procedure. In fact, teaching procedures may vary from situation to situation and from child to child in an effort to bring about effective learning. However, it would be incorrect to infer that there are no teaching procedures or methods which can be relied upon in many classroom situations. Those procedures that have been developed with due consideration for the nature of the learning process will be appropriate in many instances. The danger lies in the day to day use of the same few teaching procedures without considering the varying conditions of the learners, the environment, and that which is to be learned.

An example of the importance of considering the children and the environment of the learning experience was observed by one of the authors in an elementary school in a large Midwestern city.

It was a cold, snowy day in mid-December. The teacher of this group of fifth graders had made extensive plans for developing the interests of the children in the new unit in science. The unit was concerned with birds and their habits. In this locality there were relatively few birds remaining in December. As the discussion proceeded, the teacher attempted to stimulate interest in the characteristics of the common birds— their songs, their eggs, their nests and the like. On a cold day in December there appeared to be little genuine interest in birds of the spring and summer. It seemed reasonable to assume that the children would have been interested in the winter resident birds of their area and may have built bird feeders and shelters, if given the opportunity.

Careful planning by the teacher must include the setting as well as the children.

Children Are Different

Human beings are generally quite conscious of external physical differences between individuals, and deviating behavior is commonly noticed by the members of any society. It is not difficult to see that children are shaped differently, that they do not all weigh the same, that they differ in facial characteristics and expressions. By observation one may become aware of the differing physical strengths of children. The fact that children argue about choice of games indicates that children are different as to interests, emotions, and social development. Yet, the concept that children are different in their learning activities has been rather slowly accepted by many persons.

Man has had for centuries some concept of genius and feeble-mindedness. These conditions may have at one time been attributed to peculiar and mystical causes, but they were, nonetheless, recognized. Although today's parents recognize that one child seems to learn more rapidly than another and that some seem brighter than others, there are many who do not understand why the classroom teacher does not use the same procedures with all children. In fact, some parents believe the teacher is lowering "standards" when she does not proceed to "instruct" all children in a similar manner and insist upon uniform achievement. An illustration points up this concept:

Stuart was an eight-year-old who was experiencing considerable difficulty with the reading skills in third grade. His teacher had provided Stuart, and several other pupils, with "second" grade reading materials for instructional purposes. Stuart was happy and began to experience success. Stuart's mother was terribly upset because she was certain that Stuart should be forced to read from a "third" grade reader or he would never learn to read at that level. Since other third grade pupils were reading "third" grade material, it seemed to her that Stuart should also be expected to do as well as his classmates.

The illustration presented here is not unusual. It points out the reluctance or inability of many persons to recognize the necessity of teaching procedures being adapted to individual learning problems.

As the teacher works with children she becomes increasingly aware of the subtle differences in terms of personality, emotional stability, and mental maturity. The teacher may observe that the individual presents different reactions and abilities within himself. For example, a child may do very successful work in reading activities, but he may lag behind many of his classmates in science.

Some teachers have suggested that it is difficult to group together thirty children who appear to be fifth graders in terms of the maturity and achievements of the "typical" fifth grader. It may be equally difficult to find a single ten- or eleven-year-old who possesses all the growth and learning characteristics of the "typical" fifth grade pupil. This is one reason why the term "average" is misleading when applied to child behavior.[36]

In grouping children for instruction, teachers must be aware of the fact that there may be instances in which the child who is an accelerated reader may need to work with a slower group in arithmetic. The necessity for flexible grouping then arises. Thus it may be noted that there are variables among children in terms of their emotional, social, physical, and mental traits as well as within the individual's performance in the several areas of the curriculum. Differences which exist within the individual are generally referred to as trait variability.

How Does the Teacher Help Children Solve Problems?

Too often the abilities of children in problem solving have been limited simply to arithmetic class. Yet, an area of concern to the pupils may appear in science or spelling which requires problem solving ability quite as much as any arithmetic item. Problem solving involves the skills necessary for locating pertinent information, deciding what is important, comparing information, drawing tentative conclusions, and trying out or applying the facts.

As is the case with so many learning tasks, the child will become genuinely involved in problem solving if the problem has significance

---

[36] For a detailed treatment of individual differences see Anne Anastasi and John P. Foley, *Differential Psychology* (New York: The Macmillan Co., 1949).

or interest for him. In an effort to center instruction around problem solving activities it is possible to encounter the unrealistic or absurd situations as well as the significant and realistic learning experiences. One of the authors visited a first grade classroom in which the children were attempting to determine the value of a piece of silver the size of a human head. The cruciality of this "problem" to six-year-olds is extremely doubtful.

The measurement of the school playground by each sixth grade group is unlikely to present a pertinent problem unless there is some reason for measuring the play area. If additional bicycle parking space is needed or a new softball area is planned, then such a measuring problem may become real and of interest.

Children may engage in problem solving without reaching final conclusions. This need not detract from the value of the problem solving activity. The following problem situation of a group of third graders is offered:

> As an outgrowth of reading and discussion of the settlement of the American colonies and the growth of the United States, the third grade children wanted to bring to school any Early American articles which they might find at home. A display case was made available for the exhibit of these articles. The question soon arose as to whether all or any of the articles were actually representative of Early America. This led to a discussion concerning just when the Early American period started and ended. Some children suggested that Early America started with Columbus, others said that it began with the first colonists. Still other children thought the genuine Early Americans were the Indians, and the period must go far back in time.

The preceding illustration could have been handled too abstractly for third graders, but as it became a genuine problem to them, the teacher guided them to search in many sources for information to clear up their questions. The children finally agreed that their exhibits of "old" articles were not twentieth century, but doubted, too, that they were Early American.[37]

Children benefit from problem solving situations which have been recognized and defined by themselves. This does not eliminate the need for teacher guidance, but it does imply that the problems that are recognized, isolated, studied, and tentatively solved *by the teacher* are usually

---

[37] For other examples of problem solving situations see: Glenn O. Blough and Albert J. Huggert, *Elementary School Science and How to Teach It* (New York: Holt, Rinehart & Winston, Inc., 1951), pp. 11, 14, 16; Gerald S. Craig, *Science for the Elementary Teacher* (Boston: Ginn and Co., 1958), pp. 115-21.

no longer pertinent to children. What is the purpose in discussing how to solve any problem when the "answer" is on the chalkboard?

Problem solving should be based upon the concerns of the children and should proceed in an atmosphere of questioning and searching for information. This searching for solutions to problems is best characterized by what is sometimes called the "scientific" approach. Insofar as prejudices, opinions, and other non-factual attitudes are obstacles to the solutions of problems in a democracy, the teacher must direct the educative processes toward those problem solving patterns which make careful use of available facts. The teacher must avoid hastily formed opinions and always be open to new information.

In the role as a worker with children, the teacher will direct the pupils' search for information and skills beyond herself. In other words, the teacher is not properly conceived as a storehouse of answers, but rather as a guide to children in leading them toward independence in problem solving. The vital difference between an authoritarian system of education and a democratic approach is that the latter seeks to develop independent people who can apply problem solving techniques in life situations.

How Is Learning Organized in the Basic Skills?

There has been a tendency among some observers of modern education to believe that when attention is given to the social, emotional, and physical aspects of learning, the basic skills will be neglected. This should be far from the case, since the skills which children use as children and, later, as adults are as vital today as ever. In fact, the necessity for proficiency in reading, writing, and arithmetic is probably more pressing in an age of highly developed technology than in the time before the industrial revolution.[38]

Emphasis has shifted from memorization and rote learning to a reasonable application of the basic skills. A child will certainly function with greater efficiency in the use of numbers if he has had opportunity to practice the addition and subtraction facts. Also, his ability in multiplication and division will be improved if he has been "drilled" on these processes. However, if purposeful learning has the advantages over meaningless learning (as psychologists have reported) then it is important that children understand and see reasons behind the learning situations.

Present day teachers are aware of the need for practice sessions as children learn the multiplication facts. Such practice will be of an indi-

---

[38] See Chapter 1.

vidual or a group nature, depending upon the needs of the children. Practice sessions will be followed by application of the facts in a reasonable situation. It is a fact that children have drilled in many class sessions on the "I have dones" and the "I have gones," only to say, "I have did my work now. Can I go home since my brother has already went?"

The difficulties which many children experience with arithmetic "story" problems are often the result of drill on facts without meaningful application. If the child cannot determine whether he should use division or multiplication, his memorized facts will not help him. The arithmetic processes have value only as the means for solving problems, and in this function they are priceless. Divorced from problem solving they have little value.

Proficiency in spelling is similarly valuable only as it aids the child in communication through written symbols. The oral spelling class is an example of wasted educational effort, since the child will probably do little oral spelling as he communicates with others.

Reading, spelling, writing, arithmetic, and speaking involve skills that will be used in many situations in school and in later life. These skills have far too much value in practical application to be treated as pure memorization material for use ten or fifteen years later. Children have problems with numbers and speech long before they come to school. By age six or seven the social pressures from parents and other youngsters have made them aware of reading, writing, and spelling. Thus, teachers who seize upon reasonable opportunities for practicing and applying the basic skills will likely find their approach sound.

Basic skills are important in the school program in a democracy. The individual's ability to direct his own search for information through reading, his ability to manage his own economic problems, and his effectiveness in communicating with others are dependent upon proficiency in applying the basic skills. They are indispensable in a nation of free people only if the people are able to apply these skills. *Modern education is concerned with skill mastery and skill application.*

As psychologists and teachers learn more about the development of language and number concepts in children, the school's program may be modified in some respects in the interests of more efficient learnings. For example, whether third grade is the best place to introduce the process of multiplication may be open to debate until more research data becomes available.

An example of effective teaching.   It is not a simple matter to plan and carry out classroom activities that will be of interest to children, result in important learnings, and involve the use of basic skills. A first grade teacher who looked upon teaching-learning situations as challenges to be met with all the skills at her command provides an example for consideration:

> The first graders had been involved with a unit on "Pets." Their interests had led them to a consideration of other animals that were not necessarily good pets, but nonetheless, appealing to them. Baby chickens were looked upon with favor by many of the children.
>
> The teacher used this existing interest to extend science learnings by arranging a visit to the hatchery where the children witnessed eggs being placed in the incubators. Twenty-one days later the children returned to see the chicks hatching from the eggs that were placed in incubation during their first visit. This thoughtful planning helped prevent mistaken ideas that eggs are put in an oven to bake for a few hours in order to get the chickens.
>
> Of course, the marking of time between visits to the hatchery required the use of a calendar, recognition of numbers, counting and the like. The children wanted to record their field trips in story form so they could take the interesting facts about baby chicks to their parents. Abundant opportunity existed for oral language development and practice in the writing skill. The children worked hard—they were interested, they had purposes, and they gained accurate information on the phenomenon of the life of a chicken

Opportunities for applying the basic skills in purposeful situations are many. The teacher who is seeking such opportunities will find them in the life experiences of children. What child has not generally been awed at the progress of a snail on the side of an aquarium? Who among children does not have a desire to search for answers to his questions? The interests, the capacities and the behavior patterns of children may not be exactly what the teacher expected, but the possibilities for seeking and for learning exist wherever there are children. It is with these infinite possibilities that the teacher begins to work with children, and in guiding children toward continuous learnings, the successful teacher will never see her work completed.

Classroom climate. The role of the teacher with respect to her influence upon the social and emotional climate of the classroom has been the subject of considerable study by several researchers.[39] The results of such investigations indicate that the relationships between pupils are affected by individual pupil-teacher relationships as well as by the interaction among the children themselves. There seems to be a positive rela-

[39] Ned A. Flanders, "Personal Social Anxiety as a Factor in Experimental Learning Situations," *Journal of Educational Research*, 45 (October, 1951), 100-10; John Withall, "The Development of the Climate Index," *Journal of Educational Research*, 45 (October, 1951), 93-100.

tionship between the emotional-social climate of the learning environment and the performance of the learners, although it must be pointed out that for such comparisons pupil performance should not be confined to academics only.

It is evident that the orientation of the child in the classroom is of an individual nature, for what disturbs one child may not necessarily disturb other children. However, it seems that some conditions are more conducive to learning than others. A situation in which the teacher is sincerely interested in the child as an individual, in which the child finds success and growth within his reach, and in which children enjoy the security of a friendly atmosphere is a situation that provides a milieu for social interaction, and for personal and mental growth.

Withall has made some important contributions to the study of classroom climate as affected by the teacher.[40] It is the position of Withall that the prevailing types of statements and questions which are used by the teacher may be classified as to their apparent aim in direction of the learner, and that this aim exerts an influence upon the classroom climate. Table I presents the different types of statements and questions and their purposes, as proposed by Withall.[41]

Generally, it seems that the teacher must assess her classroom conversation in terms of the kind of responses which she believes are desired. Pupil reponses may not always be immediate and may involve far more than mere verbalization insofar as emotional health, personality development, and mental growth are jointly concerned. With this in mind, the teacher will study the situation and select the course of action which is most likely to bring about pupil responses which indicate the children accept responsibility, feel at home in the classroom, and feel free to move with considerable independence toward the solution of their learning and total behavior problems.

Occasionally one reads of a teacher who has won local acclaim for her sharp wit and her success in using it to keep youngsters on guard or even on the defensive. Lest there be misunderstanding of the use of the sarcastic rejoinder by the teacher, it should be pointed out that such verbal jabbing is genuinely appreciated only when used with persons who understand and accept one another, either socially, professionally, or intellectually. Its use in the elementary school classroom must be questioned severely. As a general procedure, the teacher will do much toward the creation of a favorable climate for learning by using statements and questions that are pupil-centered and problem-oriented.

---

[40] J. Withall, "Assessment of the Social-Emotional Climates Experienced by a Group of Seventh Graders as they Moved from Class to Class," *Educational and Psychological Measurements*, 12 (Autumn, 1952), 440-51.
[41] *Ibid.*

TABLE I

Types of Teacher Statements and Questions

Type	Aim
Learner supportive	To encourage the learner
Accepting or clarifying	To help the learner move toward the solution of a problem by removing confusing or extraneous obstacles.
Problem structuring	Neither pupil centered nor teacher centered, it helps sustain the pupil as he attempts to isolate and identify the nature of his problem.
Neutral (such as repeating a thought to oneself)	
Directive statements	To have the pupil take the teacher's point of view and follow the course of action proposed by the teacher.
Reproving, disparaging statements	To cite behavior that is socially or morally undesirable, in terms of the prevailing cultural patterns.
Teacher supportive	To defend the teacher; to support the teacher's position in the fact of contradictory evidence.

What Is the Teacher's Role?

The teacher who is informed with respect to the factors and forces which affect learning may assess his classroom setting in terms of the following characteristics of situations which are favorable to efficient learning:

1. Consideration is given to the mental maturity and learning capacity of the child.
2. Basic life needs of children are recognized in planning the classroom program for learning.
3. Motivation and incentive for learning are fostered.
4. Drill and practice are provided when necessary to maintain skills and to provide readiness for further learnings.
5. Meaningful applications of the skills learned are provided.
6. Evaluation of the learning environment is looked upon as a continuous concern of the teacher.

The teacher who has appraised the learning environment of her classroom in view of these characteristics is in a position to "bridge the gap between what a person should learn and what he wants to learn."[42] Another educational writer has suggested that the crisis which must be recognized by the teacher consists of "the disproportion between what is available and necessary to know and the capacity of the individual to know it."[43] The teacher must bring together the resources and materials for learning, and each child with his own unique experiences and capabilities. Effective citizenship and social membership in terms of economic efficiency, civic responsibility, personal integrity, and moral fitness are the goals of the teacher as she works within the role assigned her.

SUMMARY

In this chapter consideration was given to a number of factors that influence learning and to the role of the teacher in providing pertinent opportunities for learning. The following statements provide an overview of this chapter:

Theories of learning have, in the past, often been based upon speculation rather than upon careful research and experimentation. Psychologists now employ techniques of study and experimentation which lead to theories of learning based upon actual performances under controlled conditions.

A modern concept of learning involves many factors in the individual development and maturation of the learner, and does not overlook the importance of the environment. Children have certain basic physical, social and emotional needs which greatly affect their ability to succeed in a learning task. Internal forces of maturation affect the child's learning performance. A child's readiness to engage in any specific learning activity depends upon many factors of internal maturation, previous experiences, and present surroundings.

Intelligence, as evidenced by an individual's mental maturity, may be regarded as problem solving ability or adaptable behavior, which is an important factor in the learning process. *Learning has come to be regarded by many psychologists as that sequence of mental processes which leads to changes in the child's behavior.* Such changes may be expressed

---

[42] W. B. Waltjen, "Learning Now and in the Future," *Educational Leadership*, 14 (February, 1957), 269-72.

[43] P. H. Phenix, "Key Concepts and the Crisis in Learning," *Teachers' College Record*, 58 (December, 1956), 137-43.

in ideas, attitudes, emotions, physical activities, and in combinations of all of these.

Drill or practice exercises are most valuable when used in conjunction with some purposeful use of the skill being practiced. Children perform more effectively in learning situations which hold interest and purpose for them than in situations where the results and outcomes are either unknown or unrecognized as being important.

Teachers must continually be aware of the differences which exist among children as they plan learning experiences for the pupils. Similarities of interests, abilities, and purposes are important, also. Teaching procedures should be evaluated continuously in terms of the learning which occurs. Effective teaching is characterized by the classroom situation in which desirable learning results.

SUGGESTED PROBLEMS AND ACTIVITIES

1. Obtain from one or two elementary school teachers information on each child in their rooms with respect to mental age, reading age and arithmetic age. In view of the information which you obtain, how would you describe a "typical" pupil in these classrooms?

2. Using the information secured for the first activity, group together the children according to reading ages. Does it appear that these groups could be left intact for arithmetic instruction?

3. Arrange a five or ten minute visit with an elementary school teacher. Find out what views or theories she holds with respect to the manner in which children learn. As a class activity, compare the results of your interviews. Do you find some of the older theories of learning present? Do you find any eclectics among the teachers interviewed?

4. Miss Edsel insists that her fifth grade pupils need a great amount of drill on the multiplication facts. Accordingly, Miss Edsel devotes two or three separate arithmetic sessions each week to drill. Would you agree or disagree with Miss Edsel's position and procedures?

5. The "activity school" has received considerable criticism because of emphasis upon activity. How is the word "activity" frequently misunderstood as it applies to learning?

6. Certain educators have proposed that tests of mental maturity should avoid the use of "verbal" material since some children with language difficulties will be handicapped on such a test. What criticism and support can you offer for this position?

7. Intelligence plays an important part in learning. Teachers need to know something about the child's intelligence and often this information is expressed in terms of I.Q. alone. What other information must the teacher possess before the I.Q. has meaning for her?

SELECTED READINGS

Association for Supervision and Curriculum Development. *Learning More About Learning*, ed., Alexander Frazier. Third ASCD Research Institute. Washington, D. C.: The Association, N.E.A., 1959.

Baller, Warren R. and Don C. Charles. *The Psychology of Human Growth and Development*. New York: Holt, Rinehart & Winston, 1961.

Bischof, L. J. *Intelligence, Statistical Concepts of Its Nature*. Garden City, N. Y.: Doubleday & Company, Inc., 1954. (A thirty-one page review of the development of theories of intelligence.)

Bruner, Jerome S. *The Process of Education*. Cambridge, Mass.: Harvard University Press, 1961.

Burton, William H. *The Guidance of the Learning Activities*. New York: Appleton-Century-Crofts, 1962, Chapter 5.

Davis, W. Allison. *Social-Class Influence Upon Learning*. Cambridge, Mass.: Harvard University Press, 1948.

Deese, James. *The Psychology of Learning*. 2nd ed.; New York: McGraw-Hill Book Company, 1958.

Getzels, J. W. and H. A. Thelen. "The Sociopsychological Structure of the Instructional Group," National Society for the Study of Education, *The Dynamics of Instructional Groups, Fifty-Ninth Yearbook*, Part II. Chicago: University of Chicago Press, 1960, pp. 53-82.

Getzels, Jacob, and Phillip Jackson. *Creativity and Intelligence*. New York: John Wiley & Sons, Inc., 1962, Chapters 1, 2, 3, 5.

Hamachek, Don E. *Motivation in Teaching and Learning*. No. 34 of *What Research Says to the Teacher*. Washington, D. C.: Association for Supervision and Curriculum Development, 1968.

Havighurst, Robert J. *Human Development and Education*. New York: Longmans, Green and Company, 1953.

Holt, John. *How Children Fail*. New York: Dell Publishing Co., Inc., 1965.

Hull, C. L. "The Evaluation of Concepts," *Selected Readings on the Learning Process*, eds. T. L. Harris and W. E. Schwahns. New York: Oxford University Press, 1961, Rdg. No. 13.

Klausmeier, Herbert J. *Learning and Human Abilities: Educational Psychology*. New York: Harper & Row, Publishers, 1961, Chapters 1, 3 and 6.

Phi Kappa Deltan, March, 1958. Special issue devoted to "Research in Teaching and Learning."

Prescott, Daniel A. *Factors That Influence Learning*. Pittsburgh, Pa.: University of Pittsburgh Press, 1958.

Pressey, S. L. and D. C. Hanna. "The Class as a Psycho-Sociological Unit," *Educational Psychology: A Book of Readings*, ed. A. P. Coladarci. New York: Holt, Rinehart & Winston, Inc., 1955, pp. 246-53.

Seagoe, May V. *A Teacher's Guide to the Learning Process.* Dubuque, Iowa: William C. Brown Company, Publishers, 1956.

Thorpe, Louis. *Child Psychology and Development.* New York: The Ronald Press Company, 1955, Chapters 6 and 15.

Wertheimer, Max. *Productive Thinking.* New York: Harper & Row, Publishers, 1945.

CHAPTER 4

INTRODUCTION

EMERGING CONCEPTS OF METHOD
    What is the meaning and importance of method in teaching?
    What is meant by the developmental approach to improving teaching?

TEACHER-CENTRIC METHOD OF TEACHING
    The recitation method
    The discussion method

PUPIL-CENTERED METHODS OF TEACHING
    Teacher-pupil planning method
    Activity method
    How does curriculum organization affect instructional practices?

ORGANIZING LEARNING INTO MEANINGFUL WHOLES
    What is the unit approach to learning?
    How does the teacher pre-plan for children?
    How does the teacher plan with children?
    How is a unit organized?
    What is the function of the teacher in unit teaching?
    How does the teacher plan for unit teaching?
    Pre-planning
    Planning for room arrangement
    Planning for a desirable emotional tone
    Providing needed source materials
    Planning for the use of instruments for recording pupil growth
    Personal preparation
    What is the source of content in unit teaching?
    How are the basic skills taught?
    How does the teacher plan a daily schedule?
    What is individualized teaching?
    What are some ways to start individualized teaching?
    Socialized learning
    What kind of grouping will best contribute to pupil learning in the affective domain?
    Why did team teaching and cooperative teaching begin?
    What is team teaching?
    What is cooperative teaching?
    How is a school organized for team teaching?

SUMMARY

Instructional Evolution

INTRODUCTION

Early American schools were known for their read-recite-test plan of organizing learning. It was fairly common for a local examining committee to appear in a classroom for the purpose of determining if the children were mastering the content before being promoted to the next grade. In Quincy, Massachusetts, as early as 1873, the board of education, under the persuasion of Charles Francis Adams and Colonel Parker, examined the children in what was a unique approach for determining learning for the period. The children were given problems to solve which required the mastery of the subjects studied rather than mere memorization of textbook content. The examining committee was astounded at the results acquired from this procedure for determining the effectiveness of instruction. The children were found badly lacking in the ability to apply their rote learning to real situations.

Efforts have been continuous in a search for effective instructional procedures since the times of the early New England schools. Each generation has had its critics which have spurred educators and psychologists to investigate factors which affect learning.

Newspaper and magazine editors have some justification for criticizing certain statements made by educators as well as some of the practices utilized by ineffective teachers. An article written for a large city newspaper by a prominent educator has revealed the basis for criticism which results in misunderstandings. The statement pointed out that the "teacher did not teach subject matter but that she taught children." As trite as it may be, such statements do not build understandings between the school and the community because they emphasize an *either–or* approach. That is to say, *the teacher does not have to make a decision between focusing upon the development of children and the teaching of subject matter;* she must attend to both. These two factors in the learning situation are highly compatible when the desired results are being achieved by the learners. It is a fact that traditional schools did neglect recognizing the total growth of the child in a developmental process, due perhaps, to lack of research in the area. At the same time, some teachers have failed in helping the child to acquire knowledge needed in today's world.

It will be the purpose of this chapter to furnish some practical guides for organizing learning experiences in order that teaching will be more productive. The teaching process will be traced to show how a new emphasis has evolved which places the burden of learning largely on the learner. This shift to the recognition of the importance of the learner in acquiring knowledge is shown by tracing developments in instruction from the read-recite-test procedures to the recent development of programmed learning. The authors purport that teachers emerge as master teachers through a conscious effort to evaluate and modify these procedures. But they also recognize that for the most part these changes come about slowly and deliberately.

EMERGING CONCEPTS OF METHOD

Since the early efforts to "train" teachers in America, which began sometime after the War of 1812, method has occupied a very important place in teacher education. Stiles and Dorsey[1] point out that early efforts to train teachers consisted primarily of two types of experiences: (1) lectures on schoolkeeping given by teachers in service to prospective teachers, and (2) demonstration teaching in certain observation schools related to the training institution. During the past century much criticism has been recorded of the "methods schools." Some was justified but some had developed from misunderstandings of a growing profession. No doubt the mechanical nature of method, as applied to older teaching procedures, needed criticism before any real efforts could be exerted to produce concepts of method that are more compatible with the cooperative principles involved in democratic living. It is, therefore, the purpose of this section to show the development of teacher-centric methods of teaching and the emerging pupil-centric methods as means of achieving the fundamental goals of education.

What Is the Meaning and Importance of Method in Teaching?

For those elementary teachers who have had specific preparation in reading methods, arithmetic methods, and the like, method becomes a

---

[1] Lindley J. Stiles, and Mattie F. Dorsey, *Democratic Teaching in the Secondary Schools* (Philadelphia: J. B. Lippincott Co., 1950), pp. 77-8.

series of specific ways of arranging certain experiences, or systems used to produce specific learnings in particular situations. An illustration is used to point up this concept of method.

> Miss Jones decided that most of her first grade children were ready to move from concrete number experiences in addition combinations to semi-concrete concepts. The children had been experiencing counting objects which they could touch and feel. They had used the abacus and other specific objects in computing sounds. The teacher prepared some materials for the children to use at their seats. She asked the children to draw three trees and one tree. She then asked them to color two trees green and one tree black. After this the children were asked to write the number of green trees in the space provided. The same request was made for the black tree. Following this, Miss Jones asked the children to write the number of all the trees together. They counted two green trees and one black tree. Then they said two trees and one tree are three trees.

This illustration focuses on method as it relates to developing and understanding a skill, but importance here is attached to the specific devices found in the process of developing continuity in learning through a systematic approach for arranging the order or sequence of events in the learning process.

For our purpose here, however, we are concerned with method as it relates to a set of principles adaptable to any teaching situation.[2] To be effective, method, then, in the elementary classroom operates upon a philosophical and a psychological basis.[3] Those principles of learning which function outside of the classroom are also recognized as vital to successful learning within the room. The primary purpose of learning is to change the behavior pattern of the learner. This changed behavior pattern may produce negative results as well as positive or desirable learning. The principles of learning which the teacher practices may be based upon verbal learning only, or upon reward and punishment. In addition, the learning may take place in an authoritative environment. Thus, children may gain a false concept of school learning that can lead to memorizing parts without understanding the whole or seeing relationships among the parts memorized. This kind of learning is frequently the result of motivation by extrinsic rewards, such as a gold star. On the other hand, children may learn to dislike arithmetic because difficulty with it leads to their being punished. Children may fail to develop an appreciation for certain races, social-economic groups, or religious

---

[2] Stiles and Dorsey, *op. cit.*, p. 66.

[3] See George A. Beauchamp, *Basic Dimensions of Elementary Method* (Boston: Allyn and Bacon, Inc., 1959), Chapter II.

groups because of poor intergroup relations resulting from ineffective methods of the teacher. Method sets the tone of the classroom organization.

The teacher who is trying to achieve the basic purposes of education is cognizant of the need for providing learning by doing. This is not to imply that vicarious experiences are of lesser importance or that the teacher must choose between these two concepts of learning. Nothing could be further from desirable practice. The quantity and quality of learning in any given classroom depend upon the understanding the teacher has of method, since the general methods used by the teacher, to a large degree, are indicative of the teacher's understanding of the major factors in the learning situation. These factors are: (1) the nature of the learner, (2) the nature of the learning process, (3) the function of learning aids, and (4) the needs of society as they relate to the purposes of education.

What Is Meant by the Developmental Approach to Improving Teaching?

It can safely be assumed that most people are partially products of their environment. Changing a pattern of operation to a new design which affects custom or tradition is a gradual process because people are so closely related to environment. Social progress has continuously lagged behind scientific and technical advancement. To illustrate, it is easier to accept a flight in an airplane, or to get someone to volunteer to ride a rocket to the moon, than to break down barriers of social customs which have hampered human progress in solving significant social problems.

Teachers who are interested in self-improvement must progress a step at a time. A teacher who is doing acceptable work in supplementing the textbook with appropriate materials no doubt has reached the point in growth where she is ready to move to a type of unit organization. This teacher may develop a teaching unit based upon a content area which she is going to teach. Growth in teaching skill proceeds from using a textbook as the sole source of learning, to studying a topic either projected by the teacher or cooperatively arrived at by the group. The textbook then becomes a vital source of information for study of the selected topic. The important point is that the teacher has grown toward utilizing more acceptable principles of teaching which are consistent with psychological principles of learning, yet has maintained personal security. This step in the development of the teacher then requires her to:

1. Plan a topic or theme based on textbook content.
2. Stimulate the interests of children in a study of the topic.

3. Identify purposes for learning, which usually involve a series of questions for pupils to seek answers.
4. Provide supplemental books.
5. Use appropriate audio-visual materials.
6. Use individual and group reports, if appropriate.
7. Evaluate the learning activity.

The teacher who has been using this pattern of instruction needs only to appraise carefully her procedures in the light of the objectives of elementary education. That is, the entire procedure is a definite breakthrough for the textbook-limited teacher. This is to imply that while the textbook is a valuable tool for the teacher, it must not become the curriculum within itself. However, this step in instructional growth does not provide for vital decision-making by immature learners to the extent that it is desirable and necessary as a part of adult democratic living. In addition, it presupposes that the teacher can judge what segment of knowledge the learners need at their particular stage of development. Yet, in a real sense, the content which is to be learned may meet a practical need if, for example, the teacher can see and relate problems of misunderstandings in the Middle East to some vitally persistent problems which the children are basically concerned about in their community or neighborhood. What may a teacher do to meet these persistent life problems?

The teacher who now is ready to develop learning experiences with children beyond the points enumerated above will see the need to provide guidance in helping children to organize their attacks on real problems. This teacher is prepared to move to the higher instructional level which recognizes that education is not a series of separate, unrelated learnings.

It is not unlikely that teachers contribute to inadequate learnings due to restricting or compartmental subject areas. Since children's experiences are limited simply by virtue of age and maturity, the relating of content fields may result in a child finding meaning in the material to be learned. For example, a familiar song may give meaning to a study of pioneer life. A visit to an Indian museum may cause a child to feel acquainted with the American Indian culture. Thus, his learning may be aided significantly in this area of study. Cason[4] found many years ago that presenting familiar learnings before presenting unfamiliar material had a slight advantage. As the teacher understands the growth and development of the child and the basic principles which govern efficient

---

[4] H. B. Cason, "Associations Between the Familiar and the Unfamiliar," *Journal of Experimental Psychology*, 16 (1933), 295-305. See also W. A. Brownell and H. E. Moser, *Meaningful vs. Mechanical: A Study in Grade III Subtraction* (Durham, North Carolina: Duke University Press, 1949).

learning, the instructional procedures become more pupil-centered. A schematic presentation of this is presented in Figure III. This kind of teacher views the learning process as a means of enhancing maturation of the learner who seeks knowledge, which to him is vital, in solving an impelling problem.

FIGURE III

The Emerging Concept of Method

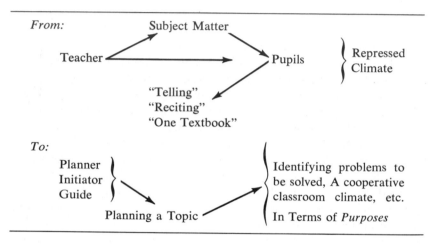

TEACHER-CENTRIC METHODS OF TEACHING

Teacher-centric methods of teaching in the elementary school are those methods which focus a major portion of the attention upon the teacher as the controlling factor in the organization of learning. Usually the methods dominated by the teacher-centric pattern of instruction are based upon an approach to learning in which the results are evaluated in terms of the number of correct responses the children can write or recite to the teacher. Thus, learning is based upon memorization of facts which are virtually never seen in relationship to each other. This may be the situation in many classrooms.

The Recitation Method

This pattern of teaching has a heritage in American education which dates back to the early schools of New England. This teaching procedure is usually characterized by using the textbook as sole determinate of the curriculum, by basing learning upon repetition and drill, and by having the teacher be the drill master seeking to produce learners who can achieve standards set by adults. Thus, the recitation pattern of teaching utilizes the assign–study–recite–test formula to achieve educational goals.

The recitation becomes the focal point of the method used by the classroom teacher. Although this method of instruction is commonly found at the secondary school level,[5] it is far from being obscure in the elementary school instructional program. One of the authors, in visiting hundreds of elementary classrooms, found this procedure being utilized at some time during the school day by a large number of teachers. Although there is a very limited and inconclusive amount of research evidence bearing upon this subject in recent years, it seems safe to assume that the recitation method is used by thousands of teachers and will continue to be used for some time to come.[6] Of importance here are some suggested guides to aid the teacher who uses this pattern of teaching to improve these procedures:

1. Differentiate assignments to provide for enrichment of the bright children and minimum requirements for the slow learners.
2. Provide questions or guides to aid the student in getting the most from his reading assignments.
3. Enrich the assignments by supplementing with films, film strips, field trips, and the like.
4. Plan questions that will relate the assignment to meaningful situations.
5. Relate assignments to contemporary times—cause, effect, current usage, etc.
6. Permit pupils to share in making a list of questions to be used during the recitation period.
7. Relate previous assignments to current recitation in such a way that continuity in learning will be facilitated.

Although space does not permit elaborating upon these guides for improving learning in the recitation procedure, the interested reader should carefully analyze the above guides in terms of the demands made upon the teacher and pupils in order to determine the degree of reorganization of teaching required to improve pupil learning. See Figure IV

---

[5] Stiles and Dorsey, *op. cit.*, p. 66.
[6] William Burton, *The Guidance of Learning Activities* (New York: Appleton-Century-Crofts, Inc., 1952), p. 336.

which presents a schematic approach to this method. Since they furnish many suggestions for enriching the learning experiences, modern text-books will also be found quite useful to the teacher who uses the recitation method.

In Figure IV, it should be noted that the line of action between the teacher and the pupils is a reciprocal sharing of questions and ideas. This improves a recitation method by helping children to feel that they have a part in the process. In such situations, the pupils may ask questions about things that they do not understand or are perplexed about as they study their assignments. It can also be seen from Figure IV that the teacher who is attempting to improve on the recitation method must consider the diversity among children and provide for them through differentiated assignments.

FIGURE IV

Improving the Recitation Method

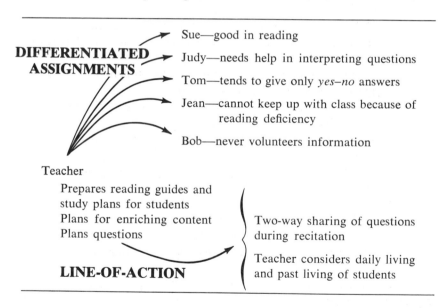

DIFFERENTIATED ASSIGNMENTS

Sue—good in reading

Judy—needs help in interpreting questions

Tom—tends to give only *yes–no* answers

Jean—cannot keep up with class because of reading deficiency

Bob—never volunteers information

Teacher
Prepares reading guides and study plans for students
Plans for enriching content
Plans questions

LINE-OF-ACTION

Two-way sharing of questions during recitation

Teacher considers daily living and past living of students

The Discussion Method

This method of instruction is an effort to improve upon the recitation by providing for individuals to interchange ideas and to ask questions. Usually in this type of organization for learning, the teacher functions much as a moderator. The effectiveness of the teacher in this method of learning is related to her ability to see that all the learners have a chance to participate and that the discussion is not monopolized by an individual or a few students. Although this method may, in some of its aspects, appear to be pupil-centered, it too frequently is controlled by the teacher. Some teachers have improved upon the discussion method to the extent that at least in their classrooms it is operating as a pupil-centered method of teaching.

Usually the discussion method follows some of the same procedures found in the recitation. That is, the teacher makes an assignment around a given topic and the children are to prepare questions for discussion. Although this method is also used extensively at the secondary school level, it is not uncommon to find the discussion method being used by elementary school teachers as a means of "covering content" in certain subjects. A survey by one of the authors indicated 97 of 110 elementary teachers stated they used the discussion method more often than any other method. This is not to imply that this procedure is not satisfactory, but to point up the need to utilize supplements for improving the learning situation.

For the teacher who is interested in improving upon her use of the discussion, some guides are also offered:

1. Seek to develop the ability to ask questions which stimulate reflective thinking and which require the learner to:
   a. compare or contrast,
   b. make application to new situations,
   c. make decisions for or against,
   d. classify data,
   e. show cause and effect relationship,
   f. give an example or illustration.
2. Release the children from seeking to determine what the teacher wants for an answer.
3. Discourage fragmentary answers to questions whether the answer is directed to the teacher or another pupil.
4. Supplement discussion with opportunities through research, use of films, and other aids, for the children to seek information which will sustain their point in the discussion.
5. Refrain from dominating the discussion, but seek to clarify meaning and promote sequence in the discussion.
6. Encourage all to participate; have a leveling effect upon those who dominate; bring those who are reluctant to share into the discussion.

Although many of the research investigations which have been conducted on the discussion method have been with college classes and in contrast with the lecture method, evidence does support the superiority of the discussion method over the lecture method if retention in learning information is the criteria. In addition, discussion has been found to be more effective in stimulating critical thinking and in helping students acquire more profound understanding.[7] This method of teaching also seems to be effective in changing attitudes and behavior patterns of the learners.[8] It becomes evident then, as we examine the developmental approach to teaching, that teachers of all levels of operation may find ways of improving upon present practices. See the schematic presentation in Figure V, which depicts the teacher's role in this method of

FIGURE V

Discussion Method

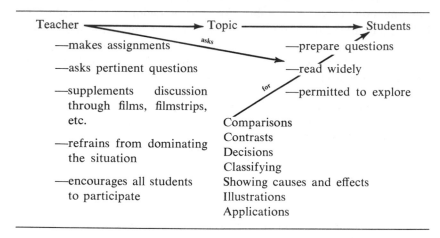

Teacher	Topic	Students
—makes assignments	*asks*	—prepare questions
—asks pertinent questions		—read widely
—supplements discussion through films, filmstrips, etc.	*for*	—permitted to explore
—refrains from dominating the situation	Comparisons Contrasts Decisions Classifying	
—encourages all students to participate	Showing causes and effects Illustrations Applications	

teaching. However, it should be made clear that it would be difficult to find a single classroom in which the teacher would rely upon any single method of teaching. This should not be construed to mean that the writers condone simply the use of an amalgamation of teacher-centered methods of teaching. These methods, along with the guides for improving them, are presented in recognition of the fact that beginning teachers and teachers in service do use them and that some teachers are interested

---

[7] Thomas F. Stoval, "Lecture vs. Discussion," *Phi Delta Kappan*, XXIX (March, 1958), 256.

[8] Franklin H. Knower, "Experimental Studies of Changes of Attitudes: I. A Study of the Effect of Oral Argument on Changes of Attitude," *Journal of Social Psychology*, 6 (August, 1935), 315-47.

in self-improvement and that improvement or change in behavior for adults is a slow and gradual process.

Pupil-Centered Methods of Teaching

During the latter part of the 19th century and the early part of the 20th century, a growing emphasis was beginning to emerge which recognized the importance of the child or the learner in the learning situation. Men such as Froebel, Pestalozzi, Dewey, Kilpatrick, and others have led the way for an attack against the teacher-dominated classroom. This philosophy is based upon new psychological understandings: a social utility philosophy which related the learner to his needs and interests. The pupil-centered method of teaching purports to develop a program of instruction which is functional, since it develops the use of principles which confront learners in their everyday life. This newer concept of teaching recognizes the teacher as a guide in helping pupils build upon their interests. Skills are developed through understanding and insight which in turn reduce the drudgery found in traditional drill practices. Stiles and Dorsey sum up pupil-centered methods of teaching by stating that they "feature developmental study, problem solving techniques, learning through experiences, and logical thinking under guidance of the teacher."[9]

Teacher-Pupil Planning Method

This method of teaching has emerged as a means of utilizing the procedures involved for providing pupils with practical experiences in democratic living.[10] This method of teaching seems to offer the widest range of advantages over those previously discussed. Some of these advantages are: (1) its consistency with democratic living, (2) individual as well as group welfare are considered, (3) group skills essential to cooperative living are fostered, (4) sound principles of learning are utilized, and (5) learning is made meaningful and its transfer or application becomes an instructional goal.

The pupil-teacher planning as a method of instruction gives impetus to the unit approach to teaching in the elementary school. Essentially, *goals or purposes* that will lead, or give direction to solving an impelling

---

[9] Stiles and Dorsey, *op. cit.*, p. 82.
[10] For a complete and comprehensive treatment of this method, see Association for Supervision and Curriculum Development, *Toward Better Teaching* (Washington, D. C.: National Education Association, 1950) and H. H. Giles, *Teacher-Pupil Planning* (New York: Harper & Row, Publishers, 1941).

FIGURE VI

Teacher-Pupil Planning

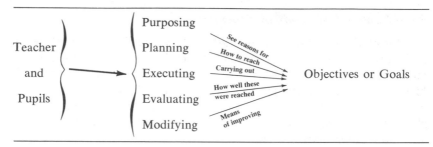

problem which has been agreed upon as being worthy of study are identified by the learners and the teacher together. Figure VI gives a graphic presentation of this cooperative approach to learning. Thus, *purposing* gives direction to establishing group-made plans by which the purposes will be achieved. This may be through large or small groups who will work on certain facets of the over-all problem. As the plans are developed, it becomes essential for the teacher to give adequate direction and guidance in helping the children to gain the most from the learning experience. At the same time, the teacher must seek to continue to challenge the thinking of the children as they become involved in *executing* their plans. It is at this point that the teacher must face the reality of democratic living. Pupils who have developed plans consistent with solving a problem must have the freedom to execute these plans. This may mean a field trip, the use of the library, or calling in a resource person. The point is, that if the teacher practices the exclusive use of the "veto," pupils may lose faith in the teacher and the plan of study since they have spent much time in setting up their purposes and developing their plans toward achieving them, only to find that the teacher isn't really democratic when it comes to permitting the children to carry out their plans. Also, the *appraisal* process which follows the achievement of the objectives must be a mutually developed plan. Pupils should evaluate the extent to which the objectives were achieved. They should determine the effectiveness of their methods used, as well as appraise the values which accrued from their group efforts to achieve new knowledge, understandings and skills.

The teacher acts skillfully in observing and analyzing the behavior of certain individuals and of the group. She continuously looks for evidence of democratic qualities inherent in the cooperative approach to learning. A more detailed description of this method of teaching will be found in a later section of this chapter under "Unit Teaching."

Activity Method

This method clearly belongs in the category of pupil-centric methods of teaching. Although many people believed this instructional pattern was developed by Dewey, the concept may be traced back to the 15th century. Michael De Montaigne, a French lawyer, was an exponent of the social-realist theory.[11] This theory concerns itself with a social adjustment of the individual with his environment in order to have a fully enriched life. Since life necessitates association with others, this becomes of paramount importance. Frederik W. Froebel also gave impetus to the activity curriculum movement. The content of a curriculum proposed by Froebel consisted of those activities which gave meaning to types of self-expression activities.[12] He further emphasized the social and intellectual aspects of play activities.

From century to century there have continued to be great leaders who were proponents of the activity-type curriculum. Dewey perhaps did give this movement its greatest impetus when he wrote that a school is not a preparation for life but is life itself. This statement has been mis-stated and misunderstood by many critics of the modern school. A curriculum based upon Dewey's concept would consist of social learnings involving problems of the learner concerning social behavior. This concept pointed the curriculum in the direction of the "here and now" type of learning and therefore departed from the traditional read–recite–test procedures. This kind of learning which took place in what were known as the "activities schools" was quite popular during the 20's and 30's. The activity curriculum was based upon certain concepts of child development which perhaps have only recently been enlarged upon through extended research and investigation in prominent child-study clinics throughout the country. One need only observe a group of children in any situation to become aware of the intense interest manifested in activities in which they are involved. Alert teachers recognize and utilize this innate interest of children in activity to direct their learnings.

The activity curriculum, when purposeful activities are chosen either by the group or by an individual, may be the basis upon which children make important personality adjustments. Such adjustments may not be possible or forthcoming in rooms where children are held under strict domination. Pupil initiative must not be inhibited or repressed if we are seeking to help each child to make the best possible use of his learning in

---

[11] Elmer H. Wilds, *The Foundations of Modern Education* (New York: Holt, Rinehart & Winston, Inc., 1942), p. 326.

[12] *Ibid.*, p. 498.

order to build a better "self" and to enhance the learner's recognition of his responsibility to society. However, during the height of the activity movement in American schools, many misconceptions of the teacher's role in the program were in evidence. These misconceptions stemmed from the inability of teachers to make such a tremendous change in their philosophy and concepts of teaching, and much of the activity in the curriculum led to disorganized teaching and false concepts of freedom. Bagley led an attack against the activity school pointing out that too much emphasis was placed upon the child and his needs.[13] Obviously, modern education has developed out of new understandings of the child and the inherent weaknesses found in the activity schools. Although the philosophy of the activity schools was no doubt sound, the developmental approach to teacher growth was not and has rarely been considered in the preparation of teachers at the pre-service level. This resulted in teachers being plunged into school situations with insecure feelings concerning their role in teaching the activity curriculum. Nevertheless, the building of a curriculum for schools situated in modern America, with its complex social, economical, political, and technological culture, demands the acceptance of some of the underlying philosophical and psychological principles adhered to by the students of the concept of the activity method.[14]

How Does Curriculum Organization Affect Instructional Practices?

Teachers have often been handicapped by rigid curriculum patterns. Due to a lack of a sound policy of curriculum organization, bright children have been kept from fulfilling their capacity to learn and slow learning youngsters have been left behind. If we are to apply the knowledge we have gained from research in child development and learning, then we must change our approach from having a curriculum with a single level of experiences to one with depth and breadth provided at each grade level. We are all familiar with the teacher of the second grade who has kept Johnny from going into arithmetic learnings beyond his grade level because the third grade teacher wouldn't know what to do with him during arithmetic period.

There must be present in the emerging curriculum a design which will provide opportunities for vertical enrichment as well as horizontal en-

---

[13] W. C. Bagley, "Progressive Education is Too Soft," *Education*, 60 (1939), 75-81.

[14] See William H. Kilpatrick, *Philosophy of Education* (New York: The MacMillan Company, 1951), Chapters 18 and 20.

richment. All children should have the opportunity to increase their knowledge about the areas being studied through the use of a wide variety of learning materials, on their own level of achievement. But it is also imperative that the emerging curriculum provide vertical enrichment for those children who are capable of learning beyond the grade level norm. Such enrichment will provide for learning in specialized areas to the extent that quantity of learning for some third graders, for example, will exceed some fifth graders. These specialized areas of the curriculum lend themselves very readily to self-teaching or at least to minimum guidance by the teacher for capable youngsters. Figure VII is an attempt to show how certain disciplines within the curriculum should provide for vertical enrichment for some pupils while others are still working at the enrichment level of the grade.

Pupils will vary in their abilities within each subject area. Horizontal enrichment, then, is provided as the basic understandings are acquired by all pupils. However, as indicated in Figure VII, whether or not certain youngsters will progress along lines A–E or A–D in arithmetic, for example, will depend upon (a) their abilities, (b) their interests, and (c) the guidance of the teacher. Thus, vertical enrichment is accomplished for some pupils at the same time horizontal enrichment is provided for

FIGURE VII

Horizontal and Vertical Enrichment

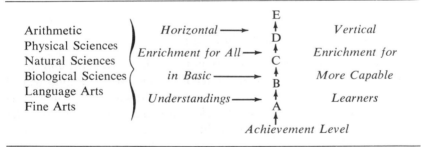

others. In a real sense then, the learner is engaged in a curriculum which provides both quantity and quality in the enrichment program. The claim is made here that teachers can provide for both types of programs in the elementary school if administrators, teachers, and the public are willing to make use of new technology in education as well as to adopt some of the novel plans for organizing elementary schools which are discussed in this chapter.

ORGANIZING LEARNING INTO MEANINGFUL WHOLES

The unit approach to teaching in the elementary school has long been recognized as a natural means of directing the learning activities of children into meaningful wholes. Yet, this task is perhaps one of the most difficult teaching methods which the elementary school teacher faces. It requires the greatest amount of professional preparation and a broad background of general education. In addition, the teacher needs to use her creative ability, imagination, and much initiative in applying her understanding of how children grow, develop and learn. Although the unit approach has been widely accepted by educators and evidenced by practices in university laboratory schools throughout the country, it has not had wide acceptance in the public schools. The writers believe that one of the fundamental reasons that the unit method is not more prevalent at the operational level is due to the need for extensive preparation and experience on the part of teachers. Thus, it becomes a question of improving undergraduate programs to the extent of helping the beginning teacher to pursue her first experience with a secure feeling in unit teaching, as well as developing in-service education programs that will build upon the preparation of the teacher as she gains in the experience of working with children. We must also be mindful of the fact that approximately 40 per cent of the nation's elementary teachers are not college graduates and, therefore, possess a limited academic background. Research investigations have proved the worth of unit teaching in the elementary school. The need now is for its application.

What Is the Unit Approach to Learning?

Like other terms peculiar to certain professions, the term *unit* in the education profession has many different connotations. Public school textbooks frequently are divided in what are termed units. This is particularly true of textbooks in the social science areas, such as history and geography. Teachers sometimes use the term to describe that portion of time devoted to a given subject. A series of stories in a reader may be called a unit. Thus, it seems feasible that a unit of learning should be defined for the purpose of giving the term a common meaning throughout this book. A unit as used here means *a series of related learning experiences which are developed around the interests, needs, and problems of children, are socially significant, and produce purposeful activities resulting in a modified behavior of the learner.*

Although there are many definitions of a unit found in the literature, most writers recognize at least five aspects of a unit as being of importance. These are (1) the relationship of the topic to the interests and problems of children; (2) the purposeful intent of the learning; (3) the need for real experiences in the learning; (4) the social understandings; and (5) the resultive behavior of the learner. As early as 1926, Morrison attempted to define a unit in an effort to refute the assign–recite–test process of teaching. However, it is not the purpose here to decide upon which definition seems to be more explicit in its meaning in the true sense of the term *unit* as it becomes operative in the classroom. Neither is it the purpose here to dwell upon the many different types of units which are in use. However, for the purpose of clarity, the pre-service student or in-service teacher should differentiate between a teaching unit and a resource unit. The teaching unit, although self-explanatory, will be dealt with at length below. The resource unit is a comprehensive study usually developed by a group of teachers or college students on some topic which is taught at a given grade level. The topic may be as broad as "South America" or as limited as "Wireless Communication." Following the same arrangement or organizational areas identified in a teaching unit, a group of teachers usually makes an exhaustive study of the selected topic. Thus, the resource unit becomes a source of ideas and materials readily available for use at the time needed by the teacher in developing some phase of learning related to the topic. Expediency becomes paramount when the teacher is involved in actual classroom teaching. Therefore, the resource unit which is usually developed during workshops or extended work days beyond the teaching year provides the teacher with an invaluable time-saving resource.

The reader will find references in other curriculum books to suggest that subject units, correlated units, fused units and experience units are opposing concepts. These lead the teacher to believe she must decide between teaching subject matter or using learning experiences exclusively. Such terms now have no contribution to make to the in-service teacher or to the prospective teacher. It is folly to try to separate these terms in view of anticipated teacher growth. Furthermore, experiences do not exist in a vacuum. Dewey pointed out in his writings that "providing an experience for children is not in itself a self-sufficient event," and he further indicated that "experiencing has no existence apart from subject matter."[15] This was basically the problem with the early efforts of the activity schools—the lack of selection and organization of subject matter to facilitate learning as well as failure to supplement the activity itself. The writers take the point of view that the learner develops and matures as he gains in knowledge and understandings. The important

---

[15] John Dewey, *Philosophy and Civilization* (New York: G. P. Putnam's Sons, 1931), p. 261.

difference is the way the knowledge is gained. That is, the learning is acquired in an ongoing effort to satisfy the need or desire as the organism matures. Figure VIII depicts this process. This concept differs from traditional teaching which suggests the accumulation of knowledge according to a preconceived plan and with little regard for the learner's needs and maturation. It becomes evident that experience and subject matter are complementary and correlative to the learning situation. It can be said that the unit approach to teaching includes worthwhile experiences and subject matter which is useful to the extent that it moves the child in the direction of achieving the objectives of elementary school education, as well as his own purposes.

How Does the Teacher Pre-Plan for Children?

In unit teaching, pre-planning for children is an essential function of the teacher. The planning required to help children meet individual needs requires much more thought and preparation than usually found in a read-recite type of teaching. Johnny's need for vocabulary building; Eddie's difficulty with map reading; Bette's need to participate in group activities—these and other similar problems reveal the many details for which the teacher must pre-plan. Such important differences which become evident through the planned use of devices for identifying pupil needs must not be left to chance. These needs must and can be met through unit teaching. However, carefully developed plans must be made in advance of each day's learning activities if each child is to progress normally. Although unit teaching provides for group work, it should not neglect the individual's needs.

To pre-plan for materials and resources which will enhance the learning situation is another function of the teacher in unit teaching. The time during the school day is valuable and the cause of efficiency demands that teachers have materials and resources at hand as the unit develops. Thus, at the close of each day, the teacher prepares for the next day's activities by reviewing the needs which have arisen. This does not mean that during the course of the school day the teacher does not seek out materials which may be useful at any given time or materials which may further the learning situation at the moment. Such occasions do arise and must be dealt with in the manner which best suits the situation at the time. Suffice it to say that pre-planning for children is essential to efficient learning in unit teaching.

Even in unit teaching there is a need to organize a plan for the daily lesson. There are certain specifics in the learning situation which require the direct attention of a professionally prepared teacher. The planning

FIGURE VIII

The Unit Approach

The Unit	"Our Weather"
The teacher guides, motivates, and plans with children. 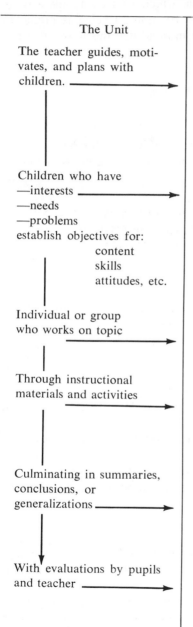	Prearranged environment such as bulletin board showing different weather conditions. *Use current events when feasible.* drought sub-zero temperatures snow storm damage to property, etc.
Children who have —interests —needs —problems establish objectives for: content skills attitudes, etc.	*Interest and needs identified for individual or group work* 1. Understand causes of weather 2. Learn effects of weather upon man (a) health (b) economic, etc. 3. Learn difference between weather and climate, etc.
Individual or group who works on topic	*Working period: topic assignment* Groups and individuals free to do research work leading to solution of problems.
Through instructional materials and activities	*Experiment, construct, dramatize* make graphs depicting temperatures construct rain gauge learn to read U.S. Weather Bureau maps.
Culminating in summaries, conclusions, or generalizations	*Ties together all learning through:* 1. Exhibits 2. Displays of projects (a) stories written (b) words or terms learned (c) construction activities, etc.
With evaluations by pupils and teacher	*Uses many techniques* teacher-made tests observations of changed behavior check lists behavior record, etc.

should be extensive enough to guide the teacher in accomplishing her objectives. At the same time, the planning must be flexible so as to permit the inclusion of ideas from situations which arise during the learning period. One plan which was used by a beginning teacher is presented. In examining this plan, it must be kept in mind that this lesson was part of an over-all unit.

How to Locate Information

General Objectives:

1. To learn to work well together and help each other.
2. To teach children the importance of locating information.

Specific Objectives:

1. To enlarge children's research background.
2. To teach children how to use different resources.
3. To learn to use the index of reference materials.

Materials:

Use of chalkboard	Atlas
Textbooks	Resource books from the library
Story books	Map
Encyclopedias	Globe

Procedure:

1. Discuss a new region in a hot, dry area.
2. Review the location of the Sahara Desert and Egypt, the largest oasis in the world.
3. Ask the class for and list on the board the various resources we can use to find information.
4. Discuss the resources and how to use them.
5. Pick one topic and go through the procedure for looking up the information.

Evaluation:

1. To show children how books help us and, when we know how to use them, how easy it is to find the information we are searching for.
2. For homework, the children will review the rules they made for writing a good report. The next lesson will include a review on how we organize and write our reports.

3. This lesson procedure will be reviewed at various stages of progress since the pupils are just learning how important the use of many resources are.

How Does the Teacher Plan with Children?

Perhaps there is no other phase of teaching which provides for planning with children in as desirable circumstances as that accomplished through unit teaching. Even the teacher who uses modified units, based upon the textbooks, will find numerous situations which will enhance placing children in decision-making situations. However, good practice dictates that children must experience democracy in action in the classroom if they are to become proficient in using cooperative skills. Since 1940, H. H. Giles[16] and others have produced excellent accounts of teacher-pupil planning. To build democratic skills within the learner requires that the teacher be skilled in handling planning sessions. These sessions should be functional to the extent that the plans developed will become a course of action for the learners and not just a method for drilling. Thus, the teacher must be an expert in understanding and utilizing cooperative group techniques. Since it is important that each pupil participate in planning sessions, the teacher must skillfully direct these sessions to be sure that they are not monopolized by a few students. Each contribution should be given consideration by the group. The timid or shy child should be encouraged to participate by the teacher. Frequently, simply asking a child who has not participated what he thinks of the idea suggested or whether he thinks it will work may be the needed incentive to start him participating.

The teacher needs to distinguish between planning *with* children and planning *for* children. For example, a teacher should plan *for* the specific skills which must be taught, such as new arithmetic processes and new words to be introduced in reading. The teacher may plan *with* children the things (goals) they would like to find out in studying Mexico. The children may also share in planning how they will go about achieving their goals. One of the authors is familiar with a teacher who professes to let children plan in a democratic fashion, but her concept of planning is far from democratic. Specifically, she will place two choices on the board and the children will select only one and then plan for carrying out

---

[16] See H. H. Giles, *Teacher-Pupil Planning* (New York: Harper & Row, Publishers, 1941); Association for Supervision and Curriculum Development, *Group Planning in Education* (Washington, D.C.: National Education Association, 1945); and Lindley J. Stiles and Mattie F. Dorsey, *Democratic Teaching in the Secondary Schools* (Philadelphia: J. B. Lippincott Company, 1950), Chapters 12, 13.

the selected choice. No alternate choice may be added to the teacher's selection. Little or no enthusiasm seems evident, perhaps due to the fact that the children have become aware of the situation and have simply accepted it.

Some of the things which children have successfully planned with teachers are:

1. Identifying problems,
2. Making room policies,
3. Planning room arrangement (furniture and physical arrangement),
4. Deciding purposes and objectives for unit study,
5. Using visual aids,
6. Planning field trips,
7. Conducting cooperative research related to unit study,
8. Evaluating learning,
9. Evaluating cooperative procedures,
10. Appraising learning plans,
11. Planning and carrying out assembly programs
12. Deciding the kinds of parent meetings
13. Developing self-evaluation rating scales

The above list could be projected into many other facets of planning with children. Important to note is the wide range of activities which have been successfully planned with children carrying out the major responsibility for the planning.

Certain basic guides are presented in summary to aid the teacher in developing planning procedures with children:

1. Establish a permissive atmosphere which will free children to express themselves without fear.
2. Arrange the room in informal seating situation, where feasible, by placing children face to face.
3. Encourage all children to share.
4. Discourage individuals from monopolizing the planning session.
5. Help children to see the need for expressing their ideas so that the best ones can become part of the plan.
6. Give direction to problems or ideas which have been omitted from the discussion.
7. Use group planning to establish standards for planning sessions. Keep guides or standards developed before the group during the process.

8. See that plans are recorded so that the final session will result in understanding decisions arrived at by the group.

9. Help the group to understand that all plans are subject to modification by the group as need arises, and

10. See that the plans result in action, with each child aware of his responsibility for his part of the plan. Understanding thus becomes the key if the action is to be successful.

How Is a Unit Organized?

Good teaching, regardless of the level of development of the teacher, necessitates planning for children as well as planning with children. Since it is highly improbable that all teachers will find that all children are always deeply involved in "centers of interest," it becomes necessary for the teacher to plan for learnings which seem desirable as indicated by studies of children's needs—social, mental, and emotional. However, whether the unit develops as a spontaneous on-going activity or is pre-planned by the teacher, a certain structural organization seems desirable. Therefore, the following approach is suggested regardless of the level of development of the teacher. The organization of a unit includes:

1. Topic or Theme
2. Development of Purposes
   (a) specific
   (b) general
3. Overview of Topic or Theme
   (a) nature of problem
   (b) scope of problem
   (c) generalizations involved
4. Initiatory or Approach
   (a) as on-going interests
   (b) pre-arranged to stimulate interest
5. Working Period
   (a) length of time per day
   (b) particular time in school day
6. Culminating the Unit
   (a) summary of learnings
   (b) accentuate activities or projects
   (c) identify related interests resulting from unit
7. Evaluation
   (a) determine the extent to which objectives were achieved
   (b) pupil self-evaluation
   (c) use variety of evaluation techniques (see Chapter XIV)

(d) make evaluation an on-going aspect of the unit from its inception

8. Instructional Materials
    (a) textbooks, reference books, bulletins, pamphlets, etc.
    (b) films, filmstrips, recordings, etc.
    (c) flat pictures, maps, globes, charts, etc.

It should become obvious to the teacher who understands the developmental approach to teaching that the unit does not have to be a highly structured plan of teaching. In fact, from the period of its inception it may be completely developed through the cooperative process with the children. It may be desirable, however, for the beginning teacher or the teacher in service who has not taught a unit previously to structure her first attempt at this kind of teaching in order to maintain a feeling of security and self-confidence. The writers, in viewing hundreds of student teachers using a unit for the first time, found that they possessed more self-assurance when they had detailed plans. However, after teaching the units, large numbers of these prospective teachers confessed that they now believed they could profitably bring the learners into the planning process. Thus, the unit method, as a teaching procedure, takes on meaning as the teacher recognizes its potential for creating harmony between the developmental processes of growth and the use of knowledge or subject matter.

The eight component parts of the above description of a unit hardly need detailed discussion here. Each item has either been discussed or will be considered in detail later on. It should be pointed out that the special methods courses in the professional preparation of the teacher will also emphasize the unit approach in the organization of instruction. Since the development of these eight parts is, or should be, basically a personal matter with the teacher, its purpose is primarily to suggest that the teacher can gain a perspective of how a unit is organized.

What Is the Function of the Teacher in Unit Teaching?

The teacher's *major function in any classroom is that of directing learning to the end that each individual moves a step nearer maturity—*emotionally, mentally, socially, and physically. This function as it relates to unit teaching becomes more realistic since unit teaching is based upon the assumption that the teacher recognizes the unilateral growth of the human organism. That is, each phase of growth is enhanced or retarded in relationship to other growth phases. For example, emotional growth may then become negative as a result of certain misunderstandings the child holds concerning changes in his physical stature. Mental growth may also lag since it is influenced by emotional or social disturbances. It can readily be seen that the nature of unit teaching requires the teacher to be concerned with the total development of the child, whereas some of the teaching procedures discussed in the earlier part of this chapter were primarily concerned with mental growth only. The teacher who envisions education as a process of fact-reciting has little or no concern for the whole organism as a learner.

A second function of the teacher in unit teaching, a corollary of the first function, is that of directing decision-making activities. The success of the unit may depend upon the extent to which the children have shared in developing the objectives, the initial activities, and their plans for achieving the objectives. The teacher must see that each child has a chance to be heard in shaping final opinion. She must guide those who dominate the discussion by helping them to recognize the rights of others to share in the discussion sessions. Thus, securing maximum participation in group discussions is a goal of the teacher. She has a particular responsibility to recognize constantly the need to clarify issues and to help children to develop critical thinking as they sharpen each issue with additional insights. In addition, the teacher must see that discussing the issues does not dwindle into wasting time or losing the point of departure. Thus, the skillful teacher may set the entire climate of the classroom as she works with children to produce sound thinking through group decision-making. This is essential if unit teaching is to project beyond the read–recite–test stage of teaching. Decision-making may well be considered the most valuable democratic technique developed by the learners in the unit process, although caution must be exercised in dealing with immature children by not requiring decision-making beyond the scope of their abilities.

A third function of the teacher in unit teaching is to direct the learning activities in such a way that individual differences are met and cared for through careful planning. The teacher must study each child meticulously in order to recognize his particular needs. For example, it may be discovered that Teddy excels in oral reading as he reads with fluency and expression. His reading rate seems to be very high. But the teacher has discovered that Teddy is not comprehending his reading. In planning the unit she may provide certain specific experiences for him which are related to this need. Teddy also needs to be aware of the purposes of these activities. That is, the teacher needs to help Teddy to see his own need in this respect in order to produce learning based upon a purpose known to the learner.

Recognizing individual differences also means putting into practice those principles which seem to produce the best results for each child. Bright children, for example, do not gain as much from group work when they are working with children of low ability on a task which only challenges the low ability child.[17] It is further indicated by research that group work affects the quality of learning more than it does the quantity of learning. Here the teacher is conscious of the differences of children within the classroom group who are capable of solving more difficult problems, and to this end groups working in the unit are geared to levels of difficulty of tasks to be accomplished or problems to be solved. Projects of mediocre construction should not become major aspects of the learning of the more able pupils. It is important for the teacher to apply sound principles in developing programs of horizontal and vertical enrichment.

Some additional functions of the teacher in unit teaching, which need little or no explanation here, are (1) to gather and classify resource material; (2) to gather and classify information concerning the progress of each child; (3) to arrange physical conditions in the room to meet the needs of children in carrying out their plans; and (4) to carry on a cooperative program of continuous appraisal with the children throughout the unit.

How Does the Teacher Plan for Unit Teaching?

It has previously been pointed out that regardless of the stage of development of the teacher in the area of teaching procedures, certain constants remain. That is, whether the teacher is using subject units, or related subject units, or is teaching directly from the textbook, *planning* is the key to producing efficient results.

Planning for unit teaching requires the highest type of ability due to the intricacies of the unit method. However, this ability can be developed if teachers will put into action certain specific suggestions which will be made here. It must be kept in mind that these guidelines to planning are not all-inclusive and should be modified in accordance with one's needs. At the same time, to modify the guides for the purpose of saving time, and sheer unwillingness to accept planning as a means to the end in teaching, will surely result in inept teaching. No one person can keep in mind from day to day all of the important aspects of teaching. In addi-

---

[17] See H. Gurnee, "Effect of Collective Learning Upon the Individual Participants," *Journal of Abnormal and Social Psychology*, 34 (1939), 529-32; G. B. Watson, "Do Groups Think More Efficiently Than Individuals," *Journal of Abnormal and Social Psychology*, 23 (1928), 328-36; B. E. Blanchard, "Recent Investigations of Social Learning," *Journal of Educational Research*, 43 (1950), 507-15; W. C. Trow, A. E. Zander, W. C. Morse, and D. H. Jenkins, "Psychology of Group Behavior; The Class as a Group," *Journal of Educational Psychology*, 41 (1950), 322-38.

tion, teaching large numbers of children and meeting individual needs makes this problem of planning paramount.

Pre-planning. In unit teaching, planning is also a developmental process, that is, pre-planning for the construction of a teaching unit may involve the actual development of a "pencil and paper unit." This type of unit is usually written out in detail by the teacher in advance of the time is to be taught. This should not be condemned if we accept the fact that growth in teaching is a developmental process. However, what we are concerned with here is the pre-planning before the unit gets under way. This important practice does not vary to any great extent even if the unit is called a "pencil and paper unit," or what some authorities term the "experience unit." Some of the guides to effective pre-planning are:

1. Planning for physical arrangement of the room.
2. Planning for desirable emotional tone.
3. Planning for needed resource materials.
4. Planning for the use of instruments for recording pupil growth.
5. Planning for personal preparation through review of content areas.

Thus, effective pre-planning is concerned with those activities and responsibilities of the teacher prior to entering into the direct learning situation with the pupils. These guides to pre-planning are essential regardless of the teaching procedure used. A further discussion of these guides should aid the pre-service or the in-service teacher in clarifying these responsibilities.

Planning for room arrangement. Essential to unit teaching is the arrangement of the physical features of the room. This arrangement must be such to facilitate the type of learning which the teacher is trying to accomplish in her room. If the classroom is to be used for unit work, certain provisions must be made. The room should be equipped with movable furniture in order to provide for flexibility of arrangement. In this way, groups can be working in various locations in the room in accordance with the nature of their activity. This type of arrangement provides for organizing the room in order that group activity will not be a disturbing factor to other groups. Ample book storage space as well as table tops for work space are essentials. Teachers frequently complain that they can't carry on unit work because of the crowdedness of their classrooms. This is undoubtedly a legitimate complaint, but, if possible, even the removal of a few permanent seats will provide room for a table or two. The flexibility found in most of the new, modern buildings provides for the needed space for unit teaching. However, even many of the older rooms can be rearranged to provide more work space if the teacher is interested. One such arrangement in a temporary building was observed by one of the writers. (This building has been temporary for 13 years!) The teacher had removed some of the old, permanent-type seats and utilized three old tables. Children were seated at the tables but were rotated as groups needed to work at a table. It should be obvious that effective unit teaching requires the furniture of the room to be movable, so that when children need to be regrouped for certain activities, the furniture and equipment can be utilized in the best possible way. Storage for projects, shelving for books, pamphlets, magazines and the like must be convenient. If the room simply cannot be improved upon and is so crowded with desks and pupils that even aisle space is at a premium, teacher initiative and leadership may be strained to utilize the classroom space to better advantage. However, in the majority of classroom situations, the teachers can improvise and plan for better utilization of space and satisfy most requirements called for in unit type of teaching.

Planning for a desirable emotional tone.   The teacher cannot leave to chance the establishing of the proper emotional climate of her room. This requires careful planning before the children first arrive, as well as after they come together. Through a careful study of the cumulative records the teacher can determine the particular emotional needs of certain pupils, plan to meet these needs, and identify others in the course of time.

The classroom teacher who utilizes unit teaching must provide for the expression of emotion as a major aspect of growth and development. The alert teacher will recognize the effect of emotion on the climate of the classroom. Healthy attitudes toward the understanding of emotion will result in more effective pupil adjustment. Suppression of emotion can only result in unhappiness and a classroom atmosphere permeated with tension and distrust. Baxter found that the teacher's behavior affected the pupils' sense of security, freedom from tension, courtesy and other basic needs.[18] Thus, the teacher provides leadership in helping children to understand emotion as a normal aspect of life and therefore assists them in adjusting to emotional experiences. The unit method of instruction should lead children to learn how to live more effectively. This approach may be contrasted with teaching procedures which emphasize the mechanics of living but fail to provide the vital experiences involving these mechanics. Jersild pointed out the large number of pupils

---

[18] Bernice Baxter, *Teacher-Pupil Relationships* (New York: The Macmillan Company, 1943.)

who may be expected to become serious problems of maladjustment and a social burden when he stated that 17 to 26 children out of a group of 40 will possess mental illnesses ranging from chronic unhappiness to criminal behavior.[19] These and other statistics emphasize the seriousness of the problem of emotional health and suggest that the alert teacher cannot disregard her responsibility for setting the emotional tone of the classroom. Even at the primary level, children are inclined toward deep rooted emotional problems. In fact, Carmichael's research focuses upon children three to eight years of age, and seems to imply that basic personality patterns are formed at very early ages.[20] It also becomes evident that modification of behavior at the elementary school level becomes increasingly more difficult unless close cooperation is achieved between home and school of the child concerned. Unit teaching, however, may provide classroom experiences for the child which will not only aid the teacher to identify basic emotional needs, but also provide an outlet for these needs. In addition, learning through the unit method can produce novel and challenging experiences, many of which will be emotional in nature, but through them the teacher must seek to balance experiences for learners based upon individual differences. It should be added that the unit approach is not the final answer to emotional problems; it can, however, provide a basis for that kind of teaching which aids in better child adjustment.

Providing needed source materials. The classroom which houses unit teaching must be a laboratory of resources. This does not mean that the room is to be cluttered with books, magazines, and other materials, but the teacher should make provisions for having on hand those materials appropriate for the unit being studied. In some schools, arrangements may be made to bring large numbers of books from the central library to the classroom for unit study. In others, there may be no central library and teachers must rely solely upon their classroom collections. Where this latter is the situation, teachers should know of the total collection housed in each room in order that they may share with each other when particular instructional needs arise.

Also, if unit teaching is to be real in the lives of the learners, construction materials and work areas must be made available. Again, the individual school organization may determine the plan. One school may provide a reasonable pupil-teacher ratio (1:25) and modern classrooms

---

[19] Arthur Jersild, *Child Development and the Curriculum* (New York: Teachers College, Columbia University, 1946), p. 145.

[20] Carmichael, Leonard, "The Onset and Early Development of Behavior," *Manual of Child Psychology* (New York: John Wiley and Sons, 1946), pp. 43-75.

equipped with work tables and the like. Others may have a central resource room for construction activities. In any event, the teacher must
plan for the materials to be on hand which will be utilized during the
unit.

Community resources and other instructional resources are discussed
at length in the next chapter. Suffice it to say here, that if resources are
going to be used to further instruction, the teacher must believe in their
value and plan in advance for their efficient utilization based upon a
real need or purpose.

Planning for the use of instruments for recording pupil growth. Although Chapter 14 is concerned with evaluation, a brief discussion is
given here as it relates to the unit method of teaching. Evaluating pupil
progress has been the "stumbling stone" for many teachers who have
attempted unit teaching. That is, after working with pupils in an elaborate
unit, the teacher concludes the experiences with a lengthy teacher-made
test based on facts requiring memorization. This is not to protest the
learning of facts, but only to emphasize that determining learning involves much more than memory testing. Hanna states that to evaluate
the change in the behavior of children during a unit of work requires
certain steps:

(1) the objectives must be stated in terms of specific and con-
    crete behaviors,
(2) situations must be provided in which the desired behavior
    can be observed,
(3) evidence of pupil behavior must be collected and recorded
    in usable form,
(4) the evidence must be interpreted and used to provide better
    learning situations, and
(5) the results must be reported to the pupils, parents, and other
    interested persons.[21]

These steps which lead to evaluating pupil behavior clearly indicate the
need for responsible utilization of instruments for evaluating behavior as
well as the interpreting of the data acquired. Every effort must be put
forth to produce evaluative data from objective sources.

There is no lack of suggestive techniques or devices for appraising
pupil growth. Some of the devices which have been found useful by certain teachers are:

---

[21] Lavone A. Hanna, Gladys L. Potter, Neva Hagaman, *Unit Teaching in the
Elementary School* (New York: Holt, Rinehart and Winston, Inc., 1955), p. 364.

Activity records
Anecdotal records
Autobiographies
Behavior journals
Case studies
Cumulative records
Charts
Checklists
Diaries
Discussion groups
Evaluative criteria
Inventories
Interviews (individual, group)

Observation (directed, informal)
Questionnaires
Profiles
Pupil graphs
Rating scales
Sociometric tests
Standardized tests
Teacher-made tests
    (a) alternate response
    (b) completion
    (c) matching
    (d) essay

The above list of devices is not complete, but includes the most representative ones. Teachers should be continuously searching for more and more objective instruments for understanding pupil growth and behavior. The teacher must recognize through use, the device which will meet her particular purpose. No single device should be used to the exclusion of all others. For example, if the teacher is trying to determine the extent of critical thinking of the group or of an individual, certain devices such as directed observation, group discussion, checklists, as well as certain standardized tests may yield the desired information. But the results accumulated from any one device in itself may be insufficient to base final judgment. Validity, reliability, objectivity and the like must all be considered in using a device for a specific purpose.

Important to the discussion here is the planning which is necessary for using the devices. Unit teaching thrives on continuous appraisal; it is part and parcel of the learning situation. Tests, both standardized and teacher-made, are important and may serve a basic purpose in the overall evaluation program; but it must be recognized that, to assay learning adequately, these tests do not always indicate changes in pupil behavior. Therefore, the teacher, in her planning for the use of instruments, or devices, must ever be on the alert to new and creative devices which may be the result of her own ingenuity. Devices must also be contrived which would assist the learner to compile information, and would record evidences of change in his own behavior.

Personal preparation. Teachers need to be ever conscious of the need to strengthen their own backgrounds of knowledge. Content areas studied in the elementary school frequently become outdated. Teachers need to read widely and be familiar with current thinking in the content areas. The areas of science, mathematics, and social studies, for example, are pregnant with new ideas, discoveries, and current problems.

Thus, the teacher who is planning unit teaching must constantly keep herself abreast of the times. She can make more and vital contributions in challenging her pupils' thinking capacity if she recognizes her need for continuous growth in knowledge.

What Is the Source of Content in Unit Teaching?

Too frequently unit teaching is misunderstood by teachers and parents alike because they see or feel that the construction or dramatic aspects of the unit are overly emphasized. Thus, they believe that content becomes subordinate to the activities. Nothing is further from the truth where good unit teaching exists. Content or subject matter is drawn upon in a meaningful way to solve problems or to achieve a purpose. An illustration of this point is presented as observed in a sixth-grade classroom:

> Mrs. Toms was involved in teaching a unit on "The Citizens' Responsibilities in a Democracy." Some of the children raised questions concerning why everyone had to vote since one vote couldn't affect a decision. Why shouldn't elected officials do what they think is best without committees? These and other questions were listed on the chalkboard. The teacher asked if anyone knew where we could find the answers to any of the questions and how we should go about this. A suggestion was made that maybe we should see if any elections were won by one vote; another suggestion was made concerning looking up ideas that lead to letting people vote. Someone then raised the question that his mother said when she was a little girl, women couldn't vote. It was not long before complete plans were made for doing research in history leading to developing a background of understanding of the unit theme. Geographical factors were studied as history led the children from one section of the country to another.

Content in unit teaching is no less important than in traditional teaching. The difference is in the way it is studied. Pupils in unit teaching use content in a meaningful and functional way as they relate it to seeking solutions to problems or achieving individual or group goals. Facts are learned only as they relate to the basic problem at hand. Facts are not learned in isolation or for the sake of reciting them back to the teacher, then to be readily forgotten. This is usually the result of teaching procedures that place an emphasis on content, with little respect for the maturity level of the learner.

Research investigations[22] have substantiated the fact that children learn as much, if not more, subject matter in unit teaching as in textbook

---

[22] J. Wayne Wrightstone, *Appraisal of Newer Elementary School Practices* (New York: Bureau of Publications, Teachers College, Columbia University, 1938), p. 257.

procedures. But accruing to this kind of learning are the many social and cooperative group skills acquired in learning the content.

How Are the Basic Skills Taught?

The basic skills are taught in most schools which utilize the unit system in separate periods during the day. Although many skills are learned during unit teaching, it seems desirable to include blocks of time in the daily schedule for developing the essential skills in reading and arithmetic.

The alert teacher, however, finds ways for the children to utilize the newly-learned skills in a functional way during the unit. This reinforces the learning in meaningful and practical ways, enables the children to see the usefulness of the newly-learned skills, and facilitates motivation for learning. It is also possible that the unit may be the basis for the learning of certain new skills that are needed in order to proceed with specific aspects of the unit. An illustration of this is found in the unit in which the children have decided to make a mural depicting the history of transportation. Each child has been assigned by the group to make a rough copy of his contribution. Thus, he needs to draw a scale model which he will later enlarge for the final copy on the mural. A need to learn proportion has arisen. Therefore, the teacher spends the next several days teaching the children the processes of proportion. Ideally, the proportion might have been taught right at the time of the need. However, due to many limiting factors in organizing a school program it seems sound to point out that separate periods for teaching the skills subjects must not be neglected. It would be naive to assume that all skill subjects can be thoroughly taught by utilizing the unit approach. Such practice will only lead to glossing over the development of basic skills.

How Does the Teacher Plan a Daily Schedule?

Many school systems provide teachers with a suggested daily schedule. Such schedules obviously reflect to some extent the philosophy of the school, although some may only reflect the principal's philosophy, especially if the schedule was prepared by him. In one school, the principal prepared a rigid schedule for grades one through six and insisted that teachers should not deviate from it. Any principal or teacher familiar with elementary school children would immediately recognize that a rigid schedule for the elementary school will not prove beneficial for the best interests of children or the teachers. Chart IV depicts a traditional schedule used in the fifth grade of a school in 1928. Chart V is a recommended daily schedule which could be found in use in a modern curriculum program today. It is readily apparent that the teachers in a modern school have considerable flexibility in developing learning experiences in accordance with their knowledge of child growth and development. Scheduling, as found in Chart V, provides for greater individualization of instruction. Programmed textbooks and teaching machines require flexibility in scheduling if these learning devices are to be used. Small group and large group instruction is also possible without disruption in the schedule, if the school is not rigidly scheduled. The basic core of the curriculum would be taught during the work periods in accordance with pupil needs. A modern curriculum design cannot emerge under rigid scheduling conditions.

CHART IV

Traditional Schedule
Grade V

Hours	*Subjects*
9:00- 9:05	Inspection of hands, hair, teeth, etc.
9:05- 9:20	Citizenship
9:20- 9:35	Spelling
9:35- 9:45	Penmanship
9:45-10:00	Oral or Written Composition or Reading
10:00-10:10	Recess
10:10-10:40	Arithmetic
10:40-11:00	Physical Education, including games
11:00-11:10	Recess
11:10-11:40	Reading
11:40-12:00	Language or Composition
1:00- 1:05	Home Room with announcements
1:05- 1:35	Art Education: Music or Drawing
1:35- 2:00	Geography and Nature Study
2:00- 2:15	Recess and Supervised Play
2:15- 2:50	Reading
2:50- 3:15	History or Civics

There is a need to develop a schedule for each grade; no single schedule can serve the needs of an entire elementary school. Children in kindergarten and grade one have varying needs which may require different scheduling, just as grade one differs from grade two or three. Although the daily schedule which is suggested in many curriculum guides will be found most helpful to teachers, some changes may prove

CHART V

Modern Flexible Schedule
Grade V

HOURS	MONDAY	TUESDAY	WEDNESDAY	THURSDAY	FRIDAY
9:00 10:00	9:00- 9:15 French 9:30-10:00 Music or Art	Work Period for Various Units	9:05-9:45 Auditorium Activity Music or Art	Work Period or French Library Guidance	Club Activities Creative Activities
10:00 11:00	Work Periods for Individual or Groups and Related to Some Unit Physical Education	10:00-10:30 Guidance in Reading 10:30-10:45 Physical Education 10:45-11:45 Work periods on units related to the program and emphasized guidance in learning			Unit Activities Physical Education
12:00 1:00	Lunch and Relaxation				
1:00 2:00	Art, Creative Writing, Laboratory Work				
2:00 3:00	Auditorium programs, Creative Work, Conferences, Reference Work in Library, Homemaking Activities, etc.				

beneficial after the teacher works with it awhile. In addition, if the teacher is not bound by administrative edict to a rigid schedule, she may permit the children to share in certain daily modifications. This is particularly true if the teacher is operating in a self-contained classroom. Here activities which fall within large blocks of time may be planned with the children.

What Is Individualized Teaching?

The success of the emerging curriculum concept will depend to a large extent on the willingness of teachers to break the rigid "lockstep" curriculum which frustrates so many children. *Individualized instruction means that the teacher as well as the school must have a definable commitment to serving the individual.* Suitable provisions must be made for individual differences. To make such provisions, each successive educational experience must be understood in terms of the child's needs at the appropriate moment of his development. *A child who is learning at his own level will then be matched with the appropriate materials, the right instructional procedure, and the time required to achieve or master the task to be learned.* These factors will, of course, vary with each learner.

The teacher needs to understand that children do not all learn according to some preconceived adult pattern. Bruner has aptly pointed out that "any subject can be taught effectively in some intellectually honest form to any child at any stage of development."[23] The important point is that the teacher needs to recognize what she is teaching in terms of the child's way of viewing things. So often what she believes to be a logical explanation is distant from the child's way of thinking. The teacher perhaps needs to discover what to do to facilitate learning and what the child can do for himself. The fact that differences in learners exist can be demonstrated in many ways, but our task is to find teaching procedures or strategies which will promote the fullest development of the individual.

One of the basic problems is expecting all children to complete a learning task in the same amount of time. Then we are able to give a weekly test and proceed to the next teaching unit. Yet, if we would vary the time according to the needs of each individual child, most of the children would eventually achieve mastery of the unit. That is, children need to be free to learn at their own rate and to use whatever learning style accommodates them. Some of the activities involved would be view-

---

[23] Jerome S. Bruner, *The Process of Education* (Cambridge, Mass.: Harvard University Press, 1961), p. 33.

ing, listening, receiving information, discussion, decision making, independent study, tutorial learning, etc. None of these activities should be used to the exclusion of others, but their use should be related to the learner's particular need at the time. The same principle regarding rate of learning applies to evaluating learning. There is little reason for all children to be tested at the same time or to be allotted the same specified number of minutes for completing a test when differences are recognized.

What Are Some Ways to Start Individualized Teaching?

One of the easiest ways to approach the individual variations found in pupils is through the use of the textbook.[24] Permit each student to proceed through his textbooks at his own pace. As the student approaches a problem which he cannot grasp, direct him to other books for alternative explanations. As the teacher uses this simplified approach to instruction, she will find a need for books below as well as above the grade level she is assigned to teach. Some pupils will not be able to work successfully in the books assigned to that grade. Since success in learning is one of the greatest motivators for learning, the teacher will need to determine the appropriate beginning level for the child. Likewise, some children will finish the assigned textbooks for the grade before the year is up, if permitted to learn at their own rate. These children will need materials beyond their grade level if they are to make progress commensurate with their abilities.

Workbooks and programmed materials may also be useful to the teacher who is individualizing instruction. The workbook might facilitate the child's ability to grasp the concept in the textbook. Since these learning aids provide different approaches to learning, the teacher will need to assist the child in determining his need, whether it be for drill or for learning in small steps or frequent reinforcement. The point to be made is that both the aids used in learning and the time permitted for mastery of the task need to be varied.

Socialized learning. The individualized program should provide for "socialized learning" experiences. This means that pupils should be grouped on certain occasions for verbalizing their learnings. Such small group discussions provide opportunities for pupils to clarify their understanding of certain processes or concepts. For some youngsters this can be a reinforcement learning experience and for others it can be a testing

---

[24] See Benjamin S. Bloom, "Learning for Mastery," *Evaluation Comment*, 1, No. 2 (Los Angeles: Center for the Study of Evaluation of Instructional Programs, University of California, May, 1968), whole issue.

of whether they have grasped the real meaning. This type of activity also eliminates the boredom which might set in if pupils are left totally to themselves. However, no individualized program is conceived which would not permit pupil interaction as they work together in similar learning experiences.

What Kind of Grouping Will Best Contribute to Pupil Learning in the Affective Domain?

The multi-age group has a place in individualized learning. Learning in the affective domain is influenced by many factors. It therefore becomes essential for the teacher to understand the growth needs of her pupils as well as the cognitive needs. To insure the child's growth, he should be given the opportunity of selecting his place in many groups as he progresses. For example, he should have the opportunity of being in a group of friends or a group without friends; he should be the oldest or the youngest of a group as well as the slowest or the fastest, depending on his needs. Thus the teacher is in a position to provide the optimum environment for the development of the child.

In this respect, the team approach facilitates the child's growth since it provides experiences with many types of teachers. Independent children need to respect differences in others; dependent children need to learn to shift their dependency to themselves. The important point to be made is that the teacher needs to recognize the different needs of youngsters and to adjust the human environment to fulfill these needs.

Why Did Team Teaching and Cooperative Teaching Begin?

During recent times, educators and critics of education have carefully scrutinized the basic values of free, universal education. With the coming of new knowledge in science, mathematics, and other disciplines has come a concern about the traditional pattern of organization in the elementary schools. The self-contained classroom has been the predominant pattern of organization. This form of organization is now showing signs of change. The question concerning the advantages of other forms of organization has not yet been fully answered by research investigations. Nevertheless, current estimates are that about 30 per cent of both elementary and secondary schools have some form of team teaching. Although the ideal concept of team teaching is probably not being achieved, it is safe to assume that schools are looking for new forms or patterns for organizing instruction.

Some sources have expressed doubts concerning the ability of a teacher in a self-contained classroom to teach all subjects in the curriculum with equal competence. This growing concern reflects the new importance of subject matter. Fundamental to the issue of self-contained classroom organization vs. team teaching organization is whether one teacher can keep abreast of the growing complexity of many different disciplines in an age of technological advancements and a period of competition for the minds of men.

Large grants of federal funds as well as funds made available by philanthropic foundations for studying gifted and talented youth reflect another growing concern for the effectiveness of instruction in a classroom where the teacher must teach all subjects. Also, some research investigations have shown that large groups can learn certain subject matter quite as effectively as small groups. Thus, it becomes economically expedient to conserve both the time of the teacher and the pupils for other valuable needs.

The many experiments now going on in various elementary schools across the nation is evidence of efforts to determine whether a new form of school organization can better meet the educational needs of individuals as well as groups. Team teaching is a new organizational pattern directed at more effective teaching and learning.

What Is Team Teaching?

Although no dictionary definition has yet emerged as to the meaning of team teaching, it is safe to say it means different things to different people. However, team teaching implies a cooperative effort of two or more teachers working together to plan, organize, implement, and appraise curriculum and instruction. Anderson states, "Team teaching is an emerging pattern of personnel utilization in the schools. Several teachers are organized into a 'team' with joint responsibility for the planning, execution, and evaluation of an educational program . . ."[25]

The team may be organized vertically (grades 1, 2, 3) or horizontally at a given grade level. The team may also be organized on a subject basis horizontally or vertically. Regardless of the organizational form used, the design is such that each member assumes responsibility for a given subject. This reduces the subject load of the teacher and provides

---

[25] Association for Supervision and Curriculum Development in Cooperation With NEA Research Division. *Team Teaching*, ed. Robert H. Anderson, CAPCI Bibliography, No. 4. (Washington: The Association, November, 1960), p. 1.

a better opportunity for her to keep abreast of her specialty as well as related research.

The heart of the concept of team teaching is found in the spirit of cooperative planning and team unity.[26] The team members, unlike the teacher in the self-contained classroom, or those teachers teaching the same subject in a departmental organizational plan, are in constant communication necessitated by mutual need for close coordination and articulation of every experience affecting the learners. The team accepts responsibility for curriculum planning, grouping practices, pupil counseling, and agrees upon instructional procedures that will best meet the needs of the group. Thus, teacher strengths are capitalized upon and utilized in meeting individual differences of children. The design provides the opportunity for a face to face relationship between teacher and pupil or a one-to-one ratio when needed. It enables teachers to provide enrichment and acceleration for pupils to progress at their own rates in any or all of the subject areas.

Cooperative teaching is, in most cases, synonymous with team teaching, although the history of cooperative teaching tends to point out a less formal structure for cooperative teaching. This form of teaching is usually voluntary, involving perhaps two teachers. One teacher might combine her group with another teacher's class for science teaching, and the other teacher might then teach some other subject which would be of special interest to her or in which she possesses special competence. Thus there is an interchange of pupils between cooperating teachers for specific learning activities. This kind of teaching does not require the formal structure attributed to team teaching, nor does it have the advantages of a team structure.[27]

How Is a School Organized for Team Teaching?

There are many different forms of team teaching. The literature abounds in describing the various innovations in team formulation.[28] However, one of the most completely organized schools for team teaching is at Lexington, Massachusetts, the birthplace of experimentation of the concept. The organizational pattern for team teaching is one in which

---

[26] Stuart E. Dean and Clinette F. Witherspon, "Team Teaching in the Elementary School." *Education Briefs*, No. 38 (Washington: Office of Education, January, 1962), p. 4.

[27] See Robert H. Anderson, *Teaching in a World of Change* (New York: Harcourt, Brace & World, Inc., 1966).

[28] See Stuart E. Dean, "Team Teaching: A Review," *School Life*, 44 (September, 1961), 5-8.

groups of teachers accept joint responsibility for instruction of a given division of the school's enrollment. In the Lexington plan, three to eight certificated teachers take the responsibility for the instruction of 75 to 240 pupils of similar age and grade status. Each team has at the base a teacher who carries the prestige and status of the usual self-contained classroom teacher. There may be as many as four teachers, each with a subject or task specialty operating at this level. In the hierarchy will be one or two senior teachers who, by experience, have achieved competence as teachers and who are subject specialists. The senior teacher assumes the leadership role in the particular area of specialization.

At the apex of this hierarchy is the team leader. The leader assumes responsibility for certain administrative functions and is largely responsible for identifying pupil needs, assigning pupils to groups, giving leadership for developing curriculum, and supervising the team. In the Lexington school, the team leaders and the principal actually formulate general

CHART VI

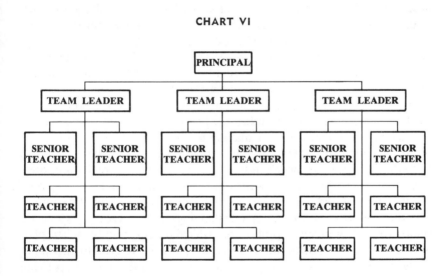

school policy and serve as an "instructional council" for continuous reappraisal of curriculum and instruction. Chart VI shows how the Lexington school is organized for instruction.[29]

---

[29] This material has been adapted from a speech presented at a conference at Ohio University in 1961 on "Team Teaching." Presented by Mrs. Ethel Bears, Principal of the Franklin Elementary School at Lexington, Massachusetts.

SUMMARY

Good teaching is the result of many combined ingredients. Learning is an intricate process which must involve each learner personally in that which is to be learned. To do this successfully, the teacher must recognize the value and functional use of subject matter as it relates to her understanding of child growth and development. Content, then, is utilized in the learning situation as it relates to the needs and maturity levels of individuals.

Method of teaching is important in the teaching situation because of *first, the need in the learning process to arrange in a series certain specifics which result in order and sequence in learning; and second, the broad meaning of method which utilizes sound psychological principles which set the tone for classroom organization.*

Growth in the teaching process implies that the same psychological processes which affect pupil learning also affect individuals at all stages of maturity. Teachers may fail to utilize the best procedures of teaching due to many causes, some of which are (1) feelings of insecurity on the job, (2) feelings of insecurity related to changing present practices, (3) lack of vision or creativity, and (4) failure of the administration to provide in-service growth and support for change. Of course, there are many other reasons for poor teaching, but the important point is that teachers can grow in understanding method a step at a time. Thus, growth in teaching procedures requires that the teacher evaluate her present stage of development in order to utilize sound steps in moving forward. Growth, then, might proceed in the following sequence: recitation, question and discussion, activity-centered procedures, and teacher-pupil planned procedures. Growth in these teaching procedures also implies that the teacher grows in her understanding of democracy. As one develops toward employing procedures which require pupil-teacher planning, the success in using these procedures will be related to the ability of the teacher to understand the rudiments of cooperative group living. These understandings are essential to the success of such instructional designs as team teaching.

The use of newer teaching procedures is based upon the need to organize learning into meaningful wholes. Unit teaching, then, becomes an effective procedure for organizing learning. Thus, some of the functions of the teacher shift in unit teaching to (1) directing learning to the end that each individual moves a step nearer maturity, (2) directing decision-making activities, (3) directing learning in order to meet individual differences through planning.

SUGGESTED ACTIVITIES AND PROBLEMS

1. Resolve: "New teaching methods have not produced evidence to justify their use."

2. Write a paper and present it to the class setting forth the difference between planning *for* children and planning *with* children.

3. From the material found in pages 99 to 109, construct a check-list which could be used to identify the various stages of teacher growth as related to methods of teaching.

4. Observe in at least three different classrooms and use the instrument you developed in Number 3 to determine the level of operation of each teacher. Discuss your results with the class, but do not identify the teachers observed. Did you find observable differences in teaching procedures?

5. Read several of the suggested references at the end of this chapter on team teaching. Plan with three other students for a day's teaching under a team organization. Present your plan to the class and discuss your reactions to this form of organizing for teaching.

SELECTED READINGS

Anderson, Robert H. *Teaching in a World of Change*. New York: Harcourt, Brace & World, Inc., 1966.

Bain, Medill and Richard G. Woodword. *Team Teaching in Action*. Boston: Houghton Mifflin Co., 1964.

Beauchamp, George A. *Basic Dimensions of Elementary Method*. Boston: Allyn and Bacon, Inc., 1959.

Bloom, Benjamin S. "Learning for Mastery," *Evaluation Comment*, 1, No. 2 Los Angeles, Cal.: Los Angeles Center for the Study of Instructional Programs, University of California, May, 1968.

Burton, William. *The Guidance of the Learning Activities*. New York: Appleton-Century-Crofts, 1956, p. 336.

Hanna, Larone A., Gladys L. Potter and Neva Hagaman. *Unit Teaching in the Elementary School*. New York: Holt, Rinehart & Winston, Inc., 1955, p. 364.

Kelner, Bernard G. *How to Teach in the Elementary School*. New York: McGraw-Hill Book Company, 1958, Chapters 7 to 12.

Kilpatrick, William H. *Philosophy of Education*. New York: The Macmillan Co., 1951, Chapters 18 and 20.

Michaelis, John U. *Social Studies for Children in a Democracy*. Englewood Cliffs, N. J.: Prentice-Hall, Inc., 1968.

Miller, Richard, I. (ed.). *The Nongraded School: Analysis and Study*. New York: Harper & Row, Publishers, 1967, Chapter 6.

Moser, E. H. and W. A. Brownell. "Meaningful Vs. Mechanical Learning: A Study in Grade III Subtraction," Durham, N. C.: Duke University Press, 1949.

Mursell, James. *Successful Teaching.* 2nd ed.; New York: McGraw-Hill Book Company, 1954, p. 10.

Shaplin, Judson T. and Henry F. Olds, Jr. (eds.). *Team Teaching.* New York: Harper & Row, Publishers, 1964.

Shumsky, Abraham. *In Search of Teaching Style.* New York: Appleton-Century-Crofts, 1965, Chapters 5 and 6.

Stoval, Thomas F. "Lecture Vs. Discussion," *Phi Delta Kappan,* XXIX (March, 1958), 256 (special issue).

Thomas, George I. and Joseph Crescimbeni. *Individualizing Instruction in the Elementary School.* New York: Random House, Inc., 1967.

Trow, W. C., A. E. Zander, W. C. Morse, and D. H. Jenkins. "Psychology of Group Behavior: the Class as a Group," *Journal of Educational Psychology,* 41 (1950), 322-38.

Watson, G. B. "Do Groups Think More Efficiently Than Individuals?" *Journal of Abnormal and Social Psychology,* 23 (1928), 328-36.

CHAPTER 5

Instructional Resources
for Learning

INTRODUCTION

It has been pointed out that learning, to be effective, first must involve the learner personally in that which is being learned. Second, the more the experience for the learner, the greater the efficiency of learning and the greater the retention; and third, productive learning in the elementary school is enhanced by skillfully employed instructional aids.

Why Are Instructional Aids an Important Aspect of the Learning Environment?

During the past three decades, the use of various audio-visual aids have become increasingly more important. World War II found the armed forces seeking effective ways of producing specific kinds of training at an accelerated pace. However, important to this acceleration was the effectiveness of the learning. At that time audio-visual aids which were available were utilized. In addition, many new instructional aids were developed to meet the challenge of a new situation. New and more effective procedures for using the aids were also brought forth. Even though improved learning efficiency seemed to result from those experiences in the armed services, the public schools have been slow to finance audio-visual equipment to the extent that it is readily available to all teachers. Dale has listed some proven contributions of visual aids to learning. He states that they:

> 1. Supply a concrete basis for conceptional thinking and reduce verbalism,

2. Produce a high degree of interest,
3. Make learning more permanent,
4. Contribute to growth and meaning in vocabulary development,
5. Provide for experiences not easily obtained through other materials,
6. Develop continuity of thought,
7. Increase concentration,
8. Provide a motive for free reading and,
9. Can be used to stimulate self-activity.[1]

Visual aids tend to reinforce and add effectiveness to the teaching-learning process. They provide for extending experiences beyond the physical limitations of the classroom. This is not to imply that reading is of lesser importance in learning; in fact, reading becomes an integral part of the visual learning experience. A brief discussion will follow concerning some of the instructional aids being used by some teachers.

Reading materials. In the elementary school, children need a wide variety of reading materials beyond the designated textbook for each subject. Good teaching implies that efforts will be made toward meeting individual differences. If this is to be accomplished, teachers must seek out and use a variety of reading materials. *Reference* materials such as encyclopedias, atlases, dictionaries, almanacs, and the like should be accessible. In addition, leaflets, pamphlets, bulletins of various kinds which are carefully previewed by the teacher, should be available. Many of these are found in lists of free and inexpensive materials. Children's magazines, weekly newspapers, daily newspapers and adult magazines contribute also to the wealth of reading material available for instructional use. Children's literature should also be made available. Thus, all reading material needs to be carefully selected and representative of a wide variety of literature including folklore, fiction, autobiography, historical materials, stories of other lands, and poetry.

Through the use of reading materials, many skills may be developed by children in the elementary school. Research skills can be acquired soon after the child gains his initial reading experiences. That is, he is ready to learn to locate information for himself. This requires knowledge of and skill in using the table of contents, alphabetical index, use of cross references, and the like. As the child becomes adept at securing information on his own, which satisfies his needs, he uses these skills to explore further for knowledge.

---

[1] Edgar Dale, *Audio-Visual Methods of Teaching* (New York: Holt, Rinehart & Winston, Inc., 1954), p. 65.

Real things. A good classroom environment is found to abound in real things. A display of authentic Indian implements, a shell collection, a rock collection, an aquarium, a bowl of frog eggs, all aid in learning about inanimate objects as well as living things. If children are to adjust to the world in which they live and gain a measure of understanding, they must come face to face with as many "real things" as can profitably be utilized from the environment. Such materials extend learnings by helping to build concepts which may lead to development of generalizations. That is, as children study "real things" they observe the characteristics, traits, qualities, and the like of the real thing. From this experience they gain new understanding which assists them to modify certain previous beliefs, concepts or even generalizations. Thus, the study of "real things" aids the child in approaching reality as he attempts to relate these things to his own understandings.

Sound and motion pictures. Motion pictures have been widely used in the elementary schools to meet many different needs. They have been found helpful in supplying concrete information of varying kinds ranging from learning to borrow in subtraction, to furnishing specific data on certain cultures. The film has been found useful in helping a child clarify a purpose as well as to give impetus to certain creative learnings. Motion pictures have been proven to be excellent for group observation and group discussion experiences. Thus, the film may serve as an instructional aid which will stimulate individuals to bring out in the discussion their varying and rich backgrounds of experiences. Such discussions will foster genuine group thinking.

In unit teaching, the motion picture may be used for many purposes, some of which are to (1) bridge the gap between present day living and historical periods in the past, (2) teach a specific skill such as working with clay, basket weaving and the like, (3) build new understandings of certain contemporary cultures, (4) enhance the learning of a tool skill—arithmetic, geography, spelling, reading, etc., (5) view situations which could not be visualized in any other way, and (6) show the development of certain scientific achievements as well as the rise of basic social, religious, and economic institutions. This list is not meant to be all-inclusive, but should help the reader to reflect upon the wide range of possibilities found within this one instrument.

Research[2] has supported the effectiveness of the use of motion pictures over verbal teaching. The more meaningful and useful information that is in the learning process, the greater the retention will be. Since the

---

[2] See Florence Reid, "Films Provide a Rich Source of Vocabulary Study," *Journal of Educational Research*, 41 (April, 1958), 617; also W. W. Charters, *Value of Motion Pictures in Formal Education, Payne Studies* (New York: The Macmillan Company, 1935).

primary purpose of using instructional aids is to make the lesson more meaningful, the teacher must make careful use of films. Important to the use of any instructional aid is the planning for its use by the teacher. Little or no planning for the use of a particular learning aid may result in ineffective instruction. Class preparation and teacher introductions of material have been found to be variables in the learning situations when using films. For example, it has been reported that a group to which a film had been introduced and shown, had an increase of 38 per cent retention over the group to which the film had been shown without introduction. Showing the film a second time after introducing it and providing for discussion questions following the showing increased the ability of the group to answer test questions 40 per cent over the group which had one showing after introduction to the film and 78 per cent over the group which had one showing without introduction.[3] It should become clear that the teacher has a major responsibility for selecting appropriate visual aids, preparing herself for their use, and orienting the children in order to produce the most favorable result possible.

Still pictures. Perhaps still pictures make up the largest number of single instructional aids used in elementary schools. This group of aids consists of filmstrips, flat pictures, photographs and the like, with each having a certain function if used with careful preparation. The filmstrip is one of the easiest to handle and saves instructional time. Dale[4] reports that the use of filmstrips with other aids results in a 35 per cent gain in learning and a 55 per cent gain in retention over those instances where filmstrips were not used. Filmstrips may be used to an advantage because they are so well adapted for discussion during their actual use. In addition, they help to provide for individual differences by permitting students to clarify points during the presentation. Teacher or pupil commentary also contributes by helping to make the viewing more effective. Many modern textbooks are being supplemented by a series of filmstrips which are quite useful in stimulating interest and building appreciation.

An interesting experiment by Flattery[5] compared the effectiveness in teaching informational and conceptional social studies material to 422 fifth grade students. She used three methods of presenting the material to be learned: (a) sound motion pictures, (b) filmstrip without participation, and (c) filmstrip with pupil participation. The results reported that

---

[3] Walter A. Wittich and John G. Fowlkes, *Audio-Visual Paths to Learning* (New York: Harper and Row, Publishers, 1946).

[4] Dale, *op. cit.*

[5] Sister M. J. Flattery, "An Appraisal of the Effectiveness of Selected Instructional Sound Motion Pictures and Silent Filmstrips in Elementary School Instruction" (Washington, D. C.: Catholic University of America, 1953), p. 67.

the filmstrip with or without participation was significantly superior to the motion picture, and there were equal results at various intelligence levels. The filmstrip with participation indicated a significant increase over the one without participation.

In addition to the use of filmstrips in the still picture category, the opaque projector also can make valuable contributions to unit instruction. This piece of equipment provides for using pictures of various kinds, materials produced by children, as well as charts, maps or other things which need to be enlarged for instructional purposes. A theme, written by a child, may be used by projecting it upon a screen for all to see. It may be that the teacher is interested in pointing out the descriptive words or adjectives which this particular student used in an effective manner. The opaque projector, although it is one of the most useful instruments, has not been utilized by teachers to the extent that it might be. Once teachers find the versatility of this equipment, however, it becomes an important instructional tool for them.

Flat pictures, which are perhaps the easiest of all materials to locate, have also been neglected as learning aids by teachers. Flat pictures have been found to be valuable as aids in initiating unit teaching. Some few years ago, the Virginia Electric and Power Company produced a series of large wall pictures which depicted domestic progress over the past century due to the use of electric power. These pictures had many implications for helping children to see the hardships which people endured without electricity. There is no limit to the many fine pictures available to teachers today. Pictures of modes of transportation, communication, conservation and industry at work, and others all contribute to building concepts and understandings.

Auditory resources. The use of records and recordings are additional aids to learning. Many fine records have been produced for use with elementary school children. Records relating to units of study from music to foreign language may be profitably used with young children. In social studies, records may provide sound effects for dramatizations, pageants, creative work, choral reading and the like.[6] Sands points out that all recordings fall into six categories. These are:

1. *Literature.* Masterpieces of drama, lyric poetry, and the essay; episodes from fiction; humor and nonsense.
2. *History.* Great events, speeches, documents; historic utterance of prime ministers, rulers, statesmen, dictators, demogogues.

---

[6] John U. Michaelis, *Social Studies for Children in a Democracy* (Englewood Cliffs, N. J.: Prentice-Hall, Inc.), 1956.

3. *Documentary Matter.* Human relations and situations; regional customs and characteristics; dialectal speech.
4. *Science.* Sounds made by birds, animals, and fish.
5. *Education.* Languages; business education; vocational guidance; calisthenics.
6. *Music.* Symphonic and chamber music; opera and oratorio; band music, art songs and folk songs.[7]

Important to the use of recordings is the skill of involving children in activities to determine the effectiveness of the listening. Pupils must listen in such a way that their minds are involved in the listening. If the children are going to become personally involved in the listening activity, then the selection of records must be geared to the on-going learning experiences of the child. That is, interest and needs of learners must be met if they are to gain effectively from this experience. Pupils must want to hear it. One of the authors observed an experience in which the pupils had requested the teacher to play "In the Hall of the Mountaing King." The first playing of this record attracted very little attention for this fifth grade class. However, after the teacher related the legend of this record to the children, they requested it time and again. Thre was little doubt that these children were living the experience.

Other uses of tapes and records.   Just as children are taught to be careful observers in the science class, they must also be taught to listen. Some authorities have pointed out that listening becomes effective when it involves participation. Support for this contention can be found in the instance where primary children, in response to rhythmic records, participate by doing what the music tells them. No one who has observed this procedure could deny the effect of participation upon listening. Choral reading, singing in unison and the like also make listening an art.

The actual making of a recording is also an effective learning activity. Tape is recommended as it is simpler to work with and cheaper to use than other types of recording equipment due to its being easily erased. Many uses have been found for tape recordings in schools. Some of these are:

(1) Plays and dramatizations taken from units developed in classrooms.
(2) Assembly programs.
(3) Speech correction, foreign language instruction.

---

[7] Lester B. Sands, *Audio-Visual Procedures in Teaching* (New York: The Ronald Press Company, 1956), p. 423.

(4) Recordings of radio programs for classroom use.

(5) Excerpts from certain selected parts of discs.

(6) Interviews with resource people.

(7) Improvement of choral reading, singing and the like.

(8) Pupils' discussions, panels, etc.

(9) Use with the reading program.

Radio and television.   Teachers in today's schools in many sections of the country have found radio a very useful aid to learning. However, the mere presence of a radio program, being aired into a classroom, is no assurance that it has instructional value. Radio, like the audio-visual medium, must be planned for in advance if the greatest value is to be received by the learners. Programs dealing with mathematics, science, geography, history, and the like must be carefully planned for in order to insure that the material to be presented will be appropriate for the maturity level of the group listening.

In school systems which utilize their own broadcasting station, such as Cleveland, it is possible to plan the programs for specific grades and with specific purposes in mind. In such situations, usually there are ample communications in the form of bulletins, memos, and monthly or weekly schedules to keep the teachers informed. It is obvious that this procedure is much more adaptable than trying to fit the school program to rigid commercial programming.

The use of radio, however, has many advantages since it is available to even the smallest and most remote school. Newscasts, weather reports, musical presentations, historical commemorations and important current reports of world conditions are only a few of the many uses of radio which can be utilized by the alert teacher. Numerous cities are experimenting with the teaching of a foreign language by radio in elementary schools. Tape recordings may be used to facilitate the scheduling of programs which will permit greater flexibility of use by the classroom teacher.

Although educational television is still in its infancy, this medium of communication has proved its worth for classroom use in many areas of the curriculum. Most of the research in this area supports the fact that television has a high motivating value for classroom use. More and more schools are acquiring television installations for classroom viewing; it must be recognized that commercial programming restricts the use of this medium for classroom use. However, the alert teacher, through the use of *T. V. Guide* and other pre-telecasting literature, can plan to take advantage of programs which will be valuable for children to view and which are scheduled during the school day.

The 1968 *Broadcasting Yearbook* reported in 1968 that there were approximately 78 million television sets in American homes, which accounts for more than one-third of the world's T.V. sets; 20 per cent of the world's T.V. stations are also found in the United States. Certainly, teachers should take advantage of this medium of communication to help make their instruction more meaningful. Homework or out-of-school assignments may be made which will require the child to view certain programs that are telecast at hours other than school time. Home-school relations should be considered in such cases so that family problems will not arise which may cause more harm than the values received. Communications with the home in advance of such assignment will aid in this respect.

Closed circuit T. V. is still very expensive and is being used only on a limited basis in certain selected communities around the country. Many of these projects are sponsored by philanthropic foundations. Preliminary reports indicate that many advantages accrue from the use of closed circuit T. V. In such cases, an outstanding teacher may present a science lesson or some other instructional material for viewing by all children of a specific grade level within the system. This excellent teacher has not only the advantages of her capabilities, but also those of a technically trained staff. In such situations, thousands of children are able to share the excellence of the one teacher who would, under ordinary conditions, have been instructing about 30 pupils. This should not be considered a threat to the classroom teacher in terms of her own security. But the classroom teacher should recognize the television program as she would any other community resource. Thus, a team approach becomes essential if the demonstrating teacher's effectiveness is to be realized.

Some of the kinds of programs which teachers will find useful are:

1. Storytelling,
2. Special events; community, nation, or world,
3. Science demonstrations,
4. Dramatic presentations,
5. Weather reports,
6. Historical presentations based upon fact,
7. Current affairs, such as inaugurations, reports to the nation, foreign events and dignitaries, catastrophies—floods, etc.

One interesting experiment in using television to instruct seventh grade children is somewhat revealing and also points to some of the precautions which must be taken when using this instructional medium. Jacobs and Bollenbacker compared achievement of three groups of seventh graders in arithmetic. Comparison was made through having some of the children partially taught by using television; some taught by the same teacher using conventional instructional methods; and some taught by a different teacher using conventional methods. The results indicated that the conventional method was superior for the high-ability children, although television was superior for the children in the average ability range. There were no significant differences between the conventional method and the television instruction for the low-ability group.[8] Obviously, a great deal more research needs to be completed before final decisions can be reached, but it is a fact that television will be used more extensively in education as more refinements are made in future years.

Curriculum becomes a vital issue when children in six states are viewing the same television lesson daily. The problem of pacing or trying to have all fifth graders, for example, ready for each day's televised Spanish lesson is a case in point. Lessons beamed for large numbers of children have the same weaknesses that exist in any given classroom where a teacher focuses attention only on the average of the class: the bright become bored and the slow get further behind. However, this and other problems will be solved as more experience is gained in using television.

Maps and other graphic representations.   Graphic aids are an essential in every classroom in the elementary school. Perhaps at no other time has there been such an abundance of commercially produced aids. Primary teachers spend much time working with children and producing their own neighborhood maps or maps showing the way to school. This experience helps children to gain their first understandings of cartography. These pictorial-type maps give meaning to the child's understanding of space and distance as well as direction.

Increased understandings are developed as the children mature. Charts and graphs which show products of the state or region help the children to refine their map concepts until they reach the stage of growth when they begin to depict physical features of a map such as boundaries, oceans, continents, roads, rivers, etc. Map symbols need to be mastered during the intermediate grades. By the time the child reaches the upper elementary grades, he should possess the skill of locating positions through the use of latitude and longitude. Modern maps and globes use a simplified grid system which assists the child at this stage of development. Through the use of numbers or letters, as found on road maps, he learns to locate horizontal and vertical lines which pin-point certain places where they intersect.

---

[8] James N. Jacobs and Joan K. Bollenbacher, "Teaching Seventh Grade Mathematics by Television," *Mathematics Teacher*, 53 (November, 1960), 543-47.

Maps, globes, charts, and diagrams have significant places in unit work. Maps are needed to relocate important historical places and events. Geography is related to historical facts in most cases. The adventure of studying the history being made at the North Pole cannot produce vital understandings without the use of maps and globes. Literature, also, can be studied in conjunction with the use of maps. Some companies have produced pictorial literary maps which virtually give life to the study of literature of early New England, the South, the western movement and the like. Still another important facet of study is air travel maps which shows the main air travel lanes as well as distances and time involved in traveling between points. All such instructional aids contribute to motivating the learner and consequently should produce pupils with better understandings and increased skills if the aids are used effectively.

Graphs and charts are of no lesser importance, and should be utilized to help children gain understandings of situations where numbers of statistics are meaningless. Graphs to depict recordings of temperatures might help the pupils to see graphically the meaning of average or mean temperature for the day, week, or month. Charts may be used in explaining the earth's layers which may be exposed through the use of a cut-away chart. Important to the development of skills in the use of any graphic aid is the significance attached to the building of concepts which lead to greater understandings. Pupils must be able to see relationships between the skills learned and the usefulness of the learning.

Pupils enjoy map making and this experience may lead to new understandings. This can be enhanced until the learner reaches the stage of being able to develop a relief map. This three-dimensional map helps pupils develop concepts of topography. Perhaps the most important experience attached to the relief map may be the tactile impressions which children receive from feelings of elevation of mountains, the curve of valleys and flatness of lakes and oceans.[9]

What Are Some Guideposts for Using Audio-Visual Aids?

Numerous other aids to learning could be added here to this brief discussion of some of the most helpful aids being used by teachers. Carpenter has produced a list of uses for audio-visual aids which are based upon psychological concepts for learning. This list, if carefully followed, will lead the teacher to more effective use of all audio-visual aids. These uses are:

---

[9] Sands, *op. cit.*, p. 216.

1. to increase and sustain attention;
2. to provide concreteness, realism and *"like likeness"* in stimulus situations calculated to instigate learning;
3. to apply and increase the meaningfulness of abstract concepts for the student;
4. to bring events, remote either in place, space or time, into the classroom;
5. to introduce opportunities for situational or "field" types of learning as contrasted with linear-order-verbal and written language communication;
6. to facilitate or advance processes of applying what is learned to realistic performances and life situations;
7. to stimulate interest, increase motivation, introduce a variety of stimulation; and generally
8. to increase the personal involvement of students in learning.[10]

TEACHING MACHINES AND PROGRAMMED LEARNING

For several decades, educators have been seeking self-motivating devices for aiding pupils in reinforcing learning. Teachers have used workbooks, duplicated materials and other aids to facilitate drill experiences for children at all grade levels. The task of trying to keep up with marking workbooks so that children would know of their progress and to work further on revealed weaknesses has almost become insurmountable. In 1954, Skinner stated,

> . . . she (teacher) spends as little time as possible on drill subjects and eagerly subscribes to philosophies of education which emphasize material of greater inherent interest. . . . Eventually, weaknesses of technique emerge in the disguise of a reformulation of the aims of education. Skills are minimized in favor of vague achievements—educating for democracy, educating the whole child. . . .[11]

It would appear that Skinner's criticism was well-founded. However, teachers of today need not be caught in the dilemma of whether to reinforce skills or to teach intangible values: both are essential ingredients to a sound educational program.

---

[10] C. R. Carpenter, "Psychological Concepts and Audio-Visual Instruction," *Audio-Visual Communication Review*, 5 (Fall, 1957), 362.

[11] B. F. Skinner, "The Science of Learning and the Art of Teaching," *Harvard Educational Review*, 24 (Spring, 1954), 86-7.

It is interesting to note that interest in and development of teaching devices occurred much earlier in educational history than might otherwise be presumed by this relatively recent consideration of their possibilities for use in our public schools and colleges. Mellan, in examining the patents registered in the United States Patent Office, learned that the earliest patent concerned with teaching and educational devices, appliances and apparatus was a contribution of H. Chard, dated February 17, 1809, which patented a "Mode of Teaching to Read." This device was followed closely by a "Mode of Teaching to Write," patented by S. Randall on October 1, 1810. These patents introduced a long series of patents concerned with educational devices, and by 1936 patents had been issued on 600 to 700 inventions on the subjects of teaching and education.[12]

These early devices, however, would not be considered today as true teaching machines because they did not present a programmed course of study to the learner or provide immediate feedback with regard to the correctness of his response.

What Are Some Recent Teaching Devices?

A modern teaching machine is a mechanical device by which a program is displayed to a learner. It usually presents one frame (item) at a time, provides some method for the student to indicate an overt response, shows whether the response is correct or not, prevents cheating by the student, maintains a record of student responses, and makes possible the use of non-verbal programs. The program contained within the teaching machine is composed of subject matter arranged in a carefully planned series of sequential items which lead the student to mastery of the subject with minimal error. Information is given to the student in small units to which he responds by completing a sentence, working a problem, or answering a question. Items are designed so that the student can make correct responses while progressing toward more and more complex material.

Porter used a teaching machine to teach spelling to elementary school children. These children used a simple mechanical device while working at their seats in class during a school year. The program used in the machine corresponded to the standard lessons used by the control group. The children were enrolled in second and sixth grade classes and were given 22 out of the normal 34 weeks of spelling instruction by machine. No spoken instruction was given to children in the experimental group.

---

[12] Ibert Mellan, "Teaching and Educational Inventions," *Journal of Experimental Education*, 4 (March, 1936), 291-300.

Results measured on standardized achievement test scores showed the experimental group to be significantly superior to the control group on both the second and sixth grade levels.[13]

At Hollins College in Virginia, the psychology department tested a beginning algebra course on eighth graders in the Roanoke, Virginia, Public School System. The subject matter was presented in the form of a programmed textbook. Students worked on the course fifty minutes a day. There was no class explanation and no homework. In less than one semester, all thirty-four students completed a full year's work. Half achieved a ninth-grade score on a standard examination. The other half averaged or exceeded the eighth grade score. At the end of the following semester, students were retested. The average retention of this group for one semester was over 90 per cent.[14]

Other research investigations have been conducted in which students at elementary, high school, and college levels and adults in industry have been instructed through the use of programmed courses of study without supplementary explanations, textbooks or homework. The results of these investigations provide evidence that programmed teaching is significantly superior to more conventional types of teaching in terms of content learned, retention of content learned, time required for learning to take place, student motivation, and student preference.[15]

What Are the Psychological Foundations for Programmed Learning?

The success enjoyed by teaching machines and programmed learning has been credited to the fact that their approach to learning is based upon sound psychological principles. Hilgard enumerated six established principles in the psychology of learning from which programmed learning derives support:

> 1. Programmed learning recognizes individual differences by beginning where the learner is and by permitting him to proceed at his own pace. It is possible that programmed learning may succeed in reducing individual differences because of these features.

---

[13] Douglas Porter, "Some Effects of Year-Long Teaching Machine Instruction," *Automatic Teaching: The State of the Art*, ed. E. H. Galanter. (New York: John Wiley & Sons, 1959), pp. 85-90.

[14] *TEMAC Programmed Learning Materials, Report Number 2* (Wilmette, Ill.: Encyclopaedia Britannica Films, 1961), pp. 18-20.

[15] Lawrence M. Stolurow, *Teaching by Machine*, Cooperative Research Monograph Number 6, United States Department of Health, Education, and Welfare (Washington: Government Printing Office, 1961).

2. Programmed learning requires that the learner be active. Learning by doing is an old educational slogan, and it is still a good one. The teaching machine (or program in other form) fights the tendency for the pupil to be passive and inattentive by requiring his participation if the lesson is to move.

3. Programmed learning provides immediate knowledge of results. Whether because it provides reinforcement, reward, or cognitive feedback, there is abundant testimony that knowledge of results is important in learning. It favors learning the right thing: it prevents repeating and fixating the wrong answers.

4. Programmed learning emphasizes the organized nature of knowledge because it requires continuity between the easier (earlier) concepts and the harder (later) ones. Again, all learning theories have some place for meaningfulness, for understandable relationships, for assimilating the new to the familiar. The program builder cannot be as arbitrary about contents as the ordinary laboratory student of learning (with his multiple-unit mazes or nonsense lists of various lengths); the programmer has to make one step fit the next and provide the hint or cue for the next. He has to examine the subject matter very carefully in order to find out what has to be known before something else can be learned, and he eliminates side issues that do not lead to cumulative learning.

5. Programmed learning provides spaced review in order to guarantee the high order of success that has become a standard requirement of good programs. Review with application, if properly arranged, permits a high order of learning on the first run through a program. While there is no rule against going through a program a second time, if there have been many errors, the aim is to produce essentially errorless learning the first time around.

6. Programmed learning reduces anxiety because the learner is not threatened by the task: He knows that he can learn and is learning, and gains the satisfaction that this knowledge brings. Lest this seems to be a trivial observation, we need only to be reminded that many children have been so frustrated by school learning tasks that they have never had the satisfaction of coming up to expectations; we have no way of knowing the costs we have to pay for this accumulated frustration.[16]

Needed research in programmed learning. Although many investigations have been conducted in the area of programmed learning, the results of these studies have been more provocative than definitive. Each finding uncovers additional areas of programmed learning which need to be explored. There is a need for research in techniques of program construction and the effects of programmed instruction upon individual

---

[16] Ernest R. Hilgard, "What Support from the Psychology of Learning?" *Journal of the National Education Association*, 50 (November, 1961), 20.

learners. Only carefully controlled, extensive research investigations will ultimately determine whether programmed learning is to be a substantial force or an ephemeral fad in the educational machinery of our nation's schools. However, preliminary reports from schools trying this innovation are indeed encouraging. It is without doubt the search will continue to find the best learning aids possible for the world's children.

What Is Computer Assisted Instruction?

Although there is at present no widespread use of computers for instruction, this innovation is just around the corner. Some corporations which have been instrumental in developing the computer for instruction have indicated another five years is needed to perfect the technology and reduce the cost so that the machinery will be marketable.

The Stanford University project is one of the best known instructional computer projects. It has student terminals in schools surrounding Palo Alto and now extends across the United States from the computer located at the University. Modern mathematics is taught via a drill-and-practice routine from text materials prepared by the project director. This is a highly sophisticated program and requires a tremendous amount of computer memory. The student enters his name via the teletypewriter keyboard as he begins the program, communicates with the computer by name, and receives tests, diagnostic branching, instruction, and daily reports of his progress via the terminal. Materials in mathematics and spelling, which have been validated over the past several years, are available now.[17]

The use of the computer will not eliminate the teacher. However, her role will become more diversified. At best, a team of teacher aides, teacher programmers, and others will be required to assist the teacher managing the learning experience. Thus Computer Assisted Instruction (CAI) will facilitate individualized instruction.

EDUCATIONAL RESOURCES OF THE COMMUNITY

The teacher has a major responsibility to know and understand the community in which she teaches. It cannot be assumed that each community is the same. Communities may possess much natural wealth, but

---

[17] See William A. Rogers and Lawrence M. Garigilio, *Toward a Computer Based Instructional System.* Washington, D.C.: U. S. Office of Education, Department of Health, Education, and Welfare, 1967.

may differ quite widely in how the wealth is utilized. The values held by the members of the community, their unselfishness and creative ingenuity will be reflected in the utilization of the natural endowments. The teacher must understand something of the level of operation within the community in order to help define its needs as well as to raise the level of aspirations of the people.

What Is the Teacher's Role in Using Educational Resources?

If the teacher begins building a foundation for understanding the community from the time she accepts a teaching position, she will waste less time on the job in getting effective teaching underway. That is, reading available materials about the community, visiting the community with the purpose in mind of building initial understanding and visiting its major social institutions will build early concepts of the available resources—human, natural and material.

This vast laboratory holds within it much of the learning of the world at work, the problems of human relationships, and the need for man to understand ways of controlling and adapting to his environment. The alert teacher will become more skillful when she finds how these resources may best be utilized for producing more efficient learning situations related to basic classroom activities. The teacher may need to exert leadership in a given school toward encouraging the administration to recognize the value of utilizing the community for improving instruction. It is hoped that the beginning teacher or teacher in service will find propitious conditions within the school relative to policies governing uses of community resources. Some of the ways which teachers may utilize the community in improving the educational program are:

1. to invite people to the school who have special talents, skills or experiences such as being a native of another land, possessing a unique collection of certain items, having a trade or profession and the like.
2. to take the children to visit a particular business, industry, agency, park or lake and the like.

Human resources. It can be readily seen that the use of community resources requires either the resource come to the school or the children go to the resource. Important then, to the successful utilization of resources relating to the community are the specific purposes for their use. These should be identified and thoroughly understood by the teacher and the group in a cooperative endeavor. Some suggested guides which will facilitate the use of bringing human resources to the classroom are:

1. to develop a purpose for the visit so that the learners will be aware of the purpose;
2. to know your visitor in terms of the specific contributions he is able to make to the purpose for the visit;
3. to plan with the visitor in advance of the visit in order to inform him of the grade level involved, the problems which lead to his invitation, and plan for his use, time, etc., and any special or particular situations which may arise;
4. to plan with the children in advance of the visit concerning ways they can acquire the most from the visit;
5. to plan for follow-up activities after the visit—clarify concepts, clear up misconceptions, appraise visit with children in terms of the purpose.

In some schools, a catalogue of resource visitors may be available. If such is available, it will facilitate work for the teacher in identifying and locating the needed resource. For example, a cataloging of names may be listed under such topics as "Hobbies" or "Agencies," under which would be the names of people in the community who have been contacted and agreed to come to the school as resource visitors. Usually this list would also contain information pertaining to the specific hobby, the extent of the collection if such is available, the days and hours during the week when it would be convenient for the visitor to come to the school. In addition, it may also be recommended that this visitor might best be utilized at a particular grade level. Although duplication is not always undesirable, time and the level of presentation may make it practical for limiting the visit to a specific grade.

Physical resources.   The field trip or excursion is rapidly becoming an important aspect of curriculum planning. Unit instruction can hardly serve the interests and needs of children in schools where resource visitors and field trips are prohibited or are not utilized by the staff. *Like the use of resource visitors, the use of the field trip should grow out of specific demands of the curriculum.* A field trip should not be taken simply because the board of education has established a policy that one trip a year is permitted. A need for the experiences involved in visiting a certain place within the community must be paramount in making the visit. Children learn from seeing new and novel situations. Their interests are intensified, and this enhances learning. Such adventures are deemed worthy because of the organized learning which is made meaningful through a carefully planned trip. Field trips may be employed for at least three purposes.[18]

---

[18] Sands, *op. cit.*, p. 56.

1. to gain an over-all view related to the area under study (usually no detailed assignments are made);
2. to involve the children in a detailed study of a certain field which involves collecting of specimens for zoological study, samples of rocks for geology, data for a study of social problems, and the like;
3. to visit, on an extended trip covering a wide geographical area, such places as historical cities within a state or nation.

Field trips must be carefully planned due to the specific nature of the place to be visited. The safety and welfare of each pupil must be cautiously considered. For example, private cars should not be utilized for such occasions. Liability insurance and other considerations are important. Teachers should, however, invite a specific number of parents to travel with the class depending upon the age of the group. For example, a parent for each five first grade children may be a desirable ratio, while a parent for each ten or twelve pupils at the seventh grade level may be sufficient. School buses then will usually accommodate the entire group. Teachers must also be aware of the administrative responsibility for such an event and thus recognize the need for basic policy. The following guide is presented for teachers to become aware of some of the planning which is essential for arranging and utilizing the field trip.

1. Evaluate the advantages in taking the field trip in order that as many contacts as possible may be utilized.
2. Determine the purpose or possible combination of purposes for conducting field trips.
3. Examine survey data for:
   (a) materials that will develop useful concepts;
   (b) situations around which activities may be organized that will assist pupils in developing desirable attitudes, skills, and understanding.
4. Make necessary arrangements in advance with:
   (a) school authorities;
   (b) owners or representatives of places to be visited;
   (c) parents;
   (d) transportation officials.
5. Pupils should be adequately prepared for the trip as to:
   (a) purpose;
   (b) need for special clothing and equipment (notebooks, field glasses, etc.);
   (c) individual or group responsibilities.

6. Final evaluation and follow-up:
   (a) teaching values; enriching, vitalizing, motivating, socializing, etc.;
   (b) constructive influence on pupils' appreciation, attitudes, understandings and skills;
   (c) application to over-all learning experience.

SUMMARY

Newer methods of teaching require the use of many materials. A knowledge of how to make effective use of materials is essential. Research has supported the thesis that learning is improved and greater efficiency is gained from prudent use of audio-visual aids. Such innovations as teaching machines, programmed textbooks, and computer assisted instruction are based upon sound psychological principles and will facilitate learning based upon individual differences if teachers will recognize their roles in the use of these innovations.

SUGGESTED ACTIVITIES AND PROBLEMS

1. Prepare a bulletin board which you believe would be useful for initiating a unit. Have the class make constructive suggestions for improving it.

2. Make a list of the types of real things which could be brought to the classroom to facilitate instruction and learning.

3. List the sources of possible field trips in your community. If you were permitted to make only one trip per year, indicate where you would take the children in each grade and justify your selection.

4. Preview and evaluate at least three films which you could use in the grade you are teaching or the grade of your interest. Discuss your evaluation with the class.

5. Demonstrate the use of three instructional aids to your class. Tell why you selected them and what you would hope to accomplish with pupils as a result of their use.

6. Organize the class according to grade level interests of each class member and assign each group: (1) the responsibility of preparing a suitable unit for class discussion; (2) the task of preparing a flexible daily schedule to show how certain phases of the unit are developed. Curriculum materials should be used freely, together with demonstrations and the like.

7. Locate a programmed textbook in your curriculum laboratory or library and bring it to class. Examine it to see if it meets the psychological principles enumerated on pages 155 and 156.

SELECTED READINGS

Brown, James W., Richard B. Lewis, and Fred F. Harcleroad. *A-V Instruction Materials and Methods*. New York: McGraw-Hill Book Company, 1959.

Dent, Charles. "Feltboards for Teaching," Austin, Texas: Division of Extension, University of Texas, 1955.

Four Case Studies of Programmed Instruction. New York: The Fund for the Advancement of Education, 1964.

Glazier, Robert C. "Television Classroom," *N.E.A. Journal*, 47 (May, 1958), 285-87.

Keislar, Evan R. and John D. McNeil. "Teaching Scientific Theory to First Grade Pupils by Auto-Instructional Device," *Harvard Educational Review*, 31 (Winter, 1961), 73-83.

Kelly, George A. "Television and the Teacher," *The American Psychologist*, 10 (October, 1955), 590-92.

Lumsdaive, A. A. and Robert Glaser (eds.). *Teaching Machines and Programmed Learning*. Washington, D. C.: National Education Association, 1960.

Skinner, B. F. *The Technology of Teaching*. New York: Appleton-Century-Crofts, 1968.

Stiles, Cordelia L. "Creative Use of Space, Time, and Materials," *Educational Leadership*, 15 (December, 1957), 165-70.

Wigren, Harold E. "Television: A Challenge to the Elementary School," *National Elementary Principal*, 36 (September, 1956), 212-24.

PART II

The Curriculum
in Action

prologue to part II

What is a significant educational experience?

This question is continually being asked by professional educators and lay persons throughout the land. The search for an answer continues as each group of specialists, educators, and laymen in all fields pressures for a new curriculum. A few years ago reading was receiving wide attention due to the criticism of "Johnny's inability to read." Recent developments in automation and in the science-centered contest for world-wide influence have made an impact upon the mathematics and science programs in the elementary schools.

No area of the curriculum has escaped the interest of the public, unless it be the fine arts. Spelling, handwriting, and phonics are but a few of the specifics within the language arts which have been singled out for an attack on the school's curriculum. Programs for the socially and economically disadvantaged, the gifted, and the slow learner have emerged. Foreign language study has begun in many elementary schools in the primary grades. In addition, the need for greater emphasis in physical education for physical fitness has been cited by the late President John F. Kennedy.

Mass revision of the mathematics programs seems to be making progress. Studies in mathematics, such as those conducted at the University of Maryland and the University of Illinois, are finding their ways into the public schools as evidenced by the completely new elementary mathematics textbooks. Less emphasis is given to the social aspects of arithmetic, as a greater emphasis is made upon scholarship, insight, and appreciation of arithmetic in our culture.

The social studies area has received increasing attention in the past decade and it now appears that concept-oriented programs using the inquiry process will emerge in the schools in the years ahead. Many issues remain to be resolved with respect to the role of the traditional social science disciplines, the selection of learning experiences that are relevant to particular age groups, and the readiness of American communities to accept the vigorous investigations by youngsters who use open inquiry in their study of man's social condition.

The discussion which follows in this part of the book is intended to inform prospective teachers of the developments which have taken place in curriculum and to present the characteristics of adequate programs in each area. Prospective teachers, like teachers in service, must continue to read popular articles that propose changes in the total program. There is, however, need for cautious judgment here. The matters of balance of objectives and supporting values must be thoughtfully considered if the emerging curriculum is to serve the needs of pupils in a democracy.

CHAPTER 6

Early Childhood Education

INTRODUCTION

Educational opportunities for the pre-primary age child are a relatively recent development in the United States. In 1965 a massive attempt was made through Project Head Start, funded by the Federal Government, to provide preschool education for millions of children who were considered socially and economically disadvantaged. However, as late as 1968[1] it was reported that only 33 states were providing financial aid of some sort to local school districts for kindergarten education. Controversy still exists, and even at the present time wide differences of opinion both within the profession and on the part of the general public continue to emerge. There is, however, little doubt that educational opportunities for youngsters of less than first grade age have been meeting with increasing favor as professional educators and the public gain broader understandings of the goals and nature of preschool education programs.

What Were the Beginnings of Kindergarten and Nursery School?

At the outset, the nursery school and the kindergarten were motivated by separate and distinct social forces. The nursery school has been, traditionally, a place where the youngest children of the poorer families were cared for. A characteristic of the nursery school has been its custodial nature. The central function of the kindergarten has been envisioned as that of educating those children who were not yet old enough to enter the first grade, the beginning reading grade of the elementary school.

Nursery school. The first nursery school of record is probably one which was opened in 1769 at Walbach, France and it was the forerunner of the Infants School in that nation. Approximately a half century later a

---

[1] See Minnie P. Berson, "Early Childhood Education," *American Education,* 4 (October 1968), 7-13.

nursery school was organized in New Lanark, Scotland, and in 1826 the first nursery school in the United States was founded in New Harmony, Indiana. The nursery school movement has gained ground in England to the point where official recognition was given to the nursery school as a part of the total educational program, as a result of the Fisher Act of 1918 and the Education Act of 1944.

In the United States the nursery school developed rather leisurely with notable exceptions during the years of the Great Depression and during World War II. In 1928 it was estimated that there were 600 nursery programs in operation and by 1940, as a result of the impetus provided by the W. P. A.-supported effort, there were 3,000 nursery units in the nation. World War II sustained the need for nursery schools due to the advent of the "working mother" in American war industries. Following the end of World War II the number of nursery school programs declined as federal support was withdrawn.

It is difficult to obtain extensive and current information regarding the number of nursery school programs in operation due to the various sponsorships of such programs and because many state agencies of education do not include this data in their reports. Moustakas and Berson[2] have reported, for example, that there are six rather common types of sponsorship, with the privately operated nursery school outnumbering all others by a wide margin as shown in Table II.

It may be observed that child care centers have not been included in this discussion to this point. The typical child care center differs in essence from the nursery school in that it provides facilities for children of

TABLE II

Nursery School Sponsorship

Type of School Sponsorship	Number
Private nursery school	1310
Cooperative nursery schools	262
Laboratory nursery schools	224
Parochial nursery schools	106
Public-school nursery schools	47
Community nursery school	18
TOTAL	1967

[2] Clark E. Moustakas and Minnie Perrin Berson, *The Nursery School and Child Care Center* (New York: William Morrow & Co., 1955), p. 18.

working parents and for children from needy families. Such centers usually operate for longer periods each day rather than for the 2½ to 4 hour period often provided in the nursery school. School age children may, also, be cared for in child care centers before and after school hours. In some presentations of pre-kindergarten programs the nursery school and child care center may be treated as one, but to the extent that they differ in terms of primary purpose and organization they are not one and the same.

The Head Start project. The Head Start project with its inception under the Federal sponsorship of the Office of Economic Opportunity emerged during the summer of 1965. While private nursery schools mainly care for upper and middle-class children, Head Start provides an expansion of early childhood education to include children of the lower class. A wide range of curriculum experiences have been tried and researched to determine the best curriculum for preschool children. Programs have included free play, language development, experiences to foster cognitive development, dramatic play, creative play, physical skill development, and a host of other activities.

Head Start was largely a program developed at the local level with no national direction dictated by the Office of Economic Opportunity. The centers were required to reflect the wide range of influence which the family and social environment exert on the child's educational development. Each center was permitted to choose the extent of emphasis it wished to place on such components as medical care, parent participation, and community involvement.[3]

In many publications the success of Head Start has been pointed out. A report by former Commissioner of Education Howe states that "through Federal programs such as Head Start, we have seen some early indications of how successful programs can give children of this age the self-confidence and language skills needed to succeed in school."[4] On the other hand, Jensen, writing on Head Start in another publication, states, "If Head Start does not produce the expected results (and so far it has not) it is because it is too little too late or is not followed up long enough and intensively enough."[5]

To add still more to the confusion of the success of Head Start, Westinghouse Learning Corporation and Ohio University conducted an *ex post facto* research study to determine "to what degree it had a psycho-

---

[3] Jerome Hellmuth (ed.), *Disadvantaged Child: Head Start and Early Intervention* (Seattle: Special Child Publications, Inc., 1968), p. 8.

[4] Harold Howe, "The People Who Serve Education" (Washington, D. C.: U. S. Department of Health, Education, and Welfare, Government Printing Office, 1969), p. 3.

[5] Hellmuth, *op. cit.*, p. 54.

logical and intellectual impact on children which has persisted into the primary grades." This study sample included children from 104 Head Start centers and compared them with similar children who did not attend Head Start programs. The study was concerned with children who attended both summer and full-year programs, beginning in the summer of 1965 and extending through the summer of 1968. On instruments such as *The Illinois Test of Psycholinguistic Abilities, Children's Self-Concept Index, Stanford Achievement Test*, and others, no significant differences were found at the end of either grade two or grade three for the total group. There was, however, a significant difference in favor of Head Start over the control group on the results of the *Metropolitan Readiness Tests*.[6] Although there will continue to be much controversy over the nature of these findings, perhaps the answer to the success of Head Start will be found in the testing of new hypotheses concerning the program. Among some questions to be answered are:

1. Why were some locally planned programs more successful than others?
2. What was the relationship of program success to staff qualifications?
3. Were local needs more specifically identified and dealt with in some programs than in others?
4. Should Head Start type programs continue on into the elementary grades one, two, and three, with formal learning based on the individual's readiness? Thus there would be a delay in abstract type learning experiences into what is normally considered the elementary grades.

The least that can be said is that we need to continue to study preschool education for deprived children, since we have not found the kind of program which produces a readiness for America's "middle-class" schools. Perhaps the answer will be found in a modification of primary education and an individual approach to learning.

The kindergarten. The kindergarten, or child's garden, is the outgrowth of the thought and practices of such people as Montessori of Italy, Rousseau of France and Froebel of Germany, the latter often considered the "Father of the kindergarten." Rousseau's emphasis upon the free

---

[6] *The Impact of Head Start: An Evaluation of the Effects of Head Start Experiences on Children's Cognitive and Affective Development*, Vol. I (Washington, D. C.: Westinghouse Learning Corporation/Ohio University, Office of Economic Opportunity, March 1969), pp. 1-11.

development of the child with little molding by adults; Montessori's emphasis upon keen development of the sensory aspects of learning; Froebel's concern for carefully planned experiences related to childrens' interests—all these may be recognized as strong influences in the modern kindergarten.

In the United States the kindergarten movement gained ground initially in the eastern part of the nation where it was soon to undergo modification from original European concepts. Patty Smith Hill was the leader of a group who held the position that the kindergarten should be involved with a more liberal and experimental philosophy than suggested by the Froebelian advocates.[7] Susan Blow led the opposition to this liberal element, but the impact upon educational philosophy of thinkers such as John Dewey lent support to the liberal experimental group and the kindergarten movement in the United States began to take on features of its own.

In terms of pupil enrollment in kindergartens in this country, there has been a sharp increase of more than one-half million pupils from 1950 to 1955. Enrollment increases may be seen in Figure IX for the years 1919-1963. Although the increases have been striking, both in public and private school kindergartens, it is worth noting that, for the school year 1955-1956, the public kindergarten enrollment accounted for 5 per cent of the total public school enrollment, grades kindergarten through twelve.[8] When this figure is compared to the first grade enrollments for that year which accounted for 11 per cent of the total enrollment, it is apparent that many five-year-old youngsters are not provided, or have no recourse to, the kindergarten experience. Only in the eleventh and twelfth grades do the percentages of total school enrollment fall near or below the kindergarten figure.

According to information available from the source cited above, the child who lives in a rural area will be less likely to attend a kindergarten than the child who lives in an urban area.[9] As an example, it has been found that of 1199 rural counties in 38 states only 477 provide kindergarten programs. In these counties the kindergarten enrollment accounted for 1.8 per cent of the total public school enrollment. When this is compared with the 5 per cent figure for the nation as a whole it may be seen that the rural areas have been comparatively slow in extending the opportunities of kindergarten education.

---

[7] For a more thorough treatment see W. S. Monroe (ed.), *Encyclopedia of Educational Research* (New York: The Macmillan Co., 1960), pp. 647-53.

[8] United States Bureau of the Census, *Statistical Abstract of the United States* (Washington: Government Printing Office, 1959), pp. 104-06.

[9] Monroe, *loc. cit.*

FIGURE IX

Kindergarten Enrollment in Public Schools

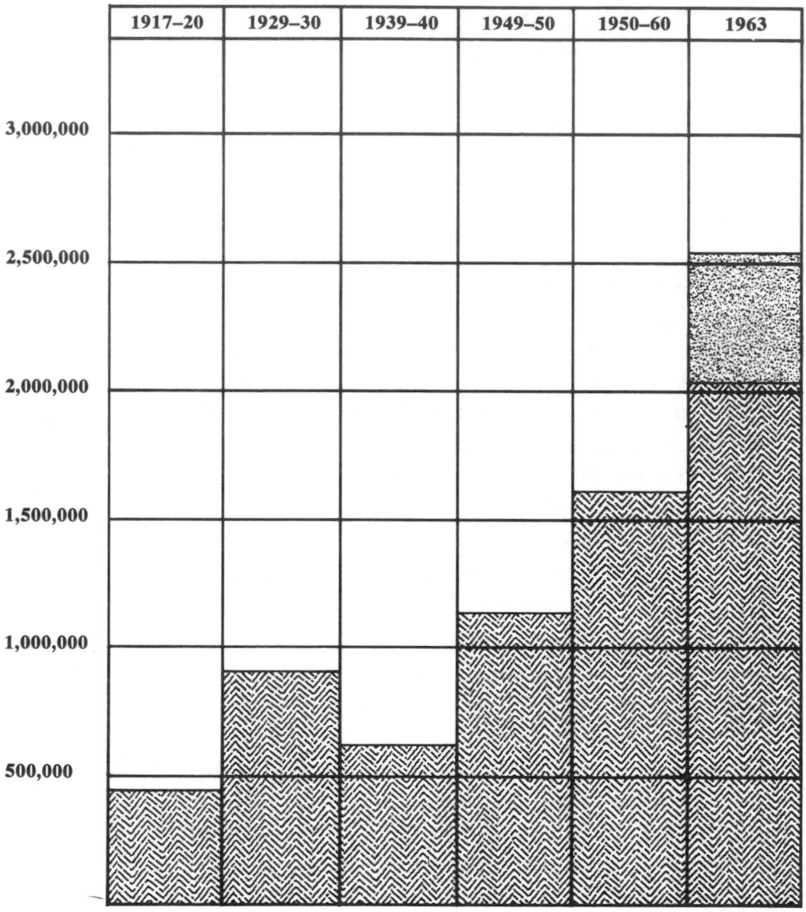
1917–20
1929–30
1939–40
1949–50
1950–60
1963
3,000,000
2,500,000
2,000,000
1,500,000
1,000,000
500,000

There is yet a long way to go in the urban areas before kindergarten opportunities are extended to all eligible children. Of some 3,647 school systems in cities of 2,500 people and over, slightly more than 60 per cent provided kindergarten programs.

Acceptance and support. From the preceding information regarding the growth of pre-primary education in the United States, one may conclude that there continues to exist the problem of public acceptance and support for the nursery school and kindergarten, especially in rural areas. The very rapid increase of the private kindergarten enrollment may be an indication that informed and interested parents do not care to wait for the public schools to provide the kindergarten.

Doubtless, some of the cause for public disinterest may be found in the misunderstanding of the nature of the nursery and kindergarten programs. The fact that the child does not appear to begin mastery of the skills commonly associated with a "beginner" grade may lead some persons to believe that the children go to the kindergarten or nursery for play experiences only, and that they can play at home at far less expense. Related to this is the possible misunderstanding of the "child development" philosophy. It is certainly a mark of modern educational controversy to find persons discussing the social, emotional, and physical factors of education, and ofttimes setting these factors in opposition to the "basic learning" experiences of the child. The nursery school and the kindergarten have traditionally held to the "whole child" philosophy and it appears that public acquaintance with that philosophy will precede or accompany the future extension of pre-primary programs.

The kindergarten has enjoyed a relatively stable relationship to public education to the extent that it has often come under the auspices of the local boards of education, whereas the nursery school has done so less frequently. This closer tie between kindergarten and elementary school is due, at least in part, to its long-standing identity as an educational rather than a child-care venture.

It is unfortunate that 21 states continue to provide no protection for children by way of regulations governing the establishment and operation of nursery schools.[10] In some states where regulations have been established there are often ambiguities and exceptions which render the directive powerless.[11] In the kindergarten area the problem of physical environment and teacher qualification is not so loosely handled as in the nursery school, again due to the relation of the kindergarten to the total elementary school as an official educational program. The kindergarten continues to have its own problems, however, in the area of large class size, suitable equipment and space, and in the use of the part-time teacher whose specialty is in another area but who teaches a half-day kindergarten in order to have a full-time job.

Certainly, the range of problems facing the extension and provision of desirable pre-primary educational opportunities is not cause for pessimism. The kindergarten movement has spread rapidly in the past two

---

[10] Moustakas and Berson, *Op. Cit.*, Chapter 12.
[11] *Ibid.*

decades and as its role in the total education of the child is more clearly conceived by educators and the public, it will continue to spread.

In the past there has been some inclination on the part of pre-primary educators to look upon the nursery and the kindergarten as separate and apart from the more formalized program of the elementary school. There has been, also, some disinterest shown by school administrators. Much progress may be expected as the professional people in school adminis-tration, elementary education, and pre-primary education work together to improve and extend the opportunities of education to youngsters. This will entail a better understanding of the role of pre-primary education in the over-all school program and an appreciation of the continuity of ex-periences from nursery through the various levels of the elementary school.

VALUES IN NURSERY AND KINDERGARTEN EXPERIENCES

To gain an adequate view of any educational enterprise it is necessary that the student inquire as to the values which are expected to accrue to the individuals who participate in the particular program. Likewise, one may well look beyond these stated values to the nature of the society which supports these values. In the nursery and kindergarten programs in the United States the value of effective *human relationships* is ex-pressed from the beginning. The values of individual intellectual, emo-tional, and physical development are not neglected, but certainly the im-portance attached to the young child's learning to get on with other children and with adults is illustrative of the high cultural value placed on social development.

What Is the Need for Sociological and Psychological Values?

Cooperation and competition may seem to be directly opposed, and in specific behavior situations this is sometimes the case. Nonetheless, competition and cooperation are interwoven into the cultural fabric of this nation and the need to orient children to this fact is recognized in the pre-primary programs for children. So it is that the 3, 4, or 5-year-old child may attend a nursery or kindergarten where he can continue to develop a feeling of individuality, to gain experience in working with other children, to further his development of educational readiness, and generally live in a stimulating and safe environment. In view of the adult responsibilities which exist in this society, it is not surprising nor improper that early educational experiences should place emphasis upon the socialization of the child.

In some respects it is superficial to attempt to clear distinction between the psychological values and sociological values found in the pre-primary programs for it is true that these values are interrelated and modify one another. Perhaps it will be helpful to look upon the sources of these values as the major difference. The sociological values are asserted by the larger cultural group, while the psychological values derive from the nature of the child as he seeks adjustment in the social milieu.

The nursery and kindergarten provide for children in the following areas of values as they:

1. Develop individuality and independence of the child;
2. Provide a setting for growing adjustment to the stress and strain of living with other children;
3. Aid the child in development of confidence in adults outside the home;
4. Provide opportunities for physical development;
5. Widen the child's interest in the world about him; guide him into habits of observation and investigation; and
6. Contribute to the general educational development of the child.

It may be observed that the values which are identified in a well-conceived program for nursery school and kindergarten continue to be important to a greater or lesser degree throughout the elementary school. The manner by which these values are realized differs with the age level and specific needs of individual children, and the specific educational values that are contained in skill development and acquisition of information are not given the emphasis here that is found in later school years.

What Is the Curriculum Design for Pre-Primary Education?

The curriculum plan puts into action the decisions made by teachers, parents, and administrators in accord with their collective judgment of the priorities to be given to the several values. It is here that balance is essential: that one or two possible values not be promoted at the expense of other values. Gans, Stendler, and Almy referred to a lack of balance in the kindergarten when they wrote: "The 3 R's approach has not only prevailed in the primary grades, but it has reached down into the five-year-old kindergarten. . . . Under such a setup the kindergarten is seen as a year of settling down for children, of adjusting to sitting still and following directions, so that they will be better prepared for a more vigorous attack on the 3 R's during first grade."[12]

At another extreme of curricular imbalance is the overemphasis on group adjustment to the point where other legitimate concerns, such as language development, may be neglected. A sensible guide in the selection of, and emphasis on, certain aspects of the curriculum is the state of readiness and need of the children, individually or generally. One of the authors has observed kindergarten teachers devoting much time and energy in the use of readiness books when a number of children appeared disinterested, restless, and not ready to engage in such activity. In such situations it is not unusual to see emphasis placed upon being quiet and sitting still, often for periods that are too long. The concern for providing for one highly regarded outcome of kindergarten may lead to practices that are neither legitimate nor rewarding in terms of later progress.

Curriculum designs for early educational programs may be generally classified as:

1. The 3 R's approach,
2. The interests and needs approach,
3. The social-psychological approach.[13]

In their discussion of these approaches to curriculum design, Gans, Stendler, and Almy pointed out the disparity between a 3 R's approach and a realistic view of the needs and interests of young children. Also, they cited the highly transient and incidental nature of the interests and needs approach, and take the position that an inclusive provision for the social-psychological factors is best suited as a curriculum design that will be balanced and sensitive to the varying natures and needs of different groups of youngsters across the nation.[14]

Any plans for working with pre-primary age children should take into account the fact that there is not a commonality of educational experience represented in the group as is the case in the later elementary grades. To be sure, the similarity or identity of school experience at any age is not safely assumed, but the entry of the child into nursery or kindergarten constitutes the beginning of an extremely important venture

---

[12] Roma Gans, Celia Burns Stendler, and Millie Almy, *Teaching Young Children* (New York: World Book Co., 1952), pp. 80-1.

[13] *Ibid.*, Chapter 4.

[14] *Ibid.*

and individual success and confidence are enhanced in the program that recognizes variety.

It must be apparent at this point that the basic philosophies which guide the teacher of the very young child have much, if not everything, in common. The fact that support for the nursery school is often derived from sources other than public, whereas the kindergarten, where it exists, is commonly an integral part of the public school program, does not dictate a difference in method of working with the children. A kindergarten program may differ from the nursery school to the extent that the five-year-old may express interest and readiness for more intensified experiences in certain areas than is the case with the three- and four-year-olds. Otherwise, there is a common foundation, philosophically and theoretically, for the development of nursery school and kindergarten programs.

At this juncture some observations will be made regarding the characteristics of an effective nursery school curriculum, to be followed by a discussion of the features of the modern kindergarten.

The nursery school program. It is important to recognize that the nursery school curriculum is planned around the same basic principles which are operative at other levels of curriculum planning. It is evident, then, that the child should be surrounded with experiences which will serve to facilitate his understandings of the world about him and that these experiences should be planned in accordance with the best available knowledge of human growth and development. Such a curriculum will provide the opportunity for each child to develop in his own natural pattern. The teacher aids this transition by carefully studying each child in order to help him make the transition from one growth stage to the next with a minimum of frustration and confusion. Yet the teacher must not over-protect the child from natural challenges which are conducive to learning.

The curriculum of the young child provides for initial learning experiences based upon the early demands of group living. Two of these demands are *learning to share* and *learning to become effective in communication*. Learning to share his ideas, materials and resources of his work and play environment becomes an important goal. At the same time the child must become aware of the needs and wants of others. Early in the life of the child, social sensitiveness to the needs of others should grow out of the curriculum experiences.

Some Alternatives for the Individual

There are many authorities who have reached at least a tentative agreement on the kind of curriculum experiences desirable in a nursery school program. But most of these programs are planned for the masses, with little or no provision for the child who does not fit the mold or the school which does not insist on all children achieving the same aims. If the emergent curriculum is to have its impact it must start at the nursery school level. Here, from the time the child enters school, he should become involved in making decisions which concern purposes and goals as well as procedures for achieving these.

Thus, curriculum is not preconceived but developed with the individual. The child answers questions concerning his own experiences with guidance from the teachers. All children will not experience the same "readiness" experiences for reading at the same time, but each child's learning will depend on his own rate. He will pace himself through an individualized program from the nursery school through all the elementary school years and, hopefully, through the secondary school. Spodek terms such a program the "transactional curriculum."[15] This curriculum then is determined for each child through transactions between the child and the professional teacher. The early childhood teacher would be charged with setting the stage for learning, providing legitimate alternatives for children's activities, and serving in a guidance capacity in the classroom. In such a program, the teacher would provide alternative goals, help clarify needs, and aid children in anticipating the consequences of their acts.[16]

Scheduling the program.   Although daily schedules will vary according to the individual school, one is offered here to provide general ideas as to the kinds and timing of certain activities:

9:00	Children arrive for greeting and health inspection
9:00- 9:45	Children are allowed free play period either indoors or outdoors depending upon weather and other factors
9:45-10:00	Personal care time
10:00-10:15	Snack time
10:15-10:30	Rest time on pallets or cots
10:30-11:00	Free play time
11:00-11:15	Personal care time
11:15-11:30	Story time, experiences in content areas and investigatory opportunities
11:30	Departure time

(Include group discussions, singing, dancing, art, and so on for the four-year-olds.)

---

15 Bernard Spodek, "Early Learning for What?" *Phi Delta Kappan*, L, No. 7 (March 1969), 396.
16 *Ibid.*

It should be kept in mind that many programs in settlement houses and laboratory schools are from 8:30 a. m. to 3:30 p. m. The schedules may vary somewhat according to the age of the nursery child. For example, the two- and three-year-olds will follow about the same kind of schedule with allowances for free play time and rest time. The four-year-olds will have a later snack time, and have time for group discussions, singing, and other planned experiences. The schedules must be planned to provide for individual as well as group needs. However, such activities as the singing and dancing may be included in the schedules of the younger children during the informal periods of free play time. Thus the schedule is flexible and designed for the maturity level of the group, but there is also a sufficient amount of stability to provide for feelings of security.

The kindergarten program. The kindergarten is the continuation and expansion of the educational plans which have been started in the nursery school, and in most instances, it is the setting for the initial school experience of children. The responsibility for orientation of young children to the new challenge of school belongs to the kindergarten, which shares with the nursery school the task of providing a secure and stimulating environment wherein the four- and five-year-old child may satisfy some immediate needs, anticipate new challenges, and move toward a broad condition of readiness for further learning activities.

Kindergarten is not looked upon as an end in itself—educational readiness may be fostered which will lead to early and satisfactory adjustments to later school experiences. This in no way implies that the kindergarten teacher takes her cues from the first grade teacher. However, she is acquainted with the on-going educational program of the school and she realizes that kindergarten is often a vital first contact with the school. In the discussion that follows, the content of the kindergarten program will be presented with accompanying comments concerning implementation.

Physical development. The kindergarten child is one who is interested in activity. He is still experimenting with bodily movement and gaining muscular control. The kindergarten teacher is well acquainted with this characteristic of her pupils and she provides a variety of opportunities for the children to engage in activities using the larger muscles and developing rhythmic movements, and activities using the smaller muscles such as puzzle work, block building, clay modeling and the like. Physical development, lingual development, and social development occur together in many activities such as cooperative block building, using play equipment, and learning rhythms. The unity of the well-planned program is perceived as one observes the several values that accrue from any one kindergarten activity.

Social-emotional considerations. The child who leaves the security of mother and home faces an emotional as well as a social adjustment when he enters kindergarten. Many kindergarten teachers prefer an arrangement whereby parents and children visit the kindergarten room and the teacher sometime before the child is to begin school. This may be, in some cases, during the late spring. The child has a concept, limited though it may be, of the situation into which he will enter.

In some instances, the kindergarten teacher brings the children into kindergarten in small groups during the first two or three days of school in order that the children may become oriented into their new environment in a friendly, relaxed way, without the confusion and insecurity involved in entering kindergarten simultaneously with twenty or twenty-five other youngsters. By admitting the children in groups of seven or eight over four- or five-day intervals, the teacher affords a more personal approach to the child's initial contact with school and with new children and adults.

Young children who have had numerous contacts with adults other than the parents may yet encounter adjustment problems as they must learn to cooperate, to share, and to work and play with a number of other children their own age.

The wise teacher will not attempt to bring about student behavior changes in children who seem to present undesirable patterns of social conduct. It may be dangerous to directly threaten the security of the child, even though his security is wrapped in aggressive behavior which is contrary to the interests of the group. Because the teacher knows that the child's behavior patterns emerge from a complex background of experiences of home and neighborhood, she looks upon behavior change as a developmental job to be approached as the child begins to understand that his purposes, and those of his friends, will be served better through mutually acceptable behavior. This in no way implies a laissez-faire attitude by the teacher and, quite obviously, the social and physical welfare of children must not be endangered as a result of extreme deviate behavior of one individual. It does imply that social learning and emotional stability must involve the child actively in terms of his own purposes and needs.

The kindergarten experiences provide opportunities for the children to find secure relationships with other children and adults as they progress along the way toward social and emotional maturity. Kindergarten provides a beginning in a setting more highly organized than that found in the typical home or neighborhood—an environment for growth and development that is professionally planned and guided.

There are numerous persons, teachers and parents, who regard the major role of the kindergarten as that of providing specific readiness experiences for the reading and number learning of first grade. The authors would prefer to view the contributions of the kindergarten to educational readiness as being more broadly conceived than reading and number readiness alone, although these are not to be denied. Language development, providing bases for conceptual development in the areas of science, number and social problems, seem to contain more fundamental implications for kindergarten than do reading and number readiness per se.

Language development. The children who come to kindergarten present a variety of experience backgrounds, a diversity of language development, and, of course, wide ranges of intelligence. It is not the function of the kindergarten experience to equalize the many differences which exist, but rather to provide access for development in all children so that they may become effective in communication and at the same time increase their skills in terms of the potential which exists.

Greene and Petty have presented five general objectives for early language development which deserve the consideration of the kindergarten teacher. They include:

1. Spontaneity of expression.
2. Socialization through language.
3. Enunciation and voice control.
4. Correct usage.
5. Organization of thought.[17]

Because the activities of the kindergarten program contribute to child development in a manner that is characterized by unity, the teacher will recognize opportunities for encouraging language development as children play with blocks, share toys, or decide upon the selection of a rhythmic game. Through sharing experiences in a group discussion, listening to a story, discussing a picture story, and engaging in dramatic play, the kindergarten child has opportunities for specific language growth. Four- and five-year-olds may continue to talk while others are talking, with little concern for the thoughts being presented by others. The young child may be timid in expressing himself or he may talk profusely and he may have difficulty expressing his thoughts in an organized manner. The kindergarten teacher assesses the language status of the child as the year progresses, and she draws upon the informal language situations as well as upon more formalized situations to stimulate and guide language development. Chart VII presents some of the more commonly occurring activities which may be used as opportunities for guiding language development in the kindergarten.

---

[17] Harry A. Greene and Walter T. Petty, *Developing Language Skills in the Elementary School* (Boston: Allyn and Bacon, Inc., 1959), pp. 66-9.

CHART VII

Language Development in the Kindergarten

Activities	Contribute to development of
1. Listening to a story; listening to other children in group situations	social awareness organizing what is heard desirable listening habits
2. Planning with the teacher and other children	social awareness organizing what is heard desirable listening habits voice control social awareness in speaking
3. Talking before the group	spontaneous expression conversational participation correct usage voice control social awareness in speaking
4. Talking with another child in a play or work situation	spontaneous expression conversational participation correct usage voice control social awareness in speaking

There are, of course, almost limitless possibilities for formal language experiences in the kindergarten. The material in Chart VII is intended to suggest the kinds of opportunities which exist in numerous kindergarten situations.

Another aspect of the kindergarten program of language development concerns proper usage and intelligible speech. Children come to school with a variety of speech patterns as a result of the kind of speech they have imitated at home, and to further complicate matters, a number of parents seem to derive pleasure from the continued use of "baby talk" long after their child should have been showing signs of beginning maturity. Speech therapists often suggest that immaturity of speech on the part of the four- and five-year-olds may be best approached through the use of correct English by the teacher and, of course, through the encouragement for correct usage which is provided by many children who have acquired desirable usage habits. Unless organic difficulties are found to be present, the informal classroom approach is preferable to special classes with children at this age level.

Children enjoy using new and colorful words and the kindergarten child is no exception. In this regard it is important that the teacher remember that the use of a socially unacceptable word is not the cause for great alarm. In some situations it is necessary to talk with a child, and perhaps his parents, in order that offensive language will not become a prevailing part of the school's language environment. Too frequently an oversensitive teacher shows alarm and great concern over unusual speech when that kind of reaction may serve to reinforce the child's language habits because of attention received. There are no recipes for such problems, but it is apparent that the teacher must act in terms of helping children rather than venting her disgust.

Reading readiness. In a general sense, the entire kindergarten program contributes to the child's readiness for reading in first grade. The social development of the child, his growing feeling of security away from home, an expanding vocabulary and increasing language facility will serve to make the child ready for reading. In a more specific manner, however, the kindergarten program may offer opportunities for the child to develop his auditory and visual acuity in order that he may become aware of differences and similarities of sounds and visual symbols. This should include experience in "reading" pictures for their stories, play with picture puzzles and the like.

A number of kindergarten teachers prefer to present a reading readiness workbook to the child during the last few weeks of kindergarten. Such prepared materials provide specific experiences which lead to the development of related reading skills such as progressing left-to-right, seeing likenesses and differences, and promoting auditory discrimination. Experience in handling a book, finding positions on a page, and other mechanical operations have been suggested as being favorable to the use of readiness workbooks.[18] It seems that readiness workbooks may be used profitably by many children during the latter part of the year, but the teacher should not regard this as the major objective for all children. It may be more desirable for the teacher to prepare single work sheets based upon current classroom themes to provide the above-mentioned experiences. In the case of kindergarten children who do not seem to be ready to work with readiness workbooks, the first grade teacher should provide additional readiness experiences.

Evidence is now accumulating that indicates some children are ready to read from the printed page while in the kindergarten. However, teachers should be cautious about getting children into reading activities before

---

[18] See Paul McKee *et al.*, *Getting Ready* (Boston: Houghton Mifflin Co., 1949), Reading Readiness Book.

they are ready. But it should be made clear that individual differences do not make themselves known arbitrarily at a certain grade level or chronological age. A few children will be advanced physically, socially, mentally, and psychologically to the extent that they should begin to read during the kindergarten year. It is as unjust to restrain these children as it is to coerce children who are *not* ready to read.

Children who show signs of wanting to read should begin an individualized program or be grouped in such a way as to facilitate this activity. Creating their own stories and putting them on experience charts has proved an effective way of developing language skills essential to beginning reading. This experience aids the children in constructing concepts and builds vocabulary which is necessary for beginning reading.

The kindergarten teacher should be acquainted with the fact that boys usually encounter greater difficulty than do girls in first-grade reading and writing. Some authorities have attributed this to natural sex differences,[19] and others have attributed the difference to cultural expectations which involve different activities for boys and girls.[20] Whatever the cause for these differences in reading performance, it is apparent that the kindergarten teacher should provide abundant experiences to serve the greater need which boys may have.

Social learnings.   The socialization of the child has been stated previously as being a major goal of pre-primary education and a considerable amount has been said of the social learning experiences which are part of all classroom activities.

More formally, it is the responsibility of the kindergarten teacher to guide the development of understandings to the end that the child becomes aware that:

1. People are different in many ways, such as color, dress, etc.
2. People do many things alike and share many feelings.
3. We depend upon many people to help us in our daily living.
4. Differences in people are not immediate reasons for disliking them.

The environment of the school can provide many experiences that will advance such understandings and attitudes. Becoming acquainted with the various workers about the school, learning about the occupations

---

[19] William Martin and Celia Stendler, *Child Development* (New York: Harcourt, Brace & World, Inc., 1953), p. 227.

[20] Donald Durrell, *Improving Reading Instruction* (Yonkers, N. Y.: World Book Co., 1956), p. 43.

of the parents of other children, working and playing with children of other races and family backgrounds are specific opportunities in the immediate environment.

Observance of national holidays may provide early experiences in the development of an awareness of history. Of course, the five-year-old is not expected to possess a sharp concept of time nor an appreciation of the significance of events which occurred in 1776. Five-year-olds are interested in sharing important occasions with older children and adults and such experiences are valuable as beginnings.

Safe living in and about the school and home is a necessary inclusion in the social learnings plan for kindergarten and may permeate the various working and playing activities throughout the day.

Much of the social learnings program of the kindergarten will be informal in nature and in many instances will grow out of other experiences of the children. In no event does this imply that the teacher does not have in mind goals of social growth and plans to structure appropriate learning situations to this end.

Teaching the skills of inquiry. With the increasing importance placed on early childhood education and the deepening insights about human behavior, we do not have to be faced with the constant either–or type of questions. It is not a question of whether we should teach young children the skills of inquiry.[21] The question is: "Can teachers be trained to use inquiry techniques to help children develop the power of critical thinking or problem solving?"

Inquiry is the process of asking questions and seeking solutions to the questions. Anyone who has had experience with very young children knows the wide range of questions they can ask and the intensely curious nature of the children. The teacher can use these questions as the basis of helping the child to acquire the beginning skills of inquiry. As this aspect of the curriculum emerges, the teacher needs to be cognizant of the differences in children. All four-year-olds or all five-year-olds are not four- or five-year-olds in all stages of development. The teacher needs to recognize the level of each child in the cognitive domain. Thus the teacher needs to assess the level of concepts, as reflected in the terms used by the child in asking a question. She must provide time for him to explore, create, and discover answers for himself, but with help and assistance from her, the teacher aides, or even other children. She must guard against the onset of frustration and redirect his activities if need be

---

[21] See Frank J. Estvan, "Teaching the Very Young: Procedures for Developing Inquiry Skills," *Phi Delta Kappan*, L, No. 7 (March 1969) 389-393.

to eliminate random actions. Continuous evaluation of the child's behavior should lead the teacher to a better understanding of the learner and his level of development.

Science experiences.   The science experiences found in the modern kindergarten are provided to help the child acquire new concepts of the world in which he lives, to extend his present knowledge of things about him, and to guide the child toward a scientific approach in solving his problems, whether they are scientific or not. It is as important that the kindergarten teacher be sensitive to the daily needs of children for science learning as it is to provide singing activities. Four- and five-year-olds are inquisitive about their world: they are ready to find out for themselves with the guidance of an understanding adult.

Science experiences in the kindergarten may evolve from the incidental happenings in the lives of the children; however, it is desirable that the teacher have some plan of her own for science learnings which can be coordinated with the incidental program.[22] For example, in the fall there are experiences involving observation of the signs of the changing season. Animal and plant life are of interest to kindergarten youngsters at all times of the year, and planting bean seeds, observing guppies in the aquarium, feeding birds in the winter, are activities which excite their interest. During the winter the children can put snow in a glass and examine it for dirt after it melts; they can also make numerous other experiments of the simplest type which involve observation.

To the extent that an important function of elementary school science is "to encourage and stimulate the natural tendencies of curiosity and experimentation found among children,"[23] it is quite within the realm of the kindergarten teacher to guide child behavior in the use of science in their lives.

Quantitative experiences.   When children indicate interest and concern with number values and relationships the teacher may be assured that learning experiences should be planned and provided. Most kindergarten children are ready to approach numbers through the manipulation of blocks, sharing of toys, counting the number of children in a group, reporting ages, and other similar activities.

In number learnings the following objectives are appropriate in the kindergarten:

---

[22] For the teacher's guidance such resources as Elizabeth M. Fuller and Mary J. Ellis, *Springboards to Science* (Minneapolis, Minn.: T. S. Denison Co., 1959), should be useful due to its appropriateness for young children.

[23] John G. Navarra and Joseph Zafforoni, *Science Today for the Elementary School Teacher* (Evanston, Ill.: Harper & Row, Publishers, 1960), p. 25.

1. to count to ten by rote;
2. to enumerate groups of ten objects;
3. to recognize groups of objects numbering three and less without counting;
4. to use partial counting for simple objects in groups of ten or less;
5. to show growth in judgment of size and quantity;
6. to become increasingly sensitive to situations involving number;
7. to apply these number skills and understandings in daily activities.

Ordinarily there is no need for any type of number workbook in kindergarten. The teacher who is aware of the many possibilities for development in the concepts of number, space, size, and time will find that kindergarten children disclose many of their own real learning needs, and that others may be structured for them. There are helpful references which the teacher should use for her own purposes as she plans for quantitative learnings for four- and five-year-olds.[24]

What Equipment and Supplies Should Be Found in the Kindergarten?

Because the kindergarten program is oriented toward working and thinking with things and activities rather than being built around abstractions, it is necessary that adequate supplies and materials be provided. Complete listings of such materials and equipment are provided in a number of publications[25] for those who desire detailed information. For the purposes of providing the teacher with a review of the materials and equipment as they relate to a curriculum design for the kindergarten, the major categories will be discussed here.

Play equipment. The physical activity of the four- and five-year-old cannot be properly scheduled into one or two ten-minute periods per day. Therefore, it is important that equipment be provided within the school day. Large rubber balls, blocks, skipping ropes, tricycles, wagons, slides, swings, jungle gyms, and teeters are representative of the equipment which should be provided for indoor and outdoor use.

---

[24] H. F. Spitzer, *The Teaching of Arithmetic* (Boston: Houghton Mifflin Co., 1949).

[25] Foster and Headley's *Education in the Kindergarten* (New York: American Book Co., 1959), Ch. 7; *Equipment and Supplies* (Washington, D. C.: Association for Childhood Education International 1955), Bulletin No. 39.

Manipulative materials. Beads, peg boards, miniature figurines, dominoes, rings, and sturdy puzzles should be available for the use of the children as they engage in smaller muscle activities.

Furniture. Movable chairs and tables rather than single, fixed desks lend themselves to kindergarten activities. In addition, the room should contain adequate bulletin board space, conveniently arranged book cases and tables, drinking fountains, toilet facilities, linoleum or tile floor covering, sand table, storage space, workbench, tool chest and the like. All such equipment should be designed for the safe use of young children, should be easily maintained and sturdy. Cots or resting mats are needed for the quiet period during the kindergarten day.

In addition to the aforementioned equipment and supplies there are numerous items needed for *science experiences*, for *dramatic play*, for *music experiences*, for *construction activities*, and for *art work*. The need for adequate supplies and equipment should not leave the impression that kindergarten is only a collection of gadgets and toys. Quite the contrary. The effective teacher is one who knows how to use these things in activities that promote child development in the fullest sense.

How Does the Kindergarten Fit into the Total School Program?

It has been emphasized that the kindergarten experience is comprehensive, and is not oriented toward one or two facets of educational readiness, but to the general development of the child. As the child gains facility in the use of language, becomes increasingly aware and observant of his natural and social environment, and grows in competence to recognize and approach his problems of living, he becomes prepared to move on to the more formalized and verbalized experiences of the elementary school. The freedom which is provided to the end that the child can discover important things about himself—socially, artistically, linguistically and the like—this freedom to grow and to learn does not work against preparation for first grade. It promotes total educational and personal readiness.

Kindergarten must remain a place free of rigid subject or skill requirements, although it provides a carefully planned program. It must take its cues from the four- and five-year-old youngsters who come with their many different levels of development. The kindergarten experience should stimulate growth in many ways—growth toward realization of the potentials which exist. Such experiences will not serve to "flatten out" individual differences. In fact, an excellent pre-school program will increase individual differences by providing optimal development of all children in all aspects. They may serve to provide a commonality of school background within which are present all the tremendous opportunities and possibilities for social, emotional, physical, and intellectual development of the individual child.

How Is Progress Assessed in Kindergarten?

In kindergarten, as in other grades, the school is concerned with progress of a continuing nature. Much of the job of assessing pupil progress may involve the use of anecdotal records concerning social, emotional, and intellectual behavior. The health record and the chart of physical growth are important sources of information for this purpose.

Inasmuch as language development is one of the major aims of the first grade, some kindergarten teachers administer readiness tests near the end of the year in an attempt to determine the status of the children with respect to probable success in first grade. It is important that information be obtained concerning mental maturity and educational readiness: this data can often be assembled by the teacher as she works with the five-year-old. If a formal measure of mental maturity is to be used, it would seem that an individual type test is to be recommended in the kindergarten. The use of such tests as the Harrison-Stroud Reading Readiness Profiles[26] are helpful as diagnostic instruments to the extent that they provide a basis for the adjustment of instruction to meet the various needs of the children.

Decisions regarding placement of pupils in first grade should be made upon the basis of what will be the best educational environment for the child. In some situations it may be deemed advisable to have the child spend another semester or year in a kindergarten if he is not ready physically, socially, and mentally for the first grade experience. In situations where the kindergarten teacher concerns herself with individual development, a second year in kindergarten need not be a dull repetition. Also, the first grade teacher who conceives of her function in the same light can offer valuable opportunities to children who come to her even though they may not be ready to read at the beginning of the year.

How Do We Develop Effective Teacher-Parent Relationships?

Educators who have successful modern school programs have found the importance of involving parents in meaningful, participating experiences. Teachers of nursery and kindergarten children usually are the first contacts parents have with the school. Each parent is vitally concerned

---

[26] Available from Houghton Mifflin Co., Boston.

when the young child leaves home for his first experience at school and being away from home alone. Teachers must capitalize upon this initial interest of parents and help them to recognize the importance of their close association with the school program. If these experiences prove valuable to a parent in appraising his child's growth and progress during the early years of school, perhaps closer identification with the child and the school will continue throughout the elementary school years.

The roles of the teacher and the parent in the educative process must be viewed as complementary and supplementary to each other. The parents' role in providing love, security, and feelings of belongingness are essential if the young child is to make an adequate adjustment away from home. This kind of home environment is reassuring to the child and leads him toward independence and maturity. The teacher must accept each child, provide a warm, friendly environment for him to work and play in, and help him to feel secure in his new relationship. The teacher also recognizes that she cannot and should not attempt to be a substitute for a parent. The teacher's relationship must remain more objective toward each child than would be possible or expected of a parent.

Of importance to the teacher is the kind of adjustment the parent is making in sending her child off to school, whether it be the nursery school or the kindergarten. Parents have different reactions about the school and its effects upon their children. It may be that their only previous contact with school was as a student and many unpleasant memories may be recalled. Or it may be that an older child in the family had a disturbing experience when he started to school. On the other hand, previous school contacts may have been very pleasant, and the parent envisions the school as the means for facilitating the child in growing toward independence, maturity, and an enriched childhood. Of importance is the recognition, on the teacher's part, of the many different kinds of parental attitudes reflected in the children and which the teacher must understand as she tries to help these children make satisfactory adjustments. Children from some homes come to school with certain fears, anxieties and apprehensions which challenge even the best-prepared teachers.

Teachers of pre-school children have more contacts with parents than have teachers at any other level in the school's program. Since parents of nursery school children must bring their children to school and come for them, these opportunities give the teacher frequent occasions to talk with the parent informally. Through these contacts the teacher may learn of certain events which have occurred at home and find reasons why a child was unable to show progress toward adjusting to certain situations today. On the other hand, these contacts may help the parent to be reassured of her child's welfare when she leaves the child with the teacher. In addition, there should be days when the teacher invites parents to visit and to see a typical school day. Such visits help the parents to see how their children work and play in a more formal setting than is found in the backyard. It is most important that parents experience the feeling of friendliness from the school personnel. Each contact with the school on the part of a parent should help him to feel that he is wanted and that the entire school staff is interested in the development of children.

A number of schools have prepared booklets or mimeographed material which is presented to parents of nursery and kindergarten children. Such material presents information about the school program, the activities of the children, goals of the program, routine matters requiring parental cooperation, and the like. In addition, there are available commercially prepared bulletins which are inexpensive but informative.[27] The teacher may have such material available for loan, or the school or the parent groups may sponsor distribution to parents of pre-primary children.

RESEARCH IN PRE-PRIMARY EDUCATION

Research that has been done in the area of nursery and kindergarten education has been directed largely to identification of the values of the pre-primary experiences as evidenced by certain behavior characteristics in the early primary grades. This is somewhat in contrast to investigations done at other levels of education where research is more commonly devoted to assessing the effectiveness of certain methods of instruction. In such situations use is often made of experimental and control groups of pupils at a particular grade level. Research in the area of nursery-kindergarten frequently looks to the first or second grade for its study of the behavior of children who have had and children who have not had pre-primary experiences.

The aforementioned direction of pre-primary research may be due in part to the status of the nursery and the kindergarten; to date, as many as 40 per cent of the school systems do not provide kindergarten and very few public schools provide nursery school. So it is not surprising that this relatively recent extension of the educational program should be searching for evidence that will provide profession and public alike with significant information upon which to base judgments concerning the value of nursery and kindergarten education.

At this point it may be emphasized that the nursery and kindergarten educators have not chosen to design their programs in order to directly affect specific pupil performances in later reading or number learnings,

---

[27] *Happy Journey*, Washington, D. C.: National Education Association.

and so to anticipate the educational tasks of the children in first or second grade. The investigations have been concerned, in the main, with the long-range effects of programs that are planned to meet the psychological and sociological needs of three-, four-, and five-year-olds.

Valuable research efforts have been made in the face of difficulties which are unique to nursery and kindergarten programs. One of the common problems encountered in nursery school research is the fact that a nursery school population is often atypical, due to the low socio-economic status of many children who traditionally attend such schools. The nursery of the university laboratory school may find its population in imbalance due to a preponderance of children of faculty people. This problem is not so pronounced at the kindergarten level, although it has been stated earlier in this chapter that the rural areas of the nation lag far behind the urban areas in provision of kindergartens and that the large majority of kindergarten children live in cities of 2,500 and above. This may produce an element of bias.

Nonetheless there is a growing fund of information coming from research efforts in the pre-primary area, and the foregoing discussion of research problems is offered to acquaint the student with the working conditions of nursery-kindergarten researchers.

Nursery School Investigations

A number of investigations have been carried on in the area of the nursery school experience and its effects on later school behavior. However, some of the most controversial studies have been devoted to the effect of pre-primary school upon the I. Q. Peterson and others have looked into this matter by studying the test performance of children at the State University of Iowa.[28] Generally, the reports of these studies indicated that children who have had pre-school experience perform significantly better on intelligence tests after the pre-school experience. This improvement in I. Q. was not in evidence in control groups of children who had not attended pre-school programs.

Other investigators[29] have reported similar findings with respect to gains made in I. Q. by children who have had nursery school experience, and that such gains were maintained after leaving nursery school. Contrary findings have been reported by Karvin and Hoefer[30] who have sug-

---

[28] Harvey A. Peterson, Stanley S. Marzolf, and Nancy Bayley, *Educational Psychology* (New York: The Macmillan Co., 1948), p. 510.

[29] E. Starkweather and K. Roberts, *Intelligence: Its Nature and Nurture*, National Society for the Study of Education (Chicago: Public Schools Publishing Co., 1940), pp. 315-35.

[30] E. Karwin and C. Hoefer, *A Comparative Study of a Nursery Versus a Non-nursery School Group* (Chicago: University of Chicago Press, 1931).

gested that there seems to be inadequate evidence to support the position that nursery or kindergarten experience will raise the I. Q. of children who attend.

Although the issue of the raising of the I. Q. may not yet be settled, there are other important considerations which deserve attention. It is inestimably more important that the pre-primary educators direct their efforts to providing a fruitful learning environment in which children may develop on a broad front. Allen and Masling[31] have looked into the matter of the social development and status of nursery school children after they have progressed into kindergarten, first and second grades. In this investigation 82 non-nursery children and 34 nursery children were administered a "near sociometric" device involving five questions. Thus, for the three grades there were fifteen choice situations and in fourteen of these situations the nursery subjects received the higher mean number of nominations. It was only at the second grade level, however, where the number of nursery children nominations was significantly higher than the non-nursery children.

Other studies on this topic have suggested that academic differences between pre-primary children and non-pre-primary subjects continue as children move through the grades; in fact, they tend to increase.[32] It may be observed that some of the studies cited were made in the 1930's and that there is certainly a need for further carefully controlled investigation.

Kindergarten Research

Studies made in the area of the kindergarten program are frequently directed to discovery of the effect of kindergarten on first grade reading and number experiences. Not infrequently, generalizations have been made on the basis of teacher observation rather than carefully controlled measures and there is a need for continued investigation here. Caution is advisable in this matter inasmuch as a growing emphasis upon higher first grade reading achievement as an outcome of kindergarten may work against the broadly conceived program of pre-first grade educational development.

Investigations into the effect of the kindergarten experience on first grade performance generally suggest that children with kindergarten

[31] G. B. Allen and J. M. Masling, "An Evaluation of the Effects of Nursery School Training On Children in Kindergarten, First and Second Grade," *Journal of Educational Research*, 51 (December, 1957), 285-96.

[32] Ruth Brandenburg, "The Effects of Preschool Attendance Upon Intellectual Development During the Elementary School Years," Unpublished study, State University of Iowa, 1931; Jean Koumin, "Effect of Preschool Attendance Upon Later School Achievement," Unpublished study, State University of Iowa, 1939.

background show evidence of being readier for reading, that they are socially more adaptable to the classroom environment, and that they will be more successful in over-all first grade performance than those children with no kindergarten experience.[33] Again, it is necessary to emphasize the need for further study of a careful nature in these areas inasmuch as there are many issues that have not been explored.

One of the more interesting investigations made in the area of kindergarten training and first grade reading was carried on by Fast[34] using 134 kindergarten and 46 "no-kindergarten experience" pupils. The children were carefully equated for I. Q. and mental age. Four tests were administered at intervals throughout the first grade and on all occasions the children with the kindergarten experience achieved significantly higher than did the non-kindergarten children. Table III presents the test information for these groups:

TABLE III

Performance of Kindergarten and Non-Kindergarten Pupils On Selected Reading Tests

MONTH	TEST	MEAN SCORES	
		Kindergarten	*Non-Kindergarten*
October	Reading Readiness	8.67	4.03
February	Word Recognition	13.71	11.83
February	Paragraph Reading	5.45	3.96
May	Paragraph Reading	13.30	9.54

Of considerable interest will be long range studies of the school performance of children with kindergarten preparation. To the extent that the kindergarten provides for a broad range of developmental opportunities it would seem that the benefits to be realized would extend beyond first and second grade and, indeed, be far more inclusive than a test of reading performance would suggest. These are matters that will receive attention of educational researchers in the future.

---

[33] S. L. Hammond, "What About Kindergarten?" *Childhood Education*, 33 (March, 1957), 314-15; Ruth Strang, "Pre-School Prelude to School Success," *National Parent-Teacher*, 50 (April, 1956), 19-21; Horace English, *Child Psychology* (New York: Holt, Rinehart & Winston, Inc., 1951), p. 344.

[34] Irene Fast, "Kindergarten Training and Grade One Reading," *Journal of Educational Psychology*, 48 (January, 1957), 52-7.

This brief reference to the research needs and findings at the pre-primary levels is intended to emphasize the use of carefully obtained information in any discussion of the status of the nursery and kindergarten program. It is intended, also, that cooperative research efforts may be suggested in which nursery and kindergarten people will work with investigators from other levels of education in a mutual effort to learn more about the contributions of pre-primary education to the lives of children.

SUMMARY

Nursery and kindergarten programs are relatively recent in the educational history of the United States. The kindergarten has enjoyed a marked growth over the years 1945 to the present both in public and private schools. The nursery school movement has undergone spasmodic development since it has been related frequently to the child-care function, rather than the educational function designated to the kindergarten.

Head Start and other programs of early intervention have not proved that the type of curriculum provided in these programs prepares the disadvantaged child for formal schooling. This might suggest that "formal" schooling should be modified and that the emerging curriculum can best serve the individual when he helps to make decisions which affect himself in terms of goals, learning activities, procedures, and self-evaluation.

Many issues remain to be resolved with respect to the specific value of pre-primary educational experiences in the lives of youngsters. With the acquisition and dissemination of information in these areas there will doubtless be a continuing spread of pre-primary educational programs throughout the nation. There is an increasing body of research information which points to positive values of the nursery and kindergarten experience. One may anticipate new problems as educators and parents speculate as to the proper function of pre-primary programs, whether they should be "child development" oriented or geared to provide specific outcomes in educational readiness.

Extending the opportunities of pre-primary education to the many youngsters who do not now receive them will depend upon the concerted efforts of the nursery and kindergarten people and the administrators and teachers from higher levels of education. This, with the support of an informed public, will serve to open the doors to about 50 per cent of the kindergarten age children who do not attend kindergarten and to extend nursery school programs far beyond their present status.

SUGGESTED ACTIVITIES AND PROBLEMS

1. Miss Deen says that her kindergarten children are too young to accept much responsibility of any sort. It is her position that four- and five-year-olds must receive adult direction in all their school experience. Miss Allen, the principal, believes that children must have opportunities to try out a number of things on their own, that the kindergarten program should help the child make a beginning toward independence and self-responsibility. What kinds of activities might Miss Allen suggest as being suitable for developing a feeling of responsibility on the part of the child? What activities might permit freedom of choice by the children?

2. Some of the research available indicates that the intelligence quotient of a child may be increased as a result of attendance in nursery school and kindergarten. Read the summaries of several of these studies and report as to your position in this matter.

3. Miss Deen uses a readiness workbook with all her pupils during the second semester of the kindergarten year. She feels that reading readiness is one of the areas which needs much attention and that the workbook more or less guarantees such attention. Inspect several reading readiness workbooks. Do you believe that they may be best used in kindergarten or grade one? If Miss Deen were to omit the use of the workbook, would she probably cease to help children get ready for first grade?

4. Do you believe that certification for the nursery school teacher is a necessity? Support your claims.

5. Show the common characteristics needed by teachers of pre-school children that are not too necessary for the elementary teacher.

7. Plan a visit to a nursery school and/or kindergarten. Indicate what items will be observed. Consolidate your findings in a total class discussion.

8. Mrs. Martin believes her five-and-one-half-year-old son should start to read. Mrs. Martin points out to the teacher that her son recognizes certain words he sees on T. V. and again when he sees them on a cereal box. What course of action should Miss White, the teacher, take and how should she deal with Mrs. Martin's request?

SELECTED READINGS

Allen, B. and Joseph M. Masling. "An Evaluation of the Nursery School Training on Children in Kindergarten, First, and Second Grades," *Journal of Educational Research*, 51 (December, 1951), 285-96.

Bain, W. E. "Teacher for Children Under Six," *Education*, 74 (February, 1954), 343-46.

Dale, D. G. "Love of Literature Begins in the Kindergarten," *Elementary English*, 35 (January, 1958), 28-9.

Eiserer, Paul E. "Children's Perceptions of School and Teachers," *Educational Leadership*, XI, No. 7 (April, 1954), 409-12.

Elias, James, and Paul Gebhard. "Sexuality and Sexual Learning in Childhood," *Phi Delta Kappan*, L, No. 7 (March, 1969), 401-405.

Foster, Josephine C. and Neith E. Headley. *Education in The Kindergarten.* New York: American Book Co., 1959.

Fuller, Elizabeth M. *Values in Preschool Education.* Washington, D. C.: National Education Association, 1960.

Fuller, Elizabeth M. "Early Childhood Education," *Encyclopedia of Educational Research.* New York: The Macmillan Co., 1960, pp. 385-87.

Gans, Roma, Celia B. Stendler, and Millie Almy. *Teaching Young Children in Nursery School, Kindergarten, and The Primary Grades.* New York: World Book Co., 1952; Chapters 3 and 4.

Headley, Neith. *Foundation Learning in the Kindergarten.* Washington, D. C.: National Education Association, 1958.

Hellmuth, Jerome (ed.). *Disadvantaged Child: Head Start and Early Intervention*, Vol. 2. Seattle, Wash.: Special Child Publications, Inc., 1968, p. 620.

Hubler, Clark. *Working with Children in Science.* Boston: Houghton Mifflin Co., 1956.

Imhoff, Myrtle. *Early Elementary Education.* New York: Appleton-Century-Crofts, Inc., 1959; Chapters 7, 8 and 9.

Lambert, Hazel M. *Teaching The Kindergarten Child.* New York: Harcourt, Brace & World, Inc., 1958.

Leavitt, Jerome A. *Nursery-Kindergarten Education.* New York: McGraw-Hill Book Co., 1958.

Leonard, Edith M., Dorothy D. VanDeman, and Lillian E. Miles. *Foundations of Learning in Childhood Education.* Columbus, Ohio: Charles E. Merrill Publishing Co., 1963.

Moustakas, Clark and Minnie P. Berson. *The Young Child in School.* New York: William Morrow & Co., Inc., 1956.

Moustakas, Clark and Minnie P. Berson. *The Nursery School and Child Care Center.* New York: William Morrow & Co., Inc., 1955.

Strickland, Joann H., and William Alexander. "Seeking Continuity in Early and Middle School Education," *Phi Delta Kappan*, L, No. 7 (March, 1969), 397-400.

Wills, Clarice D. and William H. Stegeman. *Living in The Kindergarten.* Rev. ed.; Chicago: Follett Publishing Company, 1956.

CHAPTER 7

Developing the Language Arts

INTRODUCTION

It is through the possession and use of the skills and appreciations of the language arts that man understands, acquires, preserves, and transmits thought. The language arts provide the vehicles for the passing of information from person to person, from generation to generation, and from era to era. No field of human endeavor escapes a dependency upon the language arts for the transmission of ideas and information. Philosophy, the sciences, the arts, and the daily affairs of all societies must look to the language arts for the means of common understanding and communication.

Talking, listening, reading, and writing comprise the major components of the language arts curriculum, although it is only recently in human history, that large numbers of people have become proficient in the reading and writing phases of the language arts. Oral language as a means for the expression of thought and information had its beginnings long before the time of recorded history. Indeed, the beginnings of written language are shrouded in the dimly perceived past.

With the advent of democratic institutions and a recognition of the worth of the individual, there has come a great need for all persons to be proficient in the use of the language arts skills. In any nation where the responsibilities of government rest with the voting populace, the schools must do more than provide for general literacy; they must promote the most efficient use of the language arts to the end that people may read with discrimination, write with clarity, and communicate effectively with their fellow citizens and the greater community of men around the world.

The teacher of language arts can no longer be satisified with providing only for drill in skills; reading, writing, speaking, and listening must be regarded as the avenues by which the citizen in a democracy informs himself and expresses himself in matters of a civic and a personal nature. Skill in the application of the language arts becomes an important phase of the teaching process as does the mastery of the several skills.

Proficiency in the use of language arts in the classroom must eventually find its fulfillment in the life of the citizen; the teacher who does not see this relationship may well neglect a vital part of language learning.

Aside from the implications for language arts in a democratic society, one soon recognizes the role of language proficiency in the economic life of the individual. Unless one can read and write with some measure of skill, and unless one can observe common courtesies of listening and speaking, one will encounter difficulties in earning a livelihood, managing routine business affairs, and establishing social contacts with others. It is something of an understatement to say that the people of this nation expect the elementary school to insure that each child will gain skill in reading and writing. It is probably true that before the advent of satellites the language arts areas received more popular attention than any other area of the elementary school curriculum. Even now there is a continued concern that represents a desirable interest of the people in the educational programs of their schools; it places a great responsibility upon classroom teachers and school administrators to plan, implement, and evaluate carefully and completely the language arts program at all levels.

In this chapter the several areas of the language arts will be considered as they contribute to the educational growth of the child. Practices and issues in the teaching of language arts will be discussed, and the role of the teacher in organizing the learning program in language arts will be stressed.

What Is the Scope of the Language Arts?

The language arts may be properly regarded as the common carrier of the curriculum. Reading and writing are basic to all school activities whether the child is in the wood-working shop, in science class, or in a "reading" class. Listening and speaking are likewise important in the learning activities throughout the entire school program. As the learnings of the school become a part of the child's behavior patterns, the language arts bind together experiences of a real and a verbal nature. Yet, they are more than the "glue" of the school program; they are part of all learnings. Sapir, writing of the relationship of language to any culture, said: "[Language] does not as a matter of fact stand apart from or run parallel to direct experience but completely interpenetrates with it."[1] So is language an insoluble part of the child's learnings.

---

[1] Edward Sapir, "Language," *Selected Writings of Edward Sapir in Language Culture, and Personality* (Berkeley, California: University of California Press, 1951), p. 11.

What Is the Role of Language in Learning?

Some rather pedantic questions have been raised from time to time concerning the role of language in thinking. Whether persons can think without some form of visual, mental, or auditory symbols is not a crucial topic for the classroom teacher. She is concerned with the effective use of the language arts in the social and intellectual development of children inasmuch as the wider learning experiences and extended social relationships depend so greatly upon the use of the language arts.

Terman[2] has indicated that the child's use of speech is an indication of intellectual development and has gone as far as to state that the mastery of language is suggestive of conceptual thinking and is an excellent index of the stage of mental maturity. So closely is language intertwined with all experience that its mastery seems to be evidence of intelligent perception of experience.

Thorpe[3] has proposed that the auditory and visual symbols which are the words of a language help the child to deal in an abstract manner with realities of his environment; in other words, the child thinks with the help of symbols. Instead of the child's taking his mother to the spot where he stumbled and skinned his knee, he can, with the use of words, reconstruct for her the real experience.

The many learning experiences of the school can be made available to the child only through a wide use of language. Ideas, concepts, facts, and relationships with the human and natural environment come within the daily experiences of children when they have the language skills to deal with them. It is a well-known fact among teachers that the child who has difficulty with the language arts is often handicapped as he approaches learning tasks in other areas. The child who has difficulty with reading may be expected to experience trouble with story problems in arithmetic class. The brilliant science student is due to encounter difficulty if his writing and spelling are so poor that he cannot communicate his thoughts to others through writing.

Language, then, is much more than an indicator of intelligence. Through the application of the skills it becomes a fundamental part of the continued learnings of children, and regardless of a child's capacity for learning, the language arts will play a vital role in whatever learning takes place.

---

[2] L. M. Terman, *The Intelligence of School Children* (Boston: Houghton Mifflin, 1919).

[3] Louis Thorpe, *Child Psychology and Development* (New York: The Ronald Press Company, 1955), p. 249.

CHILD DEVELOPMENT THROUGH LANGUAGE

From the moment of birth the child finds himself in contact with the world of language. The sounds and the physical actions which accompany certain vocalizations soon come to have meaning for the child. Long before he is physiologically able to use the word symbols of his native language, the small child will communicate with those who are close to him by means of facial expressions, bodily movements, and the seemingly meaningless sounds which he can produce.

As Strickland[4] has pointed out, the acquisition of language is more than the mechanical mastery of sounds; it represents the operation of a comparatively high degree of intelligence in order that meaning is related to the sound symbols of human speech.

A number of research workers[5] have pointed out that the infant seems to express purpose and needs in his vocalizations, and that inflection and intonation not only are recognized by the very young child, but they are among the elements of communication that are imitated before words are actually used.

Since language must be acquired from the surrounding cultural group, it is important that the teacher know as much as possible about the early language development of each child in her classroom. Such information may afford valuable clues to underlying causes of poor speech habits, lack of interest in reading, and similar problems. Of equal concern to the teacher will be the background of language development of the child who has difficulties in personality adjustment, who is timid and withdrawing. Sybil was a child whose problem illustrates this point.

> Sybil was an eleven-year-old pupil in a fifth grade room. Throughout her early years in elementary school she had maintained an almost unbroken silence and had remained apart from the other children.
>
> After careful study by her teacher, it was discovered that not only was she later than usual in starting to walk, but her muscular coordination seemed to be a problem for her as late as the fourth grade. However, the real clue to her language development was revealed in her father's attitude toward children in the home. Sybil was not permitted to share her daily experiences at the dinner hour nor was she encouraged to talk at other

---

[4] Ruth C. Strickland, *The Language Arts in the Elementary School* (Boston: D. C. Heath & Co., 1957), p. 69.

[5] Katherine E. Roberts, "Babies Don't Cry for Fun," *Parents' Magazine*, 21 (November, 1956), 154-57; Morris M. Lewis, *Infant Speech: A Study of the Beginnings of Language* (New York: Harcourt, Brace and World, Inc., 1936).

times. There were no suitable books or magazines in the home for children. Sybil's language development had been thwarted by the culture of which she was a part.

The teacher must then be aware and informed regarding the language culture from which her pupils come. They will present a wide variety of backgrounds in language, as in other experiences and learnings.

Is Social Development Enhanced Through Language?

It is through the use of language that the child is able to gain a concept of himself. From the time that the child is able to express his desires, ideas, and feelings to other people, he receives from their responses and actions, acceptance or rejection or unconcern for himself. Piaget[6] has made some interesting and thought provoking observations which point up the function of language in the development of a concept of self. In the classroom it is not difficult to overlook the fact that the child who finds his spoken thoughts rejected may feel that his total being has been rejected. Children who find their vocal responses rejected by teachers and peers cannot be expected to strive for oral language development; it is simpler to withdraw.

Thus the child sees himself developing into a particular kind of a person, as he finds his relations with others to be satisfying and stimulating, or dissatisfying and frustrating. Through language, the child must depend upon others to provide him with the basis for his own ideas about himself. The child will reconstruct a picture of self from pictures given by the people about him as they accept or reject, praise or criticize him.

How Does Experience Affect Language Development?

It is only as the child comes into contact with many different situations that he is able to build a background of meaning for the language symbols that he will encounter from day to day. Although all children have experience continuously, it is true that many children lack the variety and scope of experiences which provide the foundations for language development. The city child who has never seen a cow cannot verbalize adequately on the process of obtaining milk at its original

---

[6] Jean Piaget, *The Language and Thought of the Child* (New York: Harcourt, Brace and World, Inc., 1926) and *The Construction of Reality in the Child* (New York: Basic Books, Inc., 1954).

source. On the other hand, the lad who has been reared on the dairy farm may have little difficulty in this respect, but he may have no real concept of a skyscraper. In addition, the home that provides little or nothing in the way of stories, picture-books, pictures, magazines, excursions, and the like may be doing little to help the child in building concepts about books and the richness of language which helps to foster reading readiness and total language development. Many kinds of experiences are necessary if the child is to go beyond mere verbalism in his use of language.

McKee[7] has pointed out that it is necessary that the school provide for a wide variety of real experiences inasmuch as the "growth of vocabulary" and other forms of verbal expression is greatly conditioned by the experiences they gather. This is particularly important in the development of concepts which may be otherwise shallow and thus impede clear and correct comprehension of spoken or printed symbols.[8]

The presence of television in so many homes must indeed have an effect of providing visual concepts of lands, peoples, and events that were unknown to children a few years ago. The increased exposure of children to television and radio may, of course, serve to dull their sensitivity, and, in fact, impair their ability to devote their attention to the relatively quiet proceedings of the schoolroom.[9] It would seem that the children of today would have a wider variety of interests and experiences than ever before, which should be conducive to further inquiry through reading.

In this regard, Witty has reported that a study of the effects of television viewing upon academic achievement indicated that there is little or no harm done to school performance, and that viewing was not related to intelligence or scholarship. However, *excessive* viewing was associated with lower academic performance.[10]

Watts has reported that the sales of hard-bound and paper-back books has increased 500 per cent since the advent of television, and has urged that children should be encouraged to develop selectiveness and critical habits toward the television programs available.[11] Whatever is to be the ultimate role of television in the language arts program, it is

---

[7] Paul McKee, *Language in the Elementary School* (Boston: Houghton Mifflin Co., 1939), p. 89.

[8] *Ibid.*, p. 12.

[9] "Mass Communication and Education," *The National Elementary Principal*, 37 (February, 1958), 14.

[10] Paul A. Witty, "Seventh Report on TV," *Elementary English*, 33 (December, 1956), 523-28.

[11] Doris Ryder Watts, "What's Happening to Reading?" *Education Digest*, 19 (May, 1954), 46-8.

clear that careful observation and study is needed on the part of many teachers throughout the land to determine the values and problems involved.

DISADVANTAGED CHILDREN AND LANGUAGE DEVELOPMENT

If we regard disadvantagement as including those children whose learning difficulties are related to social, economic, and cultural factors that limit the child's development, effective teachers have always been concerned with the disadvantaged children in the school. However, in recent years, the incidence of disadvantaged children has been found to be much higher in those parts of the population where poverty exists and where there are concentrations of minority racial and ethnic groups.

According to Frost,[12] the problem of the limited language development of the "disadvantaged" youngster includes:

1. Limited language experiences during the pre-school years due to a working mother.
2. Dominant use of informal language which is not acceptable in many schools.
3. Limited conceptual development related, perhaps, to the restricted environments of early childhood.
4. Value systems different from those of teacher and peers.

Dean Olympia Lowe of Mississippi Valley State College has called for a realistic approach in the schools to the problem of motivating and reinforcing the language learnings of the disadvantaged child. The gold or silver star as a reward for performance in spelling is, according to Lowe, often a meaningless reward since the parents and siblings in the economically deprived home place higher value on tangible rewards. Although it is contrary to the Puritan ethic which continues to dominate the educational thought of American laymen, it appears that the award of oranges or apples for achievement would have higher impact on reinforcing desired behavior in the disadvantaged than does the gold star.[13]

In working with the socially and economically disadvantaged child, the way in which the teacher reacts to the informal and sometimes crude

---

[12] Frost, Joe L. *Developing Literacy in Disadvantaged Children* (Austin, Tex.: University of Texas, 1968), pp. 264-75.

[13] From remarks of Dean Olympia Lowe contained in a videotape prepared for a teacher conference on the educationally disadvantaged, August, 1969, Ohio University, Athens, Ohio.

language of the child is very critical. The language represents the child and the people close to him in the home and neighborhood. To reject the language of the disadvantaged child is often to reject the child and his entire cultural melieu. The way of working with the disadvantaged child is not really different from the practices which stem from long standing educational theory:

1. Differentiated instruction is of extreme importance in working with the disadvantaged.
2. Rewards and reinforcements must be meaningful to the child (as well as the teacher).
3. Language learning must first be approached for its communicative powers; its moral aspects are of secondary nature.
4. Progress is measured by the many variables in the situation rather than in terms of a fixed *a priori* standard of grade achievement.

COMMUNICATION THROUGH WRITING AND SPEAKING

Writing and speaking are the "outgoing" processes of communication. Writing depends upon (1) correct spelling of the words used, (2) a legible hand, and (3) acceptable usage or grammar in constructing the written thoughts. Speaking or talking is most effective when the individual employs good speech habits and acceptable forms of expression.

Undergirding all forms of communication are the desires and ability of the child to express his thoughts and feelings to others. In giving attention to the mechanics of written and oral expression, the teacher must be extremely careful to avoid "shutting off" or stifling the desires of children to express themselves through writing and talking. Until the child has something to express and desires to communicate this to others, there is little point in attempting to refine the skills of writing and speaking.

Strickland[14] pointed up the dilemma in this area when she discussed the problem of helping the children express their "own free spirit" while at the same time helping them to become careful writers. She has suggested that "concern with 'correct' writing has completely overshadowed and crowded out all else in the writing experience of many children."[15] The child must feel free to express himself through speaking and writing before the teacher can learn about his language development and problems.[16]

[14] Ruth Strickland, *op. cit.*, p. 273.
[15] *Ibid.*
[16] *Ibid.*, p. 131.

Writing: Skill and Creation

Children are often interested in writing before they enter school. They have observed older persons in the home making strange marks with pencil or pen on paper. Letters that have been brought by the postman may contain "writing" from grandmother, and the child may pretend to read such letters. Many children enjoy "writing" their names, or helping mother prepare the grocery list.

Since most children know what writing is, they know that it represents ideas or real things. Children want to write, and they do have ideas that they want to put on paper. It seems unfortunate that the child must await the muscular control and visual perception that will one day make it possible for him to write his ideas. In some school situations, the child will find his time so taken up with practice in writing words which have little meaning to him that he comes to associate writing with meaningless drudgery.

> The first requisite for practice is that it must be related to a meaningful purpose. The child himself must recognize the need to possess the particular skill. When a child wants to write for others to read, he is willing to practice. He attends to what he is doing, corrects mistakes, notes his successes.[17]

This statement applies to the writing of first grade children quite as much as to the writing of fifth grade children.

How Does the Teacher Begin Teaching Writing?

Children in first grade classrooms seem to get much satisfaction from helping the teacher prepare a chart story about something they have done. Early experiences in writing may involve each child's copying the chart story on his own paper in order that he can take it home to share with his family. In this, as in other learning situations, the teacher will expect to find differences among children in their writing readiness and ability.

The first writing experiences of the child will, of necessity, be brief and simple. Learning to form the letters is a new task, even though most children do not find the letters to be strange in themselves. When writing has some purpose for the child, he will see purpose in practicing on letter forms. Although it is a safe practice to provide many purposeful writing experiences, it is also true that children can benefit from much

---

[17] Association for Supervision and Curriculum Development, *The Three R's in the Elementary School* (Washington, D. C.; N. E. A., 1952), p. 59.

individual practice in writing as long as the practice does not become an end in itself.

Writing experiences of young children should be based upon both individual and group experiences. For example, the child may write, "My name is Jane," as her first writing "lesson." Before long she may take to her family a story which tells about her school life.

> I go to West School.
> My teacher is Miss Roe.
> I am in first grade.

The use of chart stories is frowned upon by some persons who fear that the child will be introduced to too many new words. From the standpoint of motivation and interest, it would seem that the early copy-writing experiences of children are best drawn from a group-developed chart story, as long as it is kept brief, simple and meaningful. Of course, the vocabulary of a chart story can be controlled to a considerable degree by the teacher, and there is no reason to avoid the use of words which the children have learned in reading.

> One of the authors visited a first grade classroom while the children were in the process of dictating a story to their teacher. They had just returned from a visit to the airport, and they insisted that the words "airplane" and "propeller" must be in the story. In a return visit by the author a few weeks later, the teacher commented that none of the children in the room had since failed to recognize the "big words" which they had wanted in their story.

In using the chart-story approach to beginning writing, the following suggestions should be considered:

(1) Develop the story from an experience of the group.
(2) Help the children use simple vocabulary by restating some of the more complicated sentences.
(3) Keep plenty of space between lines.
(4) Try to keep sentences to one line in length.

The children will see definite purpose in the copying of chart stories based on experiences of their own. Frequently these may be taken home by the child, inasmuch as they represent work in writing, reading, and actual experiences of the school day.

Manuscript or Cursive?

Manuscript writing is used in many schools in the first and second grades. The argument offered advocating the use of manuscript writing is that it is less complex in form and looks more like the printing of pre-primers and primers. It is common practice to change from manuscript to cursive sometime during the third grade.[18] Actually, this practice seems to be a rather arbitrary matter, with little regard being given to the problems of children.

Many second grade pupils have begun to feel confident and comfortable in their use of manuscript writing only to find that they must abandon it in favor of what grown-ups call "real" writing. Hildreth[19] has questioned the necessity of making the change in view of the fact that manuscript writing is usually more legible than cursive and can be written with equal speed. Tradition will probably make it necessary that children continue to change to cursive writing shortly after they have become skillful in manuscript. Writing continues to be regarded by some persons as something more than the means for communication of one's thoughts to others.

An account of one school system's use of manuscript writing through all the elementary grades has been reported by Hendricks, who stated that the learning of cursive writing was optional at the junior high school level.[20] The adoption of the manuscript form of writing was based upon the fact that it was easier for children because it has simple strokes, uses one form of the alphabet for reading and writing, causes less fatigue and eye strain, can be written as quickly as the cursive form, and is more legible.[21]

At any grade level there is only one requirement that should be placed upon the mechanics of handwriting—that it be legible. Instruction in handwriting will provide practice of an individual nature designed to correct various writing errors. Spacing, slant, letter formation, and writing on the line are the major components of legible cursive writing. Children's writing errors should be assessed in terms of these components.

An illustration follows to indicate the need for practice in handwriting even for sixth grade pupils and points out how handwriting instruction may be organized:

> Two twenty-minute practice sessions were provided each week during the time devoted to the language arts. During these practice periods, the pupils looked over written work that had been returned to them previ-

---

[18] Strickland, *op. cit.*, p. 285.

[19] Gertrude Hildreth, "Should Manuscript Writing Be Continued in the Upper Grades?" *Elementary School Journal*, 45 (October, 1944), 85-93.

[20] Archie E. Hendricks, "Manuscript and Cursive Handwriting in Brookline," *Elementary School Journal*, 55 (April, 1955), 447-52.

[21] *Ibid.*

ously. Miss Nielson, the sixth grade teacher, had written suggestions and questions on these papers regarding writing errors that needed attention. Each child spent the practice sessions on the writing problems which he recognized were his own. Drill by the entire group was used only when all the children had experienced the same writing problem, which was seldom.

Motivation was high during these practice sessions because the children were doing something of value to themselves. Practice on written forms which they had already mastered was not used.

Can Writing Be Creative?

It is an interesting paradox which finds teachers talking about the creativeness of children at the same time telling children what kinds of stories to write, how to write these stories, and whether the stories are good or bad. When friendly letters are written to proverbial cousins, the children are often told what they should write about. Poems written by children are often carefully checked for rhyme, punctuation, and the like until the child finds himself concentrating upon the mechanics of writing to the exclusion of expressing his thoughts well.

Thus the writing of stories or poems that are teacher-suggested as a means of stimulating children should not be used in connection with lessons in punctuation, grammar, and form. However, when the child gains confidence in his ability to express himself on paper, he will be ready to use self-criticism and to accept suggestions from others.

The teacher who is interested in fostering creative expression will not say, "I wouldn't write a poem like that," or "You should write about something nice instead of writing mysteries." It is true that children must have the opportunities, the time, and the necessary guidance from interested teachers if they are to express their thoughts and feelings— and realize that they are important. Self-expression through writing is much like other forms of expression insofar as the child must develop a feeling of security and satisfaction from writing. This security and satisfaction results in most cases from happy experiences in self-expression in painting, drawing, coloring, speaking and the like,[22] with a corresponding feeling of freedom in written expression during later school years.

The prime requisites to good writing experiences lie in the teacher's understanding of those factors which foster writing. In classrooms where pupils are encouraged to speak and to write their thoughts, a relaxed

---

[22] *Language Arts*, 35, No. 7 (Richmond, Virginia: State Board of Education, 1956), p. 32.

atmosphere enhances the development of these skills. Beyond this, children need a wide variety of experiences in order to have something to write about. Field trips to the nearby zoo, park, quarry, or a large industrial plant, will add to the children's experiences. Firsthand experiences aid children to gain needed insights essential to self-expression. It has often been found that prolific writers are also extensive readers.[23] While it is not the intent here to cause every child to become a Jesse Stuart or a Norman Cousins, the teacher is charged with the task of helping to surround the children with many varieties of literature for free and relaxed reading from which new ideas may emerge.

From the first days of school the child will grow in his willingness to express himself in various manners if he knows that it is fun to share his thoughts and expressions with others. In first grade classrooms the teacher may encourage language expression by writing for the children the things they want to say. The subject of their "writings" may be the flowers outside the window, the bird's nest in a tree nearby, the machinery being used to repair the street near the school—there is no end to the experiences that children wish to recall by writing them on paper.

Writing poetry is an activity which interests many children in the elementary school. Since the feeling or the word-picture which the child wants to express is the reason for poetry, it is important that teachers do not inhibit expression by insisting upon rhyming and pattern at this stage of maturity. As in other activities of the school program, there will be those children who are interested in writing poems while others are not. Creative expression in writing is not gained by forcing or pressing children into making certain responses, since a stimulating environment, free of pressure, is a necessary condition of productivity. Of course, an interested teacher who is aware of the creative possibilities in children, is the key to creative written expression in the school.[24]

Lowenfeld[25] has discussed in a thorough manner the role of the teacher and parent in providing opportunities for creative activity in the elementary school. The importance of freedom and avoidance of adult interference is pointed out: "The independent, thinking child will not only express whatever comes into his mind but will tackle any problem, emotional or mental, that he encounters in life."[26] Expression

---

[23] See "Using Reading to Teach Creative Writing," *Education Today*, Bulletin No. 25 (Columbus, Ohio: Charles E. Merrill Publishing Co.).

[24] June Fereber, Doris Jackson, Dorothy Saunders and Alvina Treut, *They All Want to Write* (Indianapolis, Ind.: The Bobbs-Merrill Co., Inc., 1939), pp. 7-9.

[25] Viktor Lowenfeld, *Creative and Mental Growth* (New York: The Macmillan Co., 1952), Chapter One.

[26] *Ibid.*, p. 7.

through writing is not unlike expression through drawing or painting in this respect.

Creative writing has been neglected by many teachers because of their being pressed for time in administering the curriculum. Programmed instruction in the language arts may serve a much needed purpose in saving the teachers' time. Fillmer[27] found that teaching irregular verbs to fourth grade children was as effective using programmed textbooks as when the teachers taught using the usual procedures. Fillmer also found that "pupils using the programmed textbooks completed the course of study in less than two-thirds of the time required by the pupils involved in the conventional classroom approach."[28] It would seem, if continued research supports the effectiveness of programmed instruction, that teachers should have more time to spend in the creative writing approach to language.

An interesting project concerning the relationships between the literature read by elementary pupils and the quality of their written compositions was carried out by Grothe as part of Project English at the University of Nebraska. In this experimental activity, selected groups of children were provided similar literature background but without specific instruction and model units. The experimental groups which were given the full treatment over a three-year period produced higher quality compositions, according to the evaluative scheme which was used, than did other groups, but it appears that other related findings are more helpful in planning for the writing experiences of middle grade children.

Grothe reported that children are generally inhibited when writing about events close to themselves, that the better quality compositions dealt with fantasy and legend. Poorer quality writing was found on topics such as exploration, sports, and future occupations. Many of the better quality compositions made use of dialogue, unusual endings, abundance of descriptive language, and new variations on old themes.

It seems that Grothe's work points up the need to provide children with a rich background of experiences before they try to write in any original manner. Such experiences would include discussions and examples of the use of words to establish an atmosphere, identify a character, build toward a climax, and perhaps surprise the reader with an unexpected ending. Unlike the advice of many successful novelists who urge that one should write about the people and events around him, it

---

[27] Henry T. Fillmer, "The Construction and Experimental Application of a Programmed Course in Verb Usage for Grade Four" (Unpublished Ph.D. Dissertation, Ohio University, Athens, Ohio, 1962).

[28] Henry T. Fillmer, "Programmed Instruction in the Elementary School," *The Elementary School Journal*, 63 (January, 1963), 200.

seems that 10- to 12-year-olds feel freer and more secure when they can write about the imagined, the unreal.[29]

EFFECTIVE TEACHING

Miss Davis had posted on the classroom bulletin board the reports written by her third grade pupils. They had been invited to write about an experience which they would like to share with the other children. She helped them with the new words which they needed to use in their reports. These are examples of the pupils' writings:

> I like to visit Jimmy. Jimmy is my cousin. He lives on a farm in Missouri. I ride Sugar. Sugar is a pony. Sometimes we play in the barn. I have fun.

Another example is Randy's report:

> We went to the show last night. It was cold at the drive-in. The show was about cowboys.

Miss Davis found that such reports sometimes provide the basis for oral conversation as the children want to know more about certain reports, and opportunities for reporting personal experiences are entered into with interest.

It is necessary to differentiate between the written report and the original or creative story. The report may or may not have a great deal of interest for other children although it is usually of personal interest to the writer. The story should draw upon the creative abilities of the pupil as he constructs an experience or experiences which contain some type of plot and involve the climactic element. Both types of written activities should have a place in the language program and both should receive guidance from the teacher.

It is apparent that some teachers have an inadequate concept of creative writing, and although there has been much said about creative writing experiences, frequently there is a lack of definition of the creative aspect. McKee has stated that creative writing "always includes ideas which represent the writer's reaction to the situation or experience about

---

[29] Barbara F. Grothe, *Literary Models and Children's Writing* (unpublished project report, Nebraska Curriculum Development Center; Lincoln, Nebraska: University of Nebraska, 1965).

which he writes."[30] Thus it is apparent that a friendly letter may contain the creative element or a poem may lack the creative element, depending upon the content of the writer's own reactions and expressions.

Where Does Spelling Belong?

There has been some disagreement among educators as to the place of spelling in the curriculum. It is doubtful that anyone has argued that spelling does not belong; rather the issue has been centered upon the place of formal spelling in the classroom of today. Should spelling be taught during separate periods throughout the week? Should spelling be taught along with reading in order that children learn to spell the new words in their reading vocabularies? Patton suggests that words children learn to spell should first be in their reading vocabularies.[31] Or should spelling be taught during the penmanship period? These questions, and others of this sort, have been voiced frequently by classroom teachers, and it is doubtful that complete answers can be supplied on the basis of research evidence. On one point there is strong agreement: *children must acquire spelling skills if they are to be able to express themselves through writing.*

How Do Children Learn to Spell?

As is the case with other areas of learning, it is difficult to determine just how various children learn to spell. It is a safe assumption that children differ in their approaches to the learning of spelling as much as they differ in reading and arithmetic. In order to find out by what means and with what materials children learn to spell in an efficient manner, the emphasis in spelling research has been placed upon the various approaches and methods which seem to work best, and upon the determination of those words which children *need* to spell.

It is possible that some children may have special ability for remembering "mental pictures" of words in the spelling list. Perhaps other children find it necessary to think through the sound elements of a word before attempting to spell it. Occasionally the teacher may work with children who seem to have no particular approach to spelling and thus

---

[30] McKee, *op. cit.*, p. 209.
For a presentation concerning the difference between reports and stories, see Paul McKee and M. Lucille Harrison, *English For Meaning—3* (Boston: Houghton Mifflin Co., 1958).
[31] David H. Patton and Eleanor M. Johnson, *Spelling for Word Mastery, Teacher's Manual* (enlarged edition; Columbus, Ohio: Charles E. Merrill Publishing Co., 1963), p. 1.

write any combination of letters that comes to mind. Thus, an important part of spelling instruction is the recognition by the teacher of the spelling procedures being used by the children.

Hanna and Moore[32] have stressed the importance of the child's hearing his own speech sounds and associating them with printed and written symbols. Speech development and good speech habits then must be looked upon as valuable assets in the learning of spelling. Teachers at all levels, particularly in the early years, must provide opportunities for practice of proper speech and should guide the child toward a consciousness of the different sounds in the spoken words. Such experiences should help bridge the gap between the child's spoken language and the language which he must put into written symbols through spelling.

Which Words Should Be Learned?

It may seem to be an extreme understatement when certain authorities suggest that the child should learn to spell those words which he needs to know how to spell. There may be some danger in oversimplifying this approach inasmuch as the spelling needs of any person cannot be ascertained at all times. As Dolch has pointed out: "Life spelling needs go far beyond any list that may be taught in school."[33]

The classroom teacher cannot rely entirely upon the mastery of the spelling list as the major objective of her instructional effort. The Denver[34] course of study for English has suggested that the child must master the words he uses very often and the words he uses less frequently. In addition, he must know where to locate correct spellings for words used only occasionally.[35]

Dolch has stated that ". . . 2,000 words have been found to include 95 per cent of adult writing."[36] However, he has further stated that: "the small percentage covered by the 'less common' words is equally, if not more, important."[37]

The investigation of spelling books which was made by Wise[38] seems to point out the lack of agreement as to the "common" words which

---

[32] Paul R. Hanna and James T. Moore, Jr., "Spelling—From Spoken Word to Written Symbol," *The Elementary School Journal*, 53 (February, 1953), 48-51.

[33] Edward William Dolch, *Better Spelling* (Champaign, Ill.: The Garrard Press, 1942), p. 22.

[34] "A Program in English" (Denver, Colorado, Public Schools, 1953) pp. 312-13.

[35] *Ibid.*

[36] Dolch, *op. cit.*, p. 17.

[37] *Ibid.*, p. 18.

[38] Carl T. Wise, "Selection and Gradation of Words in Spelling," *Elementary School Journal*, 34 (June, 1934), 754-66.

children should learn to spell. Although the spelling test publishers each claimed that their books contained the 3,000-4,000 commonest words, Wise[39] found that the combined lists from these books contained more than 13,000 words. The classroom teacher may be faced with a challenging task if she attempts to determine which 3,000 of these 13,000 words should be taught as the commonest and most used.

Of all the words included in the twenty spelling books in the Wise study, slightly fewer than 900 words were common to all spellers.[40] There can be little doubt that these words represent frequently used words that should be included for study in the elementary school.

Horn's study[41] of adult writing vocabularies revealed that 1,000 different words make up about 90 per cent of all written material. It would appear that spelling lists which teach 4,000 words for the elementary school spelling program must present many words that are hardly common or frequently used by either adults or children.

Perhaps the interest in spelling which is expressed by parents, businessmen, and others, is responsible for the extensive spelling lists provided for school use. It is not uncommon to find spelling texts which contain more than 4,500 words for the elementary school program.[42] The teacher should not permit the presence of long lists of words to prevent her from providing instruction which will help individual children who are having difficulty. It is infinitely more important that the sixth grade child be able to spell the 1,000 words which appear in the second and third grade lists, than to devote his efforts to mastery of the less commonly used words found at the sixth grade level. For the able speller extended challenges and growth are certainly desirable. For the poor speller the common words should be his concern in spelling at any grade level.

Certain advocates of spelling as a functional skill have suggested that the child's word list should be made up of words that are misspelled in daily written work. Others have recommended that the teacher draw upon words from the content areas of science, geography and the like for spelling instruction.

Blitz[43] has reported on an experimental situation in which the spelling program was individualized to help children write correctly the words misspelled on papers and the words commonly used by children and

---

[39] *Ibid.*

[40] *Ibid.*

[41] Ernest Horn, "The Curriculum for the Gifted: Some Principles and an Illustration," *Twenty-Third Yearbook of the National Society for the Study of Education*, Part I (Chicago: N.S.S.E., 1924), p. 87.

[42] Gerald A. Yoakam and Seward E. Daw, *Manual for Learning to Spell* (Boston: Ginn and Co., 1956), p. 3.

[43] Theodore F. Blitz, "An Experiment in Individualized Spelling," *Elementary English*, 31 (November, 1954), 403-07.

adults rather than words in spelling book lists. Skinner[44] has reported on a "creative" approach to spelling by which children came to be aware of the words which they needed to learn to spell and built their spelling lists with such words, thus keeping the spelling program close to the actual needs of children.

It is necessary that the teacher be familiar with spelling lists,[45] for the grade level, in order that the "incidental" or "practical" approach to spelling does not result in lists of words that will be of little importance. For example, the geography teacher may think that the word *aborigine* is an excellent one for the local spelling list. From the health lesson may come the words *aorta* and *pharynx*.

What Are Some Problems in Teaching Spelling?

Generally, spelling instruction involves diagnosing the individual's spelling problems and then assisting him to develop more effective approaches to spelling. Furness[46] has proposed that any child of normal intelligence can learn to spell with a minimum of difficulty and that spelling failures are unnecessary. Such a proposal places a heavy responsibility upon the teacher to insure: (1) that the spelling list is appropriate, (2) that the daily or weekly spelling list is not formidable or hopeless for each individual, (3) that the child's spelling difficulties have been carefully assessed and assistance toward improvement is being provided.

It is important that spelling instruction be based upon the interest, confidence, and desire of children to spell correctly.[47] The child for whom spelling is a confusing mystery is not likely to approach his task with enthusiasm and confidence. The emotional factors must also be considered in spelling as in other learning tasks.

Sandmeyer has written that "research in the field leads us to the probable conclusion that perfect spellers are born, not made."[48] She states, however, that poor spellers can become better spellers with proper help.

One might ask, "If it is impossible to teach in school all the words which may be needed in adult writing, what should the teacher do?" It is here that the teacher must plan and provide experiences in the use of

---

[44] Blanche Skinner, "Spelling—A Part of the Language Arts Program," *Elementary English*, 31 (February, 1954), 79-81.

[45] B. R. Buckingham and E. W. Dolch, *A Combined Word List* (Boston: Ginn and Co., 1936); Henry Rinsland, *A Basic Vocabulary for Elementary School Children* (New York: The Macmillan Co., 1945).

[46] Edna Lue Furness, "Some Do's and Do Not's for Spelling," *Elementary English*, 31 (November, 1954), 407.

[47] *Ibid.*, p. 408.

[48] Katharine H. Sandmeyer, "Spelling: Help or Hindrance?" *Elementary English*, 35 (January, 1958), 44.

phonetic elements in spelling. Although it is true that spelling rules have their exceptions, it is also true that the words of many spelling lists for school use are quite consistent in their adherence to "regular" spelling from the speech sound.[49]

Hanna and Moore[50] have reported that more than 80 per cent of the consonant blends and speech consonants have one spelling. These writers[51] also reported that nearly 75 per cent of the vowel sounds are spelled by their "regular letter representations" in a majority of the cases. For example, the vowel "o" as in "hope," "pole," and other syllables ending in the silent "e", is spelled by its letter representation.

It would seem then that spelling instruction should be based upon (1) lists of commonly used words, (2) careful attention to individual learning problems, (3) pupil motivation and interest in spelling, (4) functional relationship to other language arts areas, and (5) attention and instruction in the use of visual, auditory, and kinesthetic avenues in learning to spell.

What Is Effective Spelling Instruction?

The teacher who would do an effective job in the teaching of spelling must avoid the use of one method of instruction to the exclusion of others. Although it is generally agreed that it is important for the child to associate the correct letters with the sound of a word, it is necessary to give attention to the visual and kinesthetic approach to spelling. In fact, the great amount of attention that has been devoted to relationships between errors of speech and spelling may have been overdone. Carrell and Pendergast,[52] as a result of a controlled experiment with speech defectives and speech normals, concluded that there does not seem to be any positive relationship between phonetic disabilities and spelling deficiences. This does not minimize the role of auditory factors in spelling, but it does suggest that phonetic defects in speech do not affect spelling achievement significantly.

An illustration is offered to show the organization of the spelling program in the classroom, making it possible to work more effectively with the individual problems in the room.

The school system in which Miss Ellis teaches provides all classrooms above first grade with "basic" spelling textbooks. The textbook for this

---

[49] Hanna and Moore, *op. cit.*, p. 7.
[50] *Ibid.*, p. 9.
[51] *Ibid.*, p. 8.
[52] James Carrell and Kathleen Pendergast, "An Experimental Study of the Possible Relation Between Errors of Speech and Spelling," *Journal of Speech and Hearing Disorders*, 19 (September, 1954), 327-34.

fourth grade presents, on the average, thirteen words in the weekly spelling list. Miss Ellis does not require that all children study the thirteen or fourteen words on the list. There is John with an I. Q. of 78 who has extreme difficulty with spelling. Miss Ellis directs John's spelling efforts toward spelling of the three or four words in the list which have highest frequency of use. She is concerned throughout the week with John's misspelling of certain "service" words such as *from, over,* and the like. John approaches his spelling tasks by writing the words in cursive form on the chalkboard and then tracing over each word with his fingers as he pronounces the word softly to himself. John is concentrating his efforts on a spelling job that is realistic to him. The thirteen or fourteen word list was only confusing to him.

Fred does not have the difficulties experienced by John. It is not unusual that Fred spells all the words on the list correctly on the "exploratory" or "pre-test" on Monday. Miss Ellis does not have Fred devoting his efforts to the study of words of which he has mastery. Instead, Fred is developing his own list of personal spelling errors taken from his written work. He finds that a number of his written errors are due to poor letter formation and he works on that part of his spelling—a writing problem.

Miss Ellis recognizes that spelling is a functional skill. She regards spelling instruction as being important only when it helps children improve and become proficient in written communication. The weekly spelling list is not a pill to be given to all children as a "cure" for the able and the problem "spellers." To Miss Ellis, the word list provides a point of departure from which she helps children meet their own difficulties and challenges in spelling.

Increasing attention is being given to the contribution of spelling-related experiences to the total language growth of the child. A small amount of preparation by the teacher can add interest and enrichment to the spelling work. Some of the words in every spelling list will have unusual origins; they may have evolved through various spellings before becoming accepted in the present form. Word-building games can provide motivation and fun as the children seek to discover how meanings and forms have changed over many years as a by-product of technological development. This may provide as fascinating a field of inquiry as do the words which have fallen by the way. This is not to detract from the major functional purpose of spelling instruction, but it is obvious that the nature of spelling instruction provides numerous opportunities to motivate and enrich learning about the language.

A very effective way to help children to learn to spell has been proposed by Thomas Horn, who has found that the teacher-dictated, pupil-corrected lesson brings rapid improvement. Replications of the Horn study have shown that the method is also effective with older pupils and adults. This plan calls for the teacher to dictate the list of words to the pupils, then to dictate the correct spelling of each word while each child corrects his own list, drawing a line through each misspelled word and writing the correct spelling beside it. This approach does not disregard the usual attention to the pupil's needs and abilities, but as an approach to learning new words, it has much to commend it. The self-corrective aspect is helpful, particularly in view of the time-worn practice of having children exchange spelling papers for correction. It is difficult to see the value of exchanging papers if the objective is to help each youngster recognize his own spelling errors and to practice the correct form immediately.

How Is Oral Language Developed?

The effective use of oral language depends upon having (1) something to say of interest or importance, (2) a pattern of grammatical usage that makes the speech meaningful, and (3) control of the speech mechanism. Teachers are concerned with all of these aspects of effective oral communication and recognize that oral language is developed away from school as well as in the classroom. In many respects it would seem that the teacher must depend upon family and community for the reinforcement and maintenance of good speaking habits taught in school.

In the section of this chapter which dealt with language development in young children, the early appearance of meaning in gestures and vocalizations was discussed. It is from the early experiences and conceptual background that the child is able to move toward a versatile use of speech symbols.

A number of studies have been made on the growth of speaking vocabularies of children.[53] From them it appears that the typical six-year-old has a speaking vocabulary of from 2,000 to 2,500 words. By sixth grade this vocabulary size will have increased to more than 7,000 words.[54] It should be noted that a child's listening vocabulary far exceeds his spoken or written vocabulary.[55]

The teacher of kindergarten and first grade children should provide abundantly for the use of the speaking vocabularies of these pupils. During conversation periods the teacher can make tentative judgments con-

---

[53] Medorah E. Smith, *An Investigation of the Development of the Sentence and Extent of Vocabulary in Young Children* (Iowa City, Iowa: University of Iowa, 1926), p. 54.

[54] Lewis M. Terman, *The Measurement of Intelligence* (Boston: Houghton Mifflin Co., 1916), p. 226.

[55] Thorp, *op. cit.*, p. 245.

cerning the speech development of the children long before vocabulary can be observed in reading and writing. Enrichment of the speaking vocabularies can proceed rapidly in the early elementary grades even though the reading vocabulary will grow much slower by comparison. Speaking and listening constitute a major part of the child's language activity at all age levels. Thus modern classroom practices point to the values of encouraging children to make effective use of oral language instead of stifling speech development.

How May Acceptable Speech Be Taught?

Children will learn acceptable speech habits through hearing and using speech that promotes this objective. Some persons have suggested that no amount of formal instruction in good speech and correct usage can be as effective as a good language environment. Although this may be true, the classroom teacher cannot ignore the need for speech improvement. She may provide opportunities for informal conversation before classes begin. She may plan discussion sessions in which children address one another and are not limited to question-and-answer responses.

It is important that the teacher observe correct usage and employ desirable speech habits. The teacher who shouts at children cannot expect them to admire this practice. When children cannot hear the teacher with the "too quiet" voice they must not be expected to remain attentive and interested in what she is saying. The teacher's voice may well reflect her confidence and competence as she works with children. Children are quick to take note of irregularities in speech and usage. The teacher can provide valuable speech learnings through her own practices. An atmosphere of inquiry and alertness may well be a trademark of the classroom, if oral language is to be fully developed. There is no reason why the fourth grade teacher should not refer her own questions concerning correct usage to the children for solution, and the children should be mutually observant of correct usage.

One may occasionally encounter a teacher who looks upon herself as the only source of learning. Insofar as oral language is concerned, nothing could be more incorrect. The language of the home and neighborhood has provided the standard of usage for several years before the child comes to school, and it remains forceful thereafter. Children and parents do not like to have the teacher label them "illiterate" because of poor usage which may be prevalent and acceptable in the community. However, the teacher must remember that the American people have become quite mobile in modern times and children are brought to the classroom with many speech patterns which are very acceptable in certain localities.

The development of pleasant speech and correct usage will be realized only to the extent that the child becomes aware of a need or a goal in this respect. Drill in isolation on the "have been's" and "this is I" cannot be expected to result in good practice unless the child perceives the value and purpose in changing his usage.[56]

Some persons become quite concerned, and rightly so, because of the seemingly wide prevalence of poor usage among students who have had instruction in the use of their native language for 12 years and yet continue to express themselves incorrectly. Indeed, this is cause for concern among teachers of all youth; however, it should be remembered that speech is acquired and that even poor usage has been learned. The teacher must be aware of the favorable conditions for acceptable speech development and correct usage. Some suggestions for establishing such conditions are:

1. Provide opportunities for informal classroom conversation.
2. Involve the pupils in setting standards for good speech.
3. Provide opportunities for conversation in small working groups.
4. Provide situations where pupils report, plan, and discuss in a large group setting.
5. Arrange periods for telling stories and oral reading for enjoyment which are helpful in speech development.
6. Use choral speaking experiences, especially for the speech defective or the timid child.
7. Provide experiences in dramatizations.
8. Include opportunities to appear before large pupil and adult audiences as an individual or member of a group.

Obviously, the teacher who is friendly and is aware of the speech and usage problems of the pupils becomes an important, basic factor of a desirable classroom situation. In fact, certain authorities assert that the teacher who is respected and admired by her pupils is likely to influence their behavior in speech just as she influences other forms of behavior.[57]

Acceptable oral communication has serious implications for happy and successful living long after the individual has left the schoolroom. Securing and holding a job, participating in the civic affairs of the community, establishing satisfying social contacts, and providing a favorable environment for family life are some of the adult activities that require

---

[56] National Council of Teachers of English, *Language Arts for Today's Children* (New York: Appleton-Century-Crofts, Inc., 1954), p. 133.

[57] *Ibid.*, p. 128.

competency in speech. As the teacher views the speech needs of the child, she must be aware of the importance of good foundations for speech development in the school. She will provide opportunities for children to learn good speech by using it at school; she cannot teach good speech through silence and stilted recitation. She must seek a balanced program between opportunities for self-expression in communication and certain restraints placed upon children due to the nature of the organization of the elementary classroom.

TOWARD BETTER LISTENING AND LEARNING

Reading and listening are often referred to as the "intake" phases of communication. Reading is a means of listening through the use of printed symbols which represent sound symbols. Information and ideas are "taken in" by reading and listening, and both of these phases of language contribute largely to the leisure activities of many people.

As in speech and writing instruction, the school has definite contributions to make by way of providing opportunities for the development of skills, attitudes and appreciations in reading and listening. Needless to say, reading has received a great deal more attention than has listening as an important part of the child's school program. Recently, however, there has been increased interest in the role of listening in the classroom, and as many classroom situations contain much "teacher talking and children listening," it is timely that teachers should ask themselves, "How may we help children to listen and learn?"

The last sections of this chapter are devoted to the intake phases of language and to the means, materials, and conditions whereby learnings may be efficiently fostered in these areas.

What Is Listening?

Listening is more than sitting quietly in the presence of conversation, music, or other sounds. "Constructive listening in the classroom and elsewhere involves attention, interpretation, selection, and the responsibility for the selection or rejection of ideas."[58] It must be obvious to every parent and teacher that there are many times when children hear what has been said but have not been listening to the extent that they understood or responded. Perhaps it is fortunate that children are able to turn off many of the sounds that come from radio, television, playmates, par-

---

[58] *Language Arts*, op. cit., p. 27.

ents and teachers else they would be bombarded with such a multiplicity of ideas, commands, and suggestions that utter confusion would result.

Fostering better listening habits. The problem that confronts the teacher is one of directing the child's listening skills toward the selectivity and evaluation that is necessary in and out of the schoolroom. The teacher can do much to provide conditions favorable to the building of good listening habits. A few suggestions are mentioned here.[59]

1. Informal seating provides for better listening conditions.
2. The activities of the group are planned so that children have reasons for speaking and listening; confusion does not foster effective listening habits.
3. The content of the material used is on the maturity level of the listeners. Vocabulary and sentence structure must also be suited to the particular age level.
4. Opportunities should be provided for children to talk about the things they have listened to.
5. Children are given opportunities to listen more to one another rather than to teacher-pupil conversation.

The teacher must use clear, distinct speech, be sensitive to the interest span of the child listener, and observe closely for indications of poor comprehension. Unfortunately, there remain a few teachers who believe that their job has been well done as long as they talk and require pupils to sit and "listen." One of the writers visited a fourth grade classroom where the children had been making their own story problems for arithmetic. The class had been asked to listen as one of the pupils read her problem. She read so rapidly that one boy asked that she repeat the problem. Immediately the teacher interceded and informed the lad that he "should have been listening." Actually, it seemed that the boy had been listening quite closely and had concluded that he could not follow such a rapid presentation of number situations.

Children help themselves. Children may well be encouraged to build their own standards for good listening. In second and third grade classrooms where teachers are concerned with good listening habits, it is not unusual to notice posters which present the children's "Listening List." Courtesy for the speaker is included as a part of good listening and this means that interruptions by teacher or other children is not a commendable method for developing either effective listening or speaking. Younger pupils may develop a few standards for listening by remembering:

---

[59] National Council of Teachers of English, *op. cit.*, pp. 84-5.

1. We do not interrupt others.
2. We listen to what others say.
3. We do not play or read when we should listen.

Older pupils may approach the matter of good listening habits in a much more detailed and mature manner. For example, a listening guide of sixth grade children may include the following suggestions:[60]

1. Listen thoughtfully to others who have something important to say.
2. Pick out the main ideas of the speakers.
3. Wait until the speaker is finished before agreeing or disagreeing with him.
4. Be considerate of other people as they speak.
5. Try to summarize what the speaker has said.

Listening activities. It would seem that there is no dearth of listening activities in the classroom, particularly since one study indicates that the children spend about half of the school day listening.[61] Corey[62] has reported that the teachers out-talk the children by a comfortable margin, so there is much to listen to in the classroom. Some listening activities that are real to children in terms of purpose are:

1. Listening to songs, poems, stories.
2. Taking part in class discussions.
3. Listening to pupil reports.
4. Preparing and presenting dramatizations.
5. Listening to selected radio programs.
6. Listening to tape recordings of class discussions and the like.
7. Taking part in school assemblies and other large group audience situations.
8. Using the telephone.
9. Following directions.

What Are Some Issues in Listening?

Although it is commonly recognized that children receive much information by listening and that listening is an important part of the class-

[60] National Council of Teachers of English, *op. cit.*, pp. 88-90.
[61] Miriam E. Wilt, "A Study of Teacher Awareness of Listening as a Factor in Elementary Education," *Journal of Educational Research*, 43 (April, 1950), 626-36.
[62] Stephen M. Corey, "The Teachers Outtalk the Pupils," *School Review*, 48 (December, 1940), 745-52.

room situation, there is disagreement as to how listening skills can be taught. Hackett has maintained that "there is not enough evidence that listening can be taught," [63] and that "there is no evidence that knowledge *about* listening contributes to the ability to listen." [64]

Walker[65] has reported on the listening program carried on by the Nashville teachers in which it was found that (1) individuals differ in listening ability; (2) results from listening were higher at elementary school levels than were the results from reading; (3) listening for main ideas ranks high while listening for sequence ranks low.

Hogan[66] has reported that experimentation with fifth and sixth grade pupils revealed that children in the experimental groups made greater improvement in several areas of listening than did the control groups. She concluded that teachers could vastly improve the learning environment of the classroom if they gave as much attention to listening activities as to the other language skills.[67]

As with other learning activities it seems that effective listening habits must be fostered by (1) making listening a part of the regular classroom routine rather than a drill activity; (2) providing listening situations in which children can see a purpose; (3) providing opportunities for children to think critically about the things listened to and to offer their own ideas on the subject.

Listening must be looked upon by teachers as a part of the total language development of children. It is closely related to the speech development of the child, as it brings in ideas and information which form much of the background for speech. Because there is much yet to be learned about the development of listening skills of children, the classroom teacher may wish to attempt some of her own techniques in teaching for better listening and learning. Such experimentation might well be carried out by several teachers in a system-wide cooperative study, such as in the Nashville study.

READING: GATEWAY TO WIDER LEARNINGS

Reading, the process of gaining information and ideas by means of perceiving and responding to visual symbols, constitutes the gateway to

---

[63] Herbert Hackett, "A Null Hypothesis: There is Not Enough Evidence," *Education*, 75 (January, 1955), 349.

[64] *Ibid.*, p. 350.

[65] Lalla Walker, "Nashville Teachers Attack the Problem of Listening," *Education*, 75 (January, 1955), 346.

[66] Ursula Hogan, *An Experiment in Improving the Listening Skills of Fifth and Sixth Grade Pupils* (M.A. study; Berkley, Cal.: University of California, 1953).

[67] *Ibid.*

an almost infinite world of experiences by way of the printed word. Reading is a necessary skill for competent participation in the society of a modern America; it is also the means to hours of pleasure and enriched living with books, newspapers, and magazines. The person who possesses the fundamental reading skills and who has a keen interest in the world about him may recognize no limits to the acquaintances which can be made with people, places, and events in the contemporary world and in the world of history.

Despite the fact that an occasional complaint is raised because many people do not read as much as people allegedly did in the past, the newspapers, magazines, and book publications are at record highs per capita. One source has called attention to the large number of children's publications today as compared with a few years ago, and cited the advent of the children's book editor as an indication of the growing interest and market in juvenile and children's books.[68] If people are not reading as much today as they did twenty or thirty years ago, one must question what is being done with the record publications of all kinds of reading materials.

The elementary school has accepted as one of its major responsibilities the job of helping children learn to read. During the earlier years of American history the teaching of reading was regarded by many persons as the only function of the elementary school teacher. Today the thought that children should start reading as soon as they enter the elementary school is still prevalent in some areas. It is doubtful that anything causes greater concern to the parent than does the failure of his child to read with some success early in first grade. Because of the expectations of children and parents with respect to reading achievements, and because reading is the foundation for the extended learning experiences of children, it is vital that every teacher have a thorough understanding of the mechanics of reading, of the problems encountered by children in reading, and of the role of reading in the total school program. This is applicable to the teacher of older children (fourteen-year-olds) just as it is to the teacher of the six- and seven-year-olds.

What Is Developmental Reading?

Reading instruction must at all times consider three factors: (1) the reading needs of the child at the various age levels; (2) the readiness of the child for the learning of the reading skills; and (3) the capacity of the child. The teacher may look upon these three factors in terms of a series of ever-widening circles, each supporting and giving rise to the others as the individual grows in reading achievement and continues to perceive

---

[68] National Council of the Teachers of English, *op. cit.*, pp. 144-45.

greater needs for reading. Reading is more than a mechanical competency, in that it is a means to fuller living[69] and must be approached as such, if it is to have importance for the child.

A reading program that will provide experiences of a developmental nature must begin with children who come to the school with many types of language backgrounds, and then proceed to guide them through the initial stages of reading and on to the higher levels of independent search for information and ideas which characterizes the mature reader. It is in this area that the teacher must provide leadership in the classroom if each child is to benefit from the type of instructional program that will help him to become an efficient reader.

If the teacher conceives of reading instruction as being a series of steps which must be taken by every child at a certain grade level, the child will remain a secondary consideration, and the developmental reading approach will be neglected. The best teaching will assess the needs, the readiness, and the capacity of each child to move progressively toward reading maturity, and will provide the materials and the instructional activities appropriate for the situation. As the teacher operates in the developmental reading program she will:

1. Recognize and plan for the needs of the individual children.
2. Select and use pertinent materials and activities.
3. Relate the reading program to the total school program.
4. Use methods of flexible grouping for instruction.
5. Provide continuous evaluation of the child's progress in reading.

Depending upon the manner of classification, children probably move through five or six stages of reading development. Russell[70] has set forth six stages of reading development ranging from the pre-reading stage to the advanced stages of reading maturity. For the purposes of this discussion the stages of reading development are classified as follows:

1. Pre-school stage.
2. Initial reading stage.
3. The stage of rapid growth in skills.
4. The stage of growing independence.
5. The mature reading stage.

---

[69] Strickland, *op. cit.*, p. 243.
[70] David H. Russell, *Children Learn to Read* (2nd ed.; Boston: Ginn and Co., 1961), pp. 19-23.

The elementary school teacher will most generally be concerned with the first four of these stages inasmuch as the fifth stage will be approached in senior high school and college. At all levels above the pre-school stage the teacher will work with four broad parts of the total reading process: (1) recognizing printed symbols or words; (2) attaching meaning to the printed words; (3) responding to the words intellectually or emotionally; (4) incorporating into one's experience and person the major parts of that which is read. Allied very closely to the reading process are the competencies in locating information, reporting on material read, using the dictionary and other references, and the like.

A developmental approach to reading instruction places the emphasis upon the child as the learner rather than upon the materials to be read and the skills to be learned. Materials are important, as are reading skills, but they must be adapted to help the child grow into reading competence rather than becoming obstacles in his path. This would seem to be a perfectly obvious approach to reading instruction, yet one first grade teacher offered a response which typifies a common misunderstanding of the developmental reading program: It would be all right to individualize reading instruction so that each child might progress as his needs and abilities permit if it were not for the fact that some children will not get to complete all the basic reading books for the grade.

The pre-school stage. During the pre-school stage of reading development the child builds the backgrounds of experiences which will one day assist him in attaching meaning to printed words. Experiences with picture books and story books may aid the child in understanding that books have stories in them, that books are fun. The language of the home provides the child with a listening and speaking vocabulary which will affect his readiness for understanding the printed vocabulary of books. Of importance during the pre-school years are the social contacts of the child with other children and adults. Social experiences will help the child adjust to the new and stimulating classroom environment.

It is not possible to determine the exact influence of the social, emotional, physical and intellectual factors on the reading process inasmuch as children with all sorts of problems have learned to read. It is safe to assume that emotional instability, social immaturity, and serious physical defects are not going to promote reading skill and may indeed provide obstacles.[71] Therefore, it is necessary that the teacher inform herself as to the pre-school experiences and the health history of the child as he approaches initial experiences with reading.

Most children have developed an awareness of the reading process and have an interest in reading before they enter school. Children are ex-

---

[71] McKim, *op. cit.*, p. 40.

posed to a variety of words on television, cereal boxes, outdoor signs, and the like. The letters which must indeed seem strange to the first grader are not, however, completely foreign to him, because many letters and words have been seen before school age, and many children know that words mean "something."

What Are Some Initial Reading Experiences?

In the kindergarten the child makes long strides toward successful experiences with reading. He makes social adjustments with large numbers of children and acquires a sense of security away from home. He has many experiences with stories in picture books, on records, and from other children and teachers. Working with finger paints, clay, blocks, and toys, the child gains in muscular control and eye-hand coordination.

By the time the child enters the first grade he has had valuable experiences that have contributed to his readiness for reading. The teacher must not assume, however, that all children are ready to begin reading because they have completed an excellent kindergarten program. The kindergarten program may have fostered total child development in terms of each child's own developmental pattern, but it can neither force all children to fixed levels of readiness nor bring individual development to a common level.

Hildreth[72] has suggested several traits associated with readiness for reading, including: (1) mental maturity of about 6½ years; (2) linguistic maturity as evidenced in the ability to understand a story; (3) interest in stories and books; (4) breadth of pre-school experiences; (5) social and emotional adjustment; (6) auditory and visual maturity; (7) motor control and coordination. Inspection of these traits reveals that readiness for reading is not unlike readiness for other school experiences, and should not be regarded as a program separate and apart from the total learning program.

The question which confronts the teacher is: What can be done for children who are not ready to read in first grade? A careful assessment of the areas in which the child seems to lack readiness will reveal, generally, where attention must be given. Obvious problems of social and emotional maladjustment are often recognizable, and the teacher may take steps to determine what might be done to remedy or relieve the problem. However, mental immaturity does not lend itself to correction and the teacher may be perplexed as to what should be done for the first

---

[72] Gertrude Hildreth, *Teaching Reading* (New York: Holt, Rinehart & Winston, Inc., 1958), pp. 165-66.

grader who has a mental age of four years. In such instances delayed reading may be beneficial *if the child is provided learning experiences that will foster readiness for later school learnings.* When delayed reading means an idle waiting until the child becomes older, chronologically and mentally, there is reason to question its value, because the pupil may acquire negative attitudes from such a *laissez faire* approach just as through reading frustration and failure.

In many first grades the initial reading experiences are often related to daily interests and activities of children. Cards bearing the names of objects in the classroom, children's names, and simply-printed instructions are some of the devices employed to build a sight vocabulary. Regarding the use of teacher constructed materials, it is necessary to bear in mind that story charts or experience charts should be used only with great care because of the dangers involved in uncontrolled vocabulary, tendency of children to memorize rather than read the charts, and because they exact a great amount of teacher time in return for doubtful results. McKee has thoroughly discussed the advantages and the disadvantages of using the story charts for early reading experiences, and has suggested that they lead themselves better to use in other language development activities.[73]

Emphasis in the initial stages of reading development is upon reading for meaning, and attention to sound elements of words is usually directed toward beginning letter sounds and observing endings. The use of context clues will serve the child as he goes about the task of identifying words in a story. The use of configuration clues is probably limited largely to the observation of the words' "length and shortness," inasmuch as many words appear very similar in their general outline. It is likely that many words which have seemed to lend themselves to identification by the use of the configuration clue have actually been identified because of the unusual occurrence of letter patterns, such as *Mississippi, elephant,* and the like.

It is a rather common practice in the first grade to divide the class into several groups for the purpose of reading instruction. Such grouping may result in (1) an accelerated group of pupils who are ready to begin reading and who make rapid progress, (2) a group of so-called average pupils who progress at a rate typical of most six- and seven-year-olds, and (3) a group of children who are not ready to participate in a formalized reading program. There is no reason why the teacher *must* have three reading groups; she may have four or five or two, depending upon

---

[73] Paul McKee, *The Teaching of Reading* (Boston: Houghton Mifflin Co., 1948), pp. 216-24.

the nature of the reading needs of the class and the size of the class enrollment.

The children who need extended pre-reading experiences should be provided many opportunities to grow in the abilities associated with reading. They should have experiences with picture books, story puzzles, storytelling and sharing, social experiences with other children, reading-room signs and charts (when possible), and many other similar experiences. The child who does not seem to be ready to make progress in reading is too often forced into reading from pre-primers and such to the neglect of those experiences he actually needs.

Children who make typical progress in first grade may use pre-primers, primers and the first level reading books of a basal series. Teachers will do well to provide many interesting and purposeful reading activities even if the children can read from books. Although the basal reading approach has much to contribute to the instructional program, it is important to extend reading experiences as much as possible, rather than allow the basal reading materials to form a ceiling for the child's growth.

A variety of reading materials must be made available to children in the accelerated group. The practice of forbidding the gifted reader to use reading materials above his particular grade level is often defended on two counts: (1) The materials of higher grades should not be used because the child will be bored when he enters that grade and finds familiar material to be read; (2) The child, though an excellent reader, must wait until a later grade to develop certain skills for reading more advanced material. *Neither defense is justifiable in terms of a developmental approach to reading instruction.* Such a child should be provided more than regular basal reading materials; he should receive instruction in whatever reading skills he needs and is capable of using. *As for the problem of using third grade material with second grade pupils, it must be remembered that materials exist to be used when needed, regardless of grade level.*

Certainly, if the needs of the gifted and the slow learner are to be met, teachers must provide suitable materials and instruction for all pupils. To force the gifted child into a slow pace of reading growth is as unsound as forcing the slow learner to conform to the activities and materials of the more advanced readers.

Miss H. was a first grade teacher who could not accept the fact that some first grade pupils may not read all of the "required" materials by year's end. Here is an account of her reading plan.

Miss H. had placed her first grade pupils into three reading groups. Each group proceeded through the basal series at different rates. The immature group was some three months "behind" the advanced reading group. However, Miss H. believed that even the slowest child should go through all the basal materials for the grade if he were to be promoted to second grade. In practice her grouping of children did not truly provide the type of developmental program needed; it only postponed facing the problem until near the end of the year. Although Miss H. recognized individual differences during the year she somehow expected them to disappear at year's end. The advanced group was never permitted to read second grade level materials from supplementary series because that must be saved for the next grade.

What may appear to some persons to be a maintaining of "high" standards for the class is often a denial of appropriate educational opportunity to slower and brighter children alike.

A teacher in a modern elementary school who is giving direction to the emerging curriculum is one who seek to satisfy the needs of all pupils. Mrs. Wood's class illustrates this kind of a reading plan.

Mrs. Wood, a teacher of 28 third-graders, has carefully tested the reading ability of each child in her room with the basal reading test; her own judgment based on having each child sight-read from books of varying levels and take a standardized test. She then places her children in as many reading groups as best meet their needs. To Mrs. Wood, there is nothing magic about the number "three." Those children who were the "top" readers and were ready for material above the grade level were permitted to read at that level. However, Mrs. Wood was certain that sufficient reinforcement activities had been used before permitting children to go on to more difficult reading material. At the same time, Mrs. Wood was also providing reading material on a second-grade level for those pupils who were at the lower end of the scale in reading. In fact, she sought to have just the right reading matter that would challenge the ability of each child.

Rapid growth in skills. As the child enters *this stage* of reading development he will possess a sight vocabulary of several hundred words, normally the vocabulary of his earlier reading materials and other commonly used words to which he has been frequently exposed. At this stage he will know the names of the letters of the alphabet and show evidence of readiness to associate the various parts of a word with their proper sounds. This is necessary if the child is to grow toward independence in figuring out strange words by sounding the letters and letter combinations of the word. Generally, the child is ready to work with sound elements by the second grade, but there will be some first-grade youngsters who will be aware of sound elements and similarities.[74]

---

[74] E. K. Sexton and J. S. Herron, "The Newark Phonics Experiment," *Elementary School Journal*, 28 (1929), 690-701.

Children must be able to apply their reading skills toward the securing of information; they should like to read for enjoyment; they must be able to comprehend what is read; and they need to be growing in word recognition skill and vocabulary, if they are to progress toward independence in reading. In many schools the reading instruction is organized around a basal program, in order that growth in the reading skills and vocabulary will be continuous. Related activities and the use of experience charts are often used in a supplementary or complementary fashion.

Oral reading will continue to be a part of the reading experience in the second and third grades even as in the first grade. However, more emphasis is placed upon silent reading, inasmuch as the individual may be expected to do most of his reading silently since vocalization only slows up the reading process. Many opportunities may be found in which children may read orally for the entertainment of the class or to cite information needed. In all audience situations the child should first read silently that which he will read orally later.

As children develop independence in reading they usually do more reading of an individual nature. In the other activities of the school day there is a need for various kinds of information from several sources, and the child can put his reading tools to work. The teacher is in a position to provide stimulation for the expanding reading interests of children through planning activities that require wide reading and by making available the books and other materials needed. A book shelf or library corner in the room is, of course, a ready invitation to the child to read and should be provided.

Independence in reading. The reading demands of the typical elementary school become increasingly numerous from the fourth grade on, insofar as the ability to read a variety of content matter is concerned. Social studies books, science books, arithmetic texts and the like present a wide vocabulary to the pupil. In much of his school work, the child must be able to locate information, select main ideas from material, read, think critically about what he has read, seek additional information at certain times, and handle the word analysis skills with competence.

Obviously, the teacher does not find all fourth and fifth grade children able to perform in the manner described. Since some junior-high pupils may be deficient in certain reading skills, it is important that the teacher of the nine- to thirteen-year-old pupils remember that individual differences do not disappear at fourth grade. Children need instruction and opportunities to develop reading skills, even though they have been reading quite well for several years.

A fifth grade teacher met some of the reading needs of her class by arranging for small group instruction in certain areas. For example, a few pupils were having difficulty with syllabification of polysyllabic words. The children knew the individual letter sounds, but they had difficulty in trying to pronounce a strange word. Since most of the class did not have this trouble, the teacher formed a small group for several 15-minute sessions of working on this problem. She followed this plan throughout the year and reported that it was possible to keep the large group working together in many areas by providing for special needs through small group instruction.

Some persons have suggested that a reading class is unnecessary in the schedule of the sixth or seventh grade room, since the child is required to read extensively in other subject areas. In some situations a literature period is called "reading class." Actually, reading occurs in many situations outside of the "reading class," and it would be unfortunate if this were not so. However, the fact remains that the skills of reading become involved and do deserve continued attention at all levels, including high school. This is true for the slow learner and the average pupil alike. Rapid reading with high comprehension does not mean that the child needs no instruction in organizing material that has been read or in using the diacritical markings in a dictionary. Teacher responsibility for adequate instruction in the reading skills continues throughout the school program, and it is of little importance whether she uses history material or science material in teaching these skills. It is necessary that the teacher be thoroughly grounded in the reading skills and in their application if she is to work successfully with the reading needs of children. Until the teacher feels completely confident in assessing the varying reading needs at the higher grade levels, she may rely upon a basal series for the continuity of the skill-building program.

As the teacher works with children who have gained independence in the reading skills, she will be aware of the need for continuing the development of good tastes and continuing interest in reading. It is a bit discouraging to read news reports to the effect that the favorite reading material of the G. I. is the comic book! However accurate such reports may be, it is certainly desirable that adults discover and enjoy the wealth of good reading which is available through public libraries, book stores and book clubs.

Appreciation for poetry and good literature is not something that may be taught in several lessons; it must be the object of teacher concern from the early years of school. Relating poetry and prose to the regular activities of the classroom should do much to foster an interest in and appreciation of the better literature. Reading for enjoyment must be a part of the planned program for improvement of reading tastes and appreciation. Good literature provides motivation for extending reading experiences. Some reading series have been completely designed to develop class-wide reading skill and literary appreciation.[75] Through literature children can enjoy certain kinds of vicarious experiences into the world of the unreal or they may learn the folklore of their heritage. The teacher who uses every reading experience as an opportunity to test for comprehension, word recognition, and the like may expect the children to miss the fun that should be a part of reading.[76]

What Are Some Issues in Reading Instruction?

In the area of reading instruction, the issues and developments, both old and new, may be classified in terms of teaching procedures and materials and organization of the instructional program. For example, the matter of including instruction in the phonics of reading, occasionally seized upon as a weak link in reading programs, is a consideration that has to do with teaching procedures. On the other hand, the organizational aspects of the reading program are brought to the forefront with proposals for use of the Joplin Plan or the individualized approach to reading instruction which is discussed later in this chapter.

Some of the more challenging issues and developments will be presented here in order to acquaint the student of elementary education with the "growing edges" of the field of reading, although no attempt will be made to predict or prejudge the direction which change will take.

Reading materials. The criticism has been made in various quarters to the effect that commonly used instructional materials[77] do not interest and challenge the children today. The "pale" primers are cited as examples, and the use of fiction materials throughout the elementary school reading program is viewed by some authorities as a waste of valuable teaching time. "Why cannot the child learn something as he refines his reading skills?" is the question raised.

In the first instance, it must be stated that the pre-primers and primers do not provide material which challenges the thinking of the typical six-year-old pupil who has become accustomed to television plots, travel experiences and the like. However, it is only fair to point out that the problem of introducing children to the reading process involves a growing familiarity with printed symbols in a variety of combinations. Whether

---

[75] See *Treasury of Literature* readers (Columbus, Ohio: Charles E. Merrill Publishing Co.).

[76] See National Council of Teachers of English, *op. cit.*, pp. 55-63, for an excellent discussion of pupil interest and appreciation of literature.

[77] Max Rafferty, "Suffer, Little Children," *Phi Delta Kappan*, 38 (December, 1956), 90.

the child begins by learning a stock of words by sight or by learning the sounds of certain letter combinations, the process must move from the simple to the complex. Nonetheless, the matter of content in the reading textbooks is an issue of increasing importance, and the teachers and curriculum planners must give thought to this.

With reference to the use of fiction materials in grades 4-5-6, there are many persons who would have the reading skills and study skills developed in the subject areas of science, social studies, and arithmetic. The use of basal reading materials would be restricted to those pupils who continued to experience difficulties with the simplest phases of reading.

Individualized reading. A development that has gained strength since 1955 is the organization of reading on an individualized basis rather than on a small group basis. Veatch,[78] among others, has been an early student and advocate of an individualized reading program which provides for reading growth with the use of reading materials selected for each child, separately, and progresses at the child's own rate, independently of group or classroom progress.

Individualized reading programs do not eliminate all group work, inasmuch as there are opportunities for dramatizations, interest group work and the like. The main emphasis is upon complete individualization of the program wherein the pupil builds his own reading skills, and a careful record is maintained for each child in order that effective teacher planning for individual growth is assured. One of the questions which is pertinent to reading instruction is whether small group instruction is not as adequate and more economical in terms of teaching time required than is individualized reading. There are many hours of the day when the child may pursue his unique interests and further sharpen his reading skills without complete individualization of basal reading instruction, so the critics say.

Joplin Plan. Another organizational development for the instruction in reading is the Joplin Plan, so named as a result of its early use in Joplin, Missouri. In essence, the Joplin Plan provides for an approach to homogeneous grouping by assigning pupils in grades 4-5-6 to an instructional group made up of children from these three grades who are judged to have similar competencies and problems in reading growth. After the assigned reading period is over each day, the pupils return to their regular classrooms for other instruction. Numerous school systems have used

---

[78] Jeannette Veatch, *Individualize Your Reading Program* (New York: Putnam, 1959). See also, Paul Witty, "Individualized Reading; A Summary and Evaluation," *Elementary English*, 38 (October, 1959), 65-9.

FIGURE X

*Initial Teaching Alphabet**

    * New York: Initial Teaching Alphabet (i/t/a) Publications, Inc. and Pitman Publishing Corp., 1964.

the Joplin Plan for modified versions of the Plan with various degrees of success.[79] Probably the most serious question deals with the problem in reading which the children face when they return to their regular graded classrooms and meet the tasks of the various subject areas.

---

[79] E. F. Morgan and G. R. Stucker, "Joplin Plan of Reading vs. a Traditional Method," *Journal of Educational Psychology*, 51 (April, 1960), 53-7.

I.T.A. One of the recurring problems in teaching children to read has been related to the irregular relationships in the English language between graphemes and phonemes. The vowel sound in *great, late,* and *pail* is represented by three different graphemes although the phoneme is identical in all three. The Pitman Initial Teaching Alphabet (i/t/a) provides an augmented alphabet which permits the beginning reader to use a system in which any given phoneme is always represented by one grapheme. The augmented alphabet is presented here for your examination.

A number of schools have adopted the i/t/a system and materials which make use of this orthography. As of this writing, there remains a good deal of disagreement among reading authorities concerning the value of using an augmented alphabet such as i/t/a for beginning reading instruction. Research efforts have not been conclusive. At least part of the conflict arises from the purposes for which one would use the i/t/a. The following questions suggest some of the problems involved in deciding upon the merits of i/t/a.

1. Does the use of i/t/a enable children to get off to a quicker start in reading?
2. What kind of difficulties do children encounter when they make the transition to reading materials using the regular alphabet?
3. Are there long-term advantages to children who begin reading with i/t/a either in terms of attitudes toward reading or skills developed by the end of the third or sixth year of school?
4. Is i/t/a helpful to youngsters of varying abilities and levels of readiness?
5. Does i/t/a approach the most critical problem area of reading performance? In other words, is the predominant source of difficulty the phoneme-grapheme irregularity, or is the source one that lies more deeply in the total language make-up of the child?
6. Are the gains, if any, brought about by the use of i/t/a sufficiently significant to merit the time and attention given to it at the expense of other problem areas in reading?

From this discussion you might conclude that the authors are opposed to i/t/a, or to *words in color,* another system which attempts to regularize the phoneme-grapheme relationship for the beginning reader. This is not the case. It seems appropriate for prospective teachers and teachers-in-service to examine the issues involved, raise their own questions, and arrive at their own professional positions.

In the years that lie before today's elementary school teacher, there will appear innovations and issues with respect to the way that reading should be taught, the materials to be used, and the organization of the instructional program. It is desirable that classroom teachers be participants as well as observers of experimentation and research in the continuing problems of reading instruction. In this venture, as in all areas of education, the goal of the program must be kept in sharp focus: that of guiding the child toward mature reading skills and habits by the most efficient means available which are not detrimental to total development of the individual.

Does Foreign Language Instruction Have a Place?

The teaching of a foreign language in the elementary school is not a recent innovation, although relatively few schools have ever included a foreign language in their program. It is interesting to note that in the four years after 1952 when 87 communities had foreign language programs in the grades, 270 additional communities added foreign language to the program of studies.[80] Only 39 foreign language programs had been in operation prior to 1950 and only 29 of these were outside of a campus school.[81]

In certain communities where there is more than one language in common use there may be immediate justification for foreign language instruction in the grades. In every situation, however, the question of teaching a foreign language should be measured against the yardstick of acceptable educational goals and the needs and abilities of children. The advocate of foreign language instruction in the elementary school should advance sound reasons for his proposal. Frequently, foreign language is looked upon as a cultural subject, although few persons seem to recommend Russian or Japanese as the language to serve this purpose. Thompson and Hamalainen[82] have reported that foreign language programs now in existence are usually supported on the basis of one or more of the following purposes:

1. To build better human relations in a given locality.
2. To improve international relations.
3. To develop the child culturally.
4. To prepare for later language training.
5. To provide challenge for the child with high I. Q.

---

[80] K. W. Mildenberger, "Foreign Language in the Grades," *American School Board Journal*, 133 (October, 1956), 25-26.

[81] Anne S. Hoppock, "Foreign Language in the Elementary School," *Education Digest*, 22 (February, 1957), 9-12.

[82] Elizabeth Engle Thompson and Arthur E. Hamalainen, *Foreign Language Teaching in Elementary Schools* (Washington, D. C.: Association for Supervision and Curriculum Development, 1958), pp. 12-18.

With the exception of the first purpose cited here, Thompson and Hamalainen[83] raise serious doubts as to the soundness of these purposes for providing foreign language instruction in the grades.

It is pertinent to consider the relationship of foreign language instruction to the total educational experience of the child. In this regard the materials of instruction and the teacher are of great importance. Foreign language that is taught by a part-time specialist or a language teacher from the high school can hardly be expected to be related to the on-going activities of the children. Materials that approach language development in a piecemeal grammar-analysis fashion do not take into account the matter of natural language development, wherein the need to communicate and to understand are of prime importance.

Mildenberger has reported on certain promising developments with respect to the inclusion of foreign language in the elementary school. Among these are the conversational, functional approach to a second language as contrasted to the older grammatical approach; the planning for continuity of instruction through the elementary grades and into secondary levels; and the recognition of the need for teachers who are competent in the language and prepared to work with young children.[84] Mildenberger also maintains that foreign language is appropriate for elementary school children because it takes advantage of the natural gift for language learning which seems to exist in young children, and it helps develop a broad-minded attitude toward things foreign through an early venture into a different language at a time when attitudes are being molded.[85]

Other authorities who envision a significant role for foreign language in the elementary school have specified that careful planning must be provided to the end that continuity, evaluation, and adequate teaching personnel are insured.[86] Kaulfers suggests that "a foreign language is good to the extent that it contributes to the basic purposes of general education in our time."[87] However, it must be recognized that these purposes may not be the same for all pupils. Perhaps some selection of pupils should be made for foreign language programs.

Certainly the advantages of foreign language instruction for young children should be carefully assessed by each community and its school

---

[83] *Ibid.*, pp. 12-18.

[84] Kenneth W. Mildenberger, "Foreign Language in the Grades," *The American School Board Journal*, 133 (October, 1956), 25-6.

[85] *Ibid.*

[86] Gilbert C. Kettelkamp, "Curriculum Problems in Foreign Languages," *Educational Administration and Supervision*, 41 (November, 1955), 407-15.

[87] Walter V. Kaulfer, "Criteria for a Foreign Language Program," *Clearing House*, 30 (October, 1955), 78-82.

people. It is true that problems of teacher supply in this area are crucial at the present, but it is also true that unused teaching talent is being overlooked by school administrators who would do well to consider the inclusion of a second language at the elementary school level.

In order that the confusion of a progressivism—traditionalism controversy be averted, it is essential that foreign language for children be regarded by parents and school people as something more than a fad or an attempt to inflate the curriculum in an age of satellites. A statement from the Modern Languages Association states the issue thus:

> It is our further judgment that the public should be warned against the faddish element of this movement. No new venture in American education can prosper long without the wholehearted support of parents, teachers, and educational administrators in a given community.[88]

This, then, is a proper concern for the parents and school people who are desirous of providing a complete program of educational opportunities for their young children. New approaches and new possibilities for foreign language experiences have made their appearance in a number of elementary schools since 1952. Appropriate extension of such opportunities to more children deserves the study and effort of classroom teachers, administrators, and parents.

SKILLS NEEDED FOR TELEVISION USE

One area of language use which has been neglected is that of the receiver skills necessary for the rational use of television. In education the practice has been to use the television medium for conveying conventional instructional packages of arithmetic, science, and the like. Numerous studies have been made of the impact of television viewing upon children's vocabularies, reading habits, and store of information. The Children's Television Workshop provides various kinds of educational readiness experiences for young children, and other ventures have sought to provide universal kindergarten experiences to five-year-old children in rural Appalachia. The question remains: What has been done to identify and develop the *receiver skills* that are used when one watches and listens to television?

At the time of this writing, the Broadcast Research Specialists in the College of Communications are working with researchers in the College of Education at Ohio University in an effort to identify the receiver skills and to develop materials designed to increase these skills. There is some

---

[88] Mildenberger, *op. cit.*, p. 26.

reason to believe that the skills used in critical reading may not be sufficient to serve in the critical viewing of television. The combinations of sound, color, action, and expression may indeed present a unique communications problem to the viewer. The inability of the viewer to stop the action or turn back the television "page" suggests that television pulls the viewer along toward a preconceived objective and that the viewer is in control only when he turns the switch on or off.

More than 60 per cent of adult Americans receive the majority of their news from television, and television is the medium that people value the most. Each of the three major networks weekly broadcasts more than 2500 persuasive messages, the major political campaigns are waged on the tube, and a huge piece of the advertising market has moved from newspapers and magazines to television.

It is too early for the research teams at Ohio University to report anything concerning the identification and development of receiver skills. It seems fairly safe to predict, however, that the entire problem of medium will receive considerable attention by educators in the decade ahead.

SUMMARY

The language arts have an all-encompassing role in the elementary school program. The several phases of the language arts have been defined as (1) speaking, (2) listening, (3) reading, and (4) writing. As avenues for acquiring and imparting information and ideas, these phases of language arts support and reinforce each other.

Effective teaching practices recognize the value in relating language arts instruction to all aspects of the school program because it is from the practical applications of language skills that the individual will become competent in this important learning area.

Certain classroom practices and instructional materials have been discussed with regard to their contribution to a program of developmental language, an approach which regards the child as the key factor. Growth in language is measured in terms of the child's readiness, needs, abilities, and capacities. The materials and methods of instruction are adapted to help the child rather than to hinder his language development.

The objectives of the language arts program include personal fulfillment, competency in the use of communication in civic and personal affairs, and appreciation and enjoyment of the heritage of literature.

Foreign language in the elementary school may have value for all children if properly organized and presented. Foreign language should undergo the same careful study and evaluation as any other part of the curriculum and should not be included as a fashionable appendage.

Teachers and administrators must be fully informed as to the issues and problems in the language arts program inasmuch as it is the subject of continuing community concern and it does constitute the basis for the greater learnings of school and life.

SUGGESTED PROBLEMS AND ACTIVITIES

1. "Slang is usually harmless and often is evidence of healthy language development." Use this statement as a topic for "pro and con" class discussion.

2. Formulate several plans for teaching acceptable oral language in the classroom. Many teachers have recognized the powerful effect on the child of home and community speaking habits. How may undesirable language be corrected?

3. Desirable speech and correct usage by the teacher is an important part of instruction in speaking and spelling. In your own classroom, suggest to the students that each report on errors in usage and pronunciation that have been commonly observed among college students.

4. What have you experienced as a student in the way of "listening instruction?" Interview an elementary school teacher and learn what she thinks about teaching for effective listening.

5. What would you suggest to Miss H. regarding her reading program? (See pp. 234-35 of text.)

6. Examine several different spelling textbooks. Report on any evidence you find of provision for the slow learner and the brighter child.

7. Mrs. White is the parent of a child in your first grade classroom. She has come to you to object to a recent field trip to the fire station. She believes that her child needs more reading instruction and fewer frills. What will you say to her?

8. To what extent do you share the authors' position with respect to the place of television in contemporary life and the need for the school to teach "receiver skills"? Do you foresee the day when it will not be necessary to teach reading as we now know it?

9. Mr. Smythe and Mrs. Jones have requested that the school offer foreign language to all sixth grade children because, they say, it will train the minds of the pupils and increase their understandings and appreciations of other nations. What would your position be in this matter?

10. Examine the basic reading texts used in the elementary schools. How well do they meet the objectives suggested in this chapter?

11. Arrange to have a demonstration of how to teach a reading lesson using the experience chart approach. The instructor, a student, or a visiting

elementary teacher may do this. Note how this approach fits into the reading program.

12. Visit some classes and note how reading is taught and the role it plays in the curriculum. Have student reports concerning their reactions, questions, and the like.

SELECTED READINGS

Arbuthnot, May Hill. *Children and Books*. Chicago: Scott, Foresman and Company, 1957.

Betts, E. A. *Foundations of Reading Instruction*. New York: American Book Company, 1946. Chapter 24.

Brothers, Aileen and Cora Holsclaw. "Fusing Behaviors Into Spelling," *Elementary English*, XLVI, No. 1 (January, 1969) 25-28.

Chall, Jeanne. *Learning to Read: The Great Debate*. New York: McGraw-Hill Book Company, 1967.

Chase, Clinton I. "Concept Formation as a Basis for Measuring Developmental Reading," *Elementary School Journal*, 69, No. 4 (January, 1969), 210-214.

Downing, John. "Alternative Teaching Methods in i.t.a." *Elementary English*, XLV, No. 7 (November, 1968), 942-951.

Duffy, Gerald G. "Insights on the Teaching of Poetry-Writing," *Elementary School Journal*, 69, No. 1 (October, 1968), 32-37.

Entrom, E. A. "Those Questions on Handwriting," *Elementary School Journal*, 69, No. 6 (March, 1969), 327-333.

Ervin, Jane. "Will the 'New Grammer' Please Stand Up?" *A Short Guide to the New Grammar*. Los Angeles: Tinnon-Brown, Inc., 1968. Reprinted in *Grade Teacher*, 86, No. 7 (March, 1969), 138-139.

Heilman, Arthur W. *Principles and Practices of Teaching Reading* (2nd ed.) Columbus, Ohio: Charles E. Merrill Publishing Co., 1967.

Hendricks, Archie E. "Manuscript and Cursive Handwriting in Brookline," *Elementary School Journal*, 55 (April, 1955), 447-52.

Herrick, Virgil E. "Manuscript and Cursive Writing," *Childhood Education*, 34 (February, 1961), 264-67.

Hillerich, Robert L. "Linguistic Efforts in Reading: An Appraisal," *The National Elementary Principal*, XLVIII (September, 1968), 36-43.

Key, Mary Ritchie. "The English Spelling System and the Initial Teaching Alphabet," *Elementary School Journal*, 69, No. 6 (March, 1969), 313-325.

Larrick, Nancy. *A Teacher's Guide to Children's Books*. Columbus, Ohio: Charles E. Merrill Publishing Co., 1960.

MacRae, Margit. *Teaching Spanish in the Grades.* Boston: Houghton Mifflin Company, 1957.

Neubauer, Dorothy (ed.). "Spelling," *National Elementary Principal,* 38 (May, 1959), 114-118.

Ploghoft, Milton E. "Do Reading Workbooks Promote Readiness?" *Elementary English,* 36 (October, 1959), 424-426.

Shane, Harold G., June Grant Mulry, Mary E. Reddin, and Margaret C. Gillespie. *Improving Language Arts Instruction in the Elementary School.* Columbus, Ohio: Charles E. Merrill Publishing Co., 1962.

Strickland, Ruth G. *The Language Arts in the Elementary School.* Boston: D. C. Heath & Company, 1957.

CHAPTER 8

Emerging Programs in
Social Science Education

INTRODUCTION

"The American curriculum must be revised to equip Americans for survival in an age where man has found new ways to exploit the powers of nature that can be either terrifying or beneficial, in an age where the interdependence of nations forces man into new relationships with his fellows."[1] This statement by Caldwell points at the heart of the problem of human existence in these latter decades of the twentieth century, and it serves to identify a central concern of social education; for the implication is clear that man is responsible for the direction of his achievements and for the consequences that may be by-products of such achievements. *Responsibility to humanity* is a value supported by social education.

Another concern which has emerged with new vigor during the past 10 to 15 years has been expressed in the writings of such men as Aldous Huxley, David Riesman, and Erich Fromm. This concern grows from the over-organization and the over-institutionalization of people in modern societies.

Huxley has asked this question: "In an age of accelerating over-population, of accelerating overorganization and ever more efficient means of mass communication, how can we preserve the integrity and reassert the value of the human individual?"[2] The response which seems

---

[1] Oliver J. Caldwell, "Education for Survival," *Audio-Visual Instruction*, 3 (April, 1958), 101.
[2] Aldous Huxley, *Brave New World Revisited* (New York: Harper & Row, Publishers, 1958), p. 57.

simple enough to come by is difficult to implement: the integrity and value of the individual can be asserted and preserved, in part, through programs of education which focus their efforts toward identifying and utilizing the potentials of each child, efforts which must be existent in the procedures and in the applied values of the school. Society's great and justifiable concern for the advancement of the well-being of the larger community must now be viewed from another point, that of the individual. Programs in social education which have long stressed the value of the individual as a member of the larger human family are taking cognizance of the difficulties which arise when the individual strives to conform and to seek status in a group while neglecting the development of concepts regarding the individual's responsibility to self. Such difficulties are to be anticipated when the teacher implies, or states outright that, "you are a good pupil when you help the group; you are not good when you are occupied with self interests." And again, in situations where social status outside the school influences the attention given the child in school, and in instances where success is too often relative in terms of group rank or peer approval, the worth of the individual becomes a value that is muted.

Social education in a democracy recognizes that the individual is valuable beyond his membership and responsibilities to the human family. The individual has responsibilities to himself because he is a possessor of potentials for self-development and self-actualization;[3] *he will be of worth to society as he is of worth to self.* Self worth and social worth are mutually supportive; one must not obliterate the other, and it can be stated with abundant support that an individual cannot develop his potential values to society without developing his individual being. The social education of children and youth reflects the basic unity in what appears at first glance to be the paradox of asserting individual worth as the foundation of desirable social behavior.

Authoritative voices have expressed the concern for a type of social education that will meet the challenges of life in an atomic age and a space-exploring world. A committee of the National Association of Secondary School Principals stated the problem thus: "The very existence of mankind today depends upon man's control of his social environment. Man must use his vast new sources of power for constructive purposes. The alternative is the creation of a global holocaust.[4] This expression of

---

[3] See A. H. Maslow, "Some Propositions of a Growth and Self-Actualization Psychology," *Perceiving, Behaving, Becoming,* 1962 Yearbook of ASCD (Washington, D. C.: National Education Association, 1962), Chapter 4.

[4] As reported in the *Lincoln Journal,* Lincoln, Nebraska, February 14, 1961, p. 1.

concern was made in 1961, and since that time, the United States and much of the world has been caught up in a host of problems which have their roots in conflicts of a social nature.

Within the last decade a variety of forces within and outside of education has given rise to serious doubts and misgivings with respect to the adequacy of older approaches to social studies to meet the needs of present and future generations of children. One clearly identifiable shift in emphasis is revealed in the attention being given to the role of inquiry in programs that are concerned with conceptualization and generalization as opposed to older programs that were geared to rote learning of isolated facts.

In keeping with the spirit and objectives of social science education, this chapter has been designed to involve you actively in the inquiry process. Problems and questions are raised and alternatives are considered, but the solutions are left for you to discuss and formulate, individually and with your fellow students. The authors believe that changes are called for, but the extent of such changes and the manner in which you work with children to make social learnings effective and pertinent are responsibilities which you alone must choose to recognize or ignore. It is the hope of the authors that this chapter will be of value to you as you deal with this responsibility.

SOCIAL CONFLICT AND SOCIAL STUDIES

In our own land the problems of the people in our midst who are economically disadvantaged and alienated from the larger society have given rise to riots in the inner cities. On many occasions, the sources of tension and disorder appear to lie within those parts of the population that are racial and ethnic minorities. In some instances, the protests against the existing social and economic conditions have taken on violent characteristics. Some protest leaders have said in effect, "We will have our share of opportunity and the good life, or we will burn down the cities of this nation."

In the last years of the 1960's there were loud and active expressions of dissatisfaction from a segment of the young populace that has not often been regarded as disadvantaged or alienated from the larger society. Young people on numerous college and university campuses demonstrated, sometimes violently, against the administration of their schools. In some cases, student groups maintained that it was the students who should really run the college, hire the professors, and decide upon the important matters. They often expressed the feeling that the older generation was not sensitive to the "real" problems and issues of life on this planet, that the adults of the nation were more concerned with comfortable homes, backyard pools, and new automobiles than with social justice, equal opportunity, and a humanitarian approach to relations with the people of other nations. A review of the newspapers and news magazines of the spring months of 1968 will provide a broad background on the social unrest then in evidence.

Young people in other lands, especially France, were also expressing displeasure with the state of affairs. The Paris riots of early 1968 had serious effects upon the monetary stability of France and placed the de Gaulle government in a difficult position. The extent of change brought about in the educational system of France still remains a matter of question.

Student activist groups have been organized on a number of high school campuses with goals which range from changing curriculum to changing faculties. "Underground" publications, formerly found most often in Greenwich Village, appeared in colleges and high schools. The "free college" and "free high school" emerged in some places where the students set out to learn together about the "important" things in life.

Other groups in the society behaved in highly unilateral ways during the late '60's. Teachers in New York City went on strike and continued their strike in defiance of a court injunction during the fall of 1968. In early 1968, unionized professors at San Francisco State College defied a court order which called upon them to cease their strike.

The mounting tide of social unrest and the accompanying widespread concern for what this meant to the "American way of life" appeared to play a part in the presidential election of 1968. Many questions were asked which did not have easy answers:

1. Do groups of people have the right in a free nation to disobey laws and court orders when they do not agree with the laws and orders?

2. How can a highly organized society such as that of the United States continue to exist without a widespread knowledge and respect for a way of resolving problems and conflicts by due process of law?

3. How can the learning experiences provided for the youth of the nation prepare them for effective and responsible participation in the affairs of the society?

During this turbulent time in the '60's, one often heard the comment expressed that the schools had taught the children about the rights of the American citizen, but the children had been given too few opportunities to experience the problems involved in the exercise of rights when the desires of several people or groups were in conflict. The young people, it was said, were inept and awkward when they forced their way into participation in the affairs of the college administrations. The militant members of the urban ghettoes, it appeared, were not informed or skilled in the ways of social and political action that would lead to the resolution of their problems.

Had the social studies programs of the American schools turned out handicapped and disadvantaged citizens? Had certain groups of teachers, by their own defiance of court injunctions and state laws against striking, provided a working model for the young people to use in ignoring due process of law in the resolution of conflicts?

The authors do not intend to persuade you with regard to the rights and wrongs of the problems and actions which have been mentioned. These problems and many others will confront you in the years ahead, and so long as you are a teacher of the children of a nation, your readiness and ability to behave effectively and appropriately are more than matters of narrow personal concern and interest. There are those persons who argue that the social education of children is best done by the "tried and true" approach that "teaches" geography, history, and civics, using textbooks written by experts. John Dewey's conception of the school as a laboratory of life is still contested, although the advent of television has aroused in our children an awareness of a wide range of life problems around the world.

The children in your classrooms may have witnessed on the T.V. newscast the shooting of a Viet Cong suspect by a Vietnamese officer. They doubtless were among the first human beings to see, via live telecast, the view of the planet Earth as it appeared to the astronauts in Apollo VIII as they circled the moon or the astronauts of Apollo XI when they first set foot on the moon. The exciting stories of Columbus, Magellan, and the American frontiersmen may seem dull by comparison; they may seem far less relevant.

Marshall MacLuhan has said that "children now interrupt their education to go to school."[5] This raises the ire of some long suffering teachers who do not like the idea of being muscled aside by an electronic tube, but one may choose to think about it for at least a minute or two. Technology has thrust human beings into many new relationships and environments that seemed impossible a few years ago. Information has multiplied at an amazing rate. How do we help young humans prepare to behave in the changing environments and in new relationships? Will

---

[5] From the film *The Medium is the Message*, McGraw-Hill Films.

the stereotypes that are created and reinforced by our cultural biases fade in the face of rational inquiry?

What kind of social being should a child become? What should he "know"? How should he behave? These are "easy" questions if the "easy" answers are: The young American should know the "essential" or "basic" things about his nation and its history. He should be a "responsible" individual, "considerate" of others, and at all times, a "good citizen."

What Is the Place of Values and Valuing?

If you attempt to answer the questions in the preceding paragraph, you will call upon your own value system in making your response. When you work with other students and teachers in an effort to get consensus responses to the question "How does a good citizen behave?" you will likely uncover a wide range of views and values. It is a difficult job to identify at any point in time those values which the larger society *wants* to have reinforced in the school. Does society value individualism to the extent that the school should teach the child to persist against the majority will? Do the educators have a responsibility to reflect and incorporate into the schools the values of society? Should the schools attempt to modify prevailing social values and perhaps support additional or alternate values?

Several points of view are presented here for your consideration and discussion. It may be that your entire class will settle upon one position if they can decide which one is "right."

POSITION 1

The schools exist to serve the individual and the society. As the creations and servants of society, the schools and teachers are bound to reflect the wishes and hence the values of the society. It is unthinkable that any society would give its support, financial or moral, to schools which attempt to teach their youth those behaviors which are not valued in the larger society. In a society that values democratic processes, it would be heresy for its teachers to arbitrarily decide those values that should be taught or rejected in the classrooms.

POSITION 2

Values are not taught in any verbal manner. They are expressed through the behavior of people, and because of this, the teacher's verbal values will have very little impact when compared to the values which her actions present. The teacher may tell children that they should respect all human beings, but it is her behavior with children and other adults that gives strength to the values which she herself respects. There is really no problem with regard to the question "Shall we teach values?" or "Which values shall we teach?" The teacher brings to the children her own set of values which reveal themselves in her behavior in and out of the school. Her values are quite likely not too different from those of society or she would have been screened out long before getting into the teaching business. Of course, the values of society are carried into the school because children and teachers alike are part of the society. Their differences will more often be of degree rather than anything else.

POSITION 3

There is no place in the schools of a democracy for the direct teaching of values. The child should grow in his ability to develop his own value system, and the teaching concern should be with the *valuing process*. To teach a set of values as though they are sacred is no less than blind dogmatism and has no place in the schools of an open and free society. To teach the *valuing process*, and hence help youngsters to discover *how* human values come into being, is to assist in the development of rational behaviors that will serve the individual throughout his life.

POSITION 4

It is not proper to *indoctrinate* the young people in a democratic society with respect to the prevailing values. It is appropriate to learn about human values both at home and in other cultures and to understand that problems arise when nations or groups of people who hold conflicting values come into contact. In this way, young people will learn that values are important in both an individual sense and in a community or national sense. Most nations seem to value *honor* just as individuals value *respect*, although nations and individuals may seek honor and respect in quite different ways.

Use the preceding positions as the basis for class discussions of values in the school. What difficulties do you encounter in seeking agreement? What position would you develop to guide you in your work with children?

Values in conflict.   In the latter months of 1968, a certain Pennsylvania school board made the decision to go against the U.S. Supreme Court ruling on prayer in the public schools. Prayer and Bible readings were ordered in all classrooms in the district. The superintendent acknowledged that the school was acting in violation of the law of the land. The president of the Parent-Teacher Organization argued that classroom prayers would help to reduce crime in the schools across the nation and would bring God back into the school.

Do you believe that the older children would sense the conflict in values here? A law of the nation was being violated in order, so it was said, to help children become law-abiding citizens. What would you do if you were a teacher in this school?

One important way in which the United States differs from closed, authoritarian systems is said to be in the acceptance of many values among its people. This is compatible with the emphasis upon individual freedom in speech, religion, and occupation. When conflicting values become operational, even in the United States, they give rise to problems of accommodation. Some of the real life problems that have emerged in recent years include the following:

1. A militant group of students refused to stand for the playing of the national anthem; they refused to show respect for the flag.
2. An atheist mother of an elementary school pupil objected to prayer in the school and obtained a court order to stop the practice.
3. Many young men, who believed that the U.S. involvement in the Vietnam War was wrong, refused to serve in the military organization. Were they being unpatriotic in their refusal or extremely patriotic in the exercise of individual conscience?
4. The Pittsburgh Federation of Teachers in January, 1969, voted to strike to support their demands for benefits, although a strike would be in violation of state law. A professor remarked that instead of teaching the pupils a disrespect for "due process," the strike would provide a good example of how to obtain changes in the laws.

Each of these examples provides evidence of the complex task that faces the teacher in a nation where different points of view are allowed to be brought out into the open. It appears that the teacher is expected to teach patriotism, respect for law and order, individual conscience, and the like, but with situational reservations.

How do we prepare young people to cope with the problems which they and their fellow citizens will face? The psychologist Cronbach has stated that "the root of 'good behavior' is acceptance of the values of one's culture." He lists six valued behaviors:

1. accepts social values
2. takes care of his physical security
3. solves problems
4. has self-respect and self-confidence
5. has personal goals, interests
6. is effective with others

Cronbach concluded his observations on social values and the schools thus:

> The school's function is to teach pupils certain core values such as consideration for others and loyalty to their country. Then we leave the pupil to work out his own position by experience or reasoning in those areas where members of our society do not agree. More than that, however, we want him to challenge traditions and values which are harmful. *Fundamentally, each person must want to do right and be willing to defend even his heresies to his group.*[6]

Analyze the Cronbach position in terms of how helpful you believe it will be to you as a teacher. What questions does it leave unanswered?

One of the difficulties which teachers encounter with general listings of human values is in their application to specific school situations. The six valued behaviors suggested by Cronbach would be acceptable in a closed society such as that of Mainland China, and the differences remain to be found in the way that one solves problems, the kinds of problems which he has an opportunity to solve, and the way in which he seeks to attain self-respect and to accomplish his goals.

Within the context of American society there are differences among various ethnic and racial groups with respect to the attainment of certain human values. Whether the setting is in the inner city, the rural ghettoes, the Indian communities, or suburbia, the human being typically values wealth in its many forms, self-respect and dignity before his peer groups, access to the power to control some of the social forces that affect his life, and the psychological and physical security that comes from the relationships with family and friends in a peaceful environment. Recent events in the United States have shown that serious conflicts arise when people strive for the same valued things in ways that are not acceptable to the society generally.

At issue seems to be the need for a broad acceptance and involvement with a valued way of resolving problems and conflicts when human beings seek to satisfy their needs. Examination of many school approaches to the *values and valuing* aspect of the child's life will show us that frequently the examples and problems are too remote or theoretical to have impact upon the child. The child has learned to value the behaviors (processes) which appear to be successful for his parents, friends,

---

[6] Lee J. Cronbach, *Educational Psychology* (New York: Harcourt, Brace & World, 1962), pp. 44-45.

television personalities, and teachers. The verbalized values have been in conflict with operational values and the young person learns the difference. He knows when to verbalize a particular value and when to perform another.

ELEMENTS OF NEW APPROACHES

What Is the Place of Concepts and Behavioral Objectives?

The term *concept* has been used in so many ways that it may have lost its meaning. Many authors have written as though they were putting concepts on the printed page to be read and transferred into the brain of the pupil. It seems appropriate and defensible to use the psychological definition of *concept—a mental structuring of ideas or notions.* We are then in a position to consider the kinds of experiences that can be planned in order to bring about specific *concept development* in the mental processes of the child. It should be recalled that the teacher may anticipate and plan for the development of certain concepts, but the actual conceptualization by the child can be estimated only indirectly through visible behaviors.

Conceptualization on the part of the child is not easily proven. The ability to recall the words *scarcity, goods,* and *flow of capital* does not indicate that the child has conceptualized much of anything about man's economic behavior—nor does it prove that he has not. The traditional inclination of teachers to conclude that a child who can verbalize something has operational knowledge and understanding, has been challenged for many decades, but it is still in evidence in too many classrooms.

A recent emphasis on the nature and place of *behavioral objectives* in the social studies program has drawn attention to the shortcoming of verbalization as a goal of education and at the same time raises a question regarding the relationships between *learning, conceptualizing,* and *behaving.* The assumption is often made that the individual will be able to behave intelligently and rationally if he understands the broader implications of this behavior. If the individual has *conceptualized* a specific aspect of his relationship to the governmental process, he may behave effectively as a citizen. Otherwise, it could be said that the person who goes about his citizenship responsibilities out of habit and imitation of others does not, in fact, have the tools to deal with the changing nature and demands of citizenship in a free society. The person who always votes Democratic because his family did so, has quite likely, not conceptualized adequately about the responsibilities of the citizen to acquire, analyze, and interpret information before arriving at a voting decision.

Conceptualizing is viewed here as a far more complex process than memorizing bits of information or reciting pages of material, although memorization and information are parts of the conceptualizing process. Dispensing *descriptive information* in and of itself is not a sufficient goal of education, although we continue to see all kinds of tests which deal almost entirely with the recall and recognition of descriptive information which the individual has internalized. To the extent that the concepts are correctly developed with reference to the situation as it is in real life, the individual has a useful *concept.* The individual may *generalize* concepts for a number of situations, although to generalize correctly again calls for information and interpretation of the situations.

At this point, some specific examples are in order.

A DESCRIPTIVE CONCEPT STATEMENT
"Columbus discovered America in 1492."

Mallan, writing about the different levels of conceptualization, calls this statement an example of a low-level concept, a descriptive statement of a unique occurrence taking place at a particular place at a particular time. As such, Mallan contends that the concept represented is singular; it does not lend itself to functional transferability.[7] This type of low-level *descriptive conceptualizing* has occupied a large amount of school time and pupil effort and has been accepted and defended as a means of teaching the basic facts.

A PROCESS CONCEPT STATEMENT
"Large groups of people everywhere on the earth create systems for controlling the behavior and conflicts of their members. When these systems are formalized, they are called governments."

Within this statement, which Mallan would label a *process concept,* are elements of human existence which are eternal and global. People form groups for various reasons, conflicts develop, systems for resolving conflicts are essential if the life of all groups is to have any permanency, and finally, systems for regulating behavior become formalized in order

---

[7] John T. Mallan, *Conceptual Frameworks for Social Education* (Athens, Ohio, The Cooperative Center for Social Science Education, Ohio University, 1967), pp. 9-10.

to give the group some security in believing that the rules will not be changed hastily. Immediately, one can see the power and utility of the process concept statement, whereas the descriptive process statement has little functional value beyond providing partial evidence of a more complex human activity.

Teachers are sometimes overwhelmed by the task of planning experiences for children that will lead to the development of process concepts. The teaching and testing of facts seems so much simpler and less demanding that it offers a temptation to ignore the more serious goals of education in a free society. The future teacher, as well as the experienced teacher, can begin to grow in their abilities to teach higher level conceptualization by asking certain questions before they initiate any learning experience:

   1. What do I hope will happen to the children as an outcome of this learning experience? Will they
      a) acquire information?
      b) analyze or compare different sets of information?
      c) interpret information; find out what it means?
   2. How will children be able to use new information as new tools in the study of other questions and problems in and out of school?
   3. What kind of material should be used to present the pertinent data?
   4. How will I evaluate pupil growth in information and in their skill to use this information?
   5. Will the experience help children better understand (conceptualize) some aspect of human existence?
   6. Is it relevant and of concern to youngsters?

What Concepts Should Be Developed?

If we believe that thoughtful behavior will be supported by a continuous process of problem identification, information collection, sorting, analyzing, and evaluating alternatives, we will be guided in the selection of learning experiences which are calculated to develop certain high priority concepts. Teachers realize that they cannot control how many concepts and which concepts will be developed in the thought processes of the child—nor would they want to do so. Within the realm of the school's role in a society, the teachers have the responsibility for making decisions about the learning activities of the pupils and they must consequently be concerned with concept development.

Some teachers are still satisfied to teach from a few books and trust that the children will develop concepts as a result of reading, reciting, and writing. And they probably will. The growing concern in social science education today is for a more deliberate approach to the problem. It is not wise to assume that all available textbooks have been planned and written for conceptually oriented programs.

A number of attempts have been made to identify the "key concepts" or "big ideas" that should be included in the social science experiences of children. There appears to be a move toward consensus in this matter, but terminology itself seems to lend to a continuing confusion.

The Contra Costa program lists five "basic concepts" for the first level of their design, these being selected for "their power to organize and to symbolize vast amounts of information."[8] Their five basic concepts are cultural change, cooperation, interdependence, causality, and difference.[9] In the brief presentations of programs for the various grade levels, the Contra Costa writers list *main ideas* rather than basic concepts. The main ideas appear to lead to the development of the basic concepts listed above, but in some cases the main ideas seem to be statements of basic concepts, for example:

1. Environment influences many aspects of the desert people's life.
2. People develop institutions that support their way of life.
3. Natural resources and the uses made of them influence the standard of living.
4. America is a country on the move. There has always been a frontier.[10]

Which of the above main ideas expresses basic concepts? Does the last main idea (4) relate to a basic concept?

This excerpt illustrates the problems of the imprecise terminology used in writing about the social sciences. This terminology is likely to create confusion unless the problem is identified rather than dodged. In addition, some statements are incorrect or lack meaning, such as "Time has brought many changes to California," or "America is the land of many environments."[11] Both of these statements are said to express "main ideas" for a year's work. How would you restate these main ideas to give them correctness and precision?

---

[8] Hilda Taba and James L. Hill, *Teacher Handbook for Contra Costa Social Studies* (San Francisco: San Francisco State College, 1965), p. 9.
[9] *Ibid.*
[10] *Ibid.*, Appendix.
[11] *Ibid.*

Another example of the problem which confronts teachers as they examine new programs and materials may be drawn from the New York State Syllabus. For grade three, the children will study, among other things, desert communities, including typical climatic conditions and economic and social organization.[12] Why would you expect the desert environment of Needles, California to have anything to do with the political organization? Would the bright child be wrong to observe that Timbuctoo and Needles have similar governments or social systems because they are both located in the desert?

Included for the third grade is the "idea" that a relationship exists between latitude and climate. Aside from a question as to what priority this "idea" should have in the learning experiences of 8-year-olds, there are other elements that should be included if the child is to *conceptualize* accurately about a locale and its climate. What other factors influence the climate of a place? Should a child conclude that all places of the same latitude have similar climates? Jacksonville, Florida and Lahore, India? Caracas, Venezuela and Panama City, Panama?

The Syracuse University Project involved the work of a number of scholars from the several social science disciplines, directed to the task of identifying concepts that should be attended to in the social science programs of the schools. The list is offered here as an example of a multi-discipline approach to the problem of identifying major concepts.

A. *Substantive:* concepts that deal with recall or recognition of ideas from phenomena within the social sciences.
1. Sovereignty of the nation—state in the community of nations
2. Conflict—its origin, expression, and resolution
3. The industrialization–urbanization syndrome
4. Secularization
5. Compromise and adjustment
6. Comparative advantage
7. Power
8. Morality and choice
9. Security
10. Input and output
11. Savings
12. The modified market economy
13. Habitat and its significance
14. Culture
15. Institution
16. Social control

---

[12] *Ibid.*

17. Social change
18. Interaction

B. *Value:* concepts that deal with questions of attitude, beliefs, and principles.

1. Dignity of man
2. Empathy
3. Loyalty
4. Government by consent of the governed
5. Freedom and equality

C. *Method:* concepts that deal with techniques, skills, and aspects used in obtaining information. They are broader methodological concepts that cross the lines of all the social science disciplines.

1. Historical method and point of view
2. The geographical approach
3. Causation

D. *Techniques and aspects of method:* These eight techniques of skills and/or behavior are not identified as concepts as such. They are envisioned as inevitable skills coming into focus as inquiry methods and conceptual approaches are utilized.

1. Observation and measurement
2. Analysis and synthesis
3. Questions and answers
4. Objectivity
5. Skepticism
6. Interpretation
7. Evaluation
8. Evidence[13]

What is the Place of the Disciplines?

There are school systems where the social science education program is derived from the disciplines or is discipline-oriented. Again, a problem in terminology may arise. History and geography are not included in the social sciences in the view of certain authorities who hold that geography is an earth science and that history is a member of the humanities. On what grounds would you agree with this arrangement?

Traditionally, the schools have included geography, history, and civics as the major components in the social studies program. Sociology and economics are relative newcomers to the school curriculum. Anthropology is probably the most recent addition to the area at the elementary and secondary school levels.

---

[13] Warren Hickman, Roy A. Price, and Gerald Smith, *Major Concepts for Social Studies* (Syracuse, New York: Syracuse University, 1965).

The social science disciplines present examples of the methodological investigation of specific aspects of the human condition, if viewed in a broad sense. The methods used by the scholar to study the behavior of man in the economic part of his activity has brought into being an abundance of information useful for an understanding of our systems for managing wealth and resources. To what extent should the information of a discipline be taught in the elementary school? Should the child learn about the methods used in a disciplinary investigation? Should a child learn the structure of one or several disciplines? And why?

Almost as if in response to the recent developments in "modern mathematics," there has been some movement toward a somewhat restricting view of social science education. Such a view casts the disciplines at the focal point, with their structures, their methods of investigation, and their historical content or information as the major elements to be learned. Senesh has proposed the structure shown in Fig. XI for the economics education, although he calls for a "grand orchestration" of the social science disciplines in the formulation of an interdisciplinary program. Senesh is aware of the difficulties which may develop as an outcome of many specially sponsored social science projects which have comprised single disciplines. In fact, he suggests that "economics should be used as a core of the social science curriculum, since economic theory and economic analysis are the most advanced of the social sciences." What aspects of the Senesh position might arouse dissent among other discipline specialists?

The serious question that confronts the teachers who serve on curriculum-planning committees is where to start. Is it preferable to begin with the persistent problems and characteristics of human life on the earth in both a geographical and a historical sense and then move to the bodies of information and the investigative methods provided by the disciplines? Or is it better to begin with fixed bodies of content and hope that the youngsters will find the relationships between what they are learning and the contemporary nature of life? This is a difficult problem for both the new and the experienced teacher. It is always a temptation to use the materials on hand, to have the youngsters master some pieces of information, and to assume that what the child retains will be relevant to him someday, if not now. With the growing concern for behavioral objectives in all aspects of the educational program, it becomes more and more difficult to justify a learning experience on the basis that the information acquired is "good" for youngsters, or that it does them no "harm."

The task of establishing the objectives for social science education is one that must finally be accepted by the teachers and other school people at that point in time when programs are being planned and certainly

FIGURE XI

Structure of Economic Knowledge[14]

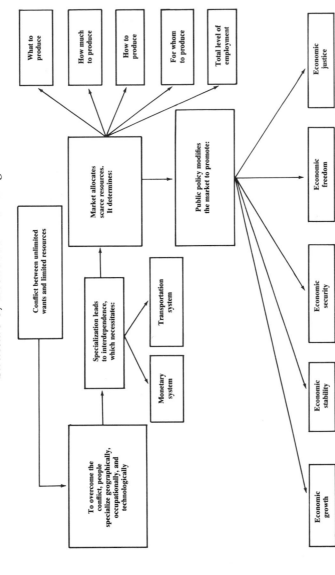

[14] Presented in a talk by Dr. Lawrence Senesh at Ohio University, Athens, Ohio, November 1, 1967.

when teachers are working with children. The abundance of objectives
and materials which have been produced by numerous social science
projects can not all be used, nor can they be chosen from in a piecemeal
fashion. In other words, it is not really the responsibility of the economics scholar or the history scholar to tell the school people what should
be put into a total program.

Recent attention to the structuring of knowledge as a means of
achieving more effective learning experiences in any discipline appears
to have left some educators with the notion that the curriculum should
be moved downward. Perhaps the developments in modern mathematics
have supported the tendency toward discipline-oriented experiences at
earlier ages. Bruner's position that the young child can learn much more
than had previously been believed possible does not automatically mean
that the child *ought* to do so.

In the social science education curriculum area, the matter of subject
placement will likely be far less an issue than will the inclusion of a
serious approach to the inquiry process. If the social science education
of the child is to be derived from the *values* and *processes* of a free
society, then the substance of the disciplines provides the information
that is the stuff of inquiry.

The search for meaning—the essence of inquiry in a democracy—
poses many questions and threats. Inquiry in mathematics is far less
threatening than is the same process when it is vigorously applied in the
social domain. In our preoccupation with discipline-oriented curriculum
we may be deferring a confrontation with the problems involved in the
use of inquiry in the social education of the child. If the events of the
1960's have shown nothing else, they have indicated many of America's
young people are ready to ask searching questions about our institutions,
our values, and our behaviors. Some questions remain concerning the
capability and readiness of American education to assist the young in
their search for meaning, if not for answers.

What Is the Place of Inquiry?

> Inquiry is essentially finding out for oneself. It is the application of pur-
> pose to data in order to develop useful knowledge. The purpose may be
> to solve a problem, answer a question, satisfy a curiosity, apply a concept
> or so on. The data may be information in any form.[15]

This definition of the process of inquiry may only serve to remind the
teacher that inquiry is not a new process. Whether it is compared to

---

[15] Barry K. Beyer, *Using Inquiry in the Social Studies—Guidelines for Teaching* (Athens, Ohio: Ohio University, The Cooperative Center for Social Science
Education, 1967).

Socratic method or to Dewey's description of critical thinking, inquiry is something that humans have been doing for many centuries. At the outset, then, it may be concluded that a new process is not being presented. The question that remains before, as it has for succeeding generations of men, is one of appropriations and practicality for use in the educational experience of the youth in a given society.

If inquiry is to be used, how open should it be? What should the children and youth inquire about? Whose purposes should be applied to data in the inquiry process? What information should be used? Who decides which problems should be investigated?

The questions that have just been raised will have varying answers depending upon time and place. In a community where coal mining is the major enterprise it may not be feasible to inquire into the high incidence of work-related injuries and the adequacy of safety legislation. In most American communities it is unlikely that the personal life of Benjamin Franklin should be used as an example of the changing public concern with the love life of important persons in government. Open inquiry can seem threatening to those persons whose feelings may be affected.

Inquiry, its purposes and its data, is affected by the values of the adult society and the representatives of that society who are charged with the education of the young. In this respect, inquiry experiences of the young in a closed society, such as Spain, Cuba, or the Soviet Union, have restrictions quite similar to those in the United States. The degrees of openness may differ, but it appears that every society has its limits of freedom to inquire and will use ways to control inquiry. During the Vietnam War the "love" children were ridiculed by many persons when these unorthodox dissenters asked whether love was not preferable to hate and peace better than war.

It is probably true that the inquiry of the classroom is usually considered "safe" to the extent that it does not deal with sensitive contemporary problems. In the elementary school one hears the argument that the youngsters are not intellectually and emotionally ready for the rigors of inquiry into sensitive problems. The inquiry process can then be directed toward the development of understandings about groups of people in other parts of the world or in other periods of time. Hence, with time and distance, the dangers of inquiry may be moderated. The assumption is made that as the child grows older, he will transfer the inquiry process from use in the safe problems to the social problems that he faces in his daily life.

Elements of the inquiry process. Again we refer to the work of Beyer[16] in considering what is involved in the inquiry process:

---

16 *Op. cit.*, p. 7.

Defining a task (purpose)
Developing a tentative answer (hypothesis)
Testing the tentative answer (testing)
Developing a conclusion
Applying a conclusion (to new situations, new data)
Generalizing

The teacher who desires to become proficient in the use of inquiry-oriented experiences will recognize the difficulties involved in guiding children to the identification or awareness of purpose, because it is true that *purpose* must be recognized by the learner. It is not sufficient to *tell* the class what their purposes are in any inquiry experience. Involving pupils in inquiry demands planning by the teacher to elicit motivation and purpose.

The objectives of the inquiry-oriented experience are more complex than those of the memorization–recite–recall lessons. Whereas data (information) possession and display is the immediate objective of the latter, the inquiry process calls for the selection of pertinent data, analysis and evaluation of data in terms of its relevance and reliability, and finally the development of a conclusion from which one may generalize.

Inquiry calls for the use of *facts* in a way not known to the read–recite method. Inquiry may be less satisfying to some persons because it is a process that calls for solutions or answers that are never more than tentative. New data may alter the conclusion. Does this mean that one should not act upon the results of inquiry until *all* information and *all* eventualities have been considered?

Applications of inquiry process in the social domain may be accepted more slowly throughout the schools than the use of inquiry in the natural and physical sciences where there is far less threat to established value systems. Accordingly, it would seem that very careful and extensive study and planning should be done by social science curriculum committees as the movement is made toward a rational program. Certainly, community groups should be brought into the development of an inquiry-oriented curriculum if misunderstandings and conflicts are to be minimized. In the final analysis, it appears that the test of a free society is, indeed, the degree to which it will support the inquiry process in all aspects of its public life. Few communities in the United States would confess that they actually oppose inquiry as a skill to be developed in the young, and the same is true of official Soviet proclamations about their educational procedures. The test is yet to be made in American communities on a wide scale, but the exposure of so many Americans to the gamut of our nation's problems, via the television medium, may be a factor that will enhance the role of inquiry in the classroom in the days ahead.

The teacher and inquiry.   A great amount of literature has appeared in recent years dealing with the *inquiry process*. Whereas *inquiry* is generally viewed in a similar manner by various authorities, there seem to exist considerable differences with respect to *how* the teacher should work with children in the use of inquiry. The following examples will illustrate this point.

Mrs. Wilson, Fifth Grade Teacher

Mrs. Wilson is regarded as one of Westwood's more effective teachers of the inquiry process. She attributes her satisfaction and success with *inquiry* to the careful structure which she provides for the children. In her words:

"With fifth grade youngsters it is not wise to expect them to identify problems or major elements of a problem. At this age the children want their teacher to tell them what the problem is and why it is important. It is also important to have materials located so that the pupils can get right to the job of finding information to answer their questions. And because young children like to complete assignments and feel that they have learned something definite, I always make sure that we all accept our conclusions and feel that the problem is settled."

Miss Welles, Middle Level Teacher

"Eleven- and twelve-year-old children are ready to confront the changing problems of everyday life and an open approach to inquiry is a good way to involve them." In this manner, Miss Welles explains her views of inquiry and its use in the classroom. "At every step of the inquiry process, including the formulation of the problem and evaluating its importance, the youngsters are active in stating opinions and supporting them with evidence. It is phony inquiry if the teacher *tells* them what their problem is. After all, in real life, people try to inquire when they are moved by a problem or conflict that means something important to them. They *feel* it before they try to solve a problem."

The teachers who work with Miss Welles do not always understand or agree with her approach to inquiry. Parents occasionally object that Miss Welles does not know where the inquiry activities take the class. Miss Welles responds to such doubts with this explanation: "In real life, people often start with the same problem but they do not always agree that the information they use will lead them to the same conclusions. Their conclusions will be influenced by the things and ideas they value. If we are helping kids get ready for adult life, I think we should give them inquiry opportunities to experience it like it is, not just the way the historian inquires."

As you think about the position of Miss Welles and Mrs. Wilson, which comes nearest to containing your own ideas? What difficulties would you expect to have in using either approach? Discuss this with other students and identify the part that you like most in each position. *A twelve-year-old boy offered the opinion that inquiry is something that you do for the teachers, but you know they don't really believe in it because they never use it themselves.*

Beyer considers the role of the teacher as one of creating a conducive climate for asking questions, suggesting possible ways of finding out, and estimating what the answer might be. He suggests that pupils must have the opportunity to find out for themselves; this includes the right to be wrong without penalty. The teacher must be an enthusiastic inquirer herself, a kind of living proof that most problems are never settled once and for all.

In summary, it appears that the inquiry activities of children and youth are typically directed at problems "far away and long ago." It is true that the elements of inquiry can be developed using almost any kind of human problem whether it is current or ancient. However, the involvement of young people in inquiry into the problems of here and now brings certain complexities that arise from strongly held values, attitudes, and emotions, and these elements make the difference between dead inquiry and lively inquiry. When persons confront contemporary issues there is feeling and conviction present in a form that is not found when the inquiry is into the big city bossism of the Pendergast machine of the 1930's or the palace politics of Louis XIV.

Accordingly, a problem that must be dealt with by teachers is the selection of areas and problems for inquiry. When the term "safe" inquiry is used, it is indeed "loaded." Only the teacher and her colleagues can decide the most promising ways to move into lively inquiry experiences with children. It should be recognized that the degrees of freedom to engage in lively inquiry make the critical difference between the open society of this nation and the closed systems of the Soviet Union, Spain, and Mainland China.

FROM SOCIAL STUDIES TO SOCIAL SCIENCE EDUCATION

How Do Emerging Programs Differ from the Old Social Studies?

It has been written that the social studies formed the foggy bottom of the curriculum and, until a well defined purpose and plan for implementation is generally accepted for social education in the United States, there will remain considerable fog. Some of the new programs that will be discussed here reveal common elements that identify them as emerging programs in social science education.

The term *social science education* itself clarifies the nature of the experiences that will be included in such programs. The domain of man and his conditions of existence are the concerns, and the rational quest for understanding of the human condition suggests that the objectivity and empiricism of science provide appropriate tools for the task. One may argue that the study of one's own social systems can never be completely objective and rational, that feeling and bias will cloud the study of our concepts of justice, freedom, and behavior on the international scene. Such limitations of perceptions and judgments are part of the fabric of human behavior, but the thrust of social science education will be in the direction of increasing rationality and objectivity.

It should be remembered that the transition from the old social studies to social science education is just now beginning, and it is easy to find some elements of the old popping up in supposedly new programs. (See Chart VIII.) There are still many teachers, and probably many more

CHART VIII

Differences Between Old and New Programs

Old Social Studies	Emerging Social Science Education
Emphasis upon descriptive concepts and information capsules.	Process- and problem-centered, with emphasis upon ways and purposes of inquiry and upon concept information.
Rote learning of facts and recall important.	Identification and analysis of facts and generalization are important.
Evaluate pupil growth in terms of demonstration of knowledge.	Evaluate pupil growth in terms of behavioral objectives which involve the skills of inquiry and use of data.
Subject oriented toward geography, history, civics.	Interdisciplinary; uses data from all disciplines as needed to study any problem.
Child was evaluated mainly on his possession of information.	Child is evaluated on his ability to identify, locate, and apply pertinent information.

parents, who maintain that all children should read and remember many facts in history and geography, even though such facts may have no operational value and may be subject to revision from time to time. This commitment to the rational inquiry of social science education may lead youngsters to ask why we prefer to study the mystical American Indian of 300 years ago rather than the disadvantaged Indian of today. There will be teachers among us who will view this as a "dangerous question," and perhaps they will decide that the old social studies with the murals, games, group poems, and information capsules is easier to teach!

The Eugene Program. A resume of the Eugene, Oregon curriculum will show some of the influences of the social science education point of view.

Grade Level	Grade Level Themes
1	The individual within the group: patterns of living
2	Man and his society: the child in many groups
3	The community structure
4	Change and continuity in society: culture concept
5	America—a land of peoples: the United States
6	People and problems in the Western Hemisphere: Latin America and Canada
7	Man and the social sciences
8	United States history: Colonial Period to 1870

At fourth grade level in the Eugene plan, the children will consider these questions: What is culture? How is culture identified? How does man use the land? How do we examine behavior? The children in fourth grade will move toward an understanding that human beliefs and behavior may differ from place to place although the problems of existence present many similar difficulties. They will learn that most major differences among humans are learned and that behavior is closely related to the system of values which surrounds the individual in his society. Which grade levels in the Eugene program appear most traditional to you?

The Greater Cleveland Social Science Program. The scope and sequence of the G.C.S.S.P. is another example of a recently developed program which emphasizes the discipline sources of its content. It appears that this program may be content-oriented rather than inquiry process-oriented.

Grade Level	Titles
1	Learning about our country, and explorers and discoverers
2	Communities at home and abroad

3	The Making of Anglo-American and metropolitan communities
4	The story of agriculture and the story of industry
5	The human adventure (ancient civilization and four world views)
6	The human adventure (rise of modern civilizations in the West, the new world and Eurasian cultures)

The Clark County, Nevada Program. The new social science education program in Clark County, Nevada has drawn together ideas from many sources and has attempted to develop interdisciplinary opportunities for the young people in their district. One of the primary sources was the Syracuse Project, which identified those major concepts from the several disciplines which were thought to be basic to understanding man and his behavior.

The Clark County Program has made use of behavioral objectives in an effort to sharpen the focus of the learning experiences in the social science area and to provide bases for evaluations. Inquiry is a key dimension in the program and the use of multi-media in the inquiry process is abundantly illustrated. An interesting aspect of the Clark County Social Science Guide is its open-ended nature. Models are provided, but the teacher is invited to make his own selection of vehicles. The guide was developed as the result of cooperative efforts of writing committees and in-service activities. But even then, the guide continues to be a document that is alive and changing, subject to the modification that use and evaluation will bring. It is viewed as more than a guide—it is an instrument that provides for communication of ideas and experiences among the total staff in the Clark County Schools.

The Clark County program does not prescribe topics or themes that are to be included at each age level; rather it presents concepts to be developed and suggests "vehicles" and materials which teachers may use. At successive age levels, this approach calls for increasingly complex development and extension of major concepts.

Some items taken from the Clark County Guide may be helpful in explaining the program. In the Level Six Guide, *conceptualization* about "habitat and its significance" will use Japan as a vehicle of experience. It is the intent in this instance to provide classroom opportunities for the child to view habitat as a resource of the society, a complex condition which will affect man and in turn be affected by man. It is anticipated that as children develop their concepts about this aspect of the human condition, they will generalize appropriately that "Each culture tends to view its physical habitat differently. A society's value system, goals, organization, and level of technology determine which elements of the land are prized and utilized."[17]

For each cluster of learning levels (Primary, Intermediate, and so on) the Clark County Guide provides a model approach to experiences designed to foster and promote conceptualization by the children. Suggested teaching techniques, learning activities, and multi-media materials are provided.

Specific *behavioral objectives* are included in the Clark County Guide, such as:

1. The child will *demonstrate* his knowledge of compass direction.
2. The child will construct drawings depicting activities of men as they relate to food, shelter, and clothing.
3. The child will describe orally what might happen if he or his group would not go to a designated area during a fire drill.

At the time of this writing, the Clark County Program was being introduced into the district. An extensive in-service program will continue to provide opportunities for the teachers to expand the behavioral objectives, to test in classroom use the procedures suggested, to modify them as appropriate, and to make recommendations, based on this experience, concerning the problems and advantages of the program presented in the Guide.

For any given learning level, then, the Clark County Guide presents this structure:

1. *To be developed:*
   Concepts, generalizations
2. *Behavioral objectives:*
   Techniques, activities
3. *Multi-media suggestions*
4. *Developmental models*

How Are the Outcomes Evaluated?

There are a number of problems that contribute directly to the matter of evaluation of child progress whether we refer to older social studies

---

[17] *Clark County Social Science Curriculum Guide* Las Vegas, Nevada, 1969 (working copy). Guides are viewed as "continuing" documents, subject to evaluation and revision in an on-going manner.

or emerging social science education. Until the objectives of emerging programs are more clearly defined and supported by the educational community than is now the case, it will be difficult to discuss generally useful evaluation procedures. Even with the more traditional social studies programs, there exists a considerable variety of opinion concerning what aspects should be evaluated.

In a recent publication of readings in the social studies,[18] the objectives proposed for the programs included almost every aspect of educational pursuit and the recommendations for evaluation ranged from one which called for continued major emphasis upon information recall to one which called for a drastic reappraisal of our methods and materials of evaluation. The conglomerate that continues to mean "social studies" to so many writers is projected in the book of readings cited above. The future teacher may well conclude that one may evaluate the child activity —including work on an Indian tepee or performance in a Thanksgiving Pilgrim skit—and feel confident that important behaviors, attitudes, skills, and knowledge have been sampled.

Teachers generally and traditionally have taken liberties with the evaluation of pupil progress. A paper which contained an excellent summary of a unit of study or a report of various readings could be graded down sharply because of a few misspellings. An extremely neat paper with no spelling errors but with scant information and innocent organization of ideas might well receive a high mark. It has been convenient for teachers to "keep the youngsters guessing" on the matter of evaluation, a practice which crops up on occasions within colleges of education, too.

In addition to an unhappy state of affairs with respect to current practices in evaluation, the social studies have added their own confusing array of poorly defined objectives. The new social science education brings with it the need to evaluate the child's progress in the use of the inquiry process and the child's development and extension of specific concepts. There is still much work to be done on evaluation instruments that will assess child growth in conceptualizing, inquiring, generalizing, and making inferences. Unfortunately, many teachers may cling to the simple programs that call for rote mastery of geography and historical information because there are standardized tests available for such programs.

The Contra Costa program has developed new and promising materials for evaluation of pupil performance in applying principles, making

---

[18] John Jarolimek and Huber M. Walsh, *Readings for Social Studies in Elementary Education* (New York: The Macmillan Company, 1969). The reader is referred particularly to the articles by Richard Gross and Dwight Allen, pp. 468-472, and by Schmuck, Lohman, Lippitt, and Fox, pp. 42-49.

inferences, and using certain skills.[19] These test materials are not yet commercially available, and other appropriate evaluative materials have not yet appeared. As Gross and Allen have pointed out, teachers should not be reluctant to consider innovations in evaluation in social science education.[20] Particularly, as we move into areas of attitude development, the valuing process, and other affective aspects of learning, we may have to abandon our obsession that paper–pencil tests are the only way to assess pupil growth and program effectiveness. It may be of some comfort to recall that teaching and learning have preceded sophisticated evaluation. New ventures in social science education should not await the development of standardized instruments. These will be helpful, indeed, and they will come in due time as experience and demand require.

What Issues Are Emerging?

It appears that the place of subject matter still continues to be an issue, although it need not be. The development of inquiry-oriented programs, which is an issue in itself, will call for a much more selective and relevant use of subject matter or content. Inquiry is not casual guessing and speculation, and as a rational activity it makes a heavy demand on data from relevant and dependable sources. Even so, it is to be expected that the inertia of traditional expectations and practices in the social studies will regard subject matter versus inquiry process as an issue.

The inquiry process itself will be an issue which will emerge as the process becomes more widely used as an open search for meaning about man and his behavior. Although the United States is popularly viewed as a place where "truth" can be sought after freely and openly, there still exist sensitive and closed areas where inquiry is seen as a threat. This condition, so typically human, is a factor to be considered and approached by parent–community groups as well as by professional educators who, quite likely, have their own sensitive areas where open inquiry seems threatening.

SUMMARY

Major changes are in the making in the social studies area and the objectives, content, and teaching strategies will all be affected. Open in-

---

[19] Curriculum Development Project (San Francisco: San Francisco State College).

[20] Jarolimek and Walsh, *op. cit.*

quiry, concept-oriented programs, and the use of data from a variety of sources are aspects of the emerging programs in the social science education that now appear likely to displace the older social studies programs with their emphasis upon two or three disciplines.

There have been "new" programs developed which are actually much more restrictive than the old—programs which are based on the assumption that young children will benefit from experiences with the methodology and content of a single discipline. On the other hand, programs in social science education seek to identify the objectives in terms of behaviors, information, conceptualizations, and inquiry skills, and the data and methods of the several disciplines are used as appropriate to the problems at hand.

Emerging programs in social science education may become controversial unless wide involvement of faculty and community is provided. Inquiry may appear threatening when it is used in the consideration of social values and customs. Teachers who have been accustomed to teaching information capsules from textbooks may feel insecure in programs that call for the use of information from many sources and the development of open inquiry, which is one of the major differences between education in the open American society and that of the closed Communist system.

SUGGESTED ACTIVITIES

1. Organize the class into study groups of not more than 4 or 5 students in each group. Ask each group to select one of the "concept areas" from the Syracuse Project and to prepare a plan for the development of the concept which has been selected. The materials and experiences as well as the teacher strategies and ideas for evaluation should be included. Then compare and critique, in a total class setting, the work of the several groups.

2. Emerging programs are often criticized because, it is argued, they neglect "current events," studies of regional geography, and international understanding. In what ways can a concept-oriented program make use of current affairs, international studies, and the like?

3. Peer teaching often prevents the limitation of being unreal when college students play the role of young children. This need not be true when you are developing your skills as a facilitator of inquiry in the classroom. If you organize into groups of 3 or 4, each student can try out an inquiry experience with fellow students. Use Beyer's guidelines and be sure to select a problem applicable to adults as well as to children so that role playing is not a limitation.

4. It has been a common practice in many schools to schedule "social studies" three times each week for 30–45 minute periods. What difficulties can you envision if you attempt to force inquiry and concept-oriented programs into a rigid time schedule?

5. Parents and other community members may be suspicious of new programs, especially in the social domain where open inquiry may seem to threaten long held values. Using the inquiry process, investigate this problem, which is common in all human societies, and suggest a plan that you believe will be helpful in gaining community acceptance and support for social science education.

6. Older programs in the social studies began with data or information in a subject area and moved toward knowledge mastery. Newer programs will begin with problems or conflict areas in the social domain and move toward understanding, conceptualization, and skill, with subject matter as only one important ingredient. It is difficult for veteran teachers to move from one approach to the other; it may be difficult for you. Develop a plan for transition from the old to the new program.

7. As a class activity, attempt to arrive at a definition of effective citizenship for the United States, including information that all should possess as well as behavior that should be observable. Why do you think that citizenship descriptions may change from time to time?

8. As an extended assignment, select one of the concept statements from the Syracuse list and plan learning activities for two different elementary school age levels designed to develop the particular concept which you choose. The assumption is made that children may conceptualize about scarcity—an item on most concept lists—at the age of seven as well as twelve. How will your teaching plan differ for the two levels even though you are concerned with the same concept?

SELECTED READINGS

Beyer, Barry. *Using Inquiry in the Social Studies—Guidelines for Teaching.* Athens, Ohio: Ohio University, Cooperative Center for Social Science Education, 1968 (monograph).

Brubaker, Dale L. *Innovation in the Social Studies.* New York: Thomas Y. Crowell Co., 1968 (Chapter 4 on game theory).

Dunfee, Maxine and Helen Sagl. *Social Studies Through Problem Solving.* New York: Holt, Rinehart & Winston, Inc., 1966 (Chapter 6 on community resources).

Jarolimek, John, and Huber M. Walsh. *Readings for Social Studies in Elementary Education.* New York: The Macmillan Company, 1969.

Mallan, John T. *Conceptual Frameworks for Social Science Education.* Athens, Ohio: Ohio University, Cooperative Center for Social Science, 1968 (monograph).

Massialas, Byron, and Jack Levin. *Creative Encounters in the Classroom.* New York: John Wiley & Sons, Inc., 1967 (Chapters 1 and 5 on inquiry and the changing role of the teacher).

Meussig, Raymond H., and Vincent R. Rogers. *Social Science Seminar Series.* Columbus, Ohio: Charles E. Merrill Publishing Company, 1965 (a six-booklet series).

Michaelis, John U. *New Curriculum Developments.* Washington, D. C.: Association for Supervision and Curriculum Development, 1965.

New York State. *Tentative Flow Chart of the Elementary Social Studies Programs.* Albany, N. Y.: State Department of Education, 1965.

Sanders, Norris M. *Classroom Questions.* New York: Harper & Row, Publishers. 1966.

Social Education, the Journal of the National Council for the Social Studies. (Suggested as a major source of information concerning issues and developments in the social studies area. See especially the issues of November, 1964, "A Forward Look at the Social Studies," and November, 1968, "International Education.")

Taba, Hilda. *Teaching Strategies and Cognitive Functioning in Elementary School Children.* San Francisco: San Francisco State College, 1966 (Cooperative Research Project No. 2404).

Taba, Hilda, and James L. Hill. *Teacher Handbook for Contra Costa Social Studies.* San Francisco: San Francisco State College, 1965.

CHAPTER 9

The Child and Mathematics

INTRODUCTION

In the phrase *elementary mathematics curriculum* one is struck immediately with a mid-twentieth century change which is far more than semantical in nature. The traditional, skills-oriented arithmetic program has given way to deeper and more challenging aspects of mathematics content, structure, and organization. Loftier goals are created. Arithmetic, the queen of the sciences, has taken up her throne at the head of a pathway which has numerous by-roads of great technological and social significance.

Once taught as a skill for its social utility, the elementary mathematics curriculum now seeks to fulfill traditional goals *at the same time* that it is seeking to accomplish other important objectives. In an age of great technological advancement and social upheaval, new uses are found almost daily for mathematics in the sciences and humanities through quantitative analysis of data gathered through carefully designed and implemented research.

Mathematics offers unlimited possibilities in helping man structure and analyze his environment. Statistical analysis has made possible the study of hyper-complex phenomena; probability concepts have enabled man to control quality in production, minimize hazards, and increase decision-making skills; computers operating on base two have made possible the calculation of problems which would have required years and even centuries to calculate by hand; logic has enabled man to become more rational in decision-making; systems analysis has been facilitated by mathematics, and so on. The contributions of mathematics to present day living could be catalogued in this manner almost indefinitely.

In an age when man progresses simultaneously in uncountable directions at "dizzying" speeds, educational institutions would be greatly remiss if they sought to teach only skills. The present age demands of its institutions foresight and wisdom—the ability to see what is not visible, to educate citizens for a world which is not yet known. Such a task can be met only by preparing new generations for a wide host of possibilities. The mathematics curriculum seeks to do this through emphasis not on skills solely but on understanding—understanding of mathematical structure, properties of systems of numeration, development of variety in problem-solving strategies, and so on. Confidence in one's ability to tackle new problems through analysis of present structures and synthesis with previously developed insights, skills, and knowledges is a goal of high priority in today's elementary mathematics curriculum.

In this chapter the forces producing this change will be considered. Knowledge of pedagogical implications and realities will be discussed, and, finally, the present and future directions of the elementary mathematics curriculum will be reviewed.

SOURCES OF THE MATHEMATICS CURRICULUM

When man imposes structure on his environment, he does so on the basis of some perceived need, either real or imagined. Educational systems are no exception. School curricula have evolved in what seem at times very accidental and unplanned ways. Currently, accepted structures have changed only when challenged by individuals or groups who think they have found strong and impelling reasons to motivate change from the *status quo*. The elementary mathematics curriculum has gone through various stages of evolution and in the '50's was said to be in a *revolution*. Why do changes occur? What are the factors which influence the minds of men to seek alternative content and pedagogical structures for the mathematics curriculum?

Morton[1] suggested that three major factors influence the structure of the mathematics program:

1. The *logical factor*, which is related to the structure of the subject matter.
2. The *social* factor, which is related to the needs of society as they are manifestly met by the subject matter.
3. The *psychological* factor, which is related to the ways in which children learn mathematics.

---

[1] Robert L. Morton, *Teaching Children Arithmetic* (Morristown, N. J.: Silver Burdett Co., 1953), p. 21.

FIGURE XII

Sources of the Mathematics Curriculum

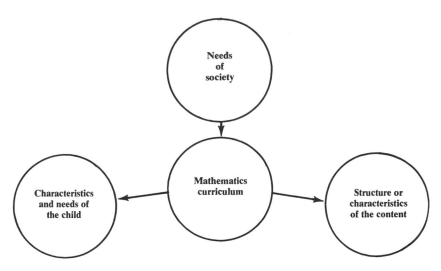

When the logical factor is disregarded, social needs and psychological factors take precedence when making programmatic decisions. Such was the case in our national history from the 1920's to the 1950's when social utility theory dominated mathematics instruction. During that time, many educators advocated that only those mathematical topics utilized in daily life should be taught in schools. A rude awakening took place during World War II when the armed services found young men grossly ill-prepared to assume the responsibilities of a technological war. Subsequently, the Commission on Post-War Plans[2] gave diligent study to the needs of American adults. Most laymen are under the impression that change was ushered in by "Sputnik"; however, several new and innovative mathematics programs had already begun to take bold new directions in the early 1950's.

When the social factor is disregarded, psychological and logical factors take precedence in the determination of programmatic decisions. This situation never actually existed in our nation's history, but there was a time when mathematics was thought to be a mind trainer. The

---

[2] "The Second Report of the Commission on Post-War Plans: The Improvement of Mathematics in Grade I to XIV," *The Mathematics Teacher*, 38 (May, 1945), 195-220.

practical significance of mathematics was more or less disregarded and the virtues of critical thinking and mind development were over-emphasized. In the early days of the modern mathematics revolution there were tendencies in this direction. Some educators were so enamored by the beauty of the logical development and structural aspects of mathematics that social needs were sometimes overlooked. The result was textbooks which were rigorous but weak in practice experiences and social applications.

When the psychological factor is disregarded, social and logical factors take precedence in the determination of programmatic decisions. To some extent rote learning and drill instruction are characteristic of this imbalance. Children would be taught process before they were capable of understanding it. This unfortunate outcome is now understandable because the research of Piaget has indicated that children pass through a constant sequence of stages of cognitive development. He has discovered that attempts to teach children in advanced levels will only lead to a lack of understanding: rote or meaningless learning.

Gradually, the stimulus-response approach to mathematics instruction, which had its genesis in the writings of Thorndike,[3] gave way to a new approach to mathematics instruction. Gestalt field theory placed greater stress on insight, relationships, and principles. The new evolutionary movement became known as the "meaning theory." William Brownell[4, 5] was one of the chief spokesmen of this movement in mathematics. His research indicated that when students understand mathematics principles their mathematics achievement is higher.

Pitfalls exist for all who do not take cognizance of all three factors. Continuing research into the nature of learning and the stages of cognitive and affective development; changing social and technological structures; new insights into structural relationships and their pedagogical implications—all these continue to reveal ramifications important to programmatic decisions. The important point is not that there exists some hypothetical point of equal tension or perfect balance. Rather, the important point is that decision-makers must remember, however strong the demands of the moment, that each component deserves very careful consideration with respect to the consequences of change.

---

[3] Edward L. Thorndike, *New Methods in Arithmetic* (Chicago: Rand McNally & Company, 1921).

[4] William A. Brownell, *The Development of Children's Number Ideas in the Primary Grades.* Supplementary Educational Monographs, No. 35. (Chicago: University of Chicago Press, August, 1928).

[5] William A. Brownell, "The Place of Meaning in the Teaching of Arithmetic," *Elementary School Journal*, 47 (January, 1947), 256-265.

PEDAGOGICAL ASPECTS OF MATHEMATICS INSTRUCTION: TEACHER CHALLENGE AND RESPONSIBILITY

Developing pupil understanding in the mathematics curriculum is a challenge which, if accepted by the teacher, can be a very rewarding experience. Certainly much is yet to be learned by educators and psychologists concerning cognition and learning styles of individuals, but even so, pioneering work has already produced implications which offer teachers opportunities to provide success experiences for all learners. What are some of the strategies and organizational schema which can be utilized by teachers to develop pupil insights and create favorable pupil attitudes toward mathematics learnings?

How Do Teachers Facilitate Cognitive Development?

Each child is unique, so it is little wonder that teachers are at times awed by their task. In a world characterized by change, both revolutionary and evolutionary, it behooves the teacher to examine and attempt to achieve new perspectives and insights into her various roles. Even a cursory glance indicates to the most casual observer that the teacher is first and foremost a decision maker. She must make countless decisions concerning the various aspects of instruction each day.

As she considers the group of youngsters she faces, she attempts to take into account the innumerable differences with which she is confronted. Reflect briefly upon the important consideration which she gives to diagnosis and planning. The teacher is inevitably faced with a wide degree of conceptual readiness. Some of the factors which she considers in making prescriptions and planning strategies include levels of abstractness, types of reinforcement, and pupil ability.

Children in the stage of concrete operations need strong associations between new learnings and the concrete world. After extensive personal exploration and class instruction, students begin to form concepts at the intuitive level. Gradually, the concrete level of operation can be replaced by visual or graphic representations of concrete ideas. This level is frequently called the semi-concrete stage. Finally, the child is able at a later time to manipulate abstract symbolism. Young children, particularly those in grades one through four, depend heavily on associations made with the concrete world for the meaning of sense impressions. Therefore, teachers in these grades rely heavily on concrete instructional aids. Teachers also realize that if each child needs these aids in the first four grades, then the child whose development is slow will need concrete learn-

ing experiences in grades five and six as well. This is frequently a youngster who is low in mathematics aptitude and low in achieving.

Teachers generally make good use of instructional aids which provide visual reinforcement of mathematical concepts. Not only are chalkboard and flannel boards widely used but inventive and creative teachers
also construct or purchase teaching aids which will help develop pupil
understanding. Verbal reinforcement is probably *over*-used! Most teachers often talk a great deal! If talking developed concepts in proportion to
its use, teachers would undoubtedly have few problems.

Other types of reinforcement should be explored and utilized in ways
which are comfortable for teachers and meaningful to students. Through
use of common individualized teaching aids such as beans, popsicle sticks,
bottle caps, and so on, teachers can allow many opportunities for students' exploration and discovery. Each child can discover meaning in the
learning situation in consonance with this level of understanding and
unique background experiences. Manipulative or tactile reinforcement
fosters student independence and creativity in problem-solving. Further,
when a child has several modes of expression available, he can solve
problems on the level of abstractness which is most meaningful to him.

Another type of reinforcement, which is a little harder to communicate, is kinesthetic reinforcement. It is similar to tactile reinforcement but
is a very special case. While tactile reinforcement has as its primary aim
the development of understanding by making concrete materials available, kinesthetic reinforcement has the aim of giving a muscular "feel"
for a concept. A couple illustrations will be helpful. Suppose the concept
of circle is being developed. A tin can with the ends cut out would provide a good visual model if we were to look at the end. By holding the
can in one hand and *tracing* a finger around the end with his other hand,
the child would get a kinesthetic reinforcement of circle. Again, suppose
the concept of "three-ness" is being developed. The child could clap his
hand three times, take three steps, pick up three pencils *one at a time*, or
hit his hand on his desk three times—these would all be kinesthetic reinforcements of "three-ness."

In many ways, the task of the teacher is similar to helping a young
child learn to eat. She is a facilitator.[6] She first spoon-feeds the young,
but she certainly does not wish to continue this forever. Her intention is
to foster independence eventually. She wants children to learn how to
learn. She can facilitate growth in this direction by designing assignments which foster independent thinking while utilizing activities which

---

[6] Educational Development Center, Inc., *Goals for Mathematical Education of
Elementary School Teachers,* The Report of the Cambridge Conference on Teacher
Training (Boston: Houghton Mifflin Company, 1967), p. 127.

encourage students to make discoveries, and by developing pupil skills in gathering information.

If the teacher perceives one aspect of her role as a stimulator, then she will use several approaches to develop pupil understanding of mathematics concepts and generalizations. She will seek to enrich the mathematics program with activities which will motivate and provide pleasurable activity, and she will seek to understand the full impact of the spiraling mathematics curriculum as she attains a more global concept of readiness.

The teacher is a model for mathematics behavior. Pursuit of precise language and notation should be her course. Frequent utilization of applications will help children see the significance of mathematics in every-day life. Finally, the teacher is first and foremost the climate controller. Her attitudes and manner exert considerable influence.

How Do Teachers Organize Children for Learning Mathematics?

Determination of the best way to organize a given class for mathematics instruction is contingent upon several variables. Among them are the characteristics of the teachers and pupils, time, available resources, school size, content, and techniques or strategies. Teachers may be very much aware of student needs and yet be able to do relatively little to accommodate them if they have no resources upon which to draw. Many trained observers have indicated that teachers must have materials other than a single textbooks series if they are to meaningfully tackle the problem of meeting individual differences in the classroom.

In a study of perceived problems in mathematics instruction a large random sample of teachers in grades K–3 and 4–6 indicated that individualizing instruction and accommodating needs of slow and high achievers were among the most pressing problems.[7] Meeting the needs of high-ability students has been the subject of much thought and research. The National Council of Teachers of Mathematics (NCTM) published a yearbook designed to help teachers recognize high-ability students. It gave helpful suggestions of both a general and specific nature to help teachers organize for instruction and select appropriate materials. In the yearbook, Glennon[8] suggested two general approaches through which provisions for high-ability students are usually made: acceleration and enrichment. Academic acceleration is inherently weak in that it pushes

---

[7] Unpublished research study of Robert G. Underhill and W. Robert Houston, Michigan State University, 1967.

[8] National Council of Teachers of Mathematics, *Enrichment Mathematics for the Grades*. 27th Yearbook of the National Council of Teachers of Mathematics (Washington, D. C.: National Council of Teachers of Mathematics, 1963), p. 26.

the student ahead in the mathematics program but generally supplies him with textbooks which were written for average children of that grade level. Horizontal and vertical enrichment is better. They provide the student with breadth and depth experiences in mathematics. In horizontal enrichment the student is challenged to look into ideas which are related to those presently under discussion by the rest of the class. Selected topics would not ordinarily occur in the curriculum at a later time. Such experiences help students gain new insights and perspectives into the ideas under study. The main problem is that materials for horizontal enrichment have been rather limited. Vertical enrichment, on the other hand, engages the pupil in the study of topics which would not ordinarily be encountered in the curriculum for a year or several years hence.

Glennon points out that a major weakness of enrichment experiences is that teachers must be rather well versed in mathematics. It is his contention that specialists are needed in the elementary school.[9] This point of view is supported by Goldberg et al.[10] They concluded after extensive study of over 2,000 New York City school children that a single teacher who can work well with slow children is effective in all curriculum areas but no teacher seems qualified or able to provide challenging work in all areas for gifted children.

Other ways in which children of differing abilities can be accommodated are through homogeneous grouping within a class and through the use of non-graded mathematics classes. In the former, the teacher may divide the class into two or three groups. She can divide the mathematics instructional time between the groups as indicated by their specific needs as shown in Chart IX. The major weakness is that none of the children gets the full benefit of the teacher's help and guidance. In nongraded instruction, children work with others of similar ability; consequently, they may be working with peers or older or younger children.

Teachers can also seek to accommodate individual differences in mathematics instruction by maximizing pupil accessibility to various concrete and semi-concrete learning devices. In this manner, children can

CHART IX

	Group I	Group II	Group III
Instructional Time for Mathematics	Instruction	Work	Work
	Work	Instruction	Work
	Work	Work	Instruction

[9] *Ibid.*, p. 27.
[10] Miriam L. Goldberg, A. Harry Passow, and Joseph Justman, *The Effect of Ability Grouping* (New York: Teachers College Press, 1966).

be encouraged to function at the cognitive levels at which they feel most comfortable. Such aids help account for differences in symbolic thought processes and perceptions. The child's ability should also be reflected in the amount and kind of assigned material. Low aptitude students should naturally work more on the development of fundamental skills and processes than would ordinarily be necessary for high aptitude students.

The teacher has an alternative which she can use in attempting to meet individual differences. She has three important factors which she can manipulate in the learning environment. These are (1) curriculum content, (2) teacher expectations for individual pupils, and (3) pedagogy. If the entire group is working on place value, she might adjust the teaching strategy to provide abstract experiences for the advanced learners in place value; at the same time the slower learners would work with bundles of sticks to determine place value. Here the teacher has adjusted or manipulated her pedagogy to meet individual differences. On the other hand, she could manipulate the content by introducing the fastest learners to more difficult concepts of place value while the slowest pupils deal with a completely different aspect of the mathematics curriculum which they are capable of mastering. Such techniques allow all teachers to provide for individual differences regardless of resources.

It has been found that if children who score low on mathematics aptitude at the beginning of a learning sequence are placed in mathematics content where they can be successful and are given a longer period of time to achieve, their achievement will nearly equal that of children who began the learning with high aptitude in mathematics. In this situation, time to achieve becomes an important variable in learning, a variable which the teacher needs to manipulate for some children. Obviously there are many unanswered questions which need to be researched, but teachers need not fear to try ideas which might lead to improved pupil learning.

For several years textbook companies have had special materials on the market for high-ability children. Concern is presently being directed towards low achievers; NCTM is preparing a new yearbook on problems and possibilities. With the increased tempo of educational discussion devoted to disadvantaged youth today, publishers are beginning to market materials designed for their specific needs. Probably the most notable characteristic of the new materials for low aptitude students is the minimal use of language. There have existed for some years now individualized programmed materials in mathematics. Fewer in number but better in concept formation and development of student understanding are those which utilize branch programming. The main characteristic of such programmed materials is rerouting. When a child reaches a point at which he cannot respond correctly, he is rerouted on the basis of *which wrong answer* he selects. Linear programs, on the other hand, have only one sequence of questions. When the child misses a question he is returned to some point in the series *through which he has already progressed.*

Oakleaf School in Pittsburgh, Pennsylvania was the location of a federally financed program to develop individualized materials for elementary mathematics instruction. Individually Prescribed Instruction (IPI) was developed by a task force of teachers and educators who wrote comprehensive lists of objectives and then proceeded to define many ways in which children could reach them. Such a program requires a considerable amount of resources from which assignments can be drawn; funds must also be secured from a commercial source.

Plans which are most likely to work for the teacher in the self-contained classroom are those which are combinations of group and individualized instruction. Buffie, Welch, and Paige[11] have described several. One consists of using class instruction for new units and then breaking down into two or three groups for continued development. Another utilizes class instruction when new material is introduced and then differentiates work for average and high-ability students while continuing to utilize group work for students with low aptitude.

How Can We Foster Desirable Attitudes Toward Mathematics?

Many children do not like mathematics. Indeed, many adults do not like mathematics either. Not only are these facts common knowledge but research has consistently found a positive relationship between the attitudes of children towards mathematics and their mathematics achievement.[12, 13] Children do not respond as easily or as quickly to those aspects of the environment which are contradictory to their attitudinal value systems. This surely accounts for some children's frustration and inability to learn mathematics. Some consideration of the teacher's role in attitude formation and change is desirable.

Several studies were cited by McDonald[14] which indicated that attitudes are greatly influenced by models. The two most significant models

---

[11] Edward G. Buffie, Ronald C. Welch, and Donald D. Paige, *Mathematics: Strategies of Teaching* (Englewood Cliffs, N. J.: Prentice-Hall, Inc., 1968), pp. 182-214.

[12] H. C. Lindgren, *et al.*, "Attitudes Toward Problem Solving as a Function of Success in Arithmetic in Brazilian Elementary Schools," *Journal of Educational Research*, 58 (September, 1964), 44-45.

[13] Esther Shapiro, "Attitudes Toward Arithmetic Among Public School Children in the Intermediate Grades" (Unpublished Ph.D. dissertation, University of Denver, 1961).

[14] Frederick J. McDonald, *Educational Psychology* (2nd ed.; Belmont, Calif.: Wadsworth Publishing Company, Inc., 1965), p. 307-85.

to the elementary school child are his teachers and his peers. If students identify closely with peers and teachers and if these two groups have favorable attitudes, then he too is likely to have a favorable attitude towards mathematics.

How can the teacher insure that the students will have favorable attitudes? First and foremost, children and adults like those things which they tend to do well: nothing succeeds like success. In mathematics instruction the teachers who really care about the development of positive attitudes toward learning in general and mathematics in particular will provide *all* children with success experiences frequently. Whether the class is developing a concept or practicing to reinforce previously developed concepts and generalizations, the teacher can utilize discovery techniques to guide children to independent insights. Through differentiated assignments the teacher can give each child success experiences on a daily basis.

Another factor which will contribute enormously to the development of positive attitudes is teacher effort directed towards making new learnings interesting and meaningful to learners. She can relate new concepts to ones previously learned; she can, through an understanding of the spiraling curriculum, show how present learnings are expansions of intuitively developed ideas and how these present ideas will enable youngsters to learn interesting new concepts later. Further, she can draw upon the real life experiences of the child for illustrations which show the applicability of present concepts; she can provide enrichment experiences for all students.

Most of all, the teacher can be interesting, enthusiastic, and warm. *The teacher needs a good attitude towards the mathematics she is teaching.* To enhance her own positive attitudes, the teacher can attempt to become well versed in the subject matter. She needs to feel comfortable. Her own peers play an important part in creating change. If the climate among colleagues is positive, she is likely to change her own feelings.

What Are Some Guides for Selecting Mathematics Materials and Teaching Aids?

Many school systems develop mathematics curriculum guides which help teachers make instructional decisions. In school systems where guides do not exist, teachers may decide through informal discussions which topics to emphasize, which ones to omit, and which ones to supplement. For these teachers the materials in textbooks are critically important.

Whether a particular school has one text or is fortunate enough to have more than one, teachers must and do rely heavily upon the ideas and concepts presented in the textbooks and accompanying materials. Careful selection of textbooks is therefore of critical importance. Generally speaking, textbooks should not be selected on the basis of criteria established by the publisher of a particular text since such criteria might be biased. This problem can be avoided by using criteria developed by more than one source. Criteria are best established by considering several important questions:

A. What are the trends in the elementary mathematics curriculum?
B. What are the special needs or characteristics of the students who will use the text?
C. What are the special needs or characteristics of the teachers who will use the text?
D. What are the important criteria for mathematics textbooks which are related to format, teachability, student factors, and so on?

The National Council of Teachers of Mathematics (NCTM) distributes a pamphlet[15] which is very helpful to those who are selecting appropriate texts. A complete summary of the NCTM publication cannot be given here, but a few major topics are listed to give an idea of the factors considered:

A. *Structure*—Does the textbook help the student understand the structure of the area of mathematics under consideration?
B. *Rigor*—Is the development of topics made on appropriate levels of rigor? Does the author attempt to cultivate and capitalize on the student's intuitive understanding?
C. *Vocabulary*—Is the vocabulary appropriate for the grade level, and are new terms introduced at a rate consonant with the ability and maturity of the student?
D. *Correctness*—Is the text free from statements which most mathematicians and mathematics educators would agree are false?
E. *Generalizations*—Are sequences of presented materials adequate and appropriate in helping the child to formulate and understand important generalizations?
F. *Illustrative examples and teachability*—Are examples meaningful and are they concisely stated? Can the student, as well as the teacher, read and understand the presentation?

---

[15] National Council of Teachers of Mathematics, *Aids for Evaluators of Mathematics Textbooks*. The Report of the Committee on Criteria for the Analysis of Instructional Materials (Washington, D. C.: National Council of Teachers of Mathematics, 1965).

G. *Optional topics*—Are enrichment topics provided? Are materials organized in such a manner that the teacher can omit certain topics without disrupting continuity?

H. *Teachers' manuals*—Are the manuals organized for convenient and effective use? Do the manuals provide information on evaluation, diagnosis, and individualization? Do they contain background information which is helpful to the teachers?

Textbooks are aids to instruction. In most classrooms they are viewed as the most important aid. Because the student and the teacher both depend on them heavily, careful selection is important.

There are many other instructional aids which teachers can make or purchase which will enhance student understanding. Kennedy's *Models for Mathematics in the Elementary School*[16] is a good example of contemporary books now available which serve as idea banks which help teachers creatively build understanding of mathematics concepts and make drill experiences more interesting and fun.

Sources on creating and purchasing instructional aids are helpful, but teachers also need criteria for the establishment of priorities. Many aids are available for purchase, and many can be constructed. For a listing of many commercial devices and, more important, for help in deciding priorities, teachers can refer to another publication of NCTM, *A Guide to the Use and Procurement of Teaching Aids for Mathematics.*[17]

Some general observations can be made concerning the establishment of priorities. Chart X below indicates four general areas by which in-

CHART X

Use	User: Teacher-Demonstrator	Student-Manipulator
Drill or Practice	a	b
Concept or Generalization Formation	c	d

---

[16] Leonard M. Kennedy, *Models for Mathematics in the Elementary School* (Belmont, Calif.: Wadsworth Publishing Company, Inc., 1967).

[17] Emil J. Berger and Donovan A. Johnson, *A Guide to the Use and Procurement of Teaching Aids for Mathematics* (Washington, D. C.: National Council of Teachers of Mathematics, 1959).

structional aids can be classified. Generally speaking, instructional aids are used by teachers for demonstration and by students for manipulation. These aids help develop concepts or generalizations in the mathematics curriculum and they provide experiences in drill practice. Decisions concerning the construction or purchase of new aids should be based on a rather careful analysis of present instruction relative to these four combinations. Mathematics instruction was formerly dominated by the teacher and drill practice (a). Present mathematics instruction emphasizes student involvement and concept and generalization formation (d). A teacher should decide what is needed by examining current teaching strategies. If most aids currently used are teacher-demonstrator models for *class* work (a,c), emphasis should probably be placed on student-manipulative materials (b,d). If most currently used aids are for drill and practice (a,b), emphasis should probably be placed on aids which will develop concepts and facilitate the formation of mathematical generalizations. An article in October, 1968 issue of the *Arithmetic Teacher*[18] contains a comprehensive list of instructional aids along with brief descriptions and uses. Versatile aids satisfy three or even all four of the combinations in the table for more than one concept.

PEDAGOGICAL ASPECTS OF MATHEMATICS INSTRUCTION: PUPIL COGNITIVE DEVELOPMENT

Some of the major considerations concerning the teacher's challenge and responsibility have been discussed. The focus will now be directed more specifically to the learner: How does he grow? What does "mathematical readiness" mean? How does this concept apply to mathematics instruction, and what is its role in the overall curriculum? How do children acquire early number concepts? What is the role of discovery learning in elementary school mathematics? These questions represent some of the vital concerns of psychomathematics and mathematics pedagogy today.

What Are the Problems Related to Mathematics Readiness?

Teachers have long been cognizant of reading readiness, and today they are increasingly becoming aware of the importance of the readiness concept as it relates to other parts of the curriculum. In some respects

---

[18] Patricia S. Davidson, "Annotated Bibliography of Suggested Manipulative Devices," *Arithmetic Teacher*, 15, No. 6 (October, 1968), 509-24.

readiness is an illusive concept. Some have facetiously stated that if a child can perform a task, he is ready; if he cannot perform the task, he is not ready! Analysis of points of view is helpful in order to clarify the meaning of readiness.

One point of view holds that readiness is determined maturationally. This point of view is supported by the research and writings of Jean Piaget.[19] Take, for example, the concept of number. Piaget states that this concept has three basic aspects: cardinal number, ordinal number, and unit. He gives criteria for determining when a child has attained understanding of each of the basic concepts. He categorized concept attainment into three states: (1) no understanding, (2) transitional understanding, and (3) complete understanding. Further, he gave age levels for the attainment of the concepts.[20] While the stages of development described by Piaget are not fixed with respect to time, they are fixed with respect to sequence. The implication is that if a child is in the stage of preconceptual and intuitive thought, then he cannot master formal operations until he has passed through the intermediate stage of concrete operations.

A second, but not dichotomous, point of view is that readiness consists of a set of experiences. *Experiences* refers loosely to those activities or events in the life of the student which have helped him learn a concept or skill; hence, a *specific* set of experiences does not exist. This point of view is supported by Robert Gagne.[21] He determines readiness by examining the structural prerequisites inherent in the subject matter. For example, if a child is approaching that point in the curriculum in which he will learn to add, those concepts prerequisite to understanding addition are delineated. Prerequisite concepts and knowledges are compared with the background of the child. If the child does not have a particular concept or knowledge, then he is deficient in his store of experiences. The teacher can build readiness for addition by supplying the child with an appropriate set of experiences. William Brownell,[22] who supports this point of view, states that children are ready for new concepts when they have an understanding of the concepts and a mastery of the skills from which the new concepts will be developed.

---

[19] John H. Flavell, *The Developmental Psychology of Jean Piaget* (Princeton, N. J.: D. Van Nostrand Co., Inc., 1963).

[20] A. F. Coxford, Jr., "Piaget: Number and Measurement," *Arithmetic Teacher*, 10 (November, 1963), 419-27.

[21] Robert M. Gagne, *The Conditions of Learning* (New York: Holt, Rinehart & Winston, Inc. 1965).

[22] William Brownell, "Arithmetical Readiness as a Practical Concept," *Elementary School Journal*, 52 (September, 1951), 481-98.

To a rather considerable extent, this latter point of view places the responsibility for development of the pupil's readiness on researchers, authors, and teachers. Support for this contention comes from Bruner in his now well-known statement as interpreted here by Michaelis *et al.*[23]

> The traditional readiness concept of deferment of instruction until children mature is rejected in favor of the principle that pupils can be introduced to a subject as early as desired, provided it is presented properly and the pupils have the prerequisite background of experience.

Today's mathematics curriculum demands a broader view of readiness than has previously existed. While the concept of preschool readiness is as needed and valuable as ever, readiness must be expanded to incorporate the full meaning of the spiraling curriculum. Some sentences extracted from *Goals for School Mathematics*, also known as the Cambridge Report, serve to illuminate, clarify, and add meaning:

> The reorganization which we refer to above has as its principal aspect the parallel development of geometry and arithmetic (or algebra in later years) from kindergarten on. . . . we want to make students familiar with part of the global structure of mathematics. This we hope to accomplish by the "spiral" curriculum which repeatedly returns to each topic, always expanding it and showing more connections with other topics. . . . The use of a spiral curriculum, in which the same subject arises at different times with increasing degrees of complexity and rigor, offers many advantages. At the first stage an intuitive or pre-mathematics approach offers the opportunity of an early introduction of important concepts. . . . The intuitive discussion should not be wrong or misleading, as it often is, but incomplete structurally. . . . When possible, the limitations involved are to be described and counter examples established. The student is given the confidence to use the results of an intuitive discussion, but with care. . . . After an interval in which the concepts have become more concrete in the student's mind through use in other contexts, the subject is brought back to formal organization. . . . The first stage of pre-mathematics training will here enable the student to see through the formal discussion to the structure and meaning of the proof. . . . The frequent use of older material throughout the course is related to the spiral technique of teaching. It also develops the theme of the unity and interdependence of mathematics. Although more and more rigor is introduced for older topics as the course proceeds, at the same time new topics and advanced concepts are being introduced pre-mathematically.[24]

---

[23] John U. Michaelis, Ruth H. Grossman, and Lloyd F. Scott, *New Designs for the Elementary School Curriculum* (New York: McGraw-Hill Book Company, 1967), p. 16.

[24] From *Goals for School Mathematics, The Report of Cambridge Conference on School Mathematics,* © 1963 by Educational Services, Incorporated. Reprinted by permission of the publisher, Houghton Mifflin Company.

This is a very powerful conceptualization of readiness. Each teacher builds upon the readiness experiences provided by the child's previous teachers and provides the requisite readiness experiences for the child's successive teachers. Jones states the case succinctly in the Twenty-Fourth NCTM Yearbook:

> Understanding and meaningfulness are rarely if ever "all or none" insights in either the sense of being achieved instantaneously or in the sense of embracing the whole of a concept and its implications at any one time. . . . the nature and generality of the pupil's conception will grow and develop and should not in general be expected to be complete at any stage. . . . Teachers must plan so that pupils continually have recurring but varied contacts with the fundamental ideas and processes of mathematics. . . . Teachers in all grades should view their tasks in the light of the idea that the understanding of mathematics is a continuum, that understandings grow within children throughout their school career.[25]

Kaplan[26] suggests that readiness must be judged in relation to the given learning context and that curricula should contain detailed behavioral specifications which tell the teacher whether a child has grasped a concept. While mathematics education has not reached this mecca, there are certain guidelines which will be helpful to teachers:

A. Identify major prerequisite concepts or skills and evaluate student attainment formally or informally.
B. Review major prerequisite concepts or skills with all students when introducing new concepts.
C. Provide individualized materials for those students who have not yet attained the desirable or necessary level of development.
D. Use a variety of methods and instructional aids to accommodate a variety of assimilative experiences by students.

Teachers should probably assume that students are maturationally ready since textbooks have generally taken this into consideration. However, if success does not come to all children regardless of the teacher's and pupil's effort expended, leave the topic and return to it later when the children are more likely to be ready.

---

[25] National Council of Teachers of Mathematics, *The Growth of Mathematical Ideas, Grades K-12*, 24th Yearbook of the National Council of Teachers of Mathematics (Washington, D. C.: National Council of Teachers of Mathematics, 1959), pp. 1, 2, 3.
[26] Jerome D. Kaplan, "What is Readiness?", *Arithmetic Teacher*, 14 (March, 1967), 216-17.

How Do Children Develop Abstract Number Concepts?

The pre-school child lives in a world which is of his own creation. His perceptions are related to past experiences and join together to form, however inexact, his concept of adult reality. Throughout his early years, he encounters mathematically-related ideas which are derived from his perceptions. "Two" may represent his age even though he has no concept of time, and "one, two, three, five, seven" may tell him "how many" even though his concept of counting is inaccurate. Throughout daily associations with members of his family, his box of toys, the coins in his bank, and other collections of things, he develops an intuitive sense of set. From various games with other children and adults he may learn to count in a rote manner; that is, he may count to ten when someone hides but may have no understanding that eight things are more than three things.

Rather crude concepts related to number are developed early in the lives of most children as they begin to notice which sibling received the biggest piece of pie, that Daddy is taller than Sue, that Bill has more marbles than Joe, and so on. The next step in the development of number understanding might well be acquired through the matching of sets of things. To see who has more marbles, he can remove one from each set in repeated succession until one set is exhausted. Through this matching process, he begins to develop rudimentary notions of *more than* and *less than* inequalities. Studies have shown that most children have had considerable informal contact with intuitive mathematics concepts before they begin formal instruction.[27,28]

The kindergarten and first grade teachers enrich the mathematics background of students and correct misconceptions which have formed. Considerable effort is spent to develop rational counting, i.e., matching each object in a collection with a subset of counting numbers. This builds the understanding that the last counting number used in the matching process is the number property of the set. For example, if the child rationally counts, "one, two, three, four," then the set which was counted had four things in it. The cardinal number of the set is four. Early in the school program teachers explore with children sets, counting numbers, simple fractions, recognition of coins and geometric shapes, use of the calender, and crude measurement concepts.

[27] Corwin E. Bjonerud, "Arithmetic Concepts Possessed by the Preschool Child," *Arithmetic Teacher*, 6, No. 4 (October, 1959), 186-90.

[28] Burdette R. Buckingham and Josephine H. MacLatchy, "Number Abilities of Children When They Enter Grade One," *Report of the Society's Committee on Arithmetic*, Twenty-Ninth Yearbook, National Society for the Study of Education (Bloomington, Ill.: Public School Publishing Company, 1930), pp. 473-524.

FIGURE XIII

Set with Cardinality Five Determined by Matching the Elements of a Set with the Set of Ordered Counting Numbers

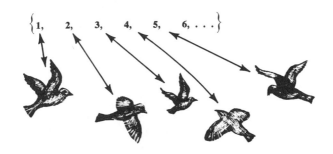

Five-year-olds are usually functioning at the preoperational stage of cognitive development, so teachers must rely heavily on intuition and make extensive use of concrete materials when engaging children in mathematical exploratory activities. Through manipulation of sets of concrete objects, children perform matching operations. A sense of "sameness" is developed when two sets can be matched, one at a time, and there are none "left over" in either set; i.e., the child exhausts both sets at the same time. This "sameness" is termed equivalence. When two

FIGURE XIV

Equivalent Sets

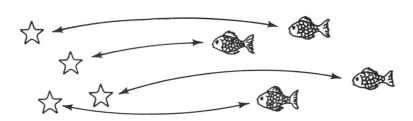

sets of objects can be matched using each element only once and no elements are left over, they are said to be equivalent sets. They have the same cardinality, or same cardinal number. Hence, through this matching or one-to-one correspondence, the child intuits that there are differences between various sets in this intuitive number sense.

FIGURE XV

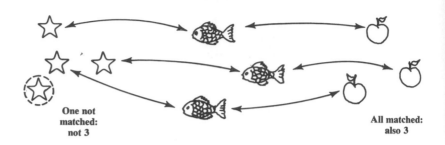

One not
matched:
not 3

All matched:
also 3

The culminating idea in the process is the introduction of the model set. The teacher presents a set which has three elements in it. The children are then taught through numerous experiences that any set which can be matched or put into one-to-one correspondence with this set also has the number property or cardinality three.

Eventually, the child no longer needs two *concrete* sets when he wants to know "how many" as in the case of the model set. He learns through the use of rational counting that in order to answer the question of "how many," he merely counts the objects in a set and the last counting number utilized represents the cardinality of the set. That cardinal number answers the question.

From this development, one can easily see why the Cambridge Conference recommended that

> . . . whenever possible, the child should have some intrinsic criterion for deciding the correctness of answers, without requiring recourse to authority. In the present work, this bed-rock foundation is generally provided by the fundamental operation of *counting*. The child's slogan might well be: when in doubt, count![29]

What is the Place of Discovery in Learning Elementary Mathematics?

Very analytical statements concerning discovery learning were made by David P. Ausubel in the *Arithmetic Teacher*[30, 31] relative to expository

---

[29] Educational Services Incorporated, *Goals for School Mathematics*, The Report of the Cambridge Conference on School Mathematics (Boston: Houghton Mifflin Company, 1963), p. 35.

[30] David P. Ausubel, "Facilitating Meaningful Verbal Learning in the Classroom," *Arithmetic Teacher* (February, 1968), 126-32.

[31] David P. Ausubel, "Some Psychological and Educational Limitations of Learning by Discovery," *Arithmetic Teacher*, 11 (May, 1964), 290-302.

and discovery teaching techniques. He addressed himself to the question of which is best. His major contribution in clarifying this educational question was undoubtedly his additional distinction between meaningful and rote learning as they apply to *both* teaching modes. An illustration to examine each is helpful:

A. A teacher says, "Addition is associative." She proceeds to explain to the class that numbers can be re-grouped when they are added, and the sum will not be affected. However, when the children add they do not use the associative property, $a + (b + c) = (a + b) + c$. Neither does the teacher use the property to show children how it can be used to make mathematics more understandable. The *teacher exposites*, and the *children memorize* her words, but neither the teacher nor the children are better off for having "learned" this property.

B. A teacher says, "Addition is associative." Through several teaching devices she makes a concerted effort to make this statement meaningful to students. When children add $26 + 7$ she shows them the associative property helps in the following way: $26 + 7 = (20 + 6) + 7 = 20 + (6 + 7) = 20 + 13 = 20 + (10 + 3) = (20 + 10) + 3 = 30 + 3 = 33$. Through repeated reinforcement of the basic concept and through repeated use in the development of mathematical understanding, the *teacher exposites* and the *students understand.*

C. Students are given six blocks with which to play. They are asked to find how many ways they can separate the blocks into three different sets and to write the mathematical sentences for each. With teacher guidance, the students can be led to discover, with the help of the associative property, that $1 + (2 + 3) = (1 + 2) + 3$ and so on. With considerable exploration the students can be led to see the generalization that numbers can be regrouped. Suppose the *teacher never capitalizes on this discovery* when she continues, then the students may have discovered the associative property but it has not become useful to them.

D. As in the preceding illustration, the children are directed in the discovery of the association property. This time, however, the teacher continues to explore the property with sets containing more than ten blocks. After a basic understanding of the associative property is developed, it is *utilized*. The *children are led to discover the property* and then *they are led to discover its implications for making* mathematical structure meaningful.

Proponents of discovery strategies frequently fail to take cognizance of the fact that all discovery learning is not necessarily meaningful.

Since teachers can teach mathematics meaningfully by expository and discovery methods, other factors must be considered when an appropriate method is sought. First, the advantages and disadvantages and then the relevance of teaching objectives should be considered.

Advantages and disadvantages. Teacher guidance is an important factor in teaching. The amount of guidance provided is determined by the objectives of the learning experience. When the teacher simply provides materials and allows children to explore without providing any assistance or direction, learning outcomes are determined entirely by the child's ability, curiosity, and previous experience. Such a pure discovery approach has its merits. In particular, the child is provided an opportunity to *ask* questions; he has the opportunity to form his own questions or hypotheses and collect data which supports or fails to support them. The student defines his own problem and creates his own structure in the learning experience. Goals are established internally.

Such an approach can be frustrating to a child who demands a structured learning environment. It is also time-consuming and has undefined outcomes. When the teacher guides student discoveries, the situation is quite different. In essence, the teacher poses the question and then the student is allowed considerable latitude in arriving at an acceptable solution. An important characteristic of this approach is that nearly every child can experience success. As a result of direct observation, the teacher can ask leading questions and structure the learning experience in such a way that nearly all students can make the discovery under observation. As with a pure discovery approach, the amount of time in making a generalization may be considerably longer than if the teacher were to explain it. However, proponents claim that the time lost in the beginning is regained later when the understandings built now facilitate new learnings by decreasing the amount of time necessary to develop skills and learn facts.

Herbert F. Spitzer[32] has observed that

> Controlled research studies, comparing pupil achievement in programs emphasizing an exploratory type of procedure with programs of a non-exploratory nature, have given a slight edge to the exploratory programs. When comparisons of outcomes are made through other data-gathering

---

[32] Herbert F. Spitzer, *Teaching Arithmetic*, No. 2 of *What Research Says to the Teacher*, Department of Classroom Teachers, American Educational Research Association of the National Education Association (Washington, D. C.: National Education Association, 1962), p. 8.

means, such as observations of pupil resourcefulness, confidence, and general interest in mathematics, the results have been even more definitely in favor of programs emphasizing exploration and discovery.

Guided discovery techniques tend to be characterized by active learning. Learning is pupil-centered because pupil thinking is stressed. Students are encouraged and guided to discover patterns and relationships in the study of mathematics. In such a way, they become more aware of the structure of mathematics.

Objectives. In addition to those considerations already mentioned, the teacher should examine the purpose of the day's lesson and the more encompassing objectives of the mathematics curriculum. A major question worthy of consideration is whether the curriculum is designed to develop skills (capabilities), as proposed by Gagne, or whether it is to develop thinking processes, as proposed by Bruner. As in the case of most such dichotomies, the truth is not either by itself but a proportion of each.

Skills can be developed by teachers most quickly and efficiently by expository instruction if understanding is not important. Skills with understanding can be developed, as indicated earlier, by either method. If skills, understanding, and problem-solving flexibility are all desirable, then guided discovery is most likely to yield the best results.

The Madison Project had as some of its goals in the directed discovery approach the following student objectives:

A. To have experience in discovering patterns in abstract situations.
B. To have experience in recognizing potentially open-ended situations by original creative work.
C. To possess an easy skill in relating mathematics to the applications of mathematics in physics and elsewhere.
D. To know that mathematics really and truly is discoverable.
E. To get a realistic assessment of his own personal ability in discovering mathematics.
F. To come to value "education intuition" in its proper place.
G. To value abstract rational analysis in its proper place.
H. To know when to persevere, and when to be flexible.
I. To have a feeling that mathematics is "fun" or "exciting" or "worthwhile."[33]

Teaching strategies are appropriate or inappropriate as they are related to the objectives of the day's lesson and the extent to which they

---

[33] Robert B. Davis, *Some Remarks on "Learning by Discovery,"* The Report of the Madison Project (Webster Groves, Mo.: Syracuse University-Webster College Madison Project, 1966), pp. 8-9.

support the broader goals of the mathematics curriculum. Strategy decisions must be made within the context of carefully defined objectives.

PERSPECTIVES

The evolution of the elementary mathematics curriculum will probably continue for many years. Meanwhile, mathematics educators are confronted by vexing questions on issues which cannot be resolved until much more research has been completed. From innovative programs have come not answers, but a new awareness of the numerous aspects of a very complex problem.

As a brief description of contributions from innovative programs is made, an assessment of current trends will be in order. What are the changes which have occurred? What are the current issues and trends?

What Have We Learned from the Innovative Mathematics Programs?

While much could be said of the new insights gained from innovative programs, much of this material would reflect the biases of writers. Proponents of new mathematics curricula assume that many fine things are being accomplished but often such feelings reflect *objectives, purposes,* and *hopes* rather than concrete data or even a concensus of opinion. Once one has filtered out the claims and hopes from those statements which are backed by research or concensus of most mathematics educators today, there is still a wealth of support for modern programs. Several of these claims will be considered.

Many mathematics topics can be lowered in grade placement. Many innovative programs have succeeded in teaching topics *meaningfully* at a lower grade level than had previously been done. A couple of notable programs of this type include the work with geometry in the Minnemast Project, formal set notation and logic in the Stanford Project, and mathematical sentences and inequalities in the School Mathematics Study Group (SMSG) materials. This trend is in agreement with Bruner's contention that material can be presented in a respectable manner at any age.

Discovery modes of instruction have several advantages. Participants in the Greater Cleveland Mathematics Program (GCMP) found that children were greatly fascinated and excited by their abilities to discover mathematics generalizations through utilization of a deductive approach.[34] Davis's experiences with the Madison Project also supported this approach. He found that children discovered generalizations through concrete experiences intended as preliminary to teaching understandings to such a great extent that frequently there was no need to teach the understandings—the children already knew what the teacher was going to teach![35] Research studies have disagreed about the positive benefits which may be attributed to discovery learning. One factor which has been well substantiated, however, is that discovery learning motivates children and this motivation is internalized. The challenges and excitement of discovery become self-rewarding.

Innovative programs seem to develop mathematical reasoning better than more traditional programs. This claim is a result of the emphasis placed by most new programs on the nature of proof, the use of discovery strategies, the presentation of logic, encouragement of pupil flexibility in problem solving, and stress on definitions and primitive or undefined terms. Work on estimation and some basic concepts of number theory also contribute to this goal.

Mathematics in K–6 is a systematically developed whole through the emphasis on structure, unifying ideas, and integration of content materials. Most innovative programs have developed within the framework of the Cambridge Conference in placing special emphasis on the structure of the real number system and extensive treatment of geometric concepts even though many such programs preceded the Cambridge Conference. Although most current textbook series limit extensive treatment to the whole numbers (counting numbers with zero) and non-negative rational numbers (positive fractional numbers with zero), the Cambridge Conference emphasizes properties of the set of real numbers and the various sets which are isomorphic to subsets of real numbers (counting or natural numbers, whole numbers, integers, and rational numbers). The concept of the spiraling mathematics curriculum has contributed greatly to the unity and structure of the curriculum; readiness experiences unfold and develop in increasing degree of depth and complexity as the child is introduced to concepts at the intuitive level and then proceeds to progress eventually to a great degree of symbolic abstraction and mathematical sophistication. Rosenbloom, the former director of Minnemast, has done a considerable amount of work with the integration of subject matter in his work with geometry and arithmetic concepts in the primary

---

[34] National Council of Teachers of Mathematics, *An Analysis of New Mathematics Programs* (Washington, D. C.: National Council of Teachers of Mathematics, 1963), p. 12.

[35] *Ibid.*, p. 17.

grades. Other unifying ideas include sets, operations, and measurement. Each has helped the child achieve an intuitive understanding of progression, continuity, and "unfoldingness" in the curriculum as he proceeds from kindergarten through the grades.

Additional support for concrete, individualized mathematical experiences has been garnered. The presence of Mueller-Willis, a student of Piaget, on the staff of the Minnemast Project is typical of the concern of nearly all innovative programs for the importance of children's characteristics and growth and development patterns. Teachers who have worked with GCMP and other new materials have been very pleased with the progress of children when they are provided with materials appropriate to their level of cognitive development. Many programs are characterized by active student participation, a variety of pupil experiences, and several methodological approaches. Teachers have become more aware that the learner must be met at his level of cognitive development *regardless of his grade level.*

The time required to cover a given amount of material can be somewhat diminished. By developing broader understanding of underlying concepts, teachers have found that less drill or practice is required. Also, by incorporating future concepts in the drill or practice exercises, the child is provided readiness experiences upon which to build understanding when new material in encountered. Again, this condensation is in agreement with the Cambridge Conference recommendations.

In-service work is important. While most educators and many teachers have always subscribed to this view, experiences with teachers in GCMP and other programs have indicated that teachers can change their attitudes and patterns of teaching when they become involved in the creative teaching fostered by understanding. They are stimulated through in-service work.

These findings support continued change and research in the mathematics curriculum. A desirable side-effect has been the creation of a climate for experimentation and change. Continued research has done a great deal to create an attitude of *evolution* in mathematics: this is very helpful in a world which is characterized by change.

What Are the Major Issues in the Elementary Mathematics Curriculum?

In the curriculum, as in so many aspects of life, issues are never clearly defined. The definitions of the issues depend upon the perceptions of the individual to whom the question is placed. Thorough analysis of current literature, however, enables one to determine those concerns expressed by leaders in the field and attempt to order and analyze them.

A list of issues is necessarily limited. When are concerns issues? When are they only of mild interest? This cannot be determined by any absolute cut-off. Some of the current professional concerns will be listed and discussed. By the very nature of the undertaking, it must be understood that the list is neither definitive nor exhaustive.

Individualized and group learning experiences in mathematics. For the past forty years, mathematics educators have been seeking acceptable solutions to the evasive problem of instructional grouping. Although most professionals agree that traditional self-contained classroom, single-group instruction is inadequate to meet the diverse needs of children, a suitable alternative has not been widely accepted. Research is currently being done with computers, most notably by Suppes at Stanford University,[36] and with Individually Prescribed Instruction (IPI); the best known work is probably that of Deep at Oakleaf School in Pittsburgh. Proponents of these methods praise these approaches for their flexibility and ability to meet the individual needs of children. Opponents have raised serious questions concerning the dehumanization of learning, social implications, and motivations. In Chapter 5 of this book there is a discussion concerning the socialization of learning. Rereading this chapter may help to sharpen up one's thinking concerning the dehumanizing of learning.

Grade placement of topics. The writings of the Cambridge Conference, the work of researchers such as Davis in the Madison Project, and the studies of prominent psychologists have raised many issues concerning children's abilities to handle more sophisticated mathematical concepts at earlier ages, including the integration of broad areas of mathematics such as arithmetic and geometry and the place of readiness experiences in the curriculum. Recently, the greatest activity has been in the development of pedagogically sound geometry materials for primary and intermediate grades. Logic, probability, and systems of numeration will probably continue as strong issues in curriculum over the next decade.

Discovery teaching and learning. While there is unquestionably a trend in instruction towards discovery modes of teaching, many professionals continue to raise questions concerning the purpose of instruction and the extent to which discovery can expeditiously be utilized within the

---

[36] Patrick Suppes, "The Uses of Computers in Education," *Scientific American*, 215, No. 3 (September, 1966), 206-20.

framework of existing time and ability structures. Perhaps more careful analysis should be made of individual learning modes. Discovery has been accepted by many as a panacea which will solve all instructional problems and develop critical thinkers. Others continue to research the impact, benefits, weaknesses, and appropriateness of discovery strategies. Mathematical understanding continues to be a goal of modern mathematics programs, but the issue is related to the manner in which this goal can be attained.

What Are the Trends in Elementary Mathematics?

Papers delivered at regional and national professional meetings and the current literature both provide indications of perceptible trends in the content and methodological aspects of the elementary mathematics curriculum. Some of the more obvious ones will be mentioned and briefly discussed.

New topics. Following the pattern established by the School Mathematics Study Group (SMSG), other innovative programs of the 1950's and 1960's, along with the Cambridge Conference, have influenced the grade placement of geometry topics. Authors are including increasing amounts of geometry in current textbooks, and teachers are becoming convinced that the trend is desirable. They are tending to omit geometry topics less and less! Considerable emphasis is being placed on an informal study of geometric concepts through the analysis of models as observed in concrete objects in the child's environment. The informal study of geometry emphasizes such aspects as the classification of various plane and solid models and the identification of members of certain sub-classes in the physical environment. Another aspect of the trend in geometry is the study of geometric concepts from a set-theoretic point of view. Lines are sets of points; circles divide plane regions into disjoint sets of points; and angles are unions of rays with common starting points.

Measurement has long been a part of the mathematics curriculum, but new emphasis is being placed on an understanding of the *characteristics* of measurement: precision, approximation, arbitrariness of units, direct versus indirect measurement, discrete versus continuous measurement, and so on. Understanding as well as skill is considered important.

All new textbooks are striving to develop mathematical readiness as represented by the spiraling curriculum model.

Individualization of instruction. In the previous two decades many individuals expressed their concern about mathematics for superior or gifted students. Presently, with the nation's concern for disadvantaged youth, considerable energy is being expended to develop appropriate mathematics and instructional strategies for slow learners in mathematics. A major indication of this trend was the 1964 Conference on Low Achievers jointly sponsored by the National Council of Teachers of Mathematics (NCTM) and the U.S. Department of Health, Education, and Welfare.[37] NCTM is presently preparing a new yearbook on low achievers in mathematics.

Laboratories are being increasingly utilized in mathematics instruction. While considerable debate concerning the focus, use, and physical set-up of laboratories in elementary schools is emerging, laboratories are helping to underscore the great need for concrete experiences in mathematics instruction. They make learnings meaningful by relating mathematics to the real world of the child and by providing experiences which are appropriate to the child's level of cognitive development. The Nuffield Project in England has been a driving force in this movement.

Individually Prescribed Instruction and computers are being used more extensively as time passes. Time and cost factors have so far limited the extent to which these modes of individualization have been utilized.

Psychomathematics. Gestalt Field Theory has been a dominant influence in mathematics instruction for quite some time. Current research tends to indicate that various degrees of discovery learning are desirable in mathematics. There are definite instructional trends in that direction. The writings of Bruner, Gagne, and Piaget are influencing mathematics instruction and the trends in mathematics education today to a great extent.

SUMMARY

Mathematics holds a position of great importance in our society. Its importance is not only reflected in technology but in the many ways it serves man in the social sciences. Through its application in statistics and computer science man progresses towards control and understanding of his environment. Mathematics serves as man's very dutiful subject. For what purposes its services are utilized cannot be said, but great potential for service which is directed at the common good is certainly present.

Mathematics serves the average man in a real, practical sense. In making daily decisions concerning buying, selling, insurance, college ex-

---

[37] Lauren G. Woodby, *The Low Achiever in Mathematics*, Report of a conference held in Washington, D. C., March 25-27, 1964, sponsored jointly by the U.S. Office of Education and the National Council of Teachers of Mathematics (Washington, D. C.: U.S. Department of Health, Education, and Welfare, 1965).

penses, saving, and so on. Each citizen calls upon his number skills to help arrive at rational decisions.

When building a mathematics curriculum, the builders of the curriculum must bear in mind the needs of the society, both technological and humanitarian. These two aspects have common and also distinct implications. The degree to which such implications should be implemented must necessarily be influenced by the needs of the child and the structural characteristics of the subject matter. To be sound, curriculum must consider relevant factors of child growth and development patterns, individual readiness patterns, and a whole host of other complexly related variables.

Teachers are truly challenged by today's mathematics curriculum. Creative approaches and flexibility in mathematics instruction are highly desirable. Since children learn in many ways, teachers are challenged to use a variety of instructional strategies in developing pupil understanding. Through extensive use of concrete materials, especially manipulatory devices for individual use, teachers can offer variety to children in the ways in which they can achieve new mathematical insights. Teachers are challenged to view textbooks as being one of many instructional tools. Textbooks are semiconcrete and abstract learning aids which should be utilized in the earlier grades only after concrete aids have been extensively explored.

Evaluation is an important aspect of the teacher's task. Not only does she evaluate daily work, but she must evaluate readiness levels of children to make decisions concerning timing, types of materials, and strategies which will be meaningful. Decisions related to review and individual attention are based on her evaluation of child needs. Also, she must make evaluative decisions concerning texts and teaching aids in resource acquisitions. All of these factors place a responsibility on the teacher to attempt to keep up to date and to know sources of help to which she can turn when the challenges of her daily program exceed her personal resources.

SUGGESTED PROBLEMS AND ACTIVITIES

1. Mrs. Jarvin discussed decomposition in multiplication on Tuesday. She explained it like this:

$$
\begin{array}{cc}
47 & 40 + 7 \\
\times\,6 & \underline{\phantom{40 + {}}6} \\
& 240 + 42 \\
& 282
\end{array}
$$

Mary worked all home work problems by utilizing the standard algorithm. She had learned it from her parents. What alternatives are open to Mrs. Jarvin? Under what conditions should each one be followed?

2. Dr. Perkins from the local college wants to teach logic to fourth graders. What questions might he expect at the P.T.A. meeting from individuals with points of view representative of each of the three curriculum criteria?

3. Cite examples of objectives from various grade levels which would most appropriately be achieved through *pure discovery* (no teacher guidance; student forms own questions), *guided discovery* (teacher poses problem and guides student toward discovery of answer or generalization), and *straight expository instruction* (lecture with appropriate teaching aids).

4. Describe two methods of accounting, to some degree, for individual differences in mathematics instruction other than those cited in this chapter.

5. Write six test items for any grade level of mathematics instruction which seek to evaluate pupil *understanding* of concepts.

6. Describe some of the major elements or activities in the K–6 mathematics curriculum which communicate the nature of the spiraling curriculum. In what way or in what sense do these elements represent the expanded view of readiness?

7. The teachers in K–6 (one in each grade) are told that a grant has been received which will enable them to purchase $250 worth of instructional materials in mathematics. List several steps they might follow in making a wise decision.

SUGGESTED READINGS

Ausubel, David P. "Facilitating Meaningful Verbal Learning in the Classroom," *Arithmetic Teacher*, Vol. 15 (February, 1968), 126-32.

Buffie, Edward G., Ronald C. Welch, and Donald D. Paige. *Mathematics: Strategies of Teaching.* Englewood Cliffs, N. J.: Prentice-Hall, Inc., 1968.

Deans, Edwina. *Elementary School Mathematics: New Directions.* Bulletin 1963, No. 13. Washington, D. C.: U.S. Department of Health, Education, and Welfare, Office of Education, 1963.

DeVault, M. Vere, and Thomas E. Kriewall. *Perspectives in Elementary School Mathematics.* Columbus, Ohio: Charles E. Merrill Publishing Company, 1969.

Educational Services Incorporated. *Goals for School Mathematics.* The Report of the Cambridge Conference on School Mathematics. Boston: Houghton Mifflin Company, 1963.

Glennon, Vincent J., and Leroy G. Callahan. *Elementary School Mathematics: A Guide to Current Research.* 3rd ed.; Washington, D. C.: National Education Association, 1968.

Houston, W. Robert. *Improving Mathematics Education for Elementary School Teachers.* Report of a two-week conference held in East Lansing, Michigan in August, 1967, sponsored by the Science and Mathematics Teaching Center, Michigan State University, and the National Science Foundation. East Lansing, Mich.: Michigan State University, 1967.

National Council of Teachers of Mathematics. *Enrichment Mathematics for the Grades.* 27th Yearbook of the National Council of Teachers of Mathematics. Washington, D. C.: National Council of Teachers of Mathematics, 1963.

National Council of Teachers of Mathematics. *The Growth of Mathematical Ideas, Grades K–12.* 24th Yearbook of the National Council of Teachers of Mathematics. Washington, D. C.: National Council of Teachers of Mathematics, 1959.

Phillips, Jo. "Teaching New Math." *The Instructor,* Vol. 77 (February, 1968), 33-40.

Spitzer, Herbert F. *Teaching Arithmetic.* No. 2 of *What Research Says to the Teacher,* Department of Classroom Teachers, American Educational Research Association. Washington, D. C.: National Education Association, 1962.

Woodby, Lauren G. *The Low Achiever in Mathematics.* Report of a conference held in Washington, D. C., March 25-27, 1964, sponsored jointly by the U.S. Office of Education and the National Council of Teachers of Mathematics. Washington, D. C.: U.S. Department of Health, Education, and Welfare, 1965.

CHAPTER 10

Implementing the Science Curriculum

INTRODUCTION

Science has played a vital role in bringing about changes in human societies, although not as an organized body of knowledge. Technology is one of the forces that has given birth to an American society that must face the realities of continuous change; there can be no turning back. New break-throughs in medical research, thermo-nuclear physics and a host of other fields will have a profound effect upon human society. Science has been thought of as a method of working, but in today's world science also contributes as a way of thinking, a way of life and even a world-wide philosophy through which men may find a common ground for furthering Democracy.[1] One authority has reconciled the unrealities of the past by advancing certain premises of science and democracy which point out the relationships between the two concepts:

> Democracy, as a way of organizing human relations, cultivates responsible freedom of choice. Science, as a method and philosophy, produces the technical basis for making that freedom responsible. Democracy sponsors the continuous development of the uniqueness of individuality; science utilizes this uniqueness for producing fresh hypotheses, new viewpoints and the discovery of new problems. Democracy rests its foundations on the dignity of man as a responsible citizen; science makes possible the dignity of man by involving him meaningfully in the painstaking accumulations of reliable knowledge and their technical applications.[2]

The above quotation serves to clarify one's thinking concerning the task of teaching science and the need to view science as a major contributing source in helping men to reconcile new knowledge to solving basic social problems.

---

[1] National Council for the Social Studies, *Science and the Social Studies*, Twenty-seventh Yearbook (Washington, D.C.: National Education Association, 1957), p. 184.
[2] *Ibid.*, p. 184.

It is also true that children live in a world of science. They ponder its wonderments each day. Any experienced teacher or parent is aware of the profound questions to which children seek answers as they try to gain new and interesting understandings about their environment. One of the authors in journeying to his home found three small chilren with a jar which had holes punched in the top. Inside were two different types of caterpillars. It was the fall season, and the children had found out from the encyclopedia that these caterpillars would soon develop into cocoons. They were hoping this phenomenon would take place right before their eyes. Science to these children (and most others) is largely a vital, dynamic world of the unknown. But each day new understandings are gained which help children to interpret more fully their environment. It should be obvious from the experience just cited that science is problem-solving in nature. Unfortunately, many teachers have not always viewed their responsibility as that of guiding children into real experiences in finding solutions to problems and interpreting these solutions in terms of their scientific and social implications.

This chapter will contribute to the teacher's understanding of science learnings as a developmental process which is in complete harmony with the development of children. A discussion of basic science objectives, the children themselves, and science experiences will relate science teaching to certain developmental concepts of child growth. Some suggestions will be made to assist the teacher in improving science teaching through relating science to compatible content areas as well as to indicate how instructional materials and resources may be utilized toward this end.

SCIENCE FOR THE ELEMENTARY SCHOOL

The American elementary school, a product of democracy, is controlled by the people. There are deep-rooted American beliefs about maintaining local control of education. This concept leaves the people of the nation responsible for preserving, perpetuating, and to a large extent, modifying our way of life. It further recognizes that communities may have different needs and thus the freedom to meet these differing needs lies within the control of the people. In a very real sense the wide disparities in science offerings in our elementary schools are the responsibilities of the people, but educators must provide the leadership for curriculum innovations and improvement.

An elementary school science program must be designed at the level of each local school to meet the needs of each child. Research by Brown[3]

---

[3] Stanley B. Brown, "Science Information and Attitudes Possessed by Selected Elementary Pupils," *Science Education*, 39 (February, 1955), 37-59.

points out how these needs differ among various groups. For example, it was found that rural pupils scored significantly higher on science information tests than urban pupils, and that boys scored higher than girls on science information. In addition, rural pupils possessed more favorable science attitudes than urban pupils. Girls, although possessing less information, had more favorable science attitudes than boys. A good science program must further the understandings of *all pupils.* Since the children attending public elementary schools will be the future medical researchers, nuclear researchers, and other types of scientists in our society, individual needs must be met with a challenge. However, this does not mean that elementary school science must become a tool for specialists only. Science must serve the needs of all in such a way that it aids in the development of the child and serves the welfare of all mankind. If our basic premise that each society recognizes the value of its schools as perpetuating and modifying its way of life is true, then science, or any other subject in the elementary school, must contribute to this end. Science can only make such a contribution as all citizens become proficient in using it as a tool for constructive—not destructive—purposes. Mankind has the responsibility for enriching life for all peoples if conditions throughout the world are to be improved. This can more nearly be accomplished when people learn to think of science as a benefit to mankind and how it can be used to shape the future.

Science and democracy are compatible to the extent that science helps the pupil to utilize democratic skills, to gain broader understandings of man and his environment, to utilize these understandings in building a better world, and to understand and appreciate the contributions of his heritage. The public elementary school science program then is not for developing specialists, but for building understandings, skills, and appreciations in the future scientists and others from all walks of life who will work and live together. It is not difficult for past generations to have known both the destructive and constructive powers of science. This knowledge alone should serve warning that any area of study which has such tremendous forces for evil must be controlled by the people. If this is to be effectively carried out, the science taught in the elementary school must provide for developing the potential of *all* pupils.

Why Has Science Taken on a New Meaning in the Elementary School?

It has been suggested that there is a world of science about us in every day living. Our way of life is shaped by man's increasing understandings of science, which are interwoven with the total living of man. His ability to continue to improve his way of life, or to destroy it, will depend upon his ability to possess necessary skills to solve ever-increasing problems of a more complex nature. His need to learn to live cooperatively with all men has become paramount. Communication and transportation advancements have brought the most remote sections of the world within easy reach. Science has become a basic tool for solving critical problems relating to world peace as well as a means of improving the living standards of all people.

Social implications. Man's knowledge in the development of civilization has resulted in a complete change of our social arrangements. What was formerly a totally independent, small group arrangement for producing those things which were needed has become a large impersonal urban community. This arrangement has resulted in the loss of the satisfying feelings of accomplishment which individuals gained from personal responsibility for producing an essential commodity for the community. Such was the case in rural America at the turn of the last century. The age of automation broadened this gap between man's identity with his own contribution and the intangible, impersonal contribution of the assembly line. That is, in the past the cobbler made a pair of shoes completely by hand and gained an intrinsic satisfaction from a task well done as well as a feeling of personal worth to the community. Today, only the finisher sees the end product. Many men contribute to making thousands of pairs of shoes a day, but the real personal feeling of contributing one's skills may be lost in this age of automation. The jet age, the rocket age, the wonders of the atomic age, all will produce a dynamic, changing world. Although it may be speculative to proceed on the assumption that living in a rapidly changing world produces large numbers of mentally ill people, there does seem to be some evidence pointing to the inability of many individuals to adjust. Cobb points out that five per cent of the general population of America is suffering from emotional disorders ranging from mild to severe cases.[4] Rogers points out that this figure is even higher, since large numbers of people are not institutionalized or being treated, and are not reported.[5]

Can Science Help Children Live Successfully in a Changing World?

Life takes place in a context of continuous change which cannot be slowed down and perhaps should not be impeded, even if it were possible. Nevertheless, the basic social adjustment essential to maintaining mental health is one of the functions of the elementary school in which science

---

[4] Stanley Cobb, *"Borderland of Psychiatry"* (Cambridge, Mass.: Harvard University Press, 1943), p. xii.

[5] Dorothy Rogers, *Mental Hygiene in Elementary Education* (Boston: Houghton Mifflin Company, 1957), p. 11.

learnings can play a major role. World events and scientific discoveries happen so quickly that it becomes increasingly more difficult for man not only to adapt mentally to these changes, but also to realize the immediate social implications. Science progress in journeying to outer space, medical advances in organ transplant, and other scientific gains are understandably accompanied by fear and anxiety. Religious beliefs have been challenged and new moral and ethical problems which need solutions have come to the forefront.

How will children in tomorrow's schools face the events ahead? Possibly we will soon have the knowledge to control human behavior, to order the weather we want, to unlock the secrets of traveling to distant planets, and to establish communication with intelligent beings from beyond our own solar system.[6] Therefore, we need elementary science programs that will release the thinking of children so that they will be able to cope with a world in continual technological change. We must help children to intelligently make decisions about the future without fear of the technology that man has created. He must realize that man has control of the technology which he produces and that he can use it for good if he so desires. The vast amount of good for mankind which can come from atomic energy is but one example that the decision rests with man.

Children who experience science learning throughout the elementary years will inevitably accept change as a necessary part of their lives. As children study science, they will learn of its inconsistencies as well as its orderliness and will come to realize that the universe itself is constantly changing. Such programs must assist children to face the events of the future and to become contributing members of a rapidly changing world.

Nevertheless, the basic social adjusting which is essential to maintaining mental health is a function of the elementary school in which science learnings can play a major role. Although children may be caught up in life's tremendous, impersonal whirl, through science they can learn some basic principles which will assist them in taking intelligent action that can lead to more favorable environmental adjustments.

How Do Children Learn Problem Solving?

The problem-solving approach is the scientific method which, with modification, should become an organized approach to living. However, it should be made clear that science has no special claim upon this method. A way of developing an orderly procedure for reaching solutions to problems has its place in the total curriculum. Basic, however, to the use of this procedure for teaching is the recognition of the fact that this

---

[6] See for further discussion Emmanuel Mesthene, "Learning to Live with Science," *National Elementary Principal* (Sept. 1968), 32-35.

method must be taught and learned as any other skill. That is, direct experiences which will place the child in situations which demand the use of the method are essential. As the pupil experiences the process, he learns to *identify and define a problem.* This may emerge as a result of his own thinking or it may be the result of group thinking with teacher guidance to insure sequential development with a minimum of inefficiency in the process. In other words, when more than one individual seeks to identify a problem, that identification will in all likelihood be more definitive.

It is important for the teacher to be aware of the need for pupils to feel that the identification of a problem is theirs, and to be certain that the problem is one of major interest to the pupils so they will want to solve it. It is not uncommon for children to be placed in situations where the teacher virtually manipulates them into accepting what she considers to be a problem. This may lead to a lack of faith in the process especially if the problem is beyond the comprehension of the group or individual.

The method of solving a problem is an important part in developing the skill of problem solving. Here again, teachers may feel that children lack experience and therefore seek to "tell" the children how to find their solutions. Children, if given a chance, will use their own ideas in search of possible solutions. These may not always be expressed in terms of a scientific solution, but they will be in terms of the pupils' experiences and understandings. Some methods which may lead the group to a solution of their problems are (1) discussion, (2) experimentation, and (3) research. Thus the teacher's role becomes clear as she guides the children in utilizing techniques which will lead to purposeful, intelligent action.

How Do Children Determine the Validity of Their Conclusions?

It was pointed out in Chapter 5 that children need to learn how to authenticate the conclusions they reach. Solutions to problems whether they be in social studies or science need to be validated. Children who work experiments to gain certain insights or information need also to recognize sources of authority to determine the accuracy of their information. Therefore, children need to become familiar with sources of scientific material, science textbooks, encyclopedias and other materials commensurate with their maturity level. Obviously, as they become older they should become more adept in securing information from the most reliable sources.

Craig points out that children need to learn how primitive explanations have grown into modern scientific ideas.[7] Children should not only

---

[7] Gerald C. Craig, *Science for the Elementary School Teacher.* (Boston: Ginn & Company, 1958), p. 120.

learn to verify their findings, but they should through this procedure come to know that scientists have not always been successful in finding answers to their questions. Thus the endless search to explore the unknown continues. As children formulate hypotheses, seek solutions to problems, and evaluate or appraise the solutions reached, they become familiar with the scientific method as a helpful tool which can be adapted for use in solving problems in their daily affairs.

THE EMERGING SCIENCE DESIGN IS BASED UPON SOUND OBJECTIVES

Science objectives, as any other set of objectives, should give direction to the kinds of teaching-learning situations which develop in the classroom. Science should no longer be thought of as an organized body of knowledge from which children are expected to memorize certain principles or a set number of generalizations relating to each experiment. Modern science teaching is problem-centered. Through a study of science, children come to a better understanding of themselves and their environment, and this cannot be accomplished through memorizing a series of what was formerly termed "universal laws." *A curriculum design for science education must concern itself with the world in which the child finds himself. That is, the child must learn skills, appreciations, understandings, and attitudes which will help him to understand the changing, dynamic nature of his social and physical environment.*

Have Elementary School Science Objectives Changed?

Elementary school science objectives as listed in various sources during the several previous decades are markedly alike.[8] Most statements of objectives emphasize structure, process, and attitudes.[9] The Illinois Curriculum Program[10] states the following purposes for teaching science:

1. To familiarize children with a basic body of knowledge.
   a. To acquaint children with the fundamental facts and ideas of science

---

[8] See Maxine Dunfee, *Elementary School Science: A Guide to Current Research* (Washington, D.C.; Association for Supervision and Curriculum Development, 1967), pp. 4-5.

[9] *Ibid.*, p. 7.

[10] Illinois Curriculum Program, *Strengthening Science Teaching in Elementary Schools* (Springfield, Illinois: Office of the Superintendent of Public Instruction, 1960), p. 184.

b. To integrate the broad subject matter areas of science as much as possible so that the child can begin to see science in total perspective

c. To correct common misconceptions relative to science phenomena in our environment and to combat superstition

d. To help children understand the scientific facts and applications regarding personal health and human survival

2. To help children develop proper attitudes toward science and the world of technology.

a. To develop the attitude that, in the physical universe, nothing happens without a cause

b. To develop an appreciation for science and its potential

c. To develop an appreciation for the inherent limitations of science and the fact that science is not a panacea for all man's difficulties

3. To help children acquire the basic skills of science so they will be able to study better about, and function within, a scientific environment. These skills are:

a. Skills in making observations

b. Skills in making comparisons

c. Skills in making relevant distinctions

d. Skills in critical thinking

In addition to the skills listed above, the following could be added:

e. Skills in experimentation

f. Skills in investigation

Elementary school science will serve its purpose only when the child sees science as being exciting and challenging and when it furthers the inquiring mind to higher states of curiosity. The objectives of teaching science must be to awaken the intellectual power of the learner so that through inquiry he will learn to use sources of information, make careful observations, develop scientific attitudes, and build classification systems, all in the process of forming supportable principles and generalizations.

Another list of purposes of science instruction points out the similarity in the science purposes of the elementary schools and those of the secondary schools. The Virginia State Department of Education conducted two state-wide workshops for the purpose of giving emphasis to improved science teaching. At these workshops contributions from the experience of many classroom science teachers were made, and a tentative guide for science teaching was formulated. The approach may be considered unique, since elementary and secondary teachers worked together in developing a guide for the total school program. The common purposes developed were:

(1) To help pupils discover, understand, and interpret their natural environment, their relationship to it, and its impact upon them.

(2) To help pupils feel at home in their environment, to appreciate it, and to use it wisely.

(3) To help pupils develop and apply those understandings which contribute to good physical and mental health.

(4) To encourage and stimulate the inquiring mind in all pupils.

(5) To develop an appreciation for scientific contributions and their benefits to mankind.

(6) To help pupils gain those understandings which will dispel fear of superstition and unsound beliefs.

(7) To assist and encourage pupils in developing certain hobbies which may contribute to the worthy use of their leisure time.

(8) To develop in pupils a knowledge and appreciation of the vocational implications of science in order that they may be better able to make a selection of their life's work.

(9) To develop such scientific attitudes as belief in cause and effect, willingness to change with new evidence, willingness to consider new facts, and willingness to withhold conclusions until all available facts have been secured.

(10) To develop an understanding of man's dependence upon natural resources and the importance of conserving them.

(11) To develop an appreciation for the Supreme Power that created the universe in an orderly and systematic manner.[11]

Many other lists of objectives could be included, if space permitted, but few differences would be noted. It should become evident after a study of the above objectives that a new kind of science must become an integral part of a new elementary curriculum design. To achieve these objectives, time must be allotted for science in the daily schedule both in a direct approach to science and in an incidental or related subject approach. To achieve these objectives children must participate—science learnings require activity. The classroom then becomes a laboratory, and the community a resource for learning as children seek to solve problems. It is not uncommon for young children to ask, "Where does the sun go when it goes down?" "Why do stars twinkle?" "Why are wings large on some katydids and small on others?" Questions are posed and answers sought when teachers establish the appropriate climate for discovery and investigation. As children study social studies, arithmetic, music and other curriculum areas, the natural relationship of science becomes clear. That is, music involves sound, sound involves tone, tone involves pitch,

---

[11] Commonwealth of Virginia State Board of Education, "A Tentative Guide for Science Grades 1-12" (January, 1956), pp. 2, 3.

and a whole gamut of science learnings may provide new and interesting understandings of music and science for the children.

THE SCIENCE EXPERIENCES AND CONCEPTS OF CHILDREN

Although the research evidence concerning the reasons why children lose interest in science is limited, there is some basis for assuming that one of the reasons is that in the upper elementary grades there may be changes in the teacher's approach. General science courses have been known to be boring, uninteresting and considered useless by seventh-, eighth- and ninth-graders. The cause may be traced to the traditional methods of teaching laws, principles, generalizations and terms with virtually no supplemental experiences provided. This lack of interest may also be found at any grade level for the same reason and due to the same causes. If the objectives which were outlined in the previous section are to be achieved, then science learnings must be organized consistent with child development characteristics—organized around a problem-centered approach that is provoked by intense interest.

Why Are Children Interested in Science?

Science in the elementary school is not considered a highly technical subject, since it is an area of learning which relates itself to the everyday experiences of the learner. A few hours spent in child observation will reveal the strong desire children have to understand their environment. Science in the elementary school should consist of meeting the challenges of helping children to learn about those things which "bother" them and to the degree that their maturity and ability will facilitate comprehension of certain phenomena. Science is the vehicle by which children reach out into their everyday lives and search for answers to constantly arising questions.

Natural investigators. Children are, by nature, curious. From the time they begin talking, their continuous flow of questions deals with why is it? what is it? and the like. What mother hasn't experienced finding her child at a very early age involved in a secret session of mixing up her best face creams with powder and other cosmetics, or climbing to the top of a chair to reach some intriguing keepsake which was supposedly put in a safe place? What adult doesn't have the urge to run his hands through the fur of a coat? To feel the texture of various things is a strong desire which helps us to learn through the sense of touch or "tactile perception." The natural curiosity of children contributes to maintaining their interest at a high level. The teacher who permits children to carry out their characteristics of being *natural* investigators has little or no cause to fear that she will have trouble motivating children to learn science. Obviously, science experiences need to be directed in such a way that the child will gain the most from them. But this does not mean that science is to become a mere textbook subject. In fact, if children are to satisfy their interests in science, they need to go beyond the limits of the textbook. This is not to imply that the textbook is not valuable as a guide, but instruction must be vertically as well as horizontally enriched. Many sources of information are required. The point is that these "natural investigators" must be reasonably free to pursue their interests—each child to his own satisfaction. That is, once a child has reached his mental limit as related to his maturity for exploring a particular area, he is ready to pursue a new science interest.

Concepts are developmental. Science learnings, like other curricula areas are, developmental in nature. It is not that these learnings take on some mythical or logical arrangement of subject matter, but that they are dealt with in terms of their concreteness as well as their relationships to the learner's immediate environment. In his quest for refining his understandings he reaches a point beyond which he is unable to comprehend. Usually, however, he has satisfied his initial motive at this point. Of importance here is the teacher's role in guiding this interest so that permanent learnings which the maturing child can build upon will result.

Firsthand experience is essential in developing concepts in early childhood. From this assumption, it can be seen that children in the primary grades must have ample opportunities to develop concepts suited to their maturity level by being permitted to investigate and explore. The vagueness of the concept of the earth's motion is evident when the child says "the sun is moving." Numerous other statements of children reveal the need for careful planning by the teacher to insure firsthand experiences and demonstrations for children in concept building. This is an essential step in helping the child to form generalizations and principles. The child who holds a cold glass of milk over a steaming bowl of soup may wonder what's happening around the outside of the glass. Thus, as children have experiences which are related to science subject matter will they gain new insights into the world of the unknown.

How Are Science Concepts Formed?

The developing of concepts is an important aspect of learning whether it be in science or any other area of learning. *A concept is an idea, or notion, or image conceived in the mind.* Thus it may be real and specific as snow, or it may be a broad generalization such as the earth's moving around the sun producing the seasons. The child who has never seen snow may have a difficult time conceiving of it. Again, the teacher's task in concept building is to provide firsthand experiences wherever possible to aid the child in gaining insights which may be recalled mentally when the situation demands.

When children have had a variety of concrete experiences, reading takes on new meanings. That is, the children are able to build concepts for themselves as they read and are able to generalize with accuracy from their many experiences about that which is being read. As children grow in the use of vocabulary, they become more capable of learning from vicarious experiences. Dewey has written that "memory is vicarious experience in which there is all the emotional values of actual experience without its strains, vicissitudes and troubles."[12] The experiences of kindergarten and first grade children are sometimes quite limited. *It might be generalized that concrete learning experiences should decrease from the kindergarten to the sixth grade. Thus, vicarious experience becomes an increasingly more important function of the teaching-learning process in concept building.* The teacher has the responsibility of helping children to reconstruct certain experiences in order to gain the most from vicarious learnings. However, the teacher must be aware of the child's need to develop his concepts in some logical order.[13]

The teacher needs to understand that logical order or sequence does not necessarily mean the way a given subject is presented in the textbook. It is true that science may be a subject which has traditionally been taught or presented in a given logical order, but the interests of children cannot be ignored in learning. That is, children do not always learn according to some adult plan. A study of energy, for example, usually starts with the nature and importance of energy. However, due to the inquisitiveness of children, instruction may start with the children's interest in a crane lifting steel to the top of a building near the school. Such was the experience of one group of first grade children. As the study developed, one little girl asked, "Is energy what makes my dolly walk when I wind her up?" This led the teacher to bring to class an old alarm clock. After she removed the back and wound up the alarm the children could see the spring being made tighter. As the teacher let a child release the alarm, the other pupils could watch the spring increase in size as it released its energy to make the bell ring. The little girl who started this inquiry by asking about her doll now questioned, "Is it food that I eat that makes the energy for

---

[12] John Dewey, *Reconstruction in Philosophy* (Boston: Beacon Press, 1948), p. 2.
[13] Clark Hubler, *Working With Children in Science* (Boston: Houghton-Mifflin Company, 1957), p. 31.

me to walk and run?" This child was now forming abstract concepts and was ready for developing deeper insights about energy than were most of the other children.

Further pursuits will depend upon the maturity of the individual learners. We can conclude that in the final analysis concept building in science may be directed through teacher-pupil planning. This procedure permits the teacher to develop the area of study as outlined in the course or curriculum guide, but leaves the sequence of experiences involved in the learning to be developed in accordance with the circumstances surrounding the learning situation. Therefore, concepts are learned in logical sequence as they are related to the comprehension of the learner. New meanings are built upon previous learnings as new understandings are continuously pursued through the interests of the children. It is necessary to keep in mind that concepts rarely develop in isolation. Science concepts are inter-related with the whole of human endeavor. Carpenter,[14] in a research study, concluded that (1) functional learning of concepts is more efficient than rote learning when measured by retention and ability to verbalize meanings; and (2) concepts of material objects are better understood when the learner is able to manipulate and study the objects rather than just dealing with factual information.

The Science Curriculum Improvement Study[15] has been concerned with the development of scientific literacy. This term refers to sufficient knowledge and understanding of the fundamental concepts of both biological and physical sciences to insure effective participation in twentieth-century life.

The child builds up concepts through a program based on a hierarchical arrangement of levels of abstraction. It is of major importance to provide the child with an intellectually free atmosphere where his ideas will be respected, where he may learn to test his ideas by experiment, and where he can accept or reject an idea not based on authority but on the basis of his own observations.[16]

In a project[17] by Atkin at the University of Illinois, the researcher indicated that there was evidence to support the opinion that children

---

[14] Finley Carpenter, "The Effects of Different Learning Methods on Concepts Formation," *Science Education*, 40 (October, 1956), 282-85.

[15] *Science Curriculum Improvement Study*, Robert Karplus, Director, University of California, Berkeley; funded by the National Science Foundation, 1962.

[16] J. David Lockard (ed.), *Sixth Report of the International Clearinghouse on Science and Mathematics Curricular Developments*, A joint project of the American Association for the Advancement of Science and The Science Teaching Center (College Park, Md.: University of Maryland, 1968), p. 332.

[17] J. Myron Atkin, Director, The University of Illinois Elementary School Science Project (Astronomy), College of Education, University of Illinois, Urbana, Illinois.

were interested in and capable of comprehending content and concepts not now included in most elementary science curricula.[18] However, the importance of helping children to build concepts in an interesting and stimulating environment cannot be over-emphasized. The common complaint of both teachers and children concerning social studies and science books has been the comprehension level of the materials.

As children build insights or concepts and as they mature, vicarious experiences may serve a useful purpose in learning. It is at this point that the child is able to relate his concrete experiences to present situations through reading, discussion, and other procedures which produce new learnings or interpretations based upon indirect experiences. *However, the elementary school teacher must guard against assuming that children have had sufficient direct, first-hand experiences at any level of learning. Each new inquiry may need careful analysis to insure that the learner has acquired the necessary concepts to proceed to new learnings.* When teachers recognize this, learning becomes more efficient and accurate.

GUIDING CHILDREN IN SCIENCE EXPERIENCES

The most important factor in guiding the science experiences for children is the attitude of the teacher. She may envision science as a wonderful subject to teach, full of new and challenging experiences for children. On the other hand, she may feel that science teaching in the elementary school requires a technically trained specialist and thus may fail to progress beyond using the science textbook as a reader. This may be the fault of the teacher's preparation in science. In working with pre-service elementary teachers, one of the authors found that some were having great difficulty in trying to relate their college science learnings to elementary school science. Since the attitude of the teacher plays an important part in developing any teaching-learning situation, it becomes clear that if the teacher is to become effective in guiding children's experiences in science, she must consider it as an exciting and challenging opportunity. The teacher need not fear the teaching of elementary school science, since it is largely concerned with interpreting those things with which the child and the teacher have daily contact. Science is an area of the curriculum which ordinarily does not present problems of motivation; however, the selecting of appropriate experiences does present a problem for the classroom teacher.

---

[18] Dunfee, *op cit.*, p. 11.

What Criteria Should Be Used for Selecting Science Experiences?

Science must contribute to meeting the basic purposes of elementary education as well as the objectives for elementary science. This means that children should learn how they are affected by the environment in their everyday living. Carefully planned science experiences are essential in developing a good science instructional program. No program which depends solely upon incidental-type teaching can be considered wholly adequate. Therefore, the teacher must have some basis for selecting appropriate science learnings for children. The criteria for selecting such experiences should:

1. Be based upon sequence as it is related to the maturity level of the learner and provide the necessary continuity from kindergarten through grade six.
2. Provide for the differing ability levels of the children to insure continuous growth of *all*.
3. Provide the kind of experiments which are rudimentary in nature and natural for children to carry out in the classroom.
4. Contribute to helping children achieve the objectives of science education which will insure growth in critical thinking and result in a better understanding of the scientific method as a process for solving problems in everyday life.
5. Aid the children in developing favorable attitudes, appreciations, skills, and habits related to developing a "democratic personality."
6. Develop skill in analyzing, appraising, and evaluating evidence before reaching decisions.
7. Help children to become familiar with and recognize the value of utilizing many kinds of resources both human and physical in seeking solutions to purposeful problems.

How May Science Teaching Be Initiated?

Since science learnings are largely concerned with those things and events which occur in the learner's environment, the teacher should be influenced by the natural curiosity of the children. Some specific suggestions are given below to aid in initiating science instruction. The order of the suggestions may be considered as developmental from the point of view found throughout this book. That is, a teacher may want to identify the technique which she has been using and then study what changes she would need to make in her personal adjustment in order to effect the new procedures as she grows toward utilizing the children's aspirations in initiating science instruction. The suggested procedures are:

1. Start with textbook or other materials (chapter dealing with weather; a weather map, etc.)
2. Begin through a lively discussion (controversy over what it means to break the sound barrier, etc.)
3. Begin by pre-arranging the environment (exhibit of rocks; bulletin board on birds, etc.)
4. Start with some event which has occurred (such as the first moon landing)
5. Begin with children's inquiries (do snakes grow from horse-hair?)
6. Begin with specimens or items children bring to school (rocks, roaches, insects, magnets, etc.)

It should become apparent that there are many other ways of initiating science teaching, and in addition, it is entirely possible that the same desired results may be achieved from the use of any one of these procedures. However, the above suggested procedures will be expanded briefly to help the interested teacher clarify how these are applied in practice.

1. *Start with textbooks or other materials.* The teacher should guard against any either-or issue relative to teaching science. There are those who believe that all science should be an outgrowth of the experiences of children and those who believe that some logical or systematic approach to science instruction is the only way to teach this important subject. The authors have assumed that both of these projected methods of science teaching have something to offer. The teacher cannot always delay instruction, even if it were desirable, by waiting for an event to occur or some item to be brought to school which would provide interest (although it seems almost impossible for a day to go by without such occurrences). The teacher must also feel secure in her undertakings, and the textbook may be her source of confidence. If this is true, she should try to select a chapter which is related to the season or some area of science which can be dealt with most easily and profitably in her situation. The interests of children may well be the deciding factor as to which chapter is to be selected for the next study. However, important to textbook teaching is still the need for direct experiences. If the teacher uses the textbook to lead the children into science study, she may well capitalize upon some content area which will be familiar to the children either from their previous study or through experiences with the environment.

For example, if the children are from a rural district, a study of soil may be a familiar area and thus lead to a natural interest. The "Weekly Reader," "Science News" and other such publications may also be used to initiate science teaching. Interest which goes beyond the printed page in the textbook may result from reading these source materials. The teacher then has the responsibility to direct this learning in such a way that it becomes meaningful and that *children become more self-directed* as they learn to weigh values in decision-making situations.

2. *Begin through lively discussion.* The teacher who utilizes good discussion techniques will be aware of the values which result from enthusiastic discussions. Frequently, these discussions are terminated without really resolving the problem in the minds of all the children. Science experiences which utilize the scientific method of attack may result in children directing their own experiment or study to find out the best solutions to their problems. Thus the alert teacher may initiate activity in science by carefully developing those discussion areas which project real issues and which are of genuine value to the children.

3. *Begin by pre-arranging the environment.* The teacher may stimulate interest in some area of science which the children have not discovered, but is within their comprehension. This may be initiated by an attractive bulletin board which will create interests and questions in the minds of the children. A display or an exhibit is equally valuable and may also be used for this purpose. As the teacher pre-arranges the environment to open up new and interesting areas of study for the children, she plans experiences with them for ways of getting the most from the study. Field trips and first-hand experiences may contribute to broadening the pre-arranged environment.

4. *Start with some event which has occurred.* Events of local, state, national or international interest may be the basis of a spontaneous unit of study in science. The launching of a rocket to the moon, a new medical discovery, the community decision concerning public fluoridation of water, and similar events may utilize the natural inquisitiveness of children as they identify problems for study under teacher guidance, and lead them to better understandings of their environment.

5. *Begin with children's inquiries.* It was pointed out in a previous section of this chapter that teachers must be alert to the many questions which children ask. These questions are usually provoked by some interest which the child has acquired from reading, listening, seeing, feeling and the like. The teacher obviously cannot pursue every question; but when sufficient interest in a given question seem to arouse the class, she may capitalize upon this interest in getting a unit of learning underway. These questions may also be outgrowths from other studies. Since science

is related to history, arithmetic and other areas of the curriculum, the best answers to questions in these areas may come from a study of science.

6. *Begin with specimens or items children bring to school.* Most teachers are aware of the vast collections of items which children assemble during a single year. In the fall of the year a child may bring to school grasshoppers, leaves, bird's nests, turtles, caterpillars and the like. Full fledged interest in all or any one of these items might develop from initial curiosity. The teacher must be adept at helping children to identify what they are concerned about as related to the item of interest. As with each of the six suggestions for initiating science instruction, the teacher will need to be aware of the need to aid children in procuring the most from their learnings. Thus it becomes essential that the teacher not let the learnings dwindle into superficial understandings or drift off into so many tangents that they become inefficient and even haphazard. Certainty of interest and careful planning with the children may lead to valuable experiences for the children. *It should behoove the teacher to be interested and enthusiastic about the items children bring to school. The reaction of the children may be the gauge which determines the extent of study subsequent to the bringing of such items to school.*

How May Science Instruction Meet the Needs of All Children?

Science can and must contribute towards meeting the needs of all children, as they continuously seek to gain a better understanding of themselves and their physical and social environment. Since children are not alike in the way they develop, certain individual differences become more evident as the children grow older. Research studies have pointed out how girls differ from boys in science attitudes and how rural children possess more knowledge of science than urban pupils. It is evident that some children are more inclined toward science activities than others, but it seems essential that all children should have certain basic experiences and gain certain knowledge from science education. Therefore, if we are to help children to adjust to a rapidly changing world and to understand some of these changes it is necessary that a functional science program must be planned for all.

The development of a program for all children should be based upon rediscovering what is already known about science, since this is an essential aspect of the developmental nature of learning. The slow or average child, as well as the gifted or bright child, might derive much from this phase of the program. That is, the child who is testing a piece of metal to determine its quality as a conductor of electricity is simply rediscovering what is already known, although this experience is essential to furthering his knowledge in the subject. Elementary school science can meet the needs of children by providing certain experiences which will contribute to answering some of their questions. Children of all abilities will ask questions which may cause them to seek possible solutions, even though the quality of the solution may depend upon the mental capacity of the learner.

Some Guides to Facilitating Individualized Science Learnings

The teacher planning science instruction must consider that children are all different and that they learn at different rates. Too often, good science experiences are destroyed for some learners because the teacher assumes that all children should experience the same activities. Special programs do not have to be set up for the slow learners or for the gifted if the teacher recognizes the differences in children. Some useful guides in meeting these differences follow.

1. *Permit the children to share in planning science learnings.* This planning will mean that each child can suggest his own activity which, through guidance, will lead to learnings related to his level of comprehension. Thus the gifted child is challenged to use his special talents and creative ability. The teacher should see that he sets for himself tasks comparable with his brightness.

2. *Demand that bright children achieve more than others.* This guide suggests that gifted children should go beyond the rediscovering stage. Children can, to a limited extent, be creative. Bright children should be expected to seek further knowledge about any given area, but these children will need assistance from the teacher in locating additional sources of information. The teacher need not fear that these children are gaining more knowledge about a given subject than she possesses, since importance is attached to the level of accomplishments of her pupils. Therefore, she must release them through helping them to pursue learning rather than setting limits arbitrarily.

3. *Recognize science as a process which leads to many ways of investigating.* The learning of science may be limited if the teacher does not see the variety of ways by which science knowledge can be acquired. The use of a textbook should not limit learning experiences, but should open doors to learning and develop good observers and experimenters. The teacher who recognizes that science information may be learned from using resources—human and physical—and that the use of many kinds of media will result in higher levels of motivation, will no doubt facilitate more effective learning.

4. *Keep a variety of reading materials on science available.* Bright children are able to profit more from abstract reading than are other children. Through reading, children are able to explore new interests and acquire new understandings. If good books and other reading materials are available to them through a continuously changing book supply, these children will progress rapidly.

5. *Permit those children who are highly motivated to pursue problems of special interests.* The teacher will find that bright children are, in most cases, the first ones finished with any given assignment. These children should be permitted to engage in projects which will lead them to new and challenging experiences. Although children who have normal intelligence, but special science interests, should also be permitted to pursue problems of their choice, obviously, the teacher must give her support and guidance to such activities. These activities may well be the kinds which in some schools are extra-curricular, the so-called "club activities." Placing such activities within the curriculum may lead other children to finding new interests through science.

It should become increasingly evident that children who are experiencing such a science program will achieve more nearly in line with their ability than those who participate in a program aimed at the so-called "average" learner. Such a program will lead only to mediocre instruction in science, or in any other subject for that matter. One precaution, however, should be taken: Teachers should not use science as a reward for completing reading, arithmetic, or other assignments early.[19] This may mean that some children would never have an opportunity to participate in science activities. However, this does not mean that free time should not be utilized in science interests; but a definite time must be provided within the school day for science for all children.

What Is the Basis of the Science Curriculum?

Science education has moved in new directions as a result of the impact of experimental projects in elementary school science. These projects, largely funded by the National Science Foundation, have examined science content, modes of inquiry, instructional materials and procedures, science concepts which children are capable of learning, estimation and measurement in elementary science, and a host of other aspects of science. The intense interest and the cooperation of scientists and educators in their endeavor to define the most effective elementary science

19 *Ibid.*, p. 263.

curriculum has led to innumerable explorations in the schools. The Arlington County Schools in Virginia are introducing children to living things—the earth, the universe, matter and energy—and they are developing materials to facilitate this curriculum. One of the unique aspects is that the program is being developed in grades K through 12.[20] Most of the major projects, however, deal only with certain grades or in some cases K–6.

The *Science Curriculum Improvement Study* (SCIS),[21] which got underway in 1962, was an attempt to simplify science for the elementary school and to change the basis of science from its logical subject matter organization to a program based on a sequence of units which foster inductive thinking.

The SCIS project builds its curriculum around sequential physical and life science learnings. The project uses a materials-centered approach which permits children to explore, observe, and manipulate selected materials and, with some teacher guidance, a scientific concept is introduced. Through a series of related experiences the concept is reinforced, and finally the children learn that this new concept has applications to many situations.

Thus three steps are followed in introducing children to the science curriculum: (1) *preliminary explorations,* where children explore the elements of the new concept; (2) *invention*—the teacher introduces the new scientific concept that explains what the children have observed; and (3) *discovery lessons*—this experience helps the child to recognize that the new concept has applications to situations other than the original, or initial meaning.[22]

A second major project which has had an impact on the science curriculum is the AAAS Commission on Science Education. A program in elementary school science, sponsored by the Commission, was developed which is known as *Science—A Process Approach.* This program provides for the continuous growth of each child in acquiring scientific knowledge about man's world. The program required teachers to know the level of understandings developed by the child to insure sequence in learning before moving on to study in the same area at a higher level. Since the program is based on behavioral objectives for each exercise, it becomes important for the teacher to determine if the specified behavior has been learned and to know what new experiences are needed to enhance the learning. Teacher guides as well as pupil kits provide for a hierarchy in

---

[20] Lockhard, *op. cit.,* p. 291.
[21] *Ibid.,* pp. 331-340.
[22] *Ibid.,* p. 332.

learning. Of major importance in this project is the process of science which is thought to be applicable in learning science concepts.[23]

A third project known as *Elementary Science Study* (ESS) was developed around meaningful science materials for use by children. The units were developed to permit the teachers to arrange the sequence to meet the children's needs or the school's own requirements. Thus no rigid curriculum structure is established. Of importance in this project is the way the materials appear to be normally accessible to children in their own environment. These materials have been used successfully, not only with middle-class, suburban children, but with children from low socio-economic areas of large cities and small towns.[24]

As a result of the many different emphases being given to elementary science through the various science projects, it would be difficult to conclude that there is but one direction for elementary science. There is general agreement, however, that the elementary school science curriculum should include three general areas of science: (1) the earth and the rest of the universe; (2) living things; and (3) matter and energy. These three areas of science encompass the basic five fields of science—astronomy, biology, chemistry, geology, and physics. Thus the important point is that the elementary science program should include a representative selection of science experiences from both the physical and the biological sciences.

What Are Some Guides for Selecting Specific Science Content?

When teachers are asked to serve on committees to determine the science curriculum for their school districts they need assistance in making basic decisions concerning science content. This is also true if they are left to their own discretion within their own classrooms. These guides should help teachers who find themselves in either of these two situations.

1. Identify from the sciences themselves the basic concepts and conceptual schemes upon which the organization and development of the science is based.
2. Explore children's interests and capacities to learn. Recognize the ability of youngsters to grasp abstract ideas and their curiosity to explore their environment as well as to understand themselves.
3. The child community should be a source of selection of content which will bring understandings about the nature of the child's

---

[23] *Ibid.*, p. 150.
[24] *Ibid.*, p. 220.

community—local terrain, climate, living things, industrial or rural, etc.

4. In selecting science content the curriculum should be correlated with the rest of the elementary curriculum wherever possible. Science content is related to music, social studies, language arts, mathematics, and art, and it should not only reinforce these learnings but the reverse should also be true.

5. And finally, the selection of science content should also involve sex education, health, safety, and conservation.[25]

Although these three areas aid in the selection and organization of science content, the teacher should not be concerned with trying to produce some learnings in each area for each grade. Importance is attached to seeing that each area is included in both the primary and intermediate programs. The teacher is more likely to find appropriate experiences for each of the areas within the divisions of the elementary grades. Maturity level, interests, and the various aspects of how children learn must be recognized as deciding factors. The organization and selection of content then provides for limited experiences in primary grades with a gradual increase in knowledge and experiences for succeeding grades.

Scope and sequence. The above discussion should point out the problem of determining scope and sequence. Yet, if our science objectives are to be achieved in any school system, it is necessary that children have those experiences which will lead them to more profound insights in science understandings. There seems to be insufficient evidence that there is a definite and particular source of content for each grade. However, if the areas just cited give direction to the scope of science experiences in the elementary school, then, from a study of children's interests and the local environment together with an understanding of their ability to comprehend certain concepts at various growth stages, the teacher should be able to plan vital experiences for the children. If a school staff makes a study of these interests as related to a knowledge of child growth, a basic sequence guide could be developed for age groups rather than separate grades. Chart XI is indicative of what could be done in a sample area.

It should be noted that this chart does not purport to be a prescription, but rather a source of ideas which could be used to supplement or expand certain science learnings. When a teaching staff begins to build a comprehensive guide for science learnings, they will help to eliminate

---

[25] Edward Victor, *Science for the Elementary School* (New York: The Macmillan Company, 1965), pp. 29-31.

needless overlapping and at the same time provide sufficient scope and sequence to broaden the child's knowledge of science in areas which are unfamiliar to him. Craig, for example, found many years ago that primary children's inquiries involved content from all the major areas of science: astronomy, biology, chemistry, geology and physics.[26] Other investigations have since supported these earlier findings. Of importance here is the need to recognize that the elementary school science sequence must provide for experiences involving both physical and biological sciences.

Chart XI can serve as a guide in developing scope and sequence for a broader age group than a single grade. To develop fully the scope and sequence for elementary science, the teacher should consider not only the three areas listed on page 338, but also the interests of children and the required comprehension level of the concepts involved. Ruth[27] found that science concepts for the sixth grade were understood by children of better than average intelligence; by children who were reading up to the grade level; and by children who come from middle to upper class homes. She also found that boys did better than girls. This kind of information makes it even more imperative that the teacher must provide a variety of activities if all children are to learn from and to be successful in science experiences. Thus mass teaching of science (teaching the same concept at the same time to all children in the classroom through a single experience) may not lend itself to achieving the desired results for all children. In summary, *scope and sequence must be thought of in terms of the range of abilities in the class, the differences of social-economic groups in learning science concepts, and the maturity differences among children.*

How May Units Be Developed in Science?

Unit teaching is applicable to all areas of the curriculum. Separate teaching units in science may be developed through related subject units may prove more valuable.[28] However, as previously stated, the teacher who is seeking self-improvement will move from one teaching procedure to a more effective procedure as she feels secure in bridging the gap.

---

[26] Gerald S. Craig, *Certain Techniques Used in Developing a Course of Study for the Horace Mann Elementary School* (New York: Bureau of Publications, Teachers College, Columbia University, 1927), pp. 33-40.

[27] Alice Kerney Ruth, "Science Concepts of Sixth Grades," *Science Education,* Vol. 38 (February, 1954), p. 30.

[28] See Arthur Carin and Robert B. Sund, *Teaching Science Through Discovery* (Columbus, Ohio: Charles E. Merrill Publishing Co., 1964), Chapter 4.

Of importance here, is the need for teachers to be cognizant of unifying learnings in science, and to recognize that science is not an isolated subject area, but one which is interrelated in the child's life. Unit teaching, in fact, may be easier for teachers to develop in science than in other aspects of the curriculum. For example, units in science at the primary level can be built around such familiar topics as "Our Pets," "The Wheel," "Our Shadows," and numerous others.

The adequate development of concepts and generalizations at the primary level should result in the children entering the intermediate grades with certain scientific abilities established. This provides for children of these grades to have experiences for reinforcing earlier learnings, and also, to explore new avenues of interests, since at this age they need experiences which will develop broader understandings of their environment. It is at the intermediate grade-level that children begin to feel more at home in their environment as a result of gaining knowledge about things which caused fears or anxiety during early childhood. Unit teaching may be helpful during this period of development as children work together in solving problems. They are older, more articulate, and able, to an extent, to reason from experience. Thus discussions may deal with science as it relates to building certain social understandings. This is not to imply that direct, firsthand experiences are lessened; to the contrary, they must be continued, both as individual and group efforts. A good unit will meet the demand for serving the needs of all. Thus the added advantage of working with children at this age is the challenge to the teacher to "stretch" the "thinking power" of the young learner.

Although there are many other possibilities for unit teaching in science, a final point to be made is that unit teaching serves the need for limitless firsthand experiences for children. The child can be robbed of real learning situations when the pressure of time obliges the teacher to tell the answers to questions. Children need to learn to seek answers themselves to such questions as, "what holds an airplane up?", "what are the bubbles in water?", "what makes my clothes stick to me when I come in from the cold?" The teacher should serve as a guide in helping children locate reference materials, equipment and material for experiments. Through careful questioning, instead of a "telling" kind of teaching, she may lead the children to new and more vital learning as they become more self-directive in problem-solving.

How Is Science Related to Other Content Fields?

To those who have not studied science it may be difficult to point out how science is related to other fields, since science is a vital aspect

CHART XI

Scope and Sequence Chart of Concepts on Air, Winds, and Weather[29]

	What is the Nature of Air?	What Makes Winds?	What Causes Precipitation?	Weather Instruments	How Do the Earth's Slant and Rotation Affect Weather?
Kindergarten— Grade 2	1. Air is real and occupies space. 2. Air is all around us. 3. There is air in soil and in water. 4. Air has weight and exerts pressure. 5. Air pressure can be made to do work. 6. Air contains dust.	1. Wind is moving air. 2. The wind shifts from day to day. 3. Winds are named for the direction *from which* they blow. 4. Warm air expands.	1. Water is in the air in the form of a gas called water vapor. 2. Warmth speeds evaporation. 3. Frozen water can evaporate directly into the air. 4. Wind speeds evaporation.	1. A thermometer is used to determine temperature.	1. The sun gives us heat.
Grade 2— Grade 4	1. Air is a mixture of gases. 2. Air is elastic. 3. The atmosphere extends many hundreds of miles	1. Air is heated primarily by contact with the ground. 2. Substances differ in their capacity to absorb radiant heat.	1. Clouds are formed by the cooling of water vapor. 2. Dew is formed by the earth's rapid cooling and the re-	1. Liquids expand when heated. This is the principle of the common thermometer. 2. A wind vane	1. The earth is heated by the sun most strongly at the equator.

above the surface of the earth. 3. Warm air is lighter than cold air. 4. Local winds are caused by unequal heating of the earth's surface.	sultant condensation of water vapor near the surface.	points into the wind. 3. A barometer is used to measure air pressure.	1. Winds shift to their right in the Northern Hemisphere because of the earth's rotation. 2. Prevailing winds in the United States are from west to east.
Grade 4— *Grade 6* — 1. Air is composed of molecules in rapid motion. 2. Air pressure is equal in all directions.	1. The atmosphere and the clouds trap heat from the sun. 2. Expansion of the air cools it. Compression warms it. — 1. Clouds are formed partly by the expansion and resultant cooling of rising air. 2. Heat loss from the earth by radiation is reduced by an overcast. 3. Frost may be formed when the earth's surface cools below the freezing point of water. (See concept 2 above, Grade 2—Grade 4.)	1. Some thermometers work on the principle of unequal rates of expansion of different substances. 2. A hygrometer is used to determine relative humidity. 3. A rain gauge is used to measure precipitation. 4. An anemometer is used to measure wind speed.	

29 Atkins and Barnett, "Air, Winds, and Weather," *Elementary School Science Activities Series* (New York: Holt, Rinehart & Winston, Inc., 1958), pp. 4-5.

of all of our living. The emerging science curriculum must consist, largely, of related experiences in science and other areas of the curriculum. Unless we are to ignore completely the interrelations of all human experiences, we must teach the children to see science as a powerful factor for the good of mankind in improving the ways of living.

It is true that some school systems have established science as a separate subject. That is, a period has been set up in the schedule to provide science instruction at specified times during the week. This, however, should not be considered a handicap in relating science to other areas of the curriculum. Blocks of time may be combined for a unit which will relate several subjects. Or, if the children are studying "How Airplanes Fly" in science, the topic may become a part of an over-all unit on the "Development of Transportation." Science learnings also may be provided during the science period. During the arithmetic period the children can relate their study of the airplane to such problems as: how are fares figured out; how much fuel is required to fly a given number of miles; how to read the airlines schedules, and the like. In addition, geography may be studied as it relates to a trip made by some member of the class or some news about air travel. The use made of the prevailing westerlies in air travel and other geographic factors may be related. The study of world air routes may lead to broad understandings of other peoples when science and the related subject approach is used. At the same time certain transitory interests may require some limited science experience which satisfies this short-lived and incidental inquisitiveness. These are necessary and important, but the entire science program would lack continuity and balance if these incidental learnings comprised the total of science experiences.

USING SCIENCE INSTRUCTIONAL MATERIALS

Good science teaching depends upon the use of a variety ·of materials. Contrary to what many teachers regard as fact and use as a defense mechanism for not teaching science is that the large majority of science materials do not need to be purchased from a commercial supply house. Materials for elementary school science should be of the simplest kind. A large part of these materials may be brought from the homes of the children and those materials which may not be thus available may be borrowed from the high school science department. This is not to say that science materials purchased from a commercial supply house are not desirable, but lack of such materials cannot be defended as a cause of ineffective science instruction in the elementary school.

Why Are Science Materials Indispensable to a Good Science Program?

Instructional aids have been widely recognized for at least a generation for their contributions to increasing the effectiveness of learning. In the late eighteenth century, Pestalozzi pointed the way for utilizing materials in the classroom when he shifted the arm of teaching from merely giving information to developing the child in accordance with his inborn faculties.[30] He recognized the use of sense impressions in gaining knowledge. Although there is a definite trend in the direction of permitting children to manipulate and observe objects, science teaching is still void of the necessary firsthand experiences in too many classrooms. Departments of education in some states are cognizant of the need for teachers to utilize materials in science learnings. An examination of two such guides reveals the following:

> . . . there is no substitute for first-hand experiences and experimentation. As children participate in planning the experiment, in working it out, in watching the results and in checking results, they have an excellent opportunity to grow in understanding the scientific method. . . . Through wise use of materials of science, a rich contribution can be made to the development of this ability.[31]

> One of the dangers in teaching elementary science is that too much time may be devoted to reading about things rather than to studying the things themselves.[32]

The importance of teaching materials in science is further emphasized by numerous investigations in the science areas. Investigators have sought to determine the factors which inhibit teachers from doing more and better science teaching. Lanimers found through extensive interviews that a lack of suitable teaching materials was the problem most often mentioned by teachers.[33] Piltz in an investigation of difficulties encountered in teaching science found that inadequate physical facilities

---

[29] Elmer H. Wilds, *Foundations of Modern Education* (New York: Holt, Rinehart & Winston, Inc., 1942), p. 469.

[30] *Science Education for the Elementary Schools of Ohio, op. cit.,* pp. 10, 12.

[31] Tennessee State Department of Education, *A Science Program for Elementary Schools: Grades Four, Five, and Six* (Nashville, Tenn.: Tennessee State Dept. of Education, 1944), p. 15.

[32] Threas J. Lanimers, "One Hundred Interviews with Elementary School Teachers Concerning Science Education," *Science Education*, 33 (October, 1949), 292-95.

were the most common.[34] Other investigations, too numerous to mention here, support the thesis that science materials are an important factor in developing good science programs.

The abundance of materials. In almost all of the science curriculum projects the importance of appropriate materials for study and experimentation have been emphasized. All types of materials have been developed for use with units in these projects. Films, filmstrips, booklets, portable laboratories, tapes, and science kits are but a few of the innovations in curriculum materials which are readily available to teachers. The availability of federal funds has made it possible for many elementary schools to acquire science equipment which they could not otherwise afford.

The need for careful selection of materials. The amount of equipment needed will largely depend upon the extent to which a teacher will permit pupils to explore or seek solutions to problems. An examination of classroom closets has often turned up unused science equipment. Nevertheless, the teacher should be prudent in selecting commercial equipment for elementary school use, since science equipment can be a very expensive outlay of public funds. Therefore, there is a need to select carefully *those materials which will be used.* It is urged that teachers regulate their ordering of supplies according to the needs of the children as those needs are identified throughout the year. Science equipment which is neither applicable for elementary school use nor within the comprehension level of the learners serves only to limit the purchasing of suitable equipment.

It is important for the beginning or new teacher to know the school's policies regarding the ordering of materials. This knowledge can be secured from the principal. The teacher should not put herself in an embarrassing situation by purchasing supplies on her own. Usually the principal compiles the requests for supplies in the spring of the year. Requests from the entire school system are then combined by the central office and ordered within budget allowances. It is paramount in selecting materials to know the school's policies, the anticipated expenditures and the most pressing needs for developing a more effective science program.

Constructing equipment. Constructing science equipment for elementary school science may serve at least two basic purposes: *First,* many pieces of useful science equipment may be improvised from inexpensive materials and *second,* constructing science materials may

---

[33] Albert Piltz, "An Investigation of Teacher-recognized Difficulties Encountered in the Teaching of Science in the Elementary Schools of Florida" (Unpublished doctoral thesis, University of Florida, Gainesville, Florida, 1954).

serve as useful learning experiences for children. Since it is not feasible to purchase all science equipment, the interested science teacher will be able to provide innumerable science experiences for children largely through improvising. Many such experiences should be omitted from the science program in classrooms where teachers do not see the value in these experiences for children. A basic psychological principle is at work when the child is encouraged by the teacher to construct that which is needed to reach a solution to his problem. The experiment in Figure XII may be constructed by an intermediate-grade child, and can

FIGURE XVI

Testing Materials to See If They Are Conductors of Electricity

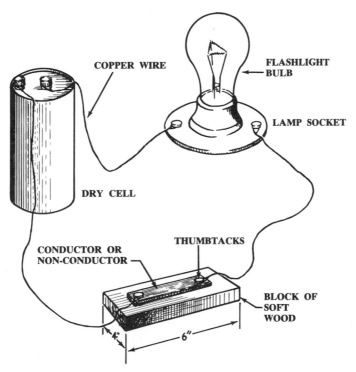

be used to test materials for their ability to conduct electricity. Such a device is easily made and can serve as a useful learning activity for children interested in studying electricity. Many different materials, such as rubber comb, piece of wood, aluminum foil, and paper may be tested for their ability to conduct electricity between the thumbtacks.

The following guides[35] may be used to aid the teacher in deciding when constructing equipment may *not* be profitable:

1. When the length of time required for construction is not justified.
2. When a good product is needed.
3. When construction skills are beyond the ability of the child.
4. When the best interests of the group will be served by not delaying the activity until the needed equipment is constructed.

It should be pointed out that the use of audio-visual aids, as indicated in Chapter VI, is equally applicable to science. Films, filmstrips, flat pictures, real objects, and the like, all aid in the learning process. Although the class, for example, may be able to see evidence of erosion from the classroom window, a good film should improve the learners' understandings of both the process and the importance of the problem as related to conservation.

EVALUATION OF SCIENCE LEARNING

Good teaching involves determining the effectiveness of the instruction. The teacher needs to be aware of the results she is achieving in science. That is, to what extent are children growing in science understandings, skills, attitudes and appreciations. To this end, teachers must recognize that evaluation is an integral part of the teaching-learning process. Assuming this statement is true, the teacher must continuously seek to determine if the learning experiences of the children are leading them to achieve the basic purposes of elementary education and to recognize the relationship between these purposes and science learnings. To determine this the teacher cannot wait for the learning experience to terminate and then administer a test. Therefore, this section is concerned only with special problems involved in evaluating science learnings.

Efforts to determine the effectiveness of science instruction have largely been those involving measurement of factual information. This may be due to the fact that science has been the least developed area of the elementary curriculum. However, there is evidence that during the past few years many school systems have been actively engaged in developing curriculum guides in science. This means that thought has been given to scope, sequence, children's interests, learning activities, materials and evaluation of science. As science becomes equal, at least

---

[34] Hubler, *op. cit.*, p. 164.

in time allotment, with other basic areas in the curriculum, teachers will need to find better ways of sensing those science needs of pupils which will lead to improved learnings. Measurement is important, but evaluation techniques which have been used successfully in other content areas will have to be adapted for science.

How Does the Teacher Evaluate Science Learnings?

The nature of science learnings virtually demands that informal evaluation procedures be utilized. Pupil progress is important as it relates to a knowledge of content, and the teacher can develop tests for this purpose or use some recognized standardized test to examine progress in basic study skills. However, the teacher must guard against using tests as ends in themselves, lest she lose sight of the true aim of science education. Determining progress in attitudes, appreciations and values acquired through science learnings demands that the teacher seek to interpret pupil behavior through the use of many techniques and devices.

Although there have been a vast number of science projects developed during the past decade in an effort to improve science instruction, no program will be any better than the way the classroom teacher implements it. The modern science program is more concerned with providing pupil experiences in the process of science. Pupils at their own level of development are expected to behave like scientists; they are to experience science rather than just to learn about it. Thus they are involved in formulating principles and generalizations. This process is quite different than simply reading about science or hearing about it through expository methods. The shift has thus been from emphasis on information for its own sake to process, inquiry, and problem solving. Elementary school science then needs new evaluation techniques which are broader than testing alone.

Carefully planned teacher-pupil objectives should serve as the guide for the techniques to be used. Facts are only useful to the learners to the extent that they are related to broader understandings which will lead to some modification in the learner's behavior. An understanding of science should help the child to adjust to changing conditions in his environment. However, the teacher must be alert to the interpretations which the learner is attaching to these changes and must determine to what extent his interpretations are leading to desirable attitudes, improved understandings, skills, and appreciations. The teacher needs to use a host of evaluation techniques such as:

1. Observation of how children function
2. Analysis of pupil's diaries

3. Interview techniques
4. Tests designed to examine the child as an inquirer
4. Tests to determine the development of science concepts

The development of these techniques and instruments calls for the creative ability of the teacher to go beyond the simple testing for facts. If individualized pupil learning is going to succeed in science, then techniques appropriate to the pupils' learning will be essential.

What Are Some Guides for Evaluating Science Programs?

Teachers must continuously examine the science curriculum K–6, and even K–12, as schools move in this direction.

There have been over 100 science projects and investigations in the United States in the past decade to determine the appropriate science curriculum for grades K–12. However, in our search for a quality science program, Zafforoni sets forth criteria which should be helpful in evaluating elementary school science programs. These criteria are:

1. Are the science program and its activities clearly aimed at developing an attitude of inquiry and encouraging carryover to other subjects?
2. Have qualified consultants helped to identify the subject matter and the teaching methods pertinent to the needs of the child and the society?
3. Do classrooms activities show promise for developing the highest quality of learning in science of which the children are capable?
4. Do programs show a sequence of learning activities that develop both the product and the processes of learning?
5. Do programs recognize and apply present-day knowledge of the behavioral patterns and growth processes of children?
6. Are appropriate facilities being made available for children to study science?
7. Are sufficient time allotments made for science study? Are enough teachers assigned to science teaching and are they adequately prepared for this assignment?[36]

SUMMARY

Science in the emerging elementary school curriculum should contribute to the total development of the child. The approach to science is made through recognizing that science may contribute to child growth

---

[35] Joseph Zafforoni, *New Developments in Elementary School Science* (Washington, D.C.: National Science Teachers Association, 1963), p. 52.

by serving as a vehicle for a way of thinking which may become universal, and thereby produce a basis for common agreement in furthering democracy.

Children are living in a dynamic world which demands the ability to interpret one's environment. Such interpretations must be satisfying to the individual if adequate adjustments are to be made. Therefore, the emerging design for elementary school science must provide firsthand experiences for all children in rediscovering basic science principles which are already known. These experiences become an essential core of all science learnings as individual differences lead children into varying learning activities. Gifted children are not limited only to the rediscovering phase of the science program, but are challenged to move beyond the normal range or scope of the basic program.

Scope and sequence in the science program are developmental. Scope may be defined in terms of experiences in learning about the universe, the earth, essentials for living, living things, physical and chemical phenomena, and how man seeks to adapt to and control his environment. Sequence may be determined according to the individual's maturity level, mental ability and interests.

Learning in science utilizes the principles of learning which place the learner in an active, energetic kind of environment. The classroom becomes a laboratory for learning to the extent that the teacher's philosophy recognizes the value of problem-solving activities for children. Materials of instruction need not limit the elementary science program. Learning may be enhanced by permitting children to share in bringing to school or constructing needed equipment and materials which are appropriate for science use.

Evaluation of science experiences must be informal and related to the objectives to be achieved. This calls for the use of a variety of techniques and devices which will produce evidences of change in pupil behavior as a result of their understandings of science. Formal tests may be used to determine the extent of science knowledge being acquired. Such tests may serve also as a guide for the teacher in determining the adequacy of the scope of the program.

SUGGESTED ACTIVITIES AND PROBLEMS

1. Jimmy brought a turtle to school one morning. It was the fall season and Mrs. Rogers had planned to introduce her fourth grade children to the chapter in their science book which started with autumn leaves. However, the

children became very excited about the turtle and asked many questions. Mrs. Rogers was not sure that the children's interest would be lasting or whether this was a transitory situation. Nevertheless, she suggested that they would study turtles in the spring and persisted in carrying out her original plans against a background of "ahs."

Discuss what you would have done in this situation if you had been Mrs. Rogers.

Is there a relationship between the turtle and the fall season?

2. Jean brought to her classroom a picture of a rocket blasting off for a trip to outer space. The children in Miss Cousins' sixth grade asked many questions concerning man's ability to live in outer space. Jean told that her father said, "man could never live in outer space because God had made the earth man's home." This provoked much discussion; Miss Cousins did participate. Religion soon became the subject under discussion. With this Miss Cousins asked the children to open their geography book and answer the questions at the end of the assignment.

Should Miss Cousins have joined in the discussion? Would you have changed the discussion by turning to another lesson? What do you think was Miss Cousins' responsibility in this situation?

3. The principal of Brookside Elementary School was interested in improving the science instruction in his school. After a discussion with the school board he sent bulletins to all his teachers stating that the School Board was interested in improving the science program and that science should be taught three times a week for not less than 20 minutes a day in the primary grades and not less than 30 minutes a day in the intermediate grades. The principal also pointed out that incidental science teaching should not be counted in the time allotted.

The principal received a number of complaints from the teachers. These complaints revealed that the teachers did not think they could do a good job of improving science teaching because the school lacked science equipment. Some teachers also said they did not have enough science background to teach elementary school science. If you were a teacher in this school could you justify these complaints? What should the principal do?

SELECTED READINGS

Blough, Glenn O., Julius Schwartz, and Albert J. Huggett. *Elementary School Science and How to Teach It*. New York: The Dryden Press, 1958, Chapters 1-6.

Butts, David P., and Howard L. Jones. "Inquiry Training and Problem Solving in Elementary Science Children," *Journal of Research in Science Teaching*, 4 (March, 1966), 21-27.

Carin, Arthur, and Robert B. Sund. *Teaching Science Through Discovery.* Columbus, Ohio: Charles E. Merrill Publishing Co., 1964, Chapters 1-3.

Carpenter, Finley. "The Effects of Different Learning Methods on Concepts Formation," *Science Education,* 40 (October, 1956), 282-285.

Craig, Gerald. *Science for the Elementary School Teacher.* Boston: Ginn and Company, 1958, Chapters 1-4.

Dunfee, Maxine. *Elementary School Science: A Guide to Research.* Washington, D. C.: Association for Supervision and Curriculum Development, 1967.

Hubler, Clark. *Working With Children in Science.* Boston: Houghton Mifflin Company, 1957, Chapter 11.

Jacobson, William J., and Harold E. Tannenbaum. *Modern Elementary School Science.* Science Manpower Project Monographs. New York: Bureau of Publications, Teachers College, Columbia University, 1961, Chapters I, II, III, VI, and VII.

Karplus, Robert, and Herbert D. Thier. "The Science Curriculum Improvement Study." *The Instructor,* Vol. 74 (January, 1965), pp. 43-84.

Lanimers, Thereas, J. "One Hundred Interviews With Elementary School Teachers Concerning Science Education," *Science Education,* 33 (October, 1949), 292-95.

Lewis, June E., and Irene C. Potter. *The Teaching of Science in the Elementary School.* Englewood Cliffs, N. J.: Prentice-Hall, Inc., 1961, Chapters 1, 2, and 3.

Livermore, Arthur H. "The Process Approach of the AAAS Commission on Science Education," *Journal of Research in Science Teaching,* 2 (December, 1964), 271-82.

Navarra, John G., and Joseph Zafforoni. *Science Today for the Elementary School Teacher.* Boston: Allyn & Bacon, Inc., 1960.

Tannenbaum, Harold E., and Nathan Stillman. *Science Education for Elementary Teachers.* Boston: Allyn & Bacon, Inc., 1960, Chapters I-IV.

Ulrich, Arthur H. "A Comprehensive Level Determination of a Basic Science Concept," *Science and Children,* 1 (April, 1964), 12-13.

Victor, Edward, *Science for the Elementary School.* New York: The Macmillan Company, 1965, Chapters 1-8.

CHAPTER 11

Art and Music for Children

Two areas of the school program that may be avoided and neglected by many classroom teachers are music and art. It is not surprising that the teacher who has attended a school where music and art were reserved for only the gifted or where special teachers were utilized, might believe that she is entirely unprepared to offer leadership in these areas. Likewise, the teacher who regards music education as a process of memorization and manipulation may dislike any contact with experiences in music. Art experiences which consist of pattern copying, color-wheel drill, and the like may be regarded by the teacher as dull, lifeless work periods to be fitted into the schedule once each week.

In modern schools, art and music have come to be regarded as experiences which offer creative and appreciative *opportunities for all children*. As educators have recognized and accepted research evidence concerning how children learn, it has become necessary to modify certain approaches and techniques employed in teaching art and music. In this chapter the emerging concepts of art and music education will be discussed in light of newer teaching-learning methods. The emphasis is upon the relationship of the teacher to these learnings and upon her leadership opportunities in these areas.

What Is Creativity?

There have been numerous disagreements on the subject of *creativity* and what types of people possess creative characteristics. A traditional outlook held that very few people were truly creative and that it was a natural fact that most people must forever be imitators because they lacked the unusual characteristics necessary for creative work.[1] A more acceptable view of creativity which has been advanced by Kilpatrick,[2] among others, suggests that all human beings engage in some form of creative thinking and acting as they approach and react to each new life situation.

It appears that these two viewpoints on creativity differ with respect to what constitutes a creative act or thought. The older viewpoint seems to be concerned with the unusual or atypical results of human effort as judged by others. The newer viewpoint seems to regard creativity as a process common to all individuals, although differing in degree in the uniqueness of the product. The dilemma in any attempt to decide who is capable of creativity occurs when it becomes necessary to locate persons who cannot only define creativity, but also recognize its presence in individuals. Too often it seems that certain work or thought has been considered to be creative only because it was so very different from the ordinary. Yet the ordinary activities of each child have resulted from the child's encountering and reacting to experiences that were, at one time, new to him and required new responses. Obviously, society will set its own standards of excellency for the products of creativity, but a democratic society should not overlook or deny opportunities for each individual to enjoy and develop his own potentials for creativity in many areas of life.

The classroom teacher finds a great challenge and a wonderful opportunity for providing the situations and the atmosphere for pupil creativity in the everyday life of the school. Although it is true that the teacher cannot prevent a certain amount of pupil creativity in thought and action, even though she tried, it is apparent that some situations are more conducive to creativity than others.[3] It is essential that each teacher be aware of this and that she provide the settings for fruitful, creative work by children. Such settings will include (1) a friendly atmosphere in the classroom, (2) an absence of vigorous interpersonal competition, (3) teacher acceptance of widely differing performances by children, and (4) opportunity for creative expression throughout the school week rather than during one or two periods each week.

---

[1] R. L. Finney, *A Sociological Philosophy of Education* (New York: The Macmillan Co., 1932), pp. 394-95.

[2] William H. Kilpatrick, "Some Basic Considerations Affecting Success in Teaching Art," *Teacher's College Record*, 32 (January, 1931), 348-59. See also Freeman G. Macomber, *Principles of Teaching in the Elementary School* (New York: American Book Co., 1954), pp. 32-3.

[3] H. O. Rugg and Ann Shumaker, *The Child Centered School* (New York: World Book Co., 1928), p. 228.

If the teacher accepts the creative activity of children in art and music as important, she cannot reasonably confine such activity to one or two periods a week. Creativity in these areas of learning will extend to other experiences in the school program, if permitted. This is not an argument against the scheduled and planned development of skills in the use of art materials or in the area of music, nor against the values of appreciation and refinement of taste. It may be desirable and in fact necessary to provide carefully planned experiences wherein children enjoy "good" music, and it is important that children have an opportunity to develop their skills in art and music in regularly scheduled sessions, particularly at the intermediate grade level. The creative aspect, however, cannot be so well scheduled; it may occur spontaneously. Pupil creativity in art, music, language, and other areas must be a continuing, daily concern of every teacher.

MUSIC EXPERIENCES FOR ALL CHILDREN

The music program in the elementary school must be concerned primarily with the music needs of all children, and to the extent of the available resources. The elementary school may also provide experiences for the musically gifted child and at the same time meet the music needs of all children. Music in the elementary school is not conceived as a *special* part of the program, valuable to only a few select pupils; it is regarded as having value for all children.

Music experiences for children should be planned with these objectives in mind:

1. To provide emotional release.
2. To provide for social unity.
3. To promote individual music skills.
4. To foster understanding of the place of music in the lives of people of other lands and times.
5. To foster desirable attitudes that will lead to an increasing appreciation and enjoyment of music by the child.

It is questionable whether vocational possibilities should be a specific objective of the elementary music program any more than the science experiences should be specifically directed toward producing nuclear physicists.

Occasionally one may encounter the suggestion that one objective of music education should be international understanding. No doubt there is some truth to the statement that "music is a universal language," but this seems a heavy responsibility to charge to the music program in the elementary school. Certainly music is a part of the life of all cultures, but it is only one part of the complex social whole and must not be mistaken for the whole. Nevertheless, it should contribute to this objective of elementary education in at least a minor way, perhaps through its relationship to the social studies program.

Music experiences at all levels of the elementary school must be developmental in nature and must be based upon sound principles of growth and learning. As Mursell has pointed out: "All power and fulfillment come through growth. It is true of every field of human endeavor, certainly including music."[4] Such an approach to music education implies that the teacher will not expect all children to perform in the same manner, nor will she reserve a greater amount of attention for those who are musically gifted. If music is to enrich the lives of all individuals, as indeed it can, the music program will be designed to meet the varying interests, needs, and capacities of children.

What Is the Place of Skills and Techniques?

The music experiences of children would not be adequately conceived without inclusion of skills in the music program. It is true that in many school situations the skills aspect of music instruction is over-emphasized and the program becomes a cut-and-dried memory experience. Care should be taken to insure that work on skills meets the needs of children, breeds enthusiasm rather than boredom, is related to individual development, and is kept secondary to the expressive and creative aspects of music.[5]

Over 20 years ago, Fox and Hopkins lamented that music reading was the major emphasis in the music program in the elementary school. They stated that such a mechanical approach to music instruction was largely responsible for the lack of music appreciation and interest on the part of children who had had six or eight years' exposure to such unrealistic music education.[6] In the time that has elapsed since the foregoing observation was made there has been a shift in the emphases in elementary school music on the part of some leading music educators.

---

[4] James L. Mursell, *Education for Musical Growth* (New York: Ginn and Company, 1948), p. 3.

[5] Bernice Baxter, Gertrude M. Lewis, and Gertrude M. Cross, *Elementary Education* (Boston: D. C. Heath & Co., 1952), p. 182.

[6] Lillian Mohr Fox and L. Thomas Hopkins, *Creative School Music* (New York: Silver Burdette Co., 1936), pp. 43-4.

Although it is difficult to determine exactly the general pattern of practice, there is evidence that in certain schools music is being taught as a means of helping children to interpret life through its meanings and that music is being utilized as a means of developing sound mental health through understanding its emotional effects.

Hartshorn has suggested that music belongs in the curriculum only as it meets basic needs of children, and he doubts that learning music merely as a body of subject matter meets any basic need.[7] Fortunately, there are many music supervisors who believe that children should enjoy music both as participants and as listeners. Thus the enjoyment and the emotional release that come from expression through music serve basic human needs. An illustration is offered to support this theory.

> It was the good fortune of one of the authors to work with an elementary music supervisor who wanted children to have fun with music. Each spring the supervisor, Mr. G., conducted a choir of all sixth-grade children in the city system at an annual music program. His predecessor had operated on the "drill-fear" theory of music instruction and the children always did a workmanlike but spiritless job of singing. Mr. G. included all sixth-grade children, whereas his predecessor selected only the best voices. Mr. G. liked children and he enjoyed music. The children expressed their satisfaction with music enthusiastically and beautifully. Teachers who worked with Mr. G. often remarked that he seemed to stimulate pupil response with a fraction of the effort and none of the drudgery exhibited by the previous supervisor. Mr. G. had several things in his favor: he never had apoplexy over a sour note, and he never needed to worry about the pupils exerting insufficient effort and interest. He accepted pupils as individuals, and they accepted him as a leader and friend of music.

Peters has pointed out that the individual should have satisfactory and meaningful experiences with music before work is undertaken with symbols and rules.[8] He has stated also that work in music theory should be related to real experiences with music and that music must have meaning for the individual if it is to be anything more than sensation.[9]

It is not uncommon to observe teachers of kindergarten and first-grade pupils hard at work on the teaching of rhythm of movement. The children may be "flying birds" or "galloping horses," and occasionally the record or the piano may stop playing in order that some little fellow

---

[7] William C. Hartshorn, "Music In General Education," *Music Educator's Journal,* 41 (June, 1955), 46-9.

[8] Darrell Peters, "Are We Teaching Music or Theory?" *Music Educator's Journal,* 41 (June, 1955), 46-9.

[9] *Ibid.*

be reprimanded because he is not skipping or galloping correctly. In many situations it will be necessary to be less zealous regarding the mastery of rhythm and to devote more attention to the developmental aspect of music learning. When the child *feels* the rhythm of music and when he is *freed* of rigid expectations of performance, he will express himself through the rhythmic movements that are uniquely his.

Children appreciate and enjoy that class where the teacher suggests that they do what they feel like doing when a musical selection is played, rather than doing only what the teacher says they *should* feel like doing with certain music. Music is the expression of emotion through tone.[10] Children must not only be allowed to enjoy music in their own individual ways, they must be encouraged to do so. They will not always have a teacher or a book at hand to tell them how to respond to certain types of music.

> Miss Peel understood that the six- and seven-year-old children in her first-grade room may, in many cases, feel subdued and self-conscious about expressing themselves with rhythmic responses to music. As she planned for activities that would help them release themselves more freely to musical responses, she arranged to invite individual pupils to lead the group in whatever rhythmic movement the particular selection suggested to them. Inasmuch as the children had previously been told by the teacher what the music suggested, she anticipated some difficulty. However, after two or three children had shown the other children how they *felt* about a particular selection, the other youngsters seemed to be more willing to try their own interpretations. Before many days it was possible for Miss Peel to play a new record, or a new piano selection, and ask that each child respond with whatever motion he wished. The results were satisfying to pupils and teacher because an environment was created in which individual children were free to *feel* their own personal responses and free to develop their own reactions. Miss Peel was able to gain much more significant information concerning the individual's status and development of musical response because she had helped free the child, to some extent at least, from the extreme imitative pressures that prevail in some situations.

However, skills and techniques must be a part of the music experiences of children when they are ready for such instruction, and when there is some legitimate purpose to be served. For example, some teachers have tried to teach music skills involving eighth notes, sixteenth notes and the like before the children were ready for the mathematical aspects of such concepts.

---

[10] Hartshorn, *op. cit.*, p. 26.

How May Appreciation Be Taught?

Teaching music appreciation may at times be analogous to "leading the horse to water, but not being able to make him drink." It seems certain that if children do not gain a feeling and interest in music experience by high school age, then any required music appreciation class will have a remarkable feat to perform. Appreciation of music can hardly be effected by administrative fiat. If one is to appreciate music he must be able to respond with something more than feeling or emotion; he must possess some awareness of the quality or worth of the musical product and have some knowledge of the intentions of the composer and the performer. Children who have come to enjoy music experiences, both as participants and listeners, will be far more receptive to learn more about a composer, an instrument, or an opera than if their experiences have been monotonous, mechanical, and personally unrewarding.

As children experience different phases of music such as composition and making music, they become better able to understand and to appreciate the work of an outstanding composer or a noted performer. Myers stated that music appreciation is actually a part of all music instruction whether it be negative or positive in value, and the wise teacher will keep this in mind.[11]

Unfortunately, in far too many schools the liberal use of "good" music ends at the kindergarten level. There the children may drink milk to beautiful music, they may dance and skip to the joy of a waltz, or they may rest with the peaceful strains of a Brahms lullaby in the background. Indeed, the five-year-old may select the color of his paints or crayons to fit his feeling with respect to a musical selection. Music is then a friend of the five-year-old. Very often this excellent music experience soon becomes limited to 15-minute periods twice a week, by assembling with a "special" teacher to perform in a certain manner with little or no time for relaxing enjoyment of music.

Music appreciation must be the concern of each teacher, whether she is a "specialist" or a third grade teacher. The teacher should enjoy music if she is to function as one who guides children toward the personal satisfactions of music appreciation.

What Belongs in the Music Program?

The learnings that belong in the elementary school music program cannot be arbitrarily classified under the headings "appreciation" and

---

[11] Louise Kifer Myers, *Teaching Children Music in the Elementary School* (Englewood Cliffs, N. J.: Prentice-Hall, Inc., 1956), p. 22.

"skills," although the skills program will contribute to greater appreciation. The activities that should be found in the music program are:

(1) Singing and playing.
(2) Writing songs and music.
(3) Listening.
(4) Rhythmic activities.
(5) Reading music.

As the teacher considers the several learning activities of the music program she will remember that it is necessary that children be ready for each new activity, that all children will not be ready at the same time, and that underlying all music instruction is value of individual expression and appreciation.

Shuster and Wetzler have developed a musical experiences chart that suggests the relative emphasis to be given to the several aspects of the music program at the various grade levels. This is presented in Chart XII.[12] It should be kept in mind that the table does not attempt to determine which experiences are *more* or *less* important at any grade level; rather it attempts to indicate at which grade levels the various music

CHART XII

Musical Skills

MUSICAL SKILLS	Grade 1	Grade 2	Grade 3	Grade 4	Grade 5	Grade 6
1. Expressive and creative bodily movement to music	XXX XXX	XXX XXX	XXX XX	XX X	XX	X
2. Listening to music	XXX XX	XXX XX	XXX XX	XX XX	XX X	XX
3. Singing	XX XX	XX XX	XXX XX	XXX XX	XXX XX	XX X
4. Making music with instruments	X	XX	XXX X	XXX XX	XXX XXX	XXX XXX
5. Creative activities with music	X	XX	XXX	XXX X	XXX XX	XXX XXX
6. Musicianship (skills)	X	X	XX	XXX X	XXX XX	XXX XXX

X Equals Proportion of Teaching Emphasis Per Grade, Per Musical Item

[12] Albert H. Shuster and Wilson F. Wetzler, *Leadership in Elementary School Administration and Supervision* (Boston: Houghton Mifflin Co., 1958), p. 264.

learnings will probably receive a large portion of the time allotted to music, thus reducing the time available for certain other activities.

Peters has suggested that children should follow a sequence of experience, expression, and experimentation in their music learnings.[13] This does not suggest that the five-year-old may not be ready to do some experimentation of his own with new words to a familiar tune, nor does it mean that the third grade child may not write a song about a winter storm. Experience, expression, and experimentation may vary as to degree of complexity at the different age levels, but the possibilities exist if the teacher is observant and resourceful in capitalizing on them.

Many elementary schools provide an excellent range of opportunities in instrumental music beginning with the kindergarten. The use of sand blocks, drums, bells, and other equipment which may be used to express rhythmic responses will be found in music programs for younger children. Piano, flutes, tonettes, and other instruments provide music opportunities as the children move into third grade and beyond. Certainly, the elementary music program should recognize no obstacles, except those imposed by lack of competent teachers and necessary funds, in its efforts to offer the broadest approach to musical experiences for children.

The use of musical instruments should be designed to advance the objectives of the total music program rather than to build material for the high school band. At fifth or sixth grade level, instrumental classes should provide exploratory and interest opportunities for children. The use of the instrumental music lesson as a mark of social prestige is to the discredit of parents, who would do better to provide pleasant music experiences in the home and permit the child to move toward his own choice of expressional medium. That is not to say that children should not be encouraged to explore many possibilities, but it is important that the activity have at least as much *value* for the *child* as it does for the *parent*. If there is any place where the parent should not seek self-glory through his child, it is in the area of personal music expression.

How May Music Be Related to Other School Activities?

Fifth grade children may catch a bit of the mood of a Latin-American holiday when they sing a Mexican folk song, or they may share the sadness of the dying soldier's words in "Loch Lomond." Such experiences with music may add to the understandings of social studies or literature. Children may be invited to write a class song about an interesting episode in history or in literature.

---

[13] Peters, *op. cit.*, pp. 46-9.

In art activities the teacher may use music to provide a background of mood. In physical education, of course, there is much need for the timely use of music in the teaching of rhythms. After a strenuous session on the playground, relaxing music may do much to help the children in the transition to quieter activity. At the end of a difficult writing session the sixth graders may benefit immeasurably from a merry, lilting record selection. Again, the physical education period may well have been a folk-dance experience as an outgrowth of a unit of study on early American settlement.

A resourceful fifth grade teacher used music from the Civil War period as a means of conveying to the youngsters the varying moods of the people of the North and South during this period of internal strife. This experience with music did not constitute a major unit in itself; it was supplementary to the social studies unit and strengthened it by helping children to sense the feelings of the people of another time.

On other occasions a unit of music activity may have a social purpose as it serves a music education purpose. An example is the familiar unit on "Music of Other Lands." Such a unit of experience may do much in the way of skill development, and it may serve as the basis for a musical presentation to other children and parents. At the same time, children who sing the festival and holiday songs of other peoples must gain a feeling of friendliness and acquaintanceship through the knowledge that other people have songs of thanksgiving, songs for festive occasions, and songs of prayerfulness, just as do the people of the United States. Social learnings and music learnings can accompany each other under the skillful guidance of the teacher who is aware of the possibilities for such rich experiences.

Music serves the child in many ways and on many occasions throughout the school experience. It must be freed from the confines of two or three brief periods of drill and allowed to become a part of the child's being so that it may meet the many needs which can be served through music. If the time devoted to careful work in singing is looked upon by the children as a time to "cut up," it is doubtful that music is being properly experienced in the regular classroom activities.

Hartshorn has called for a balanced curriculum that will provide for the use of music to support many learning activities of the school program, and provide, also, for adequate learnings in the subject matter of music.[14] Neither part of the music program mentioned by Hartshorn can stand alone and continue to be of utmost value to children.

---

[14] Hartshorn, *op. cit.*, p. 26.

What Are Some Current Problems in Music Education?

One of the most pressing problems in the program of music education in the elementary school is the securing of teachers who are sufficiently prepared to handle music instruction in the classroom. Part of the answer to this problem is the responsibility of the teacher preparatory institutions; another part lies in the proper use of the music specialist or supervisor.

Myers has reported that the prospective teacher should have (1) an understanding of the role of music in the elementary school, (2) opportunities to *observe* and *participate* in music experiences with children, (3) extensive singing, rhythmic and creative experiences *before* approaching such mechanics as music reading.[15] These prerequisites to effective music instruction should be recognized and provided by the teacher preparatory institution. The classroom teacher who feels inadequate in the area of music must seek assistance through further formal education or from the music specialist in the school—or both. Although children's experiences in music do not require that the teacher be an outstanding performer, it is necessary that the teacher enjoy music, know the subject matter of music, and understand the relation of music to the school experiences of children.

Burmeister[16] has proposed several qualifications of the teacher who would do an effective job of music instruction in the elementary school. They include: (a) a positive attitude toward the teaching of music; (b) a pleasing voice and some ability to use her voice accurately; (c) an ability to play the piano; (d) ability to teach rote songs; (e) knowledge of the elements of notation; (f) some knowledge of voices and instruments; (g) a number of good songs for use with the age group being taught; and (h) knowledge of music literature. This author has suggested that the teacher who has the assistance and guidance of a music specialist should be able to do an adequate piece of work with children.

Another problem that confronts many elementary school teachers is the use of children as performers in school and community activities. At the high school level the director of the band or the vocal music instructor often receive the brunt of such requests. At the elementary school level the classroom teacher may be called upon to provide musical entertainment for the P. T. A., the annual Arbor Day program and the like.

---

16 C. A. Burmeister, "The Role of Music in General Education," *Basic Concepts in Music Education* (Chicago: The National Society for the Study of Education, 1958), p. 226 (Chapter 9).

15 Myers, *op. cit.*, pp. 228-32.

Frequently, valuable time is devoted to elaborate costuming and rehersals out of proportion to the values that accrue to children. The classroom teacher must not assume that children never benefit from appearances before groups of people, nor must she lose sight of the purpose of music education for children. In working with parent and community groups the teacher should regard as her primary obligation the provision of the most desirable educational experiences for children.

A number of schools have abandoned the elaborate school operetta in favor of a simpler musical presentation that involves *all* the children, requires little or no special costuming and uses simple scenery. In this manner all children benefit from the experience of appearing in an audience situation, all the parents gain some understanding of the function of elementary school music, and excessive school time is not devoted to a musical extravaganza with its diminishing returns with regard to educational values.

What Are the Outcomes of Musical Experiences?

The teacher of elementary school children needs to assess the effectiveness of the program in music just as she does in other school areas. Most of the evaluation of music learnings will be done by careful teacher observation. Some of the outcomes to be desired are:

(1) Development of effective singing skills.
(2) Development of desirable music tastes.
(3) Development of instrumental knowledge and skills.
(4) Development of self-expression through music.
(5) Development of knowledge and skills in music theory.
(6) Application of knowledge and skills in many situations.
(7) Effective contribution of music to the total school program.[17]

All attempts at evaluation of the music program must be made in terms of the developmental approach which regards musical growth as highly individual, continuous in nature, and closely related to the life situations of children.

EXPERIENCES IN ART

Although there is some lack of concurrence among educators as to the major or minor purposes in art education, there is ample justification

---

[17] *Elementary Evaluative Criteria* (Boston: Boston University, 1953), pp. 51-3.

for the existence of an adequate and meaningful program. For example, Senti has offered the following reasons for art instruction in the elementary school:

(1) Emotional outlet and release from tensions.
(2) Social worth; educating intelligent consumers.
(3) Recreation; provision of hobbies and leisure activities.
(4) Appreciation of natural and man-made art.
(5) Vocational possibilities through the many uses of art skills.[18]

Other authorities in this field would place a major emphasis upon the creative and expressional aspects of the art experience. Erdt has suggested that the goals of a good art program should include:

(1) Fostering the growth of creative, spiritual and appreciative qualities, abilities and potentialities of children.
(2) Selecting appropriate materials so that the art program may meet the needs of all children.
(3) Providing favorable circumstances for art learnings and competent teaching.
(4) Giving children a deep and lasting enjoyment of art.[19]

An analysis which was made of a large number of curriculum guides in use in the larger cities of the United States has indicated that, for the most part, the teaching objectives in art involve, "(1) perceptual, manipulative, and organizational training; (2) cultural appreciation; (3) creative self-expressions; and (4) integration of art in the curriculum."[20] Lanier has pointed out that curriculum guides "do not widely reflect the recent tends in art education thought as expressed in the literature."[21]

It seems that the thoughtful teacher will recognize that providing possibilities for individual pupil adjustment, social growth, and intellectual development are important aspects of art experiences.

The many specific objectives that may need attention in the day-to-day program should, of course, be formulated by children and the teacher as they realize a particular need.

---

[18] Marvel A. Senti, "Fundamentals in Art," *Fundamentals for Children in Our Time* (Lawrence, Kansas: University of Kansas, 1954), pp. 6-7.

[19] Margaret H. Erdt, *Teaching Art in the Elementary Program* (New York: Holt, Rinehart & Winston, Inc., 1954).

[20] Vincent Lanier, "The Status of Current Objectives in Art Education," *Research in Art Education* (Kutztown, Pa.: National Art Education Association, 1954), p. 126.

[21] *Ibid.*, p. 127.

Leonard would add to the objectives proposed by Erdt and Senti, the following:

1. Help the child develop desirable work habits.
2. Provide the child with opportunities for development of co-operative, democratic attitudes in working with others in an atmosphere of freedom.[22]

It should be emphasized that a number of teachers may overlook the contributions to democratic living that are possible in the art program. Children who are provided a large measure of freedom in their expression through art are learning to assume many responsibilities for cooperative work habits. An example of democratic living and learning in art activities is the case of Joe and Bill.

> Joe and Bill wanted to use the same easel for painting. Soon they were engaged in an argument as to who got to the easel first. Miss L. asked Joe and Bill to please work out their differences so they could get on with their work. She told them that she could *tell* them what to do, but it was their problem and they needed to learn to handle this kind of problem as well as learn to paint. In a few minutes Joe and Bill re-entered the room, smiling. The boys selected different easels and the matter was settled.

The philosophy of the teacher who worked with Joe and Bill was far broader than one that considers art experiences as being limited to esthetics and techniques. Some essential requirements of all school experiences which may be found in the approach of this teacher include:

1. The development of the ability to get along well with other people.
2. The skill of working with other people in solving mutual problems.
3. The development of the ability to think and plan.
4. The necessity to make individual decisions.
5. The importance of accepting responsibility for tools and materials and their proper use.
6. The proper use of time.
7. The use of facts in solving problems.

It would have been simpler if the teacher had told Joe and Bill which easels to use. In any classroom situation it is usually simpler and more

---

[22] The authors are indebted to Mary Leonard, Assistant Professor of Art Education, Ohio University, for suggestions and criticism of this section on art.

expedient for the teacher to make most or all decisions involving selection of projects and materials, and in the solving of disputes. Such procedures on the part of the teacher do not provide opportunities for children to accept personal responsibility in many situations where growth possibilities exist. This does not mean that the teacher abandons her position of leadership in the classroom or that children are expected to assume responsibilities beyond their maturity levels; but it does imply that the teacher, as she works with children in the area of art experiences, may provide opportunities for social and personal growth that are quite as valuable as mastery of techniques, and that vital "teaching" does not necessarily involve "telling."

What Is a Point of View Toward Art Education?

It is difficult to determine nationally the nature of art education in the many elementary schools; however, there is evidence that devotion to pattern copying apparently does not dominate the teacher's approach to art instruction in a number of classrooms. But it seems that the overall art program suffers to the extent that adult standards of performance and imitation influence the art experiences of children. As was pointed out earlier in this chapter, the importance of creative expression by the individual child has come to be recognized by authorities in this area.

Each child's work will be representative of his own capacity if he is not held to adult standards of performance. The teacher may keep open the way for continual child growth in art when she accepts the child's work as indicative of himself rather than as being satisfactory or failing on an adult scale of performance. The teacher who presses the child to produce a result which is not his own but a representation of what adults think is good art is only preventing the child from expressing his own feelings and abilities through art. In such a learning situation, growth in art is hindered more than helped.

A first grade teacher who was showing samples of the pupils' art work to a group of adults remarked, "Of course, I always tell them what I want them to draw, and I usually have a picture to show them so they can get the idea." On another occasion a student teacher tearfully reported the results of her art activity thus:

> The second grade children had read a fanciful story about fairies, trolls, and elves. Since St. Patrick's Day was near the children agreed that it would be fun to draw the fabulous Irish Leprechaun. The student teacher and children observed that no one had ever seen a Leprechaun, so it was hard to tell what one would look like. No matter what each child

would draw to represent the Leprechaun, no one could say that it wasn't a good representation.

At this point, the supervising teacher intervened with a picture of a leprechaun that she had placed in her files some years ago. Now the children would have something "to go on."

One does not need to guess as to the results of this second grade art activity. All of the pupil drawings were facsimiles of the handy model which was supplied by the supervising teacher, and the student teacher's attempt to foster creative and imaginative art expression went for nought. Lowenfeld has suggested that one of the main sources of difficulty for the teacher is the "discrepancy between his own way of thinking and experiencing and that of his pupils—."[23] In the example just cited, the supervising teacher permitted her own expectancies to dominate the activity, and imaginative and child-like expression was subdued. The teacher will serve the purposes of art education best when she provides the materials and the classroom settings for art experiences and permits the child to create freely as he desires and is able. If art expression is to be viewed within the context of other human behavior, then its developmental nature must be accepted, since all children will not be equally ready and capable of using the same art materials in the same manner.

Many elementary school teachers continue to stress the craftsmanship and design aspect of art. Balance, design, color, and size take up a great amount of the art program in many schools. Yet Kusel has stated that craftsmanship and design are the concerns of adult art rather than child art.[24] He has proposed that child art depends upon an unhindered spontaneity for creativeness, that the consciousness of technique only hampers spontaneity and deadens the result.[25]

Art as a product.   It may be some time before teachers and others differentiate between art as a product or result of individual activity and art as individual experience of value primarily to the individual who is "doing." This is particularly pertinent at the elementary school level where few persons expect to find the rare or perfectly-created art objects usually found in museums. The very heart of the art program in the elementary school is the provision of opportunities for the child to grow

---

[23] Viktor Lowenfeld, *Creative and Mental Growth* (New York: The Macmillan Co., 1952), p. 57.

[24] Heinz Kusel, "Spontaneity or Prescription?" *School Arts*, 56 (May, 1957), 23-4.

[25] *Ibid.*

naturally in his understanding of self and surroundings and to accept the freedom to express himself through *many media*. The result or product of such expressional activity is not of great importance except as the child feels its importance. Too often one may overhear some teachers and parents alike discussing the results of child art work, rather than devoting their thoughts to the experiences which must be included in the art program. Thus, one may find emphasis upon art exhibits and contests wherein the child-artist may see his work rejected or rated poorly on the basis of an evaluation that is meaningless to the child.

One of the authors once worked with a second grade teacher who always "touched up" the pupil art work that was to be sent to the county fair exhibit. There were those occasions when a child could hardly recognize his own work after the retouching. There seems to be little relation between the award-giving art contests and development of art expression.

What Are the Experiences of the Art Program?

There is actually little or no reason, aside from the child's maturity, for limiting the types of activities and materials wherein children may work in a creative manner. Children of elementary school age must work with materials and tools which they can effectively control. For example, the eight-year-old would encounter considerable difficulty using the chisels necessary for carving ebony.

Aside from the physical limitations involved in the selection of materials and activities for the child, the teacher would do well to provide for experiences in using many media of art expression. Some of the art experiences suitable for elementary school children are:

(1) Painting with water colors, tempera or powder paint, and finger paint.
(2) Working with clay.
(3) Drawing with crayons, charcoals, and pencils.
(4) Working with paper; cutting, papier mâché, pasting, collages, sculpture and the like.
(5) Carving of soap, wood, and plaster.
(6) Stenciling.
(7) Printing with wood, potatoes, fingers, sponge, and linoleum.
(8) Weaving and sewing.
(9) Wood construction.

In planning the art program for the elementary school the teacher may question how much freedom should be permitted the children in the selection of materials and activities. There should be no doubt in the teacher's mind as to the necessity for deciding what materials and experiences should be introduced to children. The fact that the teacher suggests the particular activity or activities does not need to block individual initiative in expression through a certain medium. For example, the teacher who may plan for pupil experience with water colors may suggest seasonal scenes, animal scenes, and the like. The child may select freely in order to express himself as he chooses. On the other hand, the teacher may begin a period of work in paper cutting with these instructions: "We are going to use white paper cutouts on a black background, and our figures will be two Pilgrims and a turkey." Such an approach to an experience in paper cutting is little more creative than using stencils to obtain the results.

One research study has found that there is wide agreement among art teachers as to the importance of including clay work, tempera painting, colored paper work, colored chalk activities and experiences with crayons. There is also corresponding agreement that least essential are experiences with leather, silk screen printing, plastics, photographic materials and oil paint.[26] It is interesting to note that the media which demand greater technical knowledge and tend to result in more permanent products are rated low, whereas the simpler media which provide valuable experiences in the *doing* rather than in creating a lasting product are rated high. This does not mean that plastics should *never* be used as an art medium in the elementary school; rather, it indicates that the teacher think carefully through the purposes and pupil benefits involved before deciding upon the use of any particular medium.

Each child, provided with the necessary instructions for handling the materials at hand, must have the freedom to proceed with the production of something that is his own. The child will acquire skill in handling the various materials as he uses them, and more important, he will maintain his feeling of self-expression. The challenge which confronts the teacher in providing leadership in the arts may be expressed in this statement: "The teacher must know when and how much direction should be given to the child in the techniques of art expression in order that the individual's creative enthusiasm be strengthened rather than frustrated."

---

[26] Research in Art Education, Manual Barkan, ed. (Kutztown, Pa.: National Art Education Association, 1954), pp. 97-9.

How Are Techniques and Appreciation Taught?

The teacher in the elementary school gives instruction and guidance in the use of the techniques for which the child has reasonable need. The needs of the six-year-old with regard to the methods of working with clay are comparatively unsophisticated. The first grade youngster may observe that the poster paint which he has applied to a clay bowl does not provide a durable finish. This is not, however, a pressing problem with the six-year-old, although it may be a serious matter with the sixth grade child. Thus, the sixth grade child may need instruction in preparing his clay product for glazing and firing, whereas the six-year-old does not experience that need. Over thirty years ago one writer summarized the role of technique and form in art education in these words:

> Art ceases to be art—if any form or technique, no matter how good, is imposed from without. In other words, art ceases to be art if it fails to grow out of the child's own expression and feeling of need as they lead on to higher levels of appreciation and control.[27]

Just as it is futile and unrewarding to present phonetic rules to five-year-olds, so it is useless and even damaging to teach techniques of art expression before the child has developed to the stage where such instruction is needed and understandable. As Mathias has pointed out, "Training is harmful when it precedes the development of the power to be trained."[28]

Logan has suggested that the term, *art appreciation* could well be discarded because it has become far too limited in its connotation.[29] The popular concept of art appreciation has too frequently been involved with rare works of art which are located in a European museum, and has been based on the assumption that few people are capable of appreciating "good" art.[30]

The teacher needs to think of art "appreciation" from at least two points of view: one toward the child's day-to-day contacts with color,

---

[27] Margaret Mathias, *The Beginnings of Art in the Public Schools* (Charles Scribner's Sons, 1924), p. ix.

[28] *Ibid.*

[29] Frederick M. Logan, *Growth of Art in American Schools* (New York: Harper & Row, Publishers, 1955), p. 44.

[30] *Ibid.*

form, and design of clothing, furniture, buildings and the like; the other toward the child's awareness of the contribution of the great artists and architects. This outlook on art appreciation does not limit enjoyment of natural and man-made beauty to a *few* cultured people; it brings appreciation within the experiences of *most* people. Appreciation must be approached from the developmental point of view; children will grow toward an awareness of the beauty in things about them as they gain experience in working with various art materials and from observing the characteristics of art expression.

Lowenfeld has stated that one must know something of the subject matter and the means of expression used by the artist before one can begin to appreciate a particular piece of art.[31] This is particularly pertinent when the teacher views the art work of the child. She must know something of the child's subject matter. This depends, of course, upon a knowledge of his background. She must also understand his use of the medium of expression.[32]

It is doubtful that the art appreciation class is effective if it deals solely with ancient and rare art objects, and if it is not a part of the child's personal experience with art materials. The child who has worked with water colors may, when 13 or 14 years of age, appreciate a well done water color. The child who has experienced the use of color, balance and design may see beauty in the Parthenon, and it is to be hoped that the teacher will call attention to the aesthetic values of certain buildings in the child's own community. Children will appreciate the work of others as they have experiences themselves in working with various art materials.

It does not seem too utilitarian to hope that children may become, as a result of art experience, discerning and *aesthetic* in selection of clothing, setting of tableware, arranging the furniture in a room, or planning a poster display for the school corridor. At any rate, the teacher must recognize that appreciation must come from within the child; it may grow out of a well-planned art program over the years, but it cannot result from an overlay which is cast on the child by a well-meaning teacher.

How May Art Be Related to Other School Experiences?

There are many opportunities in language arts, science, social studies and physical education for the use of art expression. Posters, murals, dioramas and constructions may be of value in the development of a unit

---

[31] Lowenfeld, *op. cit.*, pp. 17-9.
[32] *Ibid.*

on Mexico, or farming, or any other area in social studies. Art abilities
are applied in such instances.

Creation of scenery for the dramatization of a favorite story calls for
art expression. Construction may come to the foreground in building a
puppet theater, an African village, or a classroom store. Class murals
which are planned by several groups of pupils may depict certain events
in history or present science information such as the various eras in mankind's biological development. Such activities should serve the purpose
of clarifying any given concept through pictorial illustration, and should
also serve to further the purposes of art education. It is a false assumption that suggests that art education can be adequately served through
the incidental functional approach in all areas of learning. Children must
have the time to experiment with art media and to express themselves in
painting, drawing, or whatever, without concern for the result being
acceptable as a mural or class display.

The classroom teacher can serve the art education of the child best
when she recognizes the difference between the use of art materials in
functional projects and the *creative* use of art materials by the individual
child as he reveals *a certain* concept of self and surrounding through an
art medium. Both have a place in the school program, but they are not
identical in purpose, and the teacher may approach them in somewhat
different manners.

What Is the Role of the Teacher in Art Education?

Much of the material of this chapter has been concerned with the
role of the teacher in the art education of the child. This section shall
serve to point out the importance of classroom teaching, cooperating
with the art specialist (if one is available in the school system), and, in
general, the teacher's having some knowledge with respect to art materials, techniques, and child development.

Some persons have decided that since art is individual expression it
is unnecessary to do anything in the way of guidance of children beyond
providing paint, brush, and paper. The teacher who has studied her
pupils is in a position to know when various individuals are ready to
benefit from suggestions. To the fifth grade child who has trouble showing movement in his baseball game scene, she may suggest that he spend
a few minutes carefully watching the pitcher or the batter. She may suggest that the child-artist observe the movement of arms and legs by the
ball players.

It should be apparent that the child must be aware of and work within
some limits and controls in creative art expression. However, the limits

and controls should derive from the capacities and developmental levels of children and from the physical aspects of the learning environment rather than from teacher-dominated selection of those activities she likes. Since it is hardly feasible for the third grade child to work with hard woods in carving or construction, the instructor should recognize that materials to be used do set limits and pose problems in terms of the physical strength of the child.

Developing art expression. Another responsibility of the teacher is that of stimulating and guiding evaluation of growth in art expression. This is most effectively accomplished by applying techniques of individual and group objectives and outcomes. The art product of the child should be evaluated in terms of the progress that he as an individual is making, and not how well he is competing with other children. Great care must be taken in the evaluation phase, inasmuch as a poor approach may well stifle individual creativity and result in all children striving to duplicate the "master copy" that the teacher wants.

The teacher provides leadership in art activities as she does in other learning activities: by being familiar with the nature and characteristics of child growth and development, child interests, and the child needs in creative expression.

Kusel has suggested that many teachers find it simpler to dictate exactly what the children will do in each art "period," inasmuch as careful study of children and much pre-planning is necessary if the art experience is to be individually creative and developmental.[33] At the other extreme is the teacher who makes the art experience completely open-ended, with few benefits of competent teacher guidance. Neither extreme is desirable.

Opportunities for *creative* art expression may be provided by the teacher at various times throughout the week. There is no reason why clay, crayons, paint, and other materials cannot be accessible for use during free times when a particular child may be "looking" for something to do. There is no reason why reading must be the only "free" choice to be made.

The teacher can do much by way of helping parents to understand and accept the child's art expression. In some situations this may be her most crucial role as was the case with Miss S., a kindergarten teacher, who was confronted by a mother who didn't want her child bringing home any more of those "hideous clay things" because they were crumbly and messed up the house. In another situation the teacher may counsel the parent regarding the critical remarks of an older brother or sister

---

[33] Kusel, *op. cit.*, pp. 23-4.

when the child proudly presents a picture that no one understands. Following is an example of the way one teacher worked with parents on this problem:

> Miss Long, a first grade teacher, used a portion of the room parents' meeting for discussion of the importance of parental and sibling attitudes in the creative development of the child. She pointed out that parents who insist upon the child's coloring and painting objects that always look like something that someone else has already created are really helping the child to become a good mimic but are hindering the child's personal creative development.
>
> Miss Long suggested that it is just as simple and far more rewarding to ask the child, "Do you want to tell me about your picture?" as it is to ask, "What is this picture you have drawn?" She helped parents understand that the young child may apply paint on paper with nothing in mind except to see what various colors look like—much as adults may "doodle" idly as they listen to an address.

Lowenfeld has delineated the crucial position of the parent as one who can do much to free the child for creative expression or to restrain and inhibit the child's individual development in this area.[34] It is difficult, if not impossible, to achieve optimum creative conditions with the child whose parents do not understand that the *expression* rather than the *result* is of the utmost concern to the child artist.

Effective working relationships between parents, teachers, and children may be fostered through the occasional room meeting where the art experiences of children may be discussed with quite as much justification as any other learning experiences of children. This is an area where teacher leadership is greatly needed.

Olson has set forth a number of desirable characteristics of the person who teaches art. They include:

1. Experience in working creatively with various media.
2. Ability to identify self with pupil needs, goals, and stages of development.
3. Sufficient psychological insight to help the student reinforce the experience he is attempting to represent.
4. A broad background of information about art forms, the history of art and its social function.
5. Knowledge of students and the social and economic forces of the world they live in.

---

[34] Viktor Lowenfeld, *Your Child and His Art* (New York: The Macmillan Co., 1954).

6. A capacity for appreciating individual differences and accepting them as essentially good for the social group.
7. Realization that ideas may be expressed in a variety of ways.[35]

It may be readily seen that there are many characteristics of the good art teacher which are essentials for all effective teachers. The teacher who conceives her responsibilities and opportunities in art *expression* as encompassing more than pattern copying and identical activities for every child has taken an important first step toward enriching leadership in the classroom.

The teacher provides valuable leadership in the art experiences of children as she encourages surroundings in the school room and in the home that are conducive to personal creativity on the part of the children. This she conceives to be as important as the materials, techniques, and tangible results of the art program. Effective integration of art experiences into the over-all program is best obtained when the classroom teacher senses the need for, and hence provides, opportunities for the expression of ideas through the art media in a variety of school situations. In this respect, the art specialist cannot replace the classroom teacher as the key person in the art experiences of children. Nor can the classroom teacher properly abdicate this responsibility to an art specialist. Working cooperatively with art supervisors and consultants, the classroom teacher can prepare herself for the vital role of leadership in the art program of the elementary school.

What is the place of handwork in the program? The experiences provided in the handwork program in the elementary school program are actually closely related to art experiences, and in many instances are considered part of the art program. The major points of differences between the art activities and the handwork activities have to do with the manipulative forms of work and the materials and tools used. Some persons have argued that the handwork program is noncreative, whereas the art program is oriented toward individual creative expression. The former point should not be considered in the practice of the elementary school, because there is room for creative expression in handwork experiences.

Newkirk has suggested that the handwork program in the elementary school has three primary objectives:

1. To give the child an objective medium for expressing his ideas.
2. To provide the child with a manipulative form of creative leisure-time expression.

---

[35] John W. Olson, "The Art Teacher," *This Is Art Education* (Kutztown, Pa.: National Art Education Association, 1951), pp. 87-103.

3. To acquaint the child with a variety of construction materials and to develop handiness with common tools.[36]

It may be observed that the objectives listed for the handwork program are not vastly different from the objectives of the elementary school program as set forth earlier in this chapter. The omission by Newkirk of the objective of acquiring aesthetic understandings may be a significant difference, although the handwork activities of the child should contribute to his desire for good form and sound construction which are qualities of appreciation.

Handwork activities should not be considered to be *art* experiences when they are confined to pattern work, teacher-prescribed designs and construction, and other similar activities where the emphasis is upon duplication rather than creative expression. For example, when the children are asked to make nut cups for the P. T. A. tea, the activity may well be handwork without the creative elements of art expression. On the other hand, the construction of the diorama depicting a colonial scene may involve creative pupil expression as well as handwork skills.

Handwork activities are to be regarded as contributing to the many learning experiences of the school program and are least effective when isolated from the work in science, social studies and other areas. Newkirk lists some of the handwork activities that may be included in the elementary school program:

(1) Book and paper making
(2) Cooking
(3) Dioramas
(4) Leather tooling
(5) Maps and charts
(6) Marionettes
(7) Metalworking
(8) Sewing
(9) Weaving
(10) Models, apparatus, and musical instruments.[37]

The classroom teacher can work most effectively with children when she considers handwork as a means to an end rather than an end in itself, and when she recognizes that certain handcraft activities do not meet the needs of children for creative expression. There is a legitimate place

---

[36] Louis V. Newkirk, *Integrated Handwork for Elementary Schools* (New York: Silver Burdette Co., 1940), p. 5.
[37] *Ibid.*

for handcraft activities that are not oriented toward creative expression, but the teacher should also provide opportunities for creative handwork. If there is a danger in the use of manuals and pattern books for handcraft instruction, it is that the teacher may permit this to dominate the total art program, and in such instances, creative art expression is lost.

SUMMARY

The experiences of the elementary school child in art and music should serve to provide (1) outlets for creative expression, (2) opportunities to acquire and develop the skills that are appropriate for the child's use, and (3) understandings and appreciation of the contributions of art and music to human society.

A rather common tendency among teachers in the past has been to treat art and music education as subject matter to be learned rather than experiences to be incorporated by the individual child as his *development* and *capacity* permit. A modern approach to music and art education is based upon the beliefs that (1) all individuals will benefit personally from music and art, (2) all individuals have something to "say" through music and art, although it may not be unusual or important to others, and (3) art and music do not provide legitimate areas of competition for children of elementary school age.

Music and art may effectively supplement other areas of learning because they are naturally interwoven with human experiences. Music and art education is not left to an incidental approach, however, because each area requires and deserves careful planning and competent teaching to be effectively incorporated into the child's learning experiences.

SUGGESTED ACTIVITIES AND PROBLEMS

1. Have a committee of four or five students interview a number of elementary school teachers to find out how they provide for *creative* experiences in art and music. The committee may word the question along these lines: "Do you provide for creative experiences in music and art? If so, how do you go about it?" The committee should report its findings to the class.

2. Develop a suggested list of social studies in which *creative* art work could be effectively used. Develop a list of activities in the social studies in which art techniques may be used, though not necessarily in a creative manner.

3. Plan a well-rounded music program for any grade level in the elementary school. Be sure that you have provided a range of experiences, a balanced program, and have considered principles of child development.

4. The local Bird Watcher's Club has asked the sixth grade to provide table decorations for their monthly dinner meetings throughout the year. A group of three or four students should role play the sixth grade teachers and present their reactions to such a project.

5. The class should arrange to visit several elementary school classrooms to observe evidences of *creative* and *non-creative* handwork. The observations should be the subject of discussion.

6. What are some ways in which the art program can help develop good work habits without stifling creative work? Why is the art activity an excellent place to provide for growth in cooperative work habits and attitudes?

SELECTED READINGS

Arberg, Harold W. *Music Curriculum Guides*. Washington, D.C.: U.S. Office of Education, 1964.

Basic Concepts in Music Education. Fifty-seventh Yearbook of the National Society for the Study of Education. Chicago: University of Chicago Press, 1958.

Conrad, George. *The Process of Art Evaluation*. Englewood Cliffs, N.J.: Prentice-Hall, Inc., 1964.

D'Amico, Victor. *Creative Teaching in Art*. New York: International Textbook, 1953.

Doig, Dorothy. "Creative Music: III, Music Composed to Illustrate Given Music Problems," *Journal of Educational Research*, 36 (December, 1942), 241-53.

Dykema, Peter and Hannah M. Cundiff. *School Music Handbook*. Boston: C. C. Brichard and Co., 1955.

Erdt, Margaret H. *Teaching Art in the Elementary School*. New York: Holt, Rinehart & Winston, Inc., 1954, Chapters 2, 7, 8.

Hartley, Joseph C. "Music-Reading Skills in the Elementary Grades," *National Educational Association Journal*, (October, 1954), 404-05.

Hartsel, O. M. *Teaching Music in the Elementary School*. Washington, D.C.: Association for Supervision and Curriculum Development, 1963.

House, Robert W. "A Definition of the Qualified Music Teacher," *Educational Music Magazine*, 36 (September-October, 1956), 8.

Keston, Morton J. "An Experimental Evaluation of the Effects of Two Methods of Teaching Music Appreciation," *Journal of Experimental Education*, 22 (September, 1952—June, 1954), 215-26.

Langan, Gene M. "Sixth Graders Replan a City," *School Arts*, 56 (May, 1957), 9.

Lark-Hororitz, Betty, Hilda Lewis, and Mark Luca. *Understanding Children's Art for Better Teaching.* Columbus, Ohio: Charles E. Merrill Publishing Co., 1967.

Logan, Frederick M. *Growth of Art in American Schools.* New York: Harper & Row, Publishers, 1955, Chapters, 2, 7.

Lowenfeld, Viktor. *Creative and Mental Growth.* New York: The Macmillan Co., 1952.

Miller, Charles E. Frederick. "Experiment in Contrasting Teaching Methods," *Music Educator's Journal*, 43 (September, 1956), 59.

Mohr, Estell Elgar. "Elementary Music Teaching Problems," *Music Educator's Journal*, 35-36 (1950), 48.

Mueller, Kate Hevner. "Studies in Musical Appreciation," *Journal of Research in Music Education*, 4 (1956), 3-25.

National Society for the Study of Education. *Art Education.* Sixty-fourth Yearbook, Part II. Chicago: University of Chicago Press, 1965.

Newacheck, Vivian. "Music and the Slow Learner," *Music Education Journal*, 40, No. 1 (November, 1953), 50.

Robinson, Donald W., Eugent Craft, and Linden Summers. "Implications of Music Program for Pupil Growth," *Elementary School Journal*, 55 (May, 1955), 158-61.

Rogers, Vincent R. "Children's Musical Preferences as Related to Grade Level and Other Factors," *The Elementary School Journal*, 57 (May, 1957), 433-36.

Schnirder, Majel Horning. "Music for Pre-School Children," *Music Educator's Journal*, 35-36 (1950), 51.

Sloat, Rosemarie G. "Science and a Seedpod Christmas Tree," *School Arts*, 56 (November, 1956), 27-28.

CHAPTER 12

Teacher Leadership in Developing Health, Physical, and Safety Education

INTRODUCTION

An aspect of national life which has received steadily increasing attention since the turn of the century has been the physical welfare of all citizens with particular emphasis upon the needs of school children. The two devastating wars which occurred during the first half of this century placed a spotlight upon the health needs and physical shortcomings of vast numbers of young men of military age. An awareness of the importance of good community health practices has emerged as a result of, or in conjunction with, the presence of dangerous diseases such as tuberculosis, poliomyelitis, typhoid fever, and other illnesses which may spread because of inadequate sanitation practices and low nutritional levels in the community and nation.

Mental illnesses, which occur in higher incidence than all other forms of disabling illnesses, have brought to the attention of the American people the vital import of emotional stability, personal adjustment, and social competence that tends to promote mental health in the individual.

With the advent of the machine age and the presence of power equipment in office, home, and factory, there has been an increasing drain on the nation's economy in terms of human and material loss due to accidents. The terrible maiming and loss of lives on the nation's highways are attributed to the absence of necessary safety practices by the automobile driver rather than to the curves and hills of the highways on which men drive.

In almost every instance of challenge to the nation's welfare, whether it come from physically unfit soldiers, from threat of epidemic, or from loss of life and limb through accident, the question is raised, "What is the responsibility of the schools in these matters?" This question has been considered by most classroom teachers who have worked with children who were poorly nourished, inadequately clothed, or ill.

What is the role of the school and the teacher in guiding the child toward a wholesome concept of his own body and its requirements? What is the purpose of a planned playground program, and where does the teacher fit into such a program? What can the school and the teacher do to help children build attitudes toward the safe use of toys, small machines and vehicles so that they will be safety conscious as children and, later, as adults?

The many aspects of the school's responsibilities with respect to the continuing physical welfare of children are represented in Figure XVII. It may readily be seen that instruction in physiology no longer makes up the sum and substance of the program. To the end that children may live and learn more effectively, both in and out of school, the range of the school's concerns for children is ever widening. The school cannot expect to carry these responsibilities alone, and the cooperation and assistance of the members of the community are necessary if an effective job is to be done.

FIGURE XVII

The School and Physical Welfare of Children

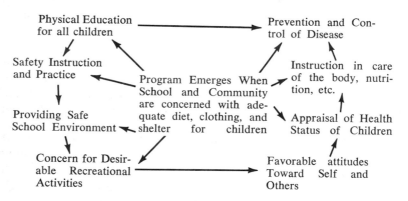

It is the purpose of this chapter to provide some guidelines which may be used in the planning and implementation of a classroom approach to effective health, safety, and physical education. It is no less important to the individual than to the national community that health, safety, and physical fitness be proper concerns of the teachers and the schools. Obviously, the prevalence of high nutritional standards and desirable health and safety practices cannot be achieved by legislative action alone, but must result from the practices, knowledge and attitudes of the individual members of society. It is in this area that the school must fulfill its role.

HEALTH EDUCATION IN THE MODERN SCHOOL

During the latter part of the nineteenth century the responsibility of the school in matters pertaining to the health of its pupils was confined primarily to providing classrooms that were properly ventilated and insuring a safe supply of drinking water. Health officers in some of the larger communities checked the school buildings for elementary health conditions. In the period following the 1920's large numbers of school systems began to perceive the nature of an inclusive health education program that would be concerned with the health maintenance and health improvement of the children.

What Is the Modern Concept of Health Education?

A modern approach to health education is oriented toward developing attitudes, providing necessary information, and encouraging desirable health practices toward the end that the individual accepts responsibility for his own physical well-being insofar as he is able. This is in contrast to an older approach to health education which was directed toward supervision, inspection, and lecturing.

Today, it is commonly recognized by people in education, and in public health services, that knowledge *about* the human body and information *about* disease control do not necessarily result in the desired kinds of individual behavior. The attitudes with which the individual regards the care of his body, the selection of his diet, and the preventive measures to be taken in disease control are quite as important as the possession of knowledge about the fundamentals of healthful living.

Wheatley and Hallock have emphasized that no child can be kept healthy and safe solely as a result of what parents, teachers and physicians plan and do for him; nor can a child relieve himself of existing defects merely by possessing and practicing good health rules.[1] The child must be guided toward a recognition and awareness of his own responsibility for behavior conducive to good health, and such guidance is indeed one of the most challenging tasks which the teacher encounters. The school health program must accept a mutual responsibility with the

---

[1] George M. Wheatley and Grace T. Hallock, *Health Observation of School Children* (New York: McGraw-Hill Book Co., Inc., 1956), p. 10.

parents and certain community agencies for observation of the physical condition of the child and for instituting the action necessary to bring about remedy and relief of any corrective defects.

In the modern health program the objectives are multiple and go far beyond traditional methods of lecture and recitation. They include:

1. Development of proper attitudes and behavior in mental and physical health.
2. Provision of a healthful school environment.
3. Observation of the health status of children.
4. Action directed toward diagnosis and remedy of existing defects.
5. Instruction in the care of the body and practice of behavior that is conducive to good health.

Why Is There a Need to Improve Health Learning Experiences?

It is doubtful that teachers and parents will ever see the day when the health practices and conditions of any community do not deserve attention and improvement. Although certain threats to the physical welfare of children have diminished such diseases as scarlet fever and whooping cough, there are constant threats from diseases which attack highly organized civilizations. For example, the great loss of time caused by the common cold and by digestive disturbances are still challenging problems to persons concerned with the health of children.

Adequate nutrition, sufficient rest, care of the teeth, bodily cleanliness and a host of other health fundamentals must be contained in the program of health education. Inasmuch as it has been accepted by many persons in the field of health education that each child is, in the final analysis, his own guardian of mental and physical health, there is an apparent need for a program that will go beyond the memorizing and reciting stage.

The school must be concerned with the total fitness of the child to participate in the learning activities of the school. The interest which the teacher has in the physical welfare of each child does not imply that the school is trying to do too many things for the pupils. Perhaps a closer home and school relationship is essential if the home is to bear the responsibility for safeguarding the child's health. In far too many situations, it seems that parents do not sense or accept the responsibility or realize the urgency of the child's physical well-being. Whatever the case may be in one community or another, the need persists for effective teaching and learning in the health program to the end that a healthier citizenry will work together in a united effort toward providing better conditions of personal and community health.

What Are Some Trends in Health Instruction?

It is not easy to determine the exact status of health education in all of the elementary schools in the nation or in any one state. A survey of the recommendations of authorities in this area indicates that the emphasis is to be placed upon a practical approach to the study of the health problems of the child, and the older practice of studying physiology as an end in itself is no longer thought to be proper for the elementary school child.

State and local curriculum planning groups have provided evidence through curriculum guides and courses of study that indicates that a much more informal yet meaningful approach is being made to health education, generally. The Nebraska Guide recommends that health education instruction:

1. Grow out of the child's needs and experiences.
2. Use all available instructional materials and activities rather than one textbook exclusively.
3. Include definite attempts to develop good health attitudes and habits on the part of the child.
4. Provide for continuous evaluation of health practices and conditions of pupils and school personnel.
5. Relate experiences in health education with other areas of the school program where this is proper.[2]

Walker has suggested that:

Programs of instruction which associate the child and his interests with his personal health needs and with community, home, and school health needs bring to him an ever-widening understanding of health problems and his relationship to them. The teacher and the pupils plan the kind of educational experiences which, at different grade levels, help to develop this understanding.[3]

From this statement it may be seen that the health education program must follow the same basic principles that foster effective learnings in other school areas.

---

[2] *A Guide for Evaluating and Improving Nebraska Elementary Schools* (Lincoln, Nebraska: State Department of Education, 1955), pp. 25-7.

[3] Herbert Walker, *Health in the Elementary School* (New York: The Ronald Press Co., 1955), p. 121.

As to the organization of health instruction, it appears that many schools follow an incidental approach in the primary grades with a formal, regularly scheduled class period allotted in the middle and upper grades.[4] The practice of alternating health education and science on an every-other-day plan or on a semester basis is not recommended as being effective as it seems to presume that the child's health problems will occur only twice a week or during one semester of the year. Obviously, a rigidly scheduled health education program suggests a "bookish" approach rather than a dynamic approach to health learnings, and will tend to place the experiences of children at a distance from their actual health understandings and problems.

One elementary school teacher made a realistic approach to the matter of cleanliness among her fifth grade pupils in the following manner:

> Miss Ames recognized that asking children whether they had washed before coming to school was not proving effective as a means of changing child behavior; the children who frequently were unwashed at the morning bell usually insisted that they *had* washed at home but had become soiled on the playground.
>
> Miss Ames was aware, also, that several youngsters came from homes where cleanliness standards did not appear to be very high. So, instead of using the morning check to find out who had washed and who had not, she discussed the proper use of the school washrooms and encouraged *all* children to wash thoroughly after coming in from the playground. Although this plan did not get 100 percent results, it did bring the matter into a realistic focus and pointed up the necessity of cleanliness at school.

If cleanliness is an important aspect of health education, and it obviously is, then few teachers will want to neglect the opportunities during the school day for pupils to learn about cleanliness. The results will warrant the time used. On the other hand, the teacher who confines her "cleanliness" teaching to a lecture and the awarding of gold stars for clean hands is hardly using the available facilities and the experience of school life to make her approach realistic and practical to children.

The *Oregon Guide for Elementary Education* states that "health education in the elementary school is a matter of helping the child to live healthfully each day . . ."[5] and proceeds to point out the functional nature of an effective program. Major areas of instruction which are mentioned in this *Guide* as suitable for intermediate grades are:

---

[4] *Ibid.*

[5] *Guide for Elementary Education in Oregon* (Salem, Oregon: State Department of Education, 1953), pp. 20-1; 48-9; 80-1.

1. Understanding and care of oneself (structure, function, and hygiene).
2. Safety and first aid.
3. Nutrition.
4. Effects of exercise.
5. Control of communicable diseases and community health and sanitation.

The subject matter of health education should be related in every conceivable instance to the daily life of the child. In this manner the attitudes, habits, and information essential to healthful living will become a part of the child.

The Health Guide for Idaho[6] provides suggested units of study to be taught in each of the elementary grades with about six weeks time being provided for each unit. The Los Angeles City Schools provide a guide[7] for elementary teachers which approaches health education from the standpoint of common experiences and problems of children. For example, in the area of mental health, some of the problems which are suggested are:

1. How can children learn to get along with others and make friends?
2. How can children learn to understand the possible causes of other people's behavior?
3. How can children learn to grow up in their behavior as they get older?[8]

Similar problems are listed for the areas of nutrition and general physical health.

The Santa Cruz guide suggests a diversified approach to the teaching of health and recommends the following methods:

1. Problem-solving	6. Pupil-conducted surveys
2. Socio-drama	7. Pupil-written plays and stories
3. Demonstration	8. Tests
4. Buzz session	9. Open-end interviews
5. Games	10. Current events.[9]

---

[6] *Idaho Study Guide in Health* (Boise, Idaho: State Department of Education.)

[7] *Experiences in Health Education* (Los Angeles: City School District, 1953), pp. 31-43.

[8] *Ibid.*

[9] *Health Guide for Elementary Schools* (Santa Cruz, Calif.: Santa Cruz County School Dist., 1952), p. 17.

There appears to be, then, a variety of practices in the many schools about the United States concerning health education; however, there seems to be a general agreement that the major goal of the schools must be to assist in changing pupil behavior rather than imparting facts alone. The classroom teacher should evaluate her health education program in terms of the behavior and attitudes of the children in her room. The Virginia guide has stated this pervading aim of health education thus:

> To develop an attitude of self-appraisal which will result in assuming responsibilities relative to a well-balanced program of personal hygiene that will enable one to live more effectively in the home, school, and community.[10]

The scope of the program. The scope of the health education program will vary as local and personal health problems require; however, there are a number of areas in which health learnings generally occur. The modern program will not rigidly place the areas of health education in any particular grade, but it is important that the teacher be aware of commonly occurring needs in the various areas.

The Fresno, California, City Schools have included in their curriculum guide a scope and sequence chart which is presented in Chart XIII. This scope and sequence guide is probably representative of the approach found in a large number of elementary schools in this nation.

Organizing the health program. Whatever the plan followed as to the scope and sequence of health education in the elementary school, the classroom teacher will have the final responsibility for the type and quality of experience in her room. With this fact in mind, it is urged that the teacher follow these guides as she plans for health education activities:

1. Provide for regular health instruction so that pupil needs and interests may be discovered and used as the basis for many learning situations.
2. Plan for activities that will be related closely to experiences and problems of the pupils.
3. Avoid a rigid curriculum plan that leaves no time for daily problems in health.
4. Use many materials and devices for health education rather than only one textbook.

---

[10] *Health Education* (Richmond, Va.: Virginia State Board of Education, 1956), p. 2.

CHART XIII

Health Education Scope and Sequence Chart[11]

Grade	K	1	2	3	4	5	6
Dental Health	x	x	x	x	x	x	x
Nutrition	–	–	x	x	–	–	–
Safety and Accident Prevention	–	–	–	x	x	–	–
Community Health							
Disease Control					x		
Public Health		–	–	–	o	o	–
Sanitation	–						
Family Life Education	–	–	–	–	–	–	–
Sense of Humor							
Getting Along with Others	–	–	–	–	–	x	x
Personality Needs							
Relaxation and Releasing Tensions							
Alcohol and Narcotics	–	–	–	–	–	–	–
School Health Services	–	–	–	–	–	–	–
Personal Health							
Grooming							
Cleanliness	–	–	–	–	–	x	x
Exercise, Rest, Sleep	x	x	x	x	x	x	x
Care of Eyes, Ears, Skin							

x Special emphasis
o Correlation with social studies and science
– Taught

5. Keep the program up to date in terms of current problems and accurate information.
6. Avoid minimizing health education through an incidental or accidental approach.
7. Evaluate the effectiveness of your health program in terms of reasonable pupil behavior with respect to cleanliness, nutrition, care of the body and the like.

An approach to planning the health education program is illustrated in Figure XVIII and incorporates the many features of a well-balanced program. As the teacher plans for the health education of children, she will keep the experiences suitable to the developmental levels of the youngsters. For example, the inclusion of alcohol and narcotics in the

---

[11] *A Tentative Guide to the Fresno City Schools Health Program* (Fresno, Cal.: Unified School District, 1954), Preface.

FIGURE XVIII

Contents of a Modern Health Program

health program is required by law in some states, but the manner in which this problem is treated varies with the age and maturity of the pupils.

Although the instructional materials and experiences will vary with the developmental level of the particular group of pupils, the basic ingredients of a modern health program are found throughout the elementary school because the health needs and interests of individuals and communities exist for all ages, and it is these elements that must receive the attention of health education.

What Are the Health Services in a Modern Elementary School?

Health services in the elementary school program have been defined to include:

1. Appraising the health status of pupils and school personnel.
2. Counselling of parents, pupils, and other persons concerning findings.
3. Encouraging the correction and remedy of existing defects, if possible.
4. Planning for the health care and education of handicapped children.
5. Preventing and controlling of disease.
6. Providing emergency care for sick and injured pupils.[12]

---

[12] "Report of the Committee on Terminology in School Health Education," *Journal of the American Association for Health, Physical Education, and Recreation*, 22 (September, 1951), 14.

In providing health services in the school it is apparent that success will be enhanced where close cooperation exists between the school, the home, and appropriate community agencies and individuals. As a result of this relationship, it is helpful to establish a School Health Committee, or Council, which will be concerned with study and coordination of school health services. Such a council or committee should have representatives of the administration (principal or assistant principal), the teaching staff and the school health office.

The school health council.   Each of the areas of the school health services requires that adequate and accurate information be made available to classroom teachers, parents, and health authorities. The School Health Council can become an important source of information and direction to classroom teachers. Although the organization of School Health Councils is an administrative matter, it is necessary that teachers be acquainted with the nature and value of such coordinating groups.

Appraisal of health status.   A number of persons are involved in the appraisal of the health status of children. The family physician, the school nurse, the dentist, the parent, and the teacher are at one time or another in favorable positions to observe casually, or examine expertly, the child's health condition.

Appraisals are obtained through the use of:

1. Medical diagnosis.
2. Screening for visual and auditory defects.
3. Height and weight records.
4. Dental examinations.
5. Psychological testing.
6. Immunization records.
7. Accident and sickness reports.
8. Careful observation by parents and teachers.

The teacher will be most directly concerned with the use of records and reports which inform her of the past and current health status of the child, and will become a careful observer of pupil appearance and behavior which may indicate attention from the school nurse or doctor. It is a rewarding situation when parents and teachers work together so that both parties are mutually aware of any health problems of the child.

Inasmuch as this chapter is concerned with the health program as it relates to teachers, it should be stated here that classroom teachers should not attempt to diagnose. Teachers are not prepared to be medical experts and it is not their responsibility to determine whether a child has mumps, measles, or a skin allergy. In every instance where the teacher suspects a condition that warrants the absence of the child from school or indicates the need for expert diagnosis, it is wise to refer the case to the school nurse or physician. In situations where there is no nurse or physician, the teacher may, with the counsel of the principal, advise the parents that the child *appears to have a skin condition or a throat condition* or whatever, and ask that they have the child checked by the family physician.

The position of the teacher as one who is in extensive daily contact with children places her next to the parents in terms of having opportunities for observing the health conditions of children. The Astoria plan[13] of school medical service places much stress upon the role of the teacher as a key observer and reference person. Such an approach places the teacher, rather than the physician or nurse who contacts the child only occasionally, in the center of the health observation plan. Experience with the Astoria plan has shown that teachers refer relatively small percentages of children who do not require medical attention, and that a far more effective observation program results when teachers recognize and fulfill their roles as key persons in this aspect of the school health service.

At the core of the appraisal aspect of the school health service is the need to provide pertinent data on the child's health, to bring about referral and possible correction of defects, to provide for classroom situations to fit the needs of handicapped children, and to offer information for use in the physical education program. All of this contributes to effective and happy living and learning in the classroom.

The role of the parent.   The parent is, in the final analysis, responsible for the health status of his child insofar as nutrition, immunization, dental care, physical checkups, and correction of remediable defects are concerned. Although this role of the parent has been widely recognized and accepted in America, many educators and health authorities maintain that adult education in the health area should be provided in order that parents will be more aware of their responsibilities and possess sufficient information to act properly in behalf of the child.

Unfortunately parent education programs of this type are not always available and the teacher is sometimes faced with the task of working with parents who apparently do not understand their responsibilities or do not choose to act. There are probably few teachers who have not worked with children forced to breathe through the mouth because of enlarged adenoids and tonsils. Another alarming problem which occurs too frequently is the neglect of the teeth, and it is not unusual to find large numbers of school-age children who have cavities or other dental

[13] Dorothy Nyswander, "Solving School Health Problems" (New York: The Commonwealth Fund, 1942).

problems that go unattended. Basically, the responsibility is that of the parent. However, the teacher who recognizes the threat to the child's present and future health, and who is aware of the effect of poor health upon school achievement, will counsel with the parent regarding referral to a physician or dentist. In schools where the services of a nurse are provided, the nurse and the teacher will pursue matters of pupil health in a joint effort to obtain parental cooperation and action.

The teacher's role. It has been mentioned earlier in this chapter that the teacher is in a very advantageous position in terms of observing the day-to-day health status of the child. In some schools the teacher is required to carry out a formal check each morning in which she observes the condition of the skin, throat, and general appearance. It seems that this should not be necessary except in times of epidemic or the like. Rather, the teacher may casually move about the room during the pre-opening minutes and after school convenes and note the appearances of the children. A flushed appearance, feverish eyes, rash, and other indications of illness may be thus observed.

The teacher is not expected to diagnose health problems and should feel free to refer the child to the school nurse or directly to the parents without determining the nature of the illness. In instances where the child must be sent home, the teacher will do well to contact the parents directly and advise them of the situation. However, school policy regarding such matters must be considered.

In cases of injury to pupils the teacher will obtain the assistance of the school nurse, if one is available, or provide emergency first aid herself. After this has been done the parent or other designated person should be notified and further arrangements made. The teacher is not expected to provide continuing treatment of wounds; in fact, the teacher must not do anything beyond emergency first aid in treating injuries and illnesses.

Providing a healthful school environment. The teacher cannot control all the health factors in the school environment; in fact, she may be unable to remedy some of the conditions in her own classroom. Such matters as water supply, ventilation, lighting, rest room facilities, and furniture fall within the realm of the teacher's concern and she is obligated to report conditions that are not conducive to child health. The teacher may do much to provide a well-ventilated classroom; she may secure the optimum use of available lighting; and she may be instrumental in bringing about more sanitary maintenance and use of school toilets, and the like.

Cooperation with the principal, superintendent, and other individuals is often necessary in bringing about improvements in lighting, drinking fountains, toilet conditions, and seating facilities. It is true that such concerns are direct responsibilities of the school administrators and the board of education, but the classroom teacher has a responsibility to children to lend her efforts in detecting, reporting, and planning for improvement of unfavorable health conditions, as well as helping to build favorable attitudes toward proper use and care of sanitary facilities.

Providing for mental health. There is one thing educators have been convinced of for many years: that the teacher will determine, more than any other single individual, the classroom climate in which the child will spend approximately six hours per day during the school year. In this respect the teacher may become a powerful force in assisting youngsters to develop habits and attitudes, or conversely, she may provide the elements which promote pupil frustration, emotional instability and socially harmful behavior.

The task of the teacher is almost overwhelming when one thinks of the individual and highly personal nature of mental health. All children do not react alike to the presence and supervision of the same teacher. Some youngsters may react favorably to certain types of pressures and urgings by the teacher; others may respond in undesirable manners. Some children can accept the responsibilities of classroom freedom; others need the security of considerable teacher direction until they feel sufficiently secure and capable of successful self-management.

Although the individual needs of pupils are different, the teacher realizes that the ultimate objectives are the same in terms of emotional balance, mental stability and personality development. This does not mean that all children must be cast alike, but that in terms of personal and social effectiveness there is a limit to the deviation which society accepts. So the teacher provides the leadership in establishing a classroom climate in which children may gain skills, information, practice in social living and confidence in themselves and others. The instructional role and the counselling role of the elementary teacher are inseparable and when wisely conceived they do much to advance the mental health status of the child.

Is There a Place for Sex Education?

Sex education as a part of the health education program is no longer as controversial as it was in the 1940's. The question is no longer: "Should sex education be included in the health education program?"; it has become one of location of emphasis and relation to other learnings. The Oregon film on Human Growth and Development and successful programs in Arlington, Virginia, and many other places, have had desirable effects upon the attitudes toward sex education. Although certain groups have taken issue with sex education in recent years, great strides have been made. Many of the Catholic schools now accept and have developed excellent courses of study in sex education.

Sex education is now being looked upon as a part of a larger learning experience which has to do with personal and social growth in relations with members of one's own sex as well as the opposite sex. Just as the care of the eyes or habits of cleanliness are not set apart as isolated areas of health education but included as integral parts of the learning experiences in health, so sex education has its proper place.

Many teachers and parents have come to recognize that sex education is far more than learning to define terms and processes. It involves, as well, knowledge of bodily functions and attitudes of social, personal and moral responsibility.

In the elementary school there is rich opportunity for the teacher to provide leadership in the development of desirable social relationships between boys and girls. Here, indeed, is a period when the teacher, through her contacts with parents, can offer guidance that will extend beyond the school. Through guidance of learning in science, health, social studies and literature, the teacher may bring to light the "facts of life" as well as an appreciation for the miracle that is life.

An important factor in working with children in the area of human reproduction and development is an approach by the teacher that is based upon factual acceptance of procreative processes and avoidance of an embarrassed or mystic treatment of children's questions.

As five- and six-year-olds play the roles of cowboys, policemen, or locomotive engineers, so will they play the roles of fathers and mothers. In this regard, it is quite natural that little girls play at taking care of babies; it is normal that they are inquisitive concerning the origin and procreation of life. In answer to children's questions it seems best that the teacher provide adequate and accurate information. It is usually not necessary that the teacher provide detailed and technical answers.

This question from a seven-year-old was directed to a teacher:

> "John told me that I was inside my mother's body before I was born, but I really wasn't, was I?" The teacher replied, "Yes, Bill, you were. That is the way that Mother Nature has of bringing little children into our world. You remember that we have taked about the little chickens that are kept safe inside the egg before they come into the world. Many animals are kept safely in this way until they are ready to live in the outside world."

Teachers, and persons who are planning to become teachers, must look upon the sexual impulse in the human being as a fundamental element in life and should understand that the richness, beauty and meaning of life are increased through the possession of the power for continuation of life. It is unfortunate that the moral values of so many persons have placed information and appreciation of the life-continuing processes at a relatively low position on the scale. Desirable attitudes toward life and toward vital family relationships are as important as the possession of facts, and it is believed that the method and emotional setting of sex learnings are crucial. It is necessary that teachers consider the following factors as they work with children in the area of human growth and development.[14]

1. Present factual information in a factual manner.
2. Avoid attaching shame or disgrace to the discussion or interest in questions relating to human reproduction.
3. Provide many opportunities for boys and girls to work and play together in purposeful and constructive activities.
4. Regard boy-girl interests as natural rather than as suspect or shady. Boys and girls regard their respective roles and relationships in the same light cast upon them by adults.
5. Always consider sex education as it fits into the larger area of human relationships and their part in building happy lives.
6. Provide information about the human body and regenerative processes to the child when he is sufficiently mature to request or show an interest in such information.

The nature of sex education emphasizes the cooperative roles of parents and teachers. To be successful, the learnings in this area are certainly made stronger when conditions exist in the home which exemplify wholesome family relationships. Although the school may be expected to proceed with the human growth and development aspect of education just as it does in other areas, it is helpful when teachers, parents, and other agencies plan together.[15] The schools in Columbia, South Carolina, have used a very extensive series of parent-teacher-child conferences as part of the sex education program.

Other programs which deal with sex education as an integral part of the total learning program may be found in San Diego, California; Denver, Colorado; Cincinnati, Ohio; and Sanford, Maine, to name but a few of the localities which have moved forward in this important area.

---

[14] See T. S. Douglas, "Just Give Your Child the Facts," *Today's Health*, 34 (August, 1956), 34-7; F. B. Strain and C. L. Eggert, "Framework for Family Life Education," *National Association of Secondary School Principals Bulletin*, No. 39 (December, 1955).

[15] Milton I. Levine, "A Sound Design for Sex Education," *The Education Digest*, 17 (May, 1952), 11-13.

In situations where parents have been involved in the planning and operation of sex education programs, the parents and teachers usually have several planning meetings in classroom groups or grade levels before the program is begun. In a few instances, children are included in the parent-teacher discussions and the undertaking becomes a well-rounded cooperative project.

The tendency in some school systems continues to place emphasis upon sex education at the junior and senior high levels. This may be justified only when sex education is conceived in a very narrow sense. A broader approach to the entire matter of human procreation and its role in human relationships must be recognized in the early elementary years. Children do not postpone their interests in the wonderful miracles of life until they are 15 or 16 years of age. School people and society can ill afford to avoid this important part of a child's education.

What Is the Leadership Role of the Teacher in Improving Health Instruction?

The teacher, next to the parent, may be more important than any other individual in guiding children in the development of habits and attitudes that will enhance their chances for healthful living. Healthful living, and health problems, cannot become a functional part of the child's learning experiences by way of a sporadic classroom approach, nor by way of a cut-and-dried curriculum that fails to take into account the opportunities for health education that are present in 25 youngsters.

Teacher leadership occurs when health education is brought out of the realm of books (where there are no health problems), and into the daily lives of people. The teacher conceives her leadership role in terms of:

1. Building desirable attitudes toward healthful living.
2. Providing accurate information on health matters.
3. Creating opportunities for children to participate in making the school and the classroom a healthful place in which to live.
4. Participating in the health services program so that children's health problems are not neglected but discovered and corrected.
5. Living with children in a healthful manner; making use of such opportunities as the school lunch program to develop desirable attitudes and habits.
6. Working with parents, nurses, and community health agencies toward safeguarding the health interests of children.

7. Organizing her personal life as a teacher to the end that good mental health is fostered as she works with youngsters.

PHYSICAL EDUCATION IN THE ELEMENTARY SCHOOL

It is not uncommon to hear the serious questions asked, "Why is it necessary to have physical education programs for children? Won't they get sufficient exercise through the incidental play of the home and playground?" To such questions one might reply: "Quite likely the children will get sufficient exercise at home, in the neighborhood, and on the playground, but there is more to physical education than exercise." Physical education has been defined by Halsey and Porter in these words:

> Physical education is the use of vigorous activity as planned developmental experience for all children and youth.[16]

In keeping with other widely accepted aims and objectives of elementary education, physical education is conceived as being of value to all children as it serves youngsters in the areas of self-realization, human relationships, economic efficiency, and civic responsibility.[17]

The physical welfare of the nation depends to a large extent upon the cooperative action of home and school. Through the carefully planned physical education program the school provides opportunities for all children to discover a variety of possibilities in bodily movement and to develop and refine many skills in accord with their levels of maturation and coordination.

What Are Some Objectives of a Good Physical Education Program?

Probably one of the most definitive statements of objectives of physical education is that offered by Knapp and Hagman:

1. To promote physical growth, development, and maintenance through activities that develop strength, vigor, vitality, skills, and coordinations leading to ability to do the day's work without undue fatigue and to have additional energy for out-of-work personal and social accomplishment.

---

[16] Elizabeth Halsey and Lorena Porter, *Physical Education for Children* (New York: Holt, Rinehart & Winston, Inc., 1958), p. 2.

[17] See *The Purposes of Education in American Democracy* (Washington, D.C.: National Education Association, Educational Policies Commission, 1938).

2. To contribute to the development of social competences in the areas of relationships with others, cooperation, competition, tolerance, ethical character, and recognition of the fundamental worth of each individual.

3. To promote emotional development through contributions toward individual adjustment, emotional self-mastery, adjustment to others, relaxation, satisfying self-expression, confidence, poise, and freedom from excessive self-confidence.

4. To provide healthful and integrating recreation for the present as well as to lay bases for wholesome, life-balancing recreation in the future.

5. To promote healthful living through contributions to health habits, attitudes, ideals, and information that lead toward elimination of unnecessary strains, drains, and illnesses, and that enable one to protect himself and others during periods of lowered vitality or illness.

6. To help each pupil to establish appropriate balances between work, play, exercise, rest, recreation, and relaxation in daily living.[18]

It is apparent, after studying the list of objectives of physical education, that the program involves more than exercise, that it holds a unifying and proper place in the school life of the child. One of the challenges to the physical well-being of people in this highly mechanized, automatic age is the dearth of physical activity required in the course of one's daily living. Added to this factor is the widespread use of television and the growing popularity of spectator sports which tend to even greater inactivity on the part of the nation's children. The fourth objective mentioned above takes on added significance as the teacher of physical education concerns herself with the attitudes, interests, and skills that will carry over into adult life.

An aspect of a good physical education program that is vital to the realization of the objectives is the participation of all individuals; certainly, the traditional concept of physical education as something for the physically gifted only cannot be a part of the teacher's thinking. The physical education program that is in the elementary school must serve every child in accord with his needs and capabilities.

What Is Included in a Modern Physical Education Program?

There are a number of excellent sources of information as to the numerous games, contests, and other activities which will be a part of

---

[18] Clyde Knapp and E. Patricia Hagman, *Teaching Methods for Physical Education* (New York: McGraw-Hill Book Co., Inc., 1953), pp. 69-70.

any well-planned physical education program.[19] An itemized list of these various activities is not included here; however, a suggested program will be provided in terms of the major types of activities that are included in the well-balanced program. These activities may be classified as to type of organization, such as:

1. Small group games
2. Circle games
3. Simple team games
4. Contests
5. Individual games
6. Mass play

Another approach to the classification of activities is in terms of the movement involved, such as:

1. Running-tagging games
2. Throwing-catching games
3. Kicking games
4. Striking games
5. Relays and races
6. Rhythm games

Still another approach to the classification of activities for the elementary school's physical education program is that of grouping together the skills which should be developed at the various levels of the child's school life. An idea of this approach may be obtained from Charts XIV and XV.

Whatever the approach to the physical education program may be it will require (1) competent leadership, (2) safe and adequate equipment, (3) space and facilities, and (4) orientation to the needs and capabilities of all children.

Competent leadership.   This will be provided in most schools by the classroom teachers, and in such situations physical education may well become an integral part of the social, emotional, and academic program.

In situations where the physical education specialist handles the instruction and direction of all playground and gymnasium activities there is the possibility that the various skills will be very well taught, that there will be an excellent variety of games and activities presented, and that

---

[19] Marjorie Latchaw, *A Pocket Guide of Games and Rhythms for the Elementary School* (Englewood Cliffs, N. J.: Prentice-Hall, Inc., 1956); Richard Kraus, *Play Activities for Boys and Girls* (New York: McGraw-Hill Book Co., Inc., 1957).

CHART XIV

Physical Skills to Be Developed by Younger Children[20]

A. Skills of Locomotion	B. Skills for Use in Games	C. Other Skills of Body Control
a. Walking	a. Stopping	a. Hanging
b. Running	b. Dodging	b. Lifting
c. Hopping	c. Tossing	c. Climbing
d. Skipping	d. Throwing	d. Carrying
e. Jumping	e. Catching	e. Pushing and pulling
f. Leaping	f. Kicking	
g. Sliding		
h. Galloping		

CHART XV

Physical Skills to be Developed in the Middle Grades[21]

A. Throwing
  a. Underhand pitch
  b. Two- or one-hand underarm pass
  c. Chest pass
B. Batting, as in baseball or softball
C. Hitting with paddles
D. Backhand swinging
E. Pivoting
F. Skills to be used in soccer, volleyball, basketball

necessary equipment will be accounted for and well maintained. The specialist will look upon his work with children as being as important as spelling and arithmetic, and physical education instruction will not be short-changed as may otherwise occur.

On the other hand, the classroom teacher is in a position to know her pupils better than any other person in the school. The possibilities for selecting classroom experiences for physical education are hers to see and to utilize. Citizenship and sportsmanship are concerns that carry over from playing field to classroom and the classroom teacher again is the one person who can effectively use the total program of the school to guide children. The desirable arrangement will have the classroom teacher working with her own pupils in the physical education program.

---

[20] This approach is presented by W. Van Hagen, G. Dexter, and J. F. Williams, *Physical Education in the Elementary School* (Sacramento, California: State Department of Education, 1951), pp. 314-23.
[21] *Ibid.*

Balance between group activities and individual participation is another aim of teacher guidance in physical education. Occasionally one may hear a teacher complain that "My pupils do not want to learn new games—they just like to play softball." It is the responsibility of the teacher to lead children into new physical activities, just as it is her responsibility to introduce them to a variety of reading materials. Teacher planning is necessary in this area in order that balance and scope of activities are assured. In this manner, physical education becomes a growing, developmental experience rather than a repetitive, static experience.

In certain larger school systems the physical education program may be handled entirely by a special teacher. There are advantages and disadvantages in such arrangements. It seems preferable to include the physical education of the child within the framework of the regular classroom program and depend upon the room teacher to make this an integral phase of the child's school life. *The contributions of the specialist must not be overlooked, however. The physical education program will be better coordinated, and achieve more balance and breadth where the specialist is available to assist with the planning of the program*, to assist teachers in any way possible, and to participate in the evaluation of the program.

Safe and adequate equipment.   In the selection of safe and functional equipment the physical education specialist may be of inestimable service. If such a person is not employed in the school system, the classroom teacher will be able to recommend a wiser selection if she seeks counsel of such a specialist.

Obviously, the selection of equipment will depend upon the use for which it is planned and the physical accommodations available. It is unnecessary to procure gymnasium mats if there is no access to the school gymnasium. A minimum list of equipment is itemized here, and the teacher who has sufficient funds available in her school budget will wish to make additional requests.

1. Climbing apparatus (Monkey climb, etc.)
2. Graduated horizontal bars
3. Basketball backstop and goal
4. Softball backstop and bases
5. Bats
6. Balls (Softballs, volleyballs, footballs, basketballs)
7. Phonograph and records
8. Whistles
9. Tricycles, wagons, wheel toys

10. Jump ropes
11. Bean bags
12. Catcher's mask
13. Nets for volleyball
14. Standards for volleyball (also may be used as standards for tether ball)
15. Indian clubs
16. Rubber balls and soccer balls
17. Shuttle cocks
18. Sand boxes

Equipment that presents unusual hazard, such as the maypole or giant stride, is better avoided. There is plenty of safe equipment which may be used to meet the needs of the children without using dangerous equipment.

Space and facilities. The provision of adequate space and facilities for the physical education program is a primary responsibility of the administration personnel of the school. The individual classroom teacher can do much by way of making the most efficient use of the space and facilities available. For example, in one relatively small asphalt area, lines for hop-scotch, shuffleboard, circle games, basketball, volleyball, and kickball were located. The teachers and a physical education specialist planned the area and worked out a schedule that would permit maximum use of the area.

A little-used storage room may become the location of the table tennis equipment, or a kindergarten sleeping room may accommodate quiet games when not being used by the younger children. The teacher with a degree of imagination and a healthy amount of cooperation can use the space of the school buildings and grounds to much greater advantage than is often realized. One school system, faced with a space problem, permitted two folding tables to be moved into the rear of the library to be used for table tennis during the noon hour. Obviously, the library was not used for free reading at this time.

How Is Physical Education Related to Other Learning Experiences?

Physical education will become a valuable part of the child's total school experience to the extent that the teacher is aware of the possibilities for relating the activities to other school learnings. Otherwise, physical education may remain in the program as an important but relatively isolated experience.

In terms of its relation to subject matter areas of the school program, physical education may contribute to the child's understanding of other people through an acquaintance with the games found in different parts of the world.[22] Physical education may relate very definitely to the citizenship and sportsmanship learnings of the social studies. Music and rhythmic activities are often so closely related to physical activity that music experiences and physical education activities may be planned together. In such instances the physical education specialist and the music supervisor can provide guidance and coordination in such related activities.

The teacher who attempts to relate physical education experiences to other school learnings should not feel obliged to search or strain for such related experiences. Cooperation, consideration for others, and fair play should be ingredients of all learning and living situations and certainly belong in physical education. However, it may not be feasible to relate every physical education activity to an activity in music, literature or history. The vital factor is the *awareness* of the teacher to such possibilities and her *willingness* to provide for related learning experiences.

An example of the relatedness of physical education to a geographical concept may be seen in Chart XVI.

CHART XVI

Physical Education and Social Studies Concepts

CONCEPT	GAME	COUNTRY
1. Children play the games which are possible in the environment. Such games may be related to living things within the child's experience.	The Fish Game	Denmark
2. Children play games that are derived from the mythology of their culture.	Catching the Dragon's Tail	China

How Should Play Days Be Used?

School "play days" may be used as an effective means for informing the parents of the nature of the total school program and providing a wholesome activity for children in which they develop the social skills of cooperation and planning. Of course, the continued development of the physical skills is an integral part of the play day.

---

[22] Nina Miller, *Children's Games from Many Lands* (New York: Friendship Press, 1943).

An opportune setting for the play day is in the springtime and out-of-doors. There are several very important considerations in planning the play day program:

1. Activities should be representative of the total school program.
2. All children should participate.
3. Pageantry and special costuming may detract from the purpose of the program.
4. Intra-school and inter-school competitions are not major objectives of the play day.
5. Pupils, parents, and teachers should cooperate whenever possible in planning and carrying out the play day program.

Friendly competition between individuals and teams reflects an American value and is, of course, present in the activities of the youngsters. The competition itself may add interest and challenge to a game or contest, but in the case of play day activities the emphasis may too easily fall upon competition rather than upon the presentation of many activities of the school program. Thus many youngsters cannot participate and the activity becomes of value only to the relatively few who are physically gifted.

The manner in which competitive activity is planned and directed is of great importance and may determine whether competitions will be friendly and constructive or hostile and damaging. One of the authors was involved for several years in a play day activity that was limited to carefully selected individuals and teams for competition between several schools of the city. The emphasis was upon victory over the rival schools and emotions became so involved that pupils, classroom teachers, and parents of each school became suspicious and envious of the members of the largest school which always emerged victorious. Instead of fostering attitudes conducive to city-wide cooperation the school play day was a divisive influence. Finally, the activity was reorganized so that competing softball teams were made up of members from the several schools, points were not scored, and school victories were not tabulated to produce a victor.

Whatever the role of avid competition at high levels of education, it is quite apparent that social, emotional, and personal development is served better at the elementary school level by friendly competition with emphasis upon the building of skills and attitudes rather than upon the emergence of a victorious individual or team. Teachers are in a position to render sound leadership as play days are planned in terms of acceptable and valuable goals of physical education.

What Is the Role of School Camping?

School camping, for a day or for more extended periods, provides opportunities for activities rich in a variety of learnings. Often, the camping experiences are included within the framework of physical education because of the recreational and craftwork features involved. However, the classroom teacher should be as concerned with the camping program as is the physical education specialist, for there are a host of science learnings and, certainly, many possibilities for social learning in such a program.[23]

Day camping programs where children plan the activities and carry out the duties about their camp may be developed in most communities, and the values involved merit the time given to the camping experience. Nature study, rock collecting, hiking, cooking, planning and working together are just a few of the ingredients of camping experiences.

Various communities have approached the camping programs in different manners due to location, population and the like. There are camping programs which have been carried out with a high degree of school-home planning,[24] and it appears that interest is increasing in this area of the schools' learning program.

Montgomery has reported on experiments in school camping which have been carried on in New Castle, Indiana.[25] In this instance the camping experience was included as a feature of the science program for sixth grade pupils and enlisted the cooperation of mothers who accompanied the children and teachers. Two plans of camping were tried; one was a day camping experience, the other was a two-day experience. Star study, hiking, fossil collecting, nature study, meal planning, and housekeeping were definite features of the educational camping program at New Castle.[26]

School camping has been organized in several ways. One of the more common types is a short period experience in which use is made of existing facilities owned by agencies other than the school.[27] Some schools

[23] William Van Til, "Schools and Camping," *Toward A New Curriculum* (Washington, D. C.: N.E.A. Association for Supervision and Curriculum Development, 1944).

[24] Edward G. Olson, *School and Community Programs* (New York: Prentice-Hall, Inc., 1949), Chapter 8.

[25] Herbert Montgomery, "Experiments in School Camping," *Instructor*, 59 (June, 1950), 25, 65.

[26] *Ibid.*

[27] Julian W. Smith, "Planning for School Community Camping," *Education*, 73 (September, 1952), 50-58. This entire issue is devoted to school camping.

own and operate their own camping facilities on a year-round basis, using full-time, trained personnel. Whatever the plan may be, it is vital from the educational viewpoint that teachers, children, and the community be concerned and active in the camping program. Because the camping program requires not only extra personnel but also space and facilities which are not always owned by the school district, it is imperative that the program be well understood and strongly supported by the greater school community.

The use of school camping programs with drop-outs and potential drop-outs has been tried in several Michigan communities, and the results of such work-learn approaches have been favorable in terms of individual readjustment.[28] There is no reason to limit the learnings of school camps to special groups of children, for there is sufficient reason to include camping for all youngsters. Aside from the immediate goals of camping which may be defined in terms of science, nature study, conservation, physical education and the like, it is the aesthetic aspect which helps the child mature in his appreciation of the world out-of-doors. It is expected that the school camper will be a better citizen and a better parent as a result of his contact with this inexpensive and richly rewarding experience.

As teachers, children, and parents plan for school camping, they shall want to remember that the plan should be designed to fit the age levels of children, to provide a definite educational experience, and to take into account the existing and potential facilities. There is no community where great possibilities for learning through camping do not exist. The classroom teacher and the school administrator are in positions to assist the community in putting such possibilities to work for children.

SAFETY EDUCATION IN THE ELEMENTARY SCHOOL

Another phase of the school program which falls within the scope of physical welfare is safety education. Safety education is not a thing to be taught as a subject nor to be related only to physical activities. Safety is a part of all the child's learnings throughout the day and it is a matter of actual life and death that children put safety learnings into practice.

---

[28] *Ibid.*

Some few persons may question the value of the teacher's concern for safety education in the elementary school. After all, the child from five to twelve years of age is not driving automobiles or working with power machines in a factory. Some persons may propose that instruction in safety learnings, first aid, or driving can wait until high school.

Why Is There a Need for Safety Education?

Safety education cannot and does not wait. The child receives his first safety lessons at home as he watches his parents work and live, and he patterns his first habits likewise. The child who has no "respect" for a knife or a pointed object cannot be permitted to wait until high school to gain information for building attitudes and developing habits of safe living.

Although child deaths resulting from accidents have declined during the past few years, accidents are still the major cause of death of children of elementary school age.[29] Traffic mishaps account for the large majority of accidental deaths of children. This fact has serious implications for teachers, parents and others who are concerned with the safe conduct of children to and from school.

Additional injuries result from falls, burns, sharp instruments, thrown objects and the like. Such accidents may occur on the playground, in the halls and stairways of the school and in the classrooms. Wherever there are people moving about in work or play, there are accident possibilities. The teacher cannot expect to prevent *all* injuries, but she must do her utmost to provide and maintain a school environment as free as possible from health and safety hazards. Part of her job will be that of helping boys and girls learn the correct and safe ways of playing and working.

What Are Some Ways of Teaching Safety?

Probably the most common way of teaching safety is by classroom discussion. In this manner information may be provided to the children. Posters, safety films, dramatizations and visiting speakers help emphasize the necessity for safe living.

A very effective approach to safety education is that of involving children in the program. The principal may wish to inspect the school grounds and buildings regularly for safety hazards, but children also

---

[29] *Accident Facts* (Chicago: National Safety Council, 1953), p. 16.

should be given responsibility for checking, reporting and discussing such problems. In other words, the use of actual situations is preferable to a non-participating type of safety program. To show films about pedestrian safety is a worthy means of instruction, but it is just as effective to take the youngsters on a walk in the area of the school to practice the preferred ways of crossing intersections, observing traffic signals and the like.

Safety patrol.   The use of pupil safety patrols has become widespread and it seems that they may be of value in promoting safety practices by children. The authors have observed some situations which call for careful planning and wise direction of the safety patrol. For example, the safety patrol members who are placed in positions of nominal authority over other children may come to be looked upon as unfriendly supervisors who spy for the teachers and principal. In such situations the large number of children may learn undesirable attitudes toward safety enforcement, and actually try to jaywalk or run on the stairs without getting caught by the patrol.

Of course, the children who are engaged in safety patrol must not be placed in positions of hazard or delegated responsibilities which properly belong to adults. The aim of a good safety education program should be to help each child become his own safety patrolman, because in the final analysis there cannot be supervision of every street crossing.

Outcomes of safety education.   A well-planned, effectively presented program of safety experiences will serve in the following manner:

1. To help children become aware and observant of hazardous situations.
2. To develop proper attitudes toward safety regulations and the officers who help people live safely.
3. To provide experiences in safe living wherever possible throughout the school day.
4. To teach the proper and safe use of the tools, machines and the like, with which the child comes in contact.
5. To provide examples of safe living through the teacher's activities in and out of school.

SUMMARY

One of the most crucial aspects of a child's learning experiences is that which has to do with the development of attitudes toward his own physical well-being so that he will be personally responsible for his health and concerned with the conditions of his larger social community. In conjunction with the development of desirable attitudes is the growth of health habits and the acquisition of the information necessary to insure that health attitudes and habits are wisely selected.

The classroom teacher encounters a great challenge in the area of health education for several reasons. First, the welfare of the individual as well as the entire nation is closely linked to the health and vigor of the citizenry. Second, the imparting of information from textbooks does not in and of itself provide an effective means for developing desirable attitudes and habits for healthful living. Community and home conditions are powerful forces in this respect, as in others, and the program of the school must involve these agencies for a strong program. Third, health education may be tested by its daily impact upon the children; it must be functional and practical.

Programs of physical education for elementary school children are provided to foster the vigor and wholesome bodily development of all children. It does not have as an objective the production of a highly specialized performer in only one or two sports. A variety of developmental activities are incorporated in the sound physical education program. Friendly competition, team cooperation, respect for regulations and fair play are important concerns. Opportunities for relating physical activities with learning experiences in music and social studies are found in the well-planned program. The classroom teacher has a part in the physical education program whether it be in the role of director of the activities or as a partner with the physical education specialist. This must be so if the child's school day learnings are to be mutually supplementary and reinforcing.

Sex education is a part of the total health program and the child is presented information when it is a proper concern. Sex education is not a separate program; it is part of the child's living and learning. It is the means to an enriching outlook on the life giving processes, and it should place this important aspect of human relations in a decent role rather than delegate it to the mystery and the shame of tradition.

Safety education is another part of the physical welfare of the child for which the school must accept its share of responsibility. This share is dependent upon the needs and conditions with which the child lives. Traffic safety, care in the use of tools and machines, proper use of playthings and sound judgment in adapting bodily movements to the surroundings are ingredients of the safety program. As in the health program, the child must see himself as the vital participant in safe living, and must be taught the attitudes and habits for safe living. Such are the challenges in the health, safety and physical education program. There can be no doubt as to their importance in the lives of our children.

SUGGESTED ACTIVITIES AND PROBLEMS

1. Enlist the assistance of a student committee and ask that they visit a school where a safety patrol is being used. Observe the behavior of children and patrol members. Present a report to the class.

2. Obtain samples of the health records used in two or three school systems. Analyze them in terms of the helpful information about the child's health status which they provide for teacher use.

3. In the community in which you live, contact an elementary school teacher and ask in what ways she works with the school nurse and community health agencies.

4. Make a list of learning experiences in the science, physical education and social studies areas which could be incorporated into a day camping activity.

5. Examine several different series of health texts to determine how the reading material might be related to the day-to-day health of children. This activity may be carried out by several student committees.

6. Evaluate the physical education program provided in an elementary school in your community in terms of the variety of activities included and the manner of teaching for cooperation and sportsmanship.

7. Develop a guide that could be used by classroom teachers in the observation phase of the school's health services. What are the most common illnesses of young children and how can the teacher detect symptoms without extensive diagnosis? This might become a committee project.

8. The class members may wish to discuss the extent to which the school should attempt to encourage correction of physical defects of children. Keep in mind that some parents may object to being asked by the teacher to have their child examined by a physician for any reason.

9. Prepare a practical plan of safety education for elementary school children. Take care to include activities that involve the safety problems that children actually encounter in their school, in their community and in their homes. What outcomes do you hope will result?

10. What would you expect to be the major problems involved if you were to include sex education in your instructional program? Discuss with other class members the nature and purposes of sex education in the elementary school.

11. Miss Jayne, the fifth grade teacher, believes that Robert needs to work on division more than he needs physical education, so she has informed him that he must stay in the room during the regular physical education period and work arithmetic. If Miss Jayne were a co-worker of yours and

had asked you what you thought of her practice, how would you respond? What justification can you offer for including physical education in every child's program?

12. For several days you have observed children jay-walking near the school when the safety patrol boy was looking the other way. On other occasions you have observed older pupils openly defying the safety patrol to report them for unsafe practices. The topic for discussion at the next staff meeting concerns the role and organization of the school safety patrol. What comments will you plan to offer?

13. Jack has come to your classroom today with a nasty looking cut on his arm. The injury was received at home, but is not bandaged and appears unclean. How would you handle this problem, assuming the school nurse is not present?

SELECTED READINGS

Browne, Evelyn. "An Ethological Theory of Play," *Journal of Health, Physical Education and Recreation*, Vol. 39, No. 7 (September, 1968), pp. 36-39.

Frederick, A. Bruce. "Tension Control in the Physical Education Classroom," *Journal of Health, Physical Education and Recreation*, 38, No. 7 (September, 1967), pp. 42-44, 78-80; special issue *Priorities for Progress.*

Morse, William C., Craig Finger and George El Gilmore. "Innovation in School Mental Health Programs," *Review of Educational Research*, 38, No. 5 (December, 1968), pp. 460-477.

Mosston, Muska. *Teaching Physical Education; From Command to Discovery.* Columbus, Ohio: Charles E. Merrill Publishing Co., 1966.

Rekstad, Mary E., James Miller and H. Edwin Lanehart. "Promising Practices in Elementary School Physical Education," *Journal of Health, Physical Education and Recreation*, 40, No. 1 (January, 1969), 36-41.

"Sex Education," *Grade Teacher*, LXXXVI (November, 1968), 60-65, 122, 128-130, 134-137 (teaching program for the sixth grade on pp. 123-127).

Stewart, Colston R., Jr. and Mary Catherine Ware. "New Methods for the New Health Education," *National Elementary Principal*, XLVIII, No. 2 (November, 1968), 40–46.

Hermiston, Ray T., Andrew J. Kozar and Henry J. Montype. "Computers at the Service of the Physical Education Teacher," *Journal of Health, Physical Education and Recreation*, 39, No. 7 (September, 1968), 30-32.

Granell, Vincent. "Schools and the Nonsmoking Society," *Journal of Health, Physical Education and Recreation*, 39, No. 7 (September, 1968), 55-56.

Tyrance, Herman J. "Cooperative Evaluation: A Method of Teaching Activities," *Journal of Health, Physical Education and Recreation*, 40, No. 3 (March, 1969), 32-35.

CHAPTER 13

A Curriculum Design for
Exceptional Children

INTRODUCTION

Every school and community faces the educational problem of providing for the child who cannot profit from ordinary instruction without provision for special education services. Unquestionably, all children require stimulating and self-motivating experiences in order to develop their full potentials; good teaching is not to be reserved only for those individuals who demand careful planning and superior techniques, such as are required for children who do not respond without specialized help. However, since it is desirable that teachers work with all types of children in the classroom, it is important that some understandings, attitudes, and techniques be acquired in order that the education of the exceptional child will be directed in the most profitable manner. The inexperienced teacher usually possesses some anxieties in working with any types of children who deviate from the norm, although the in-service instructor may have some misgivings concerning the efficacy of the instructional program in connection with the exceptional child.

The field of special education is receiving considerable attention in the public schools and institutions of higher learning. Thus the practical approach must be made to assist the regular classroom teacher who is not a specialist in the sense of being prepared to work effectively with all types of exceptional children. Yet teachers must be competent in designing a part of the school program for those who are unable to obtain an effective education without the specialized help which is not generally considered essential or is not a part of the general educational program.

Probably the clearest definition of the term "exceptional children" is described in these words:

> . . . those who deviate from what is supposed to be average in physical, mental, emotional, or social characteristics to such an extent that they

require special educational services in order to develop to their maximum capacity.[1]

Since these special services will include some modifications of curriculum, instructional methods, materials and equipment, and so on, the elementary school is usually not prepared to meet the needs of these exceptional children. However, many of the borderline cases will be found in the regular classroom and require particular teacher help or even some of the specialist's time. Therefore, it is believed that it is not necessary here to describe the incidence of exceptionality in children, but rather to concentrate on those individuals teachers are most likely to encounter in their regular classes. Thus it is evident that the teacher must be able to work with exceptional children in the regular classroom. For example, there is the task of helping the talented youth to be self-directed; the love for learning is an issue for bright children particularly; every one must acquire skills, knowledge and sound attitudes; the opportunities for expression will differ but must be present. All of these considerations, and many others, demand good teaching, proper methods and materials, and a curriculum design that will insure the meeting of these differences.

In order to clarify and give additional meaning to what is meant by the expression "exceptional child," the following outline is offered to suggest some major categories for approaching the problems. It should be emphasized at this point that this discussion will center only upon the types of exceptional child that may be found in the regular classroom. The technical aspects and terminology of those cases not generally admitted to the elementary school class must be omitted here in favor of concentrating upon the exceptional child who poses a problem for the elementary teacher and who is a member of a regular class.[2] There are at least three main categories to be used in describing this child: First, he may be considered *mentally exceptional*. The retarded child may range from a very low intelligence rating to the dull or below average. Since children with I.Q.'s of less than around 60 are generally not included in the rosters of the schools, emphasis will be given to the slow learner and particularly to the dull, borderline cases. The above-average or gifted child is considered to have an I.Q. of 130 or more. There are differences of opinion as to a cut-off point on the score, but it is believed that an I.Q. of 130 should be most generally accepted as indicative of above average mentality. Finally, there are children who have special abilities or par-

---

[1] The Forty-ninth Yearbook of the National Society for the Study of Education, *Learning and Instruction*, Part I (Chicago: University of Chicago Press, 1950), p. 3.

[2] H. A. Delp, "How Many Exceptional Children in Your School?" *School Executive*, 75 (November, 1955), 52-3.

ticular disabilities. That is, the average child, with an I.Q. of 100 or so, may possess an outstanding ability in music, which earns him the label of being an exceptional child in at least one respect. By the same token a particular mental disability may exist in conjunction with a general over-all normalcy. This circumstance creates still another problem. For example, the so-called average child may possess below-average ability in numerical reasoning. Second, the *physically* handicapped child may be described in three ways: he has sensory defects that are auditory or visual (or both); he has motor defects which are classified as orthopedically crippling, or of a low vitality nature, or he has a miscellaneous classification. Physical speech defects occur also in some 10 to 20 percent of the child population. Third, the *maladjusted* child is viewed as one who needs assistance. He may be in one or more of the other categories as well, or he may simply have a social adjustment problem. Perhaps his difficulty may be of an emotional nature. In summary, special education is concerned with the total program for all children and particularly with those who have marked differences in the areas of: hearing, vision, speech, mental ability, orthopedic handicaps, cerebral disorders, neurological impairments, social and emotional disturbances, delinquency, and giftedness. The teacher has the problem of getting many of these children into the normal stream of society, since it may be evident that they are too different, and if left to chance, may fail in making the necessary adjustment.

Having described the exceptional child in terms of three categories and cited the incidence of such problem children within the regular classroom, it is evident that the teacher must satisfy the needs of these pupils, even as ordinary, routine instruction is carried out for the total class. The major purposes of this chapter are planned to assist the regular classroom instructor by (1) presenting a philosophy for the teacher in considering the needs of the exceptional child; (2) viewing the special education needs of the child; (3) offering a guide to the teacher in identifying the exceptional child; (4) suggesting a curriculum design for the exceptional child; (5) stating ways of working more effectively with exceptional children in the regular classroom. At this point, however, an over-all plan for working with the exceptional child is offered to orient the teacher and to furnish an educational perspective that should be useful in approaching the specific objectives of this chapter, as outlined in the five purposes above. The details of this over-view are presented in the remaining discussion.

As a result of a study made in cooperation with 16 primary teachers, Noel[3] furnishes this orientation-perspective as the first steps the in-

---

[3] E. G. Noel, "A New Look at Slow Learners," *Instructor*, 67 (December, 1957), 6 ff.

structor needs to take in conjunction with providing for the exceptional child's educational welfare:

Step one: Identify and describe his behavior in detail. There are techniques and devices to be used in collecting data that are used in describing his behavior. Since this process must be thorough and complete, outside assistance is often useful in aiding the teacher.

Step two: Understand the crucial characteristics in the behavior pattern. A mere description of behavior is not enough, since understanding of what is observed and described must follow. Again, clarification of such characteristics of a behavior pattern may be made by a specialist.

Step three: Find the cluster of characteristics that seem to have the greatest bearing on the pupil's behavior. This kind of narrowing process by discovering a cluster of characteristics helps the teacher to see more accurately the causes of behavior.

Step four: Develop a hypothesis about a plan of action that could make a difference in the child's behavior. There is no assurance that the first hypothesis is right; but in light of what is known about the child, the teacher should venture some such opinion.

Step five: Plan and carry out procedures to correct behavior difficulties as well as to improve learning. This is probably as perplexing a step as any, since correcting behavior difficulties may seem impossible. However, there are ways and means of meeting most situations if the teacher is able and prepared to discover and utilize them.

In many instances the teacher may believe that it is unnecessary to use these five steps in considering the exceptional child within the regular classroom. As an example, the hard of hearing child has a real, definite, and understandable condition. Therefore, it may seem to be simply a matter of observing sensible procedures in communicating with this child. Actually, the teacher who omits the five-step approach may fail to understand other behavior problems that are not discernible. To say it differently, an analysis of this particular child may uncover behavior patterns that are certainly rooted in, or stem from an auditory condition and which present a challenge to the teacher in helping the child to make better and more effective educational, social, and personal adjustment. The thesis is that the exceptional child has the same needs as any other individual, who also needs to be understood; but it is imperative that an analysis be made because of the very nature of the deviations that exist within the child, or the environment that poses such a threat to him that he behaves differently. An actual case study is offered to illustrate the five-step analysis and to point out how a child may profit from teacher-concentrated aid and effort.[4]

David was in the intermediate grades and had a record of consistent aggressiveness, both with his classmates and teachers. He especially did not accept the idea of authority, but, incongruously, he was extremely shy in some ways. (Step one)—His teachers reported that in class he had a poor attention span. His study habits left much to be desired in that he apparently knew little about how to go about performing certain tasks. In most instances he simply gave up too easily, although he had enough ability to do the work. (Step two)—His daily pattern was to assume an aggressive and even defensive attitude toward everyone. He was particularly anxious for his share of attention and apparently believed that domineering and picking on children were in order, and continued in his refusal to accept authority but still wanted to achieve, particularly in reading. He wanted friends and friendships but he had few. The conflict in shyness persisted, while his domineering attitude suggested the pressures he was subjected to by his parents. (Step three)—His present teacher believed that he needed first of all to secure confidence in himself. He needed a challenging role to play. (Step four)—Several things were done in his particular case: he was led to help himself in setting up controls for himself; the group was led to accept him; he was placed in a higher reading group; he was furnished opportunities to talk before the group about those things he had experienced; he used his interests in collecting as a focal point in certain projects; his parents were brought into the picture more completely; he saw a need to help the class. David was on the way to becoming a better student and an improved person.

This illustration affords a glimpse of a child who was classified as exceptional in the sense that he was not profiting from the regular learning situation. All children need individual attention, of course, but there are those who must be viewed as requiring a considerable amount of assistance because of some difficulty if they are to advance and progress as they should. Not all problems can be solved, but all children can be helped to some degree when teachers understand why the child is exceptional, what he should be taught, and how he should be taught.

THE SPECIAL EDUCATION NEEDS OF ELEMENTARY SCHOOL CHILDREN

Educators are concerned with the challenge of how to identify the special educational needs of children. Moving from this phase of interest,

---

[4] Noel, *op. cit.*, p. 80.

teachers are desirous of developing the abilities and inherent aptitudes of all children, particularly those who are classified as exceptional, but are still enrolled within the typical elementary grade-level class. Many parents are concerned but are unable to do much because of lack of information or know-how. Therefore it is imperative, in view of the high incidence of children who need special help, that teachers and parents discover a philosophy that will guide their planning and actions. In addition, there is a need to be cognizant of the characteristics of certain types of exceptional children, the kinds of adjustments they make, and in general, to be aware of a great deal about the child and his individual problem.

What Is a Philosophy for the Teacher in Considering the Needs of the Exceptional Child?

It would be a relatively simple matter to present an idealistic philosophy of the exceptional child that would reflect a stimulating and challenging thesis for consideration. A more realistic account may be that of viewing the teacher who may not have the full financial and moral support of the community on many policies and practices. Again, there may be certain administrative and environmental conditions that hamper the teacher who has a clear perspective of the educational task involving the exceptional child. However, the teacher needs to have a well-defined philosophy of these childen to support her thinking, planning, and action. In the event no such philosophy is present, or is ill-conceived, the following theses are offered that may form the philosophical core of thinking of the elementary school teacher who will be working with one or more exceptional children in her classroom.

Thesis number one: Believe that all children must have equality of opportunity. This does not mean that all children can and will learn in the same way or degree, but educational opportunities must lead to a discovery of self and to a maximal realization of self.

Thesis number two: Believe that every citizen has an obligation to give some assistance in providing for the exceptional child.

Thesis number three: Believe that parents can and should cooperate with the school and other agencies more effectively. The role of the parent is often clarified and strengthened when teachers assume the lead in working more closely with them.

Thesis number four: Believe that the role of research is to be promoted more vigorously. There is much research present, but there is also a great lack of specific research evidence that is urgently needed. This alertness to principles and issues can serve as a springboard for improved classroom practices.

Thesis number five: Believe that teachers can prepare themselves more positively for dealing with the exceptional child. Forward strides have been made in teacher preparation and in-service work, but a positive attitude along these lines will contribute much to improved ways of teaching.

Thesis number six: Believe that the exceptional child should be and can be accepted and integrated into society. The attitude of the American people toward the education of these childen must be that of an informed person who knows the situation and is confident and willing to raise standards and concepts.

Thesis number seven: Believe that the contributions of all agencies of society can be employed in providing better services. The many community resources should be tapped to further the advancement of the child.

Thesis number eight: Believe that each exceptional child has the right to live the best, fullest life that is possible. These children should achieve according to ability, because educational opportunities are planned in light of such abilities. Each individual should make his contribution to society, small or great as the case may be; but the quality and welfare of living are more enhanced because their education has been more complete.

Thesis number nine: Believe that planning must be done in terms of specific purposes for the child in reaching his goals and accomplishments. The exceptional child generally does not attain his goals by chance; deliberate provisions in the classroom must be made to insure such realizations, as the child studies and lives within the environment of the regular classroom.

Thesis number ten: Believe that there is a continuity in his growth. The exceptional child does not differ from his classmates in the respect that he grows and develops according to inner patterns.

Thesis number eleven: Believe that his accomplishments are usually suitable in terms of over-all ability and the experiences he will have in life as he grows older.

Thesis number twelve: Believe that one can learn to know and recognize the exceptional child. This knowledge and early identification lead to understandings of normalcy and the seeking of contributions from all fields of learning and development in working with the exceptional child, with the administration, and the community. Evaluative sessions must certainly be made periodically to assay progress and other factors.

A philosophy expressed in terms of twelve theses should support the teacher in approaching the special education of children. It is significant to state that a philosophy which causes the teacher to be more effective in the classroom will not be time wasted. Parker[5] and Ingram[6] both report evidence to support the theme that the exceptional child does profit *from special help*, and makes a better adjustment to society. Denhoff and Holden[7] believe strongly that the key to good school adjustment for any exceptional child is found in family acceptance and understanding. Thus a combination of many factors and influences must be considered by the teacher; it is believed that the philosophical framework above can assist the teacher in moving forward to the consideration of further problems of grouping, the curriculum, and ways of working with the child.

For the purposes of this chapter it should be clear that the borderline exceptional children will be in the regular classrooms and are described here. However, there are different degrees of exceptionality within the same type. For example, in the area of the visual defects there are differing degrees, with each requiring a certain kind of education. Thus, the blind child cannot be educated in the regular grades, since his method of learning is through a modification of educational practices and not simply a difference in degree of instruction. The teacher must then recognize the kind of child in the regular classroom who has some degree of exceptionality and provide proper materials and instructions to meet the need within the framework of the curriculum.

How May the Teacher View the Gifted Child?

Although research[8] shows that there are no less than 51 different terms used to describe the gifted child, it is necessary that the teacher identify and stimulate the superior student. To assume that simply because giftedness is present the child will achieve and adjust is erroneous. There is considerable evidence[9] that these above-average children acquire desirable outcomes as a result of particular enrichment programs.[10] Significantly, the bright pupils, not the brightest, are usually classified as the best students. The special education needs of this group suggest that

---

[5] C. Parker, "Measured Experiment with Mentally Advanced Children," *American School Board Journal*, 133 (December, 1956), 23-4.

[6] C. P. Ingram, *Education of the Slow Learning Child* (New York: Ronald Press Co., 1953), p. 53.

[7] E. Denhoff and R. H. Holden, "Family Influences on Successful School Adjustment of Cerebral Palsied Children," *Journal of Exceptional Children*, 21 (October, 1954), 5-7.

[8] T. E. Newland, "Essential Research Directions on the Gifted," *Journal of Exceptional Children*, 21 (May, 1955), 293.

[9] A. H. Passow, "Planning for Talented Youth: A Research Project," *Journal of Educational Leadership*, 13 (January, 1956), 249-51.

[10] For some of the kinds of programs in existence see Jack Kough, *Practical Programs for the Gifted* (Chicago: Science Research Associates, 1960).

deliberate planning must be made to insure optimum results, and the brightest children may require even more stimulation and motivation.

The need to develop within the superior student effective motivation which will produce a drive toward high intellectual achievement may be facilitated by sound curriculum planning. It has been found through research by Hobbs that children with potential as high achievers may be low achievers due to low intensity of purpose. It was found that these children were associated with homes where the intensity of purpose was also low. At the same time, gifted youngsters who were associated with homes where there was a high intensity of purpose were high achievers.[11] It would appear that if we are to help each gifted youngster to reach his potential, then the teacher through all the resources available—human and material—must work toward helping these children to identify them-selves with a functional purpose with high intensity. Such a purpose will aid the child to see how his long-range goals may be achieved through first acquiring the skills essential to that end.

The elementary school plays a vital role in shaping the future of the gifted child, according to research reports presented by Gowan.[12] He believes that there is sufficient evidence to indicate that achievement in the high school, and even later life, stems from habits, interests, attitudes, and motivations established in the elementary school years. Furthermore, with these children the latter factors seem to be enhanced or facilitated by the presence of special curriculum provisions. In another sense, "wherever under-achievement is higher than 15 per cent, look for prob-lems in morale, anti-social trends . . . which means the curriculum."[13] Gaugh[14] insists that in his study of underachievers among the gifted, such behavior is indicative of delinquency. He even compares the two forms of behavior and believes the underachiever who is talented is de-linquent. Either form of social behavior is not in keeping with good stan-dards of conduct and is considered detrimental to the best interests of society. Thus the importance of good teaching in the elementary school is pointed out for the teacher in viewing the gifted child.

The characteristics of the gifted. There are many and varied ways of listing or describing the characteristics of the gifted child. The usual approach is to examine the score made on an intelligence test. Some authorities believe that an I.Q. of 140 or above marks the gifted child,

---

[11] *Ibid.*, p. 45.

[12] J. C. Gowan, "Dynamics of the Underachievement of Gifted Students," *Journal of Exceptional Children*, 24 (November, 1957), 98-101.

[13] J. C. Gowan, "The Underachieving Gifted Child: A Problem for Everyone," *op. cit.*, p. 248.

[14] H. G. Gaugh, "Factors Related to Differential Achievement Among Gifted Persons," mimeographed (Berkley, Cal.: University of California, 1955).

although others believe that an I.Q. of 130, or even 120, should identify the above-average person. The following terms or descriptions are made to give some insights as to the characteristics of the gifted child. It is to be noted that there are variations in every child, as each possesses characteristics in different degrees:

—usually a high academic status that is substantiated by results of standardized tests
—high verbal comprehension; superior vocabulary
—personality ratings are superior or above average
—stability in school attendance and punctuality
—physical and emotional maturity and stability are marked
—social maturity is generally advanced and good
—the ability for objective self analysis is present
—a high production rate is evidenced with a corresponding quality in the productions
—the mind is active, inquiring, curious, and alert, original, imaginative
—powers of observation are keen, coupled with an ability to make critical analysis
—creativity is evident in many, varied ways
—a longer attention span, deeper insights, and powers of discrimination mean abilities to generalize and come to conclusions
—adjustment to change is more readily, easily made
—the ability to persevere and accept responsibility is present
—a sense of humor is noticeable
—reading is a pleasure and occupies 2 to 3 hours average a day in history, folk tales, biographies, science, poetry and drama

The gifted child may not possess all of these characteristics, and may be failing to use his talents for various reasons. Another way of regarding the gifted child is to note how he achieves. Gowan finds[15] common elements from research reports to indicate that achievement versus underachievement in gifted students seems related to the following factors:

—clearness and definiteness of academic and occupational choices versus the opposite
—strong ego controls and strengths versus weak ones
—socialization and social inter-action versus withdrawal and self sufficiency

---

[15] J. C. Gowan, "Dynamics of the Underachievement of Gifted Students," *op. cit.*, p. 100.

—good use of time and money versus lack of such acceptable habits

—reading and arithmetic competencies versus lack of those abilities

—positive character integration versus psychotic or neurotic tendencies

—permissiveness, intraception, and creativity versus authoritarianism in the home, parental environment, or within the gifted himself

—parents who motivated and were interested versus the dominant, autocratic, or *laissez-faire* parent

—some tension in task demands from early childhood, the imposition by parents of goals which were clear and possible to attain versus either no goals or the impossible ones

—maturity, responsibility, and seriousness of interests versus opposites

—awareness of and a concern for others versus disinterest

—dominance, persuasiveness and self-confidence versus the opposites

—enthusiastic, socialized, activity oriented view of life versus apathetic withdrawal

It is clear by comparing the two lists of characteristics of the gifted child that he can be identified and described by the teacher. The primary child may not have clearly defined academic and occupational goals, nor strong ego controls, but he is well on the way in many respects toward developing during each year he spends in the school, providing he receives special help in some instances. It is safe to conclude that the gifted child begins early to develop these characteristics and attains them in a more positive way than those who are not as gifted. As a gifted person, he is consistently doing well whatever he sets out to achieve and is a persistent, drive-impelled individual who performs in outstanding ways, or is at least capable of doing so.

How Does the Teacher View the Slow Learner in the Regular Classroom?

Teachers will have both the mentally retarded and the dull or borderline cases within the classroom. The former have an intelligence quotient from 50 to 75, although the slow learners, comprising some 15 to 20 percent of the school population, have an I.Q. range from 75 to 90. In both instances these children do not meet regular grade standards, but the slow learners can succeed with some adaptations, particularly within a planned curriculum. The emphasis will be confined to describing the slow learners, with some implications for the mentally retarded child, since the slow learner is capable of more adequate adjustments than the mentally retarded. The child may be a slow learner because of low intelligence, maturity factors, physical development and conditions of health, social maturity, or personal makeup. It should be made clear that the child with low intelligence falls into different categories for descriptive purposes. The mental defective who is usually hospitalized and the trainable retarded child who has an I.Q. of 30 to 50 are not discussed here, since these children are placed in special environments.

The teacher should recognize that there are again varieties of slow learners within a given school or community. Doll lists[16] some principles which assist in understanding this type of pupil: (1) Learning parallels growth. When the slow learner exhibits tendencies to learn with difficulty at an early age, there is no assurance that growth in itself will mean a greater power or ability to learn. (2) Environmental factors play a role in learning. Some children are classified early as slow learners because of inadequate or poor out-of-school experiences, and having average or above-average ability the child may overcome this handicap. (3) Social experiences influence learning. Again, a paucity of social experiences may hinder the child in adjusting to the school environment and earn for him the label of the slow learner. (4) Usually all children desire to learn. The slow learner has a desire for new experiences and is ready for classroom experiences if they are designed and conducted to meet his special needs.

The following list of characteristics describes the slow learner and the mentally retarded. It should be noted that the differences are in degree and not in kind, *viz.*, the slow learners or dull borderline cases have more ability than the mentally retarded, but they are still lacking in abilities in comparison to the average child or highly talented individual. Also, those children who are slow learners for reasons other than lack of mental ability may not always be described in these terms. The slow learner is an exceptional child when he:

—is below average in physical development, generally speaking; he may have more minor defects, poorer muscular coordination, flexibility, and adaptability; he may often have defective touch, sight, and hearing; he may have learned to walk later and developed muscular abilities more slowly
—cannot think abstractly or work well with symbols; has poor reasoning and visualization powers, has weak retention and association powers; has short attention span; is incapable of concentration; and lacks intelligence to go ahead on his own
—is poor in the ability to generalize and apply; has poor judgment

---

[16] E. A. Doll, "Varieties of Slow Learners," *Journal of Exceptional Children*, 20 (November, 1953), 61-4.

—lacks aggressiveness
—has the tendency to be emotionally unstable, impatient, depressed, inattentive, or apathetic
—needs more praise than usual
—has the tendency toward social misbehavior problems—dislikes school
—has an over-all slowness in doing things
—in immature in many ways, especially in expressing himself
—does things without understanding the what and the why behind the action
—learns the simpler things and becomes baffled with new situations, lacks out-of-school experiences

It is significant to note that the slow learner has the same feelings as other children. In many instances he may have strong drives to achieve and succeed, and when frustrations become too overwhelming, he may lapse into a do-nothing condition. It is important that the teacher identify carefully the slow learner and know whether or not learning is difficult because of limited mental ability or for other reasons.

How Does the Teacher View the Physically Handicapped Child?

The children with physical problems constitute serious difficulties for the teacher, since the condition is usually beyond the professional scope and knowledge of the instructor. The definitely handicapped or incapacitated child will not be a member of the regular classroom; but there are those children with impaired vision, hearing, speech, and other defects that make up the bulk of the group who must be considered. Physical examination requirements should furnish sufficient data, but in many instances the teacher may have to discover what physical handicaps may be interfering with learning, social, and physical development. For example, teachers will recognize that the deaf child has no language to communicate with his peers who have normal hearing and must be placed in a special class with a highly trained teacher. The hard-of-hearing child can receive some help in the form of hearing aids, advantageous placement in the class, and consultary advice from state divisions of service for crippled children. In addition, the totally blind child is to be placed in a special class, while the partially blind child can remain in the regular class if he can be helped by such items as large type books, seating arrangements, consultary help, and so on. Further discussions concerning the orthopedically handicapped child and the speech defective child will be given in a later section concerned with the physically handicapped individuals.

Although the elementary teacher may be in a position to do very little in correcting the physical handicap of a child, there are at least three approaches that should guide the thinking of the instructor. First, the child should be made to feel as secure as possible within the room. By the very nature of his disability he recognizes certain limitations and restrictions placed upon him. Anxieties over his future and the kind and quality of his participation or non-participation may be kept to a minimum, as the teacher helps the child to feel secure in a classroom environment of teacher-acceptance. Guidance toward developing some measure of skill and ability in a chosen area will lead to a degree of success by the child. Second, the child will need to receive aid in gaining acceptance by his group. Soldwedel and Terrill studied[17] 32 children (10 physically handicapped and 22 not handicapped) and found that a trend was definitely apparent for the physically handicapped to receive choices from non-handicapped children as playmates. The handicapped were still fairly well received in the classroom in general, but it is conceivable that the teacher could plan and initiate particular procedures to foster greater acceptance by the other children for these handicapped pupils. Third, the teacher needs to work very closely with parents of the handicapped child. Evidence is available[18] to indicate that parents have a need to be educated to the fact that the child is actually more normal than he is handicapped. It should be obvious that as the teacher works to develop self-confidence, independence, and initiative for the handicapped, a strong relationship with the home may be necessary in order to consolidate the gains that are made in the classroom.

What Approaches Are Used in Considering the Maladjusted Child?

The maladjusted child is defined here in terms of one who has difficulty in relating the group, or has some emotional, social, or personal problem that interferes with his total adjustment. Again, the teacher must proceed cautiously in classifying these exceptional children, particularly from the professional point of view when preparation and experience are lacking in this specialized area.

Two different studies[19] agree there is a great number of problem children in need of adjustment found within the regular elementary

---

[17] B. Soldwedel and I. Terrill, "Sociometric Aspects of Physically Handicapped and Non-Handicapped Children in the Same Elementary School," *Exceptional Children*, 23 (May, 1957), 371-72 ff.

[18] *Ibid.*

[19] See Carl R. Rogers, "Mental Health Findings in Three Elementary Schools," *Educational Research Bulletin*, 21 (1942), 69-78; Ohio Commission on Children and Youth, "Children Who are Socially and Emotionally Maladjusted in School," Columbus, Ohio: Ohio Department of Education, 1951.

school class. A figure of 12 percent seems to represent the portion of the total elementary school enrollment that could profit from special help in this area. Rogers seems convinced that even the better schools show a higher incidence of the more seriously maladjusted pupils. Thus, the average elementary school class may be expected to contain one or more handicapped children.

Since there are various forms of methods of expression that characterize the maladjusted child, it may be more convenient to describe in general terms the symptoms of this child. Any excess display of the following may be symptomatic: nervousness, crying, day-dreaming, fighting, withdrawing, truancy or staying at home for no obvious reason. Within the class structure this child has little or no social relations and finds it hard to relate to the group. Perhaps his internal conflicts motivate him to play the role of the bully, to be shy and withdrawing, or in some way to act out his frustrations and conflicts. Generally there is a decline in creativity, production, or individual initiative, since he may be too pre-occupied in marshalling his energies to cope with his own personal threatening world. Many times the maladjusted child feels socially inadequate and may avoid making any normal contacts. Again, his fear of failure or of a subject matter area gives rise to other symptoms and responses. The many anxieties and fears assume different proportions and forms of expression that are difficult at times to identify and interpret. In such instances the teacher should seek professional assistance for pronounced cases.

There is one problem that is receiving increasing attention in the schools: over-conformity to the group. McCall believes[20] that the teacher must combat this tendency of the child to conform too strictly to the standards of the group. Such over-conformity is considered to be a socially handicapping factor for some children, because it stifles creativity, originality, and individuality, and creates fears and anxieties about not being accepted or losing the approval of the group.

A GUIDE TO THE TEACHER IN IDENTIFYING THE EXCEPTIONAL CHILD

The problems of the exceptional child have been discussed in terms of what special education is, the incidence of the exceptional child in the schools, some problems facing the teacher, how the instructor may accept a philosophy to guide thinking, and finally the approaches that may be

---

[20] J. R. McCall, "Socially Handicapped Children," *Education*, 76 (October, 1955), 88-90.

considered in viewing the various types of children within the regular classroom. Stress has been made upon the fact that the exceptional child can and will profit generally when special help is given. Although the varieties and characteristics of the exceptional child have been listed, many teachers do not feel competent nor prepared to identify such pupils within the classroom. To be realistic, the busy teacher may not have the time nor the resources to understand child problems, to develop the skill in diagnosis, or use insight therapeutically in pupil behavior. This section is designed to provide a framework of reference or guide for the classroom teacher in knowing more about the exceptional child, since Curry,[21] Anderson and Davis,[22] and other research studies support the statement that the teacher is usually not proficient in or capable of identifying the exceptional child.

Whatever the reason for abnormal types of behavior, the teacher should feel a concern "to study pupils and their problems and seek to promote effective learning by correcting disabilities and by providing the curricular and instructional adjustments necessary to insure mastery and success."[23] Since it may be impossible or too time consuming to give sufficient study and attention to the individual child, two approaches are offered now that should aid the teacher to be more aware of problems, to discover underlying causes, and to suggest ways of assisting the child.

What Is a Suggested Approach?

The teacher should make a detailed study of the child as time, energy, and resources will permit. In the suggested study plan that follows it will be noted that much of the data may already be on hand or can be readily secured. In many instances the teacher may find little or nothing in the files to complete the analysis and may have to proceed with little or no assistance in securing information about the child. In one sense the teacher is simply making a case study of an exceptional child, or of one who is believed to be developing toward that classification. Whatever name is given to this procedure, it is important that the teacher recognize that the troubled child is one who has a problem. Through the study of the child, conflicts, frustrations, and disabilities may be discovered and lead to a realization that the "no-problem child" is in reality an excep-

---

[21] E. T. Curry, "Are Teachers Good Judges of Their Pupil's Hearing," *Journal of Exceptional Children*, 21 (October, 1954), 15-17.

[22] W. F. Anderson and L. R. Davis, "Guiding the Gifted," *School Executive*, 76 (February, 1957), 82-3.

[23] T. L. Torgerson, *Studying Children* (New York: Holt, Rinehart & Winston, Inc., 1947), p. 26.

tional child who needs special help either now or will in the immediate future. A seven point study guide is furnished to help the teacher:[24]

1. *State the problem.* Usually the child is being studied because of observed behavior, inferior work habits of production, or for some reason that suggests he may have a problem which generally can be stated in rather definite terms.

2. *Collect educational and psychological data.* From the many educational, psychological, and maturity tests, a decision is made to select and use those instruments that should give a more complete perspective of the child. In fact, a battery of tests may be employed.

3. *Summarize school history and progress.* If the child is in the first grade, little information may be available, except material that is current. The cumulative records, conferences with other teachers, or even correspondence with previous instructors may supply a great deal of data.

4. *Compile medical information and physical condition data.* Some children have very little medical or dental information to offer in that there may have been parental neglect in these areas. The physical condition of the child may be surveyed by the teacher or school nurse, although such practices should be done continuously but with reservations.

5. *Describe personality traits and social maturity.* Many problems of laziness, inattentiveness, and so on may be symptomatic of underlying behavior problems. In a program of child study the teacher should learn to recognize that symptoms are not the same as causes.

6. *Outside-of-school information.* Again, cumulative records may supplement the study by describing family and home environment, but such information may have to be secured by the teacher. In addition, if the developmental history of the child is available a clearer perspective may be obtained.

7. *Suggested solutions and recommendations.* At this point the teacher may find it profitable to summarize the data to see if any patterns stand out and to consider some suggested plans of action or corrective procedures.

The teacher should use each of the seven items as a study plan and write brief comments concerning each child, if practicable. For many

---

[24] Note the similarity in this 7-point plan to the orientation perspective beginning on page 421. The difference may be only a matter of detail or approach.

students, the data will be easily secured, or it may be unnecessary to go into detail. Even for pupils who are already classified as exceptional, such an analysis can lead to even deeper insights concerning their situation or problems. Using the child's condition in connection or combination with other factors as a basis, the best means of adjustment for the particular child may be more easily planned. A case study[25] of an actual pupil situation illustrates how a child, viewed from the psychological approach, was found upon an examination to need a different kind of educational program, but not a special class placement.

> Tom was ten years old and attended the third grade.
> Problem: Referred because of age and inferior quality of work, especially in reading.
> School progress: Attended same school for six years. Spent two years in the first grade, one and one-half years in the second grade, and was on trial promotion to the third grade.
> Social and personality traits: Obedient, trustworthy and cooperative. Lacked leadership as he reflected timidity, inhibited, passive characteristics; able to do only first grade or beginning reading and was behind in other subjects.
> Psychological data: Binet showed an M.A. of 9 years and 6 months, an I.Q. of 96; number test score at grade level of 3.0; reading level 1.5 grade level; spelling even lower. During test situation he was at ease until reading was mentioned, then he exhibited grave concern, anxiety, nausea, and even cried, desiring to leave the room.
> Summary and recommendations: Not a candidate for special class. A study of reading difficulties and home situations was made with remedial reading plan suggested and mother to cooperate with teacher in developing self-confidence and feelings of success in the child.

What Are Some Further Aids to the Teacher in Identifying the Exceptional Child?

The second approach to aid the teacher in becoming more aware of the problems of children and to identify them as exceptional children is offered within the following framework:[26]

> —have a genuine interest in each child; the teacher must certainly be concerned with the exceptional child who can be identified, as well as with those whose problems may not actually classify them as being exceptional
> —use the local physicians to assist in making identification and diagnosis; these professional persons are generally cooperative

---

[25] Ingram, *op. cit.*, pp. 106-07.
[26] D. A. Worcester, "Clinical Services Making the Best of Resources in the Rural Community," *Journal of Exceptional Children*, 20 (January, 1954), 176-79.

with school personnel in working with the exceptional child and can provide useful information and recommendations

—use the local and state departments of health, clinics, and the welfare offices; these departments are organized to render many services to the teacher in connection with special education needs

—call upon any private agencies within the locality; there may be consulting psychologists, clinics, and other agencies which are privately owned and operated available for assistance

—ask the larger school systems for aid; most large systems are glad to share and cooperate in the use of their professional staffs in a limited way

—be prepared to transport the child if at all necessary; it may be apparent that if help is available some distance away from the school, some arrangements should be possible to take the child to that service

These generalized ways by which the teacher may improve upon the identification and diagnosis of certain problems require time and funds. However, when at all possible, the exploitation of these sources will add to the knowledge and understandings needed by the teacher, especially when some exceptional children present difficult, baffling situations.[27]

CURRICULUM DESIGNS FOR EXCEPTIONAL CHILDREN

The crucial issue at this point is that of a curriculum design for the child in the classroom. Unless the elementary school teacher brings a change into curricular practices in connection with meeting the needs of the individual child there is probably little reason for making intensive study analyses of children or deciding upon elaborate educational programs to guide development and learning. It is strongly believed that only as the curriculum is designed to meet every child's need can optimum educational progress be planned and carried out. Therefore, the following questions constitute the specific purposes of this section: (1) Should there be different educational objectives for the exceptional child? (2) What is a curricular framework for the gifted? (3) for the slow learner? (4) for the physically handicapped? (5) for the maladjusted? The discussion will center upon the exceptional child who is a member of the regular class in the elementary school.

---

[27] See Torgerson, *op. cit.*, for detailed guides and forms used in collecting specialized data about the child, especially Chapter 2, "How to Identify Problem Behavior by Observation."

Are Educational Objectives Different for the Exceptional Child?

Some teachers are confused as to the objectives the school should set up for the exceptional child. In general, these objectives[28] are to further the development of the individual's total capacities and to further his personal development in every possible way. Then if the school considers the child's life in its entirety, the educational objectives must be the same for *all* children.

The objectives of the exceptional child will differ from those of all children only to the extent they are narrowed to prepare the child to make a specific adjustment, or they are expanded to meet the specific needs of a more gifted child. In short, the handicapped child may not make as many or varied adjustments as the above-average child. The handicapped is unable to live at as high a level as the more normal, and the superior child goes more deeply and widely in achieving his objectives. However, the exceptional child should achieve educational objectives that are possible for him, and he should be led to make his contribution and enjoy living according to his ability. The specific objectives for the exceptional child are essentially the same as for all children, although the scope and the degree of attainment must differ according to the individual. This is also true for those children who are not classified as exceptional, It should be added that certain conditions found within the child will dictate a kind of curricular design that may seem unique and different, but essentially it should be the same curriculum as used for any child. It is not to be assumed that there are no special education requirements for the exceptional child and that teachers need only to give more of the same kind of instruction or stress the usual things to the child who needs special help. Certainly, a modification of educational practices is required for each kind of exceptional child. In summary, an over-all curriculum design is needed for all children, with specific curriculum patterns emerging to meet definite conditions and needs of the individual child. These specific curriculum patterns are now considered separately for the types of exceptional children who may be found within the regular classroom.

What Is a Curriculum Framework for the Gifted?

It will be noted that the following suggested curriculum implications for the above average child are not unusual or different from those for most children in the classroom. That is, all students should have some-

---

[28] See Chapter 1 for a complete discussion of educational objectives.

what the same experiences and acquire study skills, develop self understandings, and so on *according to ability.*

The curriculum implications for the superior child are presented according to content areas, with suggested activities under each for both the primary and the intermediate-upper elementary grades. In no case is each area complete in terms of activities; these suggestions are offered as illustrations and as stimulants to further creative, imaginative thinking by teachers and pupils.

Since Birch has worked with and directed curriculum programs for the gifted, a report of his curriculum organization and activities is used as a basis for this discussion.[29]

A CURRICULUM DESIGN FOR THE GIFTED AT THE PRIMARY LEVEL

Reading:
 —assist in setting up a lending library from the home to supplement regular library usage
 —encourage brief reports to the class on more difficult but interesting reading materials
 —compile bibliographies concerning special topics, class or individual projects, interests, current local events
 —prepare original stories from local environment, readings, pictures, music, art, and the like

Arithmetic:
 —use class pets as a project in budgeting and spending activities
 —keep class records of each child's weight, height in chart form
 —measure the amount of rainfall and snowfall
 —estimate distances between home and school, home and city hall, school and playground, and so on

Science:
 —investigate procedures and operations locally for control of insects and pests
 —collect rocks, minerals, plants, and so on
 —take trips to specific areas that have science implications
 —study and consider certain conservation plans and practices

---

[29] J. W. Birch, "Exceptional Children in Your Regular Classroom," *Grade Teacher*, 75 (March, 1958), 34-5 ff.

Social Studies:
- —organize and direct class parties
- —develop sensible rules for school safety
- —plan and conduct a "fair"
- —prepare certain reports concerning local areas of recreational interest and the like

INTERMEDIATE AND UPPER ELEMENTARY LEVELS

Language Arts:
- —create or select pictures to illustrate poetry which can serve as a basis for oral or written work
- —use students as chairmen for discussion groups
- —prepare glossaries
- —compile a brief history of handwriting, dialects, etc.
- —analyze the library
- —locate literary figures and authorities
- —discuss certain author's ideas, values, and the like
- —use outlining, graphs, footnotes, cataloguing, files and so on
- —read aloud, use panels, tell original stories, have choral and poetry reading

Arithmetic:
- —report on currencies used in other lands
- —analyze the uses of the school building according to areas
- —report on common measurements used with respect to food
- —budget certain school activities, *viz.*, the school newspaper

Crafts and Related Art Activities:
- —prepare a plan for re-decorating a room, building, or a home
- —create interpretative pictures of art and music
- —organize and put on an exhibit.
- —catalogue the various art objects located within the community

Music:
- —write lyrics and compose music
- —produce recorded programs
- —serve as school music librarian
- —direct orchestras and rhythm bands
- —participate in vocal-instrumental groups

Dramatics:
   —write play productions
   —produce and direct skits, plays
   —give dramatic readings

Social Studies:
   —acquire deeper appreciations of people through various sources
   —discuss how people have had to adjust to difficult situations and relate them to one's own situation

It is clear that numerous activities could be listed under each area that would challenge the gifted child. It has already been suggested that the above average child must learn to do things well; he does not simply acquire persistency, understandings, and the like only because he has talent. If he is to avoid superficialities and acquire outstanding skills, together with other aspects, he must first be motivated to work towards those goals that are commensurate with his high capacity.

What Constitutes a Curriculum for the Slow Learner?

The slow learner is considered here to be that child who is experiencing difficulty within the learning situation in connection with mental ability. Those children who are classified as slow learners for other reasons may still profit from some of the curricular experiences which will be suggested in this section. Although it is believed that the over-all curriculum must be the same for all children, the teacher must set up specific attainments for the slow learner just as must be done for other children. The chronological age, mental ability, and physical and social development of each child must be carefully reviewed, since their present learning ability, rate of growth, and even their social and personal interest help to give direction to planning. In addition, information about the environment, total needs of the child, and abilities in the skill subjects contribute to the teacher's knowledge to give further guidance to that curricular design most appropriate for the child. These suggestions for the teacher are not unique in the sense of being used only in connection with the slow learner, but they are particularly emphasized here.

The slow learner who is the dull or borderline case may need special attention in the regular class in terms of these three categories, although these are applicable to every child.

First, under the *personal* category many slow learners can make progress in developing good health habits, acquiring skills in taking care of personal needs, and developing abilities in the areas of safety, use of leisure time, and so on. Second, the *social* category means that he can acquire skills in the social graces and other behaviors involving him with people. Third, the *vocational* category emphasizes his attaining at least the simple skills which help him to live more effectively at home and in society.

It is commonly agreed and known that the slow learner begins to find learning difficult at least by the fourth grade. He may also discover that his social and personal adjustment is becoming more complicated for various reasons and is beginning to present a definite problem to the teacher and to himself in many ways. This fact does not mean that the teacher delays curriculum planning until the fourth grade, but in order to insure steady and continuous growth should make some early plans. Perhaps Ingram[30] has as complete a listing of specific attainments as is needed to gain a curriculum perspective for mentally retarded children and for the slow learner. These lists are even described in light of chronological ages for children with low mental ability. Again, the curriculum is organized under health, language arts, social studies, and science, with illustrative activities in sequential order. A detailed listing is not necessary here, since an examination of the curriculum chapters in this book alone suggests a plan that can meet the needs of these slow learners, *provided appropriate adjustments are made to fulfill their specific requirements.* Again, it should be stated that the slow learner arrives at concepts and attitudes very slowly. Often his growth comes only after many and repeated experiences. For example, the curriculum design of the normal fifth grade child with a chronological age of 11 years, may be an adequate curriculum plan for some slow learners with chronological ages of 12 or more. It should be obvious that a curriculum design for the slow learner that is approached in the manner of Ingram's organization makes sense to the child who will be able to see more associations, develop clearer understandings, and so on. That is, he is not faced with a graded curriculum, but he has an opportunity to obtain those experiences for which he is ready, interested, and capable of enjoying regardless of grade level. In summary, the slow learner has the same educational objectives as other children, but regardless of the grade level in which he is placed, specific objectives are set up that may insure attainment, pupil growth, and suitability of achievement. As a third grade class member for instance, the slow learner may be profitably presented with a curriculum design that is suited for the first grade. Educationally, the slow learner works within this plan, but in other ways he is a full participating member of his third grade group. Such a curriculum design is reasonable and intelligent, in that it will be of the most value to the child.

---

[30] Ingram, *op. cit.*, Chapter 8.

What Is a Curriculum Plan for the Physically Handicapped Child?

There are little differences, if any, required in the curriculum design for the physically handicapped. Consistent with the thesis that all children have identical educational objectives, these exceptional children may pursue the regular program in much the same way, provided no other contributing factors, such as low mental ability, are present.

Probably the most important problems to be considered in planning curriculum experiences for the physically handicapped are those of acceptance by the group, motivation, and their feelings of adjustment to situations. The teacher may find the following principles helpful in working out curriculum patterns for some physically handicapped children. These principles are based upon a study made by Mussen and Newman[31] who agree that: (1) Experiences in the class, in the home, and the community should be talked about freely with implications concerning the disability, and lead toward a realistic attitude about it. (2) Teacher goals and child selected ones should be attainable. (3) Classroom accomplishments should not be emphasized as the key factor, since they are not the major considerations in receiving acceptance. Strong achievement drives may be present, but they are not to be considered necessary in themselves for teacher-class acceptance. (4) Curricular experiences should foster independence of thought and action. By recognizing and rewarding the child for acquiring such independence, a greater fund of personal adequacy feelings is being created, leading to better adjustment. (5) Although personal and social adjustment should lead to a wider range of friendships and ability to relate to people, the curriculum design should recognize that the exceptional child may need a smaller, more select, and closer circle of friendships, rather than extensive, social, personal contacts.

Does the Maladjusted Child Need a Special Curriculum Design?

The exceptional child who has emotional problems requires educational objectives similar to those planned for other children. His perspective, aims, motivations, and feelings may be distorted and cause him to do poorly when confronted with the usual curriculum plans; but, according to Rosenberger,[32] there are at least five aspects which can be

---

[31] P. H. Mussen and D. K. Newman, "Acceptance of Handicap, Motivation, and Adjustment in Physically Disabled Children," *Journal of Exceptional Children*, 24 (February, 1958), 255-60 ff.

[32] H. T. Rosenberger, "Special Curriculum for the Brillant Student," *National Association of Secondary-School Principals Bulletin*, 40 (February, 1956), 11-338.

emphasized in curriculum designing that are particularly useful for the emotionally unstable. *First*, this exceptional child may profit from varied curricular experiences in health, hygiene, and physical education. In some cases, the stress on sportsmanship, and rivalry is an excellent approach in working with this child. *Second*, the curriculum planning should include those experiences that center on real life situations and problems that can be solved. Feelings of inner security and confidence are bolstered through group discussion. In addition to being afforded the therapeutic effects of the group, the child is led to see himself involved personally in the solving of actual situations. *Third*, the curriculum design must emphasize group attack on learning. That is, the exceptional child probably needs to be removed from isolation, to make more decisions, and to regain self confidence as a member of a group. *Fourth*, a concentration upon safety instruction is believed to be a curricular approach that is needed by the maladjusted child to a large degree. This is not to say that he is not able to handle himself effectively in this area, but apparently the development of safety consciousness is simply another avenue to more satisfied inner feelings of assurance and confidence. There is a strengthening of group loyalty ties as well, when this consciousness is easily recognized and considered important. *Fifth*, the curriculum activities must lead to observable results. As the child experiences success and sees that something favorable has happened, his personal feelings of achievement are enhanced. He is not in competition with anyone, nor is he hurried in any way. His frustrations are kept to a minimum, and it is hoped that, as an accepted member of the group, he knows that in his own right he has achieved something. It is clear then that the maladjusted child may require the feelings of group membership, but the teacher needs to remember that as a person in his own right he must also have successes.

WORKING MORE EFFECTIVELY WITH EXCEPTIONAL CHILDREN IN THE REGULAR CLASSROOM

There have been many implications for the teacher as to ways of working with exceptional children in the regular classroom from the discussion about their characteristics and curriculum designs for them. In fact, classroom techniques must emerge from out of the knowledge and understandings teachers possess in connection with the child, and from a curriculum design that is considered appropriate for them to fulfill their individual needs. It is probably unwise to separate these issues into compartmental categories, but a discussion at this point of the several aspects is needed to answer the following questions: (1) Should the exceptional child be a member of the regular classroom? (2) Does the teacher use different, unique teaching methods in working with the exceptional child? (3) What should be a mental health approach in working with this kind of child? (4) How does the teacher work with the above average child? (5) With the slow learner? (6) With the physically handicapped? (7) With the maladjusted? Each of these questions is now discussed.

How Does the Teacher View the Exceptional Child in the Regular Classroom?

The administrative and organizational aspects of providing differentiated programs for exceptional children need not be examined here. The realistic fact is that teachers do have many children enrolled within their classes who need special help. In order to further their thinking and develop additional insights in terms of this question, it is believed that the teacher should have some answer to the above question, since the borderline exceptional child will probably be enrolled within the regular classroom.

The professional literature is filled with accounts of experiments, programs, and plans, but one of the older studies is selected as a basis for the ensuing discussion. The study by Gray and Hollingworth[33] gave evidence that grouping is not the final answer; there was no significant difference in achievement between the gifted in segregated and the gifted in the non-segregated classes. The answer seems to be in the provision of enrichment opportunities. On the other hand, Terman reports[34] that the gifted accelerants are found to be doing better in their school work and total adjustment than those who had not been accelerated. Gallagher and Crowder support[35] the same thinking in a study over a two-year period with 35 children in a representative city of less than 100,000. It was found that only 29 percent of the group could be said to be making an excellent adjustment within the regular classroom. Although very few were really in any kind of difficulty, the motivation was poor, there was evidence of intellectual rigidity and sterility, and a waste of intel-

---

[33] H. A. Gray and L. S. Hollingworth, "The Achievement of Gifted Children Enrolled and Not Enrolled in Special Opportunity Classes," *Journal of Educational Research*, 24 (November, 1931), 261.

[34] L. M. Terman, "Earmarking the Talented," *Science News Letter* (April, 1954), p. 214.

[35] J. J. Gallagher and T. Crowder, "The Adjustment of Gifted Children in the Regular Classroom," 23, *Journal of Exceptional Children* (April, 1957), 306-12.

lectual power. It was significant to note that those children who come
from the schools with less gifted children were the more difficult motivational problems in contrast with those who were used to associating with
many other bright children. This fact suggests that the presence of other
above-average classmates is more stimulating and challenging. Force,[36]
Johnson and Kirk,[37] Miller,[38] and many others give evidence that the
regular classroom membership by the exceptional child is fraught with
difficulties and problems. Hunt[39] believes that educators are not in agreement as to the best ways of administratively grouping pupils for instruction, since there is lack of agreement in the areas of philosophy, seman-
tics, and even research. However, since it has already been stated that
the teacher must work with these children in spite of disagreements in
such areas, it is believed that Hunt has clarified the issue for the teacher
who works with the exceptional child in the regular classroom. The following principles are offered to guide the thinking of the teacher:[40]

1. The issue should really be how a child can best be guided and
helped to achieve his potential. The plan of instruction is the means
to the realization of this goal.

2. There should be no "either-or" controversy about special
classes, acceleration, or enrichment. It is conceivable that a special
class may provide for either enrichment or acceleration or both.

3. In the final analysis the needs of the individual child and the
available resources should decide the question of how he is to be
placed, whether he is to be in a regular class or some other organizational plan.

4. The mentally handicapped and the gifted need at least some
form of enrichment.

5. The handicapped children should not be members of the
regular class.

6. Integration into the regular classroom obligates the teacher to
provide suitable curricular experiences.

Thus the keeping of the exceptional child within the regular classroom is both defended and attacked according to different researchers.

---

[36] D. G. Force, Jr., "Social Status of Physically Handicapped Children," *Journal of Exceptional Children*, 19 (December, 1956), 304-08.

[37] G. O. Johnson and S. A. Kirk, "Are Mentally Handicapped Children Segregated in the Regular Grades," *Journal of Exceptional Children*, 17 (December,
1950), 65-8.

[38] R. V. Miller, "Social Status and Sociometric Differences," *Journal of Exceptional Children*, 23 (December, 1956), 114-19.

[39] J. T. Hunt, "Special Education: Segregation," *Education*, 77 (April, 1957), 1.

[40] *Ibid.*, pp. 1-5.

For all practical and realistic purposes the elementary school teacher must face the situation as it actually exists: to provide the best program in order that the individual will profit most in light of his special problems and needs. An education for the exceptional child can, in most instances, be provided in the regular classroom, even with a minimum of special aid from other professionally trained personnel.[41] However, Kirk[42] believes more research is needed on this problem.

Does the Teacher Use Different, Unique Teaching Methods in Working with Exceptional Children?

Although succeeding discussions will emphasize ways of working with the various types of exceptional children it is believed that a general approach to the problem deserves brief attention. The authors accept the philosophy that teachers should use some different approaches in working with the exceptional child; but, in general, the same teaching methods for all children within the regular class should be employed. This is illustrated in Figure XIX. Of course the requirements of exceptional children demand revisions and changes in teaching methods from time to time, but basically the same method is to be employed with only variations for individual needs. Perhaps the exceptional child may need more drill, if he is a slow learner, but even the gifted child requires a minimum of drill. However, there are some methods to be utilized by the instructor that have definite implications for all children, but are especially important in the case of the exceptional child:

—adopt a proper attitude toward the child; show him you are interested by noting his absences, his interests, and by being friendly at all times
—arrange matters to insure more successes than failures; the child needs fewer frustrations and may lack a great deal of self-confidence
—be careful not to stimulate feelings of guilt and anxiety
—consider his mental health outlook as paramount and arrange learning situation especially to insure security
—assist him in his social relationships, even through curricular experiences

The list of suggestions could easily be extended, but it should be apparent that the teacher uses no particularly unique techniques with

---

[41] T. E. Newland, "Helping the Exceptional Child in the Regular Classroom," *Understanding the Child*, 25 (June, 1956), 66-75.
[42] Forty-ninth yearbook, *op. cit.*, p. 323.

FIGURE XIX

Teaching the Exceptional Child in Regular Classes

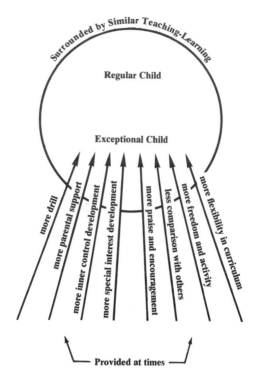

the special cases but the same ones that are used profitably with other members of the class. Though the difference is in the extent or the degree of need of the child, each pupil, regardless of his status, should be afforded opportunities to allay fears, guilt, anxieties, and so on. It should be made perfectly clear that there are unique methods of educating the exceptional child. Part of the methods used with normal children are the same, but special, additional methods may also be required. In effect, then, the general methods used with all children may still mean that special instructional techniques are used over and above those used with regular children, as illustrated in Figure XX. Thus, consultant aid, special equipment and facilities, and special educational practices are all designed to promote the welfare of the exceptional child, particularly when he is a member of a regular classroom under the direction of a teacher who is not a specialist in the area of working with exceptional children.

FIGURE XX

Working with Exceptional Children in the Regular Classroom

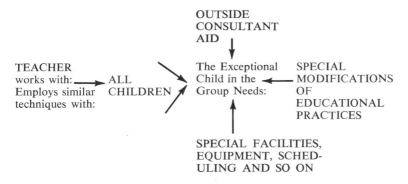

What Are the Mental Health Needs of the Exceptional Child?

The foregoing discussion implies that the mental health problems of children, especially the exceptional, are to be considered as important by the teacher. It is also obvious that a single section here can only suggest ways of working with this kind of child and further supplement the above items. Dobbs furnishes[43] perhaps the clearest frame of reference for the teacher in gaining a mental health point of view in working with exceptional children.

First, the child needs firm support by the parents, especially the mother. It is difficult to educate some parents to this fact, but often the teacher can lead the way towards improved home-child relations. *Second,* there is usually a need for the development of inner controls. The child must, of course, express himself in many ways, but he must learn self-control as well. *Third,* the development and pursuit of special interests do much to strengthen the child or insure a healthier outlook on life. *Fourth,* the lavish use of praise and encouragement increases his feelings of worthiness and stimulates a wider range of activities and attention away from the inner self. In effect, the feeling of usefulness is furthered by having interests outside of one's self, as it were. *Fifth,* comparisons with other children are scrupulously avoided, as they could lead to greater feelings of insecurity or unworthiness. *Sixth,* a mental health approach that considers a curriculum design allowing for activity and freedom in the class is beneficial, since many tensions are reduced

---

[43] M. C. Dobbs, "Mental Hygiene in the Special Class," *Instructor,* 66 (May, 1957), 49 ff.

through the activity channel. *Seventh,* the variations in activities and tempo are also conducive to better mental health in the classroom. *Eighth,* flexibility in the curriculum may insure more attention to individual needs and give rise to personal satisfactions. *Ninth,* the mental health viewpoint considers that the child needs to feel he is important and is able to make some judgment decisions, even if practiced only on a small scale.

It is implied in succeeding discussions that mental health practices are not separate and distinct operations to be followed at specific times or periods. A curriculum design that fulfills the special needs of the child emphasizes these many aspects through an integrated, continuous balanced program.

How Does the Teacher Work with the Bright Child in the Regular Class?

The teacher has many devices and techniques to be used in working with the superior child. The usual suggestion is that the regular program be enriched to care for the particular pupil who moves forward at an unusual pace. Yet many instructors are unable to perceive all the implications of an enrichment program and believe inaccurately that the above-average child simply needs more work to be piled upon him in order to insure his preoccupation and continued industry in the class. Birch[44] offers some definite ways that elementary teachers should consider in working with children. It is a good idea to develop reading and other skills as quickly as possible in order that these may be tools for further exploration. In addition, the children can more easily become independent in the sense of being able to work more completely on their own. It is important that as these children develop they learn to do things correctly and actually strive for accuracy, since they may be tempted to hurry forward and become bored with solving a problem that is really too simple for them. Of course the social, emotional, physical and other aspects of development must not be ignored.

Moving from the general and over-all ways of working with the gifted child, the following specific ideas are provided and based upon case studies which furnished the data for such suggestions:[45]

—use the idea of acceleration by allowing the child to work in higher grade level areas

---

[44] Birch, *op. cit.,* pp. 34-5.
[45] T. Crowder and J. J. Gallagher, "The Adjustment of Gifted Children in the Regular Classroom," *Journal of Exceptional Children,* 23 (May, 1957), 353-63.

—secure and make available books that have topic appeal and will challenge the gifted person; bring in supplementary and reference materials in addition to the test

—encourage creative writing; set up classroom situations that require or stimulate such activities

—stress independence of thought and action in every instance both at school and at home by showing respect for their thinking and the like

—hold frequent discussions with parents

—arrange projects in the classroom that lead to social competencies and even peer acceptance

—make it possible for some exceptional children to change from one classroom to another, or even to visit another teacher's room

—find time to have frequent personal conferences with the child, but not simply meaningless time-wasting, boring "heart-to-heart" talks

—employ role playing widely

—set time limits for work to be done

—permit greater use and freedom of the library

—plan less structured projects and assignments, *viz.*, biographies, TV analyses, cultural interpretations, etc.

—insist upon interpretation of facts that require analytical, critical thinking; stress use of reasoning

—use resource people widely

—consider the Colfax plan[46] in grouping for several hours a day or certain times during the week; under this arrangement the exceptional child is not completely segregated but still has opportunities of working with some members who have similar abilities; several grade level teachers may need to work out such an arrangement in the regular kind of classroom organization

—use the workshop approach in allowing time for such grouping; this is a variation of the above idea

—arrange for children to assume more responsibilities in the classroom and school environment

—strive to deepen and widen attitudes and appreciations in many areas by pertinent discussions, panels and the like

—set high standards in work-performance and show how to acquire good work habits by requiring their usage in every activity

—plan for the development of intelligent listening through ear phones, recorders, records with many original, student-planned activities

---

[46] See H. O. Pregler, "Adjustment Through Partial Segregation," *National Elementary Principal* (September, 1952), 241-46.

—grant privileges for pace-setting as long as the child is moving ahead in a reasonable way

—insist that tasks are completed by refusing to accept anything carelessly done or incompletely worked out

—be alert to those who have leadership potential and place them in positions within the class and the school environment so that they may gain experience in giving leadership both individually and in cooperation with other group members

This listing of ways of working with the gifted represents sound teaching methods, that, in combination with drill and variety, should challenge and stimulate the above-average child. It is of course reasonable to expect that other children who are not classified as bright may well profit from similar techniques of teaching varied according to their academic achievement, mental ability, and other conditions.

How Does the Instructor Plan Ways of Working with the Slow Learner?

The suggestion has been made that even the slow learner may profit from a learning experience that is based upon excellent teaching methods, as described above. However it is clear that some variations must be employed. According to one study[47] the use of the broad unit has been found to be workable.[48] Bishton feels[49] that even the mentally handicapped are motivated by a need to explore and extend their environment, but firsthand experiences must be a starting point. In order for concepts to be formed, many observations are required even of the same experiences. Care should be taken that the developmental approach is used and that ideas are gradually introduced and built one upon the other. More intensive drill is usually needed as well.

An important concept is presented by Birch,[50] who agrees with research evidence that delay in formal reading instruction may be useful at the primary level. However, the teacher should always plan to do what the child needs, regardless of grade placement, by determining what skill development is present and proceed accordingly. Many pictures and concrete experiences are necessary to stimulate the child, and even then he

---

[47] "A Developmental School Program for Educable Mentally Handicapped," *American Journal of Mental Deficiency*, 57 (April, 1953), 554-64.

[48] See Chapter 6 on the discussion about the unit approach to teaching.

[49] R. C. Bishton, "Why Experience is the Key to Learning," *Journal of Exceptional Children*, 23 (February, 1956), 191-93.

[50] Birch, *op. cit.*, pp. 34-5.

may have difficulty in making generalizations and applying them to life situations. Words, books, experiences and so on must be selected carefully and pace must be regulated in order for these children to learn. In the final analysis the teacher works differently with the slow learner in using more concrete terms and specific experiences; but the obligations for optimum personal, social, physical, and mental health adjustments are still present.

The following guides, suggested for the elementary teacher, are adapted from Kirk[51] and Bijou.[52]

The teacher can help the child in the regular classroom who is classified as being exceptional by:

—making clear to the child his individual goals to be reached; these goals become personalized and understandable and serve to motivate the child as well; they are short-range goals that are within his reach

—dividing the work into units; these units will reflect what he has done before and will be in keeping with his abilities

—guiding the child into using learning materials that are understandable to him and capable of being mastered

—using goal charts and other similar ideas to impress him with feelings of success as he sees his growth

—encouraging him to compete only with his own record

—bringing in much reading material that is easy, interesting, and helpful; there will be supplementary material and modifications of other materials that will be designed to meet special needs

—using concrete materials widely

—making instruction systematic and orderly

—trying to bring in as much individualized instruction as is possible to give in the regular class; consultants will be utilized extensively

How May the Teacher Work with the Physically Handicapped Child?

It has been stated that the curriculum for these children will show little if any differences from those required for most elementary school

[51] S. A. Kirk, "What is Special about Special Education? The Child who is Mentally Handicapped," *Journal of Exceptional Children*, 19 (January, 1953), 138-42.

[52] S. W. Bijou, "The Special Problem of Motivation in the Academic Learning of the Retarded Child," *Journal of Exceptional Children*, 19 (December, 1952), 103-4 ff.

children, provided there are no serious handicaps, mental, or emotional conditions of a complicating nature. The teacher may have to teach more definitely towards getting the child to be accepted by the group and maintaining this acceptance. In some cases the special interest or ability of the child may have to be stressed and used as a focal point in actual learning situations. This may well be the avenue leading to insured success for the handicapped child. However, this approach is not reserved only for this kind of pupil.

It is obvious that one of the main responsibilities is to make sure that the child is comfortable. Any teaching method may be unsuccessful if the pupil does not feel physically and emotionally comfortable and directs his energies to combating an otherwise unnecessary condition outside of his own personal problem.

In working with the physically handicapped child, the teacher needs especially to help him acquire a common-sense viewpoint in regard to himself and to life itself. Since the perspective of the child is probably distorted to some degree to begin with, the elementary teacher emphasizes through curricular experiences the down-to-earth, realistic aspects, helping the child to see how he fits into the picture at all times. This skill in teaching means giving help freely, even without the asking; but more important it enables the child to realize that requesting help is a *normal* reaction and is not reserved just for the handicapped.

In view of the fact that there are different problems for the exceptional child who is classified in the category of the physically handicapped, it is believed that separate discussions may assist the teacher in viewing and working with different types of children. Of the four categories to be described here, it should be pointed out that the severely handicapped child will not be a member of the regular classroom. In addition, some categories, such as the cardiac cases, are not discussed, since they will not usually be members of the regular class. Furthermore, it should be remembered that the borderline exceptional child who is a member of the regular class must be viewed as having a special problem unique to him and that there are varying degrees of exceptionality in any given category.

The hard-of-hearing child. Many children who may have auditory problems can become useful members of a regular classroom. Teachers can follow these suggestions as they work with children who are classified as hard-of-hearing cases:[53]

—by watching for educational and emotional problems that generally arise

---

[53] R. G. Brill, "The Education of the Deaf and the Hard of Hearing," *Journal of Exceptional Children*, 23 (February, 1957), 194-98.

—by being alert to speech and language problems that can be aggravated by failure to hear properly

—by securing professional consultant aid and advice during the school year; such constant vigilance will assure the teacher that she is doing the proper things to aid the child and help to lay out plans for future progress; hearing aids may also be recommended

—by seating the child advantageously; facing the light when talking to him may be only one of the many things that will aid the child

—by seeing that the more severe cases are furnished outside help in such things as lip reading, getting special class help, and so on

—by speaking clearly and distinctly; perhaps it will be necessary to rephrase many of the ideas given to the class

The partially blind child. Although there are varying degrees of vision problems, the teacher is not at a loss in finding specific ways of assisting the partially blind. More than likely there will be administrative and budgetary obstacles that will hinder the teacher in working more effectively with children who have difficulty with their vision. The following suggestions[54] are offered for the teacher:

—make sure that the top of the child's desk is tilted properly; correct adjustment can aid the child in viewing the materials more effectively

—keep desks away from glaring lights; avoiding sharp contrasts in brightness is one approach to this problem

—remove glossy finishes on the top of the desk

—use typewriters with large type

—utilize recording equipment

—supply magnifying devices, lenses, projection magnifiers, and the like

—use the non-glossy globes, maps, charts; furnish as many items as possible that are in large type

—stress at all times good eye hygiene

The speech problem child. It is difficult to discuss how the teacher may aid this kind of child, since there are many aspects of the problem that will require special assistance. However in general the teacher may find that:[55]

—it helps to lead the child to see some of his speech errors and particularly to realize that they can be eliminated

---

[54] F. M. Foote, "Classrooms for Partially Seeing Children," *Journal of Exceptional Children*, 22 (May, 1956), 318-20.

[55] M. Ogihue, *Speech in the Elementary School* (New York: McGraw-Hill Book Co., Inc., 1954), pp. 236 ff.

—it is important that the cause of the problem be located, particularly with the aid of the specialist; consultary advice should be
sought and followed

—it is necessary to get the errors isolated, recognized, and dissected
in such ways that correct sounds can be produced; this task usually
requires the help of a professional consultant

—it is necessary to teach the child to produce the correct sounds
in isolation

—it is important to strengthen the use of the sound by incorporating
it within a framework of familiar words

—it is necessary to arrange situations that will bring the sounds into
habitual use

It is obvious that this list of suggestions is only a partial one. The peculi-
arities of any specific speech problem will determine the formula or
prescription to be used; however, it is clear that the teacher does not need
to feel helpless when confronted by a speech case. By working in conjunction with the specialist the classroom teacher is able to make a contribution to the speech progress of a given child.

The crippled child.   Many of the severe orthopedic cases are unable
to attend the regular classroom. There are some children who are crippled
to the extent that they do not need special classes, but they must be given
consideration as they become members of the regular classroom. The
child profits when the teacher recognizes that:[56]

—children need to have some opportunity to move within the school
environment; there must be a feeling of having some freedom in
this respect, and teachers can plan ways of providing for some
mobility

—children need individual and special equipment; there are cut-out
tables, chairs, typewriters, certain crayons and the like that can
contribute something to the crippled child

—children need special schedules planned to suit their particular
problem

—children require attention to the development of physical, emotional, and social needs; the teacher can be alert to curricular experiences that will promote the best development in these areas

—children will have gaps in their experimental life; by not having
the abilities of other children they will have missed many of the
so-called normal things of life, which teachers may attempt to
bring to them at least vicariously

---

[56] R. P. Machie, "What is Special About Special Education? The Crippled
Child," *Journal of Exceptional Children*, 19 (May, 1953), 309-12.

—children need many kinds of demonstrations and excursions for enrichment purposes

—children require a flexible curriculum

—children should have strengthened relationships with parents; the teacher may assist in working carefully with the child's parents

—children may need constant contact with professional consultants; teachers can keep abreast of the child's progress and his problem by seeking consultary aid and advice

In summary, there are many steps to be taken by the teacher who is working with the exceptional child in the regular classroom. It is important that his particular problem be clearly understood, that professional aid is given to chart the child's course, and that teachers employ the best known techniques to further the progress of the child.

How Does the Teacher Work More Effectively with the Maladjusted?

The disturbed or socially handicapped child responds most readily in a friendly, warm, and permissive environment. No teaching method approach can have any suggestion of prodding or coercing, since rebelliousness, negativism or escapism may simply be reactivated or reinforced by further mechanisms. It has been already suggested that the teacher should provide classroom experiences that help the child to see his own worthiness more clearly; to work out or act out some of his internal conflicts; and to keep him involved in class projects that help him in the feeling of belongingness.

Extreme understanding and patience are required of the teacher in working with this kind of child. The mental hygiene approach which has already been discussed has many implications for incorporation into the regular teaching procedures. Perhaps one of the chief teaching techniques to be employed by the instructor in connection with these children is that of bringing them into the learning situation at every possible instance to point out their importance as individuals. Depending upon the particular need of the child, the instructor may find the socialized method more practical; she may find that the project method is the best approach for certain children, or that the research project fits into the work plan best for some children. The unit method is also highly recommended to bring some children more completely into a learning situation, and at other times the individual method may be the only approach that is feasible, particularly at the beginning of the teacher-pupil relationship. The child needs to work by himself at first and gain a measure of confidence before launching into other ways of working with his group.

In summary, the child with an emotional problem may need:[57] to develop healthy ways of meeting his problems; to receive help in seeing what other courses of action are open to him; to understand more completely his present situation; and to develop stronger relationships with his peers, parents, and others. These are general statements that can suggest to the teacher that many courses of action are open which can help this kind of problem child.

SUMMARY

The exceptional child has earned the label because he requires special help that is beyond the usual and ordinary considerations given in the classroom. The emphasis here has been upon those children who are to be found in the regular classroom of the elementary school. Most of these children do not require special institutional care, although there will be some children who apparently would profit more from being placed in special classes or schools. The point of reference is that the elementary school teacher is faced with the problem of working with these children regardless of philosophy, optimum administrative aspects, or such. These children are enrolled in the classroom and the over-all question is: How may the exceptional child be provided those experiences which help him to fulfill his special needs? For the purposes of this chapter these children have been classified as being mentally exceptional, physically handicapped, or maladjusted emotionally or socially. No attempt has been made to discuss the serious cases which require professional aid that is beyond the preparation and scope of the elementary teacher. Only those children who can be helped within the framework of the curriculum and administrative organization of the elementary school are considered.

A perspective of or orientation toward the problem of exceptional children in the regular classroom is offered and is followed by a suggested philosophy for the teacher in connection with such children. Essentially, these children require aid that the teacher is in a position to furnish, and evidence indicates they can profit from special help.

The teacher is further assisted in gaining perspectives of the gifted, the slow learner, the physically handicapped, and the maladjusted. Their characteristics and ways of expressing themselves are discussed. To supplement these discussions a guide to the teacher in identifying the exceptional child is suggested. The first approach proposes a detailed

---

[57] F. Poole, "The Child with Social and Emotional Problems," *Journal of Exceptional Children*, 22 (October, 1955), 20-23.

study of the child, according to a plan, and the second approach suggests further ways or resources which will assist the teacher in identifying the child who is exceptional.

Curriculum designs are presented for the exceptional children who are found in elementary school classrooms. The thesis here is that educational objectives are the same for all children, although variations of some kinds are to be expected. The detailed curriculum patterns listed under the section dealing with the gifted child set the theme for such patterns for any exceptional child. Of course, it is obvious that the slow learner does not follow the design in quite the same way; the key thought is that each child participates within the curriculum design according to ability and needs, although it should be added that particular recommendations for curricular activities are offered under each section concerned with the various types of exceptional child.

Finally, ways of working more effectively with exceptional children within the regular classroom are presented. In essence, no unique teaching methods are to be reserved for any one type of child, although there are different approaches and emphases recommended for certain children. The question of grouping, segregation, or enrichment is handled by stating that, realistically speaking, the children are enrolled in the regular classroom and must remain there regardless of the teacher's belief; thus specific help must be granted them. In any event, evidence is lacking and disagreement is present as to the best plan for exceptional children; but it is agreed that they can profit from special help within the regular classroom. Some definite suggestions are offered for each type of child to aid the teacher in planning better ways of arranging school and classroom situations. The elementary classroom teacher cannot escape having some type of exceptional child and she should know which specific help improves the total adjustment of the child. Some recommendations are offered. In the final analysis each child is exceptional and needs individual help, although some require specialized assistance far beyond that given the average pupil and that which is provided by the teacher in the regular class.

SUGGESTED ACTIVITIES

1. Examine the various definitions of what is meant by the exceptional child and agree as to a working definition for your class.

2. Make at least a casual survey of some elementary school classrooms to discover the incidence of exceptional children enrolled.

3. Visit a state colony for the exceptional child, or some other special schools or classes. Report back to the total class your observations, or summarize some of your findings. Be prepared to find out how the children are identified, the curriculum designed for them, and the ways of working with them, and so on. Use the orientation procedures to assist you as described on pages 421 and 422.

4. Examine the philosophy described in this chapter for the teacher to follow. Have a class discussion on each of these twelve theses.

5. Study the characteristics of each type of exceptional child.

6. Use the teacher's guide in identifying the exceptional child to make a brief study of a child. Assign several students to report their findings.

7. Debate the issue of whether or not you believe educational objectives should be different for the exceptional child.

8. Examine each curriculum design given for the exceptional child. See how well you understand these ideas and raise questions about them.

9. Study the last section of this chapter. Are there any controversial issues that should be discussed in class? Can you see how to put into practice these suggestions? Are they practical? What limitations do you see?

10. Assign to an individual or a group of students the project of consolidating some of the information collected under activity No. 3 about ways of working with exceptional children in light of this last section. If it has not been possible to visit an elementary school, have a student or a group summarize the methods suggested here and extend the discussion with illustrations and the like. Relate this chapter with the one on Evaluation to note if any further suggestions are to be offered in connection with evaluation of progress.

SELECTED READINGS

Abraham, Willard. *Common Sense About Gifted Children.* New York: Harper & Row, Publishers, 1958.

Barbe, W. B. "Homogeneous Grouping for Gifted Children," *Educational Leadership*, 13 (January, 1956), 225-29.

Barron, J. R. "The Average and the Bright Child in Regular Classrooms," *Instructor*, 67 (January, 1958), 71-2.

Birch, J. W. "Special Classes and Schools for Maladjusted Children," *Journal of Exceptional Children*, 22 (May, 1956), 332-37.

Bishton, R. C. "Why Experience is the Key to Learning," *Journal of Exceptional Children*, 22 (February, 1956), 191-93 ff.

Chace, H. "Slow Learners in the Elementary School," *Social Education*, 21 (March, 1957), 122-24.

Cruickshank, W. M. "A Review of Special Education for the Exceptional," *Journal of Exceptional Children*, 22 (February, 1956), 201.

Eisenstadt, A. A. "The Educational Challenge of the Exceptional Child," *American Childhood*, 42 (June, 1957), 32-3 ff.

Gaskill, A. R. "Helping the Mentally Retarded Child in the Regular Classroom," *Understanding Children*, 26 (January, 1957), 5-7.

Goodenough, F. L. and L. M. Rynkiewicz. *Journal of Exceptional Children*. New York: Appleton-Century-Crofts, 1956.

Justman, J. and J. W. Wrightstone. "Expressed Attitudes of Teachers Toward Special Classes for Intellectually Gifted Children," *Educational Administration and Supervision*, 42 (March, 1956), 141-48.

Kidd, J. W., "Eliminate Guesswork in Assignments to Special Classes," *Educational Administration and Supervision*, 45 (July, 1959), 220-24.

Koopman, G. R. "Curriculum Development in the Public Schools," *Journal of Exceptional Children*, 24 (November, 1957), 102-06 plus.

Kvaraceus, W. C. "Research in Special Education: Its Status and Function," *Journal of Exceptional Children*, 24 (February, 1958), 249-54.

Mase, D. J. "Emotionally Insecure and Disturbed Children," *Childhood Education*, 32 (January, 1956), 218-20.

Mullen, F. A. "How Mentally Handicapped Children Learn," *Journal of Exceptional Children*, 24 (January, 1958), 224-26.

Nelson, Henry B., editor. *Education for the Gifted*. The Fifty-seventh Yearbook of the National Society for the Study of Education. Chicago: University of Chicago Press, 1958.

Otto, H. J. *Curriculum Enrichment for Gifted Elementary School Children in Regular Classes*. Austin, Tex.: University of Texas Press, 1955.

Passow, A. H. "Planning for Talented Youth: A Research Project," *Educational Leadership*, 13 (January, 1956), 249-51.

Passow, A. H., et al. "Adapting the Curriculum to the Needs, Capabilities, and Talents of Individual Students," *Review of Educational Research*, 27 (June, 1957), 277-86.

Ray, I. I. "Enriching Backgrounds of Retarded Readers," *Instructor*, 67 (February, 1958), 36 ff.

Riley, F. C. "Grouping Gives Each Child a Chance," *Nations Schools*, 58, (August, 1956), 51-5.

Smith, D. W. (editor). *Gifted Children in Tomorrow's World: The Basic Problems and Possible Solutions*. Tucson, Ariz.: University of Arizona Press, 1959.

Sheppard, A. G. "Teaching the Gifted in the Regular Classroom," *Educational Leadership*, 13 (January, 1956), 220-24.

Thissell, B. A. "Enrichment in the Regular Classroom for the Rapid Learner," *Instructor*, 67 (September, 1957), 68 ff.

PART III

Bases for
Curriculum Modifications

prologue to part III

The final section of *The Emerging Elementary Curriculum* is concerned with those techniques and procedures which aid in modifying the curriculum. A curriculum for the elementary school in a democratic society must not only be one which is emergent but also constantly modified for each child. In the name of democratic education mediocrity cannot be tolerated in the public schools. Sufficient procedures are available for those who are concerned with implementing curriculum experiences which will satisfy children whose various demands are brought about by their differences.

Evaluation techniques and procedures are tools of the teacher; teacher; she must not only be equipped with these skills, but she must not only be equipped with these skills, but she must diligently apply them in the process of determining the effects of maturation on learning. As the teacher studies each child and identifies developmental levels of growth, the emergent curriculum needs for each child become known. Content then is learned not as an end itself, but as a means in furthering the development of the individual. The curriculum incorporates significant life experiences which enhance personality integration. The learner must feel "good" about himself, as growing perceptions lead to deeper understandings of the "self" and its relationship to the world.

Finally, Part III deals with the team approach to curriculum development. The teacher and children are the focal point of curriculum, but administrators, citizens, and curriculum workers must join together in studying the curriculum setting. It is in this social system that teaching and learning take place and from this setting emerge independent citizens.

CHAPTER 14

Evaluation in the
Elementary School

INTRODUCTION

An integral part of the elementary school program is evaluation. As teacher and principal work together to improve classroom effectiveness, they will see a need to employ certain accepted evaluative procedures. The primary emphasis is always to be upon changing the behavior of children in more desirable ways. Evaluative techniques can assist school personnel to determine how well curriculum objectives are being attained and where curriculum revision is warranted. Thus, evaluation programs within the elementary school are important for many reasons.

The major purpose of this chapter is to consider the role of the teacher in evaluation, which may be more specifically defined in light of these functions: (1) The teacher participates in the appraising of the total educational program of the school. Those factors that are generally considered to be areas of concern only for the administrators, such as school plant, supplies, classroom equipment and the like require her attention, since they are important in furthering the growth and development of children. (2) The teacher is concerned with all materials and devices that are available to set up criteria for evaluating the school. (3) She employs all possible evaluative instruments for appraising the status of or changes in pupil behavior in the classroom. She may also desire to make self-evaluations for revealing her own strengths and weaknesses as a basis for personal growth. (4) The evaluation of the curriculum receives special consideration, as the teacher is particularly concerned with the specific things that children do in the classroom. (5) The teacher assists parents and community patrons to view more intelligently and sympathetically the total school program.

These five functions of evaluation by the teacher suggest a role that is both wide and varied, one which requires certain understandings and skills that must surely be acquired to insure optimum child growth. The problems of evaluation and measurement are comprehensive and complex, but teachers can learn to use many devices in the classroom. Teachers not only need time, administrative and parental support, and efficient tools for organizing and administering an appraisal program, but they also need to know *how* to employ skills of evaluation as they work with children. It is not to be assumed that a single chapter can insure the complete acquisition of these skills, but attaining the following specific objectives can assist the teacher in developing insight, attitudes, and specific, useful skills for evaluating the child from many viewpoints:

(1) to know how to approach the problems of evaluation,
(2) to have a sound philosophy of evaluation,
(3) to work out a practical and useful pattern of evaluation within the classroom,
(4) to have some understanding of various evaluation instruments,
(5) to know how to use pupil self-evaluation in the classroom,
(6) to understand the reporting practices of pupil progress,
(7) to understand the importance of evaluating the total program of the elementary school.

THE TEACHER APPROACHES THE PROBLEMS OF EVALUATION

There are many ways of viewing the evaluative processes. The confusions and misunderstandings that do arise in connection with the nature and meanings of appraisal may lead to poor planning in school, inadequate guidance of children, faulty teaching practices, and many other inferior educational practices carried out by well-meaning persons. The following illustration points out how misunderstandings about evaluating the child's progress may lead to pupil-parent dissatisfactions:

Miss Spencer believed that her sixth grade pupils should never know where they stood in relation to their grades. Her idea was stated very simply and clearly: keep them guessing as to how they are doing, and particularly what kind of grade they are going to be given. Let them find out through their own conjectures, keep them dangling, as it were, and the youngsters will work their heads off because they are afraid they must (might) not be passing.

Thus, some teachers are using the process of evaluation as a purely motivational device, and they are apparently unaware of concomitant dangers to child growth. Additional illustrations could well be furnished to demonstrate the misuse of evaluation and measurement; other comments will deal more directly with implications for the curriculum.

Three objectives now seem important and are offered in the form of questions:

(1) What should the teacher know about evaluation?
(2) Is there a philosophy of evalaution for the teacher?
(3) What may be a pattern of evaluation to guide the teacher?

What Does the Teacher Need to Know About Evaluation?

There seems to be some agreement by educators that evaluation is a broad term that incorporates the making of value judgments. The question of measurement must enter the picture and receive some clarifications. The teacher may turn to Wrightstone to bring into focus the complete picture of evaluation:

> Evaluation is a relatively new technical term, introduced to designate a more comprehensive concept of measurement that is implied in conventional tests and examinations. Distinction may be made between measurement and evaluation by indicating that the emphasis in measurement is upon single aspects of subject matter achievement or specific skills and abilities, but that the emphasis in evaluation is upon broad personality changes and major objectives of an education program. These include not only subject matter achievement, but also attitudes, interest, ideals, ways of thinking, work habits, and personal and social adaptability.[1]

It is necessary that a distinction between measurement and evaluation be recognized. Yet, the role of each process must be considered, since one is used with the other to furnish wider concepts and complete the total picture of that aspect of the program under evaluation. It is not to be expected that teachers will alter their own classroom behavior because they are exposed to certain ways of making value judgments. There must first be an acceptance of the concepts of evaluation. These concepts must be both feasible and consistent with the elementary school educational objectives.[2]

---

[1] J. W. Wrightstone, "Evaluation," *Encyclopedia of Educational Research* (New York: The Macmillan Co., 1950), p. 403.

[2] Albert H. Shuster and Wilson F. Wetzler, *Leadership in Elementary School Administration and Supervision* (Boston: Houghton Mifflin Co., 1958), p. 345.

Teachers may find that evaluation is best understood in terms of two broad steps that they must take if there is to be a practical point of departure in arriving at a consistent set of meanings. These steps further define what teachers should know about evaluation and measurement.[3]

First, it is necessary to define the broad objectives of the school in terms of the behaviors expected from the child. This does not mean merely setting up subject matter objectives, but rather seeking behavioral patterns which may result from the curriculum design itself. Certainly there must be subject matter objectives, but these do not become ends in themselves. Content within the subject area is extremely important and should not be ignored by the teacher. For example, the emphasis is first upon such factors as critical thinking as a developmental task with subject matter used as a means of acquiring this kind of behavior. Thus, the teacher gathers data to gain evidence of the extent of behavior changes occurring within the child as he progresses through each grade level. Evaluation becomes a process that includes all appropriate techniques to assay pupil growth and development. There is a need to go beyond the measuring of information learned or skills acquired, since there is concern with the kinds of habits and attitudes children are forming; the question of concepts, thinking ability, interests, appreciations, personal adjustment; and the extent to which the child is using and applying knowledge. Although these constitute formidable problems for evaluation by the modern classroom teacher, any interpretation must certainly be based upon the best picture of the child as he progresses within the educational program. The teacher needs measurement both as an instrument for securing quantitative data and as a set of values in interpreting and appraising his data meaningfully. This is a complex process that requires professional maturity and skill on the part of the teacher.

Second, the process of evaluation is not complete until the teacher knows what behaviors are desired for the child, identifies certain learning experiences to produce these behaviors, and then provides them for the child. In a very definite sense, the teacher is using evaluation in her teaching experience, and study of classroom situations have led her to make some kind of evaluative judgments. That is, the teacher must decide *what* learning experiences are best for the child and *how* to provide them. These decisions should be made in the face of the best evaluative data available to the teacher. Then, of course, there are always decisions to be made as to how well these behaviors are being acquired, what other situations may be required and appropriate for the child, whether continuity in the work is present, and so on.

---

[3] R. P. Kropp, "Evaluation Promotes Understanding of the Total School Program," *School Review*, 63 (November, 1955), 446-47.

In summary, teachers may approach the problem of evaluation in these general ways: by evaluating how well the objectives of the school are producing the desired behaviors, and by evaluating those learning experiences that best promote these behaviors. In the process of these evaluations, such problems as grade placement of the child, the subject matter to be taught, the roles of the teacher, and so on, are all considered. Evaluation by school personnel is concerned with finding what is done in the school with children and how change may be brought about to help them realize as completely as possible their potentials. Thus, teachers need to know much about evaluation and how to use particular techniques.

What May Be a Guiding Philosophy of Evaluation for the Elementary School Teacher?

A philosophy of evaluation may be considered a way of thinking about its meanings, objectives, and processes involved. Perhaps a written philosophy of evaluation should be formulated by individual schools, even as an educational philosophy is decided in terms of objectives. Again, combined thinking of the staff should bring forth these philosophies which are the bases for the total program. Teachers may find the following tenets useful in arriving at a philosophy of evaluation:

Belief number one: If the all-inclusive goal of education is the fullest self-realization of every child, then teachers must recognize and accept the fact that there must be differences in standards for various children. There are many standards to be met by children, not one set from the instructor or some other individual.

Belief number two: Ideally, evaluation should be concerned with discovering all that one can about each child. From a practical point of view, however, the teacher may wish to decide on a starting point and delimit the evaluation. Since instruction is designed to lead the child to his maximum growth within the framework of the objectives of the school, the evaluation may begin in these areas.

Belief number three: A curriculum should be designed for the child based upon his needs, interests, and abilities. Evaluation of the child and of learning experiences can assist in defining more accurately what he needs for his growth and development.

Belief number four: The teacher should assist each child through cooperative self-evaluation to see himself and recognize his strengths, weaknesses, and possibilities. Although this evaluation relates largely to teaching methods, it should be obvious that the teacher will recognize many implications for the curriculum. In addition, the teacher is concerned with making it possible for the child to achieve the growth of which he is capable. Both pupil self-evaluation and teacher evaluations should be as complete and comprehensive as possible to assist the child in attaining his highest possible growth.

These four beliefs suggest a framework of a philosophy of evaluation that should be mutually worked out by staff personnel. From a practical viewpoint, a philosophy of evaluation may well be stated in these four useful points:[4]

> (1) Evaluation should help the teacher and the child to know what the child is going to do this year.
>
> (2) Evaluation should point up the difficulties he will face during his school term.
>
> (3) Evaluation should appraise for teacher and child the assets he brings to the classroom.
>
> (4) Evaluation should reveal what the school, the home, and other agencies are doing to help the child achieve his optimum development—and lead the way to suggested ways of improving upon past performance.

Thus, a philosophy of evaluation guides the teacher in considering the over-all curriculum of the elementary school. Not only does she understand the *content* to be taught, but it is hoped that she will gain some insights as to the pitfalls and difficulties that may be encountered by pupils. Knowledge of the child's growth patterns, needs, interests, and the like should assist the teacher in planning better curriculum experiences.

Is There a Pattern of Evaluation to Guide the Teacher?

The nature and philosophy of evaluation have suggested some ways of working with children in the classroom. A more specific pattern is now offered to crystallize the thinking of the teacher who may use a four-way approach[5] in the role of the evaluator. These four points may also serve to summarize the previous discussion and suggest further topics of interest in the remainder of this chapter.

I) The teacher *establishes criteria.* The beginning point of evaluation may be realistic in that one must know what the child needs and what behavior patterns are most desirable for him. To give structure to the thinking of the teacher there should be an understanding of the principles

---

[4] Harold G. Shane, *The American Elementary School*, 13th Yearbook of the John Dewey Society (New York: Harper and Row, Publishers, 1953), p. 82.

[5] A. F. Hansen, "How the Teacher Collects and Uses Evidence," *Educational Leadership*, 13 (April, 1956), 430-34.

of child growth and development, and of the psychology of learning, plus knowledge of what community expectations may be. Her criteria may then be specifically described in terms of certain behavior patterns, skills in reading, numbers, and the like, abilities expected at any grade level, desirable habits that can be attained, and attitudes and understandings which may be achieved. These become definite patterns to look for as every child progresses through the months of the school year. There is every reason to believe that a wiser selection of learning experiences for each child is always possible. Better organization and marshalling of all factors that contribute to learning can be expected. Finally, the evaluation of progress begins to take on meaning as both teacher and pupil become better acquainted with what the child actually *does*.

II) The teacher *collects data.* The next section of this chapter is devoted to describing the devices by which the teacher gathers pertinent information about the child. Through testing and observing behavior, the teacher obtains a better idea as to what is happening to the child and whether or not the best results are being achieved.

III) The teacher *interprets* data. Perhaps the most difficult task in evaluation is that of deciding how well the child is progressing. Is the direction of behavioral change the most desirable? Does the information on hand support the value judgment of the teacher? Many questions are raised at this point to cause the teacher to make and alter decisions concerning the child. It will be seen that the process of pupil-evaluation is an integral part of data interpretation. That is, more emphasis should be given to this aspect of evaluation, as well as to teacher guidance.

IV) The teacher *plans a course of action.* In light of collected data about the child and cooperative interpretations, that final important step of deciding upon the achievement of desirable results *by a pattern* must now follow. Changes in the the arrangement of learning may be needed. To give more definite shape to a proposed new course of action, the teacher should call upon many resource persons. Perhaps new data are needed to give additional insights. There is a possibility that a second look is needed at the quality of the interpretations. Any one or all of these steps may be taken as the teacher makes this value judgment and plans future action. Unquestionably, the process of evaluation becomes a continuous matter, calling for many skills and actions by the teacher.

Since the role of the teacher in the elementary school should be centered on the child and the learning process, it should be clear that a curriculum design is necessary that will further his optimum development. The teacher may wish to consider evaluation in terms of processes and progress.[6] (See Chart XVII.)

---

[6] Albert H. Shuster and Wilson F. Wetzler, *op. cit.,*

CHART XVII

From:

To:

1. Describing procedures in more or less precise terms for determining what the child possesses at the present moment in terms of knowledge, skills, habits, and generalizations that can be recalled.

Using procedures that help the child achieve attitudes, feelings, values, skills in human relations, quality of experiences, insights, as well as knowledge, skills, and the like which can be put to use.

2. Relying almost exclusively on teaching-learning results in terms of marks, grades, and the like, with little or no attention to so-called concomitant learnings.

Relating evaluation to the total situation, since it is an all-inclusive process centering on the learning task itself.

3. Using few if any attempts to discover the blocks to efficient learning.

Exposing those factors hindering learning and helping the child to read.

4. Emphasizing interpretation of the child's performance in the light of test norms from group measurement.

Interpreting his performance in the light of his own growth and development pattern.

5. Having teacher-centered evaluation of the child, who learns where he stands after the learning activity is completed.

Undertaking cooperative teacher-pupil evaluation and further strengthening of democratic procedures.

6. Focusing attention on the results expected by the teacher with little regard for the child's interests.

Utilizing the motives, interests, needs, and purposes of the child.

7. Stimulating excessive competition among children.

Encouraging comparison of one's own progress in the light of his capacities, with competition held to a minimum.

8. Thinking of evaluation as dealing with immediate situations and problems for a given moment only, with emphasis on the processes used in getting results.

Considering evaluation as a continuous process of looking at results and by-products of the educational program in terms of stated aims and objectives. The goals of educational achievement are clarified through evaluation.

9. Discovering only how well the child has performed the work required.

Discovering how well the school is providing necessary conditions for growth, and giving attention to the economy and efficiency of learning experiences that will get the required work done.

10. Giving no regard to a time schedule for study of the aspects of an evaluation program, and carrying out an unorganized type of evaluation not based on research.

Planning and carrying out time-budgeted study of specific items in the evaluation program which is grounded in continuous research for improvement.

11. Using only a few devices in appraising the child; mainly tests, oral or written, formal or informal.

Studying, analyzing, and employing many tools and techniques to discover the nature and course of behavior changes.

Evaluative procedures and how they are used have a definite relationship to the curriculum of the elementary school. For example, if evaluation is conceived as stimulating excessive competition among children, the teacher will not only use certain teaching methods, but she may consider only those aspects of the curriculum that will foster competition. However, if children are encouraged to compare their progress in light of their capacities, then competition is held to a minimum. Curricular experiences are selected and developed in many different ways and for different reasons depending on the teacher's philosophy of evaluation. Thus, in many ways, the curriculum is affected according to how teachers conceive and use evaluation and measurement in the classroom, although there are other factors that influence the curriculum also.

THE TEACHER USES INSTRUMENTS OF EVALUATION

The primary task of the teacher is to arrange learning situations within the classroom environment. The modern situation requires a friendly, warm climate that is created by the interested instructor who must seek ways of stimulating interest and curiosity in exploring and solving problems. There are ways of achieving the most effective arrangement of teaching-learning situations that may insure optimum student progress, but the center of interest here is upon those devices and techniques that are available to the teacher in appraising learning situations and pupil progress.

What Devices and Techniques Can Be Employed by the Teacher for Pupil Evaluation?

Since the meaning already given to the elementary school curriculum has included all the experiences of the child, the evaluative experiences become an integral part of his development. Thus, in keeping with the philosophy of instructional practices expressed in this book, and of evaluation described in this chapter, teachers may employ those instruments of evaluation that are concerned with multiple learnings. That is, evaluation goes beyond academic achievement and is concerned with the child's attitudes, his personality, how he works, his interests, physical development, and his social relationships.

Instruments are needed to evaluate the many outcomes of school-home-community interactions, and teachers must make evaluative decisions that will bring about the kind of educational experiences that promote the growth and meet the needs of children.

Readiness for learning.[7]   It is important to know when the child has reached that level which is generally considered necessary for undertaking learning, and whether he is prepared for the next step in a learning sequence. Readiness tests are available to aid in this kind of evaluation. He may be given a general mental maturity test, certain standardized tests in reading, arithmetic, and so on. Teachers may construct tests to learn if he is ready to progress to the next step in a sequence. Thus, it is clear that the specific abilities of the child must be known in order to discern the desirability and feasibility of his understanding certain learning tasks at a given level. There should be no doubt that such information is valuable in helping the child to lay foundations and create readiness interest for school. For example, the kindergarten[8] prepares the child by building his vocabulary, sensitizing him to his surrounding culture and society (particularly to the school environment), helping him to work with other persons, and by introducing him to the community. Teachers use readiness devices at any grade level, but particularly upon the child's entrance to school.

In considering the readiness for learning factor of each child for participation in the program of the school, it should be clear that the varied curriculum activities as well as the child's pattern of abilities must be evaluated. Frandsen expresses the importance of reading readiness in these words:

> . . . before a child is ready to progress from pre-reading activities to initial attempts to read, his oral-language comprehension and expression should, at least, equal the vocabulary level of the "experience reading" and primers in which he will begin to read. He should understand and speak easily in four- or five-word sentences. His experience and information background should include the concepts about which he will read and hear read to him . . .[9]

Frandsen continues to describe other readiness factors needed by the child, such as perceptual discriminations, articulations, remembering, poise and self-confidence, and so on. Thus, a gauge of these abilities is needed not only for reading but for other learning experiences. Therefore, the readiness test has a direct tie-in with the curriculum, as teachers

---

[7] See Chapter 3, p. 69.

[8] G. E. Parsons, "Readiness for School," *Elementary School Journal*, 57 (February, 1957), 272-75.

[9] A. N. Frandsen, *How Children Learn* (New York: McGraw-Hill Book Co., Inc., 1957), p. 82.

gain more understandings about the child and his adjustments in the curriculum.[10]

Mental maturity and intelligence tests. Teachers need to evaluate their pupils in order to determine where they should go educationally and how far they are able to progress. However, the controversies in education over the questions of intelligence, abilities, the influence of environment and training on intelligence, and so on, seem to have caused as much confusion as agreement among classroom teachers. Perhaps more emphasis needs to be given to the problem of what to do with the information teachers secure relating to these abilities.

The traditional approach has apparently been that of securing a single index that reflects the general mental ability of the child. This information does not lend itself very readily in assisting the teacher in the various areas of the curriculum, unless the teacher has some data concerning the special types of abilities possessed by the child. If so, she can guide the child more adequately, since her evaluations will lead her to determine as accurately as possible those curriculum experiences which will be most profitable to the child. In addition, evaluation should lead the teacher to discover the achievement that can be expected from each child, since all pupils in a given classroom do not have the same capacity or ability to achieve in any subject matter area. Probably the most prevalent problem facing teachers is that of finding the answer to this question: Is the pupil working at the level of his ability? It will be noted on page 529 that it is virtually impossible to say that a child is (or is not) working up to ability, especially when that ability is expressed merely as a single score, i.e., his I.Q. It will be seen that many factors need to be studied before the teacher can reach conclusions to guide her in working with the pupil and have a general idea of level of ability.

Achievement tests. Teachers should be aware of the fact that the curriculum of the elementary school can be evaluated to discover how well knowledge and skills are being taught in the classroom. Many testing practices have been overly concerned with *how much* information is learned, and too little concerned with *how well* it has been learned. Teachers must be interested and concerned that children acquire basic skills and facts; but they need also to know how to evaluate the child's progress, how well he is understanding, making applications of facts, seeing their relationships, and solving his everyday problems. Through evaluation, the teacher may recognize that mere memorization of facts

---

[10] Test titles will not be given here, but it is suggested that the reader become acquainted with available tests. See Oscar K. Buros (ed.), *The Fifth Mental Measurements Yearbook* (Highland Park, N. J.: The Gryphon Press, 1959).

and practicing of mechanical skills are the outstanding achievements of some children. Thus, the teacher can take steps to determine other ways of presenting curricular experiences designed to go beyond this kind of memorizing and mechanical skill practice.

The standardized achievement test is one device that can be used wisely and carefully to aid the teacher in discovering some strengths and weaknesses in the curriculum and even in teaching practices. Although the test scores of the child can be compared with norms, the teacher should know that these norms are derived from scores of children from many and varied school systems. A norm is actually a reference point that is derived from a study of the scores of a selected group. Teachers use common age and grade norms, as a comparison of pupil test results with the over-all results from certain specific groups. For example, John is in the fifth grade and scores 115 on a general achievement test, which is equivalent to a grade norm of 6.8. Then John's score is typical of pupils who have been in the sixth grade for a period of eight months. (The decimal is usually an estimate.) Thus, this norm helps the teacher in comparing the results of testing her group with all pupils in a certain classification, providing the original group is representative. The teacher recognizes that John is at a level suitable to sixth graders and must design work challenging to him. At least the norm helps the teacher to locate John on an academic achievement scale and gives a reference point in planning curriculum experiences for him. This means that John obviously cannot be challenged if he is not allowed to progress faster, say in arithmetic, than the slow members of his group. Teachers will have to find ways and means of "keeping up" with such pupils as John, and the emerging curriculum design suggests some answers along these lines.

Teachers should not consider the achievement test results as a measure of their ability to present particular textbook or content material. There could be a tendency to "teach the test," in order that children will make acceptable scores. This practice would mean that curriculum offerings would have little significance to the teacher.

Most standardized achievement tests cannot hope to meet the objectives or the grade level needs of a given school. Perhaps undue competition among the pupils may be encouraged if "passing" the test becomes paramount. It is not unreasonable to believe that teachers and even local schools may catch the competitive spirit and attempt to attain levels of achievement that are not in keeping with their situations.

In spite of the limitations, achievement tests can assist the teacher for guidance purposes. As they are used in conjunction with teacher-made tests particularly, the instructional objectives can be evaluated. Thus, some diagnosis of the learning difficulties and problems being met by the children is possible, and consideration for curriculum and teaching problems is pointed out for the teacher.[11]

The case study approach.   In making evaluative decisions concerning curriculum experiences to be brought to children, it has been suggested that teachers need to know a great deal about the individual child. The curriculum objectives may suggest what learning experiences are needed to produce favorable outcomes, but teachers must still make the proper selections in light of the children themselves. Therefore, it is important for curriculum purposes and for teaching practices in the classroom that children be studied carefully by the teacher. Although Chapter 2 is concerned with understanding the child, an important tool of evaluation that is both diagnostic and remedial in nature is that of the case study approach. By using this device, teachers are often able to discover the "why" behavior and then determine a course of action to aid the child in realizing his potentialities. This course of action will surely mean that the teacher looks to the curriculum for experiences to help the child in his development.

Data may be collected from at least three sources: the diary, the log, and the anecdotal record. The diary is a written account about the child during an unspecified period of time and records all the information deemed pertinent by the teacher. The log is a written account for a specific period and for a definite, specified purpose. The focus is on the observer's reactions or interpretations of how the child meets and solves his problems. The anecdotal record lists actual occurrences and may use all three devices in keeping a record of certain behavioral incidents. The important thing is for the teacher to be aware of the case study as a process designed device in keeping a record of certain behavioral incidents. It is important that the teacher regard the case study as a process designed to get clues from behavior patterns that will make sense to the instructor and lead him to plan some sort of action to improve the child's behavior. From the practical viewpoint, teachers have little time to make case studies and little knowledge about how to gather the data and make the interpretations. Therefore, some practical guides can be used by the teacher in learning more about children:

(1) Prepare a loose-leaf notebook, with a mimeographed sheet(s) for each child, in which to record pertinent data. As each child is observed, the teacher writes down observations and incidents. For example, on a given day, the teacher may note particular aggressive

---

[11] See D. Baron and H. W. Bernard, *Evaluation Techniques for Classroom Teachers* (New York: McGraw-Hill Book Co., Inc., 1958), Chapter 6.

behavior of a certain child and records the incident. This may further suggest an anecdotal study of this child if other incidents seem to be a part of his pattern. Other information such as family background, health, educational and mental data, personality, social behavior, and ethnic or economic status, should assist in suggesting clues to his behavior.

(2) Keep descriptions and interpretations of behavior entirely separate. However, include personal interpretation from time to time within the framework of the case study.

(3) Seek to make some recommendations. Some course of action even if it is not taken, is to be suggested as a result of the case study. These recommendations must necessarily be made cautiously and be subject to reconsideration and revision. Yet the child deserves some kind of help which may lead to an improvement of behavior.

(4) Bring in many resources in the final interpretation. This last step may involve parent-case workers, principals, and, of course, the child. Even though recommendations may be offered, it is valuable to the teacher to get as much help as possible in verifying the findings of the case study.

The case study is not just a simple task of jotting down particular incidents of behavior. Rather, it is an organization of the facts in a more systematic fashion so that the physical, social, and psychological assets and liabilities of the child may be analyzed and synthesized by the teacher. Observations should lead to interpretations and recommendations; corrective, enriching or remedial efforts should always follow.

Sociometry. In working with children, teachers believe that it is important to know the group relationships that exist in every classroom. Prescott has stated in clear terms this forming of a child society:

> When children go to school they are placed together in groups or "classes" of thirty or more to do their learning. These class groups become miniature societies with the customary characteristics of societies, namely, goals, activities, customs, codes of conduct, roles, status, and the individual strivings. Consequently each child does his curricular learning, that is, learns to read and figure and studies science and social studies, in the context of a miniature child society. This child's society becomes very important to him, for it offers him the possibility of belonging to the individual just because he exists. In the peer group, belonging must be won. It must be won by playing roles effectively and by conforming in behavior to the customs and code of the child society. For any given child in school, then, classroom experiences have two kinds of meaning: one relating to the skill, information, and attitude learnings expected and de-

manded by the child's parents and teachers, the other relating to the child's status and roles in the peer group.[12]

It should be emphasized that the child earns a role or social status in the group; he is not given status simply because he is an assigned member of the group, as in a family situation. The structure that is formed reflects how children relate to and feel about each other, and it assigns their roles and status. There are those who lead and influence group behavior: children who are not accepted by any other classmate, some who are easy to get along with in certain situations, and those who are hard to get along with in other ways, and so on. Thus, sociometric techniques are available to the teacher which reveal this structure of the relationships of children at any particular time. Specifically, the teacher can find the status of the child within the group, even though sociometry does not reveal how and why he interacts, behaves, or adjusts in the group. There are no suggestions as to particular game skills and social skills that are present or lacking, nor are there definite references as to adjustment mechanisms, roles being played, or how a new role may be won by the child. Yet a sociogram, or a graphic representation of this structured relationship, highlights those children who are the "stars" or the attractions and those who are rejected or are called isolates; it indicates where a chain of mutual attractions exists, where cliques or closed relationships are, and even where triangles prevail. The total picture of the *sociogram* shows the instructor how the group is actually integrated.

There are very definite reasons why sociograms should be used by the teacher. These reasons are summarized as follows:

—to allow children who choose each other to work together in group projects
—to aid the child who is on the fringe of being accepted by the group to build new self-concepts
—to help children get to know each other better
—to teach the values of tolerance and group membership
—to show the teacher how to begin working with children in group projects, viz., to bolster the child who is having difficulty in being accepted, and thus meet his special needs
—to investigate fully how well the child is being accepted or rejected because of certain game skills that are required by the peer group
—to know to what extent the social skills are present or lacking in the child

---

[12] Daniel A. Prescott, *The Child in the Educative Process* (New York: McGraw-Hlil Book Co., Inc., 1957), p. 277.

Then, the main reason for the construction of a sociogram is to learn which children feel wanted and accepted or feel rejected by the group. It is to be realized that curriculum objectives are better achieved in an atmosphere of acceptance. Since this technique is designed to acquaint the teacher with these classroom conditions, it is then possible to make further explorations as to what can be done for the child who must live and learn within this child society.

Turning now to the administering of a sociometric test, Bennett believes[13] that members of the class should first know each other fairly well before such an investigation is to be undertaken. Some other practical considerations: (1) state reasons why you are asking the children to make choices in the test; (2) let them know that the results will be used according to the test itself; i.e., every attempt will be made to honor the choice; (3) emphasize that choices can be made for any boy or girl; (4) present the test with interest and enthusiasm without being too formal; (5) make sure they realize the confidential nature of the test; (6) tabulate the results; (7) make the sociogram as a graphic representation of the results for teacher use only.

To give validity to the test and make it real and worthwhile in the eyes of the children, the teacher should select a legitimate situation for giving the sociometric test. For example, the group may be planning a field trip on the bus, deciding upon a seating arrangement in the room, preparing for a particular play situation, planning for a work situation, and so on. Then, depending on the approach, the teacher carefully explains that the children will be allowed to choose the names of those friends they would like to sit near, play or work with, and the like. As an example, for a seating arrangement, the teacher states that each child is to take a sheet of paper and write his name at the top. Then, he is to write the name of the person he would like *most* to sit by. In case this may not always be possible, he should be told to write down only the names of those he would like *next* to sit by. Thus, the teacher has the data to tally and can plot the relationships as shown in Figure XXI.

From the data collected by the teacher, a simple chart is made showing the choices of individuals in the group. Figure XXII is a sociogram of all the children of a given class. The boys are represented by the triangles and the girls by the circles. The number within the design, of course, refers to the name of the child. Then, the sociogram is read as follows: The arrows represent *acceptance*, and from every circle or triangle (except for No. 8) there are three lines which are marked 1, 2, 3.

---

[13] M. E. Bennett, *Guidance in Groups* (New York: McGraw-Hill Book Co., Inc., 1955), pp. 195-96.

These indicate choices of other children in preferential order. For example, No. 16 chose No. 7 first, No. 17 second and No. 19 third. Other children chose No. 16 also. The numbers *nearest* the circle represent *that* person's choices and the arrows nearest the circle show acceptance by someone else which can be traced to the child who made the choice. Within each circle and triangle are three numbers. The top one is the identification of the student as listed on the bottom of the sociogram. The bottom number to the left suggests the number of times that child was *chosen* by other children. The number to the right tells the number of mutual choices that were made by him or with him. For example, No. 16 has one mutual choice. He chose No. 17 and No. 17 chose him. Only those choices which are matched for choice (first, second, or third) can be considered mutual. For instance, No. 4 chose No. 22 third but No. 22 chose No. 4 second; hence, no mutual choice. The short line perpendicular to an arrow represents the mutual choice. The starred circles, No. 1 and No. 15 indicate the most popular boy and girl. It is interesting to note that the sex preferences are clearly defined in that few choices are made between boys and girls at this third grade level.

One of the disadvantages of using the sociogram is that no standard score has been derived from the data which could be used to show individual development. However, Thorpe and others[14] have now developed a device through which a standard score or, as they call it, a Social Score can be obtained. Thus, it is possible to note social development during the intervals between sociograms.

In summary, it must be emphasized that *one* approach, such as seating preference sociogram, does not reveal the complete picture. A child's status may change in a play situation and the like. Also, the sociogram describes the child's group status, but it does not explain it. There are various arrangements that can be made both in preparing and constructing the sociogram, but the visualization of the social status should aid the teacher in spotting the leader and the isolate, and aid the teacher in working more intelligently with the new child, the problem case, and all persons concerned with developing increased social growth.

Personal adjustment. Evaluation approaches such as the case study and the sociogram are just some of the ways that teachers gain insights into how well the personal-social adjustment of the child is progressing. It is generally agreed among teachers that progress in academic subjects must be measured, and more interest is being shown in securing informa-

---

[14] Louis P. Thorpe, Milo E. Whitson, Dennis Baron, Georgia Sachs Adams, *Studying Social Relationships in the Classroom* (Chicago: Science Research Committee, 1959).

FIGURE XXI

		1	2	3	4	5	6	7	8	9	10	11	12	13	14	15	16	17	18	19	20	21	22	23	24	25	26
John	1																	2			1	3					
Sue	2											1		2						3							
Bette	3	2							2		3					1							3				
Dick	4	2																							1		
Patty	5								3							2			1								
Jim	6																					2	1		3		
Marie	7											1											2	3			
Jean	8				3	3										2											
Robert	9	2																				1					
Karen	10	3											1				2										
Becky	11	3											1			3				2							
Ann	12	3									1						2										
Dorothy	13					3										2			1								

Name																										
Ruthann 14											1	2	3											1	3	
Doris 15		2																							1		
Dan 16	1					3	3											2	2								
Bill 17	1					3	3											2									
Treasa 18			3							1						2			3			2	1				
Susan 19			3												2				3	2							
Mark 20	1			3										2			3			2			2		1	
Pete 21				2																	1		3		
George 22	2		3												2									1		
Margaret 23					3												3	2				2				1
Eddie 24	1				3														2							
Penny 25	1										3															
1st test 3	1		1			1		3	2	1	1	3	2	1	2	2	1	1	1	1	1	3	3	2	2	2
2nd test 2	1		4	1	1	2			1	1				1	1	3	3	2	1	2	2	1	1	1	1	
3rd test 2	1		4	2	1	1			1	1				3			3	2	1	2	1	1	1	1	3	
Total 7	3		4	3	3	3		3	2	2	3	3	3	2	3	3	7	3	2	5	2	4	5	2	6	2

FIGURE XXII

Sociogram University Elementary School Ohio University

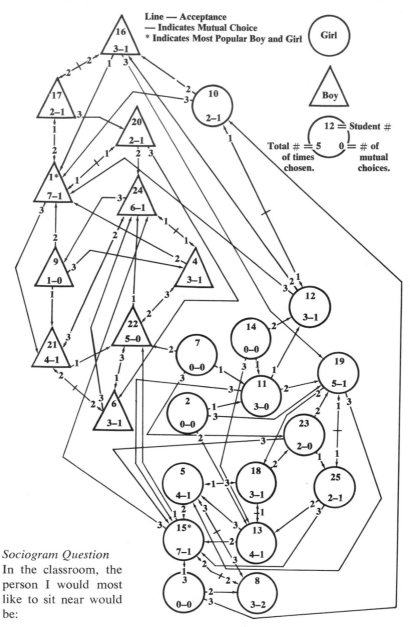

Sociogram Question
In the classroom, the person I would most like to sit near would be:

tion about the personality of the child. Thus, personality tests can yield definite results that can be useful to the teacher. In the words of Traxler:

> Most teachers and guidance officers are aware that personal qualities and interests are fully as important in a pupil's academic and out-of-school adjustment as are those more easily measured factors of intelligence and achievement.
> . . . three broad approaches to the *evaluation* of personal *adjustment* . . . tests, usually of the paper-and-pencil sort . . . informal procedures involving anecdotal records, ratings, descriptions of behavior, and sociometric devices . . . use of projective techniques of a laboratory or clinical nature.
> Under ideal conditions, anecdotal records, rating devices, and behavior descriptions undoubtedly have more to offer to a guidance program than do personality tests which, for the most part, are still in an experimental stage. . . .[15]

Teachers should rely upon competent authorities and trained personnel for guidance in the matter of personality tests and interpretations. The indiscriminate use of personality tests by teachers should be discouraged, as teachers are usually not trained in these areas of competency.

Interviews and conferences. Through the pupil-parent-teacher interviews and conferences, the teacher can secure important information about the child. From one viewpoint, the conference serves to keep parents informed about the program of the school. However, this evaluative approach that may be initiated by the teacher is designed primarily to discover such things about the child that suggest his hopes, aspirations, attitudes, interests and so on. Information relating to the plans that parents may have concerning the child is also secured. It is hoped that teachers will learn something about the child through these interviews and conferences that suggests definite curriculum experiences which will aid in the child's development.

Certainly the teacher is required to furnish evaluative information about the child to the parent and even to the pupil himself. Through a sharing of information in the interview or conference parents particularly can provide important data about the child that will make a contribution to the total picture in guiding the behavior of the child. Teachers should plan this experience carefully by knowing what purposes can be served; by interpreting appraisals to the parents; by having a check-list available for behavioral reference; by collecting pertinent evidence about the child

---

[15] A. E. Traxler, *Techniques of Guidance* (New York: Harper & Row, Publishers, 1957), p. 101.

to show to the parents; by arriving at some tentative generalizations with the parent as to proposed action and the like. In short, the teacher may find this evaluative approach extremely beneficial to all persons concerned if proper planning and thinking are done in advance.

After conducting a study of the parent-teacher conference as it was being used to report pupil progress in a number of midwestern schools, Ploghoft reported that a better understanding of the child's learning problems by parents and teachers seemed to be a major outcome.[16] From a total of 319 teachers who responded, only two indicated that parental acceptance of the conference plan was unfavorable.

The parent-teacher conference may well be extended to include the child as an active participant. Involving parents and pupils more directly in the evaluation of pupil progress should "arouse or help maintain parental interest in the educational welfare of the pupil and lead to additional beneficial guidance contacts with parents."[17]

What Is the Role of the Teacher in the Total Evaluation Program Within the School?

The emphasis to this point has been upon the process of evaluation with particular reference to the role of the teacher. By analyzing and studying the child, the teacher can evaluate his progress in terms of his individual situations. Then, the teacher can be in a better position to work within a curriculum designed for the optimum development of the child. Evaluation procedures can assist the teacher in this guidance function. Then, in summary, the elementary school teacher must:

1. Understand first what educational goals and objectives are being sought.
2. Look for changes in pupil behavior as a result of certain curricular experiences;
3. Employ those instruments of evaluation that point out the strengths and weaknesses of the child; plan learning experiences in light of the child's needs;
4. Re-evaluate the child's growth, his achievement, and his behavior in order to insure the validity of the decision made concerning either a diagnosis or a remedial program;

---

[16] Milton E. Ploghoft, *The Parent-Teacher Conference as a Report of Pupil Progress* (doctoral dissertation; Lincoln, Nebraska: University of Nebraska, 1957), pp. 138-39.

[17] Leslie L. Chisholm, *Guiding Youth in the Secondary School* (New York: The American Book Co., 1950), p. 310.

5. Appraise continuously with parent and child, and tell them enough to keep them adequately apprised of problems, progress and the like.

The role of the teacher in evaluation is only partially suggested by the five-point outline above. It should be clear, however, that teachers can use many and varied evaluative instruments and determine more accurately those particular curricular experiences which can be achieved by the child, according to what he is capable of doing.

How Does the Teacher Interpret Test Results More Effectively?

Many teachers feel concerned about the matter of interpreting test results and may believe that it is almost an impossible task, or one that requires the professional expert at all times. Certainly the prepared, experienced person can do a more adequate job in interpreting test results, and a few pages here of suggestions or guides can be no substitute for applied study and extensive experience. Yet all elementary teachers can approach the problem of interpreting and applying test results in a more adequate fashion by following the suggested procedures. First, any reliable standardized, major test will furnish a detailed manual of directions. There is generally a description of the test itself, together with some information about the authors and why the test was developed. The factors of reliability and validity will be discussed also. Then, a section on how the test results may be interpreted and used is given in detail.

Second, the teacher can interpret test results more efficiently by following the steps suggested here:[18]

1. Classify and tabulate the scores. Perhaps even a simple ranking of the scores can help to pull out significant items, such as which children scored high or low, how many in certain categories, and so on.
2. Make a statistical analysis of scores. Depending upon the kind of test data to be analyzed, the teacher may wish to apply some simple procedures, such as determining the average, the mode, the median, and the like. For example, a sharper perspective of results is gained by knowing whether the majority of pupils in the class are above or below the median score for a particular age-grade in intelligence.

---

[18] C. C. Ross and J. C. Stanley, *Measurement in Today's School* (3rd ed.; New York: Prentice-Hall, Inc., 1954), p. 234.

3. Make a graphic analysis and representation. A visual study of this nature can supplement any statistical analysis and summarization of data by attracting attention, clarifying meanings, and even helping the teacher to see the whole perspective and retain the data more efficiently.
4. Use norms and standards. One purpose of a certain test may be to determine the present status of a given class in light of national norms and standards. That is to say, in achievement tests, the fifth grade child should be expected, according to a national norm, to perform certain arithmetical manipulations.
5. Analyze errors. In some tests, such as in diagnostic instruments, the teacher is interested in seeing where the errors were made, the kinds of errors, and particularly who and how many children committed them.

The teacher will probably give some attention to all five steps in the interpretation of test results, although none will always receive equal emphasis. As an example, item five is of most importance when diagnosis is the prime purpose. It should be emphasized that even with teacher-made tests, interpretations should be made that can follow this outline. The important fact to keep in mind is that interpretations should be made from the results of the tests. Teachers should not use excuses that they have secured test data but cannot make interpretations, since they can follow the manual of directions and apply the five-step approach suggested above. Although interpretations should lead to direct applications, the fact remains that this final step is often neglected. Thus, teachers need to know what test scores mean and be prepared to plan a course of action based on the knowledge derived from the test data. If the children do not change behavior, or the teacher finds that what they are doing is correct, then there is every reason to believe that administering the tests was not really important to begin with. Both individual and group attack upon such problems is advisable.

Gordon approaches the question of test interpretation from the guidance point of view that has some limited implications for elementary teachers:

> . . . the locus of evaluation is with the self. Test scores, then, should not be used to "challenge" a student's self-concepts, but only as additional data available to him to react to and interpret in light of his own meanings . . . The interpretation of scores should be done without judgment and decision-making on the part of the counselor . . . In the long run, the interpretation of the result is the student's task, not the counselor's. It may

be accepted or rejected, denied or distorted, explained away or relied upon . . . test results can be misleading . . . subject to change.[19]

The elementary school child should be led to make self-evaluation; but because of his immaturity it is hardly feasible to expect him to react and interpret in light of his own meanings, when actually none may be present. It is important that teachers render judgments and make decisions, since the child is unable to do it alone. However, Gordon is correct in believing that too many test scores are injected improperly in counseling situations, especially for the student at the secondary level. In addition, test scores are in no sense the final evaluation to be made, and they do change with the maturity and new experiences of the child. Whenever possible, test scores should be interpreted only in light of a child's pattern of self-meanings under the guidance of the teacher.

TEACHING IS IMPROVED THROUGH PUPIL SELF-EVALUATION

The suggestion has already been made that evaluation should be concerned with the objectives of the curriculum and related learning activities. In addition, the evaluation program must be continuous, comprehensive, and cooperative. Therefore, this section is designed to emphasize the cooperative phase of evaluation, with particular reference to pupil self-evaluation. Under the guidance of the teacher, children can develop many desirable traits, especially when they are able to participate in evaluating their own progress, their own problems, and their growth. Within any kind of curriculum design of the elementary school, teachers should lead the child to discover more adequately his growth status. Both teacher and pupil are sharing and participating in the total educational process; this kind of evaluation data can assist them in making better curricular decisions. Therefore, this section is designed to furnish answers to these questions:

1. How can a pupil self-evaluation program be organized?
2. How is it administered?
3. What records are kept?

How Does the Teacher Organize a Pupil Self-Evaluation Program?

Unless the school personnel and patrons are familiar with pupils' self-evaluative procedures, the teacher may find difficulty in using this device. Therefore, the discussion that follows will center on the developmental

---

[19] J. J. Gordon, *The Teacher as a Guidance Worker* (New York: Harper & Row, Publishers, 1956), p. 285.

phases that may be necessary in order to initiate a pupil self-evaluation program.

Phase One. The teacher involves the administration, pupils, and parents in developing some understandings about the procedures of self-evaluation. In one sense, a philosophy or way of thinking is being considered before any formal steps are taken. No elaborate write-up is necessary, but the main emphasis is upon getting understandings of and insights into self-evaluation by all persons involved.

Phase Two. Setting performance standards must lead to the development of specific criteria by which children can appraise themselves. This does not mean long and involved statements in the phrasing of such criteria, since this is beyond the capabilities of young children, and to some extent, of many teachers. Yet, the group can participate in deciding upon a brief, easily understood list of criteria by which they look at their own work for evaluative purposes. First, the group has standards and specific criteria for gauging purposes, which will mean that as a group they may be concerned with group behavior. Three questions may furnish an evaluative framework: (1) What are we doing well as a group? (2) What do we need to do in different ways in order to improve? (3) How should we go about it? Second, from the individual's standpoint, these three questions are simply re-stated by using the personal pronoun "I". These questions lead the child to focus attention on himself and call for the development of evaluative self-aids, discussed in the next phase. It may be suggested again that primary children will require teacher-questions and close supervision.

Phase Three. Although standards and criteria of performance have been worked out by the group, some definite forms should be developed for recording purposes. Of course, in the primary grades, the teacher must take the lead and handle the forms personally. A separate section will discuss the details of this last phase, but such provision for self-evaluation should include progress in all areas: the degree of achievement in the basic skills, work and study habits, thinking, social development, and so on.

How Does the Teacher Administer Pupil Self-Evaluation?

It is not an easy task to expect the child to be objective and accurate in self-appraisal, and the success may well rest in how well the teacher observes the following requirements in administering the program:

1. Have each pupil accept certain educational goals. As provisions are made within the classroom for achieving them, records of progress must be kept. It will be seen that individual

folders for each child should contain plans and representative samples of both group and individual accomplishments.

2. Provide specially scheduled time periods for the pupil-teacher conference. It may be added that learning activities for the remainder of the class must be planned and carried out in order for time to be used productively.

3. Make the conference with the child the core of self-evaluation. The teacher should have the class so well organized that good planning will mean that all necessary forms will be in readiness for the conference itself. There would be little point in conferring if children consistently do not have their self-evaluations made by the appointed time.

4. Follow through on the results of the self-appraisal. It is obvious that the teacher must gain new insights from the pupil self-evaluation, or the process may simply be a bookkeeping device that leads to little or no change in behavior.

Administering the pupil self-evaluation program begins with the teacher. There is no blueprint of action that must be rigorously followed, but the four-point plan above may be considered as a framework within which any program can operate. The next section completes the discussion and shows what records may be kept by the children.

How Do Children Keep a Self-Evaluation Record?

The child keeps a record of his and the group's progress. It is advised that each child be provided with a folder that contains appropriate forms for aiding in self-appraisal. The following recommendations are given to indicate what forms may be devised and those materials and records that should prove useful.

1. *The achievement record form.* It should prove useful to the child, above the primary level, by having some record of his performance in particular areas. Administrative and teacher thinking should decide the scope and makeup of this particular form based on data from the central office. Current ideas of strengths and weaknesses of the child should become more significant as he moves through the grades.

2. *The autobiography form.* For the upper elementary school child, his written reactions about himself, according to some specified directions from the teacher, should prove helpful to him as he thinks about his interests, friendships, home life, group activities, likes and dislikes, and so on. The teacher is doubtless given useful guidance data which may be used wisely in conference to aid the pupil in his own self-appraisal.

3. *The class attitude form.* Children need to look realistically at their own attitudes in the way they adjust to the class and tackle their work.

Standardized tests may reveal how well the child is achieving at an expected level, but he should be giving attention to his own feelings outside
the test score area and consider his own attitudes and what he may need
to do to change them.

4. *Work samples.* The teacher helps the child to decide what work
and activity samples should be placed in the folder. This evidence can
be used to note progress in a definite, concrete way.

5. *The conference form.* A form should be devised which will help
the child to see what benefits were derived from the teacher-pupil conference. For example, the child may record what topics were discussed
and what steps he believes should be taken in light of suggestions and so
on. The teacher will find that much direction is needed at first to get
worthwhile reactions recorded.

6. *A check list or self-rating form.* An appropriate grade level criteria
of behavior should be worked out in advance by the group. Certain items
as cooperation, persistence, ability to face criticism, playing fair, responsibility, open-mindedness and so on are included. The child should be
able to write or talk about his own behavior, since the usual checking by
teachers on a report card means little to the child, who may not even be
aware of the implications of the word "persistence."

7. *The physical development form.* The records of health and physical growth and development may be of interest to children. In conjunction with the health and physical education personnel, the teacher may
cooperatively work out some possibilities in these areas which can be
used in the self-evaluation.

8. *The test score progress form.* Since teachers do give tests quite
frequently, it may be useful to keep some record form available that
apprises the child of his own progress. It is to be noted that his procedure can degenerate into a mechanical routine of test recording, but if
used wisely can give good results.

9. *The goal seeking form.* As children begin to discover their
strengths and weaknesses, they see a need to consider desirable goals
to be achieved. Thus, in a program of self-evaluation, the pupil is learning to identify and select meaningful goals. On this form, he may wish
to record the fact that his understanding of division by two-place numbers is fuzzy and to clarify this understanding now is his goal. To illustrate
this kind of self-evaluation, a realistic classroom situation is now presented:

Mrs. Meeks felt that her fifth grade class should begin a program of
self-evaluation. Since they had practically no experience in this venture,
she decided that the work in arithmetic could be handled more objectively
and she would "train" them more readily. Accordingly, she set about

finding out all she could about each child in terms of his past performance in other grades and achievement scores. After plotting the data, she felt she knew more about what each child could do and where he was at this particular time. Of course, to arrive at these ideas, she had used information other than just what had been accomplished in arithmetic. The administration was behind her in every respect. Then she worked out with the class some of the preliminary details. It took some explaining to get across the idea, but it was accomplished. Then, they went on to some definite goals to be accomplished. By examining the arithmetic text, they saw that at the present time they were dealing with reading charts, graphs, maps, and tables. These were special goals to be achieved. They even set up some criteria by which they could judge how well they were reading them. They were led to see that they could think through ways of improving their reading of these arithmetic skills and even how to go about it. Not only did they work as a class, but each child became interested in his own personal progress. It was interesting to see their interest and disappointments. But Mrs. Meeks was careful to schedule individual conferences. As they began to see their strengths and weaknesses in this area of arithmetic, they were encouraged to keep certain goals before them. It was difficult to get too much self-evaluation at first, but the teacher felt that this was a real start. She hoped to extend this process to other curriculum areas after a few months, and to widen the scope of the kind of self-evaluation forms being used. Of course, she was concerned with heightening the interest of the group and increasing their proficiencies in self-evaluation.

It is clear that the teacher at each grade level must decide what kind of forms are to be included within the folder of the child. The techniques will also vary. There may be a sense of frustration and futility as teachers begin pupil self-evaluation because progress is slow and painstaking. However, it is reasonable to believe that as children work with self-evaluation, beginning even in kindergarten, they will surely develop many skills even by the second and third grade levels. Thus, teachers should not find that using these devices is an overwhelming, impossible task; they need only to grasp the full possibilities of employing the techniques adapted to their needs and pupils' levels of maturity. It should be added that the teaching-learning situation may not only definitely be improved, but the pupil himself will develop skills and gain insight for solving his own problems.

THE TEACHER IMPROVES PRACTICES OF REPORTING PUPIL PROGRESS

The problem of reporting pupil growth, particularly to parents, is one that has caused school personnel to make many changes in their reporting practices in the past few years. The relevancy of this kind of evaluation to the curriculum is pointed out in these ways: first, the reporting system should cover the major areas of the curriculum; second, the teacher should be able to report progress clearly and adequately in each area of the curriculum; third, teachers should understand the reporting system in such ways that they can describe progress satisfactorily to parents; fourth, the reporting system should be accepted by the community as well as the school; fifth, the reporting system should reflect how well the child is progressing according to grade standards; and sixth, the reporting system should reflect how well the child is progressing according to his abilities. Thus, it is clear that reporting pupil progress has a definite relation with a curriculum design of the school.

If teachers are to be the most reliable agents for reporting child progress, they should have developed certain skills and abilties for this process. Therefore, the main purpose of this discussion is to help elementary school teachers to gain these skills by suggesting some patterns to be employed in reporting pupil progress. The following specific purposes are given to accomplish this major objective:

1. To help the teacher utilize certain preparational activities before writing the report or holding the conference.
2. To set up a pattern for writing the report or holding the conference.
3. To show how the letter-number type of report card may be improved.
4. To aid the teacher in personalizing any type of reporting device.
5. To furnish a check-list for teachers in looking over the finished product.

There are many kinds and combinations of reporting systems in use, but at least two major patterns furnish the beginning point of any reporting device. That is to say, a written or narrative account is made to furnish specific information regarding the child; or a planned parent-teacher interview is conducted to accomplish the same purposes. Second, a letter-grade or numerical designation is given to convey certain progress or growth concepts to the parent. Some schools use only one approach, or may attempt to combine the good features of each method of reporting. Although parents seem to prefer a more specific letter or number grade to indicate their child's standing within the class, the authors believe the teacher-parent-child conference is superior to any device used. However, general principles are offered which may be helpful both to teachers who must use a report card device as well as to those who may conduct the conference for evaluative purposes.[20]

What Preparational Activities Are Made by the Teacher Before Evaluating Child Progress?

Certain preparational activities by the teacher should benefit the evaluation of the child's progress, whether it is to be written or a conference is to be called. Some suggested activities are listed which aid the teacher in organizing the data:

1. Read professional material on the subject of reporting. New ideas are constantly appearing in the professional literature which should deepen and enlarge one's insights.

2. Determine the needs and status of each child who is to be reported. Cumulative records are an excellent source of gaining new concepts about the child. Organized and systematic records of pupil samples, test scores, and standardized test data are kept and studied.

3. Keep anecdotal records. Observations may be made concerning work habits, special abilities and interests, the way the pupil relates himself to others, his way of expressing his attitudes, and his behavior changes as they occur from time to time.

4. Get acquainted with the home environment. The teacher has various ways of securing such insights; study records, visit the home, arrange informal conferences, use the telephone for a specific purpose, ask for parent comments and interpretations, visit during PTA and other functions, and arrange definite situations with the parents to gain understandings.

5. Talk with other persons about the child. It is true that other comments and interpretations may be inaccurate, but valuable information is often available from other people who know the child.

6. Know and define goal expectations of the child. An important preliminary activity is that of knowing those "norms" or expectations for each child. These are not to be considered as rigid and definite, but only as clues for understanding the child.

7. Begin to analyze the child's progress as an individual. At this stage, the teacher is beginning to consider some tentative things that may be included in the evaluation. The prepara-

---

[20] Wilson F. Wetzler, "Reporting Pupil Progress," *Grade Teacher*, 76 (April, 1959), 20-1 ff.

tional activities have been contributing data and insights that should assist in completing the final report based on evidence and understandings.

What Pattern May Guide the Teacher Either in Writing the Report or Conferring with the Parent?

It is clear that all collected data contribute to the reporting process. However, four principles emerge that should guide the teacher in the evaluation of the child. (1) The report should reflect his background; (2) the report should point out his abilities; (3) the report should indicate his achievement in relation to standards or norms for his grade level; and (4) the report should provide a basis for continuing cooperation between parents and teacher as they provide for the educational needs of the child.

In order to satisfy the requirements stated by these principles, there are two approaches that may be utilized by the teacher. First, a pattern for reporting progress should show achievement that is *above, on* or *below* grade level standards in terms of: (a) The skills, abilities to be acquired, and knowledge to be learned. The emphasis here is upon the acquisition of certain basic skills, attitudes, appreciations, facts, and understandings from the viewpoint of actually "learning something." (b) Using effectively certain materials as learning progresses. In this respect, there are books to be read, spelling lists to be covered, maps and charts to be learned, resource materials to become familiar with to determine how well the child is learning to use these tools or materials of instruction. (c) The standardized and teacher-made tests. Many test scores help to show the above-or-below grade level perspective needed for the total picture of child progress.

Comments. In this first pattern of reporting pupil progress, the teacher learns to assay progress in light of grade level standards or norms. It is obvious that teachers must know what is expected at each grade level if they are to use state and local curriculum guides. There must be no doubt about the fact that it is impossible for *each child to be at grade level in achievement.* Secondly, if teachers believe that not every child can attain the grade level standards, then progress must be analyzed in light of his background and abilities. It follows that achievement should indicate where the child is: above or below his ability level in terms of the three categories described as skills, abilities, effective use of materials of learning, and certain individual test scores of various kinds. Both group and individual analyses are made to show how well the child is doing in light of group norms, and more particularly what he is doing in terms of his own capacities. In every instance, the teacher needs personal data about the child, scholarship records, health and physical fitness information, educational and vocational experiences, general school relationships data, intelligence and achievement test scores, personality data, special abilities, aptitudes, interests, and creative abilities data.

Comments. In the second pattern of reporting progress, the individual emphasis poses no easy task and is subject to criticism should the teacher fail to assemble sufficient supporting data. It is difficult at best to know whether or not the child is performing above or below his capabilities. It is then necessary for the instructor to look beyond the confines of her own classroom to secure a complete picture of the total educational program. One should know the child's previous experiences, as well as understanding what is expected in the school years ahead of the child. Still, the emphasis must be upon a valid, objective analysis of the individual child's ability level to determine where the child belongs on *his scale* of ability by using many, varied ways of assembling data about him. For example, Arthur receives a low grade in language arts. If both patterns of reporting his progress are employed, there would be some indication of his capacity output. Certainly he may well deserve a low grade, but a progress report should uncover factors other than a mere score or letter grade. Each pattern should complement the other in that every child is not expected to be *on* grade level either by group standards or individual ability. However, an evaluation should consider both approaches, since the usual "grade" could mean several things, none of which may be precisely clear.

How Does the Teacher Improve Upon the Letter-Number Reporting?

Since teachers are often required to give either a letter or a percentage number on a report card, some suggestions are now offered which may supplement that kind of reporting:

1. Include on the report card either space or a checklist that will indicate the progress of the pupil in such areas as personal and social habits of adjustment, work habits and so on.
2. Reserve space for teacher-parent comments.
3. List the subject areas and show a grade that indicates (a) the child's actual achievement and how well he is meeting grade standards; and (b) the child's performance according to ability. For example, a C in arithmetic in column one tells what he has achieved, but a B in column two suggests he can do better and should be encouraged to do so. The B grade is not actually

an evaluative mark, but it serves to give more meaning to the achievement grade in column one.

4. Be prepared to support the grades given in each column for each subject by having detailed evidence in a cumulative folder.

5. Encourage the use of pupil self-evaluation devices to lend further support and meaning to the two-grade approach.

How Does the Teacher Personalize the Report Card or the Parent Conference?

Up to this point, the teacher may feel that enough time and effort have been devoted to evaluation of progress. Yet parents are interested in securing as much information about their child and the class work as is possible to give. The teacher may wish to organize some evaluative. material either for conference or for mimeographed distribution several times during the school year. (1) Indicate what have been the centers of interest and write in the child's particular emphasis, or lack of it. (2) Describe the class units of work briefly. (3) Tell about certain group activities such as field trips, research projects, creative and special projects, experiments, demonstrations, and so on. (4) Point out any highlights during the year; the new processes introduced, new skills learned, the kinds of tests taken, etc. (5) Discuss any certain academic achievements of the group. (6) List the common learnings of the group, such as: attitudes, values, habits, leadership, getting along with each other, and the like. (7) Present some facts about the self-evaluation process.

A mimeographed report could be drawn up in brief terminology that would supplement the report card or conference. Pertinent notes could also be inserted to point out the child's role under particular items which give the report an even more personalized touch.

How Does the Teacher Check Up on the Finished Product?

If the progress report is to be written or talked over with the parents, the teacher can find the following criteria useful in determining how thorough and complete a job has been done:

1. Does the evaluation show specifically and clearly the pupil's relative standing in academic subjects for his particular grade level?

2. Does the analysis of progress and achievement reflect the relationships to ability as well as to grade standards?

3. Is there a mention of individual and group participation in school activities and how these are carried out? Any suggestions or recommendations?

4. Is there an analysis made of work habits and attitudes?
5. Are significant aspects of physical, social, mental, and emotional developments discussed with reference to what the school is doing to further the child's progress, together with what the home may do?
6. Is there specific information regarding special abilities, interests, and so on in terms of above-or-below grade level achievement? Any reference to what the school is doing to promote progress? What the home is doing?
7. Is there a report and interpretation of certain achievement and other test scores, clearly and sufficiently stated for parental consumption?
8. Does the teacher offer, if she is in a position to do so, specific evidence to support an evaluation made of child progress?
9. Is the language appropriate, grammatically correct, and neat appearing, if written?

In summary, there are two major patterns for reporting pupil progress: (1) a carefully planned and prepared written or oral account; (2) a letter-number grade with attempts to convey other significant aspects about the child. There are at least five factors that should be common to any type of evaluation of child progress: (1) an analysis or indication of the child's ability; (2) a background analysis; (3) an indication of achievement in relation to ability; (4) an indication of achievement in relation to standards for the grade level; (5) provision for continued cooperative effort by parents and teacher. It is important that the teacher prepare or collect information to validate the report of progress. The writing or discussion of the report should be well organized and thoughtfully done in light of definite guides or principles. Even the letter-number reporting systems can be improved upon. It is particularly useful to have some idea whether or not standards are being met—and how well—in relation to ability. Parents like a personalized account of class work since it gives meaning to the evaluation itself. Finally, teachers should have a checklist or criteria to gauge the finished product, as well as to use with parents and child. The instruments of evaluation are available if teachers will use them in organizing a more systematic kind of reporting system.

At this point, it may prove helpful to tie together the essential features of the marking or reporting process by presenting an illustration:

> The principal of the Main Street Elementary School was not convinced that the report cards sent home to parents were entirely adequate. No one seemed to be overly excited or concerned, but Mrs. Ruth was not content in allowing a poor situation to deteriorate even more. Consequently, she began to ask a few well placed questions among the staff and parents. It was not surprising to learn there was more dissatisfac-

tion than she had even thought would be present. They set to work on the problem.

One of the first steps was to study the Main Street situation. A committee took a long look at its procedures for reporting pupil progress in attempting to uncover: (a) how "up-to-date" they were, *viz.*, were they using well-proven devices; (b) how realistic they were with their reporting procedures; (c) how discerning were they in examining their procedures for making changes and improving their situation; (d) how "individualized" were they in dealing with each child, by not using the same approaches for each person, when special procedures for certain cases were needed. These were a few of the considerations given by the committee.

In due time, the Main Street Elementary School arrived at some definite purposes of evaluation which gave them direction in planning and organizing the educational work of the students. The main problem was, of course, the marking or reporting of pupil achievement, particularly in giving the parents some sort of accurate description of the way the child was progressing in school. It was agreed that the single letter grade or number (A, B, C, D, F, or 1, 2, 3, 4, 5) does not convey enough information. Such a mark simply cannot point out the student's needs, how he can improve, what the next steps for him would be, and a host of other items. The use of teacher-parent conferences or a detailed letter from the teacher were ruled out in favor of a report card. The majority of school and community personnel were not quite ready to abandon the traditional report card.

Mrs. Ruth helped her faculty to see the limitations of school marks, and they did take some forward steps in improving the marking system. First, it was agreed both teachers and parents want to know how the child has learned to read, to spell, to do arithmetic, and so on. They learned to think of marks as showing pupil development, instead of mere memorization or ability to repeat what was given by the teacher or learned in a meaningless way. It was no easy task to define these marks in terms of pupil growth, but it was obvious that teachers had to know each child and what his strengths and weaknesses were at the time he came for instruction. Thus, knowing what each child is like and why he is that way would help the teacher in guiding him to the fullest development of his ability. It meant that teachers could use certain achievement and aptitude tests in helping them in the evaluation process. For example, a score on the reading achievement test helped the teacher to see how well a child was doing, but it did not suggest how well he can perform. Then, aptitude tests may be given to suggest capacity, while the intelligence tests furnish a good guide to predict general school learning. The Main Street faculty came to know that tests must be used cautiously and that a combination or battery of tests are needed in making evaluations about the abilities, aptitudes, or even personality of any child.

The new report card at Main Street School was not the final answer, but it served in a more practical way to give more information to the parents. This is what was accomplished. First, the faculty defined in terms of activities the kind of development expected of the child with regard to the various subjects to be studied and the basic skills to be acquired, including the so-called personality and citizenship growths. These were not included in detail on the report card, but the data were at least available for conferences with parent and child. Second, a letter or number grade had more meaning to teachers than previously. It was not possible again to place all of this data on a report card, but parents were told that the grade suggests the child's individual work and development. The faculty did not believe that they should send home certain standardized test scores on the report card, but they were better prepared to talk about whether the performance of the child was typical of the group or not. They were ready to compare the purposes of the school, its facilities, curriculum, and instructional procedures in general terms with that of so-called typical or norm groups. They were cautious about comparing a child's performance with his potential based on certain scores. At best, they were thinking of his work or performance according to his ability. In the general areas of personality and citizenship, there were marks given by the teacher.

Mrs. Ruth was somewhat more satisfied after a year's work on the reporting practices in the Main Street School. Actually, the report card retained much of its traditional look at first glance. There was a new design and additional features of citizenship and personality were included. Most significantly, she knew that the school staff were more definite in their thinking and gave marks that indicated how well the child was performing, not only according to grade standards, but in terms of his individual growths as well. There was the comforting knowledge that teachers were able to talk more intelligently to parents and tell them what they really wanted to know, and that notes sent home helpfully supplemented the report card. It was resolved that continuous study would be given to this important problem, and more efforts on pupil self-evaluation in the classroom were to be made.

How May the Teacher Consider the Problem of Promoting the Pupil?

All teachers must at one time or another make a decision as to whether a pupil is to be retained and repeat the year's work, or be allowed to go on to the next grade. It is obvious that teachers face this question when they believe that a child, for various reasons, is not prepared to do the work expected of him in the next higher grade.

Caswell and Foshay[21] have presented an excellent array of convincing statements, based on research, that non-promotion practices are not based on any consistent, agreed-upon principles. Furthermore, they

---

[21] H. L. Caswell and A. W. Foshay, *Education in the Elementary School* (3rd ed.; New York: American Book Co., 1957), Chapter 13.

found no consistent relationship between the level of achievement of the student and non-promotion. That is, too few cases are recorded which show that children who are low in achievement have been promoted, while those of higher achievement have been retained. Additional false assumptions underlying non-promotion maintain:

—that higher achievement standards are possible
—that instruction is made easier by insuring a more even distribution of achievement ability in a given class
—that pupils work harder and achieve more
—that society is protected from having the so-called educated persons thrust upon them

Since evidence seems to disprove the popular notion that non-promotion has real value if rigorously practiced, teachers should be extremely cautious in rendering a decision to retain a pupil for a repetition of a year's work. In a recent study,[22] the policy of having regular promotion indicated that the number of retarded readers will actually be reduced. Thus, there is no lack of research evidence to suggest that even though *some* students do profit by repeating a grade, most pupils will not improve, while actually a few will even do poorer work. Teachers may find these guiding principles helpful in making decisions about promotion or non-promotion:

1. Survey and study each child's situation. Policies about non-promotion should generally serve as guides, but the school may or may not have defined them clearly or adequately. In every respect, the teacher needs to do research and hold conferences with all persons involved. The research should be made along the lines of securing the child's mental, emotional, academic, social and physical data. Conferences with teachers, parents, and other school personnel should both supplement this data and shed further light on the child. Thus, interpretations about what the child has accomplished and why he has failed to accomplish significantly during the year's work are made only in view of knowing a great deal about him.
2. Keep adequate records during the school year. Obviously, the teacher is in a better position to evaluate whether or not a child is to be promoted when evidence is kept systematically over a long period of time. Furthermore, teachers should begin early in the school year to discover potential failures, if for no other reason than to inform parents of the possibility.

---

[22] W. F. Hall, "Effect on Achievement Scores of a Change in Promotional Policy," *Elementary School Journal*, 58 (January, 1958), 204.

3. Recognize the potential failure in a positive way. A corollary to the second item above is the fact that teachers should take steps to prevent the failure before the end of the school year. By working with the child and the parent, it may be possible to overcome certain problems by providing skillful, adequate help. Then, a final decision may be based not only upon evidence of the child's work, but by personal knowledge from having worked closely with a potential failure.

4. Make all decisions in light of sound principles of child development. Having studied the individual child, kept adequate records and worked in a "preventive" way with him, the teacher tries to bring all of this data to bear upon what is really best for the child in the long run. If the teacher believes that there is actually evidence pointing to the fact that non-promotion cannot be practiced in a strict, uncompromising fashion, then, armed with data concerning the child in question, the teacher may decide that the best educational opportunities may favor moving the child ahead in his educational career. If not, the teacher is convinced he will make more progress by repeating the grade. In any case, when teachers have freedom in designing the curriculum for the individual student, perhaps the day is not too far distant when problems of promotion will be matters of pure academic curiosity, since children will be facing those learning experiences that are designed for them, and progress at a rate suitable for them—there is literally no failure according to the traditional use of the term.

EVALUATION IS USED TO IMPROVE THE EDUCATIONAL ENVIRONMENT AND CURRICULUM

The main concern of the classroom teacher in evaluation is that of working with the child to lead him to realize his maximum potentialities. The discussion up to now has helped to contribute certain understandings about evaluation; to suggest specific evaluative instruments; to discuss how pupil self-evaluation is organized, administered, and recorded; and to show how reporting practices can be improved upon. There are several aspects of evaluation which deserve the attention of the teacher: How does the teacher contribute to the over-all evaluation program of the school? How can the teacher work more effectively with the community in evaluation? What are some trends in evaluation that have special emphasis for the curriculum and the teacher? These three questions constitute the purposes and framework for this final section. It should be added that discussions of these questions are relevant to the area of the curriculum of the elementary school. By contributing to the evaluation program of the school, teachers may assist in curriculum revisions. By working more effectively in evaluation with the community, teachers and parents learn many things about the child, and can plan better curriculum experiences.

How Does the Teacher Contribute to the Evaluation Program of the School?

An educational environment for the child will promote growth and development and will enable him to participate in our democratic way of life. Teachers are in a position to assist in periodic evaluations of the school's educational objectives and its efforts as they are influencing the child. Specifically, the most significant task, and where the teacher makes the greatest contribution in evaluation, is in the improvement of classroom performance. Therefore, there need to be understandings of classroom environments and the interacting learning processes in which children engage. Further, the teacher can evaluate how well a classroom environment and the learning process are being experienced by the child.

There are other specific ways in which the teacher can contribute to the evaluation program of the school and these are now summarized:

1. The teacher helps to define certain issues, raises questions, clarifies purposes, and identifies problems. This approach by a staff member in the elementary school keeps both administrators and faculty personnel alert to new needs and clearer thinking.
2. The teacher needs to think in terms of particular educational values. As a faculty member begins to consider those activities of value in a given classroom, it is evident that such thinking may well lead to over-all improvements.
3. The teacher can use cooperative self-evaluation to solve common problems. The sharing of ideas by individuals leads to an evaluation of ideas and activities.
4. The teacher seeks to understand the problems of the principal and other school personnel. Such an awareness of and attitude toward other's problems should generate group-directed activity along evaluative lines of endeavor. Thus, the teacher is helping to bring about changes in policy and in behavior to improve the over-all educational program. Perhaps a stimulated concern for the school and its program of effectiveness may result. Finally, teachers help one another to develop skills in using the techniques of evaluation which should contribute to the total growth within the school and community.

How Can the Teacher Work More Effectively with the Community in Evaluation?

It has been suggested that the community gains its greatest understandings of the school through the child, and the teacher may be considered the most effective interpreter of the school in many respects. It is conceded that the community constantly evaluates the school and the effectiveness of its program as parents see the school through the experiences of children.

Teachers should be interested in learning about the expectations parents have of their children. They need to inform them more accurately and frequently of the changes of behavior they have observed in the child. The questionnaire can be used to secure more objective opinions from the parent. Above all, teachers must be clear and definite in translating to the parent the teaching-learning situation and the results as indicated in the behavior of the child. Suggestions are now offered as guiding principles to the teacher who may wish to make this kind of contribution to community evaluation of the school: Involve the parents in every conceivable, useful way. Committees may be formed for specific purposes, parents can be used in experimental projects, as resource persons, for special help days, and so on. Parents who are called upon to make a contribution to the educational program learn about what is going on. Thus, the teacher can call upon such individuals who can really make evaluate judgments based upon definite understandings. In addition, the teacher may profit from this relationship as well as aiding in the translating of the educational program to the community.

What Are Some Trends in Evaluation That Have Implications for the Teacher and the Curriculum?

If emphasis in the past has been upon the acquisition of factual knowledge as the child is confronted with curricular experiences, the concern today should go even beyond that concept. Children must be proficient in the basic skills, secure knowledge or facts, develop attitudes and understandings and the like, but the teacher should consider another role as well: she is an evaluator of what is happening to the child as he involves himself in the process, and a designer of a curriculum that will recognize many aspects of child growth and development. It must be stated clearly that children are expected to learn facts and knowledge, but there must be understandings or meanings as well as development of abilities to interpret and apply what is learned. Thus, there must be an added emphasis upon evaluation by both teacher and pupil that points out what is to be learned, how well it is being learned, and what improvements may bring about better results.

The teacher may find the following statements suggestive of trends in educational evaluation that are also indicative of realistic goals to be achieved in the modern classroom. Teachers should discover:

—how the individual child approaches the curriculum in his own way
—the effective skills of presenting and arranging learning experiences in light of (teacher) personality factors, readiness, motivations, and the like
—which kind of individual studies help to reveal the make-up of the child
—more about the child through the projective techniques that are available, but require specialized training for use and application
—those resources and aids that enhance the curriculum and teaching

Obviously, this list of generalized trends could be extended to protray the increased emphasis that is to be given to the role of evaluation in the classroom. Teachers must be primarily interested in discovering what is happening to the child as a result of his having certain curricular experiences. The use of evaluative devices should give teachers better understandings of what is happening to the child, and assist in planning better ways of meeting his needs.

SUMMARY

Teachers and administrators may find that a sound evaluative program within the school contributes both to an improvement of curriculum design, teaching practices, and to the answering of community questioning of the school's educational program and its achievement. A comprehensive evaluation program gives support for following certain educational practices and points the way toward improved changed behavior for teacher, administrator, child and parent. Thus, evaluation is considered to be the making of valid judgments plus using the measurement approach in defining school objectives or those behavioral changes desired for the child, and in identifying and providing those learning experiences that insure such behaviors. These are the approaches to be used by the teacher in evaluation. She begins with a philosophy that evaluation can help in knowing what the child may do during the year, and can point up his difficulties, uncover his assets, reveal his achievements, and provide better ways of improving upon past performance. To implement these tenets of philosophy an evaluative guide for the teacher includes: (1) the establishing of criteria of behavior expected of the child; (2) the collecting of data to see what is happening to the child; (3) the interpreting of data; and (4) the planning of a course of action in light of data.

The teacher has many evaluative instruments that aid in appraising learning situations, the child, and his progress. The varied use of these tools should contribute information to the teacher who is responsible for analyzing growth and designing better ways of helping the child to achieve.

Pupil self-evaluation is emphasized as a means of helping children to make decisions concerning many phases of their behavior. Suggestions are offered to aid the teacher in organizing, administering, and recording pupil self-evaluations. According to grade level and maturity, such programs are set up to aid the pupil in developing skills and insight for solving his own problems.

The reporting of pupil progress can be improved upon. Consistent with the philosophy of evaluation described in this chapter, the teacher begins first to carry out certain preparational activities before the actual evaluation of the child is made. In addition to this important activity, the teacher is offered the following guides for reporting pupil progress: a pattern for writing the report or holding the conference; ways of improving the letter-number type of report card; a personalizing of the reporting device; and finally, a suggested checklist for looking over the finished product.

Teachers can and must contribute to the improvement of the educational environment and program. Some specific ways in which teachers can make these contributions are summarized. Then, their evaluative role in community affairs is discussed, with some concluding remarks about the trends in evaluation with implications for teaching. Evaluation as a process is both complex and necessary if the child is to be understood, the program to be judged, and if improved teaching practices are to emerge.

SUGGESTED ACTIVITIES AND PROBLEMS

1. Examine the various evaluative approaches discussed in this chapter in light of getting class members to investigate what various surrounding schools are doing along these lines.

2. Show how the four beliefs under the philosophy of evaluation section are relevant to the curriculum of the elementary school.

3. Use the eight suggested instruments of evaluation beginning on page 474 as the basis for assigning topics for research and discussion, either by groups or selected students. The discussion then may center around this outline: (1) the purposes of the instrument; (2) how used; (3) some actual reporting of uses and results, either from research studies or by investigations from nearby schools. However, students should be free to set up their own pattern for reporting their thinking and reactions concerning each of the eight instruments.

4. Discuss the pupil self-evaluation approach. Have some students investigate: (1) Where such an approach may be used and with what criticism and results. Also report the kind of plan in operation, (2) What teachers think of the plan. Students should conduct interviews of teachers if possible. *Note:* The instructor may invite student comments particularly to get students to find weaknesses and disadvantages in certain situations. Have suggested ways of overcoming these weaknesses brought out.

5. Arrange two teams of students to debate the problem of reporting pupil progress as mentioned in this chapter. Further, examine the different reporting systems being used and compare them in light of the stated ideas here.

6. Have the group summarize the problems of evaluation. Use the final section as a focus for securing opinions as to what class members personally expect to do as teachers in a new situation or upon returning to an established position.

7. Divide the class into grade-level teams and have them investigate the evaluative activities of their given grade as practiced in nearby elementary schools. Summary reports should be made in class with total class participation. This should be a realistic and helpful experience.

SELECTED READINGS

Blanchard, B. E. "The Meaning of Evaluation in Education," *National Association of Secondary School Principals Bulletin*, 40 (May, 1956), 39-45.

Bleismer, E. P. "Using and Achieving Achievement Test Results," *Education*, 77 (March, 1957), 391-94.

Boag, A. K. "Standardized Tests: How, Why, When," *Instructor*, 65 (October, 1955), 24.

Boykin, L. L. "What is Evaluation," *Progressive Education*, 34 (January, 1957), 16-18.

Brueckner, L. J. "Diagnosis as a Basis for Further Learning in the Fundamentals," *American Business Education Yearbook* (1955), 42-55.

DeLong, A. R. "Emotional Effects of Elementary School Testing," *Understanding the Child*, 24 (October, 1955), 103-07.

Ebel, R. L. "Using Tests for Evaluation," *National Elementary Principal*, 35 (December, 1955), 29-31.

Engelhart, M. D. "Testing and the Use of Test Results," *Review of Educational Research*, 26 (February, 1956), 5-13.

Hansen, A. F. "How the Teacher Collects and Uses Evidence," *Educational Leadership*, 13 (April, 1956), 430-34.

Jordan, Thomas E. *The Exceptional Child.* Columbus, Ohio: Charles E. Merrill Publishing Co., 1962.

Kirk, S. A. *Educating Exceptional Children.* Boston: Houghton Mifflin Company, 1963.

Kooker, E. W. and C. S. Williams. "Standards Versus Evaluation," *Educational Administration and Supervision*, 41 (November, 1955), 385-89.

Kropp, R. P. "Evaluation Promotes Understanding of the Total School Program," *School Review*, 63 (November, 1955), 446-47.

Noll, Victor H. *Introduction to Educational Measurement.* Boston: Houghton Mifflin Company, 1957, Chapters 10-14.

Parson, G. E. "Readiness for School," *Elementary School Journal*, 57 (February, 1957), 272-75.

Raths, L. E. "The Role of Evaluation in Research Design," *Educational Leadership*, 13 (April, 1956), 412-14.

Rothney, W. M. "What Research Says to the Teacher," Washington: N. E. A., Department of Classroom Teachers, American Educational Research Association, No. 7, 1955.

Strang, Ruth. "Reporting Pupil Progress," *The School Executive*, 72 (August, 1953), 49.

Thomas, R. Murray. *Judging Student Progress.* New York: Longmans, Green and Company, 1954.

Thurston, E. L. "The Teacher and Personality Assessment," *Education*, 77 (March, 1957), 414-17.

Trow, W. C. "When Are Children Ready to Learn?" *NEA Journal*, 44, (February, 1955), 78-9.

CHAPTER 15

Organized Guidance
Contributes to the
Emerging Curriculum

INTRODUCTION

The future success of any individual, regardless of the criteria for measuring it, may depend upon the quality of the instructional program in the elementary school. If each child is to be given the opportunity to achieve the maximum inself-realization, then no curriculum design would be complete without a recognition of the place and function of guidance in the plan. The American elementary schools have not kept pace with the secondary schools in recognizing guidance as a major function of the school. Although secondary schools have not achieved the desired level of operation in guidance, the major accrediting agencies have insisted upon some evidence of an organized program of guidance in secondary schools if accrediting standards are to be met. However, none of these agencies, to date, has insisted upon any standards for the elementary schools which send their pupils to the high schools.

Educators have been writing for decades advocating that teachers have the responsibility for developing each pupil to the extent of his mental, physical, social and emotional potential. In recent years, some evidence has appeared which indicates that school boards and school administrators are beginning to recognize the need for guidance to become a functional aspect of elementary education. Teachers need to understand the distinctive traits and characteristics of children in order that curriculum experiences will produce the desired result—maximum growth for each child.

Krugman aptly stated the case for more adequate guidance services than are currently available in the elementary school when he wrote,

"Life doesn't begin at age fourteen."[1] A functional guidance program in the elementary school helps eliminate many of the personal and social problems of child adjustment. Many of these currently go unresolved until either the child is old enough to drop out of school or the problem has persisted so long that the secondary school personnel are faced with a severe handicap in trying to aid the child.

It will be the purpose of this chapter to relate guidance to the elementary school through consideration of its unique function in elementary teaching. Guidance will be related to the emerging design for elementary curriculum through a recognition of the complementary relationship of of guidance and teaching. Pupil personnel practices which affect the curriculum design will be discussed in detail. The role of the classroom teacher will be considered as it relates to guidance and curriculum modification.

GUIDANCE IN THE ELEMENTARY SCHOOL

What Is Guidance?

There are many misconceptions of guidance activities which may be due in part to earlier concepts which viewed guidance as basically a vocational endeavor. To aid the reader in understanding the guidance concepts of the authors, this definition is presented. Guidance activities may be thought of as *all those experiences which the child has under the direction of the school which assist him in realizing his potential to become a self-directed individual.*[2]

The comprehensive nature of this definition suggests that guidance is not a separate supplementary service offered by the school. It envisions guidance as an active, integral part of the learning experiences which the child undergoes through a curriculum design which is based upon a recognition of the inherent nature of growth and development of children.

What Is the Function of Guidance?

The paramount function of guidance is developmental in nature. This is not meant to deny the corrective aspect of guidance, but elementary school guidance should work toward preventing certain needless waste of a child's life by providing a curriculum design which envisions guidance

---

[1] Morris Krugman, "Why Guidance in Our Elementary School?" *Personnel and Guidance Journal*, 32 (July, 1954), 270.
[2] Albert H. Shuster and Wilson F. Wetzler, *Leadership in Elementary School Administration and Supervision* (Boston: Houghton Mifflin Company, 1958), p. 274.

as being compatible with instruction. Poor educational adjustment, emotional adjustment and social adjustment in addition to health and physical needs should loom in the forefront as possible areas which elementary school guidance should attack.

Gordon summarizes the functional meanings of guidance in the following five points:

1. Guidance is the organization of information by the school about the child and his community for the purpose of helping the child learn to make wise decisions concerning his own future.
2. Guidance is the organization of life experiences within the school situation so that the child is provided with situations in which he feels completely accepted, in which he is enabled to "take stock" of his potentialities, accept his limitations without threat, and develop a realistic picture of himself and the world around him.
3. Guidance is the provision for satisfactory group experiences in which successful leadership and membership roles are learned and in which the group is able to set goals and solve problems dealing with interpersonal relations.
4. Guidance is the provision of opportunities for the child to understand and value his uniqueness and his relatedness to others.
5. Guidance is the provision of the above experiences and opportunities for all children.[3]

It should become clear that the teacher is the focal point in any guidance program. The extent to which guidance functions will be translated into meaningful learnings which will aid the child in growing toward maturity depends upon the understanding the teacher has of her role in the program.

What Is a Philosophy of Guidance for the Teacher?

Guidance in the elementary school has largely been the product of the classroom teacher. Research investigations have indicated that about 35 percent of the nation's elementary schools employ some specialists to give direction to their guidance programs.[4] However, no program of guid-

---

[3] Ira J. Gordon, *The Teacher as a Guidance Worker* (New York: Harper & Row, Publishers, 1956), pp. 3-5.

[4] S. C. Huslander, "Assisting Youth Adjustment in Elementary Schools," *Personnel and Guidance Journal*, 32 (March, 1954), 392-94.

ance can be successful without the classroom teacher understanding both the role of the specialists and that of the teacher. If a guidance point of view is to give direction to the guidance program the specialists must view their role as one which aids the classroom teacher in becoming more effective. At the same time the teacher must recognize that because of limited training in the more specialized areas of guidance, her effectiveness is dependent to a large extent upon the assistance which can be rendered by the specialists. However, the effectiveness of the specialists may be limited by the failure of the classroom teacher to furnish certain pertinent data essential to the work of the specialists. Thus, *a philosophy of guidance must recognize the complementary roles of the teacher and specialists.* Essential for all guidance workers is the basic premise which brings these people into a teamwork approach. This premise is the desire by all to help the child make better adjustments in and out of school in the areas of educational, social, emotional, and physical growth.

Guidance efforts evolve from a recognition of the differences in pupils. Children grow, develop and mature at different rates and with different patterns of growth. These differences have been found to produce vast divergences in the ability of children to learn. A philosophy of guidance for the teacher must consider these differences as the basic educational need in giving assistance to all pupils. Guidance should aid the child in accomplishing his potential as he grows from childhood to manhood. This is not to be construed to mean that the child is preparing for the first fifteen or twenty years of his life to learn how to live, but that he is living as fully as he knows how during each stage of growth. Thus he moves continuously toward maturity. In summary, the teacher must develop a philosophy which recognizes her key position as it relates to guiding pupils into those enriching experiences which will enhance the development of each pupil toward self-direction as his potential unfolds.

What Is the Relationship Between Guidance and the Curriculum?

The curriculum has previously been defined in this book as being *all the experiences the child has under the direction of the school, including the child's interaction with and reaction to these experiences.* It is evident that this definition goes beyond what is frequently misrepresented by educators and lay people alike when they name subjects as the curriculum. They are thinking in terms of the school's offerings or a program of studies, but all children do not have or experience the same curriculum. This fact means that children do not "interact" or "react" in the same way to the same experience. Therefore, it cannot be assumed that all children are going to achieve the same things from a given classroom. The teacher accepts the responsibility for setting the standards of her teaching, but if she is cognizant of the differences of children, these standards become variable. When the teacher sets standards, she utilizes a vast amount of knowledge which she must secure so that Howard, who is a bright lad, is sufficiently challenged and Jean, who is average in ability, is also challenged. Each child is challenged within the range of his ability to be successful. Thus guidance and instruction are inseparable since the teacher should be the person who is able to see the need for adjustment in learning activities. Stiffening the challenge for Howard and lessening it for Jean requires the teacher to be flexible in her instructional procedures and at the same time to understand the problems faced by both children. Then, the teacher's task is to collect information and to discover as much as possible about each child.[5] In this way modifications are made in the curriculum which result in more effective living and learning for each child.

Guidance and the emerging curriculum. The emerging curriculum is based upon the compatible role of the teacher in carrying out the guidance function. Any curriculum design for the last half of the twentieth century must be projected on a premise that points the way for examining those designs which will facilitate both learning and guidance.

The traditional pattern of curriculum organization with separate subjects and yearly promotions may be a handicap even to the guidance-minded teacher. When the teacher can see the children functioning in normal situations over long periods of time, she comes to recognize the patterns of adjustments which the children are making. Since adjustment is often slow and takes place over a long period of time, a curriculum design which establishes blocks of time, such as the "primary block" which is being utilized increasingly in school systems, seems to offer a possible solution. This pattern may suggest some of the next steps in elementary school organization. In this type of program children are kept with the same teacher for a period of two or three years. Thus children are carefully studied by the same teacher who, because of her longer association with the children, is in a better position to render guidance as needed. Such innovations as team teaching can contribute to providing time for the professional team to study the particular needs of certain children. In this way they may be spared the failure complex by moving through the three year block rather than failing in the first grade.[6]

---

[5] See Chapter 13 for a discussion about techniques for studying children.

[6] Current investigations reveal that the first grade is the place in the elementary school where more children are retained than any other single grade.

A child for many reasons may make slow progress during his initial year in school, but may during the second or third year actually spurt to a very acceptable achievement level. This acceleration is facilitated by the teacher when the child is in the primary block, since the teacher is able to know the stages of readiness and the needed incentives to further the child's learning progress. The maturing process is recognized as an irregular pattern which through a longer and closer association with the teacher may be understood. *Some preliminary observations of an instructional team working with a group of second year pupils (first graders) indicates that the team is better able to help a single child when all team members observe and study the child.*

The primary block seems to offer optimum circumstances for implementing guidance and instruction as interrelated components of curriculum; experience can be modified or adjusted to meet identified needs, whether they be individual or group. The desire to provide instruction which will consider the individual differences of children has long been given lip service by educators. In recent years lay citizens have also become conscious of this instructional goal. Teachers and administrators who understand the values inherent in organizing not only the primary block, but the other elementary grades as well, into longer periods of time will be better able to explain this to parents.

Perhaps the greatest handicap in "block" organization of grades in the elementary school is teacher attitude. Teachers who have taught the same grade for years are reluctant to make the necessary adjustment of staying with the same group for two or three years. Obviously, there is also the undesirable factor of subjecting children to a poor teacher for long periods of time. However, school boards, administrators and the profession, all have a responsibility in up-grading the quality of instruction. Even one year is too long to subject children to a poor teacher.

What Are Some Guides for the Teacher in Guidance?

The extent to which the teacher understands the basic guidance function and the related instructional function of her classroom activities will bear directly upon the effectiveness of the way the teacher's role is carried out. That is, in the course of a school day the teacher makes many decisions, she reflects many attitudes, she directs numerous activities and a host of other things, all of which make some impression upon the young learners. The teacher needs to see the inter-relationships between the many activities which she performs and the teaching-learning situation. Inconsistencies on the part of the teacher, an inbalance in the curriculum, too many curriculum experiences for some children and not enough for others are all related to the decision-making process of the teacher. Thus the teacher who seeks to render a guidance function as she teaches should carefully orient herself to the following guideposts.

1. A teacher who effectively integrates guidance with classroom teaching knows that all children face a variety of adjustment problems in the normal course of growing up and that it is in the resolution of these problems that all children need guidance.
2. A teacher who effectively integrates guidance with classroom teaching knows that children of the same chronological age are at different levels of readiness for a given learning experience.
3. A teacher who effectively integrates guidance with classroom teaching is skillful in gathering and using the data needed to determine readiness.
4. A teacher who effectively integrates guidance with his classroom teaching knows that success in school work is intimately related to the way a child conceives himself as a human being and to the emotional satisfaction he is achieving in his relationships with others.
5. A teacher who effectively integrates guidance with his classroom teaching knows that children learn many things within a given context, and plans with reference to the whole constellation of possible wholesome learnings.
6. A teacher who effectively integrates guidance with his classroom teaching appreciates that the true measure of his success is the degree to which children come to understand themselves more fully and to direct themselves more wisely.
7. A teacher who effectively integrates guidance with his classroom teaching is able to accept diversity "in stride" and to retain perspective in spite of confusing variations in pupil behavior.[7]

It should become clear after reading the above guides that teaching effectiveness is largely related to the guidance function in the learning process. The focal point is that teachers must adequately fortify themselves with profound understandings and knowledge of child development.

PUPIL PERSONNEL POLICIES AND THE CURRICULUM

Teachers are in a unique situation to help shape the policies which affect children and learning. The advent of cooperative approaches to

---

[7] Association for Supervision and Curriculum Development, *Guidance in the Curriculum* (Washington, D. C.: The Association, Department of the National Education Association, 1955), pp. 14-25.

policy development in school administration has more closely related the classroom teacher to the administrator in a positive way. Although there are still far too many schools being administered by autocratic administrators with little or no regard for the feelings of teachers, great strides are being made in the direction of permitting teachers to share in making decisions which affect them. For example, in 1951, Chase,[8] in an investigation of over 200 school systems involving 1184 teachers, found that job satisfaction was related to the quality of leadership exhibited by administrators. Teachers in this study related participation in policy making for grouping, promoting and controlling of pupils and participation in curriculum making as important factors in job satisfaction. This is indicative of the need for teachers to make decisions relative to such matters based upon the best available information. Pupil personnel matters are guidance factors which have a direct bearing in most instances upon the curriculum. Therefore, these policies reflect certain values which the school imposes upon society as well as values which the society exerts upon the school. An examination of some of the pupil personnel policies should help the prospective teacher or in-service teacher to recognize how such policies affect the curriculum and the children.

What Is the Teaching-Guidance Function as Related to Curriculum?

A good pupil-personnel program is built around a sound guidance program. Since most areas of pupil-personnel are directly related to the classroom teacher, it becomes imperative that the teacher not shirk her responsibility in the sharing of policy making. In this way the teacher, who is the educator closest to the pupils, can see that policies are formulated which will enhance rather than hinder her efforts at producing curriculum experiences for pupils based upon guidance. What are some of these areas of pupil-personnel practices of which the teacher needs to be informed? Some of these are:

1. Educational placement of pupils
2. Establishing school standards
3. Marking practices
4. Promotion and retention policies
5. Grouping practices
6. Discipline and punishment
7. Extra-class activities

---

[8] Francis S. Chase, "Factors for Satisfaction in Teaching," *Phi Delta Kappan*, 33 (November, 1951), 128.

Obviously this list is not all-inclusive, but it is believed that these areas are of major importance to the classroom teacher as they affect the relationship of instruction and guidance. Therefore, a brief discussion of each of these pupil-personnel areas will be presented, emphasizing the common practices and the effect of certain practices on structuring the teaching-learning process.

Educational placement of pupils. The procedures which determine the educational placement of pupils directly affect the teaching process. Teachers need to be aware of the vast array of problems which arise from pupil placement policies. The most common practice of pupil placement is that which begins at the time the child starts school. The mode practiced in this respect is largely that of admittance according to some scheme of chronological age. Many states have established laws which state that all children between the ages of 6 and 16 must be in school attendance. Supplementing such laws are practices by local school systems of admitting children to first grade if they reach six years of age by November 15, or some such date. In New York State, a child who is admitted to kindergarten or first grade in a private or public school at any age must be accepted by another school if the child moves into the district, even though their policy regarding age is different from that school which the child first attended. The disparity in ages of children would be even greater in situations where children are admitted to first grade if they will be six years of age by September 30. Even the latter plan means that there would be as much as one full year variance in chronological ages of children admitted to school under such a plan. Thus any plan which is based upon a single factor such as chronological age will result in wide variances in pupils. Therefore, it is important to recognize that emotional maturity, social maturity, physical maturity, and mental maturity are vital growth factors which are influenced differently at various chronological ages.

Another procedure for school admission is to admit children according to mental maturity. Although this practice is not prevalent, it is being used by some school systems in Ohio and other states, in addition to their practice of admitting children according to chronological age. That is, the policy may require a child to reach age six by September 30, but if a parent desires to enter a child before age six the child must have a certain mental maturity age as derived from a clinically administered psychological test.

It should become clearly evident that no reliable admission policy has yet been found. However, it has been suggested that a combination of factors which would include information related to current status of social, mental, emotional, and physical growth could be developed. This would mean that there would be even wider disparities in chronological age, but hypothetically the children would be more ready to pursue learning, even though the problem of educating parents to accept such a plan would be overwhelming. Nevertheless, there would also be differences due to many uncontrollable factors such as background of experience. Another limitation to such a plan would be that children who need certain readiness experiences provided for them in school probably would be the last ones to be admitted. Ideally then, the kindergarten may hold some children for longer periods of time and the primary block should alleviate other obstacles.

It should be quite evident that any plan for educational placement only emphasizes the need for teachers to be more guidance conscious. The teacher has the task of placement within the classroom, whether at grade one or grade eight. Placement within the classroom group requires much information. Anecdotal records, standardized test results, health records and the like, must all be accumulated and consulted, and every possible effort made to establish objective information which will facilitate pupil placement. Poor placement may result in poor educational achievement for a child through his entire schooling. Thus guidance and teaching become inseparable as the teacher seeks to prevent major problems which may reflect upon school adjustment or life adjustment.

Establishing school standards.   Beginning teachers, or teachers in service, will hear much about school standards. One should continuously appraise his own efforts in terms of either conscious or subconscious standards which prevail in the classroom, since the teacher determines these standards. What, then, are standards for elementary children?

Figure XXIII is a schematic attempt to help the teacher envision differences in pupils and relate them to the uniqueness of children. For ex-

FIGURE XXIII

Classroom Standards and Guidance
Standards Vary for Each Child

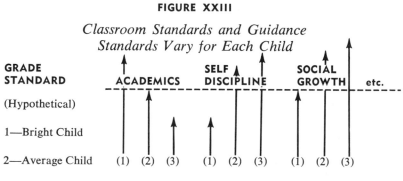

ample, child number one achieves at a high level in academic learnings, but has not achieved the hypothetical but desirable standard in self-discipline, and is barely reaching the standard in social adjustment. This may be contrasted with the extreme as illustrated for child number three.

Educational standards, or any other standards for that matter, cannot be established for every child. A teacher who is rendering guidance services as she teaches soon becomes aware of the many problems involved in setting a single standard for all pupils. As long as pupils are different (and the authors are under the impression that children will continue to come to school with growth patterns which are quite irregular) there cannot be a set standard to be achieved by all pupils at a given time. Standards must be established which will permit pupils to achieve them in their own way. Thus each child is challenged in terms of his ability.

There also seems to be little evidence that standards can be established which could be met by all children at the same time in any given area of growth. The implication is that even standards for discipline must be variable. This does not imply that there are not desirable standards for self discipline, but it implies that children have certain emotional problems and that they come from different home backgrounds which influence their behavior. Therefore, the guidance-minded teacher seeks to set her standards for each pupil as she discovers where he is educationally at a given time and where he is expected to go. In fact, the guidance-minded teacher will permit the pupil to share in setting his own standards in order that the learner is in a position to evaluate his progress. For example, a pupil who has written a letter to a friend as an assignment in communication may well compare this previous written letter with one recently written. He then has the opportunity to determine, with guidance, his own improvement during the interim between the letters. Thus when standards are individualized and the teacher carefully studies her learners, curriculum experiences will aid the learner in making progress. Provision then is made for the less apt pupil as well as the brightest child.

Marking practices.   Whether marking practices influence the child's curriculum or whether the curriculum influences the type of marking policy under which a given school is operating may be difficult to determine. Empirical knowledge leads the authors to believe that a certain philosophy about teaching tends to produce a particular type of marking, or a philosophy about marking is predicated upon certain basic assumptions about instruction. If teachers want children to memorize specific facts to be given back to them on a given day through a test, then the teaching is geared to preparing the children for such a test. That is, traditional drill will probably best serve the purpose. However, if the teacher's goals are to help the children to understand certain significant facts as related to an historical period, then the relationship between the facts requires a different kind of marking. It should be clear that a child's curriculum is influenced by any particular marking system. Each system influences, to a large degree, the extent of curriculum modifications which a teacher will make in order to meet individual needs. A few basic principles are set forth to aid the teacher in developing a philosophy of marking as it relates to curriculum practices. These principles are:

1. Marking should be based upon the goals of elementary education, the goals of the school, and the cooperatively formulated goals of the teacher and pupils.
2. The available research concerning the individual differences of children should be used in developing marking systems.
3. It should be assumed that marking serves a constructive purpose in helping the pupil, parent, and teacher to evaluate pupil growth in all areas of human behavior.
4. Marking should be the result of a carefully developed plan for gathering data and from the utilization of a variety of instruments and devices.
5. Marking should result in a cooperative approach between pupil and teacher to determine pupil progress. That is, the mark received at the end of six weeks should not be a surprise to the pupil.
6. Marking should further the pupil's growth toward self-direction and self-responsibility.

The many inconsistencies found in the day to day marking systems, as well as in the long range plans, are evidence that teachers must carefully study the many facets of this complex traditional system of categorizing pupils. Efforts on the part of some teachers to set themselves up as "little gods" who are infallible in marking pupils has had detrimental effects upon pupils. The pupil who receives a poor grade may envision this as a reprimand and thus may become antagonistic[9] toward the teacher and the school. Yet in a very real sense teachers have given pupils grades to encourage them or because they believed that the children had some kind of handicap. Thus another misuse of the grading system resulted. The point to be made here is that marking systems which do not meet the needs of *all* pupils, or in other words, systems which cause some pupils to suffer because of inconsistencies, need to be carefully evaluated

---

[9] Dorothy Rogers, *Mental Hygiene in Elementary Education* (Boston: Houghton Mifflin Company, 1957), p. 243.

in the light of their purposes. It must be recognized that grading practices do contribute in meeting some of the many psychological needs of children. The task then becomes one of relating or modifying the practice to serve the best interests of each pupil.

One of the authors, when serving as director of instruction, was called to a school by the principal to meet with five sixth grade boys. The teacher had asked that the director of instruction talk with these boys in order to find out what was hampering their progress. Each of the boys related his story. During the marking periods when the boys appeared to be working at their best they usually received a failing mark; when they were not working too hard, they received a passing mark. This was, at least, the way they felt. They did not seem to feel that their effort was either recognized or rewarded. A conference with the teacher revealed her philosophy of the marking system. She stated that she believed they would work harder if she kept them "on the fence" so they wouldn't know whether they were going to pass the grade or fail it. Such a philosophy is not uncommon when teachers can hold a weapon as dangerous as a mark over the heads of pupils. Psychologically, these pupils were defeated. Their egos had fallen so low that school held little hope for them. A few of these boys reported they had been disciplined at home because of poor report cards. Obviously, this did not add to their rapport with the teacher.

Marking has been defended for generations on the assumption that this device is a means of letting parents know the progress being made by their children. However, when marks are based upon a conglomeration of skills, attitudes, knowledge, appreciations and the like, and then are subjected to the manipulations and frailties of human beings, one is justified in wondering just what a parent does know about his child from a mark.

In a university laboratory school with which the authors are familiar, children are not inhibited by fears of poor grades. No grades as such are given to the pupils or parents. Children study their mistakes as pointed out on their papers, but grades are not given. There is evidence, however, that these children are successful in achievement as measured by standardized tests, and in many cases these children are motivated by interest in a given subject to pursue it until maximum benefit is derived. Parent-teacher conferences are used in this school and parents have a feeling of knowing a great deal about their children's progress after the conferences. Since parent-teacher conferences are practiced, there is little need for giving marks which are unreliable and poor criteria for measuring what a pupil has learned. Such conferences seem to hold out hope for better reporting procedures which could lead to modifying marking systems.

In one research investigation by Gordon concerning conferences, it was found that:

1. Children liked being included in the conferences. Conferences helped teachers to gain an insight into children's backgrounds which was beneficial in understanding problems.
2. Teachers received valuable information which helped them understand child's behavior.
3. Parents with children who had no problems were as grateful for conferences as were the parents of those with problems.
4. Parents' friendliness and genuine interest in school gave the teachers a warm feeling.
5. Conferences provided opportunity for teachers to explain methods and techniques used in teaching subject matter.[10]

Rogers[11] ably points up the many factors concerning report cards which lead to emotional disturbances or poor mental health. If the mental health of pupils is important, then it seems safe to proceed on the assumption that some substitute for present marking and reporting systems is needed which will be consistent with modern instructional goals.[12] Curriculum practices which attempt to meet pupil needs also must be based upon sound evaluation procedures. Traditional marking practices tend to curtail functional curriculum experiences in many schools.

It seems safe to assume that marking practices have been largely developed for two reasons. *First*, as a means of motivating learners to do better. Some investigations indicate that marking serves to stimulate approximately 10 to 20 percent of the pupils; others don't care about their marks or they are not concerned about them. *Second*, marking practices are used to serve as some criteria by which parents are able to judge pupil progress. It can be seen, however, from the investigation reported on page 488 and in numerous others not reported here that parent-teacher conferences[13] tend to benefit both the teacher and parent as well as the child by furnishing mutually valuable information.

Promotion policies. Promotion policies are directly related to the marking procedures used in a given school. If teachers feel that they are "all-powerful" and are able to determine the extent of learning to a

---

[10] I. J. Gordon, "Action Research Improves One Aspect of Elementary Guidance," *Personnel and Guidance Journal*, 37 (September, 1958), 65-7.

[11] See Rogers, *op. cit.*, pp. 240-45.

[12] See Chapter 13 for a complete discussion of evaluation.

[13] For a complete discussion of parent-teacher conferences, see Chapter 13.

fine degree, retention policies usually are equally as naive. That is, the authors have seen schools where children in elementary classes were retained or promoted according to some combination of performance, such as failure in arithmetic and one other subject or failure in reading and one other subject. Such plans then become the basis for retention. What is needed is a realistic promotion policy based upon a curriculum constructed from guidance information as it relates to individuals. The American common school was established with certain basic values deemed essential for all children. Modern schools must not lose sight of this aspect of our heritage. Thus a good promotion policy should insure that:

1. Children who finish the elementary school have reached their potential in the basic skills to the extent that they cannot profit from spending further time nor contribute to the elementary school environment.
2. The values of the promotion policy are weighed in terms of their effects upon the mental health of pupils.
3. Each child will be dealt with as an individual based upon all of the known information, thereby insuring the best possible placement.
4. The curriculum will be adjusted to meet the needs of all children to insure equal opportunity to experience success; even so, it will be necessary for children to adjust to certain curriculum requirements, such as basic reading, writing and arithmetic.

Although there is a downward trend in non-promotion according to Kitch, 10 to 25 per cent of the children repeat first grade.[14] Any increase or decrease in non-promotion should be accompanied by some new evidence which justifies retention and insures pupil growth. The theme of this book is to show how pupil growth can be assured through a curriculum which is based upon the best known information concerning child growth and instructional practices consistent with this knowledge of children. No policy which proceeds upon the assumption of mass promotion can serve all the needs of all the children and no policy which advocates retaining a certain percentage of each group can serve the needs of pupils or the community. Such policies are wasteful of human resources and are tremendously expensive. Physical maturity, social adjustment, educational achievement, mental maturity and emotional balance must all be

---

[14] D. E. Kitch, "What Research Says About Non-Promotion," *California Journal of Elementary Education*, 21 (August, 1952), 7-24.

carefully considered in relationship to chronological age when making decisions concerning retention which affects an entire year of a child's life.

Grouping practices. Grouping practices may affect the kind of experiences which children will have in any given school situation. Most schools practice *heterogeneous grouping.* This plan provides for children who are educable to be divided so that each team has pupils with varying abilities. Grouping takes place within the framework of the teaching unit as teachers classify the children, in some cases, according to achievement in reading or arithmetic. This plan is then varied throughout the day. Proponents of this plan contend that it is more democratic, since it provides opportunities for future leaders to work and associate with children of all abilities and social-economic backgrounds. They further maintain that if additional funds were used to reduce teacher load instead of setting up separate classrooms for the gifted and retarded, all children would make expected progress under a heterogeneous grouping plan. This is not to imply that special education is not needed for those children who, though mentally retarded, are trainable.

Efforts to narrow the range of achievement of a group of pupils has been a problem which educators have faced since the advent of the graded system. It has been commonly assumed by many teachers and administrators that homogeneous grouping, on the basis of I.Q. alone, narrows this range and thus creates a simplified teaching plan. The contention that children with similar I.Q.'s are easier to teach because their range of achievement differences are narrowed does not seem to hold true. Figure XXIV indicates that there is a range for total achievement of 5.9 to 7.4 grade levels between two fifth-grade girls with I.Q.'s of 111 and 113. Total reading indicates a still wider gap between the same two pupils, with a grade level range from 5.6 to 8.3. It should be noted that the I.Q. of these two pupils varies only two points and that these I.Q.'s were determined from clinically administered tests. When you compare Figure XXV with Figure XXIV, the problem of grouping on I.Q.'s alone becomes even more evident especially concerning the injustices and false conceptions about the narrowing of the range through grouping on this basis. For example, pupil F with an I.Q. of 94 has a total achievement record of 6.6 in comparison to pupils B and C with total achievements of 5.9 and 6.3 respectively and I.Q.'s of 112 and 111. If total arithmetic grade levels are considered, pupil F with an I.Q. of 94 should be working with pupils A and C with I.Q.'s of 113 and 112 respectively. However, when Figure XXVI is introduced, pupils G and H should be working with pupils B and C as shown in Figure XXIV. It should be made clear that no effort has been made to use scores from subtests in reading vocab-

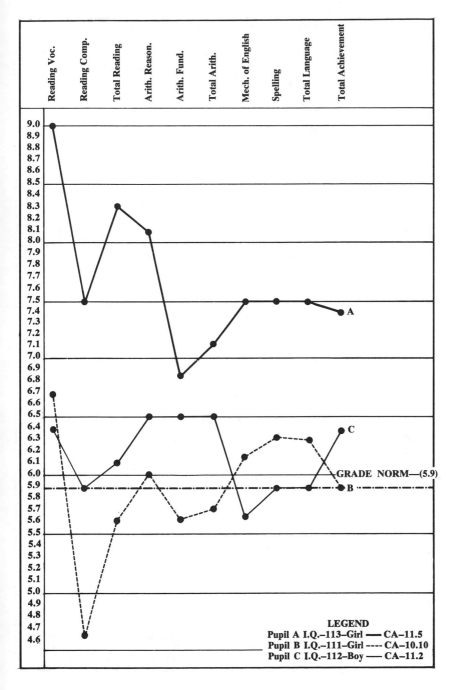

FIGURE XXIV

Achievement Scores of Three Fifth Grade Pupils

FIGURE XXV

Achievement Scores of Three Fifth Grade Pupils

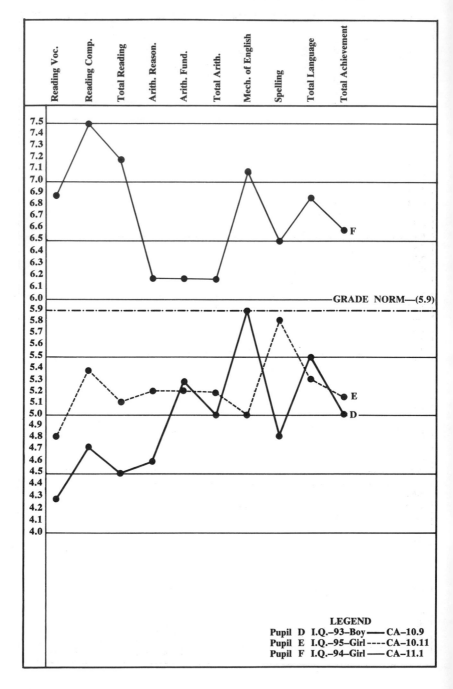

Pupil D I.Q.–93–Boy ——— CA–10.9
Pupil E I.Q.–95–Girl ----- CA–10.11
Pupil F I.Q.–94–Girl ——— CA–11.1

FIGURE XXVI

Achievement Scores of Three Fifth Grade Pupils

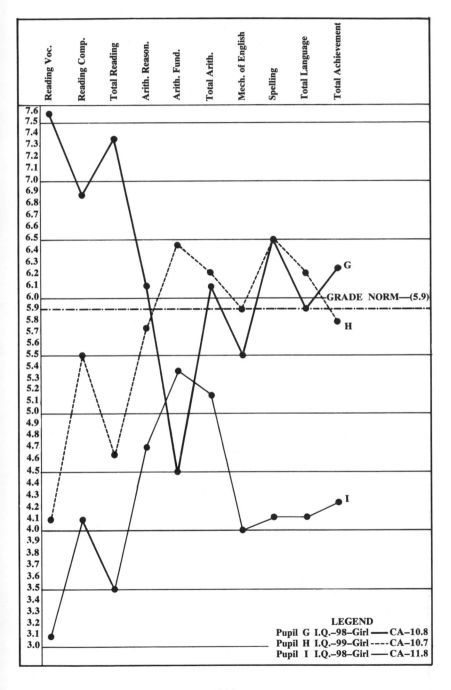

531

ulary or arithmetic fundamentals in citing these differences. Only total grade levels seem significant. Nevertheless, achievement tests which are devoted to separate subject areas such as reading, arithmetic and the like might reveal similar differences.

When such differences in achievement as those cited above are found (this appears to be the case rather than the exception), and since samples from many grades and many schools tend to support this assumption, homogeneous grouping based upon I.Q. does not seem justified. Groupings within the team should, under the influence of good teachers, meet these needs of pupils better.

It should be made clear, however, that even in the team form of organization some pupils might make better progress by being taken out of the teaching unit for portions of certain days. For example, retarded pupils who have the potential, as determined by psychological assistance, should be placed in homogeneous groups to remedy identified weaknesses. That is, pupils who for some reason other than lack of mental ability, have not made satisfactory progress should be placed in special groups for remedial help. It has been emphasized that it is democratic for each child to have the opportunity to progress to his maximum.

Heterogeneous grouping when practiced under teacher loads which are desirable according to research investigations, seems to offer:

1. Opportunity for gifted pupils to excel in *all* areas of giftedness.
2. Opportunity for all pupils to learn to work together and to understand and respect differences in individuals.
3. A stimulating environment for all children through various levels of competencies.
4. Wider opportunities for children to assess their own strengths and weaknesses with guidance from the teacher.

These and many other factors could be expanded, space permitting, and would be evidence of the many ways which pupil personnel policies affect the curriculum. The essence of guidance practices of the classroom teacher should always be the seeking of solutions to problems which prevent her from assisting the child to achieve his potential.

Discipline and punishment. Dissatisfaction on the part of teachers concerning pupil discipline has been prevalent for several years. School boards have been asked to clarify their policies concerning disciplining of children by teachers. Some teachers' associations have requested the right to use corporal punishment. The General Assembly of the State of Virginia has re-affirmed its support for corporal punishment administered by the teacher. Much of this unrest has been cast upon "progressive" education, although little or no attention has been given to identifying the basic causes. Sub-standard teachers, heavy pupil-teacher loads (55 percent of elementary classrooms have more than 30 pupils)[15] post-war insecurity, poor social environments for rearing children, broken families and numerous other factors of the environment are areas which need careful analysis if solutions are to be found.

Strict discipline by the classroom teacher may actually lead to more problems for the teacher. Some discipline problems have been caused by teachers failing to recognize when firm measures are needed and when certain situations should have been ignored. Teachers have been guilty of imposing their own wills on children. The superiority concept which a beginning teacher may hold when she stands behind the desk may result in a complete disregard of what she knows is good practice, since the feeling of being in control can sway the mind of a teacher. Thus some teachers start out with a negative view toward discipline. Beginning teachers have often asked the authors if a certain set of rules for classroom management would help maintain discipline. Such teachers seem to need a defined approach to discipline. That is, children should be guided into seeing freedom, decision-making and the like, and view these as privileges. Unfortunately, such thinking is not in keeping with modern education theory. Discipline is viewed not as a list of rules, but as a self-imposed restraint upon the individual which aids him in knowing when to conform and when to let his best judgment guide his actions.

It has been stated elsewhere in this book that a basic goal of the school is self-discipline. The acceptance of this objective of course implies that some type of classroom organization and management must be practiced which permits pupils to share in making those decisions which affect them. *However, one of the weaknesses in modern schools is the failure of teachers to see that children understand that when they make decisions they must also be willing to accept the consequences for their actions or lack of action. Decision-making implies a willingness to abide by the decision and face the consequences.* An actual illustration observed by one of the authors is presented here to focus upon this point:

> Miss Montgomery was a young beginning teacher of second grade children in a large city system. Her teaching assignment was in a school in the upper-lower social-economic section of the city. The children had been studying a unit on the farm for the past week. On the board was a list of rules which they had decided were necessary for a trip they were going to make to a farm. The rules included such things as:

---

[15] Research Division of the National Education Association, "Elementary-School Class Size," *Research Bulletin*, 36 (April, 1958), 51.

1. Stay with your buddy.
2. Don't leave the group.
3. Keep all parts of your body inside the bus.
4. Don't call out the bus windows to people on the street.

These children were not used to riding on school buses, as they walked to school. On the day of the trip mothers were present who were to be responsible for groups of eight children. The bus was boarded at the school at 9:00 a.m. Soon after the bus was underway it became evident that the children were not abiding by their rules. Some were waving their arms out the windows, others had their heads out calling to people on the corners. The teacher went to the front of the bus and had the driver return the group to the school. At the school the children went into their room quite dejected and subdued. The teacher let them spend the next fifteen minutes discussing why they did not make their trip. The trip was re-scheduled in two days and went off perfectly.

The teacher in the above illustration understood her responsibility as an adult. Her concern for the welfare of the pupils was evident, but she was also concerned about the decisions which the pupils had made and their willingness to accept the consequences. Freedom to make decisions is not a license to abide by them haphazardly. Children need to experience in school the same limitations which will be placed upon them as adult members of society. This is not to say that they should be considered little adults, but they should have experiences along adult lines in accordance with their maturity level. Children can experience punishment without the teacher resorting to corporal chastisement. Loss of approval from the teacher, group pressure, or disfavor, and the withdrawing of certain privileges have been used successfully as punishment. However, the extent to which any punishment is effective will depend upon the understanding the teacher has of her pupils. *Punishment is a remedial effort to aid a child in seeing the shortcomings of his behavior.* But the true problem the teacher faces is in determining the underlying causes of the behavior. Some guides which the teacher should consider in developing self-discipline are:

1. To place children in situations where they must accept responsibility for their actions equal to their level of maturity.
2. To exhibit faith in each child as an individual.
3. To overlook unimportant acts which can be exaggerated into problems.
4. To be adequately prepared for each day's work.
5. To appraise mental health carefully and continuously.

6. To use praise more than blame.
7. To maintain a pleasing voice and refrain from nagging or threatening.
8. To be friendly but firm in following through with actions which demand attention.

Extra-class activities. Many elementary schools have moved decidedly in the direction of providing increasing numbers of extra-class activities during the past decade. Such practices must be carefully considered before they are initiated by the school. Patrol groups, student council, science clubs, camera clubs and many other activities have been adopted from the secondary schools. Before the elementary school attempts to prolong the school day for both teachers and pupils for so-called extra curricular activities, certain values must be appraised. A brief discussion will point out the pros and cons of these values.

Safety Patrol. Many elementary schools have sought to protect the lives of the children from the dangers of traffic through the use of safety patrol groups. Boys from fourth to sixth grades are utilized in these patrols. In these schools it is believed that this is a means of developing leadership and responsibility. Patrol groups may be organized and advised by an interested teacher. This group may hold meetings after school hours, or, in the case of rural schools where children ride the bus, the group can meet during the school day. Some schools have all the boys from a given room attend the meetings which take the form of a safety instructional period. It seems that the latter practice is the most desirable where safety patrols are utilized. Safety is part of the curriculum, not some isolated or unrelated area which is practiced after school by a small number of students.

On the other hand, safety patrols which operate solely to protect children at hazardous crossings should be carefully evaluated. The burden of responsibility may be too great for ten- to twelve-year-old boys. Children are not expected to be adept at making quick decisions, nor are they expected to be mature enough to make the right decisions every time. Such tasks even adults find difficult to do. Thus many cities have seen fit to employ adults to work at hazardous crossings, which leaves the school patrol, if deemed desirable, for other types of safety activities around the school building and grounds.

Student Council. Perhaps one of the best instruments for developing leadership in children at the elementary school level is the student council. In recent years this organization has been increasingly evident in elementary schools. Perhaps no other organization exists which has more potential for developing democratic skills than the student council. Children should be given an opportunity to learn democracy from actual participation. Since democratic action involves permitting children to share in the management of those functions of the elementary school which directly affect them, this organization seems most desirable.

In one school with which the authors are familiar, council representatives are elected by each room. This council has equal representation from the kindergarten through the sixth grade. Although there is a teacher-advisor elected by the council, only students are permitted to vote. Each council representative has the responsibility to present issues that arise in the home room which he represents. Likewise the representative must report to his constituents those issues which come up at the council. In this way the social studies may become a live subject and involve real issues since the social studies period may be used for class discussion of council issues. Democratic procedures should be learned and utilized in arriving at group decisions as the groups learn to instruct their representatives to take certain action on council issues. Although the principal always maintains the veto power, in schools which have encouraged pupil leadership through student councils it has rarely been used.

The teacher plays an important role in student council organizations. Both the home room teacher and the council advisor must look upon this opportunity as a means of providing children with practical problems that can be solved democractically. Such situations foster the development of leadership skills. However, a word of caution seems essential since teachers may believe that the decision being arrived at by the group is not the one she thinks they should reach. Teachers are in unique positions to become guilty of manipulating the minds of children. Teachers who have a genuine belief in democracy do not manipulate children into believing what the teacher wants is best. Children must have the benefit of adult guidance, but it must not be biased. It is not infrequent that teachers control school elections by manipulating children into nominating for office those children whom the teacher believes are the best candidates. Children will not learn desirable values from such procedures.

The student council can be a useful organization for student participation in:

1. Developing school policy which affects them;
2. Suggesting and purchasing school equipment—playground, gym, recreational and the like;
3. Building good school citizenship;
4. Planning the school calendar;

5. Suggesting projects which will develop magnanimity of mind;
6. Evaluating the school program.

It should become clear that the student council is a device which provides opportunity for pupils to develop democratic behavior in the framework of group guidance.

GUIDANCE AND THE ROLE OF THE TEACHER

The teacher's role in guidance has been evident throughout this chapter and is described in more specific ways throughout the book. The classroom teacher is concerned with individual guidance and with group guidance. Guidance and curriculum are interrelated in these functions, both of which are duties of the classroom teacher. Group guidance is used here to refer to those activities of the teacher which involve her directly with the entire class or a portion of it. Such activities, however, are usually of the orientation type in which there is a common goal for the group. However, individual differences of the learners often prevent achieving the type of group situation in which each individual can meet personal needs.

What Kind of Classroom Climate Promotes Good Teacher-Pupil Relationships?[16]

The mental attitude of the teacher probably is the most important single factor in the development of a classroom atmosphere which is conducive to optimal learning situations. Investigations of pupils' attitudes toward teacher have been many and have consistently revealed those personality traits or general attitudes of the teacher which pupils disliked. These investigations cannot be ignored if guidance efforts are to be successful in adjusting curriculum experiences to pupils' needs. A teacher's personality may be reflected in the behavior of her pupils as shown in Figure XXVII. For example, a nervous, high-strung teacher will usually generate this same pattern of living into her pupils. Anderson points out that a worried teacher develops regressive tendencies in her pupils, and the sarcastic, sharp and bitter teacher's attitude is dangerous to timid and

---

16 See Chapter 4, p. 124.
17 See Harold H. Anderson and Joseph E. Brewer, "Studies of Teachers' Classroom Personalities: II," Applied Psychology *Monographs, No. 8,* American Psychological Association (Stanford University, California: Stanford University Press, 1946); also R. N. Bush, Teacher Pupil Relationship (New York: Prentice-Hall, 1951).

over-sensitive children.[18] Teachers must continuously be aware of the many kinds of influences they make upon children.

FIGURE XXVII

Teacher Personality Affects Child Behavior

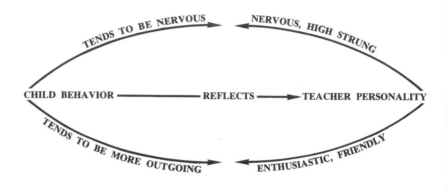

The authors have seen many teachers who have drifted into teaching and apparently have no thoughts of understanding and loving children. Teacher selection practices should be such that the mental health of the pupils or the teacher would not be placed in jeopardy. Those preparing to be teachers should carefully evaluate their attitudes toward children before making a final decision to enter classrooms as teachers of elementary children. Although in some cases student teaching may come last in the preparation program, the prospective teacher should seek counseling assistance if she has doubts about entering the teaching profession.

Teacher-pupil relationships, although in many respects unlike those of the family, are in most cases similar to any other intimate relationships which people experience. That is, those same attitudes which develop or destroy good relationships are evident. Research surveys have revealed that boys receive lower grades than girls and that more boys are retained than girls. Although this may largely be due to the failure of most female teachers in the elementary school to understand young boys, it may also be due to a dislike for boys. Or, paradoxically, the teacher, like some parents, may prefer boys to girls. Rogers points out that problems of the teacher's adjustment to her own sex role may bias her feelings for one

---

[18] V. V. Anderson, *Psychiatry in Education* (New York: Harper & Row, Publishers, 1932), p. 300.

sex over the other.[19] Such practices can only lead to poor pupil-teacher relations and in addition the children's mental health and even their entire educational career may be at stake. Poor school adjustment caused by personal feelings of teachers which result in pupils being assigned roles by the teacher such as teacher's pet, scapegoat, seat-occupier[20] and the like, may become more serious. That is, the judgment of the teacher who assigns such roles to some children is usually based upon some recognized evidence by the teacher, but if she is not emotionally stable herself, these roles may become more intensified and the problems become more profound.

Perhaps the best known analysis of the traits children preferred in teachers was the famous Quiz Kids Contest.[21] Witty, in analyzing the data, found democratic attitudes, kindliness, and patience were three traits certain children listed as being most important for a teacher. Other surveys revealed the importance of traits of a similar nature. It is evident from this and other studies that teacher-pupil relations are built upon basic laws of human acceptance. Teachers who practice democratic principles are providing fruitful experiences for children and at the same time are producing the classroom "climate" which is most conducive to effective learning. There is little doubt that pupil-teacher relations are built with lasting bonds when the teacher recognizes the worth of individuals, is fair in all her dealings with individuals and the group, and shows evidence of emotional stability by establishing a warm, friendly, and permissive climate for learning.

What Is the Teacher's Role in Developing Good Mental Health Among Her Pupils?

Like adults, children are caught up in a world of continuous change. They are growing up in a very different society from the one their parents and grandparents knew. It is predicted by anthropologists that in a comparatively short time, three out of every four mothers will be working. The mechanical processes of rearing children according to certain authorities, have tended to cause some children to have greater needs for love, security, and a feeling of belonging. These children may face even greater obstacles in adjusting to certain conditions under the teacher's control. In one first grade classroom, the following was recently observed:

---

[19] Dorothy Rogers, *Mental Hygiene in Elementary Education* (Boston: Houghton Mifflin Co., 1957), p. 163.

[20] *Ibid.*, pp. 166-69.

[21] Paul Witty, "An Analysis of the Personality Traits of the Effective Teacher," *Journal of Educational Research*, 40 (1947), 662-71.

Miss Lutz had been drilling her entire first grade class in addition and subtraction combinations through the use of flash cards. After this experience, two captains were appointed and each captain selected the members of his team. Miss Lutz commented to the observer that the captains hadn't caught on yet to selecting the best children in number work. After the teams were selected, each lined up in a row. The teacher then used the flash cards to see which member of the teams in the lead position could give the answer the quickest. The winning team was the line which had completely rotated itself first by giving the quickest answers. One little girl, who had missed five answers and was still at the head of the row when the opposite team won the game, had been so frustrated by remarks from children directly behind that she had missed at least two times because she was looking at them instead of the flashcards. When the teams went to their seats, the captain nudged her with his shoulder and said, "You dummy, you made us lose." It was really apparent from the expression on her face that this child needed some word of encouragement from the teacher, but it was not forthcoming.

Many situations of the type described above occur in classrooms each day. The teacher is the controlling factor in such situations. Mental health is an important responsibility of the teacher and tantamount to other goals of elementary education. What is mental health? *Mental health is a quality or state of being which results in a satisfactory relationship to one's environment.* The teacher is continuously seeking to help children to develop "well-rounded" personalities. Thus, what she really wants is for the child to become well-balanced, mentally, socially, and emotionally. Rogers[22] points out six traits of a mentally healthy person. These are: (1) satisfactory relationship to oneself, (2) satisfactory relationship to society, (3) ability to deal with problems, (4) ability to adapt, (5) positive satisfaction from emotions, and (6) effective way of life.

An examination of each of these six traits readily reveals the relationship between mental health and the school. The teacher is in one of the most important roles of any adult contacts that the children have and therefore must accept responsibility for helping children to mature into mentally healthy individuals.

At least two factors must be considered which are inter-related in developing the role of the teacher in creating an environment conducive to good mental health. *First*, the teacher is responsible for the quality of living that takes place within the classroom. The type of climate found with the room may be directly related to the teacher's beliefs and understandings of those factors which produce good mental health. In develop-

---

[22] Rogers, *op. cit.*, pp. 5-6.

ing a good classroom environment all aspects of the classroom must not be considered separately. For example, you cannot have one type of environment for social studies and a second type for number work and a third type for sharing period with separate sets of rules for each. The qualities which permeate a good environment are equally appropriate in all situations.

The *second* factor which the teacher must accept responsibility for in developing good mental health is instruction. This has not been placed second because it is any less important, but an environment for learning must be developed in relationship to the goals of instruction. Instructional practices may have good or bad effects upon the mental health of the children. In classrooms where instruction is aimed at the middle or average group, discipline becomes a major concern of the teacher. It is impossible to challenge every pupil in a reading lesson when all are reading the same reader. The brighter children are bored and the slow children are lost. Such is the case in reading, arithmetic, or any other subject area in the program where children are all doing the same thing. Poor mental health may be the result of such practices. Children become confused and frustrated when the curriculum is rigid and they often conform rather than become more different. Instructional practices which cause children to memorize instead of really grasping the meanings involved in the learning are apt to produce problems of mental health due to the differences in children. An imbalance of competition over cooperative learnings,[23] of blame over praise, and of punishment over reward may cause children to suffer mentally. The teacher needs to consider each of these as they are related to her instructional program if adequate attention is going to be given to producing a mentally healthy society.

What Information About Children Do Teachers Need to Facilitate Curriculum Decisions?

Guidance and teaching are compatible functions of the elementary school teacher. In fact, it would appear that guidance is inseparable from teaching. If such an assumption is supported, then elementary teachers need to be aware of their influence in this capacity since guidance may have negative as well as positive effects upon children. If guidance services are desirable and lead to improved pupil adjustment and curriculum modification, then certain services must be a normal part of the school program. These services are: (1) pupil inventory, (2) informational serv-

---

[23] May Seagoe, *A Teacher's Guide to the Learning Process* (Dubuque, Iowa: William C. Brown Co., Publishers, 1956).

ice, (3) counseling service, (4) placement service, and (5) follow-up service.

The effectiveness of the guidance services in revealing information to aid teachers and curriculum workers in curriculum development will depend upon the teacher's knowledge and understanding of her role in this phase of the educational program. Teachers must first recognize the need for the services and the usefulness of the information being accumulated. These services should lead to helping each individual become more self-reliant as he matures. To accomplish the task of adjusting the curriculum in order to meet pupil differences, guidance services must become unified and integrated into all phases of the school program.

Pupil inventory service. This service is the heart of the guidance program. A teacher-centered guidance effort requires that teachers study what information they need to facilitate their understandings of pupils. As teachers recognize the usefulness of information they should seek to gather this information and place it in the pupil's record. Most authorities are agreed as to the kinds of information which are needed in the pupil inventory. However, usefulness should be the criteria for the information to be collected. Some of the items which teachers will find helpful are:

A. Family background.
   1. Names of parents or guardians.
   2. Occupations of parents or guardians.
   3. Marital status of parents—divorced, separated, etc.
   4. If both parents are living, which one he lives with and where each lives.
   5. Economic condition of the home.
   6. Language spoken in the home.
   7. Number and age of siblings.
   8. Attitude of the family toward the individual, and other members of the family group.

B. Personal data about the student.
   1. Name and age.
   2. Personal appearance.
   3. Color and race.
   4. Place of birth.
   5. Religious affiliation.
   6. Dated picture of student, if possible (many firms take photos at no cost to schools).

C. General health status.
   1. Past illnesses.

    2. Daily schedule kept by pupil of his health habits; food included in family diet, amount of sleep, exercise, etc.

    3. Absences and tardinesses.

    4. School examinations (physical).

    5. Physical handicaps, if any.

  D. Personality traits and work habits.

    1. Continuous record of developing interests.

    2. Behavior record—kept by teacher over a period of time with regular notations made and dated.

    3. Autobiographies.

    4. Reports of interviews.

    5. Teachers' observations of work habits, etc.

    6. Reports of visits to the home, from the parents, correspondence, etc.

  E. Participation in out-of-class activities.

    1. Summer activities.

    2. Hobbies.

    3. Clubs and activities in school.

    4. Spare-time activities.

  F. Special aptitudes, interests, abilities.

    1. School grades.

    2. Results of standardized tests.

    3. Interest tests.

    4. Teachers' observations and anecdotal records.

    5. Honors and awards.

    6. Special abilities, such as music, art, etc.

  G. Work experiences.

    1. Part-time experience.

    2. Summer jobs.

  H. Vocational preferences.

    1. Student's expressed goals and purposes.

    2. Questionnaires—e.g., What would you like to be ten years from now?

    3. Essays on "My Occupation," etc.[24]

Pupil records. An efficient system of records becomes a major necessity. School records vary within schools in all sections of the country. *The Revised Standards for Elementary Schools in Ohio* now requires

---

[24] *Guidance Handbook* (Richmond: Virginia State Department of Education, 1951), pp. V-C-2, V-C-3.

each school to maintain an adequate record of each pupil. The development and maintenance of an adequate record system can only be justified when teachers realize the usefulness of the information contained therein. Such a record system should include information which has been found necessary in order to meet the demands of teachers and others who seek information about pupils. Thus, cumulative records become an important aspect of the guidance service.

What Is the Cumulative Record?

This record is the source of all information collected about a pupil from such areas as listed above. This information is placed in a folder known as the pupil-personnel folder or cumulative record. The information found in this record should assist the teacher in planning the most beneficial curriculum experiences for each learner. In addition, this information should help teachers and curriculum workers both individually and collectively to plan better for the pupils' educational and vocational needs.

The Lakewood, Ohio, public schools cumulative record folder is one which serves as a basis for other types of information which may be placed in the folder. Samples of pupil's work, anecdotal records, records of teacher conferences, parent conferences, and the like might be placed within the folder for future use. It is important to know that these folders provide for information about the child from kindergarten through high school.

Are Elementary Teachers Counselors?

Each elementary teacher does some counseling whether she is aware of it or not. The important point to be made is that since this function of guidance is carried on consciously or unconsciously, teachers need to grow in developing their effectiveness in this capacity.

Counseling requires a knowledge of special skills if it is to become a valuable service to the pupil and assist the teacher in understanding the pupil. There are two extreme forms of counseling—directive and non-directive.[25] The directive approach implies that the counselor will direct the course of the interview. In such situations the counselor identifies the problem and seeks to set the course of action to be pursued in reaching a solution. The non-directive type of counseling is the opposite

---

[25] For a detailed discussion of this form of counseling, see Carl R. Rogers, *Client-Centered Therapy* (Boston: Houghton Mifflin Co., 1950).

of the direct approach. That is, the non-directive approach gives little or no direction to the counselee about the problem of charting a course of action. The purpose of the non-directive approach is to encourage the counselee to express himself about his major concern and in so doing to let him suggest possible solutions to his own problem. In such situations the counselor's action is completely void of persuasion.

School counseling may be defined as any situation which brings the teacher together with one or more people for the purpose of solving an individual or group problem.[26] The authors recognize some values in each of the above mentioned approaches to counseling. The classroom situation is not conducive to the use of non-directive therapy. Yet, at times it would appear to be reasonable to expect that the teacher would combine these two approaches by helping the child to identify his problem then, permitting him to discuss it freely. The teacher may help him to see additional avenues beyond those suggested by the child for arriving at a solution to the problem yet leave the child free to select his own approach. At the same time the teacher may help the child to identify as many advantages and disadvantages of certain approaches as possible. It must be kept in mind, as previously stated throughout this book, that the teacher's goal is to help the child grow toward greater independence. An illustration of the counseling function is presented to help the teacher to see how certain aspects of each approach are utilized in a counseling situation.

Chip: Why did you ask me to stay in this afternoon?

Teacher: Do you remember the number of times I asked you to go back to your seat this morning?

Chip: Yes, I guess I did leave my seat too many times. May I go now?

Teacher: Why did you leave your seat?

Chip: I had to sharpen my pencil and I had to fix the window shade because the sun was coming in.

Teacher: Did you have to sharpen your pencil three times?

Chip: I guess I did go to the pencil sharpener too many times. I just didn't feel like working I guess. I was thinking of the ball game at recess.

Teacher: So you like to play ball?

Chip: Yes, I play every afternoon when I get home. If school was like a ball game I'd like it. I want to be a big-league player!

Teacher: Have you ever read about Lou Gehrig?

Chip: No, but I've heard of him. Do you know about baseball, too?

Teacher: Would you like to read about the life of Lou Gehrig? I think we have the book in our library.

---

[26] Shuster and Wetzler, *op. cit.*, p. 301.

Chip: Could I read it tomorrow in school?

Teacher: Yes, I think you might start it during pleasure reading period. Perhaps you would like to find the dimensions of a baseball field and explain them to the class during arithmetic. You know we are studying about measurement and proportions.

Chip: Gee, Miss White, I'd like to do that. I'll make a drawing tonight and have it ready to put on the board tomorrow. Could I show the other kids how to figure batting averages too? I keep my own average for each game. I didn't think we could learn about baseball in school.

Teacher: I'm sure you can explain these things to the class and maybe you could think of some other things we could study. You may go now, Chip, and I'll see if I can find the book about Lou Gehrig for you.

Chip: Good-bye, Miss White, and I can't wait to tell the other kids what I'm going to do tomorrow.

In the above interview, the teacher utilized counseling techniques when she: (1) let Chip have an opportunity to discuss his problem, (2) directed his thinking toward his problem, (3) used non-directive therapy by letting Chip discuss his interest, (4) established a friendly relationship by showing interest in Chip's interest, and (5) concluded the conference with a positive plan for action.

The counseling period proved valuable in helping Chip's teacher to discover an interest which could be utilized in curriculum modification. Although this may not be the goal or outcome of teacher-pupil counseling, a good counseling session should produce much helpful information for the teacher and it should also aid the child in growing toward independence as he matures.

How Is the Curriculum Affected by a Sound Guidance Program?

The teacher who is guidance conscious recognizes the many differences in children and does not force each child into the same pattern. Children may be working toward achieving the same objective, but they may be going about it in many different ways. Teachers who understand the physical make-up of a child and the psychological factors in learning are aware that curriculum must be flexible enough to challenge each child to learn. Therefore, the teacher should be aware of the following guides as she relates her guidance function to the curriculum.

1. The selection of learning activities must be meaningful to the learner and he must feel that they are useful to him.
2. Teacher-pupil sharing should be employed in goal-setting, planning, executing and evaluating learning.

3. Each child should gain a better understanding of himself as he identifies and evaluates his strengths and weaknesses.
4. Children should become acquainted with the resources of their community in order to understand their role more fully.
5. Curriculum experiences should proceed from the concrete to the abstract and from direct experiences to vicarious experiences.
6. Curriculum experiences should develop not only skills and abilities, but attitudes, appreciations and understandings as well.

Ostensively, the teacher's philosophy of guidance leads her to make certain adjustments in her own mind even though it may appear that all children are seeking the same objective. The teacher's expectation for one pupil should be different from that for another pupil. In addition, when groups of children are working together the teacher anticipates growth in certain areas for one child but in different areas for another child. One child may need to learn to accept the rights of others to have opinions, while another child may need to learn to express himself before the group. Thus the teacher puts her philosophy of guidance into action as it is reflected in curriculum experiences.

What Is the Role of the Elementary Guidance Specialist?

The role of the guidance specialist in the elementary school as practiced throughout the nation is not at all clear. But the need for such services seems to be recognized by the continuing demand for trained elementary guidance workers. It does seem that if such services are to be provided by the schools, the point at which the child enters school is the most logical place to begin.

The elementary guidance worker's function should be that of a consultant to the teacher, pupil, and parent. It should be the function of this specialist to facilitate the child's educative process. Basically, this function implies that the counselor should serve as a member of the instructional team. Learning problems have many different sources and the guidance worker should use his expert knowledge in working with the team to help alleviate these problems. This may mean teacher adjustment as well as pupil adjustment.

One of the major problems at the present time is the lack of elementary trained guidance workers. Some weaknesses in the training of most elementary counselors is in their lack of knowledge of the learning processes as applied to the various areas of the elementary curriculum. In spite of all the training related to social and emotional adjustment, it is recognized that most counselors are not well enough prepared to deal with the more serious problems of this nature. But they should be able to assist the classroom teacher in problems of learning related to curriculum adjustment. Hummel and Bonham point out that the specialist who should be called "elementary counselor" is a member of the school staff viewed in this light:

1. The elementary school counselor is a member of the building staff. . . . she is a team member readily available for close, intimate work with the teachers, the principal, the other special service workers, and the supervisors.
2. She is an educator, prepared and experienced in teaching in the grade.
3. She will probably serve a pupil population of 400 to 600. . . .
4. This counselor is appointed to a school only after thorough study by the staff of its needs and at least a tentative definition of functions by the staff.[27]

Suffice it to say that, as elementary guidance workers become available and as school staffs recognize the need for such personnel, the instructional teams will be enhanced and the child will be provided another valuable service to facilitate his progress.

How Does the Role of the Guidance Specialist Relate to the Classroom Teacher?

One of the purposes of guidance in the elementary school is to render preventive as well as therapeutic types of service. Although school doctors, school psychologists, and other specialists are desirable for each school, cost and availability limit their being used. Teachers need to recognize the need for the school doctor, school psychologist or trained guidance director in order that adequate utilization of these personnel may be made. The psychological structure of children's problems invariably calls for the specialists. The effectiveness of these personnel will largely depend upon the teacher's willingness to give and take in their relationships together. The guidance-minded classroom teacher does not see the specialist as a threat to her prestige, but views him as a person with special training and knowledge beyond hers. The teacher should also recognize the limitations of time which the specialist has available for the service which he renders. However, the specialist must also be aware of the unique position of the teacher in relation to her association with the pupils. The teacher sees the child under many different circumstances.

---

[27] Dean L. Hummel and S. J. Bonham, Jr., *Pupil Personnel Services in Schools —Organization and Coordination* (Chicago: Rand McNally & Company, 1968), p. 121.

She also has opportunity for counseling which, because of her propitious relationship, may be more effective.

Teamwork is essential if effectiveness of the school specialists and classroom teachers is not to be impaired. This team is working to promote pupil welfare and recognizes that adjustment or the solving of problems takes time. Teachers sometimes show a lack of faith in specialists because some miracle wasn't performed for a pupil with a problem. In other words, when Johnny returned from a conference with the specialist he was virtually the same boy who had gone into the conference. One of the first principles of behavior which the teacher should have learned in human growth courses is that complex problems which have been a part of a child's behavioral pattern for a long time are slow to be alleviated. The teacher should solicit suggestions from the specialist concerning certain things which she may do in the classroom which will aid the child. At the same time, the specialists will want to learn of any changes in the child's behavior. Thus the development and coordination of an adequate record system will be essential. When the teamwork approach is used and the central purpose is to help the child, guidance and curriculum become one.

What Community Agencies May Assist the Teacher?

The classroom teacher who envisions her role in guidance as facilitating and promoting pupil growth toward maturity must also recognize the need to utilize the many resources which are available to her from the community. These resources or agencies may be instrumental in providing certain services which may not otherwise be available to her or the pupils. Most communities have the following agencies which are interested in assisting both the teacher and the pupil.

1. Government Welfare Agencies.
2. Child and Adult Mental Hygiene Clinics.
3. United Appeals and Religious Agencies.
   (a) YMCA, YWCA, YHMA, etc.
   (b) Salvation Army.
   (c) Catholic, Jewish, and Protestant Organizations.
4. Public Health.
5. Scouts, 4-H Clubs, etc.
6. Minister and the Church.[28]

---

[28] Adapted from John A. Barr, *The Elementary Teacher and Guidance* (New York: Holt, Rinehart & Winston, Inc., 1958), pp. 364-67.

School and community relations will be reflected by the use or lack of use of these agencies to aid pupils. The teacher needs to familiarize herself with these agencies and their services. Pupils who are lacking in certain health needs cannot develop to their potential, nor can pupils who are hungry or have certain emotional problems. The teacher needs to know when and which agency should be brought into the case in order to alleviate some of the problems which handicap children. The problems a child faces in school are a part of his life problems, and his failure to meet academic or social demands of the school is part of his failure to cope with life.[29] It should be evident that the teacher has a tremendous responsibility in determining her role as it relates to utilizing certain techniques to aid adjustment, or in referring the case to an agency for assistance. It is important for the teacher to know the limitations of her potential in dealing with psychological or physical factors which lie outside of her domain.[30]

SUMMARY

Guidance and good teaching practices are inseparable. The teacher who looks upon her teaching as being guidance-centered is in a position to utilize this guidance information to improve the curriculum. It is basically the function of the American elementary school to develop each child to his potential in physical, mental, social and emotional growth. To accomplish this the fundamental function of guidance must first be preventive in nature, and second, curative.

The elementary school curriculum must be modified in relation to pupil needs as identified through good teaching-guidance. When this is the aim to be accomplished, guidance becomes effective at the elementary school level. There is no justification for assuming that guidance efforts should be delayed until children reach the secondary schools. In fact, in too many cases delays result in pupils' leaving school before guidance practices have become effective.

Teachers who seek to understand their pupils begin to recognize that curriculum experiences are related to the growth and maturity of the learners. Such teachers are cognizant of the many differences which exist between pupils in the various stages of growth. These teachers are developing a philosophy which will help to design curriculum experiences that

---

[29] Charlotte Buhler, Faith Smith, Sybil Richardson, and Franklin Bradshaw, *Childhood Problems and the Teacher* (New York: Holt, Rinehart & Winston, Inc., 1952), p. 284.

[30] *Ibid.*

are deemed essential for meeting pupils' needs. However, no single design will serve all needs.

In schools which attempt to relate curriculum experiences to guidance knowledge, pupil personnel policies reflect certain values which are consistent with their understandings of pupils. Pupil personnel matters are of concern to the classroom teacher since she is either directly or indirectly affected by these policies. Therefore, the classroom teacher needs to accept the responsibility for help to formulate policies which will enhance rather than hinder her efforts in providing sound curriculum experiences based upon guidance. Among some of the pupil personnel policies which the teacher should share in developing are: (1) educational placement of pupils, (2) establishing school standards, (3) marking practices, (4) promotion and retention policies, (5) grouping practices, (6) discipline and punishment, and (7) extra-class activities.

The guidance-minded teacher utilizes community agencies and resources to help facilitate or supplement her efforts toward promoting pupil growth. Agencies which can assist the teacher to identify pupil needs as well as those which may be able to fulfill pupil needs are brought in to assist the pupil through the teacher. The school specialist is also a major guidance worker whom the teacher recognizes as a person prepared to handle those kinds of pupil problems which go beyond the scope of the teacher. The teacher must see these relationships as a team effort; all working together for better pupil adjustment.

SUGGESTED ACTIVITIES AND PROBLEMS

1. Miss Humphries, a fourth grade teacher, found out at the beginning of the year that she was to have Tommy S———— in her room. She had studied the records passed along by other teachers and found from experience after school started that Tommy had many emotional problems which were reflected in his classroom behavior. It was learned that Tommy had a brother who was first in his class at law school. The parents were proud of this older son and continuously pointed out to Tommy that he should do as well as his brother. The vast difference in ages of the two boys was evidence that they had not much in common. Tommy's ability was just average as indicated by the California Mental Maturity test. His work was not up to the level of his ability, however, and frequently he just refused to do anything.

What should the teacher do?

Should the teacher discuss the known attitude of the parents toward their older son?

In what ways would a specialist be helpful?

2. The principal of Brookside School was interested in the teachers' attempting to meet individual needs of pupils. However, Mrs. Brown was a spokesman for several teachers when she expressed her feelings by saying that modern schools just did not teach skills, that the teachers were not going to lower the standards of their rooms, and that all pupils must reach a minimum of 75 percent on arithmetic, geography and other subjects to pass the grade.

The principal pointed out that unit teaching would help children to learn democratic skills as well as facts about subject matter, but the teachers thought unit teaching was play.

What factors of human growth were these teachers ignoring?

If you were the principal what would you have done to encourage teachers to improve?

3. Miss Agles was an elementary school teacher who believed that character education was important. When one of her fifth grade children misbehaved, she would require the child to stand facing a picture of Abraham Lincoln for 10 or 15 minutes. She believed that this would help change behavior. What is your evaluation of this method of changing child behavior? What corrective measures do you propose for unacceptable behavior?

4. Guidance of children must be a cooperative undertaking, with the parents, teachers and children working together. The teachers of Kenwood School would like to initiate a program of parent-teacher-pupil conferences either to replace or supplement the traditional report card. They believe it would serve to meet a vital guidance need. What suggestions would you offer as to ways in which parents can be involved in the planning of such a program to that the cooperative approach will not be lost?

5. Make a collection of methods of reporting pupil progress to parents. Place in one column those factors which would be conducive to good mental health, and in a second column place those factors which foster poor mental health. Justify your listings for each column with reports of research investigations in mental health.

6. Plan a mock parent-teacher conference for reporting pupil progress. Discuss the advantages and disadvantages of this form of reporting pupil progress.

SELECTED READINGS

Association for Supervision and Curriculum Development, *Guidance in the Curriculum*. Washington, D.C.: The Association, Department of the National Education Association, 1955, pp. 14-25.

Barr, John A. *The Elementary Teacher and Guidance*. New York: Holt, Rinehart & Winston, Inc., 1958.

Buhler, Charlotte, Faith Smith, Sybil Richardson and Franklin Bradshaw. *Childhood Problems and the Teacher*. New York: Holt, Rinehart & Winston, Inc., 1952, Chapter XIV.

Edwards, P. O. "Promotions: Pro and Con," *The Instructor*, 65 (September, 1955), 24.

Goodlad, J. I. "Promising Practices in Nongraded Schools," *Midlands Schools*, 75 (May, 1961), 15-16.

Gordon, Ira J. "Action Research Improves One Aspect of Elementary Guidance," *Personnel and Guidance*, 37 (September, 1958), 65-7.

Gordon, Ira J. *The Teacher as a Guidance Worker*. New York: Harper & Row, Publishers, 1956, Chapter I.

Guidance for Today's Children, Thirty-third Yearbook of the Department of Elementary School Principals. Washington, D.C.: National Education Association, 1954.

Hill, George E. *Management and Improvement of Guidance*. New York: Appleton-Century-Crofts, 1965.

Hummel, Dean L. and S. J. Bonham, Jr. *Pupil Personnel Services in Schools*. Chicago: Rand McNally & Company, 1968.

Huslander, S. C. "Assisting Youth Adjustment in Elementary Schools," *Personnel and Guidance*, 32 (March, 1954), 392-94.

Johnston, Edgar G., Mildred Peters, and William Evraiff. *The Role of the Teacher in Guidance*. Englewood Cliffs, N. J.: Prentice-Hall, Inc., 1959, p. 276.

Kelner, Bernard C. *How to Teach in the Elementary School*. New York: McGraw-Hill Book Company, 1958, Chapter IX.

MacFarlane, Jean Walker. "Some Findings from a Ten-Year Guidance Research Program," *Progressive Education*, 15 (November, 1938), 529-35.

Martinson, Ruth A. and Harry Smallenburg. *Guidance in Elementary Schools*. Englewood Cliffs, N. J.: Prentice-Hall, Inc., 1958.

"Nongrading: A Modern Practice in Elementary-School Organizations," NEA Research Division, National Education Association, October, 1961.

Rogers, Dorothy. *Mental Hygiene in Elementary Education*. Boston: Houghton Mifflin Company, 1957.

Shuster, Albert H. and Wilson F. Wetzler. *Leadership in Elementary School Administration and Supervision*. Boston: Houghton Mifflin Company, 1958, Chapters 11 and 12.

Stringer, T. A. "Report on a Retentions Program," *Elementary School Journal*, 60 (April, 1960), 370-75.

United States Office of Education, *The Gifted Student: Research Projects Concerning Elementary and Secondary School Students*. Washington, D. C.: Government Printing Office, 1960, p. 83.

Worth, W. H. and J. H. Shores. "Does Nonpromotion Improve Achievement in the Language Arts?" *Elementary English*, 37 (January, 1960), 49-52.

CHAPTER 16

Educational Leadership in Curriculum Improvement

INTRODUCTION

The theme of this book has been based upon the assumption that teachers are actually the curriculum builders. The extent to which a new curriculum design may become evident and the extent to which this new design will prepare children to live in the twentieth century world will depend largely upon three factors: (1) the willingness of teachers to grow professionally in service; (2) the extent to which educational administrators and supervisors provide sound dynamic leadership; and (3) the willingness of lay people to contribute their time and resources in working with school people to develop the best possible schools for children.

Modern schools must equip children to cope with a complex society which is faced with diverse social, economic, scientific, political, religious, and other significant problems. The use of wisdom and knowledge to reach solutions to these problems through democratic practices must be taught. There is ample evidence to support the assumption that cooperative procedures are not just absorbed from the culture. The common school is responsible for developing in children those democratic skills and procedures which will enable them to approach their world with greater understanding and hope of alleviating hunger, disease, hatred, and other factors which affect human welfare. The responsibility for exercising a positive, informed leadership rests with educators. The resulting *nonplus* rests with the citizenry. However, when democratic procedures in curriculum development are used and vigorous leadership on the part of educators is given, it can reasonably be expected that a better informed citizenry will begin to grasp the significance of what a sound school program will mean to their communities. It will, therefore, be the purpose of this final chapter to point out (1) the responsibility for curriculum improvement, (2) where leadership begins, and (3) how in-service education is related to curriculum planning.

RESPONSIBILITY FOR CURRICULUM IMPROVEMENT

Curriculum improvement is a continuous process of practicing, modifying, exploring, and evaluating pupil learning. However, we must be cautious to the extent that curriculum changes are not made just for the sake of change. Some educational leaders have been guilty of causing teachers to become confused and insecure as a result of the change concept. Curriculum change is justified when present practices have been carefully evaluated to determine the extent to which they are not leading to desirable objectives. That is, from the evaluation, areas of weaknesses will become evident and should be carefully studied to determine causes for the weaknesses. Modification of these practices may lead to better learning situations for the pupils, although it may be necessary first to explore or to experiment with certain curriculum ideas before initiating modifications. In addition, this may mean a re-examination of objectives since they change as society changes. However, the important point to be made here is that the cause for curriculum change should be identified and that the change should result in improvement of pupil experiences.

Some teachers have been led to believe that their parts in efforts to improve the curriculum were "busy-work." There are enough problems in any school system that are vital and impelling for teachers to study without using their valuable time and energy in developing ideas which the administrator knows will not be put into practice. It is therefore imperative that teachers and administrators recognize their responsibility in curriculum improvement and that they seek to broaden their own concepts of the values of curriculum improvement.

Who Is Responsible for Curriculum Improvement?

Curriculum improvement does not occur without some impetus. Furthermore, teachers who are the individuals who initiate curriculum change at the "grass roots" level many times are fearful of change due to job insecurity. The failure of the administrator or the lay public to support change has stifled ideas which teachers have preferred to disregard. In some cases, the responsibility for improving the curriculum has been abdicated by administrators and teachers alike, either because they felt their own inadequacy or because they each believed the other was responsible for initiating changes. What then is the role of the administrator in curriculum improvement?

Role of administrators. The importance of the status leader of any group cannot be over-emphasized, as it relates to the effectiveness of group operation. The teachers are eager for the administrators' active support of their efforts to improve pupil learning. It seems safe to assume that initiating curriculum improvement is basically the responsibility of the administrator. The superintendent of schools who encourages teachers to try new ideas, who supports action research projects which are carefully developed, and who realizes which part of the curriculum needs modification is accepting his role as educational leader. Nevertheless, the extent to which the superintendent or principal will be a positive force for implementing group action will depend upon his ability to clarify limitations of the group. It is at this point where many administrators fail and teachers soon lose faith in their administrator when they have worked diligently to accomplish a task only to find out that school policy as it now stands will limit the use of their efforts, or that the administrator is opposed to putting their findings into practice. The administrator must not permit groups to work without stipulating possible limitations to their efforts. Board of education policies, school law, public acceptance and the like must be considered before group action is begun. In addition, the administrator is charged with helping the group to clarify its goals, and to give as much direction as is desirable in moving the group in the direction of achieving these goals.[1]

The school administrator who lacks the knowledge of sound curriculum practices no doubt will be hesitant to permit teachers to implement new ideas. Furthermore, the administrator who lacks the understanding of how the lay citizen is involved in curriculum improvement will further hamper progress. There seems to be no substitute for knowledge of curriculum and strong, dynamic leaders who believe and practice democratic educational administration. This is not to imply that the superintendent must be an expert in every area of curriculum, but he should at least be well informed on major current practices. As in the case of large school systems, usually a curriculum director or an assistant superintendent in charge of instruction is the expert in curriculum and furnishes leadership through delegated responsibility from the superintendent. Nevertheless, the superintendent must show by his deeds and action that he supports sound advancement in curriculum.

---

[1] Othanel Smith, William O. Stanley, J. Harlan Shores, *Fundamentals of Curriculum Development* (New York: Harcourt, Brace & World, Inc., 1957), p. 658.

Some guides which the administrator should use in leading his school system in planning for curriculum improvement are:

1. The central administration, the supervisory staff, and representative teacher and community groups should determine the approach to be made.
2. The approach decided upon should recognize the autonomy of the local school, its social, economic, and cultural environment, and other characteristics peculiar to the individual school system.
3. The approach decided upon should be consistent with the democratic purposes of the school.
4. The approach should be flexible enough to provide for experimentation without jeopardizing the welfare of the pupils.
5. The teachers in the individual school should be agreeable to the approach and reassured of their individual security in the changed situation.[2]

Role of the principal.   Present trends seem to indicate the principal has taken on a new responsibility in the curriculum area. Anderson points out that "the superintendent, as the responsible head of the school, usually delegates responsibility for curriculum leadership to principals in the school buildings."[3] Numerous other authorities point to the local school as being the basic unit for curriculum improvement. This practice places the principal in a strategic position for promoting improved learning experiences. He is in close relationship with his faculty. He knows their strengths and their weaknesses and, therefore, he can involve faculty members to the best advantages. The principal maintains implicit faith in his staff and believes they will work to produce the best possible curriculum experiences for children. Those who need to grow in certain areas can be given that opportunity. Thus, as the principal leads his staff in curriculum improvement, he seeks to help each to grow in the process.

Before the principal involves his staff too deeply in curriculum improvement, he must be cognizant of the limitations placed upon him by the central administrative staff. These people should be utilized as resource personnel, but the principal must also have their support in order that proposed changes in curriculum will not be hampered and thus cause teacher morale to be lowered.

Role of classroom teachers.   The classroom teacher is the most important person in the curriculum improvement program. The success of

---

[2] Albert H. Shuster and Wilson F. Wetzler, *Leadership in Elementary School Administration and Supervision* (Boston: Houghton Mifflin Co., 1958), p. 269.

[3] Vernon E. Anderson, *Principles and Procedures of Curriculum Improvement* (New York: The Ronald Press, 1956), p. 161.

the entire effort to improve learning experiences for children may be measured by the amount of change which actually is reflected in classroom practice. Modification must come through ideas getting into the teachers' "nervous system." *Curriculum improvement is contingent upon the ability of the teacher to approach curriculum with an open mind.*

The teacher is responsible for pointing out areas of the curriculum which are not meeting pupil needs. She must bring to the attention of the principal areas which she recognizes as being starting points for studying the curriculum. These may seem to be either trivial and unimportant or they may be complex problems. The essence of the situation is found in the action taken by the staff after identifying any aspect of the curriculum that is not fulfilling its purpose.

In many school systems, the quality of administrative and supervisory leadership provided teachers in in-service education programs for curriculum improvement causes neglect of some of the basic issues. Teachers must still face up to these issues if curriculum is to be improved. For example, simply because some current idea is popular, there is no reason to focus upon it as a problem for study. Soon after "Sputnik I," many school leaders "pushed" their teachers into studying the science curriculum. In some cases, this resulted in a re-defining of the so-called universal laws of science, to determine if they were teaching these laws. Curriculum improvement must go beyond mere re-denfining of content to be learned. In fact, much good might come from studying how to improve science experiences for children that may result in broadening the entire science learnings. Of importance here is the point that the classroom teacher must be willing to face issues which may require her to change some of her practices or modify some of her valued procedures if learning is to be improved.

Role of supervisors. The term supervisor is used here to refer to director of instruction, curriculum director, or the general supervisor. The supervisor has a distinct responsibility for encouraging teachers and principals to study and improve their programs. The supervisor is a coordinator of curriculum activities. Although there are some common elements in the curriculum which need to be coordinated between schools, the supervisor must also guide individual schools in discovering their own problems. Thus, the supervisor is a resource person, a consultant to each staff in the various local schools. Because of his preparation and broad experience, the supervisor is in a position to render valuable service to the local school. Some of the functions of the supervisor in curriculum improvement programs are:

1. To encourage teachers and principals to work on individual problems;

2. To help individual school staffs identify common group problems;
3. To lead teachers and principals into exploring new ideas;
4. To help build a cooperative and permissive atmosphere conducive to work;
5. To encourage action research as a means of seeking answers to questions;
6. To encourage community participation in curriculum study;
7. To provide resource materials pertinent to the study;
8. To arrange with local or nearby universities for consultants and in-service education courses as needed;
9. To arrange for the publication of any materials which may emerge from the study.

Although there are numerous other important functions of the supervisor in curriculum improvement programs, these seem to be the most prominent. Thus, the supervisor must accept his role in curriculum development programs as a coordinator and leader. His ability to foster good human relations and cooperative procedures will no doubt be the measure of his success as a supervisor.

Role of lay citizens. Many teachers, supervisors, and school administrators have not found the key to working with lay citizens. Professional people sometimes feel that it is not the job of citizens to help develop a specialized school curriculum. In some cases, school leaders have believed they would lose prestige with lay citizens by asking them to work with them on what the school personnel considered to be a job only for a professionally competent staff. One large school has a principal who prided himself on being able to forestall any real efforts to organize a P.T.A. group during his tenure. The vast amount of indifference on the part of teachers and administrators toward involving lay citizens in determining school improvement programs is deplorable. Although there are some signs which indicate that progress is being made in this area, there are still too many school systems lagging behind.

Lay citizens have a duty and a responsibility in a democracy to help plan the type of school program they desire for their children. Willett pointed out that "out of the adversity we now face may come . . . greater unanimity as to what schools should accomplish."[4] Indeed, if the schools are to make progress, parents must be kept informed and the best way for them to be informed is through active participation in programs of

---

[4] Alpha Beta Chapter, Phi Delta Kappa, University of Virginia, Charlottesville, Virginia, *Newsletter*, 3 (November, 1958), 3.

curriculum improvement. Specifically, parents may aid the professional staff in deciding what should be taught (and in assisting in determining the effectiveness of the instruction program). But professional educators must accept the responsibility for determining the "how" in the teaching process. Parents know of the effectiveness of the curriculum as evidenced by the success or failure of the school to meet the needs of their youngsters. Thus, parents are in a position to assist in determining the effectiveness of the instructional program.

LEADERSHIP IN CURRICULUM PLANNING

It has been stated that the chief school administrator is in the key position to furnish leadership in curriculum planning. Although the administrator may have a curriculum director charged with the responsibility of improving the curriculum, teachers appreciate the school administrator who plans and works with them in bringing about improvements. Obviously, the size of the school will have some relationship to the amount of time the superintendent is able to devote to direct participation with his staff. Nevertheless, his presence at key meetings will help his staff to feel that he is interested in their efforts. Whether the superintendent in a small school system or the curriculum director in a large school system works directly with the staff is immaterial; the importance is attached to the quality of relationships which exists and the quality of the planning which goes into the curriculum improvement program.

It is essential to successful curriculum planning that those individuals charged with this responsibility seek to design a curriculum which will recognize: (1) the role of the elementary school in a democracy, (2) the developmental nature of children, (3) the principles of learning, including the materials which facilitate it, and (4) the relationships between the school and the society it perpetuates.

Each chapter of this book has been developed with these four essentials as the basic criteria for a curriculum design. The effectiveness of curriculum planners will depend upon their efforts to focus upon these as they seek to involve all who are concerned with public education in the process of planning for improvement. Administrators and teachers must accept their roles as professional personnel and they cannot afford to overlook the fact that lay people are interested in how the curriculum affects their children. The schools in a democracy belong to the people and sound school leadership recognizes that if improvement is to be accepted in the light of the basic criteria above, then parents must be actively involved.

How Do We Organize for Curriculum Development?

It has previously been stated that the chief school administrator and the professional staff are responsible for initiating curriculum study. Whether the impetus is from one teacher or many teachers, the superintendent must furnish the leadership which in the final analysis will insure its success. Principals and superintendents have a responsibility for initiating school improvement and this responsibility goes beyond improving the buildings and providing materials of instruction. The administrator who believes in cooperative administration recognizes his role is also that of initiating improvement in the instructional program. As a member of the group, his suggestions are considered with those of the staff. However, the administrator is basically responsible for establishing the organization by which the curriculum will be studied.

The instructional council. One plan for organizing a curriculum study which is meeting with success in many school systems is the instructional council or the curriculum council. This council is charged with the responsibility for continuously studying curriculum. It is the instrument by which communication lines between individual schools and the central staff may be kept open. Although the council has a coordinating function, it does not have the function of seeing that each first grade in the system is doing exactly what the other first grades or schools are doing. This is not to imply that the same good practices that are used in one school are not to be found or encouraged in a neighboring school. Specifically, the council assists schools in meeting their own peculiar needs.

The instructional council should consist of representatives from each school in the system, or in cases of large cities, a representative from each district or geographical location, together with the supervisory staff, special service personnel, the administration and lay citizens. It is important that the council is not over-balanced with supervisors and administrators; that is, at least two-thirds of the representation should be classroom teachers. Teachers should be elected by the groups which they represent. One factor which should be included in the policy which authorized the council's creation is that one-third of the representatives should be elected for one year, one-third for two years and one-third for three years. This will provide the necessary stability as well as wide participation by teachers.

Obviously, it is impossible for all citizens to participate directly in curriculum improvement. Therefore, participation may be through indirect representation. When such an organization is used it is important that the P. T. A. representatives, or those from any other interested group, understand completely the issues before taking them back to the group they represent. In this way, the interested segment of the school population has a chance to be kept informed of curriculum proposals and a chance to be heard on the issues. After the representative attends the council meetings, he is to convey the council's plans to the group he represents. He is also responsible for securing the wishes of his constituents which he brings to the council meetings. When lay groups are actively involved, then better school-community relations exist. In one school system the superintendent attempts to have the council study such problems as are identified through an annual opinionaire. The opinionaire is used each year to identify those aspects of the school program which the public seems to be concerned about at the time. In this way, school-community relations are strengthened and "smoldering embers" do not become large explosions. The superintendent, in a sense, has his fingers on the pulse of the community and can present his findings to the council for immediate action. This action immediately puts the issues directly before the people for securing suggestions and ideas as well as some possible solutions to the basic problems involved.

Perhaps the greatest problem in working with lay citizens is found in directing their efforts and energies into meaningful and useful experiences. Parents need to be aware of the need for professional guidance and help from the school's trained personnel. Parents are not expected to possess the knowledge essential for developing arithmetic processes with children, nor are they trained in understanding children and their growth patterns. Yet, they have had invaluable experiences in rearing children and should be able to furnish significant information about children which would be helpful to teachers in developing curriculum experiences. For example, parents are in a position to evaluate the effectiveness of instruction. They might investigate the answers to such questions as: What changes are evident in my child's health practices? Does my child enjoy reading as evidenced by the increase in reading for pleasure as well as reading for information from a variety of sources? Are my children showing signs of maturity through respect for all peoples and their cultures? Are my children growing in using arithmetic to solve everyday problems? Answers to such questions will make significant contributions to school leaders in determining the need for curriculum change.

Teachers recognize that parents are interested in their children and that most of them devote much time and thought to guiding their children. Close cooperation between parents and teachers will lead to improved educational experiences for children. Although parents do take the initiative when conditions at school affect their children adversely, teachers should solicit parent participation in their early contacts with children.

The school district of Cleveland Heights and University Heights, Ohio has drawn upon the interests and energies of the various groups of people who are concerned with curriculum in their schools. Students, custodians, secretaries, and townspeople are drawn into the problems of program study and development along with the customary teacher–administrator groups. A variety of viewpoints is obtained concerning any matter of concern which comes before the curriculum council, and the channels are kept open for ideas and problems to flow from any concerned individual directly to the council. If the particular problem or proposal seems to require continued study and action, specific task force committees are then set up for that purpose, and membership on any task force is obtained through application by any interested individual.

Conference for parents of pre-school children.   One plan which schools have found successful in relating parents to the schools is the conference for parents of pre-school children. Perhaps there is no other time when parents feel the impact of the public school quite as much as they do when the child first enters the school. Most parents are young and eager to help as well as to learn as much as possible about the child's adventure out of the home for six hours a day. The conference for parents of pre-school children is usually held in the spring preceding the child's actual school entrance. The goals of this conference are to promote parent interest in the schools which will continue through the years, and to provide for communication between parents and teachers.

The conference organization is rather simple in form and quite informal and establishes the kind of permissive atmosphere which will enhance mutual communication. The conference may be structured to the extent that the superintendent may make a brief formal greeting advising parents of the school board's earnest desire to provide a sound education for their children. In addition, the school doctor or nurse should explain the school health policies relating to immunization, health examinations, contagious diseases and the like. Transportation systems should also be discussed by the person in charge. Provision should then be made for parents to meet in small groups with kindergarten or first grade teachers. Supervisors and consultants may also take part in the group discussions, but the discussion leaders should encourage questions from the parents. Teachers should suggest things which parents could do at home to get their children ready for school. Explanations of the kindergarten program and the readiness program should be made so that parents will understand the purposes of these programs. It has been found to be beneficial to initiate additional meetings of this type as the year progresses; perhaps at least two other conferences during the year would serve to inform parents of instructional procedures as well as permit parents to ask questions concerning present practices. Teachers should readily recognize the accruing values to the children as an outcome of learning something from the parents about the child's home environment.

How Is Curriculum Change Implemented?

It is a recognized principle that implementation of any changes in the curriculum depends upon the attitude toward change which is inculcated into the teacher's personality. Courses of study, curriculum guides, workshops and many other such devices for improving instruction in the classroom are all planned to help the teacher to gain new concepts of the task to be done. The administrator and supervisor are usually instrumental in initiating the use of these devices as a means of improving learning experiences for children.

Teacher's attitude. The teacher's attitude toward her profession and her responsibility as a teacher for continuous self-improvement will be evidenced by the quality of learning experiences she provides for children. The teacher must be open-minded about curriculum experiences. Complacency or smugness concerning curriculum issues and curriculum improvement can lead to stagnation of the teacher's mental processes. The "open-minded" teacher reserves judgment on issues and proposals for improving curriculum until she has gathered information from many sources as well as from action research in the classroom. She seeks the cause and effect relationship of curriculum proposals as they relate to understandings of children and the objectives of education. The professional teacher has a keen desire to provide the best possible education for all pupils but she guards against needless confusion in the classroom which may result from making changes for the sake of change. Inherent in her personality is the cultivation of ideas as she seeks continuously to find better ways for achieving the educational goals of the school.

The teacher's attitude toward other teachers and the administrative staff is a vital factor in the successful implementation of curriculum change. The teacher must accept responsibility for initiating certain changes in policy in order to improve the morale of the entire staff. A faculty which has been working with administrators who dominate decision-making may not be willing to risk seeking a voice in school policy although it is the responsibility of good teachers to help to improve school operation. Group morale is improved when teachers are free to suggest new ideas or the modification of present practices. Each teacher is obligated to help in promoting cooperative school administration as it directly affects her. Teachers need not wait for administrators to invite them to participate in policy-making, but should seek the opportunity to do so.

Industrial research has discovered the values of using the psychological approach in producing change. Coch and French found, in a carefully conducted research project, that workers who participated even to a very limited degree in discussing proposed changes in work schedules, plans and piece rates were superior in production, satisfaction and adjustment, to a control group which did not actively participate in developing the proposed changes. The control group accepted the changes after they had been worked out by management, but they were dissatisfied and failed to adjust to the new conditions. Seventeen percent of the workers in the control group even quit their jobs.[5] There is reason to believe that greater job-satisfaction and increased classroom efficiency and learning may also result from high teacher morale. If teacher morale is related to active participation in policy-making, then each teacher must accept responsibility for realizing this goal.

Administrative policies and procedures. School administrators are charged with the responsibility of developing good schools. The quality of the curriculum experiences provided in a school is, in effect, a reflection of the quality of school leadership. It is the task of the administrator to implement curriculum change. Success in this endeavor, however, will depend upon the policies and procedures utilized by the administration. Administrators who attempt to implement curriculum change by mere edict or fiat are not cognizant of the morale factors which affect teachers.[6] Teachers who share in formulating curriculum improvements can be expected to be more willing to implement the improvements. It becomes important then for administrators to plan policies and procedures for implementing change which will involve teachers in the formulating stages. Even then, the administrator must allow for differences in the personalities of teachers. All teachers may not be ready to make sweeping changes in the kinds of experiences they are providing for children. Administrative policy should make provisions for implementing change piecemeal fashion through individual teachers as well as by the entire staff. If the previous experiences of teachers and their professional preparations are considered in implementing curriculum change, then administrators will permit those teachers who are ready to initiate change. However, the administrator will not discourage those teachers who are attempting to grow as evidenced by their efforts to modify their teaching.

Teachers need and deserve the support of the administrators as they seek self-improvement. Change in the curriculum which will lead to improved instruction can only come about through a change in the teacher's personality. Mindful of this, the administrator provides for the differences which are inherent in any staff.

---

[5] Lester Coch and J. R. French, "Overcoming Resistance to Change," *Human Relations*, 1 (1948), 512-32.

[6] See Francis Chase, "Factors for Satisfaction in Teaching," *Phi Delta Kappan*, 33 (November, 1951), 128.

The school administrator has many devices at his disposal which may be used to help change the philosophy of the teachers. The development of curriculum guides, workshops, in-service education courses, and the like have been found useful in helping teachers to implement curriculum change.

The curriculum guide. The curriculum guide is a resource for teachers. It is usually designed by subject areas and frequently encompasses the kindergarten through the secondary school; however, many guides have been developed only for the elementary school or even a single grade within the school. The guides are not meant to be prescriptions for each teacher to follow but may be used to give direction in building improved learning experiences for children in the area in which the guide was developed. The guide may furnish a source of suggestions dealing with many different aspects of teaching with special reference to the specific content area.

Although many people are using the curriculum guide and course of study interchangeably, these two resources have different origins and different purposes for being developed. The course of study as developed in the early part of this century was basically an outline of content which teachers were expected to cover during the year. A mandate by the Ohio General Assembly in 1958 required each school system to develop and submit to the State Department of Education a complete course of study for the entire school system.

In contrast to the course of the study, the modern curriculum guide is suggestive to the teacher and is flexible enough to provide for the various stages of growth of the teacher. The curriculum guide may be quite useful for implementing curriculum improvement since it does provide many suggestions for teachers relative to how children learn, how to study children, scope and sequence of content and many other valuable guides.

A typical example is given on page 568 to help the teacher see the content of one such guide as well as to provide the curriculum worker with an illustration of how a guide is organized. This is not meant to illustrate the only way a guide might be organized.

It should be readily observable from the contents of this state guide that much helpful material is available to teachers which could lead to improved curricular experiences for children. However, when curriculum guides are developed at the level of the local school, more teachers can be directly involved in evaluating present practices. It is obvious that teachers who participate in developing curriculum guides gain more first-hand experiences and are in a better position to initiate changes in their own classrooms. The point here is that the curriculum guide may be an effective device for aiding the teacher to grow on the job and be beneficial for the children.

TABLE OF CONTENTS[7]

Workshop.[8]   The innovation of the workshop as a device to provide for teacher growth has been a means of implementing curriculum change. Workshops have been a vehicle by which individuals with common interests in a problem could work together in seeking a solution. Colleges and universities have sponsored workshops on their campuses, and have also organized them for school systems in their local communities. Individual school systems have also taken the initiative in providing non-credit workshops of their own.

Numerous school systems have made provisions for both teachers' workshops and administrative workshops. For more than a decade, the administration of the Norfolk City Schools has recognized the values of the workshop for teachers. Each year, a post-school workshop is conducted around a topic or theme which teachers and administrators feel is important. If desired, college credit may be received by attending the workshop. The staff at the Oak Ridge Schools, Tennessee, is employed for 200 days, 180 teaching days and twenty days for workshop and other work. This arrangement is becoming a pattern throughout the country as

---

[7] State Board of Education; *Mathematics in Grades One Through Twelve* (Richmond, Va.: Commonwealth of Virginia, State Department of Education, 1950), p. v.

[8] For complete discussion, see Earl C. Kelly, *The Workshop Way of Learning* (New York: Harper & Row, Publishers, 1951).

a result of teachers being placed under contracts for longer periods of time.

Classroom teachers have a direct responsibility in the workshop program. They should be willing to share in the pre-planning stage of the workshop. Its success or failure may depend upon the extent to which plans adequately meet teacher needs. Teachers must also see that the workshop plans are flexible enough for realization of these basic interests and needs. In this respect, the interests and needs of individuals as well as groups should be considered in the plans if goals are to be achieved. Teachers also have a responsibility in sharing with the workshop planning committee for securing the kind of resource materials and consultants which will be useful to them.

The value of any device used for improving teacher growth and implementing curriculum change will obviously depend upon the efforts to improve the device. Thus, teachers have a direct responsibility to give honest opinions concerning the workshop. Each phase of the program should be evaluated in terms of its purpose and the extent that the purpose was achieved. The general meetings, group meetings, resource materials, consultants, social activities, group attitudes and the physical surroundings of the workshop all need to be evaluated carefully to determine needed modifications for future efforts. Although workshops may be sponsored by various groups for many different purposes, there seems to be no specific pattern which will achieve the goals of all persons. However, through complete evaluation, a better frame of reference may be developed in accordance with the particular needs of each group.

One of the most extensive applications of the workshop as a vehicle for curriculum development and teacher growth may be found in the Eugene, Oregon district. In that program one third of the total staff is involved in summer curriculum workshops each year. Teacher representatives, special consultants, and administrative staff cooperate in the planning of the workshop sessions. A number of imaginative curriculum guides have been produced during the Eugene workshops, but of equal value, perhaps, is the continued professional growth which is available to the teachers in the district. The Eugene workshops are of special interest because they began as a foundation funded project, but they did not end with the expiration of funding from outside sources.

Supervision. The role of the supervisor has undergone continuous change since its inception into the public school system. The supervisor in a modern school is constantly at work implementing curriculum change. His task is no longer one of trying to make individuals conform to a given pattern of teaching. The supervisor's philosophy is broad and incorporates a thorough knowledge of individual differences, group processes, human relations, human growth and development, the public school system and the content fields which will be supervised. The supervisor is cognizant of the teacher's stage of growth and therefore seeks to help the teacher improve curriculum experiences at the level of the teacher's operation. To coerce the teacher into following a vastly different teaching procedure in order to bring about uniformity in curriculum may result in staff insecurity and produce less effective instruction. The supervisor, as any other staff consultant, must be aware of the differences in people and in their personalities and attempt to implement that curriculum improvement which affects instructional procedures with such information in mind.

To implement curriculum change, the supervisor, who is a key person in the process, must set the stage for teachers to feel free to identify their problems. Then the task of the supervisor is to determine the technique or device which will best meet the situation. Some of these devices are: (1) conference, (2) workshop, (3) demonstration, (4) inter-visitation, and (5) university or extension courses.

The classroom teacher needs to be aware of the value of having a supervisor. Teachers need not fear their supervisor but should regard him as a co-worker seeking to achieve the same primary educational goals as the teacher. Frequently, the teacher is the barrier and limits the usefulness of the supervisor. Many times teachers begin their careers without a knowledge of the function of the supervisor. They should remember that the supervisor is and wants to be their friendly co-worker. Usually, the supervisor has had advanced training and wide experience in working with children and teachers. Therefore, he is in a position to use this knowledge in helping the teacher to become more effective. Yet, all the help available will not benefit the teacher who cannot accept the supervisor. There must be a mutual relationship to the effect that a common goal emerges. Each must take the other into his confidence.

The beginning teacher should take the initiative by planning and requesting an early conference with the supervisor. Then, the teacher can talk about what she is doing and the problems that she is facing. Problems of grouping, using resource materials, discipline and a host of others may lead in opening the door to securing vital assistance from the supervisor.

It is a growing practice in many progressive school districts not to use the title of "supervisor." During the past several decades, the percentage of teachers who hold bachelor's and master's degrees has risen sharply. There is no longer the great gap in preparation between classroom teacher and "supervisor"; hence it is realistic for school systems to employ special area consultants, resource teachers, and coordinators to work as equals with the teaching staff. The major difference between consultant and teacher may be only in the assignment and use of one's time to do specific tasks, or it may be due to very specialized preparation in one field such as art or social science education.

An important concept that appears to be emerging is that of teacher responsibility and involvement in the processes that were once the concerns of the persons who were designated as "supervisors." It may be a few years before the term "supervisor" disappears from the terminology of state departments and universities, but it appears to be on the way out as a useful concept in the schools.

Evaluation of teaching. Perhaps the most effective procedure for implementing curriculum study and improvement may come from cooperative programs of evaluation of teaching. When teachers are brought together for the purpose of developing criteria for evaluating their teaching, improvements may be expected. This procedure requires a careful study of the objectives the staff is trying to achieve as well as those objectives which teachers set for themselves. In addition, the task of continuously studying the school's philosophy and modifying it is an important aspect of the evaluation. Then, as teachers measure the results they are achieving through current curriculum practices against their goals and changing philosophy, they are in a position to study intensely the problems which present the greatest need.

Self-evaluation is the ability of an individual to identify objectively personal and professional weaknesses for improvement through personal growth.[9] As teachers think together and cooperatively develop the above mentioned criteria, they are able to reflect upon their own beliefs and practices in contrast to what they hear about those of others. The actual keeping of records of other points of view and itemizing certain points under broad areas of teaching and comparing these with one's own pattern of operation may be useful. Efforts to be more observant about pupil behavior and to study cause and effect may lead to improved teaching. As teachers seek to identify their teaching practices and compare them with a scale which shows levels of development, they may identify what needs to be done in order to move to the next higher level on the scale. It must be remembered that if teachers have cooperatively developed the criteria or scale and they have agreed upon the various levels to be included as well as the areas and definitive points on the scale, they will probably make greater use of it. Chart XVIII illustrates what one group of teachers agreed upon as being four levels concerning curriculum planning.

---

[9] Shuster and Wetzler, *op. cit.*, p. 213.

CHART XVIII

Levels of Curriculum Planning[10]

LEVEL I	LEVEL II	LEVEL III	LEVEL IV
The teacher believes that the curriculum is the same as an outlined course of study. This outline may be found in a textbook. The teacher feels no responsibility for curriculum planning, as she believes that the curriculum should be outlined by experts.	The curriculum is an outline of topics or units. The teacher takes little part in arranging the outline. There is little opportunity for study and planning by a school faculty. The teacher chooses from among several topics and selects supplementary materials.	The teacher develops the curriculum around problems which she and the pupils judge to be important. The program may be a study about problems rather than an attempt to solve them. The teacher has the opportunity to make many choices with her pupils. She works with other members of the faculty to make the program more effective.	The curriculum is a program based on the needs, abilities, and interests of children. The faculty of a school is responsible for studying the community and the pupils to determine the program. Curriculum-building activities are a regular part of the faculty program. The teacher provides leadership for parents, pupils and other teachers in understanding and contributing to the development of the curriculum.
Examples:	Examples:	Examples:	Examples:
The teacher depends upon a definite outline.	The teacher may serve on a city-wide committee to select textbooks or to revise course of study.	The teacher and pupils select topics or problems and plan activities for exploring them.	The teacher assumes leadership or is an active member in faculty meetings.
This outline is sent out by the central office and has been designed by supervisors, state department of education, by the department of a college, or other similar agencies.	She may seek the help of other teachers in following the course of study.	She experiments with materials, procedures, and techniques in the classroom.	She is anxious to experiment as a means of improving the program.
Experimentation in curriculum is a part of research in college centers and has no place in the classroom.	The teacher hesitates to depart from the daily routine, but is tolerant of experimentation by others.	The classroom teacher plans cooperatively with resource personnel to improve the program.	She participates in regional and division-wide activities as a means of promoting unity and securing help in developing the program.
The teacher belittles efforts of other teachers who attempt experiments.			

[10] Norfolk City Public Schools, A Guide to Teacher Growth Through Self-Evaluation (October, 1953), pp. 24-5.

It should be noted that such an illustration has not drawn fine lines of demarcation. This would not be desirable even if it could be accomplished. However, from these guides a teacher could evaluate her own efforts and determine at which level of operation she is achieving. In addition, the guide, along with the supervisor's assistance, might help the teacher to see the next approach which she should take toward achieving a higher level of operation. Self-evaluation, while leading to personal growth, should also lead to security in one's position. But this may depend upon many factors relative to the instrument used. Self-evaluation has failed to achieve its purpose if improper use of the findings causes teachers to lose confidence in themselves or the staff.

What Is the Relationship of In-Service Education to Curriculum Improvement?

The in-service education program as it has emerged is the result, at least in part, of the democratic movement in education and more particularly in supervision and curriculum development. The concept that teachers in service, if given an opportunity, would seek to grow personally and professionally has been widely accepted. Although, in at least one state, legislation has been written to compel school systems to provide for such programs.[11] Since in-service education is a personal matter to the extent that no one can force an individual to grow either professionally or personally, it would appear that local school systems should encourage and assist teachers who are interested.

In-service education must not become an either-or issue as it relates to group or individual endeavor. At times, a group effort is needed. But there is also a need for providing for the individual. It is folly to assume that all teachers need the same experiences or that they all have the same problems. One teacher may be weak in organizing her classroom for social studies and another teacher may have the same problem. Yet, the causes may be quite different. The one teacher may need to strengthen her background in the social sciences while the other teacher may lack an understanding of growth patterns of children as they relate to organizing them for learning. Be that as it may, in-service education must not be established as an either-or situation. Provisions should be made for total staff efforts as well as individual efforts.

In-service education and curriculum improvement are obviously related to the classroom. If the activities which comprise the in-service edu-

---

[11] William B. Edwards and Paul E. Spayde, *Baldwin's Ohio School Laws* (Cleveland, Ohio: Banks-Baldwin Law Publishing Company, 1958), p. 396.

cation program are classroom-oriented, then curriculum becomes inseparable from in-service education. This is true whether it be an individual or a group effort. However, the authors have seen teachers who were involved in certain in-service workshops not to improve their teaching but to learn how to invest their personal funds. Of course, it could be argued that the teacher who has learned to be a wise investor will be a better teacher, but such a statement would be difficult to defend. The point is that if a teacher's in-service education goals are pupil-centered, then curriculum development will be tantamount to in-service education.

Teachers should recognize the need for their continuous efforts to grow on the job. The changing nature of society and the changing nature of man's knowledge of the world demands that teachers keep themselves informed. These changes produce new social needs, and consequently, teachers must be cognizant of the changing needs of their pupils. The responsibility for in-service education programs which will meet teachers' needs rests not only with administrators but with the teachers.

The continuous search for improved instructional procedures and a curriculum which will more nearly meet the needs of children and youth rests with the team consisting of parents, teachers, and administrators who are dedicated to the American way of life and who see in the democratic approach to education the realization of an enriched life for a growing number of citizens.

SUMMARY

The elementary school teacher must be cognizant of the processes and personnel roles in curriculum development. The classroom teacher should envision curriculum development as a dynamic effort to improve conditions affecting pupil learning. The roles of the chief school administrator, the principal, the supervisor and the lay public are to be viewed by the teacher as a team approach to the curriculum development process.

Teachers are basically the ones who change or modify the curriculum. Administrators, however, must accept the responsibility for providing the kind of permissive climate which will encourage teachers to find better ways of promoting learning. Teachers frequently are reluctant to initiate curriculum improvement unless it is actively supported by the administration.

Supervisors are coordinators of curriculum activities and as such should aid teachers to identify those problems which will lead to improved learning opportunities for children. In addition, supervisors are charged with the responsibility of coordinating curriculum development between schools.

Lay citizens must take active parts in helping to plan the kind of school program which they believe will benefit the society. Although lay citizens should help to plan the program studies, the professional must make the decisions as to how the teaching processes are to be carried out. Parents should not inquire as to the "how" of the teaching process, and should recognize that this is the responsibility of the professional staff. However, parents should also join in the appraisal process in helping to find out how successful the teaching procedures have been.

When the team approach to curriculum improvement is initiated, certain essentials must be considered such as (1) the role of the elementary school in a democracy, (2) the nature of the children the school serves, (3) the relationship of the school and the society, and (4) the principles of learning and the materials which enhance it. Thus, an emerging curriculum design is based upon the best information available in order to produce citizens capable of surviving in the space age.

SUGGESTED ACTIVITIES AND PROBLEMS

1. Mr. Smith, who is superintendent of the Salmon View Schools, appoints a curriculum committee each year to prepare a report upon the status of the curriculum. It has been customary for the committee to meet once each year and to prepare a brief report of their meeting. Meantime, the supervisor of the elementary schools has continued to revise curriculum guides, to select new textbooks, and the like, with no contact with the curriculum committee. What recommendations would you make for improvement of this situation? Does it seem that the curriculum committee is negligent? Is the supervisor proceeding in the most effective manner?

2. A committee of teachers has been appointed by the superintendent to work on improvement of the science program. The committee began its job by gathering together many courses of study by other schools with a view toward taking parts of each for use in their own curriculum guide. This committee, also, reviewed a number of science textbooks to see what they should teach. How would you evaluate their procedure? What would you do differently?

3. Miss Allison prefers to avoid work on curriculum planning as she would rather concentrate on teaching her third grade children. What must her attitude be toward her fellow teachers? What does she apparently think of her own teaching ability?

4. Obtain a course of study and a curriculum guide from the College Curriculum Center and compare the materials in terms of usefulness for teachers. Which resource permits greater teacher initiative? What areas do you like best about each resource? Why?

5. Form a panel and discuss the following: "Parents are assets in curriculum development programs." Point out why some teachers and administrators fear parent participation in this area of the school program.

SELECTED READINGS

Alcorn, Marvin D. and James M. Lindley (eds.). *Issues in Curriculum Development.* New York: Harcourt, Brace, and World, Inc., 1959, Chapter 9.

Anderson, Vernon E. *Principles and Procedures of Curriculum Development.* New York: The Ronald Press, 1956, Chapter 8.

Association for Supervision and Curriculum Development. *Research for Curriculum Improvement.* National Education Association. Washington, D. C., 1957 Yearbook, Chapters 8 and 10.

———— *New Insights and the Curriculum.* National Education Association. Washington, D. C., 1963 Yearbook.

Beck, Robert H., Walter W. Cook, and Nolan C. Kearney. *Curriculum in the Modern Elementary School.* New York: Prentice-Hall, Inc., 2nd ed., 1960, Chapter 18.

Gwyn, J. Minor. *Theory and Practice of Supervision.* New York: Dodd, Mead & Company, 1961, Chapter 17.

Hicks, Hanne J. *Educational Supervision in Principle and Practice.* New York: Ronald Press, 1960, Chapter 9.

Kemp, C. Gratton. *Perspectives on the Group Process.* Boston: Houghton Mifflin Company, 1964.

Lucio, William H. and John D. McNeil. *Supervision: A Synthesis of Thought and Action.* New York: McGraw-Hill Book Company, 1969.

National Education Association. *Leadership for Improving Instruction*, Yearbook of the Association for Supervision and Curriculum Development. Washington, D. C.: The Association, National Education Association, 1960.

National Education Association. *Role of Supervisor and Curriculum Director in a Climate of Change*, Yearbook of the Association for Supervision and Curriculum Development. Washington, D. C.: The Association, National Education Association, 1965.

Parker, J. Cecil, T. Bentley Edwards, and William H. Stegeman. *Curriculum in America.* New York: Thomas Y. Crowell Company, 1962, Chapter 5.

Shuster, Albert H. and Wilson F. Wetzler. *Leadership in Elementary School Administration and Supervision.* Boston: Houghton Mifflin Company, 1958, Chapters 9 and 10.

Smith, B. Othanel, William O. Stanley, and J. Harlan Shores. *Fundamentals of Curriculum Development.* New York: Harcourt, Brace & World, Inc., 1956, Chapters 25 and 26.

Spears, Harold. *Curriculum Planning Through In-Service Programs.* Englewood Cliffs, N. J.: Prentice-Hall, Inc., 1957, Chapters 3, 4 and 5.
"Who Should Plan the Curriculum?" *Educational Leadership,* 19 (October, 1961), entire issue.

Name Index

Subject Index